lonely planet

WITHDRAWN

Estonia, Latvia
& Lithuania

Carolyn Bain
Neal Bedford, Brandon Presser, George Dunford

LEGEND

Primary
Secondary
Tertiary
Unsealed

0 ——— 50 km
0 ——— 30 miles

FINLAND

HELSINKI

Gulf of Finland

RUSSIA

TALLINN (p59)
A chocolate-box confection of medieval magic, with surprising modern treats too

Naissaar

TALLINN

Maardu

Paldiski

Keila-Joa
Keila

Risti

Kabernese

Loksa
Käsmu
Kolga
Palmse

Viitna
Kahala
Kiiu

Kehra

Aegviidu

Hageri
Rapla

Märjamaa

Lelle

Vändra

Rapla

Kabala

Kohila

Prangli

Paldiski

Rumsalu

Kadrina
Rakvere
Kunda

Vihula

Haljala

Viru-
Jaagupi

Tamsalu
Väike-
Maarja

Rakke

Tapa
Jõgeva

Paide
Türi

Roosna-
Alliku

Koeru
Järva-
Jaani

Põltsamaa

Võhma

Jäneda

Suure-Jaani

Viljandi

Karksi-Nuia

Abja-Paluoja

Mõisaküla

Halliste

Lake Peipsi

Mustvee

Kallaste

Alatskivi

Tartu

Elva

Otepää

Puka

Sangaste
Tõrva

Valga

Valka

ESTONIA

**SOOMAA
NATIONAL PARK (p138)**
Rivers, bogs, forests and flood plains
create a captivating, wildlife-rich park

Soomaa NP

Kilingi-
Nõmme

Narva-Jõesuu

Narva

Sillamäe
Jõhvi

Kohtla-Järve
Lüganuse

Iisaku

Rakvere

Jõgeva

Tartu

Räpina

Võru

Haanja Nature
Park

Suur Munamägi
▲ 318m

Rõuge

Mõniste

Pskov

Pechory

Värska

Põlva

Vastse-
Kuuste

Kavastu

Maardu

Ahtme

Vasknarva

Raasiku

Pühajärv

SIGULDA (p253)
Towering pine forests
peppered with crumbling
castle ruins

Ape

Alūksne

Gulbene

Valmiera

Vidzeme

Cēsis

SIGULDA

Rauna

Druviena

Smiltene

Trikāta

Strenči

Rūjiena

Mazsalaca

Staicele

Aloja

Limbaži

Skulte

Saulkrasti

Ainaži

Salacgrīva

Matīši

Igate

Tūja

Duntes

Riņģi

Lilaste

Lāde

Ligatne

Murjāņi

Piebalga

Vecpiebalga

Taurupe

Skujene

Velki

Nītaure

Allažmuiža

Mālpils

SAAREMAA (p153)
An offshore magnet for
nature lovers, holding
a spiritual appeal
for the locals

Saaremaa

Kuressaare

Kaali

Orissaare

Leisi

Salme

Kihelkonna

Karja

Kärla

Kaarma

Angla

Koguva

Muhu

Virtsu

Lihula

Kirbla

Haapsalu

Ridala

Noarootsi

Rohuküla

Vormsi

Sõru

Käina

Hiiumaa

Kärdla

Suuremõisa
Kassari

Pühalepa

**Hiiumaa Islands
Reserve**

Ristna

**Ristna
Peninsula**

**Takhuna
Peninsula**

Tahkuna

Jaihunanina

Emmaste

**Kõpu
Peninsula**

Kõpu

**BALTIC
SEA**

Torgu

Sääre

Kuivastu

Saka

Pärnu-
Jaagupi

Vändra

Sindi

Pärnu

Audru

Tõstamaa

Tali

PÄRNU (p127)
The beachside playground of
the Baltic, where sandy beaches
and leafy parks beckon

Pärnu

Häädemeeste

Tahkuranna

Munalaiu
Port

Kihnu

Pootsi

Saulepi

Ruhnu

Gulf of Riga

Rohuküla

CAPE KOLKA (p233)
A stunningly desolate and
ever-so-enchanting realm of
gnarled pines and flaxen sand

Cape
Kolka

Mazirbe

Kolka

Roja

Valdemārpils

Mērsrags

Kaltene

Talsi

Stende

Dundaga

Mikeltornis

Ventspils

Ovīši

Vārve

Ugāle

Piltene

ESTONIA

Teterata

 Alsunga

Sabile

Kandava

Vidzeme

Valki

Baki

Vilaka

E95

E262

E77

E67

E20

LATVIA

Rīga

Smiltene

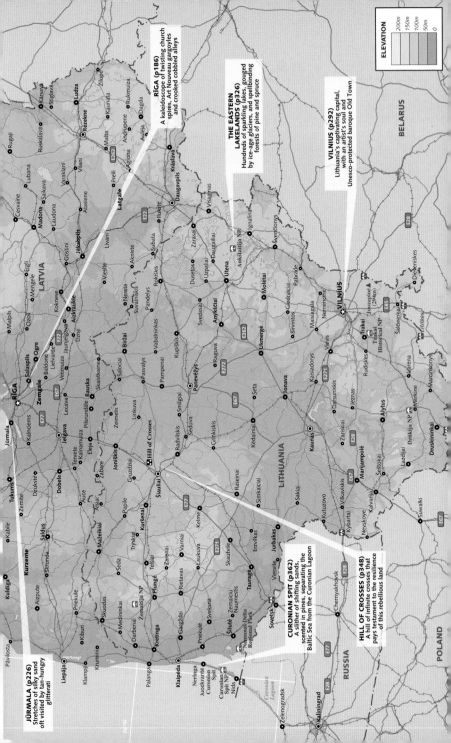

JŪRMALA (p226)
Stretches of silky sand oft visited by tan-hungry glitterati

RIGA (p186)
A kaleidoscope of twisting church spires, Art Nouveau gargoyles and crooked cobbled alleys

THE EASTERN LAKELANDS (p326)
Hundreds of sparkling lakes, gouged by ice-age glaciers, and spellbinding forests of pine and spruce

VILNIUS (p292)
Lithuania's captivating capital, with an artist's soul and Unesco-protected baroque Old Town

CURONIAN SPIT (p362)
A slither of shifting sands, scented in pines, separating the Baltic Sea from the Curonian Lagoon

HILL OF CROSSES (p348)
A hill of infinite crosses that pays testament to the resilience of this rebellious land

ELEVATION
200m
150m
100m
50m
0

LATVIA

LITHUANIA

BELARUS

POLAND

RUSSIA

On the Road

CAROLYN BAIN Coordinating Author
After the Estonia research for this book was all wrapped up, friends joined me for a Baltic city blitz, taking in Tallinn, Rīga, Vilnius, Kaliningrad and St Petersburg by plane, train and bus – a dream trip, combining business and pleasure. This was taken at fairytale-worthy Trakai outside Vilnius.

NEAL BEDFORD Happy as Larry, hanging onto a Kaliningrad border buoy. I'd caught a ride out of Nida on Hans Bastian's *Tardorna* (www.tadorna.de), a gorgeous wooden-hull yacht from 1955 he was sailing single-handedly around the Baltic Sea. We'd just released a message-in-bottle each – he to a girl back in Kaliningrad; me to my daughter in Texas. A stunning sunset and no Russian patrol boats in sight – perfect.

BRANDON PRESSER After hitching a ride with a hearty Liv sea captain, I found myself at the crimson Kolka Lighthouse floating several kilometres offshore from the tip of Cape Kolka. The manmade island had been untouched for decades, and was now home to a roaring population of seagulls. The views back towards the pine-studded shores were breathtaking; unfortunately I had to chuck my shoes after the expedition – they were drenched in guano.

For full author biographies see p432.

Estonia, Latvia & Lithuania Highlights

Look beyond the architectural treasure troves of medieval Tallinn, Art Nouveau Rīga and baroque Vilnius and the Baltic region's gentle rural character soon reveals itself in the form of quaint villages, sparkling lakes, empty coastline and all that mythical forest. Surprises abound – not least of which are the countries' idiosyncratic identities, uplifting song festivals, culinary oddities and quirky Soviet throwbacks. We asked our readers and writers what makes Estonia, Latvia and Lithuania so memorable. Here's what they had to say.

BRENT WINEBRENNER

1 BALTIC ARCHITECTURE

The individuality of each of the Baltic countries is perhaps best noticed in the capital cities. It manifests itself through the architecture, the social interaction of the people and the use of public spaces. Tallinn is gentle and totally Scandinavian in feel; Rīga is more edgy and bustling and feels like a place strongly influenced by Russia, but fiercely establishing its independence; Vilnius, with its wonderful baroque churches, feels like it's part of the Polish enclave of Eastern Europe.

Graham Harris, Traveller & Architect, UK

WITOLD SKRYPCZAK

2 LATVIA'S CASTLES

A quick glance at a map quickly reveals Latvia's key position along the ancient trade routes between Western Europe and Russia. Crumbling castle ruins abound throughout the pine-peppered terrain, each a testament to a forgotten kingdom.

Brandon Presser, Lonely Planet Author, Canada

© URMAS AARO / ALAM

3 VILJANDI, ESTONIA

We figured we'd spend just a few hours in Viljandi (p136). Two days later we left with big, relaxed smiles. The forestlike park with double moats and Teutonic castle ruins offer majestic views across the lake at the bottom of the valley. We ran down the steep hills like kids, hung out on the beach, swam and pedal-boated on the lake, even biked around it, ate at some awesome cafes and slept very soundly.

Steve Kokker, Tallinn resident for eight years (originally from Canada), Estonia

ART NOUVEAU/WOODEN HOUSES

Rīga's Art Nouveau architecture, characterised by its colourful and intricate masonry of faces, flowers and statues, is some of the most beautiful in the world. It also exemplifies the vibrant, often contradictory spirit of the city. Elaborate, lovingly restored buildings stand next to crumbling façades, still elegant in their decay. And interspersed throughout the Art Nouveau district (p198), Rīga's wooden houses have met a similar fate. The old and the new, the refined and the grit, the effort and the neglect – much of Rīga's personality can be seen through its architecture.

Ellie Schilling, Rīga resident (originally from USA), Latvia

LATVIA'S SONG & DANCE FESTIVAL

We were convinced everyone in the country was either in Latvia's Song and Dance festival, or watching it! Bewitching blondes danced their way around Milda (the Freedom Monument; p194) with flowers in their hair. They were cheered on by a crowd who truly relished being able to come together to celebrate their freedom after years of adversity.

Tess Schenberg, Traveller, Australia

JONATHAN SMITH

SAMPLING CEPELINAI

Who knew a potato dumpling could be the cherry on top of my Lithuanian adventure? The Lithuanian national dish, *cepelinai*, is hard to make but very easy to order in the quaint restaurants of Vilnius. To me those dumplings (I sampled many) represented my Lithuanian heritage, hours of learning to cook with my Lithuanian grandma and many family celebrations – and Lithuania is the one place you can order *cepelinai* from almost any menu.

**Amanda Harding,
Traveller, Australia**

6

CAPITAL CALM

All you've heard about Tallinn's chocolate-box Old Town is true – but in July you're appreciating its medieval magic alongside thousands of others. We legged it to leafy, lovely Kadriorg Park (p73) for some elbow room, a breath of fresh air, and prime people-watching – wedding parties having their photos taken, kids squealing in the playground, locals and tourists wandering and admiring. A coffee by the pond followed by a stroll around the artworks of KUMU were completely re-energising.

Carolyn Bain, Lonely Planet Author, Australia

7

BRUCE R

DEBRA HERRMANN

8

LAHEMAA NATIONAL PARK, ESTONIA

On foot follow the coastline (punctuated by 'erratic' boulders) out of Käsmu (p97), once a village for sea captains, now a burgeoning colony of artists. Survey Estonia's elite past at Palmse, Sagadi and Kolga manors and, just off the highway towards Tallinn, be sure not to bypass Bronze Age archaeological sites such as cult stones and burial cysts.

Debra Herrmann, Lonely Planet Staff

Handwritten at top: 2/3/11, 914 .79 BAM

Contents

Regional Map Contents

FINLAND Helsinki
p168

Estonia
p42

*BALTIC
SEA*

Latvia
p178

Lithuania
p278

RUSSIA

Kaliningrad
p385

Destination Estonia, Latvia & Lithuania

These are heady days for the Baltics, with the current state of play in this region unthinkable a mere two decades ago. In the space of one generation, Estonia, Latvia and Lithuania have had their prayers answered, and are scarcely recognisable from their former incarnations. After some hiccups in the early days, when self-government was being relearned, all three have politically and economically shaken off the dead weight of the Soviet era and turned their focus to the West, and to promises of a richer, shinier future. NATO and EU membership and the fastest-growing economies in Europe have been the Baltic lot since the turn of the millennium, and these three countries are now patting themselves on the back, puffing out their chests and celebrating their return to the world stage – independent, economically robust, tech-savvy and pretty damn satisfied!

And why wouldn't they be? There's certainly much to be proud about, and the world is slowly tuning in to the low-key and lovely Baltic charms. Savouring Tallinn's long white nights, scouring long Baltic shores for amber, scaling sand dunes in Lithuania's 'Sahara' and sampling local specialities – including Lithuania's infamous *cepelinai* (stuffed potato dumplings) and Latvia's Black Balzām (liqueur) – are Baltic joys to be revelled in. Vilnius boasts Eastern Europe's largest Old Town, a bohemian republic and a recommended overdose of baroque, while Rīga has the world's finest collection of Art Nouveau architecture and a market housed in a series of WWI zeppelin hangars. Elegant Estonia, with its subtle hints of Scandinavia, boasts a coastline studded with 1521 beautiful islands and a wave of outdoor pursuits. National parks provide plenty of elbow room for the locals to enjoy downtime, and for precious wildlife long gone in other parts of Western Europe. Quaint villages evoke a timeless sense of history, uplifting song and dance festivals celebrate age-old traditions and retro-Soviet recycling gives the region its quirk and its kick.

'In the space of one generation, Estonia, Latvia and Lithuania have had their prayers answered'

Still, for all their accomplishments, there's no denying that there are still issues to be addressed here. Fifty years of Soviet rule can't be erased in only one generation (if at all), and environmental and social issues remain. The environmental clean-up may indeed prove easier than solving the complex social rifts and inequalities that linger between ethnic groups, and the burden of geography makes good relations with the neighbours – particularly that big and unavoidable eastern one – vital. This trio of newbies is also coming to grips with the market economy, learning to take the good (booming growth) with the bad (slowdown and recession). There may be a bumpy financial road ahead, but the fact that they survived all that the 20th century could throw at them gives us the confidence to predict they've got what it takes to live long and prosper.

Getting Started

Astonishingly few people can pinpoint Estonia, Latvia and Lithuania on a map, giving Baltic-bound travellers an instant head start. There's more than enough here to warrant a stand-alone Baltic holiday, but equally your explorations of the region may be a northern addition to Eastern European roaming, a somewhat grittier add-on to travels in Scandinavia or a hassle-free adjunct to explorations of Russia. Either way, you'll be happy to know that communicating in English here is usually not a problem, transport is efficient and frequent between the main towns, standards of living are relatively high and you won't find the crazy crowds that blight summer travel elsewhere in Europe. One of the very few downsides is that the weather can be fickle.

Accommodation is relatively easy to find (except in the capitals and major beachside resorts in July and August, which do get tourist-busy), but is no longer the bargain it once was. Dining is another unexpectedly tasty experience, in the capitals at least, with some meals at laughable prices. To top it all off, the arts scene is hot, young and vibrant, and quirky festivals abound.

One thing to bear in mind when doing your pre-trip planning: if you're hoping to combine the Baltic countries with a jaunt into Russia (Kaliningrad, perhaps – to gain travel cred by getting a long way off the beaten path – or magnificent St Petersburg, only eight hours by bus from Tallinn), you'll make things a whole lot easier for yourself by organising your Russian visa before leaving home.

WHEN TO GO

In spring, the weather is warm, the days are long, gardens blossom and the cultural calendar oozes fun. April and May, when the stork returns to its nest, and the land and its people open up after winter, convey a real magic. June is midsummer-madness month (p20) and evokes the Baltic peoples' close ties to nature and their pagan past.

Summers are short but sweet. July and August (high season), the warmest and busiest months, and a time when many locals go on holiday too, can also be the wettest and subject to the odd thunderstorm. Coastal waters at this time average between 16°C and 21°C, and daytime highs from May to September hover between 14°C and 22°C, but can easily reach the mid- to high-20s.

Winter (November to March – essentially low season), with just a few hours of semidaylight every 24 hours, is a long, dark affair, with temperatures rarely above 4°C and frequently dipping below zero. December to March sees snow-clogged streets, icy pavements, and roofs laced with killer icicles. Ice skating, tobogganing, cross-country skiing, ice fishing and getting whipped in a sauna are this season's invigorating activities.

Avoid soggy March, when the snow thaws, bringing with it far too much slush for enjoyment. Autumn, when snow falls then melts, can be equally miserable.

See Climate Charts (p392) for more information.

COSTS & MONEY

Travellers may be surprised to find Tallinn, Rīga and Vilnius touting prices comparable to those in Scandinavia. Double-digit inflation has hit all three countries in recent years; the travel bargains of a decade ago are considerably fewer, though if you shop around you should be able to secure some good deals. Booking your accommodation online will reap discounts, while eating your main meal at lunchtime saves money. Taking public transport between major cities (perhaps hiring a car only for exploring rural areas) will also cut down your costs – petrol is relatively expensive in the Baltic countries (count on paying 15Kr/0.64Ls/3.10Lt, or just under €0.90, per litre in Estonia/Latvia/Lithuania). Discount cards in Rīga and Tallinn yield a bounty of money-savers for city-based visitors.

Accommodation in the Baltics is relatively expensive and the biggest cost for travellers, while dining in cities can be pricey (but cheap options certainly exist). Travel in the rural areas is definitely cheaper; however, in high summer popular coastal areas have room rates that may come close to those of the capitals.

At the bottom of the accommodation barrel in the capitals, you can scrape a night's sleep in a dorm for as little as 150Kr/7Ls/34Lt (€10) in a Tallinn/Rīga/Vilnius hostel. Double rooms at a midrange-standard hotel start at around 800Kr/40Ls/200Lt (€50 to €60), while top-end rates for a double room kick in at about 2000Kr/85Ls/450Lt (€125) but can easily double or triple at one of the capitals' fanciest addresses.

TRAVELLING RESPONSIBLY

Swelling tourist numbers, coupled with local property development and an ever-increasing drive towards commercialism, have accelerated the need to protect the region's fragile ecosystems, biological diversity and natural (and relatively unspoiled) treasures. Ways to avoid placing pressure on the environment include conserving water and electricity, not littering or burying your rubbish and taking care not to disturb wildlife. If you intend to camp or hike, seek permission to camp from the landowner or, in the case of national parks and protected nature reserves, pitch your tent only in designated areas. Forests – which carpet 44% each of Estonia and Latvia and 30% of Lithuania – are especially vulnerable. Do not light fires, discard cigarette butts or leave litter in these areas, and stick to assigned paths. Always observe the rules and recommendations set by park, nature reserve and forest authorities.

Erosion, fire and tourism pose an enormous threat to the unique sand spit and dunes on western Lithuania's Curonian Spit (p362) – a Unesco World Heritage natural treasure; a tableau at the foot of steps leading up to the Parnidis Dune shows just how much the mountain of sand has shrunk since 1960 (over 20m!). When walking on the spit don't blaze new trails across virgin sand or pick plant life that keeps the top sand in place; stick to the marked wooden walkways.

Cities pose a whole different set of responsible travel rules. The cobbled Old Towns of Rīga, Tallinn and Vilnius all star on Unesco's list of World

---

DON'T LEAVE HOME WITHOUT...

- Valid travel insurance (p395), ID card or passport, and visa (p399) if required
- Driving licence, car documents and car insurance (p412)
- Your sea legs
- Sunglasses, hat, mosquito repellent and binoculars (summer)
- Thermals and the thickest, warmest hat and coat you can find (winter)
- Umbrella – there's a fair chance you'll use it
- Your mobile phone – local prepaid SIM cards are cheap
- An indestructible pair of shoes or boots to combat cobblestones
- A taste for the unusual, from blood sausage to Black Balzām
- An eye mask – to help you sleep during the long nights of summer

---

DRINKING WATER

Official travel advisories detail the need to avoid tap water in the Baltic countries and drink only boiled or bottled water, but locals insist the tap water is safe to drink (if not altogether pleasant-tasting). Some visitors may wish to buy bottled water simply because they prefer the taste. If this is you, please consider the environment – buy locally sourced and bottled water, rather than imports, and look for recycling bins, where possible, to dispose of empty bottles. In Estonia (copying other Nordic countries) you can return recyclable bottles to vending machines at supermarkets for the return of a deposit (usually 0.50Kr or 1Kr) – it won't make you rich, but it will help the environment.

Heritage cultural treasures. Pay them the respect they deserve. In Tallinn, after years of Finnish 'vodka' and 'Gin Long Drink' tourism, people are fed up with rowdy drunken behaviour and blokes peeing on the streets. You'll get better treatment if you indulge in moderation. The same applies to the increasing number of British stag parties hitting the Baltic capitals for cheap weekends of binge-drinking and sex. Drink, by all means – but quietly and without offence to others.

Prostitution is rife in the capitals, particularly in Rīga (prostitution is legal in Estonia and Latvia, although pimping is illegal). Organised crime and trafficking in women and children for the purpose of commercial sexual exploitation are issues within the region. Incidents do occur where Western clients are drugged, robbed and left lying in the gutter – literally. For your personal safety and for the sake of the women at hand, please do not engage in this activity.

See also our GreenDex (p446) for Baltic attractions, hotels, restaurants, craft studios and tour operators recommended for their commitment to sustainability.

TRAVEL LITERATURE

The following page-turners have a rich Baltic flavour that evokes the region's people and places and its complex history. Some are entertaining or enlightening travelogues revealing snippets of life in another era, while others craftily use a Baltic city as a backdrop for their tale.

Among the Russians (Colin Thubron) Gloomy and resigned, yes, but that was precisely the mood when this Englishman motored everywhere he could in pre-*glasnost* USSR.

Between Each Breath (Adam Thorpe) In this witty recent novel, Tallinn and the Estonian islands are the setting for a successful Englishman's midlife crisis and infidelity, and the fallout from his actions.

Journey into Russia (Laurens van der Post) The three Baltic capitals are vividly painted in this travelogue through Soviet Russia in the 1960s.

The Last Girl and **Amber** (Stephan Collishaw) Collishaw won the heart of the literary world with these dark, haunting and highly emotive novels evoking two very different faces of modern-day Lithuania.

The Merry Baker of Riga (Boris Zemtzov) Hilarious and dry, this intuitive tale of an American entrepreneur setting up shop as a baker in Rīga in 1992 is a true story.

To the Baltic with Bob (Griff Rhys Jones) Sail with Griff (a well-known British comedian, writer and actor) and his mate Bob from London to St Petersburg via Ventspils, Rīga, Saaremaa, Vormsi, Paldiski ('a wreck') and Tallinn. There are some decent laughs and spot-on descriptions, but rather too much boating talk for our liking.

Venusburg (Anthony Powell) For a taste of 1930s Latvia and Estonia, try this amusing tale of a journalist hobnobbing with exiled Russian aristocrats, Baltic-German intellectuals and local patriots.

TOP 10

Gulf of Finland
•Tallinn
ESTONIA

FESTIVALS

The region enjoys an impressive festival calendar, embracing everything from religion and music to art, folklore, handicrafts, film and drama. For a fat-cat diary of events see the Events Calendar, p18.

1 Lake Sartai Horse Race (Dusetos, Lithuania), early February

2 Midsummer (regionwide), 23–24 June

3 Rīgas Ritmi (Rīga, Latvia), early July

4 Õlletoober (northern Saaremaa, Estonia), mid-July

5 Mākslas Festivāls (Cēsis, Latvia), mid-July to mid-August

6 Baltic Beach Party (Liepāja, Latvia), late July

7 Klaipėda Sea Festival (Klaipėda, Lithuania), late July

8 Viljandi Folk Music Festival (Viljandi, Estonia), late July

9 Visagino Country (Visaginas, Lithuania), mid-August

10 Black Nights Film Festival (Tallinn, Estonia), mid-November to early December

ACTIVITIES

There are countless ways (wild or mild) to get up close and personal with the Baltic countries' natural beauty. For more see p201.

1 Cycling the Curonian Spit, Lithuania (p362)

2 High-adrenalin high jinks in Sigulda, Latvia (p253)

3 Water sports at Surf Paradiis on the island of Hiiumaa, Estonia (p151)

4 Boating in Aukštaitija National Park, Lithuania (p326)

5 Canoeing across Latgale's silent Lakelands, Latvia (p269)

6 Cross-country skiing in Otepää, Estonia (p116)

7 Hot-air ballooning high over Vilnius, Lithuania (p309)

8 Cycling along the desolate Kurzeme coastline, Latvia (p233 to p243)

9 Bog-walking and canoeing in Soomaa National Park, Estonia (p138)

10 Berrying and mushrooming in Dzūkija National Park, Lithuania (p334)

UNUSUAL & SPECIALITY FOOD

If, like us, you consider food an essential part of travel, here are some ways (from dead-easy to summon-your-courage) to embrace the local cuisines, aside from getting the ubiquitous pork on your fork. For more information, see the Food & Drink sections of the Estonia (p57), Latvia (p185) and Lithuania (p289) chapters.

1 Try out Black Balzām in Rīga

2 Harden your arteries with Lithuanian *cepelinai*

3 Enjoy freshly picked summer berries, regionwide

4 Compare each country's version of beetroot soup, pancakes or rye bread

5 Order smoked pigs' ears as a tasty beer snack, regionwide

6 Tuck into Russian-style *pelmeni* (dumplings), regionwide

7 Sample Vana Tallinn liqueur in Old Tallinn, Estonia

8 Savour smoked fish in coastal or lakeside areas, regionwide

9 Go mushrooming in autumn, regionwide

10 Be brave and taste Estonian *verivorst* (blood sausages)

INTERNET RESOURCES

The internet is loaded with sites that can help you plan your Baltic sojourn. The following are excellent starting points; many more are listed throughout the book.

Baltic Times (www.baltictimes.com) English-language news from the region.

In Your Pocket (www.inyourpocket.com) Highly recommended insider guides to a clutch of Baltic cities (free PDF downloads are available from the website).

Latvia: The Land That Sings (www.latviatourism.lv) Latvian tourist board website.

Lonely Planet (www.lonelyplanet.com) Notes and posts on Baltic travel, plus the Thorn Tree bulletin board.

Official Lithuanian Travel Guide (www.travel.lt) Lithuanian tourist board website.

Rīga Tourism (www.rigatourism.lv) Official city site.

Tallinn Tourism (www.tourism.tallinn.ee) Official city site.

Vilnius Tourism (www.vilnius-tourism.lt) Official city site.

Welcome to Estonia (www.visitestonia.com) Estonian tourist board website.

Events Calendar

Summer festival madness peaks with midsummer celebrations on 24 June (p20); the annual Baltica Folklore Festival (p34) in July, which the three capitals take turns hosting; and the legendary Baltic song and dance festivals (p34). All three countries put on magical festivals at other times of the year, too, celebrating everything from religion to music, art to film and beer to ghosts.

Expect an extra-full calendar of events in Vilnius and Tallinn as they celebrate their status as a European City of Culture in 2009 and 2011, respectively. For more, check out www.culturelive09.lt (for Vilnius) and www.tallinn2011.ee.

FEBRUARY

LAKE SARTAI HORSE RACE 1st Saturday in February
Annual horse race (www.zarasai.lt) dating from 1865 and held on frozen Lake Sartai at Dusetos, near Utena, Lithuania. Attracts horse enthusiasts, musicians and folk artists from all over the region.

TARTU SKI MARATHON mid-February
Held outside Estonia's second city, Tartu, this 63km cross-country race (www.tartumaraton.ee) draws about 4000 competitors.

PALANGA SEALS FESTIVAL mid-February
This three-day festival (www.palangatic.lt) at Palanga, Lithuania, sees thousands of hardy swimmers frolic and squeal in the freezing waters of the Baltic Sea.

UŽGAVĖNĖS Shrove Tuesday (the day before Lent begins, ie 41 days before Easter)
Mardi Gras and the coming of Lent is celebrated in Lithuania with animal, bird and beast masquerades in towns and villages (the best is in Plateliai in Žemaitija National Park).

MARCH

ST CASIMIR'S DAY 4 March
Lithuania's patron saint's day, with the renowned Kaziukas folk arts and crafts fair held in Vilnius around this date.

HAAPSALU HORROR & FANTASY FILM FESTIVAL late March
Scare yourself silly with this showcase of altogether creepy and kooky films (www.hoff.ee) in Haapsalu, Estonia.

BIRŠTONAS JAZZ FESTIVAL late March in even-numbered years
Lithuania's top jazz festival (http://jazz.birstonas.lt/en) is this three-day event at the renowned spa town of Birštonas.

APRIL–MAY

ESTONIAN MUSIC DAYS mid-late April
In Tallinn, this weeklong event (www.helilooja.ee) features both classical Estonian performances and new, emerging works.

JAZZKAAR mid-late April
Jazz greats from around the world converge on Tallinn, Estonia, during this two-week festival (www.jazzkaar.ee); it also hosts smaller events in autumn and around Christmas.

KAUNAS INTERNATIONAL JAZZ FESTIVAL late April
The Balts clearly love their springtime jazz! This four-day Lithunanian festival (www.kaunasjazz.lt) has acts in Kaunas and Vilnius; also hosts smaller events in September and December.

TARTU STUDENT DAYS late April
Tartu's students let their hair down in this wild pagan celebration (www.studentdays.ee, in Estonian) marking the end of term and the dawn of spring in Estonia.

INTERNATIONAL BALTIC BALLET FESTIVAL late April-early May
Features stirring performances (www.ballet-festival.lv) by Latvian and international companies over three weeks in Rīga, Latvia.

NEW BALTIC DANCE early May
International contemporary dance festival (www.dance.lt) held in Vilnius, Lithuania.

INTERNATIONAL FESTIVAL
FOR PUPPET THEATRES　　　mid-late May
Viljandi's puppet theatre gathers a specialist crowd at this Estonian fest (www.viljandinukut eater.ee) subtitled 'Theatre in the Suitcase', with plenty of puppet shows to take in.

JUNE

PALANGA SUMMER
FESTIVAL　　　　　　　　　June-August
Opens on the first Saturday of June in Palanga, Lithuania, and closes with a massive street carnival, song festival and pop concert on the last Saturday in August. It's one long merry-go-round of music concerts (www.palangosvasara.lt) of all genres.

PAŽAISLIS MUSIC
FESTIVAL　　　　　　　　　June-August
Three-month classical music festival (www.paza islis.lt) held in the atmospheric courtyards and churches of Pažaislis Monastery, outside Kaunas, Lithuania.

SUMMER EXTRAVAGANZA
NERINGA　　　　　　　　　June-August
The summer season at Curonian Spit, Lithuania, ushers in this fiesta (www.muzikosfrontas.lt/en/projects) of concerts, craft days and cultural events.

VILNIUS FESTIVAL　　　　　　　　June
A month-long festival (www.vilniusfestivals.lt) involving classical music, jazz and folk-music concerts in Old Town courtyards and assorted venues (Vilnius, Lithuania).

TALLINN OLD TOWN DAYS　　　early June
Held in Tallinn's cinematic 14th-century quarters, Estonia, this weeklong fest (www.vanalinnapae vad.ee) features dancing, concerts, costumed performers and plenty of medieval merrymaking.

BALTICA INTERNATIONAL
FOLK FESTIVAL　　　　　　　　mid-July
A week of music, dance and displays focusing on Baltic and other folk traditions, shared between the capitals. In 2009 it will be in Rīga; in 2010, in Tallinn; in 2011, in Vilnius.

RĪGA OPERA FESTIVAL　　　early-mid June
The Latvian National Opera's showcase event (www .opera.lv) takes place over 10 days and includes performances by world-renowned talent in Rīga.

MIDSUMMER　　　　　　　　23-24 June
The region's biggest annual night out is a celebration of the Midsummer's Night, best experienced out in the countryside, where huge bonfires flare for all-night revellers. See the boxed text, p20.

INTERNATIONAL FOLK FESTIVAL　late June
The biggest event on Nida's calendar (Lithuania), featuring folk music (www.visitneringa.com) from around the world.

OPERETTA IN
KAUNAS CASTLE　　　late June-early July
Held for two weeks in Kaunas' scenic castle ruins in Lithuania (www.operetta.lt, in Lithuanian).

JULY

CHRISTOPHER　　　　　　　July-August
SUMMER FESTIVAL
Two-month music festival (www.kristupofestivaliai .lt) of various genres in Vilnius, Lithuania.

INTERNATIONAL FESTIVAL OF
EXPERIMENTAL ARCHAEOLOGY　early July
Three days of medieval fun and frolics (www.ker nave.org) – axe throwing, catapulting, mead making, medieval fights, music making – in Kernavė, Lithuania. Lots of fun despite the dull name.

PÄRNU INTERNATIONAL
FILM FESTIVAL　　　　　　　early July
Pärnu's big-name film fest (www.chaplin.ee) showcases documentary and anthropological films from all over the world (Estonia).

ÕLLESUMMER (BEER SUMMER)　early July
Extremely popular ale-guzzling, rock-music extravaganza (www.ollesummer.ee) in Tallinn, Estonia.

MUHU FUTURE MUSIC FESTIVAL　early July
Jazz, experimental music, progressive rock and much more, on the island of Muhu, Estonia (www .nordicsounds.ee).

CASTLE DAY　　　　　　　　early July
Lots of family-friendly medieval fanfare (www .saaremaamuuseum.ee) around Kuressaare's magnificent castle in Saaremaa, Estonia. Expect lots of food, music, and handicrafts.

RĪGAS RITMI　　　　　　　　early July
'Rīga's Rhythms' is the Latvian capital's international music festival (www.rigasritmi.lv).

MIDSUMMER MADNESS

In pagan times it was a night of magic and sorcery, when witches ran naked and wild, bewitching flowers and ferns, people and animals. In the agricultural calendar, it marked the end of the spring sowing and the start of the summer harvest. In Soviet times it became a political celebration: a torch of independence was lit in each capital and its flame used to light bonfires throughout the country.

Today Midsummer Day, aka summer solstice or St John's Day, falling on 24 June, is the Balts' biggest party of the year. On this night darkness barely falls – reason alone to celebrate in a part of the world with such short summers and such long, dark winters. In Estonia it is known as Jaanipäev, in Latvia Jāņi, Jāņu Diena or Līgo and in Lithuania Joninės or Rasos (the old pagan name).

Celebrations start on 23 June, particularly in Latvia, where the festival is generally met with the most gusto. Traditionally, people flock to the countryside to celebrate this special night amid lakes and pine forests. Special beers, cheeses and pies are prepared and wreaths strung together from grasses, while flowers and herbs are hung around the home to bring good luck and keep families safe from evil spirits. Men adorn themselves with crowns made from oak leaves, and women, with crowns of flowers.

Come Midsummer's Eve, bonfires are lit and the music and drinking begins. No one is allowed to sleep until the sun has sunk and risen again – anyone who does will be cursed with bad luck for the coming year. Traditional folk songs are sung, dances danced and those special beers, cheeses and pies eaten! To ensure good luck, you have to leap back and forth over the bonfire. In Lithuania, clearing a burning wheel of fire as it is rolled down the nearest hill brings you even better fortune. In Estonia, revellers swing on special double-sided Jaanipäev swings, strung from trees in forest clearings or in village squares.

Midsummer's night is a night for lovers. In Estonia the mythical Koit (dawn) and Hämarik (dusk) meet but once a year for an embrace lasting as long as the shortest night of the year. Throughout the Baltic region, lovers seek the mythical fern flower, which blooms only on this night. The dew coating flowers and ferns on midsummer's night is held to be a purifying force, a magical healer and a much sought-after cure for wrinkles! Bathe your face in it and you will instantly become more beautiful and more youthful. However, beware the witches of Jaanipäev/Jāņi/Joninės, who are known to use it for less enchanting means.

ŽEMAIČIŲ KALVARIJA CHURCH FESTIVAL   early July

Thousands of pilgrims from all over Lithuania flock to the Žemaičių Kalvarija (Samogitian Calvary) in Žemaitija National Park.

VÕRU FOLKLORE FESTIVAL   mid-July

It's full of dancers, singers and musicians decked out in colourful traditional dress (www.werro.ee /folkloor), celebrating the culture in Võru, Estonia.

HANSA DAYS FESTIVAL   mid-July

Crafts, markets, performances and more commemorate Tartu's Hanseatic past (Estonia; www .hansapaevad.ee).

ÕLLETOOBER   mid-July

Saaremaa's long history of home-brewed beers is celebrated at this beer festival (www.olletoo ber.ee), alongside live music and festivities in Northern Saaremaa, Estonia.

JOMA STREET FESTIVAL   mid-July

Jūrmala's annual city festival (www.jomasiela.lv) in Latvia. Don't miss the sand sculpture contest.

MĀKSLAS FESTIVĀLS   mid-July–mid-August

Cēsis in Latvia comes alive on the weekends with performances ranging from symphonies to storytelling, held at a variety of venues (www.cesu festivals.lv).

KLAIPĖDA SEA FESTIVAL   3rd weekend in July

Klaipėda, Lithuania, celebrates its rich nautical heritage with a flamboyant five-day festival (www .jurossvente.lt), which includes sailing excursions on the Baltic Sea.

NEW WAVE SONG FESTIVAL   late July

This soloist song contest (www.newwavestars .com, in Russian) in Jūrmala, Latvia, attracts competitors from around the world.

VILJANDI FOLK MUSIC
FESTIVAL   late July
Hugely popular four-day festival (www.folk.ee/festival) featuring bands from Estonia and abroad, and around 20,000 attendees (Viljandi, Estonia).

WINE FESTIVAL   late July
The village of Sabile, Latvia, is famed for its vineyard – the world's most northern open-air grape grower. The only chance to taste local wine is at this festival (www.sabile.lv).

HANDICRAFTS SHOW   late July
Kuldīga, Latvia, hosts an enormous handicrafts show (www.visit.kuldiga.lv) with hundreds of artisan booths lined up along Liepājas iela.

FESTIVAL OF ANCIENT MUSIC   late July
Music festival (www.bauska.lv) held at Bauska Castle and Rundāle Palace, Latvia.

BALTIC BEACH PARTY   late July
Fast becoming a must-stop of the Eastern Europe party circuit, featuring live music, discos, carnivals, fashion shows, sporting events and other hoopla on the beach at Liepāja, Latvia (www.balticbeachparty.lv).

OPERA MUSIC FESTIVAL   late July
Open-air festival (www.sigulda.lv) held in Sigulda's castle ruins, Latvia.

AUGUST

BIRŽAI TOWN FESTIVAL   August
Biržai, the heart of Lithuanian beer country, hosts a madcap fiesta where the town's breweries sell their wares on the street; expect plenty of beer swilling and general drunken behaviour.

LIEPĀJAS DZINTARS   early August
'Amber of Liepāja' rock festival (www.liepajasdzintars.lv, in Latvian), Latvia.

MARITIME FESTIVAL   early August
Kuressaare (Saaremaa, Estonia) celebrates its island status with lots of sea-related activities (www.merepaevad.ee).

VISAGINO COUNTRY   mid-August
Visaginas, Lithuania, rocks bizarrely with a bunch of cowboys – hats, boots and all – who groove on into town from across Europe for this two-day, international country-and-western music festival (www.visaginocountry.lt).

BIRGITTA FESTIVAL   mid-August
An excellent place to experience Estonia's vibrant singing tradition, with choral, opera and classical concerts (www.birgitta.ee), held at the atmospheric ruins of the Convent of St Birgitta, Tallinn, Estonia.

TARTUFF   mid-August
This weeklong open-air film festival (www.tartuff.ee) has its screenings in the atmospheric Town Hall square, Tartu, Estonia.

BALTĀ NAKTS   late August
This 'white night' event (www.baltanakts.lv), sponsored by the Contemporary Art Forum, mirrors Paris' night-long showcase of artists and culture around the city (Rīga, Latvia).

DAY OF THE
WHITE LADY FESTIVAL   late August
On Haapsalu's castle grounds, Estonia, this festival (www.haapsalu.ee) culminates in the appearance of a ghostly apparition.

DANCE FESTIVAL   late August
Contemporary dance festival (www.saal.ee) featuring troupes from all over Europe and the Baltics (Tallinn, Estonia).

SEPTEMBER

CAPITAL DAYS   early September
Three days of musical and cultural events (www.vilniusfestivals.lt) in theatres, concert halls and the streets of Vilnius, Lithuania.

ARSENĀLS INTERNATIONAL
FILM FORUM   mid-September
Film festival (www.arsenals.lv) showcasing over 100 movies relating to experiential and interactive themes in Rīga, Latvia.

MATSALU NATURE
FILM FESTIVAL   mid-late September
One of the more unusual film festivals (www.matsalufilm.ee) in the Baltics (Lihula, near Matsalu National Park, Estonia), this one features nature films submitted by a variety of filmmakers.

SIRENS   mid-September–mid-October
International theatre festival (www.sirenos.lt) in Vilnius, Lithuania.

MUSHROOM FESTIVAL   late September
More mushrooms than you'll ever want to eat at Varėna, outside the Dzūkija National Park, Lithuania (www.varena.lt/en/events).

OCTOBER

FUTURE SHORTS
mid-late October

Kino Rīga hosts several film festivals, including the international Future Shorts (www.futureshorts.lv), celebrating short films (Rīga, Latvia).

ARĒNA NEW MUSIC FESTIVAL
mid-October–early November

Contemporary music festival (www.arenafest.lv) showcasing various genres held at venues throughout Rīga, Latvia.

GAIDA
late October

This festival showcases new music from Central and Eastern Europe in Vilnius, Lithuania (www.vilniusfestivals.lt).

NOVEMBER–DECEMBER

BLACK NIGHTS FILM FESTIVAL
mid-November–mid-December

Estonia's biggest film festival (www.poff.ee) showcases films and animations from all over the world (held in Tallin).

CHRISTMAS MARKETS
December

Festive decorations, arts and crafts, traditional foods and entertainment brighten the dark days in the leadup to Christmas, in the capitals' Old Towns (and many other towns around the region).

NEW YEAR'S EVE
31 December

Fireworks and revelry on the main squares of Tallinn, Rīga, Vilnius in the countdown to midnight.

Itineraries
CLASSIC ROUTES

BEST OF THE BALTIC
Two Weeks/Vilnius to Tallinn

Embark on the grandest of Baltic tours in the Lithuanian capital, **Vilnius** (p292). Take a day trip to castle-clad **Trakai** (p322) and/or the Soviet sculpture park at **Druskininkai** (p332), then push west to **Klaipėda** (p353) and the Unesco-protected **Curonian Spit** (p362). Next, hit Rīga: take the 3½-hour speed route via **Šiauliai** (p347) and the **Hill of Crosses** (p348), or the slow route of a few days along the tranquil Latvian coast via chilled-out **Pāvilosta** (p243), **Cape Kolka** (p233) and **Jūrmala** (p226). In **Rīga** (p186), revel in Europe's best Art Nouveau architecture, then delve into **Sigulda** (p253) and the Gauja Valley en route to university-driven **Tartu** (p106) and swampy **Soomaa National Park** (p138). Those with bags of time could detour to the lazy old spa town of **Pärnu** (p127) or the fabulous islands of **Saaremaa** (p153) and **Hiiumaa** (p146).

The final leg is north to the Estonian capital, **Tallinn** (p59), where old-town medieval splendour jockeys for pride of place with hip wine bars and a dizzying choice of cuisine. From Tallinn, a ferry trip across the Gulf of Finland to **Helsinki** (p167) is too easy to be ignored.

Vilnius to Tallinn direct is only 588km, but throw in the slow route and detours cooked up by this itinerary to cover the very best of the Baltic region and you'll easily clock up 1400km. The trip – minus deviations – can be done in a whirlwind fortnight, but definitely merits as much time as you can give it.

ROADS LESS TRAVELLED

GO GREEN   Three Weeks/Southeastern Latvia to northern Estonia

The starting point is southeastern Latvia. Here, among Soviet-era stains on the landscape, are the hushed forests and lakeside villages of the ultrabucolic **Latgale Lakelands** (p269). From Latgale, trek south for fishing, boating and berrying in Lithuania's paradise, **Aukštaitija National Park** (p326).

At the opposite end of the country, the combination of disused nuclear missile silos and sunsets over lake and pine woodlands bewitch visitors to **Žemaitija National Park** (p377). Witness the vulnerability of nature around the nearby 'Sahara of Lithuania', the unforgettable **Curonian Spit** (p362), where elk mingle with wild boar and Lithuania's largest colony of cormorants and grey herons. From Nida sail into the desolate **Nemunas Delta** (p370) to witness birdlife at the Ventės Ragas Ornithological Station. Zip up the Latvian coast to experience the rugged beaches and enchanting desolation of **Cape Kolka** (p233), then tour east to explore the castle-dotted **Gauja National Park** (p253), where walking, biking, hiking and canoeing – and the rare black stork – thrill outdoor-lovers.

Head northeast to **Otepää** (p116) for skiing or summer swimming, and midsummer celebrations around Estonia's most sacred lake. Continue via pretty **Viljandi** to the swampy, wildlife-packed **Soomaa National Park** (p138), and explore myriad forested waterways by traditional *haabjas* (canoe). West of here, **Matsalu National Park** (p146) is the Baltic's best bird-watching terrain. From here the solitude of the Estonian islands beckons, or you can steer north, bypassing Tallinn, to unwind in **Lahemaa National Park** (p94), an alluring bayside haven of nature trails, coastlines, and old-fashioned seafaring villages.

Three weeks gives you time for battery-recharging alongside glimpses of the extraordinary Baltic flora, fauna and landscapes. A breath of fresh air after the tourist madness of the three capitals' Old Towns, this green itinerary covering some 1300km guarantees a foolproof getaway from the crowds.

PAINT THE TOWN RED
Three Weeks/Tallinn to Daugavpils

Tracking the Baltic's Soviet past is an eclectic trip. First, brush up on history in Tallinn (p59) at the Museum of Occupation & Fight for Freedom, followed by coffee at the timewarp Narva Kohvik. Speed east next, through the USSR's first national park, **Lahemaa National Park** (p94), to **Sillamäe** (p102), an intriguing seaside museum of Stalinist architecture, and downbeat border town **Narva** (p103), with its moody castle and majority Russian population.

Head south to Latvia and make a beeline for **Sigulda** (p253), where you can rip down the artificial bobsled track built for the Soviet team before touring a top-secret Soviet bunker at nearby **Ligatne** (p259). In **Rīga** (p186) meet die-hard reds in Victory Park, gawp at Stalin's birthday cake, fire Kalashnikovs, dine retro-Soviet style, and learn about Soviet occupation in the Museum of Occupation. Next, play 'I spy' at the huge radio telescope in **Irbene** (p242), 24km north of Ventspils, designed to eavesdrop on Western satellite communications. Stroll around **Liepāja** (p243), taking in Karosta and its Soviet prison, where diehards can kip for the night.

In Lithuania, a tour of the underground Soviet missile base at **Žemaitija National Park** (p377) is terrifying. Sleep in the old Soviet barracks, then push east past the huge former USSR military base outside **Šiauliai** (p347) to **Vilnius** (p292), with its disturbing Museum of Genocide Victims and poignant reminders of bloody 1991. A sidetrip south to **Grūtas Park** (p336), aka Stalin World, east of Druskininkai, is a must. Afterwards, bear north to bizarre **Visaginas** (p329), where you can heed the dangers of a Soviet-designed nuclear power plant. Then it's north of the border to Latvia's grey and gritty **Daugavpils** (p266) with its 'fortress' where Soviet troops were stationed. If the theme of this itinerary has you itching for more, pop across the border to Belarus (prearranged visas essential), where the Soviet era is alive and well.

This trip takes you the length and breadth of the region, west to east and back again. Coastal security bases and the more industrial, Russian-influenced east provide relics of an era most locals would rather forget. You'll travel close to 2500km, with plenty of greenery en route for when the concrete gets too much.

TAILORED TRIPS

THE AMBER ROAD

Amber has been traded since before the birth of Jesus, and there's nowhere finer to feel its subtle magic than in the Russian-controlled **Kaliningrad Region** (p383), source of almost all Baltic amber. Stunning amber-studded jewellery and the world's second-largest hunk of amber add a sparkle to the Kaliningrad Amber Museum, while the amber cabin aboard the *Vityaz* at the World Ocean Museum is an interesting port of call. A tour of the industrial **Yantarny Amber Mine** (p384) from the capital is a must for serious amber-admirers.

The region's finest amber gallery in **Nida** (p365), Lithuania, is a hop, skip and a jump – across sand dunes on the **Curonian Spit** (p362) – from the Russian province. Amber treasure was found in **Juodkrantė** (p363) in the 1850s but today you'll find only specks washed up on the shore after fierce storms; professional amber-fishers frequent **Karklė** (p359) and **Šventoji** (p377) beaches. **Palanga** (p372) sports a palatial amber museum and an innovative amber-processing gallery, while wacky **Nida** (p376), across the border in Latvia, presents amber-fishing from a homespun perspective.

Latvia's **Liepāja** (p243) boasts the largest piece of amber art in the world (an enormous dangling tapestry) and an amber sundial. There are fine amber displays inside the Livonian Order castle in **Ventspils** (p239), the northern end of the Amber Road. More on these sights can be found at www.balticamberroad.net.

Even if you don't make it out to the Baltic coast, you'll be able to souvenir-shop for 'Baltic gold' in the stores of Vilnius, Rīga and Tallinn.

WORLD HERITAGE SITES

Estonia, Latvia and Lithuania safeguard a handful of Unesco-protected world treasures (http://whc.unesco.org), kicking off with each capital's extraordinary Old Town, inscribed on the World Heritage list since at least 1997. **Rīga** (p186) is a mind-blowing plethora of medieval, neoclassical and Art Nouveau buildings dating from the 13th to 19th centuries; its Art Nouveau collection is Europe's best. Church-studded **Vilnius** (p292) is medieval, Gothic, Renaissance and classical, and has Europe's biggest baroque Old Town to boot. And nowhere better reflects the fabric of a medieval northern European trading city than **Tallinn** (p59).

The archaeological site of **Kernavė** (p325) near the Lithuanian capital is another world gem, as is the extraordinary slither of sand linking Lithuania with Kaliningrad, the **Curonian Spit** (p362), sculpted over millennia by the Baltic Sea's winds and waves.

The region's intangible treasures are safeguarded by Unesco with a 'Masterpiece of the Oral and Intangible Heritage of Humanity' stamp: cross-crafting and its symbolism in Lithuania; the cultural and natural heritage on Estonia's tiny **Kihnu Island** (p134); and the magnificent Baltic song and dance festivals.

Snapshots

CURRENT EVENTS

Two issues dominate current affairs in the Baltic these days. The first is the bursting of the economic bubble; the second is the ever-fraught relationships with Russia. Geography and history conspire to ensure that young, newly cashed-up and strongly westward-focused Estonia, Latvia and Lithuania are always looking over their shoulders to check on the behaviour of their prone-to-bullying eastern neighbour. Events in Georgia in 2008 spooked the governments of all three nations, which immediately went on the anti-Russian offensive.

Latvia and Estonia are home to large populations of Russian speakers, and deep down is a fear that Moscow could agitate separatist feeling within those Russian minorities in the same way it has done in the breakaway Georgian enclaves of South Ossetia and Abkhazia, generating a pretext to send tanks in to protect what it would claim were in effect 'Russian citizens'. But do they need to fear the worst? The ghosts of history certainly linger, but as Estonia, Latvia and Lithuania are now paid-up members of NATO and the EU since 2004, could this sort of thing really happen on Baltic soil without invoking a huge reaction from the West? Does this mistrust, and the associated inflammatory commentary from parts of the government and media, only serve to hinder what are, at best, strained relationships with the world's largest country? And what does it do to the often-fragile relationships between ethnic groups within Estonia and Latvia's own borders?

Russia makes no bones about its opposition to NATO's eastward expansion and its increasing influence on old USSR territory. Wrangles over shared borders, WWII legacies, language laws and the citizenship rights of the region's sizable Russian-speaking community further exacerbate relations between the Baltic countries and Russia. In mid-2008 Lithuania approved a law banning the public display of Soviet symbols. Never mind that the law also covered the symbols and icons of Nazi Germany – Russia took offence at the law anyway. Moscow was similarly offended when Estonia relocated a Soviet war memorial from the centre of Tallinn in 2007 – that incident culminated in violence and the death of a protester.

The news on the economic front is not too cheery, although for a time this was very much a good-news story. After the crisis brought on by Russia's financial collapse in 1998, the Baltic countries implemented important economic reforms and liberalisation, which, coupled with their fairly low-wage and skilled labour force, attracted large amounts of foreign investment and economic growth. Between 2000 and 2007, the so-called 'Baltic Tiger' economies had the highest growth rates in Europe (in 2006, Estonia and Latvia had GDP growth rates of over 11%; Lithuania lagged a little at 7.5%). Accompanying these figures were high inflation rates, meaning that the three countries missed their targets for adopting the euro as national currency (the euro adoption is now looking more likely between 2010 and 2013). The brakes have come on, however, with the worldwide economic turmoil of 2008. If the pessimists are right, dark times lie ahead as the Baltic economies slow sharply; optimists, however, feel that the bursting of the bubble might simply mean the countries are en route to a more sustainable pace of development. Time will tell.

PRESIDENTIAL LINE-UP

Estonia: Toomas Hendrik Ilves (www.president.ee); elected in 2006 for five years.

Latvia: Valdis Zatlers (www.president.lv); elected in 2007 for four years.

Lithuania: Valdas Adamakus (www.president.lt); elected in 2004 for five years.

All three countries are parliamentary democracies run by a parliament (Estonia: *Riigikogu;* Latvia: *Saeima;* Lithuania: *Seimas*) and a president, both elected by universal suffrage for a four- or five-year term.

BALTIC LEXICON

Balkans Absolutely nothing whatsoever to do with the Baltic, beyond the fact that a shocking number of people confuse the two. (If you're one of them, the Balkan countries are in southeastern Europe.)

Baltic countries Estonia, Latvia and Lithuania.

Baltic states A generic term used to refer to the Soviet Baltic-Sea Republics of Estonia, Latvia and Lithuania. Since independence, this has become a misnomer of convenience, but it is considered to be outdated and politically incorrect by some – a better term is Baltic countries.

Baltic region The entire Baltic Sea catchment area, of which Estonia, Latvia and Lithuania make up approximately 11%. Finland, Sweden, Denmark, Germany, Poland and the Kaliningrad Region (Russia) are all in the Baltic region – but are not Baltic countries.

Balts A derivative of Mare Baliticum, the Latin for 'Baltic Sea' (coined by the German chronicler Adamus Bremen in the 11th century). Its technical definition is people of Indo-European ethnolinguistic groups (Latvians and Lithuanians) who settled in the southeastern Baltic Sea area from 2000 BC, but it may also be used to cover people from any of the Baltic countries. (Technically Estonians are not Balts, as they are derived from Finno-Ugric tribes.)

Nordic countries Traditionally understood to be Scandinavia and Finland, but seen by many as also including Estonia (Estonia has closer historical and cultural ties to Finland than to Latvia and Lithuania), as expressed in a 1999 speech by former foreign minister and current president Toomas Hendrik Ilves, entitled 'Estonia as a Nordic Country'.

Post-Soviet countries Assumed to be an indisputable tag, yet one that the Lithuanian parliament clearly rejected in early 1999 when it urged NATO not to describe Lithuania as 'former Soviet' or 'post-Soviet'. This, the parliament argued, implied that the Baltic legally belonged to Moscow in the Soviet era, as opposed to being 'illegally occupied'.

HISTORY

Hard Landing – the Fairy Tale of the Rise & Fall of the Estonian Economy (Claudio Zucchelli and Dag Kirsebom; www.hardlanding.ee) gives a fascinating insight into how and why this 'Baltic Tiger' economy boomed, then went bust, and what lies in store.

Until the early 20th century the ethnic identities of Estonia, Latvia and Lithuania were denied or suppressed. They emerged from the turmoil of WWI and the Russian Revolution as independent countries and enjoyed two decades of statehood until WWII, when all three fell under Soviet influence. Occupation by Nazi Germany in 1941 was followed by Soviet reconquest and the region was forcibly merged with the USSR. In 1991 Estonia, Latvia and Lithuania again won independence.

Ethnically speaking, Latvians and Lithuanians are closely related. The Estonians have different origins, with closer linguistic links to Finland than to their immediate Baltic neighbours.

However, in terms of the history of the past 800 years, Latvia and Estonia have more in common with each other than with Lithuania. The latter was once a powerful state in its own right – at its peak in the 14th to 16th centuries – but Latvia and Estonia were entirely subject to foreign rule from the 13th to the early 20th century. By the late 18th century the entire region had fallen under Russian rule. Until emancipation in the 19th century, most of its native people had been serfs for centuries.

From Settlers to Serfs

UNEMPLOYMENT

Latest official figures from 2007 list unemployment at the following levels:

Estonia: 4.7%

Latvia: 5.7%

Lithuania: 4.3%

EU: 6.8%

Human habitation in the region goes back to at least 9000 BC in the south and 7500 BC in the north, with the forebears of the present inhabitants – Finno-Ugric hunters from the east (the forebears of present-day Finns and Estonians) and the Balts from the southeast (ancestors of Latvians and Lithuanians) – settling between 3000 and 2000 BC. The region rapidly became known as a rich source of amber, and local tribes traded the substance with German tribes, the Roman Empire and, later, Vikings and Russians.

The region was dragged into written history by the expansionist *Urge to the East* of Germanic princes, colonists, traders, missionaries and crusading knights. In 1201 the Bishop of Rīga, Albert von Buxhoevden, built the region's first Germanic fort and established the Knights of the Sword, an order of crusading knights whose white cloaks were emblazoned with blood-red swords and crosses. Their mission? To convert the region by conquest. And indeed, within a quarter of a century these knights had subjugated and converted all of Estonia and most of Latvia, baring some regions in the west, which they would snatch in 1290. Cēsis became their castle-clad base. In 1237 they became a branch of the Prussian-based crusaders the Teutonic Order, and renamed themselves the Livonian Order.

By 1346 Germanic rulers controlled the Baltic seaboard from west of Danzig (modern-day Gdansk in Poland) to Narva in northeastern Estonia. They divided the region into fiefdoms headed by Teutonics, Livonians or their vassals. In trade-rich towns like Rīga, Dorpat (Tartu), Pernau (Pärnu), Windau (Ventspils) and Wenden (Cēsis), a wealthy German nobility emerged to enjoy the good life while natives were reduced to feudal serfdom. This remained the case until the 20th century.

The Germanic invaders made repeated attacks on Lithuania during the 14th century but were restricted to a thin coastal strip around Memel (Klaipėda), allowing this Baltic country to emerge as a powerful state in the 14th to 16th centuries. But its subsequent union with Poland saw Lithuanians play second fiddle to the Polish, with Lithuania's gentry adopting Polish culture and language and its peasants becoming serfs.

Swedish, Polish & Russian Rule

As German control in Latvia and Estonia wavered in the mid-16th century, other powers cast interested eyes over the region. Ivan the Terrible of Muscovy seemed to ravage every town in mainland Estonia and eastern Latvia during the 25-year Livonian War and, after the war's end, the Baltic lands were fought over by Protestant Sweden and Catholic Poland-Lithuania, with Sweden the eventual victor. Seventeenth-century Swedish rule is regarded as an enlightened episode in Estonia and Latvia's long histories of foreign oppression: Swedish kings Gustaf II Adolf and Carl (Charles) XI raised Estonian and Latvian peasants from serfdom and introduced universal elementary education.

In the long term, however, Russia emerged as the victor. Peter the Great destroyed Sweden as a regional power during the Great Northern War (1700–21) and established Russian rule once and for all in Estonia and much of Latvia. A few decades later the Partitions of Poland gave Lithuania to Russia. The Baltic region's fate was sealed.

Russian rule brought privileges for the Baltic-German ruling class in Estonia and Latvia but greater exploitation for the peasants. In 1811 and 1819 respectively, Estonian and Latvian peasants were emancipated (Lithuanians, involved in the Polish rebellion against Russian rule during 1830–31, weren't freed until 1860), giving the native Baltic peoples the opportunity to slowly but surely crawl out from under the doormat of history to express their own cultures and senses of nationality; to teach, learn and publish in their own languages; to hold their own song festivals and stage their own plays. The policy of Russification pursued by Russian rulers only strengthened the determination of nationalist Balts.

Brief Independence

The 1917 Russian Revolution overthrew the tsar, allowing Estonia, Latvia and Lithuania to declare independence; their position as independent countries was officially recognised by Soviet Russia in 1920.

But all three countries – caught between the ascendant Soviet Union and the openly expansionist Nazi Germany, which glorified the historic *Urge to*

Using original German and Soviet wartime newsreels, International Historic Films has produced an enthralling DVD depicting the true horror of WWII for the occupied Baltic nations. Buy *The Baltic Tragedy* online at www .ihffilm.com/22023.html.

the East – lapsed from democracy into authoritarianism in the 1930s, ruled by regimes that feared the Soviet Union more than the Third Reich.

WWII & Soviet Rule

On 23 August 1939 Nazi Germany and the USSR signed the Molotov-Ribbentrop Pact, secretly dividing Eastern Europe into Soviet and German spheres of influence. The fate of the Baltic was sealed, putting Estonia, Latvia and, soon after, Lithuania under Soviet control. Baltic Germans who hadn't already left for Germany departed, and by August 1940 the three countries were USSR republics. On 14 June 1941 mass deportations to Siberia began.

Hitler's invasion of the USSR and the subsequent Nazi occupation of the Baltic region between 1941 and 1944 created one of the most sensitive periods in Baltic history, as many Balts collaborated with the Nazis in their slaughter of Jews and other local people. Nearly all of Lithuania's Jewish population were killed.

Between 65,000 and 120,000 Latvians, about 70,000 Estonians and 80,000 Lithuanians succeeded in escaping to the West in 1944–5 to avoid the Red Army's reconquest of the Baltic. Thousands more – known as 'forest brothers' – took to the woods rather than live under Soviet rule.

The postwar Soviet era saw the collectivisation of agriculture, the repression of religion and the death or deportation of thousands of Estonians, Latvians and Lithuanians. There was also a huge influx of migrant workers from Russia, Belarus and Ukraine, causing many Balts to fear that they'd become minorities in their own countries.

The Singing Revolution

Soviet leader Mikhail Gorbachev's encouragement of glasnost and perestroika in the late 1980s prompted the Baltic countries' pent-up dreams of independence to spill into the open. Popular fronts, formed in each republic to press for democratic reform, won huge followings, while rallies in 1988 saw thousands of Balts gather in the capitals to voice their longing for freedom by singing previously banned national songs. Several big rallies on environmental and national issues were held in Latvia, with 45,000 people joining hands along the coast in one antipollution protest; an estimated 300,000 Estonians – about 30% of the population – attended one song gathering in Tallinn. On 23 August 1989 – the 50th anniversary of the Molotov-Ribbentrop Pact – two million people formed a human chain stretching from Tallinn to Vilnius, demanding secession from the Soviet Union.

Moscow granted the Baltic republics economic autonomy in November 1989 and a month later the Lithuanian Communist Party left the Communist Party of the Soviet Union – a landmark act in the break-up of the USSR. Lithuania became the first Soviet republic to legalise noncommunist parties and to declare its independence. Events turned bloody in Rīga and Vilnius in January 1991, but this didn't deter all three states voting overwhelmingly in favour of secession from the USSR in referenda a month later. Although there was little enthusiasm in the West for the Baltic independence movements, the 19 August 1991 coup attempt against Gorbachev in Moscow changed everything: on 6 September 1991 the West and the USSR recognised Estonian, Latvian and Lithuanian independence.

A couple of weeks later, Estonia, Latvia and Lithuania joined the UN, the first step to consolidate their new-found nationhood. In 1992 they competed independently in the Olympic Games for the first time since before WWII, and Estonia held its first elections under its own system (followed later that year by Lithuania, and by Latvia in June 1993). The pope visited all three

Altogether, Lithuania lost around 475,000 people during WWII. Latvia lost 450,000 and Estonia, 200,000.

The Singing Revolution (1992) by Clare Thomson tracks Estonia, Latvia and Lithuania's path towards independence through an account of the author's travels in the region in 1989 and 1990.

countries in September 1993 but, such landmarks apart, the Baltic countries dropped out of the world's headlines.

Postindependence

Zealous one-upmanship between Estonia, Latvia and Lithuania marked the immediate postindependence years as the three countries suddenly found themselves vying for the same foreign investment and aid. Each established its own currency, army and police force, and started the painful process of switching from a centralised economy to the free market. Runaway inflation topping 1000%, soaring unemployment, plummeting purchasing power, the collapse of several banks (wiping out life savings) and the end to the rudimentary-but-universal Soviet social-welfare system provided a harsh introduction to the 'joys' of consumer capitalism.

In politics a succession of coalition governments came and went, with no single party managing to form a mandate strong enough to gain an overall parliamentary majority.

Free-trade agreements with the EU were established in 1995, a watershed for the region; nervous of Russian sabre-rattling and hungry for economic stability, the Baltic countries also changed tack around this time, joining forces to present a united front to the world. In 1998 the USA signed the US-Baltic Charter of Partnership, pledging its support for Baltic integration into Western institutions, including NATO (which all three joined in 2004). The same year the three Baltic presidents publicly condemned Russia's political and economic pressure on Latvia, warning it was posing a danger to the region's future unity and integration with Europe.

In October 1999, with the dismantling of the Skrunda radar site in Latvia, the last Russian military personnel left Baltic soil.

Citizenship, abolishing the death penalty, prosecuting Nazi and Soviet criminals and resolving border disputes with Russia were among the thorny issues the three countries were forced to tackle before starting accession talks with the EU in 1998 (Estonia) and 1999 (Latvia and Lithuania). For Latvia and Estonia, the question of how to treat its substantial Russian-speaking minority was (and still is) particularly contentious. All three countries were invited to join the EU in 2002 and became fully fledged members in 2004. The move was clearly not liked by Russian nationalists, who saw it as a huge step in the wrong direction – ie away from Moscow.

PEOPLE
Lifestyle

Postindependent Estonia, Latvia and Lithuania are young societies in every sense of the word. Large chunks of all three economies are in the hands of energetic young dynamos with mobile phones and fast, flash cars. For them, the world – certainly Europe – is their oyster. They speak at least a couple of languages, are comfortable mixing with most nationalities and are as at home on holiday in Spain or Greece as they are in their own country. Flitting off to the seashore to kitesurf at the first sign of good wind, regularly jetting abroad for work and indulging in the odd weekend shopping spree in London or Barcelona is what life is all about for this sizable group of city dwellers in their mid-30s.

But a fair few of the older generation look back with nostalgia to the Soviet era, when a certain equality of poverty prevailed. And indeed, stalling the ever-widening gap between rich and poor by 2015 is one of the Millennium Development Goals set for all three countries by the UN. Unless social policies are changed, life will only become harder for many people, including those living in rural areas (where the GDP per capita is generally half that

Walking Since Daybreak: A Story of Eastern Europe, World War II and the Heart of our Century (1998) is a family history of an acclaimed historian, Latvian-born Modris Eksteins, who spent most of his childhood in displaced-persons camps.

The Baltic Revolution (1994) by Anatol Lieven is a classic. Half Irish, half Baltic-German, Lieven was the Baltic correspondent for the London *Times* in the early 1990s and is a mine of information.

in the capitals), families with several children or a handicapped child, and single-parent families.

In all three countries, the birth rate is steadily declining and the mortality rate is rising. Male life expectancy in particular is notably lower than in the rest of Europe; 2005 statistics revealed that, on average, Baltic men only live until the age of 66, compared to 75 in the EU. Traffic accidents, alcoholism, violence and suicide remain higher-than-average forms of death.

Marriage and divorce trends reflect those in the rest of Europe: fewer people are marrying, more couples are having children out of wedlock and more are divorcing (around 60% of marriages end in divorce). Balts still marry quite young – when they are around 25 (women) or 27 (men), and the average age for women having their first baby in all three countries is 25.

The population is ageing and it's shrinking. The birth rate per 1000 inhabitants in Estonia/Latvia/Lithuania is 10.3/9.6/9.

Multiculturalism

Ethnic identity is a sticky subject in the Baltic countries. Large-scale immigration of workers from Russia and other Soviet republics during the Soviet period dramatically changed the population make-up of Latvia and Estonia; ethnic Estonians and Latvians are barely in the majority (67.9% and 57.7% respectively), Latvians are a minority in Latvia's largest cities, and Russians easily swamp Estonians in industrial Narva (northeastern Estonia), where they account for 95% of the population.

The inability of some native Russian-speakers to speak Latvian or Estonian has only added fuel to the fire. Citizenship requirements in both countries are equally controversial, and the Russian government regularly voices its concerns over the status of the Russian minority in Latvia and Estonia, making indigenous locals nervous (especially in light of the 2008 Russia–Georgia skirmishes in South Ossetia, where Russian President Dmitry Medvedev defended Russia's involvement,

The long, cold, hard Baltic winter casts a definite dampener over some Balts, who appear unnervingly glum, pessimistic and brusque during this dark time of year.

TIPS ON MEETING LOCALS

Don't lump Estonians, Latvians and Lithuanians into the one melting pot. They share common traits, but first and foremost they are three separate nationalities.

The stereotypical Estonian is reserved, efficient, polite and short on praise, similar to the stereotypically taciturn Finns. Lithuanians are typically more gregarious, welcoming and emotional. Dubbed the 'Italians' of the region, they have a greater confidence in their national identity, being the only Baltic country to show its toppled Lenin to the world rather than keeping it under wraps. Latvians in general fall somewhere in between these two extremes, being least at ease with foreigners (partly because of ethnic tensions between Latvians and Russians) and probably the most entrepreneurial.

Baltic people do not greet each other with a hug or kiss. Most people are quite formal, and it takes a while to get onto first-name terms. Men always shake each other's hands and some women shake hands, too. Don't mistake lack of smiles or a reserved attitude for indifference or hostility (Estonians are especially poker-faced – one national saying is 'May your face be as ice').

Flowers are a universal gift, but only give odd-numbered bouquets, as even-numbered offerings (including a dozen red roses!) are for mournful occasions. If you are invited to a private home, take flowers or a bottle of wine – but never money – as a gift for your host. Take your shoes off when you enter and do not shake hands across the threshold. Do not whistle inside, either. Both actions bring bad luck and will be severely frowned upon.

Muttering just a few words in the local language will raise instant smiles. In Latvia and Lithuania, speaking Russian as a foreigner is generally (but not always) acceptable. In Estonia, you should try every other language you know first – be it English, German or Finnish – as speaking Russian can be met with a hostile response, or no response at all.

PAGANISM

Czech bishop Albert Waitiekus, the first Christian missionary to venture into the region, came here in the 10th century. Unfortunately for him, he wandered into a forest dedicated to pagan gods and was killed – leaving paganism to run rife in the region for another two centuries.

To pagan Latvians and Lithuanians the sky was a mountain and many of the leading gods lived on it, among humans: Dievs the sky god, Saule the sun goddess, Perkūnas (Pērkons in Latvia) the thunder god, who was particularly revered, and Mēness the moon god. There was also an earth-mother figure called Žemyna in Lithuania and Zemes māte in Latvia. In Latvia the Christian Virgin Mary has many of the attributes of Žemyna, and the two figures seem to be combined in the mythological figure of Māra. Also important were Laima the goddess of fate, Medeinė (Meža māte in Latvia) the forest goddess, and Velnias (Velns in Latvia) the guardian of wizards and sages, who was transformed into the devil in the Christian scheme of things. Many lesser deities presided over natural phenomena and objects, or human activities.

Today the pagan gods are enjoying a marked revival among those known as the Dievturība (literally 'Holding the Gods') in Latvia, and among the Romuva in Lithuania. The Romuva is particularly strong, perhaps because Lithuania was the last European stronghold of paganism until 1385, and the organization has congregations in Vilnius, Kaunas and in Lithuanian communities in Canada and the USA. It is named after an ancient temple site near Chernahovsk (in today's Kaliningrad Region) that attracted Lithuanian, Latvian and Prussian worshippers alike prior to Christianity's arrival in the Baltic. Founded as an organised pagan revival movement, it was banned under the Soviet regime but revived in the late 1980s. Read more at www.romuva.lt.

stating that he would 'protect the life and dignity of Russian citizens wherever they are').

Other ethnic groups present in smaller numbers include Poles, Jews, Roma, Tatars and Germans (in Lithuania), as well as nationals of the former Soviet Union.

Religion

Prior to the arrival of Christianity, all three countries clung firmly to their nature-worshipping pagan ways (see above). Today the biggest celebrations in the region take place on Midsummer Day and hark back to these pagan roots (see p20).

Lithuania was the last pagan country in Europe, not baptised into Roman Catholicism until 1387. Today it is the most religious of the three Baltic countries; Latvia and Estonia share Lutheranism as the predominant religion, though there's little sense of either country being particularly religious – only 4% and 7% of residents attend church services once a week in Estonia and Latvia, respectively (the figure is around 16% for Lithuania). In Estonia's 2000 census, only 31.8% of the population claimed any religious affiliation (of those about 180,000 are Lutheran and 170,000 Russian Orthodox), in contrast with close to 80% of the population claiming Roman Catholicism as their religion in Lithuania's census of 2001.

FOLK CULTURE

The Balts' treasure-trove of oral folklore – inspired by the seasonal cycle, farming and the land, family life, love and myths – is considered the largest collection in the world. Latvia alone boasts more than 1.5 million *dainas* (short poetic songs somewhat like the Japanese haiku), vast collections of which were written down in the 19th century by people like Krisjānis Barons in Latvia and Jakob Hurt in Estonia. The first folkloric musical score was published in Lithuania, now guardian of some 600,000 folk songs and stories, as early as 1634.

Folk rhymes and music are very much living traditions, with numerous societies and groups devoted to them. Particularly unusual are chants of northeastern Lithuania, known as *sutartinės*, and of the Setumaa region in southeast Estonia. More immediately impressive are the national song and dance festivals, evidence of the age-old power of song in Baltic culture – if your visit coincides with a festival, move heaven and earth to attend. Folk music and dance performances are also regularly held at Tallinn's Open-Air Museum (p75), the Latvian Ethnographic Open-Air Museum (p200) in Rīga, and the Open-Air Museum of Lithuania (p346) at Rumšiškės near Kaunas.

Baltic literature draws heavily on folklore. Modern Estonian and Latvian literature got going in the mid-19th century with the writing of national epic poems based on legends and folk tales that had been part of the oral tradition over preceding centuries – see p52 for more on the Estonian national epic poem *Kalevipoeg*.

> The Balts are big drinkers: annual beer consumption per capita is 87L in Lithuania, 81L in Estonia, and 58L in vodka-fuelled Latvia.

Song Festivals

Song is the Baltic soul. And nowhere is this expressed more eloquently than in the national festivals that unite Estonians, Latvians and Lithuanians worldwide in a spellbinding performance of song. The crescendo is a choir of up to 30,000 voices, singing its heart out to an audience of 100,000 or more, while 10,000-odd folk dancers in traditional dress cast a bewitching kaleidoscope of patterns across the vast, open-air stage.

Festivals are held every four years in Lithuania and every five years in Latvia and Estonia – the next take place in Tallinn in 2009, Vilnius in 2009 (held only two years after the last event, to coincide with the city's status as European City of Culture in 2009) and Rīga in 2013. To help ensure their survival, these Baltic song and dance celebrations were recognised by Unesco as one of 47 precious 'Masterpieces of the Oral and Intangible Heritage of Humanity' in 2003. As rural communities (and thus choirs) dwindle and city dwellers get increasingly wrapped up in modern life's frenetic pace, there are fears that these precious celebrations, which evoke the Balts' age-old relationship with nature, could die off.

Although the first song festival did not take place in the Baltic region until the late 19th century, the Balts' natural lyricism and love of singing can be traced to pre-Christian times. Ancient Baltic beliefs in the pagan powers of sky god Dievs, god of thunder Perkūnas/Pērkons, and the mythological family of the sun, moon and stars found their way into Baltic folk rhymes, the lyrics of which were passed down orally between generations. Lines like 'once we sang so that the fields resounded with our songs' and choral titles like 'Song of Pain and Sun Disc', 'Lilac, Do You Bring Me Luck' and 'Blow Wind, Blow' remain an essential part of festivals. Dance, equally inspired by the agrarian cycle, relies on simple choreography, with dancing couples creating circles, lines, chains and other symmetrical formations. In the 'fisherman dance', giant ocean waves of dancers wash across the stage.

With songs, legends and proverbs being committed to paper in the 19th century, a political tool emerged. The revival of national spirit in Estonia and Latvia saw the first festivals in Tartu in 1869 and Rīga in 1873. In Lithuania,

---

BALTICA FOLKLORE FESTIVAL

The annual, week-long Baltica Folklore Festival is another potent splash of music, dance, traditional costumes, exhibitions and parades focusing on Baltic and other folk traditions. The festival takes place in each Baltic capital in turn, usually in mid-July. In 2009 the Baltica will be held in Latvia; in 2010 it's due in Estonia; and in 2011, in Lithuania.

BALTIC ARCHITECTURE 101

The three capitals are architectural wonders. Their impressive collections of historical buildings prompted Unesco to protect the Old Towns in all three cities as World Heritage sites in 1997; Tallinn is particularly rich in medieval architecture, Vilnius in baroque and Rīga in Art Nouveau.

City rejuvenation has created some noteworthy examples of contemporary architecture: Vilnius has a new skyline of skyscrapers; the new KUMU art museum in Tallinn is striking; and Lielais Dzintars ('The Giant Amber') is the exciting new concert hall due for completion in Liepāja (in Latvia) by Austrian architects Giencke & Company. The most exciting architectural event for the region is certainly the new museum planned for Vilnius, a joint project between the state, Russia's renowned Hermitage museum and America's Guggenheim. The museum (estimated to be costing some €75 million) is due to open in 2013, in an astoundingly futuristic building designed by the acclaimed Anglo-Iraqi architect Zaha Hadid.

---

song filled interwar capital Kaunas for the first time in 1924. Lyrics praising Stalin and later the USSR replaced many of the original Baltic songs during the early Soviet era. Following WWII's mass deportations, displaced Balts turned to song for solace in the refugee camps: the first song festival outside the region was held in 1946 for the estimated 120,000 Latvians in UN camps in Germany. Until 1991 loss and love of homeland dominated the festivals celebrated among Baltic immigrants in the USA, Canada and elsewhere. In Estonia and Latvia the power of song reached fever pitch during the 1990 national song festivals – two highly charged affairs climaxing with choirs of 30,000 singing in unison. The return of many Baltic exiles to the subsequent festivals in 1993–94 – the first since independence – was also incredibly emotive.

In Latvia today, the week-long festival peaks with a candlelit performance to an audience of 100,000 in Rīga's Mežaparks. Estonia's four-day festival kicks off with the centenary flame being brought by horse-drawn carriage from Tartu to Tallinn's song bowl. Lithuanians, meanwhile, sing for six days, parading along the streets from Vilnius Cathedral to the open-air festival stage in Vingis Park. For tickets and information contact festival organisers:

Estonian Song & Dance Foundation (☎ 627 3125; www.laulupidu.ee; Suur-Karja 23, Tallinn)

Lithuanian Folk Culture Centre (☎ 5-261 1190, 5-261 2540; www.llkc.lt, in Lithuanian, http://dainusvente.lt; Barboros Radvilaitės gatvė 8, Vilnius)

Song & Dance Celebration Office (☎ 722 8020; www.songcelebration.lv; Pils laukums 4, Rīga)

> The Eurovision Song Contest – won by Estonia in 2001, staged in Tallinn in 2002; won by Latvia in 2002, staged in Rīga in 2003 – served as a huge publicity campaign for the relatively unknown countries.

FOOD & DRINK

Did someone say 'stodge'? Baltic gastronomy has its roots planted firmly in the land, with livestock and game forming the basis of a hearty diet. Potatoes add a generous dose of winter-warming carbs to national cuisines that are all too often dismissed as bland, heavy and lacking in spice.

Food preparation is plain and simple, and sauces are rarely used to brighten up meat and fish. In autumn, fruits of the land – mushrooms, cabbage, herrings and sausages – are salted, smoked or pickled and stored in cellars for the long hard Baltic winter. The national cuisines are meat-based and not for the faint-hearted. Be it an animal's tail, blood or balls, the Balts eat every last bloody morsel – literally. *Šiupinys* (hodgepodge, alias pork-snout stew) and *kraujinė sriuba* (blood soup) are Lithuanian delicacies, while Estonians deem *verivorst* (blood sausages wrapped in piggy intestines) to be a real treat. Four common ways of cooking meat are as a *shashlik* (shish kebab), *carbonade* (a chop but in practice any piece of grilled meat), beefsteak (fried meat) and stroganoff (cubes of meat in stew).

Bread tends to be black, rye and dry. Other staples include pancakes filled with sweet fruit, jam, curd, sour cream or meat; sausage, usually cold and sliced; and a variety of dairy products – milk is turned to curd, sour cream and cottage cheese as well as plain old butter, cream and cheese. Mushrooms are popular, especially in August and September when forests are studded with dozens of different varieties; in spring and early summer the same forests buzz with berry-pickers.

At the end of 2007, the average monthly old-age pension in Estonia/Latvia/Lithuania was €240/156/181.

The capitals burst with sophisticated restaurants, funky eateries, cool bars and cosy cafes (often commanding Western European city prices, but eating in the provinces is cheap). International cuisines abound and there's ample choice; places dishing up the Balts' meaty national cuisines are equally prevalent, with prices to suit budgets big and small.

For more on the local delicacies and oddities you'll encounter in the region, see the Food & Drink sections of the Estonia (p57), Latvia (p185) and Lithuania (p289) chapters.

ENVIRONMENT
The Land
...is small and flat: it's just 650km from Estonia's northernmost point to Lithuania's southern tip, and the highest point, Suur Munamägi in Estonia,

---

THE BALTIC AMBER ROAD

Amber – fossilised tree resin – was formed in the Baltic region 40 to 60 million years ago. Yet it was not until the mid-19th century that the trail for the so-called Baltic gold began in earnest.

Early humans burnt amber for heat, and in the Middle Ages it served as cash. For the tribal Prussians inhabiting the Baltic Sea's southeast shores around 12,000 BC, rubbing it was the best way to generate static electricity. During the 12th century, it was said to contain mystical qualities – amber worn next to the skin helped a person become closer to the spirits. In true crusader fashion, the Teutonic knights claimed Baltic amber as their own in the 13th century, yet they too failed to understand where amber was to be found and just how much there really was.

In 1854–55 and 1860 substantial amounts of amber were excavated near Juodkrantė on the Curonian Spit in Lithuania. Three separate clusters weighing 2250 tons in total were uncovered during the 'amber rush' to the sleepy seashore village, yet by 1861 the amber had dried up. Since 1869 amber has been excavated at the Yantarny mine in Kaliningrad (Russia), the place where most amber sold in the Baltic region today actually comes from!

Treasure seekers trailed Juodkrantė's shores once more in 1998, this time in search of the legendary Amber Room – a room comprising 10,000 panels (55 sq metres) of carved, polished amber given to Peter the Great by the Prussian king in 1716. For decades opportunists have been trying to track down the missing panels, which graced the Catherine Palace near St Petersburg until 1942, when invading Germans plundered the palace and shipped the jewels either to Königsberg (Kaliningrad) or, as the mayor of Neringa told the world in 1998, to the shores of the Curonian Lagoon, where wartime residents allegedly saw the SS burying large crates. Predictably, the search yielded few results.

Amber comes in 250 colours, ranging from green, pale yellow and black to brown or golden. White amber contains one million gas bubbles per cubic millimetre. Some pieces sold are heated or compressed, combining pieces; others are polished (to test if a polished piece of amber is real put it in salt water – if it sinks, it's a dud). Rubbing unpolished amber should yield a faint pine smell. Old-fashioned ways of treating it include boiling in honey to make it darker, or in vegetable oil to make it lighter. Original pieces with 'inclusions' – grains of dirt, shell, vegetation or *Jurassic Park*–style insects – are the most valuable.

The **Baltic Amber Road** (www.balticamberroad.net), an EU-funded tourism project, steers amber-curious tourists along a 418km route tracing the region's unique amber sights and experiences. See p26 for an itinerary.

peaks at a paltry 318m. Lakes are rife – there are 9000 in all, of which Lake Peipsi in eastern Estonia is the largest.

The coastline clocks up 5000km, much of it either fronting the Gulfs of Finland and Rīga, or protected from the open Baltic Sea by islands. Estonia has over 1000 islands, but Latvia and Lithuania have none. The coast's most remarkable feature is the Curonian Spit, a Unesco-protected 98km sand bar divided between Lithuania and Kaliningrad (Russia). Lithuania and Estonia each have five national parks, Latvia four – and they all have dozens more nature reserves that are protected to various degrees.

For more on the environment in each country, including environmental issues such as energy production and greenhouse gas emissions, see p54 for Estonia, p183 for Latvia and p287 for Lithuania.

For pointers on green travel, see p14; see also our Greendex (p446) for Baltic attractions, hotels, restaurants, craft studios and tour operators recommended for their commitment to sustainability.

Forest covers 51% of Estonia, 45% of Latvia and 33% of Lithuania.

Wildlife

There are more large mammals here than anywhere else in Europe, although spotting them invariably requires the help of a local guide. Forty-eight types of mammal alone live in Latvia's Gauja National Park, and 50 in Estonia's Lahemaa National Park. Elks, deer, wild boars, wolves, lynxes and otters inhabit all three countries, but brown bears, seals and beavers are found only in Estonia and Latvia.

Some of Estonia's islands and coastal wetlands, as well as Lake Žuvintas in southern Lithuania and Ventės Ragas at the edge of the world in western Lithuania, are key breeding grounds and migration stops for water birds. Around 280 bird species have been counted at Matsalu National Park, on Estonia's west coast; Latvia and Lithuania harbour more white storks (see p287) than all of Western Europe, while the rare black stork nests in western Lithuania's Nemunas Delta and Latvia's Gauja National Park. The eagle owl and white-backed woodpecker – rare in the rest of Europe – also nest in abundance in the latter.

Estonia

Estonia

If Estonia ever makes it into the world's press, it's invariably prefaced by the word 'tiny' (eg 'Tiny Estonia wins a medal/defies its eastern neighbour/holds online elections…'). But don't be misled. It's true the country is no geographical giant (although it is bigger than the Netherlands or Denmark) and yes, its population is low (around 1.3 million). But credit where credit's due: it's big on charm. Apart from the obvious allure of the capital Tallinn and its enchanting Unesco-protected Old Town, the country boasts the knockout combination of low population and stretches of fabulous nature. That means you can enjoy Estonia's unspoilt seaside or be alone on an island or forest path, all while enjoying the comforts of a thoroughly modern e-savvy country that's hell-bent on catching up with its Nordic neighbours in the quality-of-life stakes.

The last century has been full of twists and turns for the country: it went from being a province of the Russian empire to an independent country, then an unwilling republic of the Soviet Union, an independent nation once again and now an EU member with a steadfast focus on the future. Anxious to accent what distinguishes it from the rest of Europe and keen to educate interested visitors, Estonia's primped and primed and waiting to shine in the spotlight. Travellers will find plenty to be seduced by in the new, shiny, revamped Estonia.

FAST FACTS

- **Area** 45,226 sq km
- **Birthplace of** Skype and Kazaa; Carmen Kass, supermodel; Kalevipoeg, mythological hero
- **Capital** Tallinn
- **Country code** ☎ 372
- **Departure tax** none
- **Famous for** song festivals, a tech-savvy populace, lush woodlands, saunas
- **Money** Estonian kroon; €1 = 15.65Kr; US$1 = 11.15Kr; UK£1 = 15.65Kr
- **Population** 1.3 million
- **Visas** not needed for most nationalities. See p399 for details.

HIGHLIGHTS

- **Tallinn** (p59) Find medieval bliss exploring the Old Town's nooks and crannies, then unwind among the artistic eye candy at leafy, lovely Kadriorg Park.
- **Pärnu** (p127) Get sand in your shorts at Estonia's summertime mecca, then join fellow holidaymakers at a spa or nightclub.
- **Saaremaa** (p153) Escape to Estonia's largest island for castle-admiring, coastline-combing, soap-making and spa opportunities worth savouring.
- **Soomaa National Park** (p138) Have a natural encounter worth writing home about – bog walking, canoeing and wildlife spotting – then sweat it out in a floating sauna.
- **Tartu** (p106) Further your local education in Estonia's second city and admire a student population flourishing among first-rate museums, cafes and bars.

HOW MUCH?

- **Cup of coffee** 35Kr
- **Taxi fare (10 minutes)** around 100Kr
- **Bus ticket (Tallinn to Tartu, one way)** 150Kr
- **Bicycle hire (daily)** 150-200Kr
- **Litre bottle of Vana Tallinn** 180Kr

LONELY PLANET INDEX

- **Litre of petrol** 15Kr
- **Litre of bottled water** 14-20Kr
- **Half-litre of Saku beer in a bar** 35-50Kr
- **Souvenir T-shirt** 200Kr
- **Packet of roasted nuts** 40Kr

ITINERARIES

- **Three days** Concentrate on the capital, soaking up the splendour of Tallinn's Old Town, and venturing outside the ancient walls to the bustling city centre to contrast the old with the new. On the third day, explore the sights of leafy Kadriorg, and Pirita if the weather's warm.
- **One week** After Tallinn, aim for the island of Saaremaa, where spa resorts, windswept beaches and a castle await. Alternatively, head eastward for the bucolic splendour of Lahemaa National Park.
- **Two weeks** To the above, add Tartu, a vibrant university town and gateway to the lush, lake-dotted southeast, and/or Pärnu, a picturesque, park-filled seaside town near quirky Soomaa National Park and charming Viljandi.

CURRENT EVENTS

In many ways, Estonia has been the outstanding economic success story of the Baltic region, having made a remarkable transition to capitalism. Its large-scale privatisation, free-trade agreements and low corporate taxes have brought in enormous foreign investment, mainly in the finance, manufacturing and transport sectors. The effect on economic growth has been pronounced: from 2000 to 2007, real GDP growth averaged 8.8% per year, a remarkable achievement for such a tiny newcomer. With it came better living standards than those of most new EU member states. Still, the global economic slowdown and the bursting of the Baltic property bubble has seen a sharp turnaround, and in August 2008, after negative growth in two consecutive quarters, Estonia entered a recession, and is expected to remain in one until 2010, according to official forecasts.

Meanwhile, as Estonia looks more and more to the West, its ongoing disputes with its large neighbour to the east have continued apace, and tensions between the ethnic Estonian population (69%) and the ethnic Russian minority (26%) won't go away. These were brought to the fore in April 2007, when the Estonian government relocated the Bronze Soldier (a Soviet WWII war memorial) from downtown Tallinn. Differences between Russophone and ethnic Estonian communities, as well as between the Russian Federation and Estonia, over the interpretation of events in the war has led to other controversies. The Russian government continues to maintain that the Soviet annexation of the Baltic countries was legitimate, and that the Soviet Union liberated the countries from the Nazis. In 2005, during the 60th anniversary of the Allied victory in WWII, the Estonian president at the time, Arnold Rüütel, snubbed an invitation to attend the celebrations in Moscow.

Many Estonians considered the Bronze Soldier in the city centre a symbol of Soviet

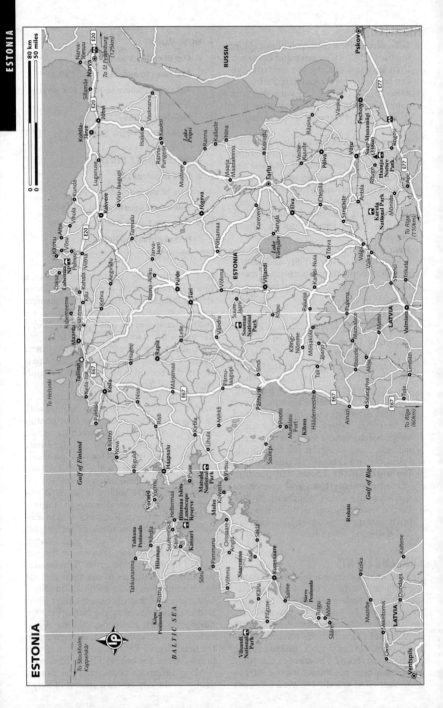

THE SOURCE OF EESTI

In the 1st century AD the Roman historian Tacitus described a people known as the 'Aestii'. In rather crude fashion he depicted them as worshipping goddess statues and chasing wild boars with wooden clubs and iron weaponry. These peoples collected and traded amber. Although Tacitus was describing the forerunners to the Lithuanians and Latvians, the name 'Aestii' was eventually applied specifically to Estonians.

---

occupation and repression. At the same time, the monument has significant value to Estonia's ethnic Russians, symbolising not only Soviet victory over Nazi Germany in the 'Great Patriotic War', but also their claim to better treatment within Estonia. The disputes surrounding the relocation peaked with two nights of riots in Tallinn (including one death) and besieging of the Estonian embassy in Moscow for a week.

Russian nationalists were blamed for a cyber attack on Estonia that same month, which took out much of the country's internet infrastructure. Websites for the country's government departments, banks, newspapers and other commercial operators were all forced offline. As a result, NATO set up an anti-cyber-terrorism centre in Tallinn, which opened in May 2008. The centre, in an old military barracks, brings together experts from Western countries to analyse cyber threats and develop counterstrategies.

Russia–Estonia cross-border and internal tensions were further exacerbated by the Georgian crisis of 2008, when the government was accused by local Russians of immediately going on the anti-Russian offensive and making overinflated, inflammatory remarks.

HISTORY
Beginnings

Estonia's oldest human settlements date back 10,000 years, with Stone Age tools found around Pulli near present-day Pärnu. Finno-Ugric tribes from the east (probably around the Urals) came centuries later – most likely around 3500 BC – mingling with Neolithic peoples and settling in present-day Estonia, Finland and Hungary. They took a liking to their homeland and stayed put, spurning nomadic ways that characterised

most other European peoples over the next six millennia.

The Christian Invasion

By the 9th and 10th centuries AD, Estonians were well aware of the Vikings, who seemed more interested in trade routes to Kyiv (Kiev) and Istanbul than in conquering the land. The first real threat came from Christian invaders from the west.

Following papal calls for a crusade against the northern heathens, Danish troops and German knights invaded Estonia, conquering the southern Estonian castle of Otepää in 1208. The locals put up fierce resistance, and it took well over 30 years before the entire territory was conquered. By the mid-13th century Estonia was carved up between the Danish in the north and the German Teutonic Order in the south. The Order, hungry to move eastward, was powerfully repelled by Alexander Nevsky of Novgorod on frozen Lake Peipsi (marvellously imagined in Eisenstein's film *Alexander Nevsky*).

The conquerors settled in at various newly established towns, handing over much power to the bishops. By the end of the 13th century cathedrals rose over Tallinn and Tartu, around the time that Cistercian and Dominican religious orders set up monasteries to preach to the locals and (try to) baptise them. Meanwhile, the Estonians continued to rebel.

The most significant uprising began on St George's night (23 April) in 1343. It started in Danish-controlled northern Estonia when Estonians pillaged the Padise Cistercian monastery and killed all of the monks. They subsequently laid siege to Tallinn and the Bishop's Castle in Haapsalu, and called for Swedish assistance to help them finish the job. The Swedes did indeed send naval reinforcements across the gulf, but they came too late and were forced to turn back. Despite Estonian resolve, by 1345 the rebellion was crushed. The Danes, however, decided they'd had enough and sold Estonia to the Livonian Order (a branch of the Teutonic Order).

The first guilds and merchant associations emerged in the 14th century, and many towns – Tallinn, Tartu, Viljandi and Pärnu – prospered as trade members of the Hanseatic League (a medieval merchant guild).

Estonians continued practising pagan rites for weddings, funerals and nature worship, though by the 15th century these rites became interlinked with Catholicism, and they began using Christian names. Peasants' rights disappeared during the 15th century, so much so that by the early 16th century a peasant became a serf.

The Reformation

The Reformation, which originated in Germany, reached Estonia in the 1520s, with Lutheran preachers representing the initial wave. By the mid-16th century the church had been reorganised, with monasteries and churches now under Lutheran authority. In Tallinn authorities closed the Dominican monastery (of which some impressive ruins remain); in Tartu both the Dominican and Cistercian monasteries were shut.

The Livonian War

During the 16th century the greatest threat to Livonia (now northern Latvia and southern Estonia) came from the east. Ivan the Terrible, who crowned himself the first Russian tsar in 1547, had his sights clearly set on westward expansion. Russian troops, led by ferocious Tatar cavalry, attacked in 1558, around the region of Tartu. The fighting was extremely cruel, with the invaders leaving a trail of destruction in their wake. Poland, Denmark and Sweden joined the fray, and intermittent fighting raged throughout the 17th century. Sweden emerged the victor.

Like most wars, this one took a heavy toll on the inhabitants. During the two generations of warfare (roughly 1552 to 1629), half the rural population perished and about three-quarters of all farms were deserted, with disease (such as plague), crop failure and the ensuing famine adding to the war casualties. Except for Tallinn, every castle and fortified centre in the country was ransacked or destroyed – including Viljandi Castle, once among northern Europe's mightiest forts. Some towns were completely obliterated.

The Swedish Era

Following the war Estonia entered a period of peace and prosperity under Swedish rule. Although the lot of the Estonian peasantry didn't improve much, cities, boosted by trade, grew and prospered, helping the economy speedily recover from the ravages of war. Under Swedish rule, Estonia was united for the first time in history under a single

ruler; this period is regarded as an enlightened episode in the country's long history of foreign oppression.

The Swedish king granted the Baltic-German aristocracy a certain degree of self-government and even generously gave lands that were deserted during the war. Although the first printed Estonian-language book dates from 1535, the publication of books didn't get under way until the 1630s, when Swedish clergy founded village schools and taught the peasants to read and write. Education received an enormous boost with the founding of Tartu University in 1632.

By the mid-17th century, however, things were going steadily downhill. An outbreak of plague – and later the Great Famine (1695–97) killed off 80,000 people – almost 20% of the population. Peasants, who for a time enjoyed more freedom of movement, soon lost their gains and entered the harder lot of serfdom. The Swedish king, Charles XI, for his part wanted to abolish serfdom in Estonian crown manors (peasants enjoyed freedom in Sweden), but the local Baltic-German aristocracy fought bitterly to preserve the legacy of enforced servitude.

The Great Northern War

Soon Sweden faced serious threats from an anti-Swedish alliance of Poland, Denmark and Russia – countries seeking to regain lands lost in the Livonian War: war began in 1700. After a few successes (including the defeat of the Russians at Narva), the Swedes began to fold under the assaults on multiple fronts. By 1708 Tartu had been destroyed and all of its survivors shipped back to Russia. By 1710 Tallinn capitulated, and Sweden had been routed.

The Enlightenment

Russian domination of Estonia was bad news for the peasants. War (and the 1710 plague) left tens of thousands dead. Swedish reforms were rolled back by Peter I, destroying any hope of freedom for the surviving serfs. Conservative attitudes towards Estonia's lower class didn't change until the Enlightenment, in the late 18th century.

Among those influenced by the Enlightenment was Catherine the Great (1762–96), who curbed the privileges of the elite while instituting quasi-democratic reforms. It wasn't until 1816, however, that the peasants were finally liberated from serfdom.

They also gained surnames, a greater freedom of movement and even limited access to self-government. By the second half of the 19th century, the peasants started buying farm-steads from the estates, and earning an income from crops such as potatoes and flax (the latter commanding particularly high prices during the US Civil War and the subsequent drop in American cotton export to Europe).

National Awakening

The late 19th century was the dawn of the national awakening. Led by a new Estonian elite, the country marched towards nation-hood. The first Estonian-language newspaper, *Perno Postimees,* appeared in 1857. It was pub-lished by Johann Voldemar Jannsen, one of the first to use the term 'Estonians' rather than *maarahvas* (country people). Other influen-tial thinkers included Carl Robert Jakobson, who fought for equal political rights for Estonians; he also founded *Sakala,* Estonia's first political newspaper.

Numerous Estonian societies emerged, and in 1869 the first song festival was held, a major event foregrounding Estonia's unique choral traditions. Estonia's rich folklore also emerged from obscurity, particularly with the publication of *Kalevipoeg,* Friedrich Reinhold Kreutzwald's poetic epic that melded together hundreds of Estonian legends and folk tales. Other poems, particularly works by Lydia Koidula, helped shape the national conscious-ness – one imprinted with the memory of 700 years of slavery.

Rebellion & WWI

The late 19th century was also a period of rampant industrialisation, marked by the rise of large factories and an extensive rail-way network that linked Estonia with Russia. Socialism and discontent accompanied those grim workplaces, with demonstrations and strikes led by newly formed worker parties. Events in Estonia mimicked those in Russia, and in January 1905 as armed insurrection flared across the border, Estonia's workers joined the fray. Tension mounted until au-tumn that year, when 20,000 workers went on strike. Tsarist troops brutally responded by killing and wounding 200.

Tsar Nicholas II's response incited the Estonian rebels, who continued to destroy the property of the old guard. Subsequently, thousands of soldiers arrived from Russia,

quelling the rebellions; 600 Estonians were ex-ecuted and hundreds were sent off to Siberia. Trade unions and progressive newspapers and organisations were closed down, and political leaders fled the country.

More radical plans to bring Estonia to heel – such as sending thousands of Russian peasants to colonise the country – were never realised. Instead, Russia's bumbling tsar had another priority: WWI. Estonia paid a high price for Russia's involvement – 100,000 men were drafted, 10,000 of whom were killed in action. Many Estonians went off to fight under the notion that if they helped defeat Germany, Russia would grant them nation-hood. Russia, of course, had no intention of doing so. But by 1917 the matter was no longer the tsar's to decide. In St Petersburg Nicholas II was forced to abdicate, and the Bolsheviks seized power. As chaos swept across Russia, Estonia seized the initiative and on 24 February 1918, effectively declared its independence.

The War of Independence

Estonia faced threats from both Russia and Baltic-German reactionaries. War erupted as the Red Army quickly advanced, over-running half the country by January 1919. Estonia fought back tenaciously, and with the help of British warships and Finnish, Danish and Swedish troops, it defeated its long-time enemy. In December Russia agreed to a truce and on 2 February 1920 it signed the Tartu Peace Treaty, which renounced forever Russia's rights of sovereignty over Estonian territory. For the first time in its history, Estonia was completely independent.

Fleeting Independence

In many ways, the independence period was a golden era. The economy developed rapidly, with Estonia utilising its natural resources and attracting investments from abroad. Tartu University became a university for Estonians, and the Estonian language became the lingua franca for all aspects of public life, creat-ing new opportunities in professional and academic spheres. Secondary education also improved (per capita the number of students surpassed most European nations), and an enormous book industry arose, with 25,000 titles published between 1918 and 1940 (again surpassing most European nations in books per capita).

On other fronts – notably the political one – independence was not so rosy. Fear of communist subversion (such as the failed 1924 coup d'état supported by the Bolsheviks) drove the government to the right. In 1934 Konstantin Päts, leader of the transitional government, along with Johan Laidoner, commander-in-chief of the Estonian army, violated the constitution and seized power, under the pretext of protecting democracy from extremist factions. Thus began the 'era of silence', a period of authoritarian rule that dogged the fledgling republic until WWII.

The Soviet Invasion & WWII

Estonia's fate was sealed when Nazi Germany and the USSR negotiated a secret pact in 1939, essentially handing Estonia over to Stalin. The Molotov-Ribbentrop Pact of 23 August 1939, a nonagression pact between the USSR and Nazi Germany, secretly divided Eastern Europe into Soviet and German spheres of influence. Estonia fell into the Soviet sphere. At the outbreak of WWII, Estonia declared itself neutral, but Moscow forced Estonia to sign a mutual assistance pact. Thousands of Russian soldiers subsequently arrived, along with military, naval and air bases, between 1939 and 1941. Apparatchiks (Communist Party members) orchestrated a sham rebellion whereby 'the people' demanded to be part of the USSR. President Päts, General Laidoner and other leaders were sacked and sent off to Russian prison camps, a puppet government was installed, and on 6 August 1940 the Supreme Soviet accepted Estonia's 'request' to join the USSR.

Deportations and WWII devastated the country. Tens of thousands were conscripted and sent not to fight but to work (and usually die) in labour camps in northern Russia. Thousands of women and children were also sent to gulags.

When Russia fled the German advance, Estonia welcomed the Nazis as liberators. Fifty-five thousand Estonians joined home-defence units and Wehrmacht Ost battalions. The Nazis, however, would not grant statehood to Estonia and viewed it merely as occupied territory of the Soviet Union. Hope was crushed when the Germans began executing communist collaborators; 7000 Estonian citizens were shot. To escape conscription into the German army (nearly 40,000 were conscripted), thousands fled to Finland and joined the Estonian regiment of the Finnish army.

In early 1944 the Soviet army bombed Tallinn, Narva, Tartu and other cities. Narva's baroque Old Town was almost completely destroyed as Russia exacted revenge upon 'Estonian traitors'.

The Nazis retreated in September 1944. Fearing the advance of the Red Army, many Estonians also fled and around 70,000 reached the West. By the end of the war one in 10 Estonians lived abroad. All in all, Estonia had lost over 280,000 people in the war (a quarter of its population): in addition to those who emigrated, 30,000 were killed in action; others were executed, sent to gulags or exterminated in concentration camps.

The Soviet Era

After the war Estonia was immediately annexed by the Soviet Union. This began the grim epoch of repression, with many thousands tortured or sent to prison camps and 19,000 Estonians executed. Farmers were brutally forced into collectivisation, and thousands of immigrants flooded the country from different regions of the Soviet Union. Between 1945 and 1989 the percentage of native Estonians fell from 97% to 62%.

As a result of the repression, beginning in 1944, Estonians formed a large guerrilla movement. Calling themselves the Metsavennad, or 'Forest Brothers', 14,000 Estonians armed themselves and went into hiding, operating in small groups throughout the country. The guerrillas had little success against the Soviet

---

TALLINN'S CHECHEN HERO

In January 1991 Soviet troops seized strategic buildings in Vilnius and Rīga, and soldiers were ordered to do the same in Tallinn. The commander of the troops at the time, however, disobeyed Moscow's orders and refused to open fire upon the crowd. He even threatened to turn the artillery under his command against any attempted invasion from Russia. That leader was Dzhokhar Dudayev, who would go on to become the president of Chechnya and lead its independence movement. He was brutally assassinated by the Russian military in 1995. In Estonia he is fondly remembered for his role in bringing about Estonian independence.

army, and by 1956 the movement had been effectively destroyed.

Although there were a few optimistic periods during the tyranny (notably the 'thaw' under Khrushchev), Estonia didn't see much hope until the mid '80s. With the ravaging war in Afghanistan and years of disastrous state planning under its belt, the Soviet Union teetered on the brink of economic catastrophe.

The dissident movement in Estonia gained momentum, and on the 50th anniversary of the 1939 Molotov-Ribbentrop Pact, a major rally took place in Tallinn. Over the next few months, more and more protests were held, with Estonians demanding the restoration of statehood. The song festival was one of Estonia's most powerful vehicles for protest. The biggest took place in 1988 when 300,000 Estonians gathered on Tallinn's Song Festival Grounds and brought much international attention to the Baltic plight.

In November 1989 the Estonian Supreme Soviet declared the events of 1940 an act of military aggression and therefore illegal. Disobeying Moscow's orders, Estonia held free elections in 1990. Despite Russia's attempts to stop it, Estonia regained its independence in 1991.

Postindependence

In 1992 the first general election under the new constitution took place, with a proliferation of newly formed parties. The Pro Patria (Fatherland) Union won a narrow majority after campaigning under the slogan 'Cleaning House', which meant removing from power those associated with communist rule. Pro Patria's leader, 32-year-old historian Mart Laar, became prime minister.

Laar set to work transforming Estonia into a free-market economy, introducing the solid Estonian kroon as currency and negotiating the complete Russian troop withdrawal. (The latter was a source of particular anxiety for Estonians, and the whole country breathed a collective sigh of relief when the last garrisons departed in 1994. Unfortunately, the Russians left a few things behind: ecologically devastated lands in the northeast, polluted ground water around air bases and nuclear waste in naval bases.)

Despite Laar's successes, he was considered a hothead, and in 1994, he was dismissed when his government received a vote of no confidence by the Riigikogu

(National Council). Laar returned to the political arena in 1999, when he was elected prime minister a second time. During this time in office, he helped correct the Estonian financial crisis brought on by Russia's financial collapse in 1998. Laar cut business taxes and reduced social benefits, and continued the march to privatisation. His remedies worked, pulling Estonia out of its negative growth in 1999, which allowed it to begin accession talks with the EU. There was much political wrangling, however, among the coalition government, and in 2002 Laar resigned.

To some degree Estonia found it hard to escape its past, notably when Arnold Rüütel, the former head of Estonia's Soviet parliament, won the 2001 presidential election. Viewed by many as a politically inept communist dinosaur, 73-year-old Rüütel won on his dedication to social problems (such as unemployment) – an issue given short shrift as EU hysteria swept the country. His communist credentials and agricultural background were particularly deficient compared with the skills of his predecessor, the brilliant and charismatic Lennart Meri.

Still, Rüütel had no intention of leading Estonia astray – and had little opportunity to do so, since the president has little involvement in the day-to-day running of the country (the domain of the prime minister). Rüütel's administration ended in 2005, marked by a few scandals. Yet more important than the setbacks were the enormous twin achievements. Following a referendum in September 2003, approximately 60% of Estonians voted in favour of joining the EU. The following spring, the country officially joined NATO and the EU.

In 2006 a popular new president, former diplomat and foreign minister Toomas Hendrik Ilves, was elected. He was born in Sweden to Estonian refugees, and raised in the USA. In 2007 parliamentary elections were held, in which citizens were able to vote via the internet (a world first). The resulting centre-right coalition government comprises three major parties, with Andre Ansip (chairman of the Estonian Reform Party) at the helm as prime minister. Recurring post-EU-accession themes are the growing economy, and strained relations with Russia (see p41 for more).

TALLINN SUMMER SCHOOL

Fancy spending some of the summer learning more about Estonian culture, or making sense of the local language? **Tallinn University's summer school** (☎ 619 9599; www.tlu.ee/summerschool) is a good place to start. You can undertake study of Estonian, or any number of foreign languages, plus various cultural programs. In 2008, a three-week Estonian language course cost 6100Kr; for 9230Kr, you participate in the language course and a cultural component that involves lectures and discussions, delving into aspects of Estonian culture, history, art, music and traditions. Lest that sound a little dry, it also involves visiting local museums, weekends away (to Lahemaa National Park, Hiiumaa or Viljandi) and handicraft workshops. Check out the details online.

Note that the summer school offers other great ways to incorporate learning into your vacation – eg a three-week intensive short-film production course in conjunction with the Baltic Film and Media School (14,900Kr), or a one-week creative workshop, drawing and painting in Tallinn's Old Town (4500Kr), in cooperation with the Estonian Academy of Arts.

THE CULTURE

The National Psyche

Despite (or perhaps because of) centuries of occupation by Danes, Swedes, Germans and Russians, Estonians have tenaciously held onto their national identity and are deeply, emotionally connected to their history, folklore and national song tradition. The Estonian Literary Museum in Tartu holds over 1.3 million pages of folk songs, the world's second-largest collection (Ireland has the largest), and Estonia produces films for one of the world's smallest audiences (only Iceland produces for a smaller audience). Despite this inward-focus, Estonians are equally interested in what's happening in the outside world, particularly now that they're part of the EU. Having politically and economically shaken off the dead weight of the Soviet era, their view is very much to the west and the north: to Western Europe, the Nordic region and the EU. They view themselves as having more in common (linguistically and culturally) with their Finnish neighbours than they do with the Baltic countries to their south, and see the lumping of Estonia, Latvia and Lithuania under the 'Baltic countries' label as a handy geographic reference but not much more. There's even talk of further cementing ties with Finland by building a tunnel under the Gulf of Finland to connect the two countries, but the cost of such a measure is likely to be prohibitive.

Estonians have a reputation for being reserved and aloof, but visitors may not feel this reputation is warranted (many may adhere to an alternative view, that the women are charming and effusive and the men stoic and humourless). Some believe it has much to do with the weather – those long, dark nights breeding endless introspection. This reserve also extends to gross displays of public affection, brash behaviour and intoxication – all frowned upon. This is assuming that there isn't a festival under way, such as Jaanipäev, when friends, family and acquaintances gather in the countryside for drinking, dancing and revelry.

Lifestyle

The long, grey days of Soviet rule are well behind Estonia. Today, first-time visitors are astonished to find a thriving society that has embraced the market economy with gusto. The new economy has created previously unimagined possibilities. Entrepreneurship is widespread (the developers of Kazaa, the peer-to-peer, file-sharing software, and Skype, which allows free telephone calls over the internet, are Estonian), and the economy has diversified considerably since 1991.

Estonians are known for their strong work ethic, but when they're not toiling in the fields, or putting in long hours at the office, they head to the countryside. Ideal weekends are spent at the family cottage, picking berries or mushrooms, walking through the woods, or sitting with friends soaking up the quiet beauty. Having a countryside sauna is one of the national pastimes.

In the realm of education, Estonia has made enormous steps in ensuring students are prepared for the future, and today its schools and towns are among the most wired-up in the world. Internet and mobile-phone usage per capita is higher here than it is in many other parts of the EU; Estonians pay for parking using their mobile phones, and in 2005 even began voting online.

Yet despite the ongoing IT revolution, the country has some nagging social problems. Although the number of people living below the poverty line has fallen in recent years, wage disparities continue to grow, and the cost of goods continues to rise faster than salaries. Pensioners have been the hardest hit, as Estonia's social-welfare infrastructure doesn't meet the demands. Many ethnic Russians (particularly the older generations) feel alienated from the new Estonia, facing what they feel are enormous obstacles – one of the most daunting being the requirement to learn Estonian – in order to succeed in the new economy.

On a positive note, in recent years Estonia has experienced huge economic growth (see p41). Inflation, income levels and standards of living have correspondingly risen – Estonia is catching up to the average European living standard faster than anybody expected. One fascinating statistic indicating the local level of satisfaction comes from World Bank estimates that only around 1% of the Estonian workforce has emigrated to richer EU member states following accession in 2004 (considerably higher proportions of Latvians and Lithuanians have travelled to the UK and Ireland for work). Finland is the most popular destination for Estonian workers, with the added benefits of geographic proximity and cultural similarities.

Population

Estonia ranks near the bottom of the world scale in terms of population (with slightly fewer residents than the Gaza Strip, but a fraction more than Mauritius). The country also has a low population density, with only around 32 people per sq km, compared with 380 people per sq km in the Netherlands – good news for those sick of wading through crowds (although it's a statistic not exactly obvious in the Old Town in July).

Only 69% of the people living in Estonia are ethnic Estonians. Russians make up 26% of the population, with 2% Ukrainian, 1% Belarusian and 1% Finnish. Ethnic Russians are concentrated in the industrial cities of the northeast, where in some places (such as Narva) they make up around 95% of the population. Russians also have a sizable presence in Tallinn (37%).

Despite their deep and abiding love of the countryside, Estonians are city slickers – 70% reside in cities (nearly one-third of the national population lives in the capital). Literacy is almost universal in Estonia (99.8%).

Multiculturalism

The ethnic make-up of present-day Estonia differs markedly from that of 70 years ago. In 1934 native Estonians comprised over 90%

EESTI CITIZENSHIP

When Estonia regained independence in 1991, not every resident received citizenship. People who were citizens of the pre-1940 Estonian Republic and their descendants automatically became citizens. Those who moved to Estonia during the Soviet occupation (mostly Russian-speakers, many of whom didn't learn the local language) could choose to be naturalised, an ongoing process that required applicants to demonstrate knowledge of Estonia's history and language to qualify. (One alternative was to apply for Russian citizenship, as all citizens of the former USSR were eligible; another was to remain in Estonia as noncitizen residents.) Only citizens may vote in parliamentary elections. Noncitizens can vote in local government elections providing they have legal residency.

The naturalisation process, and the perceived difficulty of the initial language tests, became a point of international contention, as the government of Russia, the EU and a number of human rights organisations (including Amnesty International) objected on the grounds that many Russian-speaking inhabitants were being denied their political and civil rights. As a result, the tests were somewhat altered and the number of stateless persons has steadily decreased. According to Estonian officials, in 1992, 32% of residents lacked any form of citizenship. In 2003, that figure was 12%, while in early 2008 the figure was 8.2%. (One consequence of Estonia's citizenship policy is that 8% of the population holds the passport of another state, mostly the Russian Federation, Ukraine or Finland. Around 84% of the population of Estonia holds Estonian citizenship.)

of the population. This began to change a few years later with the Soviet takeover (see p46). Migration from other parts of the USSR occurred on a mass scale from 1945 to 1955, with many of the immigrants arriving with military troops. Over the next three decades, Estonia had the highest rate of migration of any of the Soviet republics.

Estonia's restrictive citizenship law (implemented post-1991; see the boxed text, p49) has caused conflict both within the country and in the country's dealings with Russia. It's hard to deny that there are tensions between ethnic Russians and Estonians, and while instances of overt hostility based on ethnicity or race are infrequent, they do occur. The tension, and ultimately violence, that was sparked by the government's decision in 2007 to move a Soviet-era monument from the centre of Tallinn (see p41) demonstrated that fissures remain between the country's ethnic Russians and the rest of the population, and there are regular complaints (from the Russian government, and the ethnic Russian population) that Russian-speaking minorities in Estonia are being denied basic rights.

The statistics highlight the plight of the ethnic Russians. Unemployment is twice as high among Russian speakers as among Estonians; there is also a significant pay gap between the two groups. Russian-speakers account for 58% of Estonia's prison population and approximately 80% of HIV-positive cases. They have a higher incidence of alcoholism and drug addiction, and significantly higher rates of suicide than native Estonians or Russians in Russia. A drive through some of the crumbling towns of the northeast, where work and hope are both in short supply, gives some clue to the Russian plight. The greater social problems in the Russian commu-

nity in turn feeds the negative stereotypes that some Estonians have of ethnic Russians.

One of the most overlooked ethnic groups in Estonia is the Setu people (called the Seto in their own language), a native group of mixed Russian-Estonian ancestry who live in southeastern Estonia and in neighbouring Russia. They are a Finno-Ugric people with rich cultural traditions, and they speak their own language (Võru Seto). There are an estimated 10,000 Setu, though their numbers continue to dwindle. Worst of all is the border that separates the two countries, cutting whole communities in half.

SPORT

Basketball and football are Estonia's most popular sports, while the country's reigning sporting heroes are Gerd Kantler, who won a gold medal at the Beijing 2008 Olympics for discus, and Kristina Šmigun, recipient of two gold cross-country skiing medals at the 2006 Winter Olympics. Another well-known name in the sports world is Erki Nool, the decathlon gold-medal winner at the 2000 Olympics in Sydney (he is now a parliamentarian); up-and-comers include tennis player Kaia Kanepi, who reached the quarter finals of the French Open in 2008.

Football is on the up as the national team's performances improve. There has been little joy, however, for the domestic Estonian clubs competing in the new Baltic League (www .balticleague.com). This annual competition began in 2007 and brings together the four best clubs from Latvia, Estonia and Lithuania according to the results of the domestic championships. In its first two years, the Latvian and Lithuanian clubs have proved superior to the Estonian entrants.

WIFE-CARRYING WORLD CHAMPS

Forget decathlons and cross-country skiing: Estonian wife carriers rule! Since the traditional Finnish sport of wife carrying was revived in 1992 in the northern Finnish village of Sonkajärvi, Estonians have upstaged their Nordic cousins by winning all world championships since 1998 and capturing the world record (yes, there is such a thing).

Men must carry their wives (or a suitable substitute) any way they wish through a difficult, 253m-long obstacle course – through water, over barriers. Even former NBA star Dennis Rodman, visiting the 2005 championships, only managed to do the final 100m of the race, noting that it was too gruelling to complete without practice. The current record – 55.5 seconds – belongs to five-time world champion, Estonian Margo Uusorg. Sadly there are few Estonia-based wife-carrying competitions – this may just be the excuse you need to visit Finland. The event is held annually in early July; see www.sonkajarvi.fi for more details.

KIIKING – WHAT THE?

Is it only the Estonians who could turn the gentle pleasure of riding a swing into an extreme sport (frankly, we're surprised the New Zealanders didn't think of it first)? From the weird and wacky world of Estonian sport comes kiiking, invented in 1997. Kiiking sees competitors stand on a swing and attempt to complete a 360-degree loop around the top bar (with their feet fastened to the swing base and their hands to the swing arms). The inventor of kiiking, Ado Kosk, observed that the longer the swing arms, the more difficult it is to complete a 360-degree loop. Kosk then designed swing arms that can gradually extend, for an increased challenge. In competition, the winner is the person who completes a loop with the longest swing arms – the current record stands at a fraction over 7m! If this concept has you scratching your head, you need to go to www.kiiking.ee to get a more visual idea of the whole thing. And to find out where you can see it in action (or even give it a try yourself).

RELIGION

Historically, Estonia was Lutheran from the early 17th century, though today only a minority of Estonians profess religious beliefs, and there's little sense of Estonia as a religious society. The Russian community is largely Orthodox, with beautiful brightly domed churches sprinkled around eastern Estonia. There are approximately 10,000 Muslims in Estonia, and about 2500 Jews. In 2007 the Jewish community celebrated the opening of its first synagogue since the Holocaust; it's a stunning modern structure (at Karu 16, Tallinn) and home to a kosher restaurant.

One of Estonia's most intriguing religious groups arrived over 300 years ago. In 1652 in Russia, Patriarch Nikon introduced reforms to consolidate his power and bring Russian Orthodox doctrine into line with the Greek Orthodox Church. Those who rejected his reforms suffered torture or were executed, and many homes and churches were destroyed. Over the next few centuries, thousands fled to the western shores of Lake Peipsi, where they erected new villages and worship houses. Although they escaped persecution, they were still governed by tsarist Russia and weren't allowed to openly practise their religion until Estonia gained its independence in 1918. Sadly, the Soviet occupation led to the destruction of more churches, and religious persecution. Since 1991 they've been left alone to live a peaceful existence along the bucolic shoreline. Today there are around 10,000 Russian Old Believers living in 11 congregations, primarily along the shore of Lake Peipsi.

ARTS

Most travellers are likely to notice paintings and ceramics of bright pastel colours and fanciful animal compositions as emblematic of contemporary Estonian art, especially works by one-man industry Navitrolla (www.navitrolla.ee), whose playful world adorns postcards, coffee mugs, posters and cafe walls. The arts and crafts world in Estonia is much wider than that, however.

Music

Estonia has a strong and internationally well-respected classical music tradition, most notably its choirs. The Estonian Boys Choir has been acclaimed worldwide. Hortus Musicus, formed in 1972, is probably Estonia's best known ensemble, performing mainly medieval and Renaissance music.

The main Estonian composers of the 20th century all wrote music dear to the heart of the people, and remain popular today. Rudolf Tobias (1873–1918) wrote influential symphonic, choral and concerto works as well as fantasies on folk song melodies. Mart Saar (1882–1963) studied under Rimsky-Korsakov in St Petersburg but his music shows none of this influence. His songs and piano suites were among the most performed pieces of music in between-war concerts in Estonia. Eduard Tubin (1905–82) is another great Estonian composer whose body of work includes 10 symphonies. Contemporary composer Erkki-Sven Tüür (1959–) takes inspiration from nature and the elements as experienced on his native Hiiumaa.

Estonia's most celebrated composer is Arvo Pärt (1935–), the intense and reclusive master of hauntingly austere music many have misleadingly termed minimalist. Pärt emigrated to Germany during Soviet rule, and his *Misererie Litany*, *Te Deum* and *Tabula Rasa* are among an internationally acclaimed body of work characterised by dramatic bleakness, piercing majesty and nuanced silence.

Bridging the gap between old and new is one of Estonia's more clever groups. Rondellus, an ensemble that has played in a number of early music festivals, performs on medieval period instruments and isn't afraid of experimentation. Its well-received album *Sabbatum* (2002) is a tribute album of sorts to Black Sabbath – the only difference being the music is played on medieval instruments, and the songs are sung in Latin!

Hard rock thrives in Estonia with groups like Vennaskond, the Tuberkuloited and the U2-style Mr Lawrence (very popular in the 1990s). Also popular (heavy, but timelessly Estonian) is Metsatöll, whose song titles and lyrics make heavy use of archaic Estonian language and imagery. The more approachable Ultima Thule, Genialistid and Smilers are among the country's longest-running and most beloved bands.

The pop and dance-music scene is strong in Estonia, exemplified by Estonia's performances in that revered indicator of true art, Eurovision (it won the competition in 2001 and hosted the contest in 2002). The tough-girl band Vanilla Ninja became a hot ticket throughout central Europe (singing in English and Estonian) early in the millennium. Koit Toome, Maarja-Liis Ilus and Tanel Padar are popular pop singers, while Hedvig Hanson blends jazz and rock with surprising results. Exciting names in electronica are the mesmerisingly talented Paf and house kings Rulers of the Deep.

See www.estmusic.com for detailed listings and streaming samples of Estonian musicians of all genres – a worthwhile site, despite not being particularly up to date.

Literature

The history of written Estonian is little more than 150 years old. Baltic-Germans published an Estonian grammar book and a dictionary, but it wasn't until the national awakening movement of the late 19th century that the publication of books, poetry and newspapers began. This elevated Estonian from a mere 'peasants' language' to one with full literary potential.

Estonian literature grew from the poems and diaries of a young graduate of Tartu University, Kristjan Jaak Peterson. Also a gifted linguist, he died when he was only 21

CAN I BUY A VOWEL PLEASE?

Intrigued by the national language? Fancy yourself a linguist? If you're keen to tackle the local language, bear in mind that Estonian has 14 cases, no future tense, and no articles. And then try wrapping your tongue around the following vowel-hungry words:

- jäääär – edge of the ice
- töööö – worknight (can also be öötöö)
- kuuuurija – moon researcher
- kuuüür – monthly rent

And then give this a go: 'Kuuuurijate töööö jäääärel', or 'a moon researcher's worknight at the edge of the ice'!

---

years old in 1822. His lines 'Can the language of this land/carried by the song of the wind/not rise up to heaven/and search for its place in eternity?' are engraved in stone in Tartu and his birthday is celebrated as Mother Tongue Day (14 March).

Until the mid-19th century Estonian culture was preserved only by way of an oral folk tradition among peasants. The national epic poem *Son of Kalev* (*Kalevipoeg*), written between 1857 and 1861 by Friedrich Reinhold Kreutzwald (1803–82), made brilliant use of Estonia's rich oral traditions; it was inspired by Finland's *Kalevala*, a similar epic created several decades earlier. Fusing hundreds of Estonian legends and folk tales, *Son of Kalev* relates the adventures of the mythical hero, which ends with his death and his land's conquest by foreigners, but also a promise to restore freedom. The epic played a major role in fostering the national awakening of the 19th century.

Lydia Koidula (1843–86), the face of the 100Kr note, was the poet of Estonia's national awakening and first lady of literature.

Anton Hansen Tammsaare (1878–1940) is considered the greatest Estonian novelist for *Truth and Justice* (*Tõde ja Õigus*), written between 1926 and 1933. A five-volume saga of village and town life, it explores Estonian social, political and philosophical issues.

Eduard Vilde (1865–1933) was an influential early-20th-century novelist and playwright who wrote *Unattainable Wonder* (*Tabamata Ime*). *Unattainable Wonder* was to be the first play performed at the opening of the Estonia Theatre in 1913 but was substituted with *Hamlet*, as Vilde's scathing critique of the then intelligentsia was deemed too controversial. In most of his novels and plays, Vilde looked with great irony at what he saw as Estonia's mad, blind rush to become part of Europe. For Vilde, self-reliance was the truest form of independence.

Paul-Eerik Rummo (1942–) is one of Estonia's leading poets and playwrights, dubbed the 'Estonian Dylan Thomas' for his patriotic pieces, which deal with contemporary problems of cultural identity. His contemporary, Mati Unt (1944–2005), played an important role in cementing the place of Estonian intellectuals in the modern world, and wrote, from the 1960s onwards, quite cynical novels (notably *Autumn Ball* or *Sügisball*), plays and articles about contemporary life in Estonia.

The novelist Jaan Kross (1920–2007) won great acclaim for his historical novels in which he tackled Soviet-era subjects. His work has been translated into over 20 languages, making him Estonia's most internationally acclaimed author. His most renowned book, *The Czar's Madman,* relates the story of a 19th-century Estonian baron who falls in love with a peasant girl and later ends up in prison. It's loosely based on a true story, though the critique of past- and present-day authoritarianism is the crux of his work. The semi-autobiographical *Treading Air*, Kross' 13th novel, was translated into English in 2003.

Estonia also has a number of outstanding contemporary poets. Jaan Kaplinski (1941–) has had two collections, *The Same Sea in Us All* and *The Wandering Border,* published in English. His work expresses the feel of Estonian life superbly. Kross and Kaplinski have both been nominated for the Nobel Prize for Literature.

Tõnu Õnnepalu's *Borderland* (Piiri Riik, published under the pseudonym Emil Tode) is about a young homosexual Estonian who travels to Europe and becomes a kept boy for an older, rich gentleman. This leads him down a tortuous road of self-discovery. Not a mere confessional, *Borderland* is a clever and absorbing critique of modern Estonian values. In popular fiction, Kaur Kender's *Independence Day* tells the misadventures of young and ambitious entrepreneurs in postindependence Estonia.

Theatre

Many of the country's theatres were built solely from donations by private citizens, which gives an indication of the role theatre has played in Estonian cultural life. The Estonian Drama Theatre in Tallinn, the Vanemuine Theatre in Tartu and the Drama Theatre in Rakvere (the last civic building erected in Estonia before WWII) were all built on proceeds from door-to-door collections.

The popularity of theatre is also evidenced in theatregoing statistics: in 2007 the Eurobarometer found 93% of Estonians go to concerts, the theatre and watch cultural content on TV (the EU average is 78%). Estonia is second to the Netherlands in theatre attendance, with 49% of the population attending plays or musicals.

Modern Estonian theatre is considered to have begun in 1870 in Tartu, where Lydia Koidula's *The Cousin from Saaremaa* became the first Estonian play to be performed in public. The Vanemuine Theatre (an outgrowth of the Vanemuine Society, an amateur troupe) launched professional theatre in 1906. Quickly thereafter the Estonia Theatre opened its doors in Tallinn, and the Endla Theatre in Pärnu followed suit in 1911. Within the first decade, theatre took off with talented directors and actors performing the works of August Kitzberg and Eduard Wilde.

During the country's independence days (1918–40), Estonian theatre thrived; however, by the 1930s there was a noticeable retreat from experimentation. Theatre, like the other arts, suffered heavily during Soviet rule, with heavy-handed censorship and a dumping of lifeless Soviet drama onto the stage. Things began to change after Stalin's death in 1953, as theatres gained more poetic freedom in stage productions. Although the '60s were still a time of repression in other spheres of life, on the stage the avant-garde emerged, with the staging of plays wild in subject matter and rich in symbolism. Paul-Eerik Rummo, perhaps Estonia's most famous poet of the time, wrote *The Cinderella Game,* a brilliant satire of Soviet-era repression that was performed in 1969. It was later performed at New York's La Mama theatre and in playhouses throughout Europe.

With the return to independence in 1991 and the disappearance of censorship, the stage once again held wide-open possibilities. Yet some critics contend that along with Estonia's new-found freedom, radicalism died in the theatre – for the very reason that the object of satire (Big Brother) had also died. Whatever the case, stage life continues to flourish, and today the halls are rarely empty. The most original directors currently on the theatre scene are Jaanus Rohumaa, Katri Kaasik-Aaslav and Elmo Nüganen, who often work out of Tallinn's City Theatre (Linnateater); travellers, however, will have trouble tapping into the scene without any knowledge of the local language.

Cinema

The first 'moving pictures' were screened in Tallinn in 1896, and the first theatre opened in 1908. Estonia's cinematographic output has not been prolific, but there are a few standouts. It's also worth noting that Estonia produces films for one of the world's smallest audiences – far more than the output of the neighbouring Baltic countries, and with domestic films capturing an impressive 14% of the filmgoing market share.

The nation's most beloved film is Arvo Kruusement's *Spring* (*Kevade*, 1969), an adaptation of Oskar Luts' country saga. Its sequel, *Summer* (*Suvi*, 1976), was also popular though regarded as inferior. Grigori Kromanov's *Last Relic* (*Viimne Reliikvia*, 1969) was a brave and unabashedly anti-Soviet film that has been screened in 60 countries.

More recently Sulev Keedus' lyrical *Georgica* (1998), about childhood, war, and life on the western islands, and Jaak Kilmi's *Pigs' Revolution* (*Sigade Revolutsioon*, 2004), about an anti-Soviet uprising at a teenager's summer camp, have made the rounds at international film festivals.

One of Estonia's most popular locally made films is *Names in Marble* (*Nimed Marmortahvlil*, 2002), which tells the story of a group of young classmates and their decision to fight in the fledgling nation's War of Independence against the Red Army in 1918–20. It was directed by acclaimed Estonian stage director Elmo Nüganen and it's based on the book of the same name (by Albert Kivikas) that was banned during Soviet times.

In 2007, 10 feature films were made in Estonia and a number have been shown at international film festivals, garnering recognition and minor awards. Notable among them is *Autumn Ball* (*Sügisball*, 2007), based on the novel by Mati Unt and directed by Veiko Õunpuu – 'fragments of six lonely lives, stuck in the humdrum world of Soviet-era tower blocks' – and *The Class* (*Klass*, 2007), a disturbing drama about high school students who take revenge against bullies.

ENVIRONMENT
The Land

Slightly larger than Switzerland, Estonia is the smallest Baltic country at 45,226 sq km. It is part of the East European plain, extremely flat though marked by extensive bogs and marshes. At 318m, Suur Munamägi (Great Egg Hill; p122) is the highest point in the country – and in the Baltic (a mere molehill for those of you from less height-challenged terrain). Along with swamps and wetlands, forests make up half of Estonia's territory.

Although it's smaller than the other Baltic countries, Estonia gets the lion's share of coastland. Along with Hiiumaa and Saaremaa – Estonia's biggest islands – the country boasts over 1500 islands (to Latvia and Lithuania's

---

WWOOF-ING

If you don't mind getting your hands dirty, an economical and enlightening way of travelling around Estonia involves doing some voluntary work as a member of **Worldwide Opportunities on Organic Farms** (WWOOF; ☎ 5342 2378; www.wwoof.ee) – also known as 'Willing Workers on Organic Farms'. Membership of this popular, well-established international organisation (which has representatives around the globe) provides you with access to the WWOOF Estonia website, which at the time of research listed 17 organic farms and other environmentally sound cottage industries throughout the country (bear in mind that WWOOF only got started here in 2007, so this number should increase). In exchange for daily work at these farms, the owner will provide food, accommodation and some hands-on experience in organic farming. You must contact the farm owner or manager beforehand to arrange your stay; don't turn up at a farm without warning. Check the website for more information.

ETHICAL ESTONIA

In 2008 Estonia was included in a list compiled by the Ethical Traveler website highlighting the 'Developing World's 10 Best Ethical Destinations'. While we're not sure about branding the country a 'developing' one (statistics on wi-fi coverage and prestige car-ownership would indicate otherwise), we applaud its inclusion. (And indeed the website later included a caveat: 'Contrary to several of the sources used for this report, Estonia is no longer considered a developing nation.')

Ethical Traveler considers three general categories in making its selections: environmental protection, social welfare and human rights. For each of these categories, it looks at information past and present in order to understand both the current state of a country and its forward direction. This helps the organisation select countries that are 'actively improving the state of their people and environment' – read more at www.ethicaltraveler.org/destinations/2008.

---

none), making up 10% of the landmass and 2500km out of its 3800km of coastline.

The coast is also where one of Estonia's most outstanding geographical features, the Baltic Glint, lies; a long stretch of raised limestone banks, the glint extends 1200km, from Sweden to Lake Ladoga in Russia. Although 500km of this lies underwater, there are some stretches of impressive cliffs along Estonia's north coast – at Ontika (p102) the cliffs rise over 50m above the coast.

Estonia has the biggest lakes in the Baltic region; Lake Peipsi, straddling the Estonian–Russian border, is the fifth largest in Europe, at 3555 sq km (though its maximum depth is only 15m). The deepest lake, believed by some to emit magical energy, is the 38m-deep Suurjärv in Rõuge.

One of the more fascinating effects of the last ice age can be seen in various places; the march of glaciers and continental ice across the country deposited some truly gigantic rocks (called 'erratic' boulders), some of which were large enough to warrant a name – Kabelikivi (Chapel Boulder) east of Tallinn, for instance, stretches 19m long and 7m tall and hails originally from Scandinavia.

Perhaps proof of its powers of attraction, Estonia has one of the world's highest concentrations of documented meteor craters. At Kaali (p156), in Saaremaa, lies the country's most famous meteor crater.

Wildlife
ANIMALS

Estonia has its share of mammals, with 64 recorded species. Some animals that have been declining elsewhere are doing well here. The brown bear, Estonia's largest mammal, faced extinction at the turn of the 20th century (when the killing of large carnivores was all the rage). Today Estonia has around 500 bears, making it one of Europe's highest populations. The European beaver, which was hunted to near extinction, was successfully reintroduced in the 1950s, and today the population is well over 10,000. Other animals haven't fared so well. Roe deer and wild boar numbers are dwindling, which some chalk up to predators – though these animals, along with elk, are commonly hunted and may appear on the menu in more expensive restaurants. Estonia still has grey wolves (thought to number around 150), though our favourite four-legged local is the lynx (around 900), a handsome furry cat with large, impressive feet that act as snowshoes. Sadly, lynxes, bears, wolves and beavers are just a few of the animals that are hunted each year. Wolves, which numbered over 500 in the mid-1990s, are in particular danger of disappearing from Estonia.

Estonia also has abundant birdlife, with 363 recorded species. Owing to the harsh winters, most birds here are migratory. They typically arrive at the end of April (some arrive as early as March) and begin the return migration as early as August (though some birds stay until December). Although it's found throughout much of the world, the barn swallow in Estonia receives an almost regal status and is the 'national bird'; it appears in April or late May following its winter retreat. Another bird with pride of place in Estonia is the stork; while their numbers are declining elsewhere in Europe, here they are on the increase.

PLANTS

Estonia's rich flora includes 1470 varieties of indigenous plants. If you go down to the woods today, pine trees represent the dominant species in forests, making up 41% of the woodlands. Silver and downy birch are also common (28%), followed by Norway spruce (23%), alders and aspen. Oak, willow, linden and maple are also found. Juniper groves are most common on the western islands. Many species of rare northern orchids can be found in western Estonia's wooded meadows.

Mushroom-munchers be advised: fungi are found throughout Estonia's forests, meadows and bogs. The quest for some of the 400 edible species, particularly prominent in the north and southeast, is a widely enjoyed pursuit come autumn.

National Parks & Reserves

Some of Europe's few remaining original landscapes have been preserved within Estonia, much of this inadvertently through isolation under the Soviet regime. Almost 20% of Estonia's lands are protected to some degree (more than double the European average). Estonia has five national parks, three of them established since independence, and a number of nature reserves. Some of the most popular for visitors are Lahemaa and Soomaa national parks, and Haanja Nature Park.

Environmental Issues

The Soviet regime's disregard for ecology was staggering; it left a populace traditionally bound to nature with a heightened sensitiv-ity to the dangers of pollution. Large-scale clean-up programs, often foreign-funded, greatly reduced pollution as well as the concentration of dangerous emissions in industrial areas throughout the 1990s, while in recent years EU funding and assistance has seen the establishment of numerous environment-friendly initiatives. According to the website of the Estonian Environment Information Centre (EEIC; www.keskkon nainfo.ee), Estonia's greenhouse gas emissions decreased by 54% by 2005 in comparison with 1990.

Still, Estonia is among the biggest per-capita emitters of carbon dioxide in the world, thanks to oil shale-related emissions, which in 2005 accounted for 71% of the country's total carbon-dioxide emission. Estonia's greatest obstacle to a cleaner environment is the burning of oil shale (a fossil fuel) for its energy needs. Ida Virumaa county (near the power plants of Narva) reveals the ecological damage: rivers are polluted, with artificial hills made of ash from the oil-shale power plants, and barren trees silhouetted against the sky. Modern filter systems and the adoption of more environmentally friendly techniques have seen cleaner energy being produced, but there is still a long way to go.

On a brighter note, the general populace is taking green matters seriously and doing what

NATIONAL PARKS & RESERVES

National park or reserve	Area	Features	Activities	Best time to visit
Haanja Nature Park (p121)	170 sq km	forests, hills, lakes and rivers, traditional villages; highest peak in the Baltic	hiking, wildlife-watching, cross-country skiing	May-Sep
Karula National Park (p123)	111 sq km	lakes, ancient stone burial mounds, nature trails, rich fauna	hiking, wildlife-watching, swimming	May-Sep
Lahemaa National Park (p94)	725 sq km	striking Estonian coast and hinterland with beaches, rivers, lakes and waterfalls	hiking, wildlife-watching, swimming	May-Sep
Matsalu National Park (p146)	486 sq km	wetlands and major bird habitat (280 bird species)	birdwatching	Apr-Oct
Soomaa National Park (p138)	390 sq km	swampland, forests and flat meadow	hiking, canoeing, bog shoe experience, wildlife-watching	Jun-Sep
Viidumäe Nature Reserve (p161)	19 sq km	forest with rare plant species	nature trails, birdwatching	May-Sep
Vilsandi National Park (p162)	238 sq km	small islands and bird sanctuary (ringed seals, rare orchids, 247 bird species)	wildlife-watching	May-Sep

they can, as demonstrated by a grassroots initiative in May 2008 to clean up the forests. Two internet entrepreneurs were behind the idea, which saw hundreds of illegal dump sites photographed and mapped online to aid the mass clean-up. In all, 50,000 volunteers turned out to collect 10,000 tonnes of illegally dumped garbage – see www.teeme2008.ee for more.

The webpage of EKO – the Estonian Council of Environmental NGOs (http://eko .org.ee) – has links to the big organisations dealing with nature conservation, including the Estonian Green Movement, Estonian Fund for Nature and Estonian Institute for Sustainable Development.

FOOD & DRINK

Although Tallinn has a fantastically diverse dining scene, many parts of Estonia offer visitors little variety beyond what type of meat they'd like with their potatoes. This owes much to Estonia's roots. For centuries Estonia was largely a farming country, and folks who worked the fields (serfs prior to emancipation in the 1800s) sought heavy nourishment to fuel their long days. Food preparation was simple and practical, using whatever could be raised, grown or gathered from the land. Daily fare was barley porridge, cheese curd and boiled potatoes. On feast days and special occasions, meat made its appearance. Coastal dwellers also garnered sustenance from the sea, mainly cod and herring. To make foods last through the winter, people dried, smoked and salted their fish. They also ate canned and preserved foods.

Traditionally the seasons played a large role in the Estonian diet. When spring arrived, wild leek, rhubarb, fresh sorrel and goat's cheese appeared, and the spring lambs were slaughtered. During summer there were fresh vegetables and herbs along with berries, nuts and mushrooms gathered from the forests – still a popular pastime for many Estonians. Autumn was the season of the traditional goose; it was also the prime hunting season – elk, pheasant, boar and even wild goat. To sustain themselves through the long harsh winters, Estonians would eat hearty roasts and stews, soups and plenty of sauerkraut.

Despite its simple culinary roots, or perhaps because of them, Estonia has a growing world dining scene. In Tallinn, and to a lesser extent Pärnu, Tartu and Kuressaare, you'll find French, Italian, Japanese, Thai and Indian cuisine. The hunger for innovation has led to an ever-changing scene in the capital. At last count, sushi bars were the latest rage.

Staples & Specialities

Although it was a rarity in the diet of 19th-century peasants, meat is an integral part of most meals. Beefing out most menus are red meat (particularly pork), chicken and sausage, alongside which you'll see cabbage and the beloved potato.

Although Estonia has an extensive coastline, fish doesn't take pride of place. Smoked-fish lovers, however, have much to celebrate. Lake Peipsi is a particularly good place for tracking down *suitsukala* (smoked fish, usually trout or salmon); look for roadside stands along the shore road.

In summer fresh fruits and vegetables are particularly plentiful. Be sure to take advantage of the local *turg* (market) and load up on superbly flavoured strawberries (make sure you're buying the local stuff, not imports).

Given Estonia's rustic origins, it's not surprising that bread is a major staple in the diet, and that Estonians make a pretty good loaf. Rye is by far the top choice. Unlike other ryes you may have eaten, here it's moist, dense and, yes, delicious (assuming it's fresh).

Drinks

Beer is the favourite alcohol in Estonia, and the local product is very much in evidence. The best brands are Saku and A. Le Coq, which come in a range of brews. On Saaremaa and Hiiumaa, you'll also find homemade beer, which is flatter than traditional beer, but still the perfect refreshment on a hot day. In winter Estonians drink mulled wine, the antidote to cold wintry nights.

Estonia's ties to Russia have led to vodka's long-time popularity. Viru Valge is the best brand, and it comes in a range of flavours, which some Estonians mix with fruit juices (try the vanilla-flavoured vodka mixed with apple juice).

Vana Tallinn is in a class of its own. No one quite knows what the syrupy liqueur is made from, but it's sweet and strong and has a pleasant aftertaste. It's best served in coffee, over ice with milk, over ice cream, or in champagne or dry white wine.

Even without any vineyards to call their own, Estonia has a burgeoning wine culture.

ESTONIA

Wine bars are quite fashionable, especially in the larger cities. The capital also boasts the largest wine cellars in the Baltic and plenty of medieval settings in which to imbibe (see p87).

Celebrations

At Christmas, sausages are made from fresh blood and wrapped in pig's intestine – joy to the world indeed! These *verivorst* (blood sausages), which locals insist are delicious

---

EAT YOUR WORDS

Don't know your *kana* from your *kala*? Your *maasikas* from your *räim*? Get a head start on the cuisine scene by learning the words that make the dish. For pronunciation guidelines, see the Language chapter.

Useful Phrases

May I have a menu?	*kas* mah *saahk*·sin me*nüü*	*Kas ma saaksin menüü?*
I'd like ...	ma *saw*·vik·sin ...	*Ma sooviksin ...*
The bill, please.	*pah*·lun *ahrr*·ve	*Palun arve.*
I'm a vegetarian.	mah o·len *tai*·me·toyt·lah·ne	*Ma olen taimetoitlane.*
Bon appetit!	head *i*·su	*Head isu!*
To your health! (when toasting)	*ter*·vi·seks	*Terviseks!*
breakfast	*hom*·mi·ku·serrk	hommikusöök
lunch	*lyu*·na	lõuna
dinner	*er*·tu·serrk	õhtusöök

Menu Terms

menüü	*me*·nüü	menu
eelroad	*ehl*·oahd	starters
salatid	*sa*·la·tid	salads
supid	*su*·pid	soups
pearoad/praed/liharoad	*pea*·roahd	main dishes
lisandid	*li*·san·did	side dishes
magustoidud	*ma*·gu·stoy·dud	desserts

Food Glossary

biifsteek	*beef*·stehk	steak
juust	yoost	cheese
kaaviar, kalamari	*kaa*·vi·ah, ka·la·*mah*·rri	caviar
kala	*kah*·lah	fish
kana	*kah*·nah	chicken
kapsas	*kahp*·sahs	cabbage
karbonaad	*kah*·bo·noahd	grilled 'chop'
kartul	*kahrr*·tul	potato
kilud	*ki*·lud	sprats
köögivili	*kerrg*·vi·li	vegetables
leib	layb	rye bread
liha	*li*·hah	meat (red)
lõhe	*ly*·he	salmon
marjad	*mahrr*·yahd	berries
maasikas	*maah*·si·kas	strawberry
pannkook	*pahn*·kawk	pancake
puuviljad	*poo*·vil·yahd	fruit
räim, heeringas	rraim, *heh*·rrin·gahs	herring
sai	sai	white bread
šašlökk	*shash*·lerk	kebab
sealiha	*sea*·li·ha	pork
seened	*seh*·ned	mushrooms
vorst	vorrst	sausage

ESTONIA

and healthy, are served in most traditional Estonian restaurants, and sold in shops all year-round. For the bloodthirsty, *verileib* (blood bread) and *verikäkk* (balls of blood rolled in flour and eggs with bits of pig fat thrown in for taste) will surely satisfy.

Where to Eat & Drink

For a meal, you can eat in a *restoran* (restaurant) or *kohvik* (cafe); a *pubi* (pub), *kõrts* (inn) or *trahter* (tavern) will usually serve hearty, traditional meals. Nearly every town has a *turg* (market), where you can buy fresh fruits and vegetables, as well as meats and fish. For standard opening times, see the Regional Directory, p391.

Habits & Customs

Estonian eating habits are similar to other parts of northern Europe. Lunch or dinner may be the biggest meal of the day. Tipping is fairly commonplace, with 10% the norm.

If invited over to an Estonian's house, you can expect abundant hospitality and generous portions. It's fairly common to bring flowers to the host. Just be sure to give an odd number (even-numbered flowers are reserved for the dead).

TALLINN

pop 396,200

Today's Tallinn fuses medieval and cutting-edge to come up with an energetic new mood all its own – an intoxicating traveller mix of ancient church spires, glass-and-chrome skyscrapers, cosy wine cellars inside 15th-century basements, lazy afternoons soaking up sun and beer suds on Raekoja plats, and bike paths to beaches and forests – with a few Soviet throwbacks in the mix, for added spice. Despite its fiercely forward focus and the boom of 21st-century development, Tallinn remains loyal to the fairytale charms of the Old Town, and compact enough to explore on foot (or there's the option of an easy tram or bus ride should you seek leafy parks or beachside downtime).

The jewel in Tallinn's crown remains the two-tiered Old Town, a 14th- and 15th-century jumble of turrets, spires and winding streets. Most tourists see nothing other than this cobblestoned labyrinth of intertwining alleys and picturesque courtyards. Tallinn's

modern dimension – its growing skyline, shiny shopping malls, cutting-edge new art museum, wi-fi that bathes much of the city – is a cool surprise and harmonious counterbalance to the city's old-world allure.

HISTORY

The site of Tallinn is thought to have been settled by Finno-Ugric people around 2500 BC. There was probably an Estonian trading settlement here from around the 9th century AD, and a wooden stronghold was built on Toompea (*tom*-pe-ah; the hill dominating Tallinn) in the 11th century. The Danes under King Waldemar II (who conquered northern Estonia in 1219) met tough resistance at Tallinn and were on the verge of retreat when a red flag with a white cross fell from the sky into their bishop's hands. Taking this as a sign of God's support, they went on to win the battle; the flag became their national flag. The Danes set their own castle on Toompea. The origin of the name Tallinn is thought to be from *Taani linn,* Estonian for 'Danish town'.

The Knights of the Sword took Tallinn from the Danes in 1227 and built the first stone fort on Toompea. German traders arrived from Visby on the Baltic island of Gotland and founded a colony of about 200 beneath the fortress. In 1238 Tallinn returned to Danish control, but in 1285 it joined the German-dominated Hanseatic League as a channel for trade between Novgorod, Pihkva (Russian: Pskov) and the West. Furs, honey, leather and seal fat moved west; salt, cloth, herring and wine went east.

By the mid-14th century, when the Danes sold northern Estonia to the Teutonic Order, Tallinn was a major Hanseatic town with about 4000 people. A conflict of interest with the knights and bishop on Toompea led the mainly German artisans and merchants in the Lower Town to build a fortified wall to separate themselves from Toompea. However, Tallinn still prospered and became one of northern Europe's biggest towns. Tallinn's German name, Reval, coexisted with the local name until 1918.

Prosperity faded in the 16th century. The Hanseatic League had weakened, and Russians, Swedes, Danes, Poles and Lithuanians fought over the Baltic region. Tallinn survived a 29-week siege by Russia's

Ivan the Terrible between 1570 and 1571. It was held by Sweden from 1561 to 1710, when, decimated by plague, Tallinn surrendered to Russia's Peter the Great.

In 1870 a railway was completed from St Petersburg, and Tallinn became a chief port of the Russian empire. Freed peasants converged on the city from the countryside, increasing the percentage of Estonians in its population from 52% in 1867 to 89% in 1897. By WWI Tallinn had big shipyards and a large working class of over 100,000.

Tallinn suffered badly in WWII, with thousands of buildings destroyed during Soviet bombing in 1944. After the war, under Soviet control, large-scale industry was developed in Tallinn – including the USSR's biggest grain-handling port – and the city expanded, its population growing to nearly 500,000 from a 1937 level of 175,000. Much of the new population came from Russia, and new high-rise suburbs were built on the outskirts to house the workers.

Not surprisingly, the days of Soviet occupation (1940–91) were hard on the capital. The explosion of Soviet-style settlements in the suburbs meant a loss of cultural life in the centre. Old Town by the 1980s was run-down, with most people preferring to live in the suburbs rather than the centre. Old Town began to be renovated in the late '80s, with independence largely playing out on the streets of Tallinn.

The 1990s saw the city transformed into a contemporary midsized city, with a beautifully restored Old Town and a modern business district. Today a look around the centre and the skyline of the business district indicates that the city is booming. Tallinn shows a taste for all things new, extending to IT-driven business at the fore of the new economy, and an e-savvy, wi-fi connected populace embracing a brighter future.

Tallinn continues to cement its reputation as a weekend getaway (although it seems to have fallen slightly off the radar for marauding British stag parties). In addition to the close ties with Finland and thousands of Finnish visitors arriving by ferry (Helsinki is a mere 90 minutes away by hydrofoil), discount airlines carry passengers from Western Europe, curious about this re-emerging part of the world, or already sold on its charms.

Meanwhile, the outskirts of the city have yet to get the facelift that the centre has received.

NAMI-NAMI

A read through Pille Petersoo's website will have you salivating – there's plenty of talk about foraging for local ingredients in season, and using them in traditional Estonian (and international) recipes, accompanied by superb photos. Pille kindly let us in on her tips to eating well in Estonia.

Tell us about Estonian food. Traditional Estonian food is simple and hearty, a mixture of Nordic, Russian and German influences. Pork and potatoes feature heavily, though during the summer the diet is a lot lighter, with barbecued meats and salads. Surprisingly, there's not a strong fish culture here, and our food isn't very strongly seasoned.

There's a growing food culture here, and the trend (in the upper-end restaurants, cookbooks and amongst foodies) is to embrace and experiment with our Estonian roots. Foodies are getting excited about local seasonal produce like nettles and dandelions, stuff that our grandparents would have been excited about. There's also a growing market culture. In Tallinn's Central Market (p87) there are lots more things available now – Estonian-grown asparagus, white garlic, nettles, all the berries (lingonberries, bilberries, cloudberries, sea-buckthorn, wild strawberries), mushrooms in their pickled, salted, dried and fresh state. A visit here is worthwhile, especially if you're not going out with a local to forage for your own berries or mushrooms. The market's open daily, and is busiest on weekends.

What are some of your best picks for eating out in Tallinn? Top-end restaurants: Ö (p86) and Stenhus (at Schlössle Hotel; p82). Stenhus is more conservative, a dress-up place, while Ö's atmosphere is more casual.

Estonian food: I like Vanaema Juures (p82) and Olde Hansa (p82). I've been going to Olde Hansa for years, I take all my foreign visitors there and I haven't had a bad meal. While it's not a huge

In these parts of the city, that few tourists see, you'll find poverty, unemployment and less infrastructure.

ORIENTATION

Tallinn spreads south from the edge of Tallinn Bay (Tallinna Laht) on the Gulf of Finland. Just south of the bay is Old Town (Vanalinn), the city's heart. It divides neatly into Upper Town and Lower Town. Upper Town on Toompea hill was the medieval seat of power, and it still features the parliament buildings. Lower Town spreads around the eastern foot of Toompea, and a 2.5km defensive wall still encircles much of it. The centre of Lower Town is Raekoja plats (Town Hall Sq).

Around Old Town a belt of green parks follows the line of the city's original moat defences. Radiating from this old core is New Town, dating from the 19th and early 20th centuries. Vabaduse väljak (Freedom Sq) is today's city centre on the southern edge of Old Town. In late 2008 this square became home to a long-awaited and somewhat controversial new freedom monument.

The airport lies 4km southeast of the centre on the Tartu road. It's best reached by bus 2.

ON THE STREETS

- maantee – highway (often abbreviated to mnt)
- puiestee – avenue/boulevard (often abbreviated to pst)
- sild – bridge
- tänav – street (usually omitted from maps and addresses)
- tee – road
- väljak/plats – square

The passenger-ferry terminal lies just 350m from the edge of Old Town, reachable on foot or by tram or bus. For more details on getting into town, see p92.

Maps

EO Map (www.eomap.ee) produces a good map of Tallinn (50Kr), with detailed coverage of Old Town and the modern centre. Many sights are marked, as are public transport routes, and it includes a useful street index. Walking tour and basic orientation maps are available from the tourist offices and throughout Old Town, some free of charge.

---

culinary experience, it's good fun. Their wild mushroom soup is wonderful, and the spicy sugared almonds they make are delicious.

Cafes: Park Café at Kadriorg (p86). The cafes at the bookshop in Viru Keskus (Bestseller and Boulangerie; p86) are in such a handy location if you have any shopping or business in the city. And the Old Town has loads of good cafes, especially Café-Chocolaterie de Pierre (p85), and its sister cafe, Josefine (with the same owner, on the same street). The Kehrwieder 'chain' (p84) is good, it's spreading its wings and opening in different locations.

Food shopping: NOP (p86) and Stockmann (p87) for more unusual stuff, and of course the Central Market (p87).

What should visitors try? If they're brave, blood sausage (call it black pudding and it seems more palatable), or jellied pork. I'm a great fan of *kama* – a traditional dish made from a roasted powdery mixture of boiled, roasted and ground peas, rye, barley and wheat. Traditionally, buttermilk or *kefir* (fermented milk) is added to it, and it's seasoned with salt and sugar. In its traditional form, it's a light meal or drink, especially in summer. But you can add, say, curd cheese, sugar, vanilla and chopped strawberries for a dessert dish. (The basic and more glammed-up dessert-style recipes using *kama* are on Pille's website.)

And finally, what's a good edible Estonian souvenir? Vana Tallinn, especially the cream version (it has more flavour than Baileys, and isn't as sickly sweet). People might like to take home *kama* and make it themselves, or foodies could search out some more obscure gifts: pollen chocolate, for instance, or dried berry powders to mix into drinks or porridge.

Pille Petersoo is the Tallinn-based foodie and cook extraordinaire behind the wonderful Nami-Nami blog at http://nami-nami.blogspot.com (nami-nami is an Estonian colloquialism for 'yum')

ESTONIA

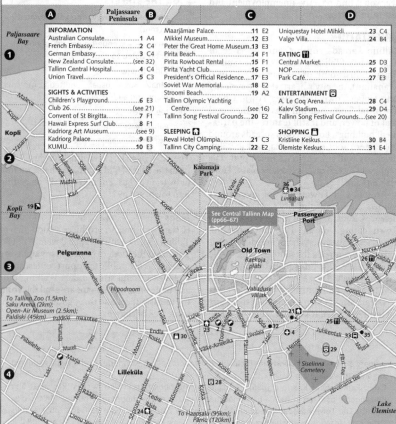

TALLINN

Paljassaare
Peninsula

INFORMATION
Australian Consulate.....................**1** A4
French Embassy............................**2** C4
German Embassy...........................**3** C4
New Zealand Consulate............(see **32**)
Tallinn Central Hospital...............**4** C4
Union Travel................................**5** C3

SIGHTS & ACTIVITIES
Children's Playground...................**6** E3
Club 26....................................(see **21**)
Convent of St Birgitta...................**7** F1
Hawaii Express Surf Club.............**8** F1
Kadriorg Art Museum..................(see **9**)
Kadriorg Palace............................**9** E3
KUMU......................................**10** E3

Maarjämäe Palace.....................**11** E2
Mikkel Museum..........................**12** E3
Peter the Great Home Museum..**13** E3
Pirita Beach...............................**14** F1
Pirita Rowboat Rental.................**15** F1
Pirita Yacht Club........................**16** F1
President's Official Residence.....**17** E3
Soviet War Memorial..................**18** E2
Stroomi Beach............................**19** A2
Tallinn Olympic Yachting
  Centre.................................(see **16**)
Tallinn Song Festival Grounds....**20** E2

SLEEPING
Reval Hotel Olümpia...................**21** E2
Tallinn City Camping..................**22** E2

Uniquestay Hotel Mihkli.............**23** C4
Valge Villa.................................**24** B4

EATING
Central Market...........................**25** D3
NOP...**26** D3
Park Café..................................**27** E3

ENTERTAINMENT
A. Le Coq Arena........................**28** C4
Kalev Stadium............................**29** D4
Tallinn Song Festival Grounds....(see **20**)

SHOPPING
Kristiine Keskus.........................**30** B4
Ülemiste Keskus........................**31** E4

INFORMATION
Bookshops

Note that central bookshops stock city and regional maps covering most destinations in Estonia.

Apollo (Map p70; ☎ 683 3400; www.apollo.ee; Viru 23) Loads of Lonely Planet and other travel titles as well as foreign-language novels and periodicals (it sells *In Your Pocket* guides and the *Baltic Times* newspaper). There's a comfy cafe on the 2nd floor and a few computers for internet access.

Rahva Raamat (www.rahvaraamat.ee) Pärnu mnt (Map p70; ☎ 644 3682; Pärnu mnt 10); Viru Keskus (Map pp66–7; ☎ 644 6655; www.rahvaraamat.ee; Viru Keskus, 3rd & 4th fl, Viru väljak) The branch inside Viru Keskus is huge, well stocked and has great decor, with the added bonus of two excellent cafes (see p86).

Cultural Centres

British Council (Map p70; ☎ 625 7788; www .britishcouncil.ee; Vana-Posti 7)
French Cultural Centre (Map p70; ☎ 627 1190; www .france.ee, in French & Estonian; Kuninga 4)
German Cultural Institute (Goethe Institute; Map p70; ☎ 627 6960; www.goethe.de/tallinn, in German & Estonian; Suurtüki 4b)

Emergency

See also p165 for countrywide emergency numbers.
Central police station (Map p70; ☎ 110, 612 4200; Pärnu mnt 11)

Internet Access

There are over 1170 wireless internet (wi-fi) areas throughout Estonia, with 372 in Tallinn

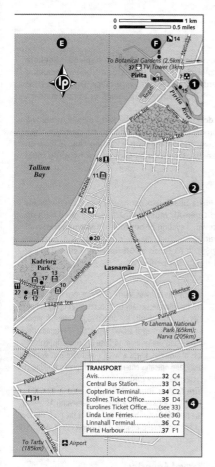

0 1 km
0 0.5 miles
E
F
14
8
To Botanical Gardens (2.5km); TV Tower (3km)
37
Pirita
16
7
1
15
Regati
Pirita River
Pirita tee
Rummu tee
Kose tee
Merivälja
18
Tallinn Bay
11
Pirita tee
2
22
Narva maantee
Smuuli tee
20
Kadriorg Park
9
17
13
10
Weizenbergi
27
6
12
Lasnamäe
Lasnamäe
Vikerlase
3
Laagna tee
Punane
To Lahemaa National Park (65km); Narva (205km)
Asunduse
Pae
Pallasti
Peterburi tee
31
4
Tartu maantee
To Tartu (185km)
Airport
TRANSPORT
Avis 32 C4
Central Bus Station 33 D4
Copterline Terminal 34 C2
Ecolines Ticket Office 35 D4
Eurolines Ticket Office (see 33)
Linda Line Ferries (see 36)
Linnahall Terminal 36 C2
Pirita Harbour 37 F1

alone; many of these are free. Visit www.wifi.ee for a complete list of locations.

If you're not packing a laptop, you'll find Tallinn light on internet cafes (with all that wi-fi around there's not so much demand for them). Most hostels and hotels will offer a computer for guests to connect to the internet, or you can try the following places:

Apollo (Map p70; ☎ 683 3400; Viru 23; per min 1Kr; 🕑 10am-8pm Mon-Fri, to 7pm Sat, 11am-5pm Sun) On 2nd floor of bookstore.

Bookingestonia.com (Map p70; ☎ 712 2102; Voorimehe 1, 2nd fl; per hr 45Kr; 🕑 10am-8pm Mon-Fri, 10am-6pm Sat & Sun) Booking agency with computers, nicely hidden just off Raekoja plats.

Estonian National Library (Map pp66-7; ☎ 630 7611; www.nlib.ee; Tõnismägi 2; per hr 40Kr; 🕑 10am-8pm Mon-Fri, noon-7pm Sat Sep-Jun, noon-6pm Mon-Fri Jul-Aug)

Metro Internet Café (Map pp66-7; ☎ 610 1519; Viru Keskus, Viru väljak; per hr 40Kr; 🕑 9am-11pm) By the bus terminal, on the basement level of Viru Keskus.

Laundry

Sauberland (Map pp66–7; ☎ 661 2075; Maakri 23; self-wash & dry 5kg 75Kr; 🕑 7.30am-8pm Mon-Fri, 8am-6pm Sat) Wash and wait, or pick-up services in ultra-clean surroundings.

Left Luggage

If you're looking to store luggage, the bus and train stations both have left-luggage offices, while Terminal A at the port has lockers; and there are also lockers at the basement level of Viru Keskus (p91), near the supermarket checkouts (close to the local bus terminal).

Media

In Your Pocket (www.inyourpocket.com) Tallinn's best listings guide, this bimonthly publication contains up-to-date info on hotels, restaurants, clubs and what's on in the city. Buy it at bookshops or the tourist office (35Kr), or download it for free from the website.

Medical Services

You'll find English-speaking staff at all of the following places.

Apteek 1 (Map p70; ☎ 627 3607; Aia 7; 🕑 9am-8.30pm Mon-Fri, 9am-8pm Sat, 9am-6pm Sun) One of many well-stocked pharmacies in town.

First-Aid Hotline (☎ 697 1145) English-language advice on treatment, hospitals and *apteek* (pharmacies).

Tallinn Central Hospital (Map pp62-3; ☎ 620 7070, emergency department 620 7040; Ravi 18) Just south of Liivalaia, some 300m west of the Reval Hotel Olümpia, this hospital has a full range of services, a polyclinic and a 24-hour emergency room.

Tallinn Dental Clinic (Tallinna Hambapolikliinik; Map pp66–7; 611 9230; Toompuiestee 4)

Tõnismäe Apteek (Map pp66-7; ☎ 644 2282; Tõnismägi 5; 🕑 24hr) Pharmacy south of Old Town, open 24 hours.

Money

Currency exchange is available at all transport terminals, exchange bureaus, the post office and inside all banks and major hotels, but check the rate of exchange (for better rates, steer clear of the small Old Town exchanges). Banks *(pank)* and ATMs are widespread. You can also receive wire transfers through the central post office, a Western Union agent.

TALLINN IN...

Two Days

To begin, get your bearings over the city by climbing up the town hall tower on splendid **Raekoja plats** (opposite). Follow this by an in-depth exploration of the streets down below (including Toompea) – museums, shops, churches, courtyards, whatever takes your fancy. That night treat yourself to dinner at the candlelit **Olde Hansa** (p82), a medieval restaurant, or sample modern Estonian cuisine at **Kaerajaan** (p82) or **Ö** (p86).

On the second day, do what most tourists don't – step out of the Old Town. Explore the **Kadriorg** (p73) neighbourhood, with its old homes, sprawling park and superb museums (see our Walking Tour, p76, for directions). Another worthwhile option is a **cycling tour** (p78) with the folks from the Travellers Info Tent or City Bike. Book a **sauna** (p76) or go **bar-hopping** (p87) before calling it a day.

Four Days

Follow the two-day itinerary, then add a trip to **Pirita beach** (p74) or have a picnic on the lawns of the **Botanic Gardens** (p75). The **zoo** (p75) and **Open-Air Museum** (p75) make a good back-up if the sun's not shining. On day four, get out of town: a cycling or bus tour of **Lahemaa National Park** (p94) is a great way to work up an appetite for dinner, maybe dumplings and vodka at **Troika** (p84), or a fancy-pants feast at **Chedi** (p83). A nightcap at **Gloria Wine Cellar** (p87) or among the locals at **Hell Hunt** (p87) will round things out perfectly.

Estravel (Map p70; ☎ 626 6266; www.estravel.ee; Suur-Karja 15; ⏰ 9am-6pm Mon-Fri, 10am-3pm Sat) Travel agency and official Amex agent.

Tavid (Map p70; ☎ 627 9900; Aia 5; ⏰ 9am-7pm Mon-Fri, 9am-5pm Sat, 10am-5pm Sun) Reliably good rates. Outside the regular opening hours a night exchange window is open 24 hours, but rates aren't as good as during business hours.

Post

Central post office (Map pp66-7; ☎ 661 6616; Narva mnt 1; ⏰ 7.30am-8pm Mon-Fri, 9am-6pm Sat) Full postal services, opposite Viru Keskus. Note that stamps can be purchased from any kiosk.

Tourist Information

Ekspress Hotline (☎ 1182; www.1182.ee; per min 14Kr) This pricey English-speaking service has telephone numbers, transport schedules, theatre listings etc. The website is also useful – and free.

Port Tourist Office (Map pp66-7; ☎ 631 8321; Terminal A, Tallinn harbour; ⏰ 8am-4.30pm)

Tallinn Tourist Office (Map p70; ☎ 645 7777; www.tourism.tallinn.ee; cnr Kullassepa & Niguliste; ⏰ 9am-5pm Mon-Fri, 10am-3pm Sat Oct-Apr, 9am-7pm Mon-Fri, 10am-5pm Sat & Sun May-Jun, 9am-8pm Mon-Fri, 10am-6pm Sat & Sun Jul-Aug, 9am-6pm Mon-Fri, 10am-5pm Sat & Sun Sep) A block south of Raekoja plats, the main tourist office has a full range of services and loads of brochures and maps, concert schedules and other info.

Traveller Info Tent (Map p70; www.traveller-info.com; Niguliste; ⏰ 9am-9pm or 10pm Jun–mid-Sep) Be sure to stop by this fabulous source of information for independent travellers (especially backpackers), set up by young locals in a tent opposite the official tourist office. It produces an invaluable map of Tallinn with loads of recommended places (and similar maps to Tartu & Pärnu), dispenses lots of local tips, keeps a 'what's on' board that's updated daily, and operates entertaining, well-priced walking and cycling tours (see p78).

Viru Keskus Tourist Office (Map pp66-7; ☎ 610 1557; Viru Keskus, Viru väljak; ⏰ 9am-9pm) As well as the main Old Town branch and desk at the port, the tourist office maintains an information desk inside Viru Keskus shopping centre.

Travel Agencies

City tours, guided trips to provincial Estonia and accommodation in other towns are most travel agencies' stock in trade. Most have branches throughout Estonia.

Bookingestonia.com (Map p70; ☎ 712 2102; www.bookingestonia.com; Voorimehe 1, 2nd fl) Nicely hidden just off Raekoja plats, this small, helpful agency can book bus, train and ferry tickets (no commission), and help arrange accommodation and car rental.

Estonian Holidays (Map p70; ☎ 627 0500; www.holidays.ee; Rüütli 28)

Estravel (Map p70; ☎ 626 6266; www.estravel.ee; Suur-Karja 15)

Union Travel (Map pp62-3; ☎ 627 0627; www.uniontravel.ee, in Estonian; Lembitu 14) Close to the Reval Hotel Olümpia. Smaller than most, but friendly and down-to-earth. It can arrange visas to Russia, but these take 10 working days to process and there are restrictions on who can apply outside of their country of residence (you'll save yourself a good deal of stress if you arrange your Russian visa before you leave home).

SIGHTS

There are loads of sights inside Old Town to keep you occupied, but sadly only a fraction of visitors make it outside the medieval town walls to see other city attractions. Chart-topping drawcards to get you out of Old Town are leafy Kadriorg Park (p73) and the stunning new KUMU art museum (p73).

Old Town

The medieval jewel of Estonia, Old Town (Vanalinn) has to be one of the country's prettiest spots, and is an ambler's paradise. Picking your way along the narrow, cobbled streets is like strolling back to the 14th century. You'll pass old merchant houses, hidden medieval courtyards, looming spires and winding staircases leading to sweeping views over the city. It's everyone's favourite tourist trap, but wears this remarkably well, remaining untacky and genuinely chic without being exclusive. No matter which direction you take, you'll see plenty of cafes, restaurants and bars en route.

If it's your first day in town, here's a tip: read the following section, then put your book away and head into town. One of the best ways to approach this old city is simply to lose yourself among its enchanting old lanes. If you happen to get lost (which is also recommended), a useful landmark is the 64m-high town hall tower.

RAEKOJA PLATS & AROUND

Raekoja plats (Town Hall Sq) has been the pulsing heart of Tallinn life since markets began here in the 11th century. All through summer outdoor cafes implore you to sit and people-watch; come Christmas time, a huge pine tree stands in the middle of the square (a tradition some 550 years old). Whether bathed in sunlight or sprinkled with snow, it's always a photogenic spot (as many postcards will attest).

Rising over the square is the imposing **town hall** (Raekoda; Map p70; ☎ 645 7900; www .tallinn.ee/raekoda; Raekoja plats), the only surviving Gothic town hall in northern Europe. Built between 1371 and 1404, it was the seat of power in the medieval Lower Town.

According to legend, its minaretlike tower was modelled on a sketch made by an explorer following his visit to the Orient. **Old Thomas** (Vana Toomas), Tallinn's symbol and guardian, has been keeping watch from his perch on the weathervane atop the town hall since 1530.

Inside the town hall, the **Citizens' Hall** (adult/concession 40/25Kr; ☿ 10am-4pm Mon-Sat Jul-Aug, by appointment Mon-Fri Sep-Jun) has an impressive vaulted roof, while the fine bench-ends (built in 1374) in the **Council Hall** are Estonia's oldest woodcarvings. Up or down? You can climb the 115 steps to the top of the 64m **tower** (adult/concession 30/15Kr; ☿ 11am-6pm Jun-Aug) for excellent views; the **cellar hall** (admission 15Kr; ☿ 10am-4pm Tue-Sat May-Sep) has an exhibition on Tallinn's fortifications.

On the northern side of the square is another ancient Tallinn institution, the **Town Council Pharmacy** (Raeapteek; Map p70; ☎ 631 4860; Raekoja plats 11; ☿ 9am-5pm Tue-Sat). There's been a pharmacy or apothecary's shop here since at least 1422, though the present facade is 17th century. It's still busy with the business of dispensing medications and is worth a peek inside.

Duck through the arch beside the pharmacy on Raekoja plats, leading into the charming, narrow **White Bread Passage** (Saiakang), once filled with the aromas of a popular bakery. At its end is the striking 14th-century Gothic **Holy Spirit Church** (Püha Vaimu Kirik; Map p70; ☎ 644 1487; Pühavaimu 2; adult/concession 15/7.50Kr; ☿ 9am-5pm Mon-Sat May-Sep, 10am-2pm Mon-Fri Oct-Apr). Its luminous blue and gold clock (on the facade, just to the right of the entry) is the oldest in Tallinn, with carvings dating from 1684, and the tower bell, made in 1433, is the oldest in Estonia. The exquisite wood-carved interior features a wooden altarpiece dating back to 1483, 16th-century carved bench-backs and a 17th-century baroque pulpit. Johann Koell, a former pastor here, is considered the author of the first Estonian book, a catechism published in 1535. Classical music concerts are held here on Monday at 6pm.

The former **town jail** (Raevangla), in a lane behind the town hall, is now home to the **Museum of Photography** (Fotomuuseum; Map p70; ☎ 644 8767; www.linnamuuseum.ee; Raekoja 4/6; adult/concession 15/7Kr; ☿ 10.30am-5.30pm Thu-Tue Mar-Oct, 10.30am-4.30pm Thu-Tue Nov-Feb), which has a small exhibition spanning photography's earliest

ESTONIA

CENTRAL TALLINN

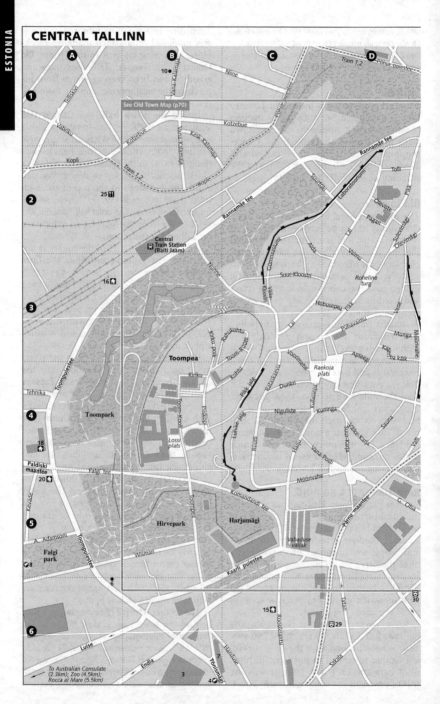

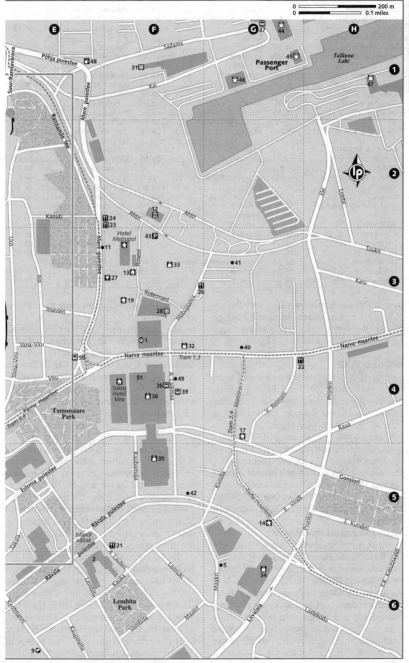

days in Estonia. Those travelling with finicky children can point out the irons still hanging outside the Town Hall. This is where lesser offenders were shackled in ye olden times.

AROUND VENE

Several 15th-century warehouses and merchant residences surround Raekoja plats, notably when heading towards Vene (the Estonian word for Russian, named for the Russian merchants who traded here centuries ago). Vene is now one of Old Town's favourite restaurant precincts, and is home to some lovely passageways and courtyards – the loveliest being **Catherine's Passage** (Katariina Käik; Vene 12), with artists' studios and a decent Italian restaurant, and **Masters' Courtyard** (Meistrite Hoov; Vene 6), a cobblestoned delight, some of it dating from the 13th-century, filled with craft stores and a sweet chocolaterie.

Set in a medieval merchant's house, the **City Museum** (Linnamuuseum; Map p70; ☎ 644 6553; www.linnamuuseum.ee; Vene 17; adult/concession 35/10Kr; ☽ 10.30am-6pm Wed-Mon Mar-Oct, 10.30am-5pm Wed-Mon Nov-Feb) traces the city's development from its earliest days, and its displays of clothing, furnishings and curios help take you back in time. The 3rd floor presents an insightful (and quite politicised) portrait of life under the Soviet yoke, and there's a fascinating

video of the events surrounding the collapse of the regime.

Also accessed from Vene is one of Tallinn's oldest buildings: the **Dominican Monastery** (Dominiiklaste klooster; Map p70; ☎ 515 5489; www .kloostri.ee; Vene 16; adult/concession 90/45Kr; ☽ 10am-6pm mid-May–Aug, visits other times by appointment), founded in 1246, once housed Scandinavian monks who aimed to convert Estonians to Christianity and educate the local population. In its glory days the coffers were full, and the monastery had its own brewery and hospital. Once the reformation began, however, its days were numbered. A mob of angry Lutherans torched the place in 1524, and the monks fled town. The monastery languished for the next 400 years until its restoration in 1954. Today the complex houses Estonia's largest collection of stone carvings (dating from the 15th to the 17th centuries), and the inner garden is a peaceful refuge from the summertime crowds.

Next door to the monastery is the 1844 **Sts Peter & Paul's Church** (Peeter-Paul Kirik; Map p70; ☎ 644 6367; Vene 16; ☽ 5-7pm daily, also 7-10am Mon, Wed, Fri & Sat). A handsome whitewashed church looking like it belongs in Spain, it was designed by the famed architect Carlo Rossi, who left his mark on the neoclassical shape of St Petersburg. It still functions as one of Tallinn's only Catholic churches, largely for the Polish and Lithuanian community. Not far away is **St Nicholas Orthodox Church** (Map p70; ☎ 644 1945; Vene 24; ⏱ 9.30am-5pm Mon-Thu, 9.30am-6.30pm Fri, 9am-7pm Sat, 9am-3pm Sun), built in 1827 on the site of an earlier church that was the focal point for the Russian traders the street was named for. Its interior is not as overwhelming as that of the Alexander Nevsky Cathedral on Toompea hill; it's known for its treasured iconostasis.

PIKK & LAI

Pikk (Long Street) runs from the base of Toompea hill towards Tallinn port and is lined with the houses of medieval German merchants and gentry. Many of these were built in the 15th century and contained three or four storeys, with the lower two used as living and reception quarters and the upper ones for storage.

Also on Pikk are the buildings of several old Tallinn guilds (associations of traders or artisans, nearly all German dominated). The Great Guild, to which the most eminent merchants belonged, is set in a striking building dating from 1410. Its vaulted halls now contain the **Estonian History Museum** (Ajaloomuuseum; Map p70; ☎ 641 1630; www.eam.ee; Pikk 17; adult/concession 25/15r; ⏱ 11am-6pm May-Aug, closed Wed Sep-Apr), with a rather dry permanent exhibition of Estonian historical artefacts dating from the 14th to the 18th centuries. (Coin-collectors, don't miss this place.) Changing temporary shows, however, are often quite interesting: check the website to see what's on.

Another old artisans guild on this street is the 1860 **St Canutus Guild Hall** (Kanuti Gildi Saal; p70; Pikk 20), with its zinc statues of Martin Luther and St Canute looking down from

their 2nd-storey perch. The adjoining buildings of the **Brotherhood of the Blackheads** (Mustpeade Maja; Map p70; ☎ 631 3199; Pikk 26) and **St Olaus' Guild** (Olevi Gildi Hoone; Map p70; Pikk 24) are closed to the public except for regular concerts. The Blackheads were unmarried merchants who took their name not from poor dermatology, but from their patron saint, Mauritius, a legendary African warrior whose likeness is found between two lions on the building facade (dating from 1597), above an ornate, colourful door. St Olaus' Guild – probably the first guild in Tallinn – began in the 13th century, and developed a membership of more humble non-German artisans and traders.

In amongst the guilds, behind a fabulous sculpted facade, is **Draakoni Gallery** (Map p70; ☎ 646 4110; Pikk 18; admission free; ⏱ 10am-6pm Mon-Fri, 10am-5pm Sat), which hosts small, sometimes stimulating, exhibitions of contemporary art.

While Pikk was the street of traders, Lai, running roughly parallel, was the street of artisans, whose traditions are recalled in the **Museum of Applied Art & Design** (Tarbekunstija Disainimuuseum; Map p70; ☎ 627 4600; www.etdm.ee; Lai 17; adult/concession 40/20Kr; ⏱ 11am-6pm Wed-Sun). Inside you'll find an excellent mix of historical and contemporary ceramics, glass, rugs, metal and leatherwork.

At the northern end of Pikk stands **St Olaf's Church** (Oleviste Kirik; Map p70; Pikk 48; admission free), its 124m spire being yet another of Tallinn's icons (once the tallest spire in the world, and formerly used as a surveillance centre by the KGB). The entrance is on Lai. Anyone unafraid of a bit of sweat should head up, way up, to Tallinn's best views, at the top of the 258-step **observation tower** (☎ 621 4421; www.oleviste.ee; adult/concession 30/15Kr; ⏱ 10am-6pm Apr-Oct). Although dedicated to the 11th-century King Olaf II of Norway, the 13th-century church is linked in local lore with another Olaf – its architect who ignored the prophesies of doom to befall the one who completed the church's construction. Accordingly, Olaf fell to his death from the tower, and it's said that a toad and snake then crawled out of his mouth. The incident is shown in one of the carvings on the eastern wall of the 16th-century **Chapel of Our Lady**, adjoining the church.

You can only imagine the horrors that went on at the **former KGB headquarters** (Map p70; Pikk 59), just south of the church. The building's basement windows were bricked up to

---

TALLINN CARD

Flash a good-value Tallinn Card to get free or discounted entry to most of the city's sights, discounts on shopping, dining and entertainment, and free travel on Tallinn's buses, trolleys and trams. Prices for one-/two-/three-day cards are 375/435/495Kr (200/225/250Kr for children under 14) and include a free 2½-hour city sightseeing tour (by bus and on foot), and a free two-hour cycling tour of the city. Cards are sold at tourist offices, hotels and travel agencies. For further details, see www.tallinncard.ee.

prevent the sounds of violent interrogations being heard by those passing by on the street. The small memorial on the wall translates as: 'This building housed the headquarters of the organ of repression of the Soviet occupational power. Here began the road to suffering for thousands of Estonians.' Locals joked, with typically black humour, that the building had the best views in Estonia – from here you could see all the way to Siberia.

The **Great Coast Gate** (Map p70), the medieval exit to Tallinn port, lies just north of St Olaf's. It's joined to **Fat Margaret** (Paks Margareeta), a rotund 16th-century bastion that protected this entrance to the town. Fat

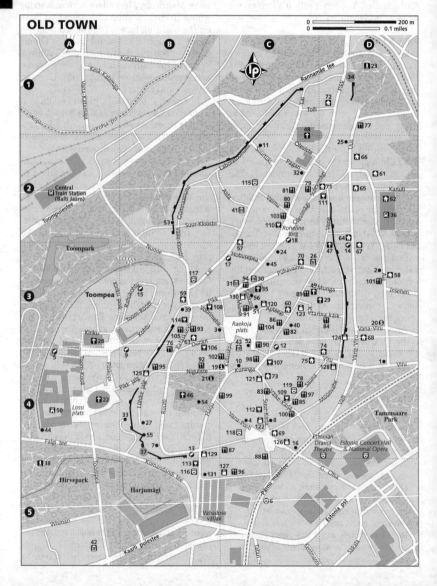

OLD TOWN

Margaret's walls are more than 4m thick at the base; inside the corpulent lady is the **Maritime Museum** (Meremuuseum; Map p70; ☎ 641 1408; Pikk 70; adult/concession 40/20Kr; ☯ 10am-6pm Wed-Sun), with displays of old charts, model ships, antiquated diving equipment and other artefacts from Estonia's seafaring his-

tory. There are good views from the platform on the roof.

Just outside the bastion stretch two strands of a long, poignant sculpture entitled *Broken Line*, which is dedicated to the victims of the *Estonia* ferry-sinking, Europe's worst peacetime maritime tragedy (see the boxed text, p151). Nearby, a 3m-long granite tablet lists the 852 people who died the night of 28 September 1994, travelling from Tallinn to Stockholm.

LOWER-TOWN WALLS

The longest-standing stretch of the Old Town wall, with nine towers, spans from Väike-Kloostri, along Laboratooriumi to the northern end of Lai.

At the northern end of Aida is a tiny passageway through the town wall; on the other side there's a picturesque spot to photograph a line-up of four **towers** (another can be found along Kooli). To access the walkway atop the walls, visit the **town wall** (Linnamüür; Map p70; Gümnaasiumi 3; adult/concession 15/10Kr; ☺ 11am-7pm Jun-Aug, shorter hr & closed Thu Sep-May), not far from the Baltic Hotel Imperial. Three empty towers are connected here and visitors can explore their nooks and crannies for themselves, with cameras at the ready for the red-rooftop views.

NIGULISTE MUSEUM

The Gothic St Nicholas' Church (Niguliste Kirik) is another of the city's medieval treasures. Dating from the 13th century, St Nicholas' is now known as the **Niguliste Museum & Concert Hall** (Map p70; ☎ 631 4330; Niguliste 3; adult/concession 35/20Kr; ☺ 10am-5pm Wed-Sun) and houses artworks from medieval Estonian churches. Its most famous work is the eerie *Dance Macabre,* Berndt Notke's 15th-century masterpiece. Other artefacts here include baroque chandeliers, a 15th-century altar and a silver chamber. The church was badly damaged by Soviet bombers in 1944 and a fire in the 1980s, but today stands fully restored. The acoustics are first-rate, with organ recitals held most weekends (beginning at 4pm on Saturday and Sunday).

TOOMPEA

A winding stairway connects Lühike jalg, off Rataskaevu, to Toompea. According to Estonian legend, Toompea is the burial mound of Kalev, the heroic first leader of the Estonians, built by his widow Linda. In German times this was the preserve of the feudal nobility and bishop, looking down on the traders and lesser beings of the Lower Town.

Although the most impressive – and until the 17th century the only – approach to Toompea is through the red-roofed **Long Leg Gate Tower** (Pikk jalg; Map p70), which dates from 1380, **Short Leg** (Lühike jalg; Map p70), at the western end of Pikk, is not without character. A number of ghostly apparitions have been reported inside the **Gate Tower** (Lühike jalg 9), including a crucified monk and a black dog with burning eyes. It's thought to be the most haunted building in Tallinn.

At the top of Lühike jalg is Estonia's parliament building, the **Riigikogu**, housed in the photogenic **Toompea Castle** (Map p70; ☎ 631 6357; www.riigikogu.ee; Lossi plats 1; ☺ tours by appointment only, 10am-4pm Mon-Fri). Nothing remains of the Danish castle built here in 1219, but three of the four corner towers of its successor, founded between 1227 and 1229, still stand. The pink baroque facade dates from the 18th century when, under Catherine the Great, it was rebuilt and the moat was filled.

The finest of the castle towers is the 1371 **Pikk Hermann** (Map p70) at the southwest corner, topped by the national flag. The two other surviving towers, plus most of the northern wall of the old castle, can be seen from the yard of Toom-Kooli 13.

Toompea is named after the Lutheran **Dome Church** (Toomkirik; Map p70; ☎ 644 4140; Toom-Kooli 6; ☺ 9am-4pm Tue-Sun) founded in 1233. The edifice dates from the 15th and 17th centuries, with the tower added in 1779 (there is actually no dome – the nickname is a corruption of the Estonian word *toom,* itself borrowed from the German word *Dom,* meaning cathedral). The impressive, austere and damp church was a burial ground for the rich and noble, and the whitewashed walls are decorated with the coats-of-arms of Estonia's noble families. From the Dome Church, follow Kohtu to the city's favourite **lookout** over the lower town.

The location of the Russian Orthodox **Alexander Nevsky Cathedral** (Map p70; ☎ 644 3484; Lossi plats; ☺ 8am-8pm), opposite the parliament buildings, was no accident: the church was one of many Orthodox cathedrals built between 1894 and 1900 as part of a general wave of Russification in the Russian Baltic provinces in the last quarter of the 19th century. Orthodox believers still come here in droves, alongside tourists ogling the interior's striking mosaics and icons.

A path leads down from Lossi plats through an opening in the wall to the view-enriched **Danish King's Courtyard** (Map p70), where artists set up their easels in summer. One of the towers here, the **Virgin's Tower** (Neitsitorn;

Lühike jalg 9a), is said to have been a prison for medieval prostitutes.

One of Tallinn's most formidable cannon towers is the tall, stout **Kiek in de Kök** (Map p70; ☎ 644 6686; www.linnamuuseum.ee; Komandandi 2; adult/ concession 25/8Kr; ☺ 10.30am-5pm Tue-Sun). Its name is Low German for 'Peep into the Kitchen'; from the upper floors medieval voyeurs could peer into the houses of Lower Town. Built around 1475, it was badly damaged during the Livonian War, but it never collapsed (nine of Ivan the Terrible's cannon balls remain embedded in the walls). Today it houses a ho-hum museum tracing the birth and development of Tallinn. Staff here also arrange tours of 17th-century tunnels connecting bastions, built by the Swedes to help protect the city. They're newly opened to the public. **Tunnel tours** (☎ 644 6686; www.linnamuuseum .ee; adult/concession 50/25Kr; ☺ 11am-4pm Tue-Sun) need to be booked in advance.

From Kiek in de Kök, a pleasant downhill stroll southwest leads to the grassy **Hirvepark** (Map p70) with a small **statue** of Linda (Kalev's widow) grieving. This has come to symbolise the tragic fate of those deported from Estonia during and after WWII. Continuing along Toompea brings you to the thought-provoking Museum of Occupation & Fight for Freedom (p75).

East of the Centre

Trams 1 and 3 go to the Kadriorg stop right by Kadriorg Park. Buses 1A, 8, 34A and 38 all run between the city centre and Pirita, stopping on Narva mnt near Kadriorg Park, and at Maarjamäe. Bus 34A and 38 go on to the Botanic Gardens (Kloostrimetsa stop).

ARCHITECTURE MUSEUM

Not far east of Old Town, and not far from the port, the Rotterman Salt Storage is a restored limestone warehouse that once served the unpoetic but utilitarian function as the city's salt cellar. Today the space houses the modest **Museum of Architecture** (Arhitektuurimuuseum; Map pp66-7; ☎ 625 7000; www.arhitektuurimuuseum.ee; Ahtri 2; adult/concession 30/15Kr; ☺ 11am-6pm Wed-Sun), with plenty of building and town models to enable you to see just how the city skyline has changed in recent years.

KADRIORG

The lovely wooded **Kadriorg Park** (Map pp62-3; Narva mnt) lies about 2km east of Old Town, and remains a long-time favourite of city dwellers seeking a bit of green space. Oak, lilac and horse chestnut trees are the setting for strollers, cyclists, picnickers, kids and wedding parties, and the park's ample acreage never makes the paths feel crowded. Together with the baroque Kadriorg Palace, it was designed for the Russian tsar Peter the Great for his wife Catherine I (Kadriorg means Catherine's Valley in Estonian) by the Italian Niccolo Michetti, soon after Peter's conquest of Estonia in the Great Northern War.

The original centrepiece of the park is **Kadriorg Palace**, built between 1718 and 1736 – with the help of Peter himself who laid no fewer than three sturdy bricks. The palace houses the **Kadriorg Art Museum** (Kadrioru Kunstimuuseum; Map pp62-3; ☎ 606 6403; www.ekm.ee; Weizenbergi 37; adult/concession 55/30Kr; ☺ 10am-5pm Tue-Sun May-Sep, 10am-5pm Wed-Sun Oct-Apr), which holds Dutch, German and Italian paintings from the 16th to the 18th centuries, along with Russian works from the 18th to 19th centuries. The Great Hall is a baroque bonanza; the collection makes for a dreamy hour or two strolling among the mostly Romantic works, and there's a handsome flower garden at the back. In the 1930s the palace was the private domain of the president of independent Estonia; in 1938 a purpose-built residence was built nearby, and since Estonia's re-independence it is again the home of the country's president. It's not open to the public, but you'll see the honour guards out front.

Close to Kadriorg Palace, in the former kitchen building, the petite **Mikkel Museum** (Map pp62-3; ☎ 601 5844; www.ekm.ee; Weizenbergi 28; adult/ concession 25/15Kr; ☺ 11am-5pm Wed-Sun) has a small but interesting assortment of art. Russian and Chinese paintings, 15th-century icons and works in porcelain are all part of the eclectic collection. Joint admission with the Kadriorg Art Museum is adult/concession 70/40Kr.

Nearby is the humble cottage Peter the Great occupied on visits to Tallinn while the palace was under construction. Today it houses the **Peter the Great Home Museum** (Peeter I Majamuuseum; Map pp62-3; ☎ 601 3136; www.linnamu useum.ee; Mäekalda 2; adult/concession 15/7Kr; ☺ 11am-7pm Wed-Sun May-Aug, 11am-4pm Wed-Sun Sep-Apr), filled with portraits, furniture and artefacts from the era.

And finally, the grand new showpiece of Kadriorg (and Tallinn): **KUMU** (Kunstimuuseum; Map pp62-3; ☎ 602 6000; www.ekm.ee; Weizenbergi 34;

adult/concession 80/45Kr; ☺ 11am-6pm Tue-Sun May-Sep, 11am-6pm Wed-Sun Oct-Apr), also known as the Art Museum of Estonia. It opened in this futuristic, Finnish-designed, seven-storey building to rave reviews in early 2006, and in 2008 won the title 'European Museum of the Year' from the European Museum Forum. It's a spectacular structure of limestone, glass and copper, nicely integrated with the landscaping, and it contains the largest repository of Estonian art as well as constantly changing contemporary exhibits. The Treasury (3rd floor) houses classics of Estonian art from the beginning of the 18th century until the end of WWII; on the 4th floor, 'Difficult Choices' showcases local art during the Soviet era and includes intriguing propaganda posters and disturbing images by Johannes Saal. Don't miss KUMU – and note that the complex is wheelchair accessible, and houses an excellent shop, cafe and restaurant.

TALLINN SONG FESTIVAL GROUNDS

The **Tallinn Song Festival Grounds** (Lauluväljak; Map pp62-3; Narva mnt), site of the main gatherings of Estonia's national song festivals (and assorted rock concerts and festivals), is an open-air amphitheatre said to have a capacity of 150,000 people. In September 1988, 300,000 squeezed in for one songfest and publicly demanded independence during the 'Singing Revolution'. Approximately half a million people, including a large number of Estonian émigrés, were believed to have been present at the 21st Song Festival in 1990, the last major fest before the restoration of independence. An Estonian repertoire was reinstated and around 29,000 performers sang under the national flag for the first time in 50 years.

PIRITA TEE

This coastal road curving northwards alongside Tallinn Bay is an ideal walk, affording a sea view that's particularly striking during late-night summer sunsets. It's a popular stretch for joggers, cyclists and skaters.

A kilometre north of Kadriorg Park, the seldom-visited **Maarjamäe Palace** (Maarjamäe loss; Map pp62-3; Pirita tee 56) is a neo-Gothic limestone palace built in the 1870s as a summer cottage for the Russian general A Orlov-Davydov. It's home to a second branch of the **Estonian History Museum** (Ajaloomuuseum; ☎ 601 4535; www .eam.ee; adult/concession 25/15Kr; ☺ 11am-6pm Wed-Sun Mar-Oct, 10am-5pm Wed-Sun Nov-Feb) – the first is in

Old Town's Great Guild (p69). Until 2010 the major exhibit is 'A Will to Be Free: 90 years of the Republic of Estonia', celebrating 90 years since Estonia's independence in 1918 and detailing the desire of the people to be free from Soviet rule.

Heading further north along Pirita tee, you pass the foreboding **Soviet obelisk** rising in its concrete glory to a sharp point on the eastern side of the street (it's locally dubbed 'the Impotent's Dream'). It's the focal point of a 1960 Soviet war memorial that's now more crumbling than inspiring.

PIRITA

Approximately 1.5km beyond Maarjamäe, just before Pirita tee crosses the Pirita River, a short side road leads down to **Pirita Yacht Club** and the **Tallinn Olympic Yachting Centre** (Map pp62-3; ☎ 639 8800; www.piritatop.ee), near the mouth of the river. This was the base for the sailing events of the 1980 Moscow Olympics, and international regattas are still held here. If you're just passing through, the Yacht Club is a relaxing spot for a drink alfresco-style.

Just behind the main Pirita bus stop are the ruins of the **Convent of St Birgitta** (Pirita kloostri varemed; Map pp62-3; ☎ 605 5044; Kloostri tee; adult/concession 20/10Kr; ☺ noon-4pm Nov-Mar, 10am-6pm Apr-May & Sep-Oct, 9am-7pm Jun-Aug). Only the Gothic gable still stands, which is the last remnant of this early-15th-century convent; the rest was destroyed courtesy of Ivan the Terrible during the Livonian War in 1577. In 1996 Birgittine nuns in Estonia were granted the right to return to and reactivate the convent. The convent's completed new headquarters are adjacent to the ruins, which are the perfect place for a ramble. Atmospheric concerts are occasionally held here in summer.

In summer **Pirita Rowboat Rental** (Map pp62-3; ☎ 621 2175; Kloostri tee 6a; rowboats/canoes per hr from 200/150Kr; ☺ 10am-10pm Jun-Aug), beside the road-bridge over the Pirita River, close to the convent ruins, rents rowboats and canoes. It's an idyllic place for a leisurely float, with thick forest edging towards the water.

North of the bridge is **Pirita beach** (Pirita rand; Map pp62-3), *the* place to shed your clothes in Tallinn summertime. It's easily the city's largest and most popular beach (and it's only 6km from the city centre). Although it's no Bondi beach (or Pärnu, for that matter), Pirita is a quick getaway for urbanites; there are plenty of young, bronzed sun-lovers filling the sands, with a handful of laid-back cafes nearby. It's a bleak and windswept place if the weather's not good, but if the wind conditions are right there are plenty of wind- and kite-surfers providing visual entertainment. If you fancy getting the wind in your hair and the salt spray in your face, talk to Toomas at **Hawaii Express Surf Club** (Map pp62-3; ☎ 503 6172; info@surf .ee; Merivälja tee), at the south end of the beach (by the car park), to arrange lessons for beginners (four hours is 1000Kr) or gear rental for experienced folks (450Kr for an hour).

BOTANIC GARDENS & TV TOWER
Need more greenery? Set on 1.2 sq km fronting the Pirita River and surrounded by lush woodlands, the **Botanic Gardens** (Tallinna Botaanikaaed; off Map pp62-3; ☎ 606 2666; www.tba.ee; Kloostrimetsa tee 52; park free, palm house & glasshouses adult/concession 45/25Kr; ☯ park 11am-7pm) boast 8000 species of plants scattered in a series of greenhouses and along a 4km nature trail. The gardens lie 2.5km east of Pirita.

The 314m **TV Tower** (off Map pp62-3; Kloostrimetsa tee 58a) is 400m further east and was once home to a panoramic viewing platform at the 170m point. At the base there are still a few bullet holes from events during the August 1991 attempted Estonian breakaway (it was as violent as things became in Estonia's bid for independence). Due to safety concerns, the tower was closed to the public in late 2007. It's worth asking at the tourist office if it has been renovated and reopened.

Southwest of the Centre
Gain some sort of understanding of the hardships and heroism involved in the 20th-century Estonian struggle for independence at the worthwhile **Museum of Occupation & Fight for Freedom** (Map pp66-7; ☎ 668 0250; www.okupa tsioon.ee; Toompea 8; adult/concession 20/10Kr; ☯ 11am-6pm Tue-Sun). Photos and artefacts illustrate five decades of oppressive rule, under both the Nazis, briefly, and the Soviets. Displays are good, but it's the videos (lengthy but enthralling) that leave the greatest impression – and the joy of a happy ending. Head to the basement toilets to check out the graveyard of Soviet-era monuments.

The impressive, monumentalist facade of the **Estonian National Library** (Map pp66-7; ☎ 630 7611; www.nlib.ee; Tõnismägi 2; ☯ 10am-8pm Mon-Fri, noon-7pm Sat Sep-Jun, noon-6pm Mon-Fri Jul-Aug) is one example of the mini-renaissance Estonia's

national stone, dolomite limestone, has undergone in recent years. Built in 1985–93 by Raine Karp (who also designed the enormous Linnahall concert hall by the port), the library is worth seeing for its cavernous interior. Frequent exhibitions take place on the upper floors (though you may need a 5Kr day pass from reception).

About 4km due west of the centre (or a 15-minute ride on bus 40 or 48) is **Stroomi beach** (Map pp62-3) in the Pelguranna district, a favourite of Tallinn's Russian community and with a distinctly local feel. The backdrop of Soviet-style apartment blocks is a real contrast to the nature of Pirita beach.

Tallinn Zoo (Loomaaed; off Map pp62-3; ☎ 694 3300; www.tallinnzoo.ee; Paldiski mnt 145; adult/concession/ family May-Sep 90/45/134Kr, Oct-Apr 50/25/95Kr; ☯ 9am-7pm May-Aug, 9am-5pm Sep-Oct & Mar-Apr, 9am-3pm Nov-Feb) boasts the world's largest collection of mountain goats and sheep (!), plus around 350 other species of feathered, furry and four-legged friends (including polar bears, leopards, elephants and rhinos). It's a good place for your kids to meet other kids – it feels like the entire child population of northern Estonia is here on summer weekends. The zoo is best reached by bus 22 or trolleybus 6.

North of the zoo is the Rocca al Mare neighbourhood and its **Open-Air Museum** (Vabaõhumuuseum; off Map pp62-3; ☎ 654 9100; www .evm.ee; Vabaõhumuuseumi tee 12; adult/child/family May-Sep 80/35/95Kr, Oct-Apr 35/20/50Kr; ☯ buildings 10am-6pm, grounds 10am-8pm May-Sep, grounds only 10am-5pm Oct-Apr). Most of Estonia's oldest wooden structures, mainly farmhouses but also a chapel (1699) and windmill, are preserved here. If you're not heading to villages in the south, this is a good place to see traditional wooden architecture and get an overview of 150 years of rural life. There are also views back to the city and you can walk through the woods and down to the sea. Every Saturday and Sunday morning from June to August there are folk song-and-dance shows; if you find yourself in Tallinn on Midsummer Eve (ie the eve of Jaanipäev, 23 June), come here to witness the traditional celebrations, bonfire and all. There's also the old wooden tavern Kolu Kõrts (open daily year-round), serving traditional Estonian cuisine. Most kids love this place, particularly for the pony rides. Bus 21 runs here. Note that you can purchase a family combo ticket that takes in the zoo and the Open-Air Museum for 199Kr.

ESTONIA

ACTIVITIES

See the Pirita section (p74), for information on summertime rowboat rental or wind-surfing classes, and under Tours (p78) for sightseeing options on two wheels. For a whole range of energetic, eco-friendly activities, from kayaking to kicksledding, contact **Reimann Retked** (☎ 511 4099; www.retked.ee). The company offers a wide range of sea-kayaking excursions, including guided overnight trips, or a four-hour paddle out to Aegna island, 14km offshore from Tallinn (450Kr). Other interesting possibilities include diving, rafting, bog walking and snowshoeing, and kicksledding on sea ice, frozen lakes or in snowy forest; most arrangements need a minimum of eight to 10 people, but smaller groups should enquire (you may be able to tag along with another group).

Bowling

If wet weather has you wondering what to do, **Ku:lsa:l** (Map pp66-7; ☎ 661 6682; www.kuulsaal.ee; Mere pst 6; ☒ 11am-11pm Mon-Thu, 11am-2am Fri, 10am-2am Sat, 10am-11pm Sun) has ten-pin bowling (lanes for six people 165Kr to 275Kr per hour) over two floors, plus bars and plenty of billiards tables (45Kr to 75Kr per hour).

Ice Skating

Rug up warm in winter to join the locals at the outdoor ice rink, **Uisuplats** (Map p70; ☎ 610 1035; ww.uisuplats.ee; Harju; per hr 50-60Kr; ☒ 10am-10pm Nov-Mar), close to Niguliste Church-Museum. You'll have earned a *hõõgvein* (mulled wine) by the end of it.

Saunas

Locals attribute all kinds of health benefits to a good old-fashioned sweat out, and truth be told a trip to Estonia just won't be complete until you've paid a visit to the sauna. You won't have to look far: most places listed in the Sleeping section have one. For something a little different, try the following:

African Kitchen (Map p70; ☎ 644 2555; www.africankitchen.ee; Uus 32; per hr 350Kr; ☒ noon-1am Sun-Thu, noon-2am Fri & Sat) This restaurant (p83) has a private sauna (holding up to 10 people) with funky lounge; you can self-cater or have the restaurant provide the drinks and nibbles.

our pick **Club 26** (Map pp62-3; ☎ 631 5585; www.revalhotels.com; 26th fl, Liivalaia 33; per hr before/after 3pm 300/600Kr; ☒ 8am-11pm) On the top floor of the Reval Hotel Olümpia (p81) and with correspondingly

outstanding views, this is one of the most luxurious choices in town. There are two private saunas, each with plunge pool and tiny balcony. Food and drink can be ordered to complete the experience.

Kalev Spa Waterpark (Map p70; ☎ 649 3370; www.kalevspa.ee; Aia 18; per hr 550-770Kr; ☒ 6.45am-10.30pm Mon-Fri, 8am-10.30pm Sat & Sun) Three private saunas at the big waterpark, with the largest holding up to 20 of your closest hot-and-sweaty mates. Prices include waterpark entry. Catering available.

Kalma Saun (Map pp66-7; ☎ 627 1811; www.bma.ee/kalma; Vana-Kalamaja 9a; admission 95-130Kr; ☒ 10am-11pm) In a grand building behind the train station, Tallinn's oldest public bath still has the aura of an old-fashioned, down-at-heel, Russian-style *banya* (bath-house). Private saunas available (180Kr to 300Kr per hour).

Swimming Pools & Gyms

Club 26 (Map pp62-3; ☎ 631 5585; www.revalhotels.com; 26th fl, Liivalaia 33; per visit 75-160Kr; ☒ 7am-10pm) Atop the Reval Hotel Olümpia (p81), this small health club is open to all and has a gym and 16m swimming pool with superb views over the city. Good choice for a workout without breaking the bank.

Kalev Spa Waterpark (Map p70; ☎ 649 3370; www.kalevspa.ee; Aia 18; 2½hr visit adult/family 150/405Kr; ☒ 6.45am-10.30pm Mon-Fri, 8am-10.30pm Sat & Sun) For serious swimming in an indoor pool of Olympic proportions; there are also plenty of other ways to wrinkle your skin here – waterslides, Jacuzzis, saunas and a kids pool, plus gym and day spa. Prices vary according to time of day, length of stay etc.

WALKING TOUR

We've sung the praises of areas outside the Old Town walls, so here's a little tour to help you on your way, with plenty of pit stops en route. Start at the focal point for most visitors to Tallinn, Old Town's **Raekoja plats** (**1**; p65), and head east along Viru, past Olde Hansa restaurant and the tourist-filled shops and cafes (yep, it's a well-worn route). After about 250m you'll exit Old Town through the dramatic twin gate towers of the 14th-century **Viru Gates** (**2**). Continue straight along, admiring the colourful flower stalls on your right.

You'll soon come to pedestrian lights to take you across busy Pärnu mnt, through **Tammsaare Park** (**3**), to the heart of the retail district and the shiny showpiece **Viru Keskus** (**4**; p91) shopping mall, which opened in 2006 and is visited daily by over 30,000 (having the main city bus terminal in the basement must help those figures along). Cut through the mall and exit onto Narva mnt, and head

TALLINN WALKING TOUR

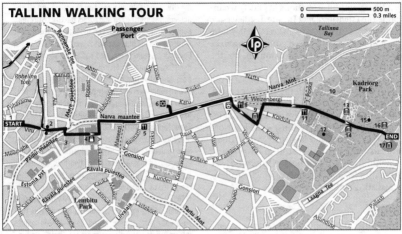

east. You'll pass slick new shopping malls and eateries before a dose of faded Soviet-style decor pulls you up short – visit **Narva Kohvik** (**5**; p86) for a taste of yesteryear.

Continue along Narva mnt, maybe taking a detour up Aedvilja (next to Café Peterson) to admire Tallinn's stunning new **synagogue** (**6**; Karu 16), which opened in 2007 (the first synagogue built in Estonia since the Holocaust).

Turn right down Köleri – note **Bally's Casino** (**7**; Köleri 2) in a grand old wooden building on your right, and a little further on, on your left, the organic grocers and cafe *du jour*, **NOP** (**8**; p86). Take a left onto Faehlmanni and you'll see the last home of the great Estonian novelist Anton Hansen Tammsaare (1878–1940), which now contains the small **Tammsaare Museum** (**9**; Koidula 12A; 10am-5pm Wedn-Mon) with period furnishings from the 1930s. The house lies on a tree-lined street among other charming 19th-century villas. Between the wars, this was Tallinn's most affluent area, and today it's undergoing some impressive gentrification.

Take a right at Weizenbergi. Following this street you'll reach the western entrance of **Kadriorg Park** (**10**; p73); on your left is an information office, on your right the inviting **Park Café** (**11**; p86), with outdoor seating by the Swan Pond. Continuing on Weizenbergi through the park at a leisurely pace in keeping with your surrounds, you'll reach a large children's **playground** (**12**) on your right, the scene of much underage merriment; **Kadriorg Palace** (**13**; p73) on your left; the **Mikkel Museum** (**14**;

WALK FACTS

Start Raekoja plats
Finish KUMU art museum
Distance approximately 4km
Duration two to six hours, depending on stops

p73) further up on the right; and the **president's residence** (**15**). As you reach the end of road, Peter the Great's unassuming **cottage** (**16**; p73) is tucked away, while **KUMU** (**17**; p73) makes a grand visual statement and is all primped and primed for your artistic explorations.

When you've finished, continue northeast to find more tourist-worthy gems (the Song Festival Grounds, Pirita etc), or retrace your route through the park, and jump on tram 1 or 3 to take you back along Narva mnt to the Viru Keskus area (the tram stop is on Weizenbergi, close to the Restoran & Spaghetteria Kadriorg at number 18).

TALLINN FOR CHILDREN

If you're travelling with kids, Tallinn's Old Town with its medieval setting, colourful restaurants and lively street scene is pure eye candy for the under-12 crowd. The touristy **Toomas the Train** (☎ 525 6490; departs from Kullassepa; adult/concession 60/30Kr; ☼ noon-5pm Jun-Sep) departs from a point between Raekoja plats and the tourist office on a 20-minute loop through Old Town, and is a favourite of little nippers and footsore adults.

Other youthful attractions in Old Town include the **Estonian Puppet Theatre** (Eesti Nukuteater; Map p70; ☎ 667 9555; www.nukuteater.ee; Lai 1), where the animator's art has been going strong since 1952. Performances are in Estonian, but the visual fun is multilingual.

Outside Old Town, the Open-Air Museum (p75) is always a hit with the younger crowd. In the same area, you'll also find Tallinn Zoo (p75). At Pirita (p74) there are plenty of kid-friendly beachside diversions, while Kadriorg Park (p73) has a lovely large playground (there are also playgrounds around Hirvepark, downhill from Toompea). Otherwise, see Activities (p76), for details of bowling alleys, ice-skating rinks and waterparks.

TOURS

The tourist office (p64) and most travel agents can arrange tours in English or other languages with a private guide; advance booking is required. The tourist office charges 450Kr per hour (with a minimum booking of 1½ hours).

There is a growing number of operators offering organised tours, below are some of the highlights.

Audioguide Old Town Walking Tour (www.audio guide.ee; audio tour 300Kr) On this self-guided tour, you follow a prescribed route through the medieval quarters, listening to historical details and anecdotes along the way. You can find the audio player at the tourist office and at some hotels and attractions. There are a number of similar audio guides on offer – see also www.euroaudioguide .com, which offers iPod downloads.

City Bike (Map p70; ☎ 683 6383; www.citybike.ee; Uus 33) Has a great range of Tallinn tours, by bike or on foot, as well as tours (cycling or bus) to Lahemaa National Park. Two-hour cycling tours (250Kr) of the capital run year-round and cover 16km out towards Kadriorg and Pirita. A two-hour walking tour (210Kr) of Old Town takes in Oleviste Church and a tour of the passages under the bastions of Toompea. See p98 for Lahemaa options.

EstAdventures (☎ 5385 5511; www.estadventures.ee) Small company offering fabulously diverse and occasionally offbeat walking tours of Tallinn (Soviet Tallinn, haunted Tallinn or 'View with a Brew', a casual walking tour of Old Town that involves a few pub stops; from 300Kr). Full-day excursions further afield include Lahemaa National Park, Haapsalu and Soviet-throwback Paldiski.

Tallinn City Tour (Map pp66–7; ☎ 627 9080; www .citytour.ee; adult 24/48/72hr pass 250/300/350Kr; ☺ 10am-4pm May-Oct) These red double-decker buses won't exactly help you blend in with the locals. They will, however, give you quick and easy access to a number of the city's top sights, allowing you to hop on and off at numerous stops. The red line covers the city centre and Kadriorg; the green line travels to Pirita and the Botanic Gardens; and the blue line heads west to the zoo and Open-Air Museum. A recorded audio tour accompanies the ride (English, German, French, Spanish etc). Buses leave from Viru väljak (the eastern end of Viru, just outside Old Town); concession and family passes are available. The open-top bus tours operated by a different company don't have the same city coverage as these guys.

Traveller Info Tent (Map p70; ☎ 5814 0442; www .traveller-info.com; Niguliste) The young guys (mainly local students) behind this info-dispensing tent run tours in English, on foot or by bike. The two-hour Chill-out Tour (100Kr) is an entertaining walking tour of Old Town conducted by a local musician. Three-hour bike tours (150Kr) take in the town's well-known eastern attractions (Kadriorg, Pirita etc), or the more off-beat areas to the west – the port, a former prison, down-at-heel suburbs (places very few travellers ever get to). There's also an evening pub crawl (200Kr, including drinks). From June to August the tours run daily from the tent itself; the rest of the year they start from Euphoria hostel (opposite) and need to be booked in advance, via email, phone or through the hostel. Winter tours are weather dependent.

FESTIVALS & EVENTS

For a complete list of Tallinn's festivals, visit www.culture.ee and the events pages of www .tourism.tallinn.ee. Big-ticket events:

Jazzkaar (www.jazzkaar.ee) Jazz greats from around the world converge on Tallinn in mid-April during this excellent two-week festival; it also hosts a smaller event in autumn, and around Christmas.

Old Town Days (www.vanalinnapaevad.ee) This weeklong fest in early June features dancing, concerts, costumed performers and plenty of medieval merrymaking on nearly every corner of Old Town.

Õllesummer (Beer Summer; www.ollesummer.ee) This extremely popular ale-guzzling, rock-music extravaganza takes place over five days in early July at the Song Festival Grounds.

Birgitta Festival (www.birgitta.ee) An excellent chance to enjoy some of Estonia's vibrant singing tradition, with choral, opera and classical concerts held at the atmospheric ruins of the Convent of St Birgitta in Pirita over a 10-day period in mid-August.

Black Nights Film Festival (www.poff.ee) Featuring films and animations from all over the world, Estonia's biggest film festival brings life to cold winter nights from mid-November to mid-December.

SLEEPING

Tallinn has wide-ranging accommodation, from charming guesthouses to lavish five-star hotels. Old Town undoubtedly has the top picks, with plenty of atmospheric rooms set in beautifully refurbished medieval houses – though you'll pay a premium for them. Midrange and budget hotels are scarcer in Old Town, though apartment rental agencies have the best deals. There's been an explosion of hostels in recent times, competing for the attention of backpackers. Most of them are small, friendly and full of laid-back charm; they're largely found in Old Town, but few offer private rooms. The website www.tourism .tallinn.ee has a full list of options.

Whatever your preference, in summer be sure to book in advance: Tallinn's medieval charm is no longer a state secret. As ever, look for good deals on the internet.

Budget

CAMPING

Tallinn City Camping (Map pp62-3; ☎ 613 7322; www .tallinn-city-camping.ee; Pirita tee 28; tent & caravan site 200Kr, plus per car/adult/child 100/50/25Kr; ☯ mid-May–mid-Sep; ⓟ ⌨) Right by the Song Festival Grounds, this well-equipped site is an amble away from Pirita beach and Kadriorg Park, and just a short bus ride into town (bus 1A, 8, 34A and 38 to Lauluväljak stop), or you can rent bikes here.

HOMESTAYS

Rasastra (Map pp66-7; ☎ 661 6291; www.bedbreakfast .ee; Mere pst 4; s/d 375/650Kr, apt 800-1200Kr) Rasastra can set you up in rooms in private homes (with shared bathrooms) in major towns in Estonia (Pärnu, Kuressaare) and all three Baltic capitals. It also has private apartments in central Tallinn. Prices listed here are the average rates; breakfast costs an additional 50Kr.

HOSTELS

All of the following (except the €16 Hostel) have shared bathrooms. Wi-fi and computer access are standard.

City Bike Hostel (Map p70; ☎ 683 6383; www.city bike.ee; Uus 33; dm 150-300Kr, d & tw 500-600Kr; ⌨) The friendly, knowledgeable guys behind the very efficient City Bike shop (with rental, tours and loads of info for cyclists) have a tiny (nine-bed) hostel adjoining the bike shop, plus a more welcoming option at Nunne 1, close to Raekoja plats. The Nunne option (on the 3rd and 4th floors – no lift) includes dorms and private rooms and has a more social vibe and roomier kitchen.

You're bound to meet two-wheeled travellers at both places.

Euphoria (Map pp66-7; ☎ 5837 3602; www.euphoria .ee; Roosikrantsi 4; dm/d 200/600Kr; ⓟ ⌨) So laid-back it's almost horizontal, this new backpackers hostel, just south of Old Town, has adopted some very '60s hippy vibes and given them a modern twist, creating a fun place to stay with a sense of traveller community – especially if you like hookah pipes, bongo drums, jugglers, musos, artists and impromptu late-night jam sessions (pack earplugs if you don't). Light breakfast is included, and there are plenty of kitchens and the expected chill-out areas.

Old Town Backpackers (Map p70; uus14tallinn @hotmail.com; Uus 14; dm 200Kr; ⌨) Cosy and intimate is taken to extremes at this option, and many backpackers love the slacker atmosphere. There are only 10 beds in two dorms, and one dorm shares its space with the kitchen and living room. There's a sauna, internet and wi-fi (all free), which helps to combat the lack of privacy.

Tallinn Backpackers (Map p70; ☎ 644 0298; www .tallinnbackpackers.com; Olevimägi 11; dm 200-225Kr; ⌨) Staffed by backpackers who are more than happy to go drinking with guests, and in a perfect Old Town location, this place has a good global feel and a roll-call of traveller-happy features: free wi-fi and internet, lockers, free sauna, snazzy bathrooms, big-screen movies in the common room, a foosball table and day-trips to nearby attractions.

The Monk's Bunk (Map p70; ☎ 644 0818; Müürivahe 33-15; dm 200-225Kr) A second option run by the guys behind Tallinn Backpackers offers austere lodging.

Viru Backpackers (Map p70; ☎ 644 6050; 3rd fl, Viru 5; s/d/tw/tr 350/600/600/825Kr) Another offshoot of Tallinn Backpackers that offers less atmosphere in a central location.

Vana Tom (Map p70; ☎ 632 3252; www.hostel .ee; Väike-Karja 1; dm 235-260Kr, tw/tr/q 750/900/1200Kr; ⌨) True, the strip club upstairs isn't geared toward wholesome fun, but this hostel is in a prime pub-visiting location and is modern, clean and well set-up (dorms of varying sizes on one floor, private rooms – something of a rarity in Tallinn hostels – on another). The downside: private rooms are pricey, given what you'll pay at the cheaper midrange options. Some guests complain about the noise – light sleepers beware.

Old House Hostel (Map p70; ☎ 641 1464; www .oldhouse.ee; Uus 26; dm/s/tw 290/550/690Kr; ⓟ ⌨)

More like its sister establishment (Old House Guesthouse, below) than some of the party places listed here, this 34-bed place has a more mature feel: wooden floors and old-world decor, plus no bunks, and a choice of private rooms. In summer it expands into a nearby local school. Kitchen, living room, wi-fi and parking are good extras.

€16 Hostel (Map pp66-7; ☎ 501 3046; www.16eur.ee; Roseni 9; s/d/tw 400/500/500Kr; P) We salute a hostel that tells you what you'll pay upfront. Opened in mid-2008 and lacking in atmosphere, but rooms (spartan but with private bathroom) are good for the price. Downsides – no kitchen, noisy location on weekends. Entry is next door to Hotel Metropol, off Ahtri.

HOTELS & GUESTHOUSES

Hotell G9 (Map pp66-7; ☎ 626 7100; www.hotelg9 .ee; 3rd fl, Gonsiori 9; s/d/tr from 550/670/850Kr) A few blocks from Old Town in the business and shopping district, Hotell G9 is a good choice for budget travellers who don't feel like bunking in a hostel. There's little by way of atmosphere (it's on the 3rd floor of a nondescript building), but the no-frills rooms are simple and clean, with TV and private bathroom.

Old House Guesthouse (Map p70; ☎ 641 1464; www.oldhouse.ee; Uus 22; s/tw/q with shared bathroom incl breakfast 490/690/1300Kr) This cosy six-room guesthouse with wooden floors and tasteful old-world furnishings offers warm, friendly hospitality in a low-key Old Town neighbourhood, close to everything. There's a guest kitchen and TV room, plus free wi-fi.

Midrange

APARTMENT RENTAL

For our money, apartments give you the best bang for your midrange buck in Tallinn. You get much more space than a hotel room offers, plus a fully equipped kitchen, lounge and often a washing machine. True, you're unlikely to meet other travellers, but you have the chance of scoring a prime Old Town location. Prices for apartments drop in the low season, and with longer stays.

Ites Apartments (Map p70; ☎ 631 0637; www .ites.ee; Harju 6; per night 1100-2500Kr) This friendly and efficient bunch offers several too-good-to-be-true apartments in the Old Town and surrounds for 1100Kr to 2500Kr per day, with discounts for stays of more than one night. Car rental can be arranged.

Old House (Map p70; ☎ 641 1464; www.oldhouse .ee; Uus 22; per night 1100-3900Kr) As well as a guesthouse and hostel, this company has 16 beautifully furnished apartments scattered through Old Town, including two spectacular three-bedroom options, perfect for groups.

Red Group (Map p70; ☎ 644 0880; www.red group.ee; Vana-Viru 4; per night from 1200Kr) Specialising in Old Town accommodation, this friendly outfit has a number of modern apartments in excellent locations (some overlook Raekoja plats). Sizes range from studio to three bedrooms. Airport pick-up included.

Erel International (Map pp66-7; ☎ 610 8780; www .erel.ee; Tartu mnt 14; per night from 1400Kr) Has three blocks of modern apartments at its disposal (two in the Old Town, including one on Raekoja plats) and offers dozens of handsomely furnished apartments.

HOTELS & GUESTHOUSES

With some notable exceptions, the best midrange options are generally found just outside Old Town.

ourpick Villa Hortensia (Map p70; ☎ 641 8017; jaan .parn@mail.ee; www.hoov.ee, in Estonian; Masters' Courtyard, Vene 6; apt s 600-1200kr, d 800-1600kr) Villa Hortensia is a small collection of studio apartments in the Masters' Courtyard, off Vene. This sweet, cobblestoned courtyard has been a labour of love for Jaan Pärn, architect-turned-jeweller (his studio-shop acts as reception) and the man responsible for the restoration of the ancient buildings. There are six apartments here (the website is in Estonian, but click on Villa Hortensia and you'll see pics) – four standard ones, with private bathroom, kitchenette, table and chairs and access to a shared communal lounge. The two larger suites are the real treats – with balconies, TVs, kitchenettes and loads of character. This place offers unbelievable value in a superb location – book ahead, and don't tell too many people about this hidden gem, OK?

Hotel Schnelli (Map pp66-7; ☎ 631 0100; www .gohotels.ee; Toompuiestee 37; r 800-1350, f 1625Kr; P 🖵) The modern hotel at the train station isn't just for train travellers. The block-boring building is home to small but fresh and functional rooms and offers very decent value a short walk from Old Town (rates include buffet breakfast, parking and wi-fi). Non-trains-potters should opt for a room in the Green Wing, with views to the park opposite and

Old Town beyond; Blue Wing rooms overlook the station.

Valge Villa (Map pp62-3; ☎ 654 2302; www.white -villa.com; Kännu 26/2; r 790-1190Kr; P) A villa in more than name only, this three-storey, 10-room home in a quiet residential area 3km south of the centre is a great option, somewhere between a B&B and a hotel. All rooms boast antiques or wooden furniture, some have fireplace, sloping roof, balcony, kitchenette, bathtub, and all have coffee machine, fridge and wi-fi. Take trolleybus 2, 3 or 4 from the centre to the Tedre stop; parking makes it a good option for those with cars.

Bern Hotel (Map p70; ☎ 680 6630; www.bern .ee; Aia 10; s/d from 1173/1330Kr) One of a rash of new hotels on the outskirts of Old Town, Bern is named after the Swiss city to indicate 'hospitality and high quality'. It's nothing special from the outside, but rooms are petite and modern with great attention to detail for the price – nice extras include robes and slippers, air-con, minibar, hairdryer and toiletries. And traveller reports indicate that the service is living up to the ideal.

Hotell Braavo (Map p70; ☎ 699 9777; www .braavo.ee; Aia 20; s/d/f 1204/1405/1565Kr; P) No calming, neutral tones to help you nod off here. Once the shock of the bright citrus colours wears off, you can appreciate the set-up at Braavo, hidden on the edge of Old Town. Spacious rooms are the cheaper option, but we particularly like the family suites – mini-apartments with kitchenette and a fold-out couch downstairs, plus an upstairs bedroom.

Kalev Spa Hotel (Map p70; ☎ 649 3300; www .kalevspa.ee; Aia 18; economy d from 1500Kr, spa class d from 1700Kr, f from 2500Kr; P 🖳) The faint smell of chlorine as you enter hints at the all-important neighbour – the huge waterpark (entry included in room rates). The neighbour makes this a popular choice with families, but everyone will enjoy the edge-of-Old-Town location. 'Economy' rooms are indeed economical with space, but are OK if you don't mind the squeeze. 'Spa class' rooms are the standard, and are Scandi-streamlined and modern.

Uniquestay Hotel Tallinn (Map pp66-7; ☎ 660 0700; www.uniquestay.com; Toompuiestee 23; s/d from 1565/1956Kr); 🖳 Here local traditions and folk elements merge where Japanese sparsity, quirky eccentricity and modern furnishings to create an excellent midrange place to lay your head. The pricier 'Zen' doubles are worthwhile for the extra harmony (whirlpool baths, anti-

gravity NASA-designed chairs). All rooms come with their own computer and internet connection. Check the website for deals – in high season rooms were going for 1175Kr.

Uniquestay Hotel Mihkli (Map pp62-3; ☎ 666 48000; www.uniquestay.com; Endla 23; s/d from 1565/1956Kr) From the people behind Uniquestay Hotel Tallinn and with the same fresh features and prices, but a more out-of-the-way location (a 15-minute walk from Old Town).

Top End

Reval Hotel Olümpia (Map pp62-3; ☎ 631 5333; www .revalhotels.com; Liivalaia 33; standard d 1700-2660Kr) If you prefer your hotels big and facilities laid on thick, this massive 26-storey hotel (built for the 1980 Moscow Olympics, when Tallinn hosted the sailing events) is for you. Sure, it lacks the character of the Old Town gems, but it does have plenty going for it – the standard rooms are good (the larger, schmicker Reval Class rooms are a better choice and cost an extra 300Kr), and on-site distractions include a cafe, restaurant, pub and nightclub. The *pièce de résistance* is the health club, swimming pool and sauna on the top floor – the views might actually entice you to work out! It's about 700m south of Old Town.

Savoy Boutique Hotel (Map p70; ☎ 680 6688; www.savoyhotel.ee; Suur-Karja 17/19; s/d/ste from 2034/2425/3990Kr) Soft creams and caramel tones make these rooms an oasis of calm off one of the Old Town's busy intersections (request a room on a higher floor for the rooftop views). Nice boutiquey touches in this tasteful newcomer include robes and slippers in every room, free local phone calls, and attentive staff. Downstairs in the art deco–styled building are a cosy bar, popular alfresco terrace and Med-themed restaurant.

Viru Inn (Map p70; ☎ 611 7600; www.viruinn .ee; Viru 8; s/d/ste from 2815/3130/5150Kr) Another new boutique Old Town offering, this one with rich colours (maroons and golds) and plenty of original features (timber beams, stone walls) behind its powder-blue facade. Some rooms can be snug (especially rooms 5 and 7), so check out specs for each of the 15 rooms on the hotel's website. And note the free airport pick-up, sauna and Jacuzzi area, and on-site cafe and pizzeria too.

Hotel Telegraaf (Map p70; ☎ 600 0600; www .telegraafhotel.com; Vene 9; s/d/ste from 3455/3943/6489Kr; P 🛱) This sister hotel to the Three Sisters (p82) opened in 2007 and delivers style in

ESTONIA

spades, in a converted 19th-century former telegraph station. It boasts a spa and small swimming pool, gorgeous black-and-white decor, pretty courtyard, an acclaimed restaurant (the Tchaikovsky), parking (an Old Town rarity!) and smart, efficient service. 'Superior' rooms are at the front of the house, with a little more historical detail (high ceilings and parquet floors), but we preferred the marginally cheaper executive rooms, in the newer wing, for their bigger proportions and sharper decor.

Schlössle Hotel (Map p70; ☎ 699 7700; www .schlossle-hotels.com; Pühavaimu 13/15; d/ste from 4000/7700Kr) Individually designed rooms are nothing less than breathtaking in this five-star medieval complex in the heart of Old Town. This lovingly restored hotel features details from the original 17th-century building (such as original wooden beams and old stone walls) and its sumptuously decorated rooms are among the country's finest. If you manage to make it out of your room, you can enjoy the fireplace in the antique-laden great hall, the courtyard garden and the historically set cellar restaurant, Stenhus (mains 420Kr to 490Kr), one of Tallinn's finest, and priciest.

Three Sisters Hotel (Map p70; ☎ 630 6300; www.threesistershotel.com; Pikk 71; s/d/ste from 5245/5790/8295Kr) Offering sumptuous luxury in three conjoined merchant houses dating from the 14th century, Three Sisters has 23 spacious rooms, each unique but with uniformly gorgeous details, including old-fashioned freestanding bathtubs, original wooden beams, tiny balconies and canopy beds. Outside of the rooms, there are plenty of romantic nooks to secrete yourself on chilly nights: the wine cellar, the fireside seats in the lounge, the inviting library, the warmly lit lounge and the lavish restaurant.

Also recommended:

Merchant's House Hotel (Map p70; ☎ 697 7501; www.merchantshousehotel.com; Dunkri 4/6; s/d/ste from 1909/2237/4146Kr) More Old Town boutique style, offering good internet deals.

Meriton Grand Hotel Tallinn (Map pp66-7; ☎ 667 7000; www.meritonhotels.com; Toompuiestee 27; s/d/ste from 2340/2652/3900Kr) Large hotel of the ilk of the Olümpia, downhill from Toompea and offering superb views from its upper floors. A new 300-room conference and spa hotel is being built next door, under the same management, and is expected to open in mid-2009.

EATING

Tallinn has an enormous variety of cuisine, from Estonian to French, African to Japanese. Headquartered in Old Town, the restaurant scene has unbeatable atmosphere: whether you want to dazzle a date or just soak up the medieval digs alfresco, you'll find plenty of choices, but not many bargains – expect to pay the kind of prices you'd pay in any European capital. A word to the wise: lunchtime specials offer the best deals.

Old Town
ESTONIAN RESTAURANTS

Vanaema Juures (Map p70; ☎ 626 9080; Rataskaevu 10/12; mains 110-260Kr; ☿ noon-10pm Mon-Sat, noon-6pm Sun) Food just like your grandma used to make, if she was a) Estonian, and b) a really good cook. 'Grandma's Place' was one of Tallinn's most stylish restaurants in the 1930s, and still rates as a top choice for traditional, home-style Estonian fare. The antique-furnished, photograph-filled dining room has a formal air, and the menu has plenty of options aside from pork and sauerkraut.

Kaerajaan (Map p70; ☎ 615 5400; www.kaera jaan.ee; Raekoja plats 17; mains 135-325Kr; ☿ 11am-midnight) Named after a traditional song and dance, this new place on the main square has quirky decor and an intriguing menu of modern Estonian cuisine, taking traditional dishes and giving them an international, 21st-century twist – gravlax (salmon) with cucumber-lemon sorbet and forest cranberries, pork tenderloin marinated with juniper berries, or tiramisu made with *kama* (a powdery meal made from different grains) and berries. The jury's out on herring lasagne, however!

Olde Hansa (Map p70; ☎ 627 9020; www.olde hansa.ee; Vana Turg 1; mains 155-365Kr; ☿ 11am-midnight) Amid candlelit rooms, with peasant-garbed servers labouring beneath large plates of wild game, medieval-themed Olde Hansa is the place to indulge in a gluttonous feast. Juniper cheese, forest mushroom soup and exotic meats (such as wild boar, elk and even bear) are among the delicacies available (as well as honey beer and spiced wine). And if the medieval music, communal wooden tables, and thick fragrance of red wine and roast meats sound a bit much, take heart – the chefs have done their research in producing historically authentic fare. It may sound a bit cheesy and touristy, but even the locals rate this place. Besides, where else are you going to see wandering chamber musicians playing 14th-century ballads?

EUROPEAN RESTAURANTS

Controvento (Map p70; ☎ 644 0470; www.controvento.ee; Katariina käik; pizzas 60-150Kr, mains 95-360Kr; ☺ noon-11pm) Hidden away on Tallinn's most atmospheric alleyway (accessed from Vene or Müürivahe), this long-time favourite serves up Italian dishes to diners lucky enough to score an outdoor table in the sun, or upstairs under wooden beams. Most people are here for the large, thin-crust pizzas, but service can be slow.

In Studio Vinum (Map p70; ☎ 683 0783; Suur-Karja 18; mains 95-320Kr; ☺ noon-midnight Mon-Thu, noon-2am Fri & Sat) Under vaulted arches, with draped fabrics and high-backed Louis XV chairs in seductive reds and blacks, this romantic spot is a good place to feel like you're splurging, but the prices aren't hitting the high notes of others in this category (mains average 200Kr). The wide-ranging menu runs from inexpensive papardelle with duck confit to veal tournedos, and the wine choices are equally generous.

Bocca (Map p70; ☎ 611 7290; www.bocca.ee; Olevimägi 9; pasta & risotto 175-295Kr, mains 345-425Kr; ☺ noon-midnight) Sophistication and style don't detract from the fresh, delectable cuisine served at this much-lauded Italian restaurant. Creative dishes such as cauliflower with black truffle soup, or sea bass and giant-prawn tortellini in saffron sauce, are matched to a strong wine list. Bocca also has a cosy lounge and bar, where Tallinn's A-list gathers over evening cocktails.

Bonaparte (Map p70; ☎ 646 4444; www.bonaparte.ee; Pikk 45; mains 260-380Kr; ☺ noon-midnight Mon-Sat) The general himself would've been hard-pressed to find fault with this venerable French restaurant in a 17th-century merchant house. The delectable dishes are French with Estonian notes (asparagus velouté with fried mushrooms, Pernod-flamed tiger prawns, pan-fried duck breast with rhubarb confit), the service is impeccable and the dining room is restrained but elegant – not unsuitable for captious aristocrats, in other words. There's also a handsome cafe (p85) in the foyer, and a superb deli (p85) next door.

Gloria (Map p70; ☎ 644 6950; www.gloria.ee; Müürivahe 2; mains 280-420Kr; ☺ noon-11.30pm) Once voted as one of the world's 100 best restaurants by *Condé Nast*, it's no surprise that this Old World wonder, the *crème de la crème* of Estonia since the 1930s, lives up to expectations on all levels: a sumptuous prewar dining room, professional service and deluxe dishes such as beluga caviar, seared foie gras and oven-baked guinea fowl. For the best wines in the city served with lashings of ambience, visit the wine cellar downstairs (p87).

INTERNATIONAL RESTAURANTS

African

African Kitchen (Map p70; ☎ 644 2555; www.africankitchen.ee; Uus 32; mains 95-250Kr; ☺ noon-1am Sun-Thu, noon-2am Fri & Sat) This place offers something different with its authentic African cuisine, but earns mixed reviews for its efforts. In summer the upstairs roof terrace is a great place to linger over a snack or meal, while at night a fun atmosphere prevails in the funky, loungelike rooms, festooned with animal and tribal prints. Dishes feature flavourings of coconut cream, peanuts and red pepper (did someone say peri peri?), and there's a good selection of meat (including some unusual options like antelope and camel), seafood and vegetarian options.

Asian

Silk (Map p70; ☎ 648 4625; www.silk.ee; Kullassepa 4; sushi 40-50Kr, mains 90-290Kr; ☺ noon-midnight) Just off Raekoja plats, this sleek Japanese restaurant has a sparkly charcoal-tinted interior that wouldn't look out of place in a nightclub. The lengthy menu hits all the right sushi notes, and throws in some *gyoza* (dumplings), *ramen* (noodle dishes) and more substantial Japanese meals for good measure. We can't decide if the sweet *gyoza* (with banana and honey or apple and cinnamon) are gimmicky or genius.

Chedi (Map p70; ☎ 646 1676; www.chedi.ee; Sulevimägi 1; dishes 120-450Kr; ☺ noon-midnight) If you can't get a booking at London's top Asian restaurants, console yourself here. From the folks behind neighbouring Bocca (left) comes Chedi, a similarly sexy restaurant serving innovative pan-Asian cuisine. UK chef Alan Yau (he of London's Michelin-starred Hakkasan and Yauatcha) consulted on the menu, and indeed some of his trademark dishes are featured here (the sublime roasted silver cod with champagne and Chinese honey). The food is exemplary – try the delicious crispy duck salad – and the sleek surrounds are first-rate.

Fusion

Pegasus (Map p70; ☎ 631 4040; www.restoran pegasus.ee; Harju 1; breakfast 55-110Kr, lunch mains 150-200Kr, dinner mains 180-360Kr; ☺ 8am-midnight Mon-Thu, 8am-1am Fri, 9am-1am Sat, 10am-6pm Sun) Over three design-driven floors, Pegasus serves reliably tasty, modern dishes such as roasted corn-fed chicken breast with mango and avocado salsa; pasta, salads, curries and grilled meats round out the menu. It's one of the best places in town for breakfast or brunch (eggs Benedict, muesli, smoothies), and by night the party people converge, especially for Friday-night salsa and mojitos in summer, or Saturday-night jazz.

Angel (Map p70; ☎ 641 6880; www.clubangel.ee; Sauna 1; mains 70-160Kr; ☺ from noon Mon-Fri, from 2pm Sat & Sun) One of Tallinn's most ebullient and diverse crowds gathers at this stylish 2nd-floor restaurant, upstairs from Tallinn's best gay nightclub, Angel (p89). Exposed brickwork, great B&W photography and a loungelike feel provide a warm setting to the small but eclectic menu (salads, pastas and an unbeatable cheeseburger). Best of all, the kitchen stays open until late – perfect for those craving chicken curry or a fruity cocktail at 3am Wednesday night.

Aed (Map p70; ☎ 626 9088; www.restoranaed.ee; Rataskaevu 8; mains 85-280Kr; ☺ noon-10pm Mon-Sat, 3-9pm Sun) From the pots of herbs framing the doorway to the artwork screens on the walls, a lot of care has gone into creating this beautiful, plant-filled restaurant (the name means 'garden'). The menu of complex dishes (all organic produce) wins fans by noting gluten-, lactose- and egg-free options, and there are creative vegetarian choices too. We like the weekday lunchtime dish of the day – great value at 95Kr.

Georgian

Must Lammas (Map p70; ☎ 644 2031; www.must lammas.ee; Sauna 2; meals 120-260Kr; ☺ noon-11pm Mon-Sat) After something a little different? Meals at Must Lammas (the Black Sheep) are a rewarding experience – tasty plates of traditional meaty fare go down nicely with the Georgian wine. Try an entrée of *hartšo* (spicy lamb soup) or dolma (stuffed vine leaves) before diving into a sizzling kebab. Some veg options.

Indian

Elevant (Map p70; ☎ 631 3132; www.elevant.ee; Vene 5; mains 97-298Kr; ☺ noon-11pm) Great aro-mas assault your senses as you ascend the wrought-iron staircase of this 2nd-floor restaurant. In its large, warm space, diners linger over expertly prepared Indian cuisine – including a wide selection of vegetarian dishes and some curiosities (moose korma, wild boar and spinach curry, crocodile in mango sauce). At 75Kr, the weekday lunch is great value.

Russian

Troika (Map p70; ☎ 627 6245; www.troika.ee; Raekoja plats 15; mains 154-594Kr; ☺ 10am-11.30pm) Tallinn's most cheerful Russian restaurant is an experience in itself, with wild hunting-themed murals, live accordion music, and an old-style country tavern upstairs. Even if you don't opt for a plate of delicious *pelmeni* (Russian-style dumplings), *bliny* (pancakes) or a bowl of heavenly borscht, make sure you stop in for an ice-cold shot of vodka. Or try stroganoff of bear (594Kr), should your heart desire it and your wallet stretch that far.

Tex-Mex

Texas Honky Tonk & Cantina (Map p70; ☎ 631 1755; www.texas.ee; Pikk 43; mains 109-199Kr; ☺ noon-midnight) Decked out like an old Texas saloon – complete with creaky wooden floors and the smell of sawdust in the air – this lively restaurant is the best place in Old Town to load up on tacos, burritos, pork ribs and other dishes you wouldn't expect to find this side of the Mason-Dixon Line. Kitschy ambience and a fun crowd.

CAFES

Forget Paris and Rome – Tallinn's Old Town is so packed with absurdly cosy cafes that you can spend your whole trip wandering wide-eyed and jittery from one coffee house to the next. In most the focus is on coffee, tea (leaves, not bags, hooray!), cakes and pastries – and the latest craze, handmade chocolates. There's usually considerably less effort put into savoury snacks (a few token sandwiches and salads), but these places often stay open until midnight dispensing post-dinner sweets and treats.

Kehrwieder (Map p70; ☎ 505 258; www.kehr wieder.ee; Saiakang 1; ☺ 11am-midnight) Sure, there's seating on Raekoja plats, but inside the city's cosiest cafe is where the real ambience is found in spades – you can stretch out on a couch, read by lamplight and bump your head on the arched ceilings.

Tristan ja Isolde (Map p70; ☎ 680 6083; www
.bonaparte.ee; Raekoja plats 1; 🕑 10am-10pm Oct-Apr,
9am-midnight May-Sep) This Lilliputian cafe built
into the town hall features heavenly scents
and a splendid medieval setting. It's run by
the folks behind Bonaparte Café (below), so
you know the pastries, quiches and cakes
are first-class.

Café-Chocolaterie de Pierre (Map p70; ☎ 641 8061;
www.pierre.ee; Masters' Courtyard, Vene 6; 🕑 8am-mid-
night) Nestled inside the picturesque Masters'
Courtyard and offering respite from the Old
Town hubbub, this snug cafe seems like a
hideaway at your granny's place (but one
where you can touch the good china). Filled
with antiques, it's renowned for its delectable
handmade chocolates – impossible to resist.
The cobblestoned courtyard also hosts occasional music performances (jazz, classical)
in summer. Pierre has a sister cafe, Josephine,
nearby at Vene 16, but for atmosphere you
can't beat the original.

Maiasmokk (Map p70; ☎ 646 4066; www.maias
mokk.ee; Pikk 16; 🕑 8am-8pm Mon-Sat, 9.30am-6pm Sun)
Open since 1864, the city's oldest cafe still
draws a crowd of greying admirers who appreciate the classic decor, elaborate ceiling
mirror and colourful cakes and marzipan
treats. The pastries may taste like they were
made on opening day, but who cares – the
atmosphere's great!

Matilda Café (Map p70; ☎ 681 6590; Lühike jalg 4;
🕑 9am-7pm Mon-Sat, 9am-6pm Sun) There's a dearth
of cafes in Upper Town, so fuel up en route.
On Lühike jalg, among the craft galleries, this
pretty pit stop offers old-world charm to go
with its savoury bites and plethora of cakes:
pavlova, wild cherry cake or lemon meringue
tart should sort out any sugar craving.

Bonaparte Café (Map p70; ☎ 646 4444; www
.bonaparte.ee; Pikk 45; pastries 14-20Kr, meals 55-130Kr;
🕑 8am-10pm Mon-Fri, 9am-10pm Sat, 10am-6pm Sun)
Flaky croissants, raspberry mousse cake,
warm *pain au chocolat* – just a few of the
reasons why Bonaparte ranks as Tallinn's best
patisserie. It's also a supremely civilised lunch
stop, with the likes of French onion soup,
green-pea risotto and salad Niçoise on the
menu. And the quiches – *tres magnifique*! For
more indulgence, try dining at the restaurant
(p83). The deli next door (right) will let you
take treats away.

C'est La Vie (Map p70; ☎ 641 8048; www
.cestlavie.ee; Suur-Karja 5; meals 65-130Kr; 🕑 noon-11pm
Sun-Thu, noon-1am Fri & Sat) The all-day menu of light

meals goes down a treat at this swanky cafe,
among the art deco–flourishes and with jazz
on rotation. Coffee lovers might like to rate
the output of the award-winning barista.

QUICK EATS
Needless to say, you'll dine alongside students
and travellers who know how to sniff out a
bargain at the following options.

EAT (Map p70; ☎ 644 0028; www.eat.ee; Sauna 2;
pelmeni/donuts per 100g 10/7Kr; 🕑 11am-11pm) You
serve yourself at this bright, no-frills cafeteria, where seriously cheap grub is the
name of the game. Fried *pelmeni* are priced
according to the weight of your bowl, or
you can opt for soup (20Kr) or the dish of
the day (35Kr). Donuts are also available,
priced by weight.

Pizza Grande (Map p70; ☎ 641 8718; www.pizza
grande.ee; Väike-Karja 6; small pizzas 39-69Kr; 🕑 11am-
11pm) The local students we polled all voted
this their favourite pizza spot. Enter from
the courtyard and admire the lengthy menu,
where some left-of-centre topping combos
(chicken, shrimps, blue cheese and peach?)
stand alongside the tried-and-true. It's a good
budget option, with salads and pasta dishes all
coming in under 70Kr.

Kompressor (Map p70; ☎ 646 4210; Rataskaevu 3;
pancakes 50-55Kr; 🕑 11am-1am) Under an industrial ceiling you can plug any holes in your
stomach with cheap pancakes of the sweet
or savoury persuasion. The smoked cheese
and bacon is a treat, but don't go thinking
you'll have room for dessert. By night, this is
a decent detour for a drink.

SELF-CATERING
Kolmjalg (Map p70; Niguliste 2; 🕑 7am-11pm Mon-Wed,
7am-midnight Thu, 24hr Fri & Sat, midnight-11pm Sun) A
large Rimi supermarket (p87) is just on the
eastern edge of Old Town, but this is a handy
small grocery store, next door to the tourist
office and open long hours.

Bonaparte Deli (Map p70; ☎ 646 4024; Pikk 47;
🕑 10am-7pm Mon-Sat) For first-rate picnic fodder, stock up on pastries, baguettes and other
Gallic-style goodies at this deli.

Outside Old Town
There are a number of eateries worth leaving the Old Town walls for, from a delightful park cafe to a great-value Italian
restaurant that seems to be every local's
new favourite.

ESTONIA

ESTONIAN RESTAURANTS

Eesti Maja (Map pp66-7; ☎ 645 5252; www.eestimaja
.ee; Lauteri 1; mains 65-195Kr; ☽ 11am-11pm) This fun,
folksy restaurant is a good place to sample
authentic Estonian fare. Traditional favourites such as blood sausage, jellied pork and
marinated eel aren't for the timid, but there
are plenty of tasty dishes for the less adventurous (baked salmon, pepper steak, lamb chops
etc). There's a small weekday lunch buffet
(adult/child 125/55Kr) that's a good place to
start the tastebud-touring, without the need
for a full-plate commitment.

our pick **Ö** (Map pp66-7; ☎ 661 6150; www.restoran-o
.ee; Mere pst 6e; mains 310-395Kr; ☽ noon-4pm & 6pm-
midnight Mon-Fri, noon-midnight Sat, 1-10pm Sun) No,
we can't pronounce it either, but award-winning Ö has certainly carved a unique space
in Tallinn's culinary world. The dining room,
with its angelic chandelier-sculptures and
charcoal and white overtones, is an understated work of art – no less so than the plates
of modern Estonian cuisine coming out of the
kitchen. You can't fault the restaurant's mission, set out in the menu, to harvest and promote seasonal Estonian produce – it makes
sorbets from collected berries and smokes its
own meats and fish. The result is something
quite special; bookings are advised.

EUROPEAN RESTAURANTS

Vapiano (Map pp66-7; ☎ 682 9010; www.vapiano.ee;
Hobujaama 10; pizzas & pasta 50-125Kr; ☽ 10am-midnight)
This European chain of Italian restaurants
has just hit Tallinn. Vapiano is doing huge
business with a great concept – choose your
pasta or salad from the appropriate counter
and watch as it's prepared in front of you. If
it's pizza you're after, you'll receive a pager to
notify you when it's ready. This is 'fast' food
done healthy, fresh and cheap (without sacri-
ficing quality), and the restaurant itself is big,
bright and buzzing, with huge windows, high
tables and shelves of potted herbs. We like.

INTERNATIONAL RESTAURANTS

NOP (Map pp62-3; ☎ 603 2270; Köleri 1; sandwiches &
meals 40-110Kr; ☽ 8am-8pm) Well off the tourist
trail and a favourite with Tallinn's hipsters,
NOP is the kind of neighbourhood deli-cafe
that drives up real-estate prices. To your right
as you enter is a deli stocked with organic
groceries and hard-to-find produce; to your
left is a charming cafe. White walls, wooden
floors and a kids' corner set the scene, while

a blackboard menu (in Estonian only, but
the helpful staff should be able to guide you
through it) highlights fresh soups, salads and
wraps. It's not far from Kadriorg Park.

Spirit (Map pp66-7; ☎ 661 5151; www.kohvikspirit.ee;
Mere pst 6e; mains 115-245Kr; ☽ noon-11pm Mon-Thu, noon-
1am Fri & Sat, 1-10pm Sun) This cafe-lounge is blessed
with model good looks and rich textures:
stonework walls, fur rugs, marble tabletops, a
fire in the fireplace, and some poor creature's
antlers on the wall. It looks like a page torn
from a Scandi fashion mag and draws a stylish
crowd, who hold court here regularly over
cocktails and/or sushi. Spirit is next to Ö restaurant (left) but there is no entrance on Mere
pst – cut through any of the street-front establishments to get to the back alley.

CAFES

Park Café (Map pp62-3; ☎ 601 3040; A Weizenbergi 22;
☽ 10am-8pm Tue-Sun) At the western entrance to
Kadriorg Park, not far from the tram stop, is
this sweet slice of Viennese cafe culture. If the
sun's shining, the alfresco tables by the pond
might just be our favourite place in town; in
poor weather retreat upstairs to enjoy your
cuppa and cake/pastry/chocolate truffle.

Narva Kohvik (Map pp66-7; ☎ 660 1786; Narva mnt
10; meals 40-75Kr; ☽ 9am-8pm Mon-Sat, 10am-6pm Sun)
Toto, I have a feeling we're not in Kansas
anymore. One of the only places left in Tallinn
where you can step back into the USSR, this
cafe is kitsch without being aware of it. The
decor is decidedly brown and faded red,
the service dismissive and the menu full of
Russian staples from times of yore.

Bestseller (Map pp66-7; ☎ 610 1397; Viru Keskus, 3rd fl,
Viru väljak; meals 60-120Kr; ☽ 9am-9pm) Located inside
the city's best bookstore (Rahva Raamat, p62),
this is more than just a place where beautiful
people come to pop open their Macs. Some
very fine food (in delicate, French portions) is
served here, including fresh, tangy salads and
decadent sweets. Upstairs, also in the bookshop, is a second cafe, Boulangerie; it keeps
the same hours and has similar prices and
a similarly appealing menu, but with more
baked goods on offer.

Moskva (Map p70; ☎ 640 4694; www.moskva.ee;
Vabaduse väljak 10; mains 75-275Kr ☽ 9am-midnight Mon-
Thu, 9am-4am Fri, 11am-4am Sat, 11am-midnight Sun) An
attractive mix of Estonians, Russians and a few
out-of-towners gather at this chic cafe-night-
spot on the edge of Old Town. In addition to
cocktails and cappuccinos, Moskva serves

tapas, salads and other light fare. The upstairs lounge is a swankier place to imbibe, with DJs spinning to young crowds most weekends.

SELF-CATERING

Load up on provisions at the city's best grocery stores – and don't forget NOP (opposite), near Kadriorg Park, for picnic supplies.

Rimi (Map p70; Aia 7; ⊙ 9am-10pm) On the outskirts of Old Town.

Stockmann Kaubamaja (Map pp66-7; Liivalaia 53; ⊙ 9am-10pm Mon-Fri, 9am-9pm Sat & Sun) At the Stockmann department store.

Tallinna Kaubamaja (Map pp66-7; Viru Keskus, Viru väljak; ⊙ 9am-10pm) Inside Viru Keskus, at basement level.

There are also a couple of markets, which are excellent for cheap produce (and loads of tat), but just as good for people-watching:

Central Market (Keskturg; Map pp62–3; Keldrimäe 9; ⊙ 8am-6pm) Popular food market. Take tram 2 or 4 to the Keskturg stop.

Train Station Market (Balti Jaama Turg; Map pp66–7; Kopli; ⊙ 8am-7pm Mon-Sat, 8am-5pm Sun) A taste of old-school Russia, behind the train station. It's a bit seedy in parts – watch your bag.

DRINKING

You've probably heard by now that Tallinn has a pretty vibrant nightlife. It's also diverse: whether you seek a romantic wine cellar, a chic locals-only lounge or a raucous pub full of pint-wielding punters, you'll find plenty to choose from.

Gloria Wine Cellar (Map p70; ☎ 640 6804; Müürivahe 2; ⊙ noon-11pm Mon-Sat, noon-6pm Sun) This maze-like wine cellar has a number of nooks and crannies where you can secrete yourself with a date and/or a good bottle of Shiraz. The dark wood, antique furnishings and flickering candles add to the allure; if you're struggling to hear your lover's sweet nothings over a rumbling tum, there's a menu of light dishes too.

Déjà Vu (Map p70; ☎ 645 0044; www.dejavu.ee; Sauna 1; ⊙ 5pm-5am Wed-Sat) This stylish lounge bar bathed in red is cosier than others of its ilk and boasts a stupendous cocktail list and extra-long drinks menu (including, for teetotallers, one of the most interesting tea menus in Estonia). Tasteful live music most evenings adds to the sophisticated atmosphere.

Hell Hunt (Map p70; ☎ 681 8333; Pikk 39; ⊙ midday-late) See if you can't score a few of the comfy armchairs out the back of this trouper on the pub circuit, beloved of discerning locals of all ages. It boasts an amiable air and reasonable prices for local-brewed beer and cider – plus decent pub grub. Don't let the menacing-sounding name put you off – it actually means 'gentle wolf'.

Von Krahli Teater Baar (Map p70; ☎ 626 9096; www.vonkrahl.ee; Rataskaevu 12; live music cover charge 75-150Kr; ⊙ noon-1am Sun-Thu, noon to 3am Fri & Sat) One of the city's best bars, Von Krahli hosts live bands and the occasional fringe play, plus serves inexpensive meals. It's a great place to meet some of Tallinn's more interesting locals.

Beer House (Map p70; ☎ 644 2222; www.beerhouse.ee; Dunkri 5; ⊙ 10am-midnight Sun-Thu, 10am-2am Fri & Sat) Tallinn's only microbrewery offers up the good stuff (seven house brews) in a huge, tavern-like space where, come evening, the German oompah-pah music can rattle the brain into oblivion. Fun and sometimes raucous, it's for those who have had an overdose of cosy at other venues.

Levist Väljas (Map p70; ☎ 507 7372; Olevimägi 12; ⊙ 3pm-3am Sun-Thu, 3pm-6am Fri & Sat) Inside this cellar bar (usually the last pit stop of the night) you'll find broken furniture, cheap booze and a refreshingly motley crew of friendly punks, grunge kings, has-beens and anyone else who strays from the well-trodden tourist path.

Stereo (Map p70; ☎ 631 0549; Harju 6; 10am-2am or 3am) It's like walking into a giant iPod. White vinyl is the texture of choice at this painfully stylish bar on the edge of Old Town. By night the sleek cube-like interior becomes the backdrop to DJs spinning a mix of global tunes. Love it or hate it, Stereo is worth checking out.

Depeche Mode Bar (Map p70; ☎ 644 2350; Voorimehe 4; ⊙ noon-4am) For fans of the '80s New Wave band, this is liable to be the holy grail of drinking establishments. Recently moved from its old location but staying true to the format (red, dark, loud), the bar itself is small and fairly nondescript – aside from the DM played in heavy rotation. You've got to be grateful the owner didn't develop an obsession with other British bands, say, Bros or Bucks Fizz.

St Patrick's (Map p70; ☎ 641 8173; www.patricks.ee; Suur-Karja 8; ⊙ 11am-2am Sun-Thu, 11am-4am Fri & Sat) One of a chain of four dotted around town, this lively, good-looking bar has plenty of beer to go round, and attracts a surprising number of Estonians. Expect plenty of tourists in the warmer months, decent-value meals and a regular roll-call of deals, including four beers for the price of three. There are quite a few boisterous, tourist-heavy sports bars along this strip, popular with stag groups.

Clazz (Map p70; ☎ 627 9022; www.clazz.ee; Vana turg 2; ☿ noon-3am) Behind the cheesy name (a contraction of 'classy jazz') and slogan (don't ask) is an increasingly popular restaurant-bar, featuring live music almost every night of the week (cover charge varies). Wednesday night is usually an open jam session (all musicians welcome), while Sunday is Latin night (with free dance classes starting at 8.30pm). On other nights it could be DJs or bands – jazz, reggae, Brazilian etc (check the website).

Scotland Yard (Map pp66-7; ☎ 653 5190; Mere pst 6e; ☿ 9am-midnight Sun-Wed, 9am-2am Thu-Fri, 9am-3am Sat) As themed pubs go, this is actually quite well done, right down to the electric-chair toilets and staff dressed as English bobbies. There's a big menu of all-day pub grub, a small outdoor terrace and clubby leather banquettes. The only thing that doesn't seem to fit with the theme is the large fish tank, but the heaving weekend crowds don't seem to mind (they're usually here for the live bands).

A few other stylish places where the beautiful people tend to flock include Spirit, Moskva, Bocca and Pegasus (see reviews under Eating, p82); late-night coffees, wines and treats are served by many town cafes (p84).

ENTERTAINMENT

It's a small capital as capitals go, and the pace is accordingly slower than in other big cities, but there's lots to keep yourself stimulated, whether in a nightclub, laid-back bar or concert hall. Buy tickets for concerts and main events at **Piletilevi** (www.piletilevi.ee) and its central locations, including inside Viru Keskus (p91). Events are posted on city centre walls, advertised on flyers found in shops and cafes, and listed in newspapers as well as in *Tallinn in Your Pocket*. To tap into the nightlife scene, check out www.heat.ee as well, or pick up one of the *Heat* guides around town (it also covers the action in Tartu and Pärnu).

Nightclubs

Most of Tallinn's nightclubs have an entrance fee, ranging from 50Kr to 200Kr. Be sure to check out dance parties at Moskva (p86), as well as everyone's favourite club, Angel (opposite).

Club Hollywood (Map p70; ☎ 627 4770; www .club-hollywood.ee; Vana-Posti 8; ☿ from 11pm Wed-Sat) For a big night out, Hollywood is the obvious choice for most. A multilevel emporium of mayhem, this is the one to draw the largest crowds, especially foreigners. Plenty of tourists and Tallinn's young party crowd mix it up to international and local DJs. Wednesday night is Ladies Night (free entry for women), so expect to see loads of guys.

Terrarium (Map pp66-7; ☎ 661 4721; www.terrarium .ee; Sadama 6; ☿ from 11pm Wed-Sat) A more down-to-earth club experience is ensured here; prices are lower and there's less attitude than in the posher Old Town clubs. But the DJs still kick out the disco and the 20-something, mostly Russian crowd laps it up.

Bon Bon (Map pp66-7; ☎ 661 6080; www.bonbon.ee; Mere pst 6e; ☿ 11pm-5am Fri & Sat) With enormous chandeliers and a portrait of Bacchus, the god of decadence, overlooking the dance floor, Bon Bon is a favourite on the club circuit and is renowned for its chichi attitude. It attracts a 25- to 30-something A-list clientele who still want to party, in style. Frock up to fit in.

Club Privé (Map p70; ☎ 631 0545; www.clubprive .ee; Harju 6; ☿ 11pm-5am Wed-Sat) Tallinn's most progressive club gets busiest on Saturday. Despite – or perhaps because of – the high prices (cover is generally 150Kr to 200Kr), good DJs attract a club-savvy local and foreign crowd after something more cutting-edge than the likes of Club Hollywood can provide. Note the oxygen bar for a quick, healthy pick-me-up.

Cinemas

Films are shown in their original language, subtitled in Estonian and Russian. Night-time and weekend tickets cost around 100Kr to 120Kr (daytime sessions around 50Kr to 70Kr).

Kino Sõprus (Map p70; ☎ 644 1919; www.kino.ee, in Estonian; Vana-Posti 8) Set in a magnificent Stalin-era theatre, this art-house cinema has an excellent repertoire of European, local and independent productions. The website is in Estonian, but generally easy enough to follow.

Coca-Cola Plaza (Map pp66-7; ☎ 1182; www.super kinod.ee; Hobujaama 5) Supermodern 11-screen cinema playing the latest Hollywood releases, behind the post office.

Gay & Lesbian Venues

See www.gay.ee for more on the (small) gay scene in Tallinn.

Angel (Map p70; ☎ 641 6880; www.clubangel.ee; Sauna 1; Wed free admission, otherwise 95-175Kr; ◷ 10pm-5am Wed, Fri & Sat) Open to all sexes and orientations (but with strict door control, particularly on Friday and Saturday when ladies may struggle to get in), this mainly gay club has become one of the liveliest spots in town for fun of all kinds. A heady mix of dark corners, sweat, Madonna impersonators and throbbing beats – amongst other things. Check the website for party nights.

X-Baar (Map p70; ☎ 692 9266; www.zone.ee /xbaar; Sauna 1; admission free; ◷ 2pm-1am) The only place in the Old Town actually flying the rainbow flag is Tallinn's premier gay bar, whose minuscule dance floor comes alive late at weekends.

G-Punkt (Map pp66-7; ☎ 644 0552; www.gpunkt .ee; Pärnu mnt 23; admission free; ◷ 6pm-1am Mon-Thu, 8pm-6am Fri & Sat) Retro heaven. To see what Eastern European gay clubs were like 15 years ago, head to this underground bar, mainly attracting lesbians, with no sign advertising itself (tricky to locate, as the G-Spot is wont to be). It's hidden in an alley behind Pärnu mnt, or accessed across a parking lot from Tatari.

Theatre & Dance

The places listed tend to stage performances in Estonian only, save of course for modern dance shows or the rare show in English or other language. *Tallinn in Your Pocket* lists major shows; other good sources of information are www.culture.ee, www.concert.ee and www.tea ter.ee.

Estonia Concert Hall & National Opera (Map pp66-7; ☎ concert hall 614 7760, opera 683 1201; www.concert .ee, www.opera.ee; Estonia pst 4) The city's biggest concerts are held here, in this double-barrelled venue. It's Tallinn's main theatre, and also houses the Estonian national opera and ballet. The box office times vary – the opera box office is open 11am to 7pm daily, the concert hall's opens noon to 7pm Monday to Friday, noon to 5pm Saturday, and one hour before start times on Sunday.

City Theatre (Tallinna Linnateater; Map p70; ☎ 665 0800; www.linnateater.ee; Lai 23) The most beloved theatre in town always stages something memorable. Watch for its summer plays on an outdoor stage or at different Old Town venues.

Estonian Drama Theatre (Eesti Draamateater; Map pp66-7; ☎ 680 5555; www.draamateater.ee, in Estonian; Pärnu mnt 5) Flagship company stages mainly classical plays and tends to avoid contemporary fare.

Von Krahli Theatre (Map p70; ☎ 626 9090; www.vonk rahl.ee; Rataskaevu 10) Known for its experimental and fringe productions.

St Canutus Guild Hall (Map p70; ☎ 646 4704; www.saal.ee; Pikk 20) Tallinn's temple of modern dance also hosts the rare classical dance performance.

Teater No99 (Map pp66-7; ☎ 660 5051; www.no99 .ee; Sakala 3) More experimental productions happen here, but definitely come by for the jazz bar downstairs on Friday and Saturday evenings – a true jazz club the likes of which Tallinn has been sorely lacking for years.

Live Music

See under Drinking (p87) for pubs and bars featuring live music, particularly Clazz, Von Krahli and Scotland Yard; and under Theatre & Dance for details of jazz at Teater No99 (above).

For major concerts, see what's on at the **Estonia Concert Hall** (Map pp66-7; ☎ 614 7760; www.concert.ee; Estonia pst 4).

Chamber, organ, solo and a few other smaller-scale concerts are held at several halls and churches around town, such as the town hall, the Brotherhood of the Blackheads and Niguliste Museum.

Major international acts usually perform at one of the following venues, or at A. Le Coq Arena (below).

Saku Arena (Saku Suurhall; off Map pp62-3; ☎ 660 0200; www.sakuarena.com; Paldiski mnt 104b) West of the centre (close to the zoo); 7000-seat arena hosts concerts and sports events.

Tallinn Song Festival Grounds (Lauluväljak; Map pp62-3; ☎ 611 2102; www.lauluvaljak.ee; Narva mnt 95) See p74 for the history of these grounds, which play host to big outdoor festivals and big acts (from James Brown to Metallica).

Sport

A. Le Coq Arena (Map pp62-3; ☎ 627 9940; Asula 4c) About 1.5km southwest of town, this arena is home to Tallinn's football team FC Flora, Estonia's largest sporting club. If you have the chance, don't miss a lively match.

Kalev Stadium (Kalevi Spordihall; Map pp62-3; ☎ 644 5171; Juhkentali 12) Basketball ranks as one of Estonia's most passionately watched games, and the best national tournaments are held in this stadium just south of town.

SHOPPING

Antiques

Whether you're looking for that brass pocket watch with Stalin's profile, the Lenin-head belt buckle or perhaps an old marching uniform, you'll find plenty of Soviet nostalgia buried in Tallinn's antique shops. There are tons of other gems waiting to be unearthed (gramophones, furniture, silverware, icons, amber pieces); you just have to dive in.

Good spots in which to fossick are **Antiik** (Map p70; ☎ 631 4725; www.oldtimes.ee; Raekoja plats 11), in the same building as the Town Council Pharmacy, and **Reval Antique** (Map p70; ☎ 644 0747; www.reval-antique.ee; Harju 13), with its entrance at Muurivahe 2. Both stores list their current treasures online.

Department Stores

Tallinna Kaubamaja (Map pp66-7; ☎ 667 3100; Gonsiori 2; ☉ 9am-9pm) Established in 1960 and with the regulation departments over a large space. It spills into the connected Viru Keskus shopping mall (where you'll find women's wear, beauty products and cosmetics, and kids' clothing).

Stockmann Kaubamaja (Map pp66-7; ☎ 633 9539; www.stockmann.ee; Liivalaia 53; ☉ 9am-9pm Mon-Fri, 9am-8pm Sat & Sun) Upmarket Finnish department store, which set up in Tallinn soon after the events of 1991 to enable Estonian consumers to enjoy all the luxuries afforded their Finnish cousins.

Fashion

Estonian high-street fashion stores are Monton, Mosaic (both offering men's and women's clothing) and Baltman (menswear), all owned by the same company and offering decent mainstream fashion. You can find branches of these inside Viru Keskus (opposite), and some of their ranges in local department stores. Viru Keskus is also home to many of the standard Euro labels – Zara, Diesel, Esprit, Vero Moda etc. For more one-of-a-kind items, head to the following places.

IIDA (Map p70; ☎ 5394 8342; www.iidadesign .eu; Suur-Karja 2) The Estonian Textile, Design & Fashion Store is a worthy stop for a browse, with some intriguing fabrics and designs, and beautiful crocheted-lace pieces (including, when we stopped by, some rather fetching but revealing bathing suits). There's a small range of jewellery, homewares and accessories too.

Ivo Nikkolo (Map p70; ☎ 699 9875; www .ivonikkolo.ee; Suur-Karja 14) Classic-with-a-twist women's fashion that's a mix of floaty and fun, or muted and professional, but all made with natural, high-quality fabrics. This Old Town address has two floors of womenswear and accessories, or you can find it in Viru Keskus.

Nu Nordik (Map p70; ☎ 644 9392; www.nunordik .ee; Vabaduse väljak 8) Unafraid of the avant-garde, this small boutique has youthful, edgier creations from up-and-coming local designers (including a small range of men's and women's clothes, plus bags, ceramics, CDs of local artists and homewares).

Reet Aus (Map p70; www.reetaus.ee, in Estonian; Müürivahe 19) Quirky one-off pieces (dresses, shirts, coats), handmade by a popular local designer with a conscience – most are made from recycled fabrics.

Handicrafts & Artwork

You'll be tripping over handicraft stores in Old Town – look for signs for *käsitöö* (handicrafts), and pick up a copy of the *Tallinn Handicraft Map* from the tourist office. Dozens of small shops sell Estonian-made handicrafts, linen, leather-bound books, ceramics, jewellery, silverware, stained glass and objects carved from limestone, or made from juniper wood. These are all traditional Estonian souvenirs – these and a bottle of Vana Tallinn, of course! In summer a souvenir market sets up daily on Raekoja plats.

Katariina Gild (Map p70; Katariina käik, at Vene 12) This lovely laneway is home to a number of artisans' studios where you can happily browse and potentially pick up some beautiful pieces – stained glass, ceramics, textiles, patchwork quilts, hats, jewellery and beautiful leather-bound books.

Knit Market (Map p70; cnr Müürivahe & Viru) Along the Old Town wall, there are a dozen or so vendors praying for cool weather and selling their handmade linens, scarves, sweaters, mittens, beanies and socks.

Lühike jalg (Map p70; Lühike jalg) En route up to Toompea, this alleyway has a good selection of galleries. Galerii Kaks at No 1 has striking ceramics, jewellery and glassworks; Helina Tilk at No 5 is known for her fun painted porcelain, although we particularly like her work with linen (kids aprons and dresses, soft toys). There's another good gallery, Lühikese Jala Galerii, at No 6.

Masters' Courtyard (Map p70; Vene 6) Rich pickings here, with the courtyard not only home to the cosy Café-Chocolaterie de Pierre (p85), but also small stores selling quality ceramics, jewellery, knitwear, wood and felt designs and candles.

Navitrolla Galerii (Map p70; ☎ 631 3716; www.navitrolla.ee; Suur-Karja 21) Find Navitrolla's bright, fanciful paintings as original artworks or on T-shirts, mugs, gift cards, posters etc.

Zizi (Map p70; ☎ 644 1222; www.zizi.ee; Vene 12) This store (one of three Zizi stores in Old Town) stocks a rainbow-hued range of well-priced linen napkins, placemats, tablecloths and cushion covers. Other stores (at Mündi 4 and Suur-Karja 2) stock bedding too.

Shopping Malls

Estonia has an ever-growing number of shiny monuments to capitalism. The supermarkets within them are usually open slightly longer hours than the centre itself.

Kristiine Keskus (Map pp62-3; ☎ 665 0341; www.kristiinekeskus.ee; Endla 45; ⏲ 10am-9pm) Southwest of the city centre and pretty generic in its offerings, but large and handy for travellers staying at Valge Villa, for example.

Ülemiste Keskus (Map pp62-3; ☎ 603 4999; www.ulemiste.ee; Suur-So amae 4; ⏲ 10am-9pm) Estonia's largest mall, right by the airport (for any last-minute purchases), and considered a must for serious local shoppers, though the offerings are pretty mainstream. Plenty of eating options. Take Bus 2.

Viru Keskus (Map pp66-7; ☎ 610 1400; www.virukeskus.com; Viru väljak 4; ⏲ 9am-9pm) Tallinn's showpiece shopping mall (aka Viru Centre) lies just outside Old Town. See Fashion (opposite) for an idea of retailers, and note the on-site treats of cafes, bookshops and a tourist information desk. The bus station lies underneath.

There are a few smaller, more exclusive shopping centres popping up nearby, including **Foorum** (Narva mnt 5) and **Rotermanni** (Rotermanni 5).

GETTING THERE & AWAY

This section concentrates on transport between Tallinn and other places in the Baltic. For listings of useful travel agencies, see p64.

Air

For information on international flights (including helicopters to Helsinki), see p401; information on the limited domestic scene is on p410. **Tallinn Airport** (Map pp62-3; ☎ 605 8888; www.tallinn-airport.ee; Tartu mnt) is 4km southeast of Old Town.

Boat

See p408 for information about the plethora of services available between Tallinn and Helsinki or Stockholm. Tallinn's sea-passenger terminal (Map pp66-7) is at the end of Sadama, a short, 1km walk northeast of Old Town. Bus 2 runs every 20 to 30 minutes between the bus stop by Terminal A and A Laikmaa in the city centre (to get to the ferry terminal, catch the bus from out the front of the Tallink Hotel). Trams 1 and 2, and bus 3 go to the Linnahall stop, by the Statoil Petrol Station (Map pp66-7), five minutes' walk from terminals A, B and C. Terminal D is at the end of Lootsi, better accessed from Ahtri (bus 20 runs every hour or two to/from Terminal D, along Narva mnt and Pärnu mnt). A taxi between the centre and any of the terminals will cost about 60Kr.

Note that Linda Line hydrofoils arrive and depart from the Linnahall Terminal (Map pp62-3), a huge Soviet-era concrete monstrosity north of the harbour – take tram 1 or 2, or bus 3, to the Linnahall stop.

For yachting information, yacht hire and activities contact the Tallinn Olympic Yachting Centre (p74).

Bus

Town buses leave from the bus terminal under Viru Keskus shopping centre or the surrounding streets (just east of Old Town). It's unlikely most travellers will need their services, but suburban buses (those numbered over 100) run to places within 40km or so of Tallinn (within Harjumaa county) and depart from the platform next to the Central Train Station (Balti Jaam; Map pp66-7). Timetables for these services are also at www.tal linn.ee.

For detailed bus information and advance tickets for all other destinations, go to the **Central Bus Station** (Autobussijaam; Map pp62-3; ☎ 680 0900; Lastekodu 46), about 2km southeast of Old Town. Tram 2 or 4 will take you there, as will bus 17, 23 or 23A. Ecolines and Eurolines offices are here, but Bookingestonia .com (p64) in Old Town can book and issue your bus tickets for no commission.

For information regarding bus travel to other countries, see p404. For travel within the Baltic countries, see also p411.

ESTONIA

Here's the low-down on daily services from Tallinn to major Estonian destinations (note that all prices are one way). Times, prices and durations for all services can be found at www.bussi reisid.ee.

Haapsalu (85Kr to 105Kr, two hours, around 18 buses)

Kärdla (185Kr, 4½ hours, two buses)

Kuressaare (205Kr to 250Kr, 4½ hours, around 12 buses)

Narva (135Kr to 170Kr, three to four hours, around 25 buses)

Pärnu (115Kr to 125Kr, two hours, around 30 buses)

Rakvere (70Kr to 95Kr, 1½ hours, around 20 buses)

Tartu (125Kr to 160Kr, 2½ to 3½ hours, over 35 buses)

Valga (180Kr, four to 4½ hours, seven daily)

Viljandi (140Kr to 150Kr, two to 2½ hours, around 12 buses)

Võru (150Kr to 180Kr, 3½ to 4½ hours, around nine buses)

Car & Motorcycle

There are 24-hour fuel stations at strategic spots within the city and on major roads leading to and from Tallinn. The Pärnu mnt Neste (petrol station) has a car-repair service.

Car hire in Tallinn is pricey (if you're booking with one of the large international companies, expect to pay around 1000Kr a day; smaller local companies usually offer cheaper rates). You could hire cars in Tartu or Pärnu instead and save a bundle – the tourist offices in both cities have extensive lists of rental agencies.

If you prefer to rent in Tallinn, try one of the following (or ask at your accommodation for recommendations). All the major players have desks at Tallinn airport.

Avis (www.avis.ee) City Centre (Map pp62-3; ☎ 667 1515; Liivalaia 13/15) Tallinn Airport (☎ 605 8222; Tallinn Airport)

Budget (☎ 605 8600; www.budget.ee; Tallinn Airport)

Bulvar (☎ 503 0222; www.bulvar.ee) Will deliver cars to you; from 500Kr daily.

Europcar (www.europcar.ee) City Centre (Map pp66-7; ☎ 610 9317; Narva mnt 7) Tallinn Airport (☎ 605 8031; Tallinn Airport)

Hansarent (☎ 627 9080; www.hansarent.eu) Will deliver cars to you; from 600Kr daily.

Hertz (www.hertz.ee) City Centre (Map pp66-7; ☎ 611 6333; Ahtri 12) Tallinn Airport (☎ 605 8923; Tallinn Airport)

R-Rent (www.rrent.ee) City Centre (Map pp66-7; ☎ 661 2400; Rävala pst 4) Tallinn Airport (☎ 605 8929; Tallinn Airport) From 500Kr daily.

PARKING

Parking in Tallinn is complicated, even for locals (and often involves paying via your mobile phone). Look for signs (not that you'll necessarily make any sense of them), and expect a fine (around 500Kr) if you don't obey them. If you have your own wheels, our best advice is to leave your car somewhere safe and walk or catch public transport into/around the city. The first point for information is your accommodation provider – some will provide parking (rarely free), or will point you in the direction of the nearest parking lot. Two central ones are at **Viru Keskus** (Map pp66-7; per hr 30Kr; 24hr), entry next to Sokos Hotel Viru, on Narva mnt; or underground below the **Rotermanni complex** (Map pp66-7; per hr/24hr 15/150Kr; 24hr), entry from Ahtri, just past Hotel Metropol.

Train

The **Central Train Station** (Balti Jaam; Map pp66-7; ☎ 615 6851; www.baltijaam.ee, in Estonian; Toompuiestee 35) is on the northwestern edge of Old Town, a short walk from Raekoja plats via Nunne, or three stops on tram 1 or 2, north from the Mere pst stop.

The station has been modernised in recent years and offers a cafe, an adjacent hotel (p80) and even a day spa, but neither the station signage nor the station website offers any information in English. Still, you should be able to find someone at the ticket booths to help you in English (or you can buy tickets for domestic routes on the trains themselves). International services from here begin and end with overnight trains to Moscow (see p406); these are operated by **GoRail** (www.gorail.ee, in Estonian).

Train travel is not as popular as bus travel in Estonia, so domestic routes are limited. Following are some places you can still reach by train (note that prices listed are one-way fares); these services are operated by **Edelerautee** (www.edel.ee) – on the Estonian-language page, click on Sõiduplannid jahinnad to access the timetables and prices.

Narva (100Kr, 3½ hours, one daily)

Pärnu (75Kr, 2¾ hours, two daily)

Rakvere (62Kr, two hours, two daily)

Tartu (95Kr to 140Kr, 2¼ hours, three to six daily)

Viljandi (85Kr to 95Kr, 2½ hours, two to three daily)

GETTING AROUND
To/From the Airport

Bus 2 runs every 20 to 30 minutes (6am to around 11pm) from A Laikmaa, next to Viru Keskus (the bus stop is opposite, not out front of, the Tallink Hotel). From the airport, bus 2 will take you via five bus stops to the centre. Tickets are 20Kr from the driver (cheaper from a kiosk, see below); journey time depends on traffic but rarely takes more than 20 minutes.

A taxi between the airport and the city centre should cost about 100Kr to 120Kr.

Bicycle

As well as offering hostels and tours (by bike or on foot; see p78), **City Bike** (Map p70; ☎ 683 6383; www.citybike.ee; Uus 33; rental per hr/day/week 35/200/765Kr) can take care of all you need to get around by bike, whether it's within Tallinn, around Estonia or through the Baltic region. It also rents panniers, kids bikes/seats/trailers etc, and dispenses maps and advice etc. For longer journeys, you have the option of one-way rentals too, for a fee.

Public Transport

Tallinn has an excellent network of buses, trams and trolleybuses that usually run from 6am to midnight. The major bus terminal for local buses is at the basement level of Viru Keskus shopping centre, on Viru väljak (just east of Old Town). All public transport timetables are online at www.tal linn.ee.

The three modes of local transport all use the same ticket system. Buy *piletid* (tickets) from street kiosks (13Kr, or a book of 10 single tickets for 90Kr) or from the driver (20Kr). Validate your ticket using the hole puncher inside the vehicle – watch a local to see how this is done, but generally it involves slipping your ticket down the green slot at the top, then pulling the top towards you (which leaves a pattern of holes punched on the ticket). One-/three-/10-day tickets are available for 40/70/125Kr (these are bought from kiosks, not drivers). The Tallinn Card (p69) also gives you free public transport in the city. Travelling without a valid ticket runs the risk of an 800Kr fine – inspectors regularly board vehicles to check tickets, so keep yours at hand.

Few of the suburban electric rail services from the central station in Tallinn go to places of much interest in and around the city.

Taxi

Taxis are plentiful in Tallinn. Oddly, taxi companies set their own rates, so flag fall and per-kilometre rate vary from cab to cab – prices should be posted in each taxi's right rear window. Rides are metered and usually cost from 7Kr to 12Kr per kilometre during the day (slightly more between 11pm and 6am), with a 35Kr to 45Kr flag fall. However, if you merely hail a taxi on the street, there's a chance you'll be overcharged. To save yourself the trouble, order a taxi by phone. Operators speak English; they'll tell you the car number (licence plate) and estimated arrival time (usually five to 10 minutes).

Here are some good choices:

Krooni Takso (☎ 1212, 638 1111; flag fall 40Kr, per km 7.50Kr)

Laki Takso (☎ 666 9999; flag fall 25Kr, per km 5.90Kr) The cheapest in town.

Linnatakso (☎ 1242, 644 2442; flag fall 45Kr, per km 9.40Kr) It also has vehicles for the disabled.

Reval Takso (☎ 621 2111; flag fall 35Kr, per km 7Kr)

Tulika Takso (☎ 1200, 612 0000; flag fall 45Kr, per km 9.40Kr)

PEDI-CAB

Throughout central Tallinn, the ecologically sound **Velotakso** (☎ 508 8810) offers rides in egg-shaped vehicles run by pedal power and enthusiasm. Rates are 40Kr for anywhere within Old Town; you'll generally find available vehicles lingering just inside the town walls on Viru.

NORTHEASTERN ESTONIA

The crown jewel of Estonia's national parks, Lahemaa occupies an enormous place – literally and figuratively – when talk of the northeast arises. Lahemaa, the 'land of bays', comprises a pristine coastline of rugged beauty, lush inland forests rich in wildlife, and sleepy villages scattered along its lakes, rivers and inlets.

The park lies about one-third of the way between Tallinn and the Russian border. Travelling beyond the park's eastern borders, the bucolic landscape transforms into an area of ragged, industrial blight. The scars left by Soviet industry are still visible in towns such as Kunda, home to a mammoth cement plant; Kohtla-Järve, the region's centre for ecologically destructive oil-shale extraction; and Sillamäe, once privy to Estonia's very own

ESTONIA

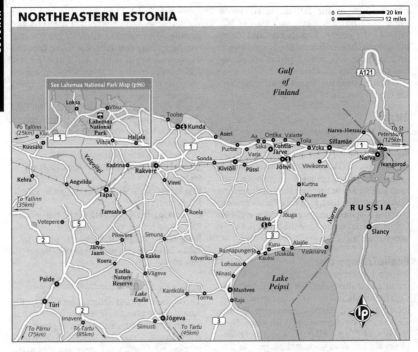

NORTHEASTERN ESTONIA

uranium processing plant. Those willing to take the time will find some rewarding sites here, including the youthful city of Rakvere, the picturesque limestone cliffs around Ontika, and the curious spectacle of the seaside city of Sillamäe, a living monument to Stalinist-era architecture. The most striking city of this region is Narva, with its majestic castle dating back to the 13th century.

For those seeking a taste of Russia without the hassle of visas and border crossings, north-eastern Estonia makes an excellent alternative. The vast majority of residents here are native Russians, and you'll hear Russian spoken on the streets, in shops and in restaurants. You'll have plenty of opportunities to snap photos of lovely Orthodox churches, communist-bloc high-rises and other legacies left behind by Estonia's eastern neighbour.

LAHEMAA NATIONAL PARK

The perfect country retreat from the capital is Estonia's largest *rahvuspark* (national park), Lahemaa – an unspoiled section of rural Estonia with an array of picturesque coastal and inland scenery. It takes in a stretch of deeply indented coast with several peninsulas and bays, plus 475 sq km of pine-fresh forested hinterland. Visitors are well looked after: there are cosy guesthouses, restored manor houses, remote camp sites along the sea and an extensive network of pine-scented forest trails.

A microcosm of Estonia's natural charms, Lahemaa's coast, forests, lakes, rivers and bogs encompass areas of historical, archaeological and cultural interest. Roads traverse the park from the Tallinn–Narva highway to the coast, with a few parts accessible by bus. Walking, hiking and cycling trails encourage active exploration that gets you close to nature, plus horse treks offer a different perspective.

Around 300,000 people visit the Lahemaa National Park every year, but only a small number go out of season, when the park is transformed into a magical winterland of snowy shores, frozen seas and sparkling black trees.

The Land

The landscape is mostly flat or gently rolling, with the highest point just 115m above sea level. Stone fields, areas of very thin topsoil called alvars, and large rocks called erratic boulders, brought from Scandinavia by glacial action, are typically Estonian. There are as many as 50 large boulders in the country – eight in Lahemaa. The biggest one (580 cubic metres) is the House Boulder (Majakivi), while the Tammispea boulder is the tallest at 7.8m. The best known stone field is on the Käsmu Peninsula.

Wildlife

Almost 840 plant species have been found in the park, including 34 rare ones. There are 50 mammal species, among them brown bear, lynx and wolf – none of which you're likely to see without specialist help, sadly. Some 222 types of birds nest here including mute swan, black stork, black-throated diver and crane and 24 species of fish have been sighted. Salmon and trout spawn in the rivers.

History

When it was founded in 1971, Lahemaa was the first national park in the Soviet Union. Though protected areas existed before that, the authorities believed that the idea of a national park would promote incendiary feelings of nationalism. Sly lobbying (including a reference to an obscure decree signed by Lenin which mentioned national parks as an acceptable form of nature protection) and years of preparation led to eventual permission. Latvia and Lithuania founded national parks in 1973 and 1974 respectively, but it wasn't until 1983 that the first one was founded in Russia.

Information

Lahemaa National Park visitor centre (Lahemaa Rahvuspargi Külastuskeskus; ☎ 329 5555; www.lahemaa .ee; ☾ 9am-7pm May-Aug, 9am-5pm Sep, 9am-5pm Mon-Fri Oct-Apr) is located in Palmse, 8km north of Viitna in the southeast of the park (next door to Palmse manor). Here you'll find the essential map of Lahemaa, as well as information on hiking trails, island exploration and guide services. Staff also have details of accommodation possibilities. It's worth starting your park visit here – you can also view a free 17-minute film introducing the park, entitled *Lahemaa – Nature and Man*.

Sights

PALMSE

The restored **manor house** (☎ 324 0070; www.svm.ee; adult/concession 60/30Kr; ☾ 10am-7pm May-Sep, 10am-6pm Wed-Sun Oct-Apr) and park at Palmse, 8km north of Viitna, is the showpiece of Lahemaa. In the 13th century a Cistercian monastery occupied the land, and it was later developed as a private estate by a Baltic-German family (the von der Pahlens) who ran the property from 1677 until 1923 (when it was expropriated by the state).

Fully restored to its former glory, the manor house, dating from the 1780s, contains period furniture and fittings. Other estate buildings have also been restored and put to new use: the *ait* (storehouse) has an exhibition of old vehicles; the *viinavabrik* (distillery) houses a hotel and restaurant; the *kavaleride maja* (house of cavaliers), once a summer guesthouse, is now a souvenir and bookshop; and the sweet *supelmaja* (bathhouse), which overlooks a pretty lake, is now a cafe, the Isabella. At the time of research a new guesthouse and tavern had opened on the estate, in what were once the steward's house and the home of farm labourers. For sleeping and eating options at Palmse, see p98.

OTHER MANORS

There are more old German manors, at Kolga, Vihula and Sagadi, the latter the most impressive of the bunch (but with Vihula set to be a strong contender). For details on accommodation and eating possibilities at these estates, see p99.

Now fully restored, the striking, pink-and-white neoclassic **Sagadi Manor** (☎ 676 7878; www .sagadi.ee; adult/concession incl entry to Forest Museum 35/15Kr; ☾ 10am-6pm May-Sep, by appointment Oct-Apr) was built in 1749 and has been beautifully restored to its former glory; the accompanying notes for visitors (in English) are well done. On the estate is a **Forest Museum** (☎ 676 7882; ☾ 10am-6pm May-Sep, by appointment Oct-Apr), with exhibits on the park's flora and fauna (primarily in Estonian). Also here is an excellent hotel, hostel and restaurant.

The estate of **Vihula Manor** (www.vihulamanor .com) has begun a huge overhaul that will turn it into 'the first genuine country club in the Baltic countries'. By 2011 there should be all manner of eateries and guest rooms, a camping area, log cabins for rent, a spa, nine-hole golf course, beach club, hot-air balloon rides, nature trails, equestrian centre and even a helicopter landing area. When we stopped in, the first rooms were ready and it promises big things ahead.

ESTONIA

LAHEMAA NATIONAL PARK

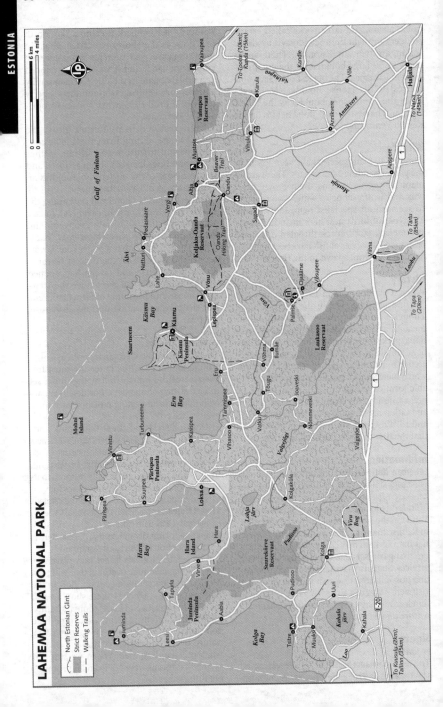

Legend:
- North Estonian Glint
- Strict Reserves
- Walking Trails

The classical-style manor house at **Kolga** dates from the end of the 17th century but was largely rebuilt in 1768 and 1820, and is long overdue for restoration. This photogenically tumbledown mansion has one renovated area that's home to a restaurant, and also on the estate (in the former stables) is a decent guesthouse. There's an interesting summertime museum here too, exhibiting local history.

BEACHES, PENINSULAS & COASTAL VILLAGES

With their long sandy beaches, the small coastal towns of **Võsu** and, to a lesser extent, **Loksa** are popular seaside spots in summer. During peak season Võsu fills up with young revellers, which can detract from the park's natural beauty. There are also good beaches at **Käsmu** (Captains' Village), a charming old sailing village across the bay from Võsu with decent accommodation options (p99); and between **Altja** and **Mustoja**. A scenic hiking and biking route runs east along the old road from Altja to **Vainupea**.

Peninsulas that make for lovely exploration include **Juminda** and **Pärispea**. Juminda has an old 1930s **lighthouse** at its northern tip; nearby is a WWII monument to the several thousand civilians who were killed (by mines and German ships) trying to flee Estonia in 1941.

The main town on the Pärispea Peninsula, Loksa, is a rather down-at-heel place, but the 9km drive northeast of here, to Viinistu, is pretty. The **Viinistu Art Museum** (Kunstmuuseum; ☎ 608 6422; www.viinistukunst.ee; adult/concession 30/15Kr; ☒ 11am-6pm Jun-Aug, 11am-6pm Wed-Sun Sep-May) houses the remarkable private art collection of Jaan Manitski, who was born in the village but left when he was a baby. Jaan is reputedly one of the country's richest men; much of his fortune was made as the business manager for Swedish supergroup ABBA, and he has returned to his roots to share his wealth. He has transformed this village with his art museum (displaying some 300 pieces, all Estonian artists, traditional and modern) and neighbouring hotel and restaurant (p100), housed in what was once a fish factory on the waterfront.

The former Soviet coastguard barracks at Käsmu now shelters the eclectic **Sea Museum** (Meremuuseum; ☎ 323 8136; Merekooli tee 4; admission by donation; ☒ 9am-7pm). In the 1920s a third of all registered boats in Estonia belonged to this village; at one time there were 62 long-

distance captains living here. From 1945 to 1991 the entire national park's coastline was a military-controlled frontier, with a 2m-high barbed-wire fence ensuring villagers couldn't access the beach or sea. The museum has photographs and memorabilia tracing the history of the village and exhibits on marine life from the area.

The fishing village of **Altja** was first mentioned in 1465, though today no building older than 100 years is left. The park has reconstructed traditional net sheds here and set up an open-air museum of stones along the protected coastline. Altja's Swing Hill (Kiitemägi), complete with traditional Estonian swings, has long been the centre of Midsummer's Eve festivities in Lahemaa, and the neighbouring tavern (see p99) is a favourite of locals and tourists. Other coastal villages with an old-fashioned flavour are **Natturi** and **Virve**.

Although technically outside the park, there are three lakes near **Viitna** that make lovely settings for a swim or hike along the pine-covered shoreline.

ISLANDS

Until 1992 **Hara island** was a Soviet submarine base and hence a closed area. Soviet-era maps of the park did not mark the island. During the 1860s, Hara enjoyed a successful sprat industry and about 100 people worked there. If you're interested in a trip over, the visitor centre can help find someone to take you. When the water's low enough, you can walk (check with the visitor centre for best times).

From Viinistu it's possible to catch a boat to **Mohni island**, privately owned by Jaan Manitski, and guided tours are available to help you appreciate the island's flora and fauna, as well as the lighthouse. Talk to the folks at Viinistu Art Museum (left) for more details.

Activities
BIKING

Lahemaa is a splendid place to cycle. You can work up a sweat along forest-lined roads, then take a dip in a lake or in the sea. The hotel at Sagadi Manor and the Kolga guesthouse (p99) both rent bikes (150Kr to 180Kr per day), but priority goes to their guests. If you're serious about exploring the park on two wheels, your best bet is to rent a bike and arrange transfers to/from the park with City Bike (p98) in Tallinn.

ESTONIA

HIKING

Some excellent hikes course through the park's diverse landscapes. Pick up maps and trail information from the visitor centre.

Altja Nature & Culture Trail A 3km circular trail beginning at 'Swing Hill' on the coast at Altja, taking in traditional net sheds and fishing cottages, and the open-air museum of stones.

Beaver Trail A 1km trail, 900m north of Oandu; a beautiful trek past beaver dams on the Altja River, although you're unlikely to see the shy creatures.

Käsmu Nature & Culture Trail A 4.2km circuit from Käsmu village, taking in coast, pine forest and erratic boulders; a longer route (stretching 14km and suitable for cycling) takes you to Lake Käsmu (Käsmujärv).

Majakivi Nature Trail A 7km trail on the Juminda Peninsula taking in the 7m-high Majakivi erratic boulder.

Oandu Old-Growth Forest Nature Trail A 4.7km circular trail, 3km north of Sagadi, that is perhaps the park's most interesting. Note the trees that wild boars and bears have scratched, bark eaten by irascible moose and pines scarred from resin-tapping.

Viru Bog Nature Trail A 3.5km trail across the Viru Bog, starting at the first kilometre off the road to Loksa, off the Tallinn–Narva highway; look for the insectivorous sundew (Venus flytrap, Charles Darwin's favourite plant).

HORSE RIDING

Feel like slow-and-steady exploration? Saddle up at **Kuusekännu Riding Farm** (Kuusekännu Ratsatalu; ☎ 325 2942; www.kuusekannu.maaturism.ee), which arranges horse riding for all levels, and trail rides through Lahemaa. Two-day/one-night treks into the park, to either Sagadi Manor, Käsmu or Altja, cost around 3500Kr; a three-day/two-night option taking in all three highlights costs around 5500Kr. Prices include meals and guesthouse accommodation. To reach the farm, head 68km east of Tallinn along the Tallinn–Narva highway. Take the turn-off to Tapa city, drive 300m and turn right at the first intersection, then follow the signs to the farm. Be sure to call before showing up.

Tours

Many tour operators offer excursions to Lahemaa out of Tallinn; these are a great option for those without their own wheels. **City Bike** (☎ 683 6383; www.citybike.ee; Uus 33, Tallinn) in particular is worthy of mention, with tours of the park by bus or by bike. Daily in summer (and four times a week from mid-October to mid-May), City Bike runs a minibus tour of Lahemaa that takes in Palmse, Sagadi, Altja, Võsu and Käsmu villages (759Kr). If you feel like getting closer to nature, City Bike also offers bus transport to the park and supply of a bike and maps, and the option of guided (920Kr) or self-guided (759Kr) exploration. Staff will even prepare a picnic lunch for you to take along, if you so desire. Talk to them about itinerary building and transfers if you fancy spending a few days discovering the park by bike.

Sleeping & Eating

Käsmu, set near a tiny beach, has plenty of low-key guesthouses. If you want rowdier beach action, head to Võsu, a popular summertime hang-out for Estonian students. Other guesthouses are sprinkled throughout the region. The visitor centre in Palmse keeps lists of options. Also, many small guesthouses have dogs (big ones). Keep that in mind before vaulting over fences.

The camping is fantastic in Lahemaa, with lots of free, basic RMK-administered camp sites. You will find them near Tsitre at Kolga Bay, at the northern tip of Juminda and Pärispea Peninsulas, and by the Sagadi–Altja road, 300m south of the Oandu trail. When looking for these sites, keep your eyes peeled for the small wooden signs with the letters 'RMK'. All camp sites (free RMK ones and private ones) are marked on the excellent *Lahemaa Rahvuspark* map available in the visitor centre.

If you're staying at a tourist farm, don't bypass the traditional home cooking. Just ask your host in advance. If you're camping, you can load up on your provisions at the small, crowded **food shop** (◷ 9am-9pm) in Võsu (which has an ATM inside) or in Loksa at the much bigger **Loksa Kauplus** (◷ 9am-10pm) store on the main road.

PALMSE

Palmse Guesthouse (☎ 5386 6266; www.svm.ee; d/tr/q with shared bathroom 580/870/1160Kr, d/tr 780/1170, ste 1190-1490Kr) So new we actually interrupted its opening ceremony, this guesthouse on the estate (in what was once the steward's house) is a fresher, shinier option than the long-running Park Hotel Palmse. On offer is a variety of rooms for all budgets, from family rooms with shared facilities, to plush suites with plasma TV.

Park Hotel Palmse (☎ 322 3626; www.phpalmse.ee; s/d 790/990Kr) This hotel offers pine-fresh rooms inside the Palmse Manor distillery – they're comfy but looking a little dated (and over-priced) compared with the newer offerings throughout the park.

Café Isabella (meals 40-80Kr) In the grounds of Palmse Manor, this pretty cafe in the estate's former bathhouse overlooks a swan-filled lake. Neither the food nor the service matches up to the lovely setting – the menu is pretty basic.

Palmse Kõrts (☎ 5300 5885; mains 65-90Kr) Brand-spanking-new for summer 2008 and just a short walk south of the manor, this rustic tavern evokes yesteryear under heavy timber beams with a short, simple menu of traditional Estonian fare. The creamy, eggy potato salad is stodgy and delicious.

OTHER MANORS

Sagadi Manor Hotel & Restaurant (☎ 676 7888; www .sagadi.ee; dm 250Kr, hotel s/d from 900/1200Kr) With its whitewashed exterior and hanging baskets of geraniums, this hotel on the Sagadi estate of-fers a cheerful welcome. On the ground floor are new and fresh rooms opening onto small patios and a courtyard. Upstairs rooms are older and marginally cheaper, under sloping roofs. Sagadi also has a 35-bed hostel in the old steward's house, with spotless rooms rang-ing in size, and you can enjoy breakfast at the hotel for an extra 100Kr. The hotel's 2nd-floor restaurant (mains 95Kr to 235Kr) offers smart decor and a menu of international and local dishes, from elk stew to Caesar salad. Bike rental is available.

Kolga Mõis Guesthouse (☎ 607 7477; www.kolga hotell.ee; d 500-800Kr; 🖳) This quiet guesthouse, in the manor's former stables, offers comfy, good-value rooms – those upstairs, under a sloping roof, have more character. Prices vary depending on the ablutions facilities – the cheapest rooms have a toilet (shared showers in the hall), while the priciest have full private bathroom. There's a small, basic cafe here too, and a summertime restaurant (mains 90Kr to 200Kr) inside the crumbling manor itself.

Vihula Manor (☎ 322 6985; www.vihulamanor.com; s/d/ste 1200/1400/2150Kr) As part of its transfor-mation into a spiffy country club and spa, this estate has recently opened up its guest quarters and raised the bar for manor ac-commodation. The team behind Tallinn's Uniquestay hotels (p81) is involved, whip-ping the rooms into slick, elegant places to bed down, while keeping the character of the historic outbuildings in which they're housed. The suites are a knockout, and worth considering if you're in the mood to splurge.

ALTJA

ourpick Toomarahva Turismitalu (☎ 325 2511; www .zone.ee/toomarahva; sites per person 25Kr, d incl breakfast 500Kr) A gem of a place, offering a gorgeous taste of rural Estonia – a farmstead with thatch-roofed wooden outhouses and a gar-den full of flowers and sculptures. There's a yard for camping, a barn full of beds serving as a summer dorm (largely used by groups), plus rooms with private bathroom (the 'suite' has kitchen facilities). The friendly owner also offers catering, and there is a rustic sauna, plus bikes for rent. Signage is minimal – look for it opposite the yard of the tavern, close to the swing.

Altja Kõrts (☎ 326 8681; www.altja.ee; mains 65-190Kr; 🕑 11am-11pm May-Sep, 11am-8pm Oct-Apr) Set in an old wooden farmhouse with thatched roof and large terrace, this charming place serves delicious plates of home cooking (in sum-mertime to busloads of tourists). Don't be deterred by the menu's first page, listing crisp pig's ears and black pudding as starters. Read on for more appetising options like juniper-grilled salmon, or pork roulade flavoured with horseradish and herbs. End on a high note with fresh blueberry pie (in season).

KÄSMU

Uustula B&B & Campsite (☎ 325 2965; www.uustalu .planet.ee; Neeme tee 78; sites per person 30Kr, d 650-700Kr) At the end of the Käsmu road/start of the hiking trail, this complex has simple, cheer-ful rooms (all with private bathroom) on a waterfront property. Campers are welcome to pitch a tent on the grassy lawn, and sauna and bike rental are available. Rooms share a common kitchen.

Merekalda Guesthouse (☎ 323 8451; www .merekalda.ee; Neeme tee 2; d 690-990Kr, apt 990-1290Kr) In an idyllic waterfront setting, just on the right as you enter Käsmu, is this peaceful, adults-only retreat comprising rooms and apartments set around a lovely large garden. Ideally you'll plump for lodgings with a sea view and balcony, but you'll need to book ahead. If funds are running low, you can also stay in a super-basic cabin (290Kr) and still enjoy the surrounds. Boat and bike hire are available.

Note that there are no eating establishments in Käsmu.

VÕSU

Eesti Karavan (☎ 324 4665; sites 50Kr, caravan 190Kr; ✆ May-Oct) In Lepispea, 1km west of Võsu, this place caters to campers and caravaners, with plenty of trees and decent facilities, including wi-fi.

O Kõrts (☎ 516 5115; Jõe 3; meals 70-200Kr; ✆ 11am-midnight) Just off the main road in Võsu (opposite the police station), this tavern has a flower-filled outdoor terrace perfect for catching the late-afternoon sun, or a cosy wooden interior. The menu covers plenty of ground from beer-drinking snacks to predictable mains of pork, steak and salmon. There's live music some nights.

VIINISTU

Viinistu Hotel & Restaurant (☎ 608 6422; hotell @viinistu.ee; s/d 825/990Kr) More of Jaan Manitski's artworks are on display in this bright waterfront hotel, next door to his private art museum (p97). There's a fresh nautical flavour to the decor, but the rooms are decidedly low on frills. Definitely opt for a sea-facing room with balcony. You can also enjoy the watery views from the restaurant (mains 55Kr to 155Kr), with big picture windows and a menu that ranges from club sandwich to pork cutlet by way of salmon tagliatelle and deep-fried pike.

VIITNA

Viitna Kõrts (☎ 325 8681; www.viitna.eu; mains 65-150Kr; ✆ from noon daily) Almost opposite the eastbound bus stop at Viitna (and a good pit stop if you're simply en route from Tallinn to Narva or beyond) is this reconstruction of an 18th-century tavern. The huge menu has some tempting traditional offerings such as honey-roasted pork or warm salmon pie; next door is a basic cafeteria open from 7.30am, serving up the essentials (coffee, sandwiches, etc).

Getting There & Away

Hiring a car is a good way to reach and explore the areas inside the park; tours from Tallinn offer a good alternative (p78).

Visit www.bussireisid.ee for all bus timetables, with details including journey time and ticket price. The best starting point for buses into destinations within the park are Tallinn,

Viitna and Rakvere (most Tallinn–Rakvere buses stop in Viitna). From Tallinn a bus runs daily to Käsmu, Võsu and Altja. Rakvere has the most frequent services to the most villages – see opposite for details.

Getting Around

A car is extremely handy for getting around; this is also a great cycling region, though distances between points can be great. Hiking and cycling routes are marked in blue and red respectively; maps and trail information are available from the visitor centre. Some tourist farms and hotels rent out bikes. You can rent a bike in Tallinn and take it on the bus to Viitna as cargo, or have it transported with City Bike (see p98).

You can also use the buses running to the coastal villages to get around the park, though these are infrequent.

RAKVERE

pop 16,700

Set with a magnificent castle – and very large bull sculpture – Rakvere is a small but confident city, transforming into one of the fastest-growing places in the country. The small town centre contains pleasant streets, nicely manicured parks and a lively, youthful population, plus a growing army of new hotels and restaurants.

Your first stop should be the **tourist office** (☎ 324 2734; www.rakvere.ee; Laada 14; ✆ 9am-6pm Mon-Fri, 10am-3pm Sat & Sun mid-May–mid-Sep, 10am-5pm Mon-Fri mid-Sep–mid-May), where you can pick up a town map and walking-tour guide from the affable staff. It's right by the main square (Turuplats), surrounded by supermarkets, banks and other services.

Sights & Activities

Rakvere's star attraction, **Rakvere Castle** (Rakvere Linnus; ☎ 322 5500; www.svm.ee; adult/concession/family 60/40/125Kr; ✆ 11am-7pm May-Sep, by appointment Oct-Apr) was built by the Danes in the 14th century, though the hillside has served many masters over its 700 years: Danes, Russians, Swedes and Poles. The fortress was badly damaged in the battles of the 16th and 17th centuries, and later turned into an elaborate manor in the late 1600s. Extensive reconstruction was completed in 2004, and today the castle contains exhibits related to its history with medieval-style amusement that's aimed mostly towards children (make a candle, make a nail at the blacksmiths, pony rides), though the adults can try their hand at archery. There are also artisan studios, and an inn serving medieval food. Don't miss the torture chamber. Concerts and plays are held at the castle in summer; ask at the tourist office to see what's on.

In front of the castle is Rakvere's other icon – a massive seven-ton **bull statue**, which was completed by local artist Tauno Kangro to commemorate the city's 700th-year anniversary. (The 1226 *Chronicle of Livonia* included a description of an ancient Estonian wooden castle on Rakvere hill, called Tarvanpea. In Estonian, Tarvanpea means 'the head of an aurochs', an aurochs being an extinct large, long-horned wild ox – hence the statue of the bull, or more accurately, an aurochs.)

In town, the **Rakvere Museum** (☎ 322 5503; Tallinna 3; adult/concession 30/15Kr; ☺ 10am-5pm Tue-Fri, 10am-3pm Sat), housed in a late-18th-century building, contains modest expositions related to the town's history. A few blocks south, on one of Rakvere's most historical streets (great for a stroll), is the **Citizen's House Museum** (☎ 322 5506; Pikk 50; adult/concession 20/10Kr; ☺ 11am-5pm Tue-Sat). Displays here show what an early-20th-century apartment looked like; several workshops tap into Rakvere's rich artisan tradition.

Sleeping

Hotell Wesenbergh (☎ 322 3480; www.wesenbergh .ee; Tallinna 25; s/d 600/890Kr) This unprepossessing hotel has comfy, spotless rooms but little by way of flair (the newer wing is nicer). It's more than adequate but looking old-school next to the glossy new competition in town.

Art Café Külalistemaja (☎ 323 3060; hotell@artcafe .ee; Lai 18; s/d 600/900Kr) Under the same ownership as the smart cafe opposite, this newly opened, 2nd-floor guesthouse has crisp, understated style – attic ceilings, orchid plants, black bedspreads and flat-screen TVs. Good prices make it even more attractive. Breakfast at the cafe costs an extra 50Kr.

Aqva Hotel & Spa (☎ 326 0000; www.aqvahotels .ee; Parkali 4; d 1290-1690Kr) Newly opened in mid-2008, not far from the main square, is this large complex housing a hotel, day spa and indoor waterpark, proving to be a big hit with Finnish families. The water theme is taken to the max here, from the fabulous swirly purple carpet to the aquarium and water wall in the lobby. Standard rooms are on the small size,

but modern and stylish (with flat-screen TVs and assorted extras, including robe and slippers to keep); rates are higher on weekends. There's a swank restaurant and family cafe on-site too.

Eating & Drinking

Art Café (☎ 325 1710; Lai 13; meals 40-100Kr; ☺ 9am-11pm Mon-Thu, 9am-1am Fri, 11am-1am Sat, 11am-10pm Sun) With a big-city feel inside, plus inviting rear garden and diverse clientele, this place serves as the ideal all-day drop-in centre, from breakfast through to late-night drinks. The menu is only in Estonian, but friendly staff will help you select from a range of salads, soups, pancakes and other creative dishes. The salad of trout, blue cheese and melon comes recommended.

Old Victoria (Inglise Pubi; ☎ 322 5345; Tallinna 27; meals 50-105Kr; ☺ 11am-midnight or later) Amid antique wallpaper, dark timber and leather sofas, this place does a good impersonation of an English pub, and the beer garden is a great spot in which to sink a pint. The basic, no-surprises menu of schnitzels, pork chops and cottage pie lends authenticity.

Turuplats (☎ 327 0600; www.turuplats.eu; Turuplats 3; mains 55-150Kr; ☺ 11am-midnight) The huge wicker teapots hanging from the roof of this lounge bar-cafe on the main square may have you perusing the tea menu – but the cocktail list is also a winner, and the kitchen concocts a range of international meals, from *pelmeni* to stir-fries, salads and pastas. The black velvet booths among mirrored walls and dwarf orange trees give the place an offbeat nightclub feel.

Virma Pubi (☎ 322 3907; Tallinna 8; dishes 60-150Kr; ☺ 11am-midnight or later) When you're not exactly sure what you're hungering after, this handsome old pub can come to the rescue with its huge, ambitious menu – categories include Chinese, Thai, Indian, sushi and Estonian dishes. We can't vouch for the quality of all cuisines, but we give them brownie points for trying. There's live music Friday and Saturday nights, karaoke (shudder) on Tuesday, and pool tables.

Getting There & Away

The bus station is on the corner of Laada and Vilde, one block south of the tourist office. Rakvere is well connected by bus to Tallinn (70Kr to 95Kr, 1½ hours, about 20 daily), 100km away, and Narva (90Kr to 115Kr, two

ESTONIA

to 2½ hours, nine daily). There are also decent links to Lahemaa towns, as follows. Times, prices and durations for all services can be found at www.bussi reisid.ee.

Altja (25Kr, one hour, one daily except Sunday)

Käsmu (30Kr to 35Kr, one to 1½ hours, three or four daily)

Palmse (25Kr, 50 minutes, four weekly)

Sagadi (21Kr to 25Kr, 45 minutes, one to three daily)

Vihula (21Kr, 40 minutes, one or two daily except Sunday)

Viitna (25Kr to 35Kr, 25 minutes, 15 buses daily)

Võsu (27Kr to 35Kr, one hour, four to six daily)

Rakvere has two trains daily to Tallinn (62Kr, two hours), and one train to Narva (63Kr, 1¾ hours). The train station is on Jaama pst, 1200m northeast of the main square.

ONTIKA, VALASTE & TOILA

The coast between Aa and Toila is lined by cliffs where it coincides with the edge of the Baltic Glint (see p54). At **Ontika**, north of Kohtla-Järve, these cliffs reach their greatest height of 56m. The views out to sea are excellent, though getting a good look at the cliffs is near impossible as they're obscured by trees, and climbing down can be a deadly affair. To save lives, a metal staircase was built, 5km east at **Valaste**, facing Estonia's highest waterfalls (33.8m), which, depending on the month, may be a mere trickle (or photogenically frozen in winter). Climbing down the staircase is free, but there's the requisite ice-cream stand and 24-hour cafe to take your money, and a small, modern hostel that accepts campers (but given that you're miles from anywhere here, you'd have to use this as a last resort). There's a second staircase down to the shore at Saka Cliff Hotel & Spa (right).

Continue 12km along the coastal road from Valaste to reach the spa town of **Toila** (12km northeast of Jõhvi), renowned for its parklands. Here stood the majestic Oru Castle, built by famous St Petersburg businessman Yeliseev in the 19th century, which was later used by President Konstantin Päts' summer residence between the wars and subsequently destroyed. Parts of the park have been reconstructed, including the old terrace, making it a pleasant place for a stroll or picnic. The views from the Baltic Glint in the Toila region are good, and here the glint forms part of the Saka-Ontika-Toila landscape reserve.

Sleeping & Eating

Both of the following are home to restaurants open for lunch and dinner.

Toila Spa Hotell (☎ 334 2900; www.toilaspa.ee; Ranna 12; sites per person 50Kr, caravan 155Kr, cabins 400-1000Kr, s/d from 800/1200Kr) Toila Sanatorium has rebranded itself as a spa hotel (it has a nicer ring to it, wouldn't you agree?) but this big, institutional place can't escape its past, no matter how hard it tries. Inside, it's a real timewarp, with small, dated and overpriced rooms over nine floors, plus various spa and health packages (for the 'manly man' and 'caring woman') and an adjacent waterpark. The camping area amongst the pines (open May to September) is a nicer option, and simple wooden cabins are available here.

Saka Cliff Hotel & Spa (☎ 336 4900; www.saka.ee; Saka; sites per person 50Kr, caravan 180Kr, s/d 900/1200Kr) In a peaceful cliff-top setting signposted off the highway just east of Varja is this manor estate, home to a pleasant hotel and spa, as well as a camping area. It's set among hiking trails and walking paths, with a new metal staircase leading from the cliff edge to the seashore below. It's a good choice if you're after something well off the tourist trail.

SILLAMÄE
pop 16,600

Located on the coast between Kohtla-Järve and Narva, Sillamäe is one of the few places in Estonia where the aura of the USSR still lives on, and it feels caught between two worlds. It's a rarely visited town with a tree-lined main street that functions as a living museum of Stalinist-era architecture. Planned by Leningrad architects, the town features grand, solid buildings with gargoyles and a cascading staircase ornamented by large urns. Around the central square, there's a **town hall** specially designed to resemble a Lutheran church, a **cultural centre** (constructed in 1949) that still has reliefs of Marx and Lenin on the walls inside, and a very Soviet-style monument erected in 1987 to commemorate the 70th anniversary of the October Revolution. Read more on www.sill amae.ee.

The region's fate was sealed in the post-WWII years upon the discovery that oil shale contains small amounts of extractable uranium. The infamous uranium processing and nuclear chemicals factory was quickly built by 5000 Russian political prisoners, and the town centre by 3800 Baltic prisoners of war who had previously served in the German army. By 1946 the city was strictly off limits; it was known by various spooky code names (Leningrad 1; Moscow 400) and was often omitted from Soviet-era maps.

Only unfinished uranium was processed at the plant, though the eerily abandoned buildings on the city's western border are testament to Soviet plans to process pure, nuclear reactor-ready uranium; only the disbanding of the USSR saved Estonian ecology from this. The plant was closed in 1991 and today the radioactive waste is buried under concrete by the sea. Fears of leakage into the Baltic Sea have alarmed environmentalists; EU funding has been channelled towards ensuring the waste is stable and safe, at enormous cost.

The **Sillamäe Museum** (☎ 397 2425; Kajaka 17a; 🕑 10am-6pm Mon-Fri May-Sep, 10am-6pm Tue-Sat Oct-Apr) details the history of the area. But the real attraction of this town is wandering its classical alleys and leafy boulevards.

The only hotel in town is **Krunk** (☎ 392 9030; www.krunk.ee; Kesk 23; s/d/tr 580/725/1050Kr), in an attractive yellow building on the main street. It's a sombre place but well located on the town square, with simple, agreeable rooms and a nicely positioned restaurant (open noon to 9pm or later, Monday to Saturday). Visit on Sunday, when the restaurant is closed, and Sillamäe feels like a ghost town.

At least 20 buses travel daily between Tallinn and Sillamäe (135Kr to 160Kr, three hours); and more than 40 buses run between Narva and Sillamäe (20Kr to 40Kr, 30 minutes).

NARVA
pop 66,900

Estonia's easternmost town is separated only by the thin Narva River from Ivangorod in Russia. Narva, which has the look and feel of a Russian city (and a population that's around 95% Russian), has a magnificent castle and a captivating history that spans centuries. Although the most outstanding architecture was destroyed in WWII, Estonia's third-largest city is an intriguing place to wander, as you'll find no other place in Estonia quite like it. The centre has a melancholy, downtrodden air; the prosperity evident in other parts of the country is harder to find here (though it does exist in

some pockets, most notably the brash shopping centres along Tallinna mnt). Narva's a place that will have you scratching your head at times – is it a Russian city on the wrong side of the border? Estonia (and Europe's) easternmost point, or possibly Russia's westernmost town? Be prepared, too, for limited English spoken in shops and services.

History

People have lived here since the Stone Age, and it was a fortified trading point in 1172. It was embroiled in border disputes between the German knights and Russia; Ivan III of Muscovy built a fort at Ivangorod in 1492. In the 16th and 17th centuries Narva changed hands often from Russian to Swede, until falling to Russia in 1704.

Narva was almost completely destroyed in 1944 during its recapture by the Red Army. Afterwards it became part of the northeastern Estonian industrial zone and one of Europe's most polluted towns. Today emissions have been greatly reduced, with investment in cleaner technology well under way.

Orientation & Information

The castle, Narva's biggest landmark, is by the river, just south of the Russia–Estonia bridge. The train and bus stations are next to each other on Vaksali 2, at the southern end of the main street, Pushkini.

From the stations it's a 500m walk north along Pushkini to the castle. En route you'll pass the **tourist office** (☎ 356 0184; http://tourism.narva.ee; Pushkini 13; 🕑 10am-6pm Mon-Fri, 10am-3pm Sat & Sun mid-May–mid-Sep, 10am-5pm Mon-Fri mid-Sep–mid-May), where you can get maps and city information from friendly and efficient English-speaking staff. A currency exchange window is next door; other neighbours include a pharmacy and ATM. A block east is the **public library** (2nd fl, Malmi 8; 🕑 11am-7pm Mon-Fri, plus 10am-5pm Sat Sep-May), with free internet access. The **New York Café** (☎ 356 7423; Astri Keskus, Tallinna mnt 41; per hr 20Kr; 🕑 10am-9pm), inside the Astri Keskus shopping centre, also has internet access – it's on the 3rd floor, by the cinema and bowling alley.

Sights

The imposing **Narva Castle**, guarding the Friendship Bridge over the river to Russia, is a must-visit. Built by the Danes at the end of the 13th century, it faces Russia's matching

Ivangorod Fortress across the river, creating an architectural ensemble unique to Europe. This picturesque face-off is best captured from the **Swedish Lion monument**, in a small park behind the Narva Hotel at Pushkin 6.

Restored after damage during WWII, Narva Castle houses the **Town Museum** (☎ 359 9245; www .narvamuuseum.ee; adult/concession 60/35Kr; ☹ 10am-6pm). The pricey admission gives you the opportunity to climb the tower here and enjoy great views, while checking out the exhibits on each level of your climb (of varying degrees of interest, not all with labelling in English).

North of the castle, the baroque **Old Town Hall** (Raekoja väljak), built between 1668 and 1671, is impressive, as is the 19th-century **home of Baron von Velio** (cnr Sepa & Hariduse), two blocks north. The Russian Orthodox **Voskresensky Cathedral** (Bastrakovy), built in 1898, is northwest of the train station. On the square in front of the train station is a monument to the Estonians who were loaded into cattle wagons here and deported to Siberia in 1941.

Also worth a visit is the **Kunsti Galerii** (☎ 359 2151; Vestervalli 21; adult/concession 20/10Kr; ☹ 10am-6pm), an art gallery some 500m north of the border point.

Sleeping & Eating

If the town's heavy mood has you longing for a bit of 21st-century modernity, your best bet is to head west along Tallinna mnt to malls such as Astri Keskus, with a few options here for a quick bite. Our best picks are the restaurants at hotels King and Inger, both open for lunch and dinner.

Hostel & Restoran Lell (☎ 354 9009; www.narva hotel.ee; Partisani 4; s 275Kr, d 550-750Kr) If you're after budget digs, don't be put off by the grey concrete exterior of this option. The rooms are well worn but decent (the cheaper options share shower facilities). It's about 20 minutes' walk west of the centre, south of Astri Keskus shopping centre.

King Hotel (☎ 357 2404; www.hotelking.ee; Lavretsovi 9; s/d 690/890Kr; ☐) Not far north of the centre (and with a few sleeping and eating options in the immediate vicinity) is Narva's best hotel choice, with snug modern rooms and an excellent on-site restaurant (mains 109Kr to 249Kr). For something different, try the lamprey, a local fish from the Narva River, or the tasty trout shashlik with bacon.

Hotell Inger (☎ 688 1100; www.inger.ee; Pushkini 28; s/d/f 950/1200/1500Kr) The newest and biggest hotel

in town has obliging staff, sizable rooms and inoffensive decor (though the carpet hasn't worn well). Some rooms have private sauna, and the themed suites are fun.

Salvadore (☎ 688 1105; www.inger.ee; Pushkini 28; mains 135-255Kr) The restaurant at Hotell Inger offers a surprisingly stylish, modern dining room with Dalí-esque murals on the wall. Creative salads and Italian specialities (pasta and risotto dishes for under 110Kr) are hit-and-miss, and there's international dishes ranging from Caesar salad to pan-fried foie gras, roasted rack of lamb to *tiramisu*.

Aleksandr Kohvik (☎ 357 1350; Pushkini 13; snacks & meals from 40Kr; ☹ 10am-11pm) Serving up melancholy music alongside its bland cafe fare, this no-nonsense coffee shop and restaurant is a blast from the USSR past. Pop into the shop next door to browse the Soviet memorabilia.

Getting There & Away

Narva is 210km east of Tallinn on the road to St Petersburg, a further 150km away. Around 25 daily buses travel between Tallinn and Narva (135Kr to 170Kr, three to four hours) and one train (100Kr, 3½ hours) runs daily, stopping in Rakvere.

There are also up to 10 daily Tartu–Narva buses (125Kr to 160Kr, 3½ hours), and buses to nearby cities such as Sillamäe and Rakvere. See http://transport.ida-virumaa.ee for timetable info for the region.

NARVA-JÕESUU
pop 2700

About 13km north of Narva, the holiday resort of Narva-Jõesuu is a pretty but slightly scruffy town, popular since the 19th century for its long, golden-sand beach backed by pine forests. There are a number of unique, impressive early-20th-century wooden houses and villas throughout the town, which makes a good base for exploring Narva if you're after a more relaxing approach. Here you'll find a half-dozen hotels and spas to choose from, all overlooking a fine sandy beach, with plenty of new development going on, largely catering to holidaying Russians.

The busiest area appears to be the little cluster of action centred on the new Meresuu hotel (1.5km west from the turning to Narva). If you stop here, be sure to admire the breathtaking intricacy of the historic villa on Aia, next to Pansionaat Valentina.

Sleeping & Eating

Pansionaat Valentina (☎ 357 7468; keeping@hot.ee; Aia 49; s 400-500Kr, d 600-800Kr) Behind the slick new Meresuu Spa & Hotel is this handsome, salmon-pink-coloured guesthouse in immaculate grounds, family-friendly and with plenty of facilities (bike rental, tennis courts, sauna, barbecue, nice on-site cafe). It offers a smaller, more personalised option than the Meresuu; rooms are pleasant, neat and simply furnished.

Meresuu Spa & Hotel (☎ 357 9600; www.meresuu.ee; Aia 48; s/d 1721/1878Kr) Only one week old when we stopped by, this shiny seven-storey hotel offers service with a smile, alongside a roll-call of extras: attractive rooms in browns and creams, an 'aqua centre' (seven pools!), saunas, wellness centre, kids' playroom, bike and even yacht rental, and the requisite restaurant, serving up buffets and à la carte dining. Outside summer, room rates drop by 630Kr.

Getting There & Away

Bus 31 runs about hourly to connect Narva with Narva-Jõesuu (25Kr, 20 minutes), as do numerous *marshrutkas* (minibuses), without set timetables. The bus station in Narva is by the train station, but a more central bus stop is close to the tourist office on Pushkin.

KUREMÄE

Originally the site of ancient pagan worship, the village of Kuremäe, 20km southeast of Jõhvi, is home to the stunning Russian Orthodox **Pühtitsa Convent** (☎ 339 2124; www.orthodox.ee; admission free; ☙ noon-6pm Mon-Fri) – the name *pühtitsa* means blessed place in Estonian. Built between 1885 and 1895, the magnificent nunnery has five towers topped with green onion domes and is a place of annual pilgrimage for Russian Orthodox believers. Murals by the convent gate depict the Virgin Mary, who, it is said, appeared to a 16th-century shepherd by an oak tree in these parts. An icon was later found in the area and it is still in the main church of the convent. There is also a revered holy spring that never freezes. The nuns work the surrounding land and are self-sufficient; they will give tours to visitors for a small fee.

Downhill from the monastery is a coffee shop, where you can enjoy cakes and caffeine on the outdoor patio.

Two weekly buses connect Kuremäe with Tallinn (130Kr, 3½ hours), via Rakvere and Jõhvi. Local bus 116 connects Kuremäe with Jõhvi about eight times a day.

LAKE PEIPSI (NORTH)

Some of Estonia's finest (and least crowded) beaches are found on the northern coast of Lake Peipsi; 42km of clean, sandy dunes hug the shoreline of what appears to be a sea rather than a lake. The area had popular resorts during Soviet times but many of them have been left to crumble. Development is very slowly arriving to this beautiful area with enormous tourism potential, but is largely in the shape of new allotments for summer houses, rather than traveller accommodation.

On the northeastern shore of the lake (south on the road past Kuremäe) is **Vasknarva**, an isolated fishing village with about 100 residents. There is an evocative Orthodox church here that, according to some, once held a KGB radio surveillance centre. Also in Vasknarva, scant ruins of a 1349 Teutonic Order castle stand by the shore of Lake Peipsi. At **Alajõe** is the area's main Orthodox church and a shop. **Kauksi**, where the Narva–Jõhvi–Tartu road reaches the lake, is the area's most popular beach.

From **Lohusuu** extending southwards is Old Believers' territory (for more details, see p126). Further south, towards Jõgeva, are the lakeside towns of Mustvee and Raja. **Mustvee**, a town of just 2000, has four **churches** (there used to be seven): Orthodox, Baptist, Lutheran and Old Believer. There is also a forlorn WWII memorial by the sea, the **Mourning Lady**, a young woman with her head hung low. Some 8km south is the one-street village of **Raja**, where a wooden church contains some rare icons dating from the 19th century when a prestigious school of icon painting was founded here by famed icon painter Gavrila Frolov.

The southern half of Lake Peipsi is covered in the Southeastern Estonia section (p126).

Sleeping & Eating

There are a couple of resorts around Alajõe, but many are in dire need of repair. The following are off the main road that follows the shoreline. Remember to bring mosquito repellent.

Kauksi Telklaager (☎ 339 3840; www.tisler.ee; Kauksi; sites/cabins per person 30/100Kr) At Kauksi beach, this popular camp site gets packed with young partygoers on weekends. It has tiny two-person cabins and a very basic, tepee-shaped cafe on the grounds. Showers cost 30Kr.

Kuru Puhkemajad (☎ 5690 6876; www.kurupuhkema jad.ee; Kuru; sites/cabins 100/500Kr, r 300-750Kr) At Kuru, a couple of kilometres east of Kauksi (off the road from the lake to Iisaku), this complex, offering camping, rooms in red-painted, barn-like buildings, or new wooden cabins (with communal kitchen and bathroom). It's set in pretty grounds, with a barbecue area, plus bike and boat rental. There's also a *pood* (grocery shop) in Kuru.

Peipsi Lained Külalistemaja (☎ 339 3723; www .peipsi-lained.ee; d 500-700Kr) At Ninasi, about 5km north of Mustvee, this friendly guesthouse offers clean, cosy, pine-lined rooms (a mix of private and shared bathrooms). There's a kitchen for guest use, a restaurant on-site, a sauna for hire, and the chance to hire boats (in summer) or snowmobiles (in winter). The lake is 50m from the door.

Locally caught and smoked fish (trout or salmon) is a speciality of the area. Some would say the delicious catch alone warrants the journey. Look for *suitsukala* (smoked fish) stands scattered all along the main road curving around the lake. There's a large supermarket next to the bus station in Mustvee.

Getting There & Away
Getting to this area is tricky without your own wheels. There are up to 10 daily Tartu–Narva buses, many of which will stop in Mustvee, Kauksi and Jõhvi. Local buses from Jõhvi will also help you reach your destination – see http://transport.ida-virumaa.ee for timetable information (note that this covers the county south of Narva to just north of Mustvee).

SOUTHEASTERN ESTONIA

Set with rolling hills, picturesque lakes and vast woodlands, the southeast boasts some of Estonia's most attractive countryside. It also contains one of Estonia's most important cities: the heart of this region, the vibrant university centre of Tartu.

Beyond the city – no matter which direction you head – you'll find resplendent natural settings. In the south lie the towns of Otepää and Võru, the gateway to outdoor adventuring: hiking and lake-swimming in summer and cross-country skiing in winter. Quaint towns set on wandering rivers or in picturesque valleys add to the allure. For a serious dose of woodland, head to Haanja Nature Park, with its crisp lakes and gently rolling hills, or Karula National Park.

To the east stretches Lake Peipsi, one of Europe's largest lakes. Along its shores are beautiful sandy beaches and a surprisingly undeveloped coastline. Aside from swimming, boating, fishing and soaking up the scenery, you can travel up its western rim stopping at roadside food stands and in tiny villages.

One of Estonia's most intriguing regions is also among its least visited. In the far southeast, clustered in villages near Lake Pihkva, live the Setus, ancestors of Balto-Finnic tribes who settled here in the first millennium.

If you plan only to dip into the region, then you'll be fine getting around by bus. For more in-depth exploring – particularly around Haanja Nature Park, Setumaa and Lake Peipsi – bus services are infrequent and you'll save loads of time by renting a car.

TARTU
pop 101,700

If Tallinn is Estonia's head, Tartu may well be its heart (and in some ways its university-educated brains trust, too). Tartu lays claim to being Estonia's spiritual capital – locals talk about a special Tartu *vaim* (spirit), encompassed by the time-stands-still, 19th-century feel of many of its streets, lined with wooden houses, and by the beauty of its parks and riverfront.

Small and provincial, with the quietly flowing Emajõgi River running through it, Tartu is also Estonia's premier university town, with students making up nearly one-fifth of the population. This injects a boisterous vitality into the leafy, historic setting and grants it a surprising sophistication for a city of its size.

Tartu was the cradle of Estonia's 19th-century national revival and it escaped Sovietisation to a greater degree than Tallinn. Its handsome centre is lined with classically designed 18th-century buildings, many of which have been put to innovative uses by the city's idealists. Today, visitors to Estonia's second city can get a more authentic depiction of the rhythm of Estonian life than in its glitzier cousin to the north (accompanied by far fewer tourists, too). In addition to galleries

SOUTHEASTERN ESTONIA

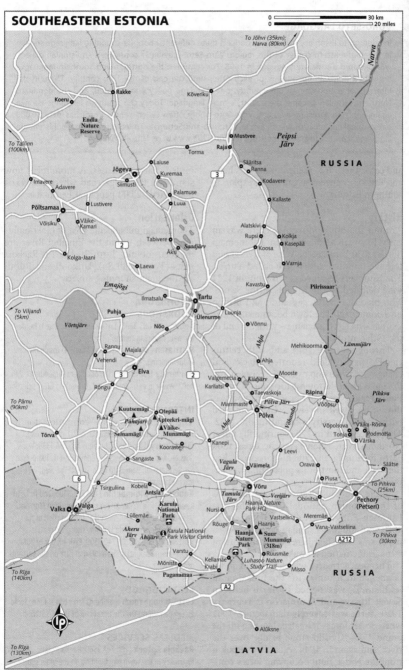

0   30 km
0   20 miles

To Jõhvi (35km);
Narva (80km)

Narva

Koeru

Rakke

Köveriku

Endla
Nature
Reserve

To Tallinn
(100km)

Mustvee

Peipsi
Järv

RUSSIA

Raja

Torma

Sääritsa
Ranna

Laiuse

Jõgeva

Kuremaa

Kodavere

Imavere

Adavere

Siimusti

Palamuse

Kallaste

Põltsamaa

Lustivere

Luua

Võisiku

Väike-
Kamari

Alatskivi

Tabivere

Rupsi

Kolkja

2

Äksi

Saadjärv

Koosa

Kasepää

Kolga-Jaani

Laeva

Varnja

Emajõgi

Kavastu

Piirissaar

Ilmatsalu

Tartu

To Viljandi
(5km)

Puhja

Ülenurme

Luunja

Võnnu

Lümmijärv

Võrtsjärv

Nõo

Mehikoorma

Rannu

Majala

Ahja

Pihkva
Järv

Vehendi

3

Elva

2

Valgemetsa

Ahja

Rõngu

Karilatsi

Kiidjärv

Mooste

To Pärnu
(90km)

Puka

Kuutsemägi

Pühajärv

Otepää

Apteekri-mägi

Väike-
Munamägi

Seinamägi

Mammaste

Taevaskoja

Põlva Järv

Räpina

Põlva

Võõpsu

Võpolsova

Väike-Rõsna

Tõrva

Kanepi

Tonja

Podmotsa

Kooraste

Ahja

Värska

Sangaste

Leevi

Vagula
Järv

Väimela

Orava

6

Tsirguliina

Kobela

Võru

Piusa

Säätse

Valka

Valga

Antsla

Tamula
Järv

Verijärv

Obinitsa

To Pihkva
(25km)

Lüllemäe

Karula
National
Park

Nursi

Haanja Nature
Park HQ

Pechory
(Petseri)

Aheru
Järv

Ähijärv

Karula National
Park Visitor Centre

Rõuge

Vastseliina

Meremäe

Vana-Vastseliina

Haanja

To Pihkva
(30km)

Varstu

Haanja
Nature
Park

Suur
Munamägi
(318m)

Ruusmäe

A212

Mõniste

Kellamäe

Luhasoo Nature
Study Trail

Krabi

Misso

RUSSIA

Paganamaa

A2

To Rīga
(140km)

Alūksne

To Rīga
(130km)

LATVIA

ESTONIA

VÕRO-SETO LANGUAGE

In addition to Estonian, visitors may notice a quite different, choppier-sounding language spoken in the southeastern corner of this region. Võro-Seto, previously considered an Estonian dialect, was declared a separate language in 1998. For centuries, the northern and southern languages flourished quite independently of each other until the end of the 19th century. Then, in the interests of nationalism, a one-country, one-language policy was adopted, and the dominant Northern Estonian became the country's main language. Today the southern language is once again enjoying a resurgence, and Võro-Seto (more often called simply Võro) has over 50,000 native speakers, most of whom live in Võrumaa and Setumaa. To learn more about this unique language, contact the **Võro Institute** (☎ 782 1960; www.wi.ee; Tartu 48, Võru).

---

and cafes, there are excellent museums here, and Tartu is a convenient gateway to exploring southern Estonia.

History

Around the 6th century AD there was an early Estonian stronghold on Toomemägi hill. In 1030 Yaroslav the Wise of Kyiv is said to have founded a fort here called Yuriev. The Estonians regained control, but in 1224 were defeated by the Knights of the Sword, who placed a castle, cathedral and bishop on Toomemägi. The town became known as Dorpat – its German name – until the end of the 19th century.

Throughout the 16th and 17th centuries Dorpat suffered repeated attacks and changes of ownership as Russia, Sweden and Poland-Lithuania fought for control of the Baltic region. Its most peaceful period was during the Swedish reign, which coincided with the university's founding in 1632. This peace ended in 1704, during the Great Northern War, when Peter the Great took Tartu for Russia. In 1708 his forces wrecked the town and most of its population was deported to Russia.

In the mid-1800s Tartu became the focus of the Estonian national revival: the first Estonian Song Festival was held here in 1869, and the first Estonian-language newspaper was launched here – both important steps in the national awakening.

The peace treaty, which granted independence to Estonia (for the first time in its history), was signed in Tartu between Soviet Russia and Estonia on 2 February 1920. Tartu was severely damaged in 1941 when Soviet forces retreated, blowing up the grand 1784 Kivisild stone bridge over the river, and again in 1944 when they retook it from the Nazis. Both occupying forces committed many atrocities. A monument now stands on the Valga road where the Nazis massacred 12,000 people at Lemmatsi.

Orientation

Toomemägi hill and the area of older buildings between it and the Emajõgi River are the focus of 'old' Tartu. Its heart is Raekoja plats (Town Hall Sq). Ülikooli and Rüütli are the main shopping streets.

Information

BOOKSHOPS

Apollo (☎ 683 3400; Tartu Kaubamaja, Riia 1) Inside the new shopping centre.
Mattiesen (☎ 730 9723; Vallikraavi 4) Inside the Café Wilde building.
University Bookshop (Ülikooli Raamatupood; ☎ 744 1102; www.ut.ee/raamatupood; Ülikooli 1) Great selection.

INTERNET ACCESS

The tourist office has computers for free internet access (maximum 20 minutes).
City Library (Linnaraamatukogu; ☎ 736 1379; www .luts.ee; Kompanii 3; ☺ 9am-8pm Mon-Fri, 10am-4pm Sat Sep-late Jul, 9am-6pm Mon-Fri late Jul-Aug) Free internet upstairs.
Kaubamaja Digimaailm (☎ 731 5100; 2nd fl, Tartu Kaubamaja, Riia 1; per hr 25Kr; ☺ 9am-9pm Mon-Sat, 9am-6pm Sun) Computers in the music section of the department store within the new shopping centre.
Kohvik Virtuaal (☎ 740 2509; Pikk 40; per hr 30Kr; ☺ 11am-midnight) A sleek internet cafe on the east side of the river.

LEFT LUGGAGE

Left-luggage room (pakihoid; Tartu bus station, Soola 2; ☺ 6am-9pm) Off the ticket hall at the bus station.

MEDICAL SERVICES

Raekoja Apteek (☎ 742 3560; Raekoja plats; ☺ 24hr) Pharmacy in the town hall building on the main square.

TARTU

0 | 300 m
0 | 0.2 miles

INFORMATION
Apollo..(see 58)
City Library...................................**1** C4
Kaubamaja Digimaailm...........(see 58)
Kohvik Virtuaal.............................**2** D4
Mattiesen......................................(see 33)
Post Office....................................**3** C4
Raekoja Apteek............................(see 18)
Tartu University Information
  Centre..(see 17)
Tavid...**4** C5
Tourist Office...............................(see 18)
University Bookshop.....................**5** C5

SIGHTS & ACTIVITIES
19th-Century Tartu Citizen's Home
  Museum......................................**6** B4
A Le Coq Beer Museum................**7** A3
Aura Keskus...................................**8** D6
Cornflower Monument..................**9** B6
Estonian National Museum........**10** A5
KGB Cells Museum.....................**11** B6

Museum of University History...**12** B5
St John's Church.........................**13** C4
Student's Lock-Up......................(see 17)
Tartu Art Museum......................**14** C5
Tartu Cathedral..........................**15** B5
Tartu Sports Museum.................**16** C4
Tartu University Art Museum.....(see 17)
Tartu University Building...........**17** B4
Town Hall....................................**18** C5
Toy Museum................................**19** B4

SLEEPING
Domus Dorpatensis....................**20** C5
Herne...**21** A3
Hostel Terviseks.........................**22** C5
Hotell Dorpat.............................**23** D5
Hotell Tartu................................**24** D5
London Hotell.............................**25** C4
Pallas Hotell...............................**26** C6
Park Hotell.................................**27** B5
Tampere Maja.............................**28** B4
Tartu Student Village Hostel
  (Narva)....................................**29** D4
Tartu Student Village Hostel
  (Pepleri)..................................**30** B6
Tartu Student Village Hostel
  (Raatuse).................................**31** D4
Uppsala Maja..............................**32** B4
Wilde Guest Apartments...........(see 33)

EATING
Café Wilde..................................**33** C5
Crepp..**34** C4
Gruusia Saatkond.......................**35** C4
Indoor Market............................**36** D5
La Dolce Vita..............................**37** C4
Maailm.......................................**38** A5
Moka...**39** C5

Outdoor Market..........................**40** D5
Pierre Chocolaterie.....................**41** C5
Püssirohukelder...........................**42** B5
Supermarket...............................(see 58)
Tsink Plekk Pang........................**43** C4
University Café............................**44** B4

DRINKING
Noir...**45** C5
Rotunda......................................**46** B5
Wilde Irish Pub..........................(see 33)
Zavood..**47** B4

ENTERTAINMENT
Atlantis.......................................**48** D5
Cinamon.....................................(see 59)
Club Illusion...............................**49** D4
Club Tallinn................................**50** D4
Ekraan..**51** C6
Sadamateater.............................**52** D5
Vanemuine Theatre & Concert
  Hall..**53** C6
Vanemuine Theatre (small
  stage)......................................**54** B6

SHOPPING
Antoniuse Gild...........................**55** B4
Pille-Resa Nukumaja..................**56** C4
Pits...**57** C5
Tartu Kaubamaja.......................**58** D5
Tasku..**59** D5

TRANSPORT
Bus Station.................................**60** D5
Central Bus Stop........................**61** D5
Eurolines Ticket Office..............(see 60)
Jalgratas.....................................**62** A3
Sixt...**63** C5

To Narva
(185km)

Emajõgi

Botanical
Gardens

Emajõgi

To Viljandi
(80km)

Sacrificial
Stone

Toomemägi

Angel's
Bridge

Raekoja
plats

Devil's
Bridge

Kuperjanovi

Train
Station

To 123 Rent (2km);
Valga (88km);
Rīga (250km)

To Otepää (44km);
Võru (65km)

To Aleksandri Hotell (250m);
Hansa Tall (300m);
City Car (400m)

ESTONIA

MONEY
Tavid (☎ 730 1170; Rüütli 2; ⏱ 9am-5pm Mon-Fri, 10am-5pm Sat & Sun) The best place to change cash.

POST
Central post office (Vanemuise 7; ⏱ 8am-7pm Mon-Fri, 9am-4pm Sat)

TOURIST INFORMATION
Tartu tourist office (☎ 744 2111; www.visittartu .com; Raekoja plats; ⏱ 9am-6pm Mon-Fri, 10am-5pm Sat, 10am-3pm Sun mid-May–mid-Sep, 9am-5pm Mon-Fri, 10am-3pm Sat mid-Sep–mid-May) This friendly office inside the town hall has local maps and brochures, and loads of other city info. It can also book accommodation and tour guides, sell you souvenirs and get you online (free internet access is available here). Be sure to pick up the excellent *Tartu in Your Pocket* guide (25Kr), published twice a year and available free online (www.inyourpocket.com).

Sights & Activities
RAEKOJA PLATS
At the town centre on Raekoja plats is the **town hall** (built between 1782 and 1789), topped by a tower and weather vane, and fronted by a statue of lovers kissing under a spouting umbrella. The building's design came courtesy of the German architect JHB Walter, who modelled it on a typical Dutch town hall. A clock was added to encourage students to be punctual for classes.

Nearby is the wonderfully crooked building housing the **Tartu Art Museum** (Kunstimuuseum; ☎ 744 1080; www.tartmus.ee; Raekoja plats 18; adult/concession 30/20Kr; ⏱ 11am-6pm Wed-Sun), former home of Colonel Barclay de Tolly (1761–1818), an exiled Scot who distinguished himself in the Russian army's 1812 campaign against Napoleon. The building receives more interest than its contents – foundations laid partially over an old town wall have given it the pronounced lean.

UNIVERSITY & OLD TOWN
The university was founded in 1632 by the Swedish king Gustaf II Adolf (Gustavus Adolphus) to train Lutheran clergy and government officials. It was modelled on Uppsala University in Sweden. The university closed during the Great Northern War around 1700 but reopened in 1802, later becoming one of the Russian empire's foremost centres of learning. Its early emphasis on science is evidenced by the great scholars who studied here in the 19th century, including physical

chemistry pioneer and Nobel-prize winner for chemistry, Wilhelm Ostwald; physicist Heinrich Lenz; and the founder of embryology, natural scientist Karl Ernst von Baer, whose image adorns the 2 kroon note.

Fronted by six Corinthian columns, the impressive main building of **Tartu University** (Tartu Ülikool; ☎ 737 5100; www.ut.ee; Ülikooli 18) dates from 1804–09. Stop in at the information centre if you have the sudden urge to become a student. There are two other sites here that warrant a visit. The **University Art Museum** (Ülikooli Kunstimuuseum; ☎ 737 5384; www.ut.ee/art museum; adult/concession 10/5Kr; ⏱ 11am-5pm Mon-Fri) contains mainly plaster casts of ancient Greek sculptures, made in Europe in the 1860s and 1870s, and an old mummy. The rest of the collection was evacuated to Russia during the war and has never returned. More fascinating is the **Student's Lock-Up** (admission 5Kr; ⏱ 11am-5pm Mon-Fri), where 19th-century students were held in solitary confinement for various infractions. Back then, if you failed to return library books on time, you'd net two days in the attic; insulting a lady, four days; insulting a (more sensitive?) cloakroom attendant, five days; duelling, up to three weeks. Today, one of these rather comfy rooms, with walls covered in original graffiti, is open for viewing.

North of the university, on the continuation of Ülikooli, stands the magnificent **St John's Church** (Jaani Kirik; ☎ 744 2229; www.jaanikirik .ee; Jaani 5; ⏱ 10am-7pm Tue-Sat). This brick church dates back to at least 1323, and is unique for its rare terracotta sculptures in niches around the main portal. It lay in ruins and was then derelict following the Soviet bombing raid in 1944. Today, after 16 years of restoration, it is once again open. Climb the 135 steps of the 30m **observation tower** (adult/child 25/15Kr) for a great bird's-eye view of Tartu.

The **Botanical Gardens** (Botaanikaaed; ☎ 737 6180; www.ut.ee/botaed; Lai 38; greenhouse adult/concession 25/10Kr; ⏱ grounds 7am-7pm, greenhouses 10am-5pm), founded in 1803, nurtures 6500 species of plants and a large collection of palm trees in its giant greenhouse. A wander through the grounds is both pleasant and free (open until 9pm in summer).

A number of smaller museums dot the town, catering to specialised interests. The **Tartu Sports Museum** (Spordimuuseum; ☎ 730 0750; ww.spordimuuseum.ee, in Estonian; Rüütli 15; adult/concession 35/25Kr; ⏱ 11am-6pm Tue-Sun) chronicles more than Estonian Olympic excellence. There's a display of the life of early-20th-century bodybuilders, early wooden skis, medals, and an interactive tug-of-war on the 2nd floor. Next door is a postal museum.

In an old wooden house amid period furnishings, the **19th-century Tartu Citizen's Home Museum** (☎ 736 1545; Jaani 16; adult/concession 10/5Kr; ⏱ 11am-6pm Wed-Sun Apr-Sep, 10am-3pm Wed-Sun Oct-Mar) shows how a burgher from the 1830s lived. A booklet for visitors explores the town's history in various languages.

The best place to pass a rainy few hours is the **Toy Museum** (Mänguasjamuuseum; ☎ 736 1550; www.mm.ee; Lutsu 8; adult/concession/family 25/20/60Kr; ⏱ 11am-6pm Wed-Sun), a big hit with the under-eight crowd (and you won't see too many adults anxious to leave). Set in one of Tartu's oldest buildings (dating from the 1770s), this excellent museum showcases dolls, model trains, rocking horses, toy soldiers and tons of other desirables dating back a century or so. If all those unobtainable toys have unearthed your inner child, there's a playroom upstairs for more hands-on activity. And be sure to wander through the adjacent TEFI House, home to an outstanding collection of theatre and animation puppets.

TOOMEMÄGI

Toomemägi (Cathedral Hill), rising to the west of the town hall, is a splendidly landscaped park, with walking paths meandering through the trees. This hill is the original reason for Tartu's existence, functioning on and off as a stronghold from around the 5th or 6th century. The approach from Raekoja plats is along Lossi, which passes beneath the **Angel's Bridge** (Inglisild), which was built between 1836 and 1838 – follow local superstition and hold your breath and make a wish as you cross it for the first time. A bit further up the hill is **Devil's Bridge** (Kuradisild).

Atop the hill is the imposing Gothic **Tartu Cathedral** (Toomkirik). It was built by German knights in the 13th century, rebuilt in the 15th century, despoiled during the Reformation in 1525, used as a barn, and partly rebuilt between 1804 and 1807 to house the university library, which is now the **Museum of University History** (Ülikooli Ajaloo Muuseum; ☎ 737 5674; www.ut.ee/ajaloomuuseum; Lossi 25; adult/concession 25/15Kr; ⏱ 11am-5pm Wed-Sun). Inside you'll find a range of exhibits, from a reconstructed autopsy chamber to displays chronicling student life. Start at the top and work your way down.

Nearby is the pretty-as-a-picture **Rotunda**, a summertime cafe perfect for an alfresco drink or ice cream.

SOUTH OF TOOMEMÄGI

Tartu, as the major repository of Estonia's cultural heritage, has an abundance of first-rate museums; among them is the absorbing **Estonian National Museum** (Eesti Rahva Muuseum; ☎ 742 1311; www.erm.ee; Kuperjanovi 9; adult/concession 20/15Kr, free entry Fri; ⏱ 11am-6pm Wed-Sun). Small, sweet and proud (much like the country itself), the museum gives a great insight into the history, life and traditions of the Estonian people. Don't miss the regional displays of folk costumes and exhibits of uniquely handcrafted tankards. Temporary exhibits here are also noteworthy.

The former KGB headquarters, known infamously as the 'Grey House', is now the sombre and highly worthwhile **KGB Cells Museum** (KGB Kongide Muuseum; ☎ 746 1717; http://linnamuuseum.tartu.ee; Riia mnt 15b; adult/concession 12/8Kr; ⏱ 11am-4pm Tue-Sat). Chilling in parts, the museum's new displays and commentary give a fascinating rundown of deportations and life in the gulags. In 1990 the **cornflower monument** was erected beside the KGB building in memory of the victims of Soviet repression; the blue cornflower is Estonia's national flower. The entrance to the museum is on Pepleri.

BEER MUSEUM

North of Toomemägi, the **A. Le Coq Beer Museum** (☎ 744 9711; www.alecoq.ee/eng/activities/museum; Tähtvere 56; admission 25Kr; ⏱ tours 2pm Thu, 10am, noon & 2pm Sat), at the brewery, briefly covers the history of beer-making, but focuses mainly on the machinery and brewing techniques. A. Le Coq has churned out its trademark beverage since 1879. Free samples at the end of tours.

SWIMMING

If the sun's beating down and you can't make it to Pärnu, there's a pleasant **beach** (with sand volleyball court) along the northern bank of the Emajõgi, a 1km walk west of Kroonuaia bridge (walk along Ujula).

Alternatively, a 50m indoor pool and family-friendly waterpark with all the trimmings can be found south of the bus station at **Aura Keskus** (☎ 730 0280; www.aurakeskus.ee; Turu 10; admission pool 40-70Kr, waterpark 70-105Kr; ⏱ 6.30am-10pm Mon-Fri, 9am-10pm Sat & Sun, closed Jul).

ESTONIA

Tours

Elina Aro (☎ 5360 3810; www.beneficium.ee) conducts a daily walking tour of Tartu from June to August. Fittingly, the meeting place is by the symbol of the town, the kissing students fountain on Raekoja plats. There's no need to book for these tours, which begin at 5pm, last 1½ hours and cost 75Kr. Elina can also provide tailored guiding services, and the tourist office can put you in touch with other guides.

In previous years there have been river cruises on the Emajõgi, but two operators have ceased operation. It's best to enquire at the tourist office about any current services.

Festivals & Events

Tartu regularly dons its shiniest party gear and lets its hair down – good events to circle in your travel calendar include the following. The lead-up to Christmas is also full of cheer, with a market set up at Antoniuse Gild (p115). Check out http://kultuuriaken.tartu.ee for more.

Tartu Ski Marathon (www.tartumaraton.ee) In mid-February the city hosts this 63km race, drawing around 4000 competitors to the region's cross-country tracks (actually starting in Otepää and finishing in Elva). The same organisation hosts a range of sporting events (cycling road race, mountain-bike race, running race) in and around Tartu throughout the year.

Tartu Student Days (www.studentdays.ee, in Estonian) You can catch a glimpse of modern-day student misdeeds at the end of April. Students take to the streets to celebrate term's end (and the dawn of spring) in every way imaginable. A second, smaller version occurs in mid-October.

Hansa Days Festival (www.hansapaevad.ee) Crafts, markets, family-friendly performances and more commemorate Tartu's Hanseatic past over three days in mid-July.

Plink Plonk (www.plinkplonk.ee) The university city makes the perfect setting for this one-day festival of independent music, in mid-July.

tARTuff (www.tartuff.ee) The Tartu open-air film festival has free screenings over a week in mid-August at the 1000-seat 'screening hall' set up on Raekoja plats.

Sleeping

Tartu lacks the capital's range of accommodation – there are fewer backpacker-oriented places, and none of the boutique hotels that Tallinn does so well. That said, there are reasonable hotels and some lovely guesthouses. The website www.visittartu.com gives a comprehensive rundown of options.

BUDGET

Hostel Terviseks (☎ 5353 1153; www.hostelterviseks .blogspot.com; apt 6, 4th fl, Ülikooli 1; dm 200-250Kr; 🖳) A

real travellers hostel (run by an Australian and a Canadian) that's best described as staying at your mate's place (albeit a mate with quite a few bunks in their apartment). There are 14 beds spread over two dorm rooms, plus a decent kitchen and cosy, orange-coloured lounge, but only one bathroom. Light breakfast is provided, as is plenty of travel advice for Tartu and surrounds. It can be a little tricky to find – check directions on the website, or call if you're lost.

Herne (☎ 744 1959; www.hot.ee/supilinn; Herne 59; campers per person 100Kr; s/d with shared bathroom 275/500Kr) A 15-minute walk northwest of the city through a traditionally poor neighbourhood of charismatic wooden houses brings you to this homey guesthouse with four pleasant rooms and clean shared bathrooms. There's a kitchen, outdoor grill, and plenty of grass on which campers can pitch a tent. Campervans also welcome. Breakfast costs an extra 50Kr.

Tartu Student Village Hostels (☎ 740 9955; www .tartuhostel.eu; s/d from 350/600Kr) Pepleri dorm (Pepleri 14); Raatuse dorm (Raatuse 22); Narva dorm (Narva mnt 27) These student dorms offer cheap, clean, central accommodation (only Pepleri is south of the river). The Raatuse dorm is newest but somewhat institutional; it's the cheapest, as every three rooms share a kitchen and bathroom. The Narva option has two rooms sharing kitchen and bathroom. The Pepleri dorm is the best pick – it's older but a bit cosier, and there's a private kitchenette and bathroom in each room (there are also larger suites here that are excellent value). Advance reservations are a must.

Aleksandri Hotell (☎ 730 3009; www.aleksandri.ee; Aleksandri 42; s/d/tr/q from 500/600/800/900Kr) A recently expanded hotel offering good-value prices for its rooms (modern, all with private bathroom). The 'lux' doubles with Jacuzzi make a nice splurge at 1400Kr. Service is friendly and efficient – the downside is that it's a 15-minute walk southeast of the town centre.

See also Hotell Tartu (opposite) for its budget rooms.

MIDRANGE & TOP END
Apartment Rental

Domus Dorpatensis (☎ 733 1345; www.dorpatensis .ee; Raekoja plats 1; apt s 500-990Kr, d 700-1190Kr) This foundation rents out 10 apartments ranging from small to large in an unbeatable location next to the town hall. Apartments are simple, comfortably furnished affairs that offer great value for money. No credit cards; parking is available. Entrance is on Ülikooli.

Wilde Guest Apartments (☎ 511 3876; www.wilde apartments.ee; Vallikraavi 4; apt d 1120-1500Kr, extra person 310Kr) Rents four beautiful apartments (two have sauna and balcony) with old-world details. All are within a short distance of the Wilde pub and cafe (p114), and can sleep four.

Hotels & Guesthouses

Hotell Tartu (☎ 731 4300; www.tartuhotell.ee; Soola 3; hostel dm/tw/tr 325/800/900Kr, hotel s/d/f 750/1150/1650Kr) Being across from the bus station doesn't make for the most charming of locations (or views), but this hotel's modernised rooms are sleek, bright and comfy. The 'hostel' is actually six spotless, older-style hotel rooms (shared bathrooms in the corridor) sleeping only three. Hotel guests have breakfast included, and there are hotel discounts for students and for online bookings. For hostel guests, breakfast is an extra 90Kr. Sauna available.

Uppsala Maja (☎ 736 1535; www.uppsalamaja.ee; Jaani 7; s/d from 535/1020Kr; 🖳) Maintained by the Swedish city of Uppsala (Tartu's sister city), this effortlessly pretty guesthouse in the town's old quarters features five warm, light-filled guestrooms; from two single rooms sharing a bathroom and lounge, to a two-room suite (room 3). Breakfast is included, and there's a kitchen for guest use. This place is deservedly popular, so book ahead.

Tampere Maja (☎ 738 6300; www.tamperemaja.ee; Jaani 4; s/d/tr/q from 600/900/1320/1650Kr; 🖳) Equally as appealing and attractive as the nearby Uppsala Maja, this welcoming guesthouse (from Tartu's Finnish sister city) offers six neat and cosy rooms ranging in size. Breakfast is included, and each room has cooking facilities; two-room suites can sleep up to four. And it wouldn't be Finnish if it didn't offer a sauna (open to nonguests).

Park Hotell (☎ 742 7000; www.parkhotell.ee; Vallikraavi 23; s/d 800/1080, ste 1300-1800Kr) Things move a little slower at this sweet-natured hotel nestled to the side of Toomemägi, but we don't think that's a bad thing. It's the oldest hotel in town, with creaky old parquet floors to prove it. You won't be dazzled by the pastel-flavoured decor, but the large comfy rooms enjoy parkland views. Access is best from Liivi.

Hotell Dorpat (☎ 733 7180; www.dorpat.ee; Soola 6; s/d/f 960/1160/1700Kr) The newest kid on the hotel

block is the Dorpat – and it's big (200 rooms over six floors), busy and shiny, complete with riverside restaurant and spa. Rooms are crisp and smart (some are set up for allergy sufferers and the disabled), and the spotty carpet offers some fun amongst the clean, modern minimalism. A nice choice, especially with its glossy new neighbour, Tasku (housing a convention centre, cinema and shops).

Pallas Hotell (☎ 730 1200; www.pallas.ee; Riia mnt 4; s/d/ste 1060/1375/2100Kr) On the top three floors of a renovated central building that used to house a famous art school, the Pallas has some of the most uniquely decorated rooms in Estonia, with vibrantly colourful walls and decent furnishings. Some rooms boast floor-to-ceiling windows that give sweeping views over the city. Request a city-facing room on the third floor, for space, size and artworks, or one of the six art-filled suites and deluxe doubles.

London Hotell (☎ 730 5555; www.londonhotel.ee; Rüütli 9; s/d 1300/1750, ste 2100-2700Kr) This handsome modern hotel makes a good top-end choice and is in a prime location. Elegant minimalism is the keyword here, although we found the standard rooms quite plain after the refinement of the serene lobby, complete with very Zen water feature.

Eating & Drinking

University Café (Ülikooli Kohvik; ☎ 737 5405; www.kohvik .ut.ee; Ülikooli 20; buffet per 100g 13Kr, snacks & meals from 50Kr; ⏱ cafeteria/buffet 7.30am-7pm Mon-Fri, 10am-4pm Sat & Sun, 2nd-fl cafe 11am-11pm Mon-Thu, 11am-1am Fri & Sat, 11am-9pm Sun) Some of the most economical meals in town are waiting at the 1st-floor cafeteria, which serves up decent breakfasts and a simple daytime buffet. Upstairs is a labyrinth of elegantly decorated rooms that create worlds unto themselves, both old-world grand and embracingly cosy. Here, delicious, artfully presented dishes are served, from chanterelle soup to duck fillet.

Crepp (☎ 742 2133; Rüütli 16; crepes 40-45Kr, salads 60-95Kr; ⏱ 11am-midnight) Locals seem to love this place, and its warm, stylish decor belies its bargain-priced crepes (of the sweet or savoury persuasion, with great combos like cherry-choc and almonds). Sad to report – we found the crepes on the dry side and think the salads are a better option.

our pick Tsink Plekk Pang (☎ 730 3415; Küütri 6; dishes 50-150Kr; ⏱ noon-midnight) Behind Tartu's funkiest facade (look for the stripy paintwork) and over three floors (plus a rooftop sun terrace) is this cool Chinese-flavoured restaurant-lounge. It's named after the zinc buckets that are suspended from the ceiling as lampshades. You may need some time to peruse the huge, veg-friendly menu – there are plenty of well-priced noodles and soups, plus a decent Indian selection and even a handful of Japanese dishes. Or simply stop by to enjoy drinks with a DJ-spun soundtrack on weekends.

Moka (☎ 744 2985; Küütri 3; meals 65-100Kr; ☯ 9am-midnight) Decor-wise, this cafe is all over the place – we think it's aiming for African tribal chic. Still, one in-the-know local votes it the best value in town, and with creative main courses coming in under 100Kr, we can't argue. Try coq au vin, trout chowder or pork fillet medallions (yep, all under 100Kr), or seafood pasta (with truffle-lobster sauce, mussels and crab claws – a steal at 69Kr).

Pierre Chocolaterie (☎ 730 4680; www.pierre.ee; Raekoja plats 12; meals 65-195Kr; ☯ 8am-11pm Mon-Thu, 8am-1am Fri, 10am-1am Sat, 10am-11pm Sun) From Pierre, Tallinn's favourite choc-meister, comes a new branch on the main square of Tartu. There's the same refined atmosphere, old-world decor and all-ages crowd – plus the all-important truffles. This is a prime spot for coffee and a sugar fix at any time of day, or for something more filling – there's a surprising range of salads, plus heftier mains.

Hansa Tall (☎ 730 3400; Alexandri 46; meals 65-220Kr; ☯ 9am-midnight) Slick bars and cafes are all well and good, but what if you want to look at a menu and really know you're in Estonia? Head to this super-rustic, meticulously decked-out, barnlike tavern southeast of the centre. You need not try the smoked pig's ears or blood sausage to enjoy the diverse, hearty menu, live music and even livelier locals; it draws a more mature crowd.

Maailm (☎ 742 9099; Rüütli 12; mains 70-115Kr; ☯ noon-1am Mon-Sat, noon-10pm Sun) The old wooden floors, beamed ceilings and mismatched furniture of artlessly hip Maailm (meaning 'world') stand in contrast to its downstairs neighbour, the awkwardly fashion-themed Catwalk cafe. Maailm is a chilled-out place for a bite and/or a beer, with a cheap-and-cheerful menu of eclectic options, from Irish stew to chilli con carne.

La Dolce Vita (☎ 740 7545; www.ladolcevita.ee; Kompanii 10; pizza & pasta 70-120Kr; ☯ 11.30am-10pm) Thin-crust pizzas come straight from the wood-burning oven at this cheerful, family-friendly pizzeria. It's the real deal, with a big Italian menu of bruschetta, pizza, pasta, gelati etc and classic but casual decor (red-and-white checked tablecloths, Fellini posters).

Püssirohukelder (☎ 730 3555; www.pyss.ee; Lossi 28; mains 70-260Kr; ☯ noon-2am Mon-Thu, noon-3am Fri, noon-midnight Sun) Set in a cavernous old gunpowder cellar under a soaring, 10m-high vaulted ceiling, this is both a boisterous pub and a good choice for tasty meat and fish dishes. When the regular live music kicks in later in the night (sometimes with a cover charge), you'll find the older crowd withdrawing to the more secluded wine cellar, which serves tapas-style snacks.

Café Wilde & Wilde Irish Pub (☎ 730 9764; www.wilde.ee; Vallikraavi 4; pub meals 75-210Kr; ☯ café 9am-7pm Mon-Sat, 10am-6pm Sun, pub noon-midnight or later) Choose grace and elegance in the cafe here or something more lively at the upstairs pub (with a killer summer terrace and great menu of snacks and meals). Its namesake is Peter Ernst Wilde, who opened a publishing house on the premises in the 18th century, though the pub also pays tribute to two literary Wildes: Oscar Wilde and Estonian writer Eduard Vilde; there's a statue of the two 'meeting' out front.

Gruusia Saatkond (☎ 744 1386; www.gruusiasaatkond.ee; Rüütli 8; mains 90-195Kr; ☯ noon-midnight Mon-Sat, noon-10pm Sun) The name means 'Georgian Embassy' and this place does a fine job representing its country on the food and wine front. A rustic, colourful dining room sets the scene for feasting on hearty Georgian cuisine: eggplant with walnuts, hatšapuri (cheese bread), trout and shashlik are among the favourites.

Noir (☎ 744 0055; Ülikooli 7; mains 120-180Kr; ☯ noon-midnight Mon-Sat) Definitely a place to impress a date, this sexy, black-walled restaurant-cum-vinoteque is a fine place for wining, dining and reclining. It's tucked away in a courtyard off Ülikooli, with outdoor tables too (but we think the inside lounges are more conducive to supping your way through the international wine list).

Zavood (☎ 744 1321; Lai 30; ☯ 11am-4am Mon-Fri, 6pm-4am Sat & Sun) This is not where you'd expect to find an Estonian-speaking Uruguayan pulling beers, but friendly Mario opened the battered cellar bar Zavood in 1995. Unpretentious decor (think car seats and industrial pipes) combined with cheap beer and the occasional student band make it a beloved drinking den of the town's alternative set.

SELF-CATERING

The **outdoor market** (Soola; ☿ from 7am), just east of the bus station, is a fun place to browse for fresh produce, flowers and other goodies. There's a more extensive **indoor market** (Vabaduse pst; ☿ from 7.30am) by the river, out front of the Kaubamaja shopping centre (look for the pig statue out front).

The most central **supermarket** (Riia 1; ☿ 9am-10pm Mon-Sat, 9am-7pm Sun) is in the basement of the Kaubamaja shopping centre.

Entertainment

NIGHTCLUBS

Wednesday is the traditional party night for students. Club doors open at 10pm or 11pm, and things kick on until around 3am or 4am. Admission at the following ranges from 40Kr to 150Kr, depending on the event.

Club Tallinn (☎ 740 3157; www.clubtallinn.ee, in Estonian; Narva mnt 27; ☿ Wed-Sat) Tartu's (and possibly Estonia's) best nightclub is a multi-floored dance fest with many nooks and crannies. Top-notch DJs spin here, drawing a fashionable, up-for-it crowd. It's open only during the school year; during the summer, Club Tallinn relocates to Pärnu.

Club Illusion (☎ 742 4341; www.illusion.ee; Raatuse 97; ☿ Wed-Sat) Close to the student dorms and built into an ex-movie theatre (a venue famous for its underground cult parties in the 1990s), Illusion has a lavish interior and first-class DJs drawing a stylish, club-savvy crowd (themed nights include retro grooves, R'n'B, hip hop, house – check the website for info).

Atlantis (☎ 738 5485; www.atlantis.ee; Narva mnt 2; ☿ Tue-Sat) Overlooking the Emajõgi River, Atlantis is a popular, mainstream place that's pretty short on style; the riverside setting, however, is nice, and if you're in the mood, the retro hits make for a cheesy good time.

CINEMA

In mid-2008 a shiny new cinema came to town – **Cinamon** (☎ 1925; www.cinamon.ee; Turu 2; tickets 45-70Kr), inside the Tasku centre down by the bus station and Hotell Dorpat. There's a smaller cinema, **Ekraan** (☎ 740 4020; www.super kinod.ee; Riia 14; tickets 45-85Kr), close to the KGB Cells Museum.

THEATRE

Vanemuine Theatre & Concert Hall (☎ 744 0165; www .vanemuine.ee, www.concert.ee; Vanemuise 6) Named after the ancient Estonian song god, this theatre hosted the first Estonian-language theatre troupe, which performed here in 1870. The venue still hosts an array of classical and alternative theatrical and musical performances. It also stages performances at its **small stage** (☎ 744 0160; Vanemuise 45) and **Sadamateater** (Harbour Theatre; ☎ 734 4248; Soola 5b). The latter has a prime location on the banks of the Emajõgi and tends to stage the most modern, alternative productions.

Shopping

The central **Kaubamaja** (Riia 1; ☿ 9am-9pm Mon-Sat, 9am-6pm Sun) shopping centre opened in 2005 and can fulfil most of your retail needs; and it's worth popping in to check out the brand-new shopping centre **Tasku** (www.tasku .ee; Turu 2; ☿ 10am-9pm), by the bus station. You'll probably have more fun discovering the handicrafts stores scattered about the old streets, however.

Antoniuse Gild (☎ 742 3823; www.antonius.ee; Lutsu 5; ☿ noon-6pm Tue-Fri) Here you'll find around 20 artisans' studios where local craftspeople make ceramics, stained glass, jewellery, textiles, woodcarvings, dolls etc. It's well worth a visit.

Pille-Resa Nukumaja (Munga 14) Behind a faded orange facade, this sweet small store sells handmade dolls and toys for the young and young-at-heart.

Pits (☎ 5620 1536; 2nd fl, Rüütli 4) A small studio showcasing original clothing from young Estonian designers, plus jewellery, accessories and music.

Getting There & Away

BUS

International bus tickets are sold from the **Eurolines** (☎ 12550; www.eurolines.ee) office inside the **Tartu bus station** (Autobussijaam; ☎ 733 1277; Turu 2). From here, daily buses run between Tartu and Tallinn (125Kr to 160Kr, 2½ to 3½ hours) about every 15 to 30 minutes from 6am to 9pm (with a few later services out of Tallinn). Times, prices and durations for all Estonian services can be found at www.bussi reisid.ee.

Some direct daily bus services to/from Tartu:

Haapsalu (180Kr, 4½ hours, one bus)
Kuressaare (250Kr, six to 6½ hours, three buses)
Narva (125Kr to 160Kr, 3½ hours, seven to 10 buses)
Otepää (35Kr to 50Kr, 45 minutes to 1½ hours, about 10 buses)
Pärnu (135Kr to 150Kr, 2½ to three hours, 10 buses)

Rakvere (100Kr to 120Kr, two to three hours, six buses)
Rīga (210Kr, four hours, one morning bus)
St Petersburg (370Kr, seven to eight hours, one overnight bus)
Valga (70Kr to 85Kr, 1½ to two hours, seven to 10 buses)
Viljandi (70Kr to 85Kr, 1½ hours, 12 to 16 buses)
Võru (60Kr to 75Kr, one to 1½ hours, 16 buses)

TRAIN

The seemingly abandoned **train station** (☎ 385 7123; Vaksali 6) is 750m southwest of Toomemägi. Timetables are posted outside; tickets are sold on the train. Services are operated by **Edelerautee** (www.edel.ee) – on the Estonian-language page, click on Sõiduplannid jahin-nad to access the timetables and prices.

Three to six trains make the daily journey to Tallinn (95Kr to 140Kr, 2¼ hours). One daily train also travels from Tartu to Valga (36Kr, two hours).

Getting Around

The central stop for city buses is on Riia mnt, between the glossy new Tasku shopping centre and the old, tired Kaubamaja. Buy a single-use ticket from any kiosk for 13Kr (8Kr for students), or 16Kr from the bus driver, and be sure to validate the ticket once on board or risk a fine. Also from kiosks, buy a one-hour/day ticket for 16/40Kr.

Bikes can be rented from **Jalgratas** (☎ 742 1731; Laulupeo 19; per day 150Kr).

The tourist office keeps up-to-date lists of car-hire agencies with prices. Among the many options are **City Car** (☎ 523 9669; www.citycar .ee; Jõe 9a) and **Sixt** (☎ 744 7260; www.sixt.ee; Ülikooli 8), which is handily located in the Barclay Hotel but isn't the cheapest. The guys at the backpackers hostel (who can usually sniff out a good deal) recommend **123 Rent** (☎ 735 6422; www.123rent.ee; Lõunakeskus, Ringtee 75), where Fiat Pandas start at 400Kr per day, and there are campervans available for rent too. Call first before stepping out, as most car-hire places can deliver your car to you (many have offices on the outskirts of town).

Local taxis include **Takso Üks** (☎ 1300) and **Tartu Taksopark** (☎ 1555).

OTEPÄÄ

pop 2100

The small hilltop town of Otepää, 44km south of Tartu, is the centre of a picturesque area of forests and lakes, scenic hillsides and crisp rivers. The district is beloved by Estonians for both its natural beauty and its many possibilities for hiking, biking and swimming in summer, and cross-country skiing in winter. It's certainly Estonia's winter capital – winter weekends here are busy and fun. Some have even dubbed this area (tongue-in-cheek) the 'Estonian Alps' – a teasing reference not to its 'peaks' but to its lovely ski trails.

Orientation & Information

The point where Valga mnt and Tartu mnt meet is the epicentre for the town, with the bus station here, alongside the new **tourist office** (☎ 766 1200; www.otepaa.ee; Tartu mnt 1; ☿ 9am-6pm Mon-Fri, 10am-3pm Sat & Sat mid-May–mid-Sep, 9am-5pm Mon-Fri, 10am-3pm Sat mid-Sep–mid-May), with well-informed staff who can distribute maps and brochures, and make recommendations for activities, guide services and lodging in the area.

Behind the bus station and tourist office is the triangular main 'square', Lipuväljak; in this neighbourhood you'll find the **post office** (Lipuväljak 24), ATMs, pharmacies and a supermarket.

Sights

CHURCH & MUSEUMS

Otepää's pretty 17th-century **church** (Võru mnt; ☿ 10am-4pm mid-May–Aug) is on a hilltop about 300m east of the bus station. It was in this church in 1884 that the Estonian Students' Society consecrated its new blue, black and white flag (see the boxed text, opposite), which later became the flag of independent Estonia. Facing the church's west door is a small mound with a monument to those who died in the 1918–20 independence war. The former vicar's residence now houses two museums: the **Flag Museum** (Eesti Lipu Muuseum; ☎ 765 5075; admission free; ☿ 9am-2pm Tue-Fri, 10am-1pm Sat) and **Ski Museum** (Suusamuuseum; ☎ 766 3670; adult/child 10/7Kr; ☿ 9am-2pm Tue-Fri, 10am-1pm Sat); both museums can be viewed by appointment outside regular opening hours.

LINNAMÄGI

The tree-covered hill south of the church is Linnamägi (Castle Hill), a major stronghold from the 10th to 12th centuries. There are traces of old fortifications on top, and good views of the surrounding country.

THE BLUE, BLACK AND WHITE: THE BIRTH OF A NATIONAL SYMBOL

Estonia's tricolour dates back to 1881, when a theology student named Jaan Bergmaan wrote a poem about a beautiful flag flying over Estonia. The only problem, for both Jaan and his countrymen, was that no flag in fact existed. Very clearly, something had to be done about this. This was, after all, the time of the national awakening, when the idea of independent nationhood was on the lips of every young dreamer across the country.

In September of that year, at the Union of Estonian Students in Tartu, 20 students and one alumnus gathered to hash out ideas for a flag. All present agreed that the colours must express the character of the nation, reflect the Estonian landscape, and connect to the colours of folk costumes. After long discussions, the students came up with blue, black and white. According to one interpretation, blue symbolised hope for Estonia's future; it also represented faithfulness. Black was a reminder of the dark past to which Estonia would not return; it also depicted the country's dark soil. White represented the attainment of enlightenment and education – an aspiration for all Estonians; it also symbolised snow in winter, light nights in summer and the Estonian birch tree.

After the colours were chosen, it took several years before the first flag was made. Three young activist women – Emilie, Paula and Miina Beermann – carried this out by sewing together a large one made out of silk. In 1884 the students held a procession, which went from Tartu to Otepää, a location far from the eyes of the Russian government. All members of the students' union were there as the flag was raised over the vicarage. Afterwards it was dipped in Pühajärv (a lake considered sacred to Estonians, see below), and locked safely away in the student archive.

Although the inauguration of the flag was a tiny event, word of the flag's existence spread, and soon the combination of colours appeared in unions and choirs, and hung from farmhouses all across Estonia. By the end of the 19th century the blue-black-and-white was used in parties, and at wedding ceremonies. Its first political appearance, however, didn't arrive until 1917, when thousands of Estonians marched in St Petersburg demanding independence. In 1918 Estonia was declared independent, and the flag was raised on Pikk Hermann in Tallinn's Old Town. There it remained until the Soviet Union seized power in 1940.

During the occupation the Soviets banned the flag, and once again the blue-black-and-white went underground. For Estonians, keeping the flag on the sly was a small but hopeful symbol of one day regaining nationhood. People hid flags under floorboards or unstitched the stripes and secreted them in bookcases; those caught with the flag faced severe punishment – including a possible sentence in the Siberian gulags. Needless to say, as the Soviet Union teetered on the brink of collapse, blue-black-and-white returned to the stage. On February 1989, the flag was raised again on Pikk Hermann. Independence had been regained.

PÜHAJÄRV

The islets and indented shore of 3.5km-long Pühajärv (Holy Lake), on the southwest edge of Otepää, provide some of the area's loveliest views. A 12km nature trail and a bike path encircle the lake, making it a lovely spot for a walk. The lake was blessed by the Dalai Lama when he came to Tartu in 1991, and a **monument** on the eastern shore commemorates his visit.

According to legend, Pühajärv was formed from the tears of the mothers who lost their sons in a battle of the *Kalevipoeg* epic. Its islands are said to be their burial mounds. Major midsummer St John's Day (Jaanipäev) festivities take place here every year. If energy levels are low after the walk to the lake, recharge at the **energy column** down Mäe (closer to the

town centre). The column was erected in 1992 to mark the long-held belief of psychics that this area resounds with positive energy.

The northern tip of the lake is around 2km southwest of Otepää, reached via Pühajärve tee (about a 30-minute walk from Otepää township). Also here is a **beach park**, very popular with summer visitors.

Activities

It would be a shame not to take advantage of some of the excellent outdoor activities this scenic region has to offer.

There's lots to do and see in the **Otepää Nature Park** *(looduspark)*, which incorporates 224 sq km of the region's lakes, forest and well-marked hiking trails. The tourist office

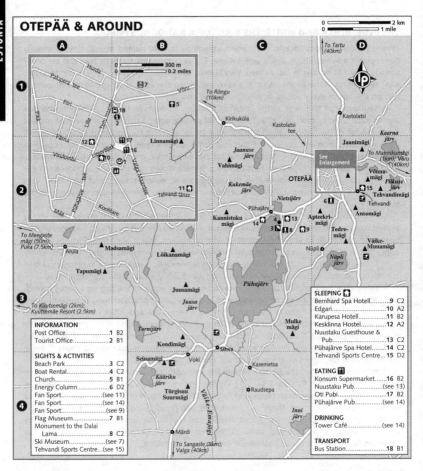

OTEPÄÄ & AROUND

INFORMATION
Post Office...................1	B2
Tourist Office..............2	B1

SIGHTS & ACTIVITIES
Beach Park.................3	C2
Boat Rental................4	C2
Church.......................5	B1
Energy Column............6	D2
Fan Sport................(see 11)	
Fan Sport................(see 14)	
Fan Sport.................(see 9)	
Flag Museum..............7	B1
Monument to the Dalai	
Lama........................8	C2
Ski Museum...............(see 7)	
Tehvandi Sports Centre..(see 15)	

SLEEPING
Bernhard Spa Hotell........9	C2
Edgari........................10	A2
Karupesa Hotell............11	B2
Kesklinna Hostel...........12	A1
Nuustaku Guesthouse &	
Pub...........................13	C2
Pühajärve Spa Hotel.......14	C2
Tehvandi Sports Centre..15	D2

EATING
Konsum Supermarket......16	B2
Nuustaku Pub............(see 13)	
Oti Pubi.......................17	B2
Pühajärve Pub...........(see 14)	

DRINKING
Tower Café..................(see 14)	

TRANSPORT
Bus Station.................18	B1

has maps and information on trails in the park, which range from short and sweet and kid-focused, to a 20km hiking/skiing track.

Ask at the tourist office for other activities on offer in the region, including horse riding and golf in warmer weather; snowtubing, sleigh rides and snowmobile rental and safaris in winter. Note too that the activities and facilities at hotels (notably the Pühajärve Spa Hotel) are open to the public for a fee.

The 63km **Tartu Ski Marathon** begins in Otepää every February.

CANOEING & RAFTING

If you're considering a trip, call these firms at least a day or two ahead of time. They can pick you up from your hotel, take you to the river and drop you back afterwards. All-day trips cost about 300Kr for an adult and 150Kr for a child.

Veetee (☎ 506 0987; www.veetee.ee) Offers a range of canoeing and rafting trips along the Ahja River, the Võhandu River and around the small lakes of the Kooraste River valley, about 15km southeast of Otepää.

Toonus Pluss (☎ 505 5702; www.toonuspluss.ee) Specialises in canoeing trips in similar areas as Veetee; tailor-made trips can combine canoeing with hiking and mountain-biking tours.

In addition to canoe rentals, **Fan Sport** (☎ 5077 537; www.fansport.ee), with a handful of branches around town, also offers canoeing excursions.

If you want to just get in a boat and go, you can rent **rowboats** (☎ 5343 6359; ◷ 10am-7pm Jun-Aug), canoes and water-bikes at the beach on the north shore of Pühajärv.

CYCLING & ROLLERBLADING

To hire bikes, rollerblades, skis and snowboards, contact **Fan Sport** (☎ 5077 537; www.fansport.ee; blades/skis/bikes/snowboards per day 80/200/200/275Kr), which has three offices in Otepää: one at Karupesa Hotell (right), one at Bernhard Spa Hotell (right), and the third office at the Pühajärve Spa Hotel (right); they will also deliver to your hotel. Loads of other operators can get you kitted up for winter fun, or on a bike, for similar rates – the tourist office has details.

SKIING

For cross-country skiing, the closest trails are near the **Tehvandi Sports Centre** (Spordikeskus; ☎ 766 9500; www.tehvandi.ee; trail use per day 50Kr), just outside town. You can also find some good trails near **Kääriku järv**. Both have guesthouses conveniently nearby, and rent skis. The 34m **viewing platform** (☎ 5302 1115; adult/concession 25/15Kr; ◷ 10am-7pm) in Tehvandi's grounds is worthwhile for great views of the landscape below.

Most skiing is cross-country here, but there are a few places for downhill skiing, including **Kuutsemägi** 14km west of Otepää, the area's most developed ski centres. There, the **Kuutsemäe Resort** (☎ 766 9007; www.kuutsemae.ee; 1-day lift ticket weekdays/weekend 220/300Kr, ski/snowboard rental 300/400Kr) operates seven runs; there's also a guesthouse here overlooking Kuutsemägi, plus three-bedroom chalets and a tavern.

Sleeping

Low season here is April to May and September to November; at this time hotel prices are about 10 to 15% cheaper. Higher rates are charged on weekends in high season; visit midweek for better deals.

Edgari (☎ 766 6550; karnivoor@hot.ee; Lipuväljak 3; s/d from 250/400Kr) One of the cheapest places to stay right in town, this is a guesthouse that feels like a hostel, with thin walls, a shared kitchen and communal lounge. More expensive 2nd-floor rooms are more like mini-apartments, with kitchenette and private bathroom. Downstairs is a tavern and small food shop.

Kesklinna Hostel (☎ 765 5095; www.kesklinnahotell.ee; Lipuväljak 11; s/d from 300/600Kr) In the centre of town, Kesklinna has clean, no-frills rooms,

each with private bathroom and TV. The place doesn't exactly ooze character, but it's central, represents decent value, and there's a pleasant communal kitchen and sauna.

Nuustaku Guesthouse & Pub (☎ 766 8208; www.nuustaku.ee, in Estonian; Nüpli; d 550-1500Kr) Better known for its cosy pub, the Nuustaku (formerly known as the Setanta) has eight pleasantly furnished rooms 3km southwest of Otepää. The best is room 5, with a living area and its own terrace, with splendid views over the lake. On the minus side, the pub's weekend discos are clearly heard in the rooms.

Pühajärve Spa Hotel (☎ 766 5500; www.pyhajarve.com; Pühajärve tee; s/d/ste weekdays 750/900/1550Kr, weekends 900/1200/1790Kr; ☒) With its 85 rooms and sprawling lakeside grounds, this is not somewhere you're likely to feel the personal touch. But you'll no doubt be happy with the sports and recreation facilities laid on thick: tennis courts, bike rental, day spa, indoor pool, boat trips, beach, bowling alley, gym. Modern rooms are nothing flash; the activities and on-site eating options go a long way towards compensating for this.

Bernhard Spa Hotell (☎ 766 9600; www.bernhard.ee; Kolga tee 22a; s/d/ste from 1050/1350/3100Kr; ☒) Tucked away in a private setting and worth seeking out for a peaceful retreat, this handsome hotel offers balconies and forest views from all of its rooms. There's a good on-site restaurant and a beautifully appointed spa, newly opened in 2007; the *pièce de résistance* is the small, heated outdoor pool – a delight in winter as the snow falls. The suite here is huge and comes complete with sauna and Jacuzzi – a worthy splurge.

Also recommended:

Tehvandi Sports Centre (☎ 766 9500; www.tehvandi.ee; s/d/tr 450/600/800Kr; ☒) Neat, functional rooms, in a somewhat foreboding, bunkerlike structure surrounded by hiking and skiing trails. It's off Tehvandi.

Karupesa Hotell (☎ 766 1500; www.karupesa.ee; Tehvandi 1a; s/d from 700/900Kr) Bland but OK rooms, right by the Tehvandi Sports Centre.

Eating & Drinking

The dining scene here is disappointing; your best options for something special are the restaurants at the Pühajärve Spa Hotel or Bernhard Spa Hotell. For self-caterers, there's a busy Konsum supermarket on Lipuväljak.

Oti Pubi (☎ 766 9840; Lipuväljak 26; mains 50-230Kr; ◷ 10am-midnight) In an octagonal-shaped building in the centre of the township, this casual pub has a loyal following and is a decent spot for a drink and a snack or meal, so long as you're not expecting any surprises from the menu.

Nuustaku Pub (☎ 766 8210; Nüpli; mains 85-219Kr; ☜ 11am-midnight) Offering a far nicer outlook than the Oti, this lively wooden pub 3km southwest of Otepää township has a popular outdoor terrace overlooking the lake, and some eclectic dishes: pesto pasta, paella and salmon steak among the options. Live music on weekends brings in the punters.

Pühajärve Pub (☎ 766 5500; www.pyhajarve.com; Pühajärve Spa Hotel, Pühajärve tee; mains 90-250Kr; ☜ 11am-11pm Sun-Wed, 11am-1am Thu-Sat) At the lakeside hotel's casual, all-day pub, everyone is catered for thanks to an extensive menu – kids, vegetarians, snackers, carnivores. The sunny outdoor terrace is the place to be, but the brick-lined interior, with pool tables and open fire, is not a bad wet-weather option. Also at the hotel is an evening à la carte restaurant (mains 90Kr to 250Kr), offering the likes of beef tenderloin and grilled butterfish.

Tower Café (Tornikohvik; ☎ 766 5500; Pühajärve Spa Hotel, Pühajärve tee; ☜ noon-8pm Sun-Thu, noon-11pm Fri & Sat) After the climb up all the stairs (no lift), sink into the white leather chairs and enjoy the leafy, lake views with a coffee, wine or cocktail (no food is offered, save for cake).

Getting There & Around

Buses connect Otepää with Tartu (35Kr to 50Kr, 45 minutes to 1½ hours, 10 daily) and Tallinn (175Kr, 3½ hours, one daily).

See p119 for details of bike rental.

VÕRU

pop 14,600

A small pleasant town on the eastern shore of Lake Tamula, Võru has a bucolic feel with its leafy parks and picturesque churches, and 19th-century houses lining its old lanes. Võru's sandy shoreline is its most attractive feature, and its lake attracts plenty of beachgoers in summer.

The town was founded in 1784 by special decree from Catherine the Great, though archaeological finds here date back several thousand years. Its most famous resident, however, was neither a tribesman nor a tsarina, but the writer Friedrich Reinhold Kreutzwald (1803–1882), known as the father of Estonian literature for his folk epic *Kalevipoeg*.

One of the biggest and brightest events in the local calendar is the mid-July **Võru Folklore Festival** (www.werro.ee/folkloor), full of dancers, singers and musicians celebrating the local culture, decked out in colourful traditional dress.

Information

The **tourist office** (☎ 782 1881; www.visitvoru.ee, www.voru.ee; Tartu 31; ☜ 9am-6pm Mon-Fri, 9am-3pm Sat & Sun mid-May–mid-Sep, 10am-5pm Mon-Fri mid-Sep–mid-May) is a good place to pick up a map and get information about festivals, attractions and tourist farms throughout Võru and Setu counties.

Banks, including **SEB** (Tartu 25), are scattered about town. Free internet access is available at the **public library** (Jüri 54; ☜ 11am-6pm Mon-Fri, plus 10am-4pm Sat Sep-May).

Sights & Activities

Võru's most interesting museum is the **Kreutzwald Memorial Museum** (☎ 782 1709; Kreutzwaldi 31; adult/concession 15/5Kr; ☜ 10am-5pm or 6pm Wed-Sun), set in the former house where the great man lived and worked as a city doctor from 1833 to 1877. In addition to personal relics, there's a lovely garden at the back. There's also a lakefront monument to the writer.

In front of the 18th-century **Lutheran church** (Jüri 9) overlooking the central square is a granite **monument** to 17 locals who lost their lives in the 1994 *Estonia* ferry disaster. Up the road is the classical yellow and white Russian Orthodox **Jekateriina kirik** (Tartu 26), built in 1793 and named in honour of Catherine II.

Marring the pretty 'boulevard' named Katariina allee is one of the town's ugliest buildings, housing the **Võrumaa Regional Museum** (☎ 782 4479; Katariina allee 11; adult/concession 10/5Kr; ☜ 10am-5pm or 6pm Wed-Sun), which has mildly interesting exhibits on regional history and culture.

The garden behind the **Cultural Centre** (Liiva 13) hosts occasional concerts and folk festivals, while the centre itself acts as the town's cinema. Check the tourist office to see if anything is on when you're in town.

Karma (☎ 782 5755; www.antiques.ee; Koidula 14; ☜ 10.30am-6pm Tue-Fri, 10am-2pm Sat) is one of Estonia's best antiques stores, and a fun place to browse, even if you already have enough WWII helmets, scythes, sleigh bells, Soviet matchbooks and wooden beer steins.

If you fancy getting out in the surrounding countryside, contact Võru-based

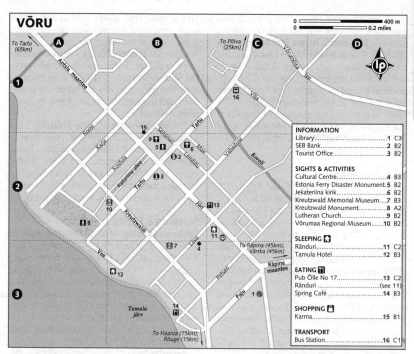

VÕRU

INFORMATION	
Library.................................1	C3
SEB Bank............................2	B2
Tourist Office......................3	B2

SIGHTS & ACTIVITIES	
Cultural Centre..................4	B3
Estonia Ferry Disaster Monument.5	B2
Jekateriina kirik................6	B2
Kreutzwald Memorial Museum..7	B3
Kreutzwald Monument........8	A2
Lutheran Church................9	B2
Võrumaa Regional Museum..10	B2

SLEEPING	
Ränduri..............................11	C2
Tamula Hotel.....................12	B3

EATING	
Pub Õlle No 17..................13	C2
Ränduri.........................(see 11)	
Spring Café 14	B3

SHOPPING	
Karma................................15	B1

TRANSPORT	
Bus Station........................16	C1

Haanjamatkad (☎ 511 4179; www.haanjamatkad.ee), which has canoes and bikes for rent, or can arrange guided rafting, canoeing, cycling and hiking adventures.

Sleeping & Eating

Ränduri (☎ 786 8050; www.randur.ee; Jüri 36; s/d/tr with shared bathroom 450/600/700Kr, with private bathroom from 480/650/800Kr) Ränduri has handsomely set 2nd-floor rooms, each decorated around a different motif and colour scheme (Japanese, Egyptian, Russian etc). Third-floor rooms are pleasant but more basic, with shared bathrooms. Downstairs, the rustic, timber-lined pub serves fairly good food: you want pork, you've got it (mains 45Kr to 110Kr).

Tamula Hotel (☎ 783 0430; www.tamula.ee; Vee 4; s/d 750/900Kr) Right on the lakefront beach, Võru's shiniest hotel has a modern exterior and bright, spacious, minimalist rooms. Ask for a balcony room with lake outlook.

Pub Õlle no 17 (☎ 782 8461; Jüri 17; mains 50-150Kr; ☘ 11am-midnight) This convivial, Irish-style pub is a popular meeting place and drinking hole for locals, with a pool table, big-screen TV, back terrace and comprehensive pub-grub menu.

Spring Café (☎ 782 2777; Petseri 20; mains 80-110Kr; ☘ 11am-10pm Mon-Thu, 11am-midnight Fri & Sat, 11am-9pm Sun) If you're longing for something a little less pubby, a little more cafe-bar, this slick new lakeside spot should put a smile on your dial. It has a pretty terrace, modern brick-and-timber dining room, and loungey 2nd floor with big windows. There's a good, modern menu too, with plenty of salads and filled pancakes. Ask about the sauna for hire.

Getting There & Away

Approximately 17 daily buses connect Võru and Tartu (65Kr to 75Kr, 1¼ hours). Buses also connect to Tallinn (150Kr to 180Kr, 3½ to 4½ hours, nine daily), Rõuge (11Kr to 17Kr, 20 minutes, nine daily), Haanja (11Kr to 20Kr, 30 minutes to one hour, six daily) and Krabi (20Kr, 45 minutes, five daily). The **bus station** (☎ 782 1018; entrance on Vilja) has the latest schedules.

HAANJA NATURE PARK

This 17,000-hectare protected area south of Võru includes some of the nicest scenery in the country (thick forests, rolling hills and

ESTONIA

sparkling lakes and rivers), and is where several of the best tourist farms in the region are located. The **Haanja Nature Park headquarters** (☎ 782 9090; www.haanjapark.ee, in Estonian) in the village of Haanja can provide detailed information about the area, hiking and skiing opportunities, and the multitude of tourist farms offering rustic accommodation, though you're more likely to get information in English at the tourist offices in Tartu (p110) or Võru (p120). A great website devoted to the area is www.haanja kompass.ee.

Suur Munamägi

Suur Munamägi (literally Great Egg Hill!), 17km south of Võru, is the highest hill in the Baltic at just over 318m. Still, the tree-covered 'summit' is easy to miss if you're not looking out for it. The best way to enjoy the Great Egg is to ascend its 29m **observation tower** (☎ 787 8847; www.suurmunamagi.ee; adult/child stairs 35/20Kr, elevator 60/60Kr; ☼ 10am-8pm Apr-Aug, 10am-5pm Sep-Oct, noon-3pm Sat & Sun Nov-Mar). On a clear day you can see Tartu's TV towers, the onion domes of Pihkva (Pskov), Russia, and lush forests stretching in every direction (binocular rental 15Kr). There's a pleasant indoor-outdoor coffee shop on the ground floor, and a large cafe back on the main road.

The summit and tower are a 10-minute climb from the Võru–Ruusmäe road, starting about 1km south of the otherwise uninspiring village of Haanja.

RÕUGE

In one of Estonia's most picturesque settings, the tiny village of Rõuge lies among gently rolling hills, with seven small lakes strung out along the ancient valley floor. The village itself sits on the edge of the gently sloping Ööbikuorg (Nightingale Valley), which is named for the nightingales that gather here (for their own songfest) in the spring.

Rõuge is a good base for exploring the countryside, enjoying fresh strawberries in summer and going for swims in the pristine Suurjärv, in the middle of the village. This is Estonia's deepest lake (38m) and is said to have healing properties.

You can pick up maps and obtain regional information at the log-cabin **Ööbikuorg Keskus** (☎ 785 9245; raugeinfo@hot.ee; ☼ 10am-6pm mid-May–mid-Sep), signposted about 1.5km east from Rõuge's church. Here there's a desk dispensing details on local walking trails,

and a handicraft shop; behind the centre is an observation tower you can climb for great views of the valley and lakes.

Opposite **St Mary's**, Rõuge's attractive 18th-century village church, stands a **monument** to the local dead of the 1918–20 independence war. The memorial was buried in one local's backyard through the Soviet period to save it from destruction.

Rõuge's **Linnamägi** (Castle Hill), by Lake Linnjärv, was an ancient Estonian stronghold during the 8th to 11th centuries. In the 13th century Rougetaja, a man who healed people with his hands, and to whom the ailing travelled from afar to see, lived here. There's a good view from the hill, across the valley.

Sleeping & Eating

Ööbikuoru Kämping (☎ 509 0372; info@visit.ee; sites per person 40Kr, cabins per person 100-150Kr, cottages sleeping 2 400-550Kr) Set on a lovely spot overlooking Nightingale Valley, this outfit offers lodging in simple wooden cabins and cottages. You can also bunk in a 'winterised cottage' with a private bathroom (or rent the whole cottage yourself, for 1500Kr). Rowboat rental is available. Located 600m from the main road, signposted as you head south.

Rohtlätte Talu (☎ 787 9315; www.rohtlatte.ee; sites per tent 70Kr, r per person 350Kr) About 6km northeast of Rõuge near the village of Nursi (12km from Võru on the Valga road), this comfortable, family-friendly tourist farm lies in a lush, photogenic setting overlooking a creek. There are hiking trails (guided excursions available), a sauna and trout fishing.

our pick **Rõuge Suurjärve Guesthouse** (☎ 524 3028; www.hot.ee/maremajutus; Metsa 5; s/d/ste 400/700/1200Kr) The perfect place to unwind and enjoy the lovely surrounds. This big, yellow, family-run guesthouse has views over the valley and a range of fuss-free rooms (most with private bathroom, some with TV, a few with balcony). The gardens (and sauna) offer a pretty retreat, and the breakfast will fuel your explorations. The turn-off to the guesthouse is opposite Rõuge's church.

Aside from the small supermarket by the southern end of Suurjärv, at the time of research there were no eateries in Rõuge. If the situation hasn't changed, to eat out you'll need to travel to Haanja (8km) or Võru (16km).

Getting There & Away

Rõuge lies 10km west of Suur Munamägi, or southwest of Võru; bus access is from Võru, with about nine connections daily (11Kr to 17Kr, 20 minutes).

LUHASOO TRAIL & KARULA NATIONAL PARK

Located in wild swampland on the border with Latvia, some 15km south of Rõuge, the **Luhasoo Nature Study Trail** provides a fascinating glimpse into Estonia's primordial past. The well-marked 4.5km trail passes over varied bogs and along a velvety black lake, with Venus flytraps, water lilies and herbivorous shrubs among the scenery. To get there, take the Krabi road from Rõuge and, after the Pärlijõe bus stop, turn right towards Kellamäe, then continue another 5km.

About 12km along dirt roads north of the village of Mõniste is an area of round, wooded hills dotted with many small lakes and ancient stone burial mounds, which forms Karula National Park. The **Karula National Park visitor centre** (☎ 782 8350; www .karularahvuspark.ee; ☽ 8am-5pm Mon-Thu, 10am-6pm Fri-Sun mid-May–Sep, 8am-5pm Mon-Thu, 8am-3pm Fri Oct–mid-May) in Ähijärve, past Lüllemäe, 25km east of Valga, distributes maps and hiking trail information. The highlight is Ähijärv, a 3km-long lake with several bays, inlets and promontories. This area can also be reached via Antsla to the north.

Set in the 'Forest Fairy Park' (Metsamoori Perepark), **Veetka Farm** (☎ 786 7633; www.metsa moor.ee; Mähkli; sites 50Kr) is one of several tourist farms in the area offering some unusual attractions. In addition to hiking trails, you can camp here, spend a night out on a raft floating in the lake, and learn about healing herbs and forest spirits.

VALGA
pop 13,900

The once-battered border town of Valga is enjoying a slow process of gentrification, and its old wooden houses and curious history make it an interesting place to wander through before moving on. The town, contiguous with Valka in Latvia, is set in the only region that was seriously contended between Estonia and Latvia after WWI. A British mediator had to be called in to settle the dispute and suggested the current border line, effectively splitting the town in two.

The helpful **tourist office** (☎ 766 1699; www.va lgalv.ee; Kesk 11; ☽ 9am-6pm Mon-Fri, 10am-3pm Sat & Sun mid-May–mid-Sep, 10am-5pm Mon-Fri mid-Sep–mid-

May), near the border crossing in town, can provide you with a town map and recommend inexpensive homestays in the area.

Sites of interest include the 19th-century **St John's Church** (Jaani Kirik), close to the tourist office, and a local history **museum** (Valga Koduloomuuseum; ☎ 766 8862; Vabaduse 8; adult/ concession 10/5Kr; ☽ 11am-6pm Tue-Fri, 10am-3pm Sat & Sun). An estimated 30,000 Russians were murdered at the Nazi POW camp Stalag-351, which was located in converted stables at Priimetsa on Valga's outskirts. Nothing remains of the camp, but a simple, moving monument is located close by. You'll need a town map before setting off.

In town, you can stay in the lovely, well-priced **Metsis Hotell** (☎ 766 6050; www.hotellmetsis .com; Kuperjanovi 63; s/d from 600/800Kr), which also has a good restaurant (mains 105Kr to 195Kr) decorated with hunting trophies (the area is a popular spot for hunting tourism). On the same road is **Voorimehe Pubi** (☎ 767 9627; Kuperjanovi 57; mains 70-85Kr), an atmospheric dark-wood pub serving filling salmon, schnitzel, pork and the like.

Seven to 10 daily buses connect Valga with Tartu (70Kr to 85Kr, 1½ to two hours), and two buses daily go to Võru (85Kr, two to 2½ hours). Until late 2008, a daily train travelled from Tallinn to Valga via Tartu – this rail line is now closed indefinitely, and the bus is your best option. However, once you get to Valga, from here it's possible to catch a Latvian train on to Rīga (2.83Ls, 3½ hours, three daily); see the Latvian rail website, www.ldz.lv, for more information.

VASTSELIINA CASTLE

Vastseliina Castle (Vastseliina linnus) was founded by the Germans on their border with Russia in the 14th century. The evocative ruins stand on a high bluff above the Piusa River on the eastern edge of the settlement of **Vana-Vastseliina** (Old Vastseliina), 4km east of the newer town of Vastseliina, itself 12km southeast of Võru along the road to Pihkva (Pskov). The area prospered from its position on the Pihkva–Rīga trade route until the mid-19th century and was also the scene of many battles.

The castle stands on the Meremäe road out of Vastseliina – look for signs to 'Vastseliina piiskopilinnuse varemad' (bishop castle ruins). Opposite the site is a small information centre and handicrafts store, and a thatch-roofed tavern, Piiri Kõrts. A map near the ruins details the region's hiking and mountain-biking routes.

A few kilometres east of the castle ruins, on the road to Meremäe (Meremäe is, in turn, 7km south of Obinitsa), is the excellent **Setomaa Turismotalu** (☎ 508 7399; www.setotalu.ee; sites/r per person 50/400Kr). With your own wheels, this makes a great base for exploring the southeast region, and the owners will help you plan your explorations and tap into the Setu culture. In idyllic surrounds, it's possible to partake in traditional Setu arts and crafts here, have a smoke sauna and stay in a log house decorated with natural textiles (rooms have shared bathrooms and access to a guest kitchen). The food's great (dinner 90Kr to 120Kr), staff friendly and you have the impression of partaking in tradition without feeling touristy. You'll need to book, as this place is popular with groups (you can book an entire house, sleeping up to 14, for 4000Kr).

About five buses run daily between Võru, Vana-Vastseliina and Meremäe.

SETUMAA

In the far southeast of Estonia lies the (politically unrecognised) area of Setumaa (in Estonian; called Setomaa in the local language), stretching over into Russia. It's one of the most interesting and tragic areas of the country, politically and culturally. Its native people, the Setus, have a mixed Estonian-Russian culture. They are originally Finno-Ugric but the people became Orthodox, not Lutheran, because this part of the country fell under Novgorod and later Pihkva's (Russian: Pskov) subjugation and was not controlled by Teutonic and German tribes and barons, as was the rest of Estonia. They never fully assimilated into Russian culture and throughout the centuries retained their language (today known as Võro-Seto), many features of which are actually closer in structure to Old Estonian than the modern Estonian language. The same goes for certain cultural traditions, for instance leaving food on a relative's grave; this was practised by Estonian tribes before Lutheranism.

All of Setumaa was contained within independent Estonia between 1920 and 1940, but the greater part of it is now in Russia. The town of Pechory (Petseri in Estonian), 2km across the border in Russia and regarded as the 'capital' of Setumaa, is famed for its fabulous 15th-century monastery, considered the most breathtaking in Russia (it looks more like an Italian villa than a monastery).

Today the Setu culture looks to be in the slow process of disappearing. There are approximately 4000 Setus in Estonia (and another 3000 in Russia), which is half the population of the early 20th century. While efforts are made to teach and preserve the language, and promote customs through organised feasts, the younger generation are being quickly assimilated into the Estonian mainstream. The impenetrable border with Russia that has split their community since 1991 has further crippled it.

A rough look at the Setu landscape illustrates how unique it is in the Estonian context. Notably, their villages are structured like castles, with houses facing each other in clusters, often surrounded by a fence. This is in stark contrast to the typical Estonian village where open farmhouses are separated from each other as far as possible. Here, the Orthodox tradition has fostered a tighter sense of community and sociability.

Aside from the large, silver breastplate that is worn on the women's national costume, what sets the Setu aside is their singing style. Setumaa is particularly known for its women folk singers who improvise new words each time they chant their verses. Setu songs, known as *leelo*, are polyphonic and characterised by solo, spoken verses followed by a refrain chanted by a chorus. There is no musical accompaniment and the overall effect archaic.

Information on the region can be found online at www.set omaa.ee.

Obinitsa & Piusa

The village of Obinitsa, near a pristine lake, makes for a pleasant stop. The chief attraction is the charming one-room **Setu Museum House** (Seto Muuseumitarõ; ☎ 785 4190; adult/concession 15/10Kr; ⏲ 10am-5pm Mon-Fri year-round, plus 11am-5pm Sat & Sun mid-May–mid-Sep), which has a few folk costumes, tapestries, cookware and some old photos. It also functions as the **tourist office** (☎ 785 4190; setotour@hot.ee). The town also has a church (built in 1897), a cemetery and a sculpture to the Setu 'Song Mother', which stares solemnly over Lake Obinitsa. There's a swimming platform by the lake.

DAY OF THE SETUS

Peko, the pagan god of fertility, is as important to the Setus as the Orthodox religion they follow. The 8000-line Setu epic *Pekolanõ* tells the tale of this macho god, the rites of whom are known only to men. The epic dates back to 1927 when the Setus' most celebrated folk singer, Anne Vabarna, was told the plot and spontaneously burst into song, barely pausing to draw breath until she had sung the last (8000th) line.

According to folklore, Peko sleeps night and day in his cave of sand. So on the Day of the Setu Kingdom – proclaimed around 20 August each year – an *ülemtsootska* (representative) for the king has to be found. The Setus then gather around the statue of their 'Song Mother' in search of someone worthy of bearing the crown of the sleeping king's royal singer. Competitions are also held to find a strongman for the king.

The Setu king's dress, and the bread, cheese, wine and beer he consumes are also important. On the same day that his kingdom is declared for another year, people from the Setu stronghold are selected to serve the king as his mitten and belt knitters, and bread, beer, wine and cheese makers.

And so completes the royal throne. Amid the day's celebrations, traditional Setu songs and dances are performed and customary good wishes exchanged. The women are adorned with traditional Setu lace and large silver breastplates and necklaces, said to weigh as much as 3kg each. Later in the day respects are paid to the dead.

Obinitsa has several big Setu celebrations, the most important being the 19 August **Feast of the Transfiguration**. Hundreds of Setus come for a procession from the church to the cemetery, which ends with a communal picnic and the leaving of food on graves for the departed souls.

The road north from Obinitsa to Piusa passes under a railway bridge after some 5km. The first dirt road east will take you to one of Estonia's more intriguing sights, the **Piusa sand caves** (Piusa Koopad), the result of a sand-mining industry that began in the area in 1922. (Sand is still mined for glass production 1km north of this spot.) Up until recently visitors could wander through the manmade, cathedral-like caves free of charge, but in summer 2008 a new arrangement came about, and the only access is now via the half-hour **tours** (adult/concession 35/20Kr), leaving every half-hour or so from 11am to 7pm (tickets and information from the cabin with the '*piletid*' sign). Tour times were not set in stone – this system was only weeks old when we visited, so it would pay to ask at the Obinitsa tourist office for an update. Tours were only offered in Estonian at the time of research, and new guidelines mean that the caves are off limits, and visitors admire them from the entrance only. You can still scramble about the sand dunes behind the caves, but overall, it's a disappointing experience.

Also at the caves site is a small, poorly stocked shop selling drinks and ice creams, and a handicrafts store and potter's studio – all open for the summer months.

SLEEPING & EATING

See opposite for information about Setomaa Turismotalu, offering excellent accommodation 7km south of Obinitsa near the village of Meremäe.

Seto Seltsimaja (☎ 786 1412, 5620 3374) A private Setu home doubling as Obinitsa's community centre. If you call the day before, you can order a very filling home-cooked meal. You can also buy a few handicrafts.

Värska & Around

The town of Värska is known for its mineral water, sold throughout Estonia, and its healing mud. There's plenty of rural charm here, including a picturesque stone church and a leafy cemetery surrounding it. The best reason for coming here is the **Setu Farm Museum** (Setu Talumuuseum; ☎ 505 4673; www.setomuuseum.ee, in Estonian; Pikk 40; adult/concession 30/15Kr; ⏰ 10am-5pm mid-May–mid-Sep, 10am-4pm Tue-Sat mid-Sep–mid-May) on the south edge of town. Presided over by a wooden carving of Peko, the museum comprises a re-created 19th-century farmhouse complex, with stables, granary and the former workshops for metalworking and ceramics. Don't bypass the charming restaurant here or the excellent gift shop – the region's best – selling handmade mittens, socks, hats, dolls, tapestries, books and recordings of traditional Setu music.

Stop in at Värska's **tourist office** (☎ 796 4782; www.verska.ee; Pikk 12; ☺ 10am-6pm Tue-Sat mid-May–mid-Sep, 10am-5pm Mon-Fri mid-Sep–mid-May) for information about the area.

Võpolsova and **Tonja**, a few kilometres north of Värska on the west side of Värska Bay, are classic Setu villages. In Võpolsova there's a monument to folk singer Anne Vabarna, who knew 100,000 verses by heart. Võpolsova homesteads typically consist of a ring of outer buildings around an inner yard, while Tonja's houses face the lake from which its people get their livelihood.

Other exotic features of this area are the borders. There are only a few official border crossing points with Russia; the rest are abandoned control points, or seemingly unguarded wooden fences, creepy dead ends or lonely plastic signs. One road, from Värska to Saatse, even crosses the zigzagging border into Russian territory for 2km. You're not allowed to stop on this stretch.

Near the tiny, ancient village of **Podmotsa**, northeast of Värska, a beautiful Orthodox church in the Russian village of Kulje is visible across the inlet – as is the border-guard watchtower. Be aware that crossing the border at any nonofficial point (even if you have a Russian visa) is illegal and can lead to your arrest.

SLEEPING & EATING

Hirvemäe Holiday Centre (☎ 797 6105; www.hirve mae.ee; Silla 4; sites/cabins 50/180Kr; s/d incl breakfast 500/800Kr) Set on a pretty lake on the main route into town, this attractive guesthouse has comfy, wood-floored rooms and a cafe on its extensive grounds, plus plenty of activities to choose from, including a tiny beach, tennis courts, boat rental, sauna and a playground. The cafe menu is short, simple and cheap (soup, salad, meat – you know the drill). There are few other options round these parts!

Setu Farm Restaurant (Tsaimaja; ☎ 505 4673; Pikk 40; meals 48-64Kr; ☺ 11am-7pm Tue-Sun mid-May–mid-Sep, 11am-5pm Tue-Sat mid-Sep–mid-May) Next door to the museum, in an atmospheric log cabin, this makes an unbeatable setting for a home-cooked meal. The fare is nothing fancy – cold Seto soup, smoked or stewed pork, herring with sour cream, fried chicken – but it's a real gem nonetheless.

Getting There & Away

There are four to five buses daily between Tartu and Värska (85Kr, 1½ to two hours) via Räpina, two of which continue to Koidula, 2km across the Russian border from Pechory. To reach Obinitsa from Tartu, you'll need to travel via Võru.

From Võru, four to six buses run to Obinitsa (20Kr to 36Kr, 45 minutes); many of these stop at Vana-Vastseliina and Meremäe too. There are only two weekly services between Võru and Värska.

LAKE PEIPSI (SOUTH)

In the 18th and 19th centuries Russian Old Believers, a sect of the Orthodox Church persecuted for refusing to accept liturgical reforms carried out in 1666, took refuge on the western shores of Lake Peipsi (Chudkoye Ozero in Russian), particularly in Kallaste. They founded several coastal villages, namely Kolkja, Kasepää and Varnja, and settled the island of Piirissaar.

About 40km north of Tartu, signposted off the main road (look for 'Loss ja park'), lies **Alatskivi Castle** (Alatskivi loss; ☎ 528 6598; loss@alat skivi.ee; adult/concession 30/20Kr; ☺ 11am-6pm Jun-Aug, 11am-5pm Wed-Sun May & Sep), which was built in the late 1500s, though its neo-Gothic centrepiece dates from the 19th century. Its design is based on Scotland's Balmoral Castle, and it's set in lovely parkland.

Three kilometres south of Alatskivi, in the hamlet of Rupsi, is the **Liiv Museum** (☎ 745 3846; info@muusa.ee; adult/concession 20/10Kr; ☺ 10am-6pm Jun-Aug, 10am-4pm Tue-Sep-May), housing exhibitions on Juhan Liiv (1864–1913), a celebrated writer and poet. Occasional concerts and poetry competitions are held at the museum; it's a lovely rural setting, with the 19th-century farmhouse (where the Liiv family once lived) and smoke sauna open to the public.

From Alatskivi, opposite the turn-off to the castle, a road heads 7km southeast to **Kolkja**, a village of Russian Old Believers with a dainty, green wooden Orthodox church and an **Old Believers' Museum** (☎ 745 3431; admission 25Kr; ☺ by appointment) in the new schoolhouse (the museum is tricky to find – turn left at the Estonian flag, and continue past the blue-painted restaurant). The restaurant is also a worthwhile stop – see opposite.

Kallaste (pop 1150), 8km north of Alatskivi, is where a settlement of Old Believers has existed since 1720, when the area was known as Red Mountains (Krasniye Gori) because of the red sandstone cliffs, up to 11m high, that surround this town. Nearly all the villagers are Russian-speaking. From June to August there's a **tourist office** (☎ 745 2705; info@kallaste.ee; Oja 22; ☼ daily) dispensing local information; there's also a supermarket, an Old Believers' cemetery at the southern end of town, and a sandy beach with small caves.

The northern half of Lake Peipsi (p105) is covered in the Northeastern Estonia section.

Sleeping & Eating

Hostel Laguun (☎ 505 8551; www.hostel-laguun.ee; Liiva 1a, Kallaste; sites/r per person 50/250Kr) In a prime lakeside spot in Kallaste, the main town of the region, Laguun is a small (10-bed) guesthouse offering simple rooms with shared bathroom, plus space for campers. There's a large garden and barbecue area, plus a communal kitchen. Try for a room with lake views.

Aarde Villa (☎ 776 4290; www.aardevilla.ee; Sääritsa; sites/r per person 75/440Kr) In the village of Sääritsa, halfway between Mustvee and Kallaste, is this lakeside estate, offering comfy rooms (with TV and bathroom) in the main house, or large grounds for camping. There's a plethora of activities, too, including sauna, boat (with fishing equipment) and bike rental.

Kivi Kõrts (☎ 745 3872; Alatskivi; mains 30-85Kr; ☼ 10am-midnight) Probably the most atmospheric place in the region for a hearty meal (the menu has patchy English translations and is *very* pork-heavy), this cosy, dimly lit tavern has taken an antique-shop-meets-junkyard approach to decor (much of what you see is for sale).

Fish & Onion Restaurant (Kala ja Sibul; ☎ 745 3431; Kolkja; ☼ noon-6pm daily, by appointment in winter) In tiny Kolkja, this simple, blue-painted restaurant offers you the chance to try the Old Believer cuisine, largely based around locally caught fish and onions grown in the villagers' gardens. It's worth calling ahead to confirm opening hours.

Getting There & Away

A car is the handiest way of getting around this area. Ten buses go daily between Tartu and Kallaste (45Kr, 1¼ to two hours), with fewer runs on Saturday and Sunday. Around 15 buses go from Tartu to Alatskivi (36Kr to 45Kr, one to 1½ hours), again with limited service on weekends. About five daily buses go from Tartu to Kolkja (43Kr, 1½

hours), most via Varnja and Kolkja en route to Alatskivi.

SOUTHWESTERN ESTONIA

Southwestern Estonia contains the country's most popular resort town, as well as charming country villages, a vast national park and two remote islands that see few foreign visitors.

Perched along a lovely, sandy coastline, Pärnu attracts legions of holidaymakers during the summer. Young partygoers appear from Tallinn and Tartu en route to the city's nightclubs, cafes and restaurants, just as busloads of elderly out-of-towners arrive seeking spa treatments and mud cures.

East of Pärnu stretches Soomaa National Park, a biodiverse region of meandering rivers, wooded meadows and swamp forest. Among the most charming country towns, Viljandi lies just beyond Soomaa. It has a tiny but historic centre, old castle ruins and breathtaking views over a forested valley and the pristine Lake Viljandi.

PÄRNU
pop 44,200

Local families, young party-goers and German and Finnish holidaymakers join together in a collective prayer for sunny weather while strolling the golden-sand beaches, sprawling parks and historic, picturesque centre of Pärnu (*pair*-nu), Estonia's premier seaside resort.

Come summer, the town acts as a magnet for party-loving Estonians – its name alone is synonymous with fun in the sun in these parts (one local described it to us as 'Estonia's Miami' – we think he was tongue-in-cheek!). Yet youth and bacchanalia aren't the only spirits moving through town. Most of Pärnu is actually quite docile, with wide leafy streets and expansive parks intermingling with grand, turn-of-the-century villas that reflect the town's rich past as a resort capital of the Baltic region. Pärnu is still a popular health resort for older visitors from across the Baltic, Finland and Eastern Europe who come seeking rest, amelioration and Pärnu's vaunted mud treatments, available in both old-school Soviet-style sanatoriums (shrinking in number) and more modern, glitzier spa resorts.

ESTONIA

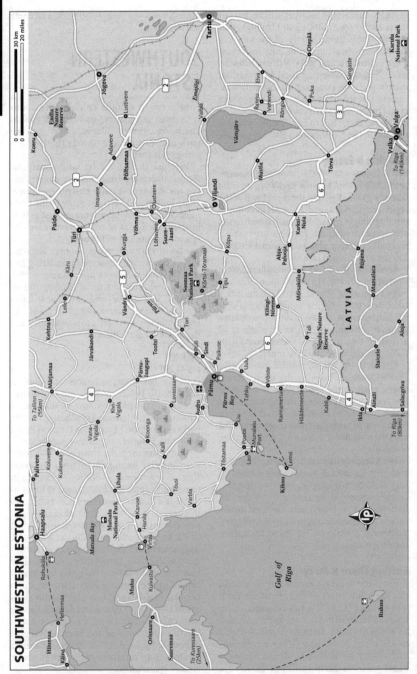

SOUTHWESTERN ESTONIA

History

There was a trading settlement at Pärnu before the German crusaders arrived, but the place entered recorded history when the Pärnu River was fixed as the border between the territories of the Ösel-Wiek bishop (west and north) and the Livonian knights (east and south) in 1234. The town, joined by rivers to Viljandi, Tartu and Lake Peipsi, became the Hanseatic port of Pernau in the 14th century. (Sinking water levels have since cut this link.) Pernau/Pärnu had a population of German merchants from Lübeck origin till at least the 18th century. It withstood wars, fires, plagues, and switches between German, Polish, Swedish and Russian rule, and prospered in the 17th century under Swedish rule until its trade was devastated by the Europe-wide blockades during the Napoleonic wars.

From 1838 it gradually became a popular resort, with mud baths proving a draw as well as the beach. Only the resort area was spared severe damage in 1944 as the Soviets drove out the Nazis, but many parts of Old Town have since been restored.

Orientation

Pärnu lies on either side of the Pärnu River estuary, which empties into Pärnu Bay. The southern half of the town contains the major attractions, including Old Town (beginning a few blocks south of the river), and the beach, which lies half a kilometre further on the far southern end. Between Old Town and the shoreline are a series of parks extending westward towards the bay.

The bus station is at the eastern end of Old Town, on the corner of Pikk and Ringi and walking distance to many hotels. The main shopping strip is the pedestrianised Rüütli.

Information

Apollo (☎ 683 3400; Rüütli 41) Sells books, maps and limited English-language books.

Central Library (Keskraamatukogu; ☎ 445 5706; www .pkr.ee; Akadeemia 3; ☷ 10am-6pm Mon-Fri, 10am-4pm Sat) Free internet at this spiffy new library, undergoing expansion at the time of research.

Central post office (Akadeemia 7; ☷ 8am-6pm Mon-Fri, 9am-3pm Sat)

Left luggage (pakihoid; ☷ 8am-7.30pm Mon-Fri, 8am-5pm Sat, 9am-8pm Sun) At the southern end of the bus terminal, near platform 8.

Pärnu New Art Museum (☎ 443 0772; Esplanaadi 10; per 30min 15Kr; ☷ 9am-9pm) Internet access.

Pärnu tourist office (☎ 447 3000; www.visitparnu .com; Rüütli 16; ☷ 9am-6pm Mon-Fri, 10am-4pm Sat, 10am-3pm Sun Jun-Aug, 9am-5pm Mon-Fri Sep-May) Pick up maps, brochures and the helpful *Pärnu in Your Pocket*, published annually (25Kr). Helpful staff will book accommodation for a 25Kr fee.

SEB Bank (Rüütli 40a) With ATM; behind the bus station. More banks are nearby.

Sights & Activities

The wide, golden-sand beach and Ranna pst, whose buildings date from the early 20th century, are among Pärnu's finest attractions. Note especially the handsome 1927 neoclassical **Mudaravila** (Ranna pst 1), a symbol of the town's history. The legendary mud baths that once operated here have closed. At the time of research it housed a summertime information desk and a few random exhibitions, but new owners are planning to restore the building and add an adjacent new spa hotel (does Pärnu need more?). Stay tuned.

A fine new beach promenade was opened in 2006, with a curving path stretching along the sand, lined with fountains and park benches. It's the perfect place for an ice-cream-licking stroll, and fun people-watching. The beach is littered with volleyball courts and tiny change cubicles. At the far end, Estonia's largest waterpark, **Veekeskus** (Waterpark; ☎ 445 1166; www.tervise paradiis.ee; Side 14; adult 115-290Kr, concession 75-205Kr; ☷ 10am-10pm), beckons with pools, slides, tubes and other slippery fun. It's a big family-focused draw, especially when bad weather ruins beach plans. It's part of the huge Tervise Paradiis hotel complex (p132), and has a complex array of prices depending on whether you're staying three hours or the day, visiting on weekdays or weekends, and using the waterpark and/or the separate 25m swimming pool.

The main thoroughfare of the historic centre is **Rüütli**, lined with splendid buildings dating back to the 17th century. Just off the main street is the **Red Tower** (Punane Torn; Hommiku 11; ☷ 10am-5pm), the city's oldest (and despite its name, white) building, which dates from the 15th century. Originally bigger, this was the southeast corner of the medieval town wall, of which nothing more remains. At one stage the tower was used as a prison. Today a small gallery is housed on the top floor, and a craft market fills the courtyard.

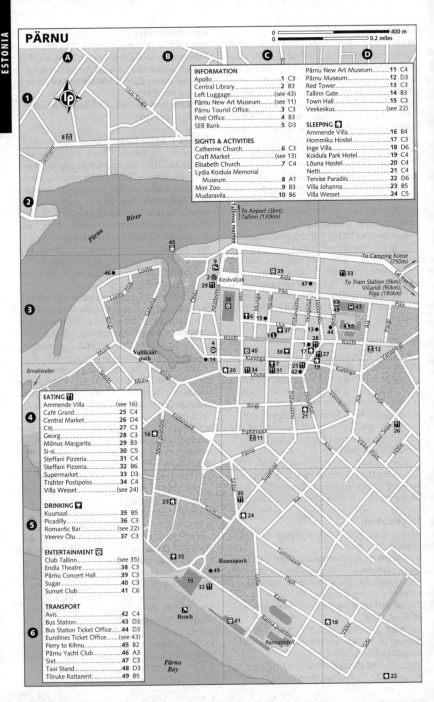

PÄRNU

INFORMATION				Pärnu New Art Museum	11	C4
Apollo	1	C3		Pärnu Museum	12	D3
Central Library	2	B3		Red Tower	13	C3
Left Luggage	(see 43)			Tallinn Gate	14	B3
Pärnu New Art Museum	(see 11)			Town Hall	15	C3
Pärnu Tourist Office	3	C3		Veekeskus	(see 22)	
Post Office	4	B3				
SEB Bank	5	D3		SLEEPING		
				Ammende Villa	16	B4
SIGHTS & ACTIVITIES				Hommiku Hostel	17	C3
Catherine Church	6	C3		Inge Villa	18	D6
Craft Market	(see 13)			Koidula Park Hotel	19	C4
Elisabeth Church	7	C4		Lõuna Hostel	20	C4
Lydia Koidula Memorial				Netti	21	C4
Museum	8	A1		Tervise Paradiis	22	D6
Mini Zoo	9	B3		Villa Johanna	23	B5
Mudaravila	10	B6		Villa Wesset	24	C5

EATING	
Ammende Villa	(see 16)
Café Grand	25 C4
Central Market	26 D4
Citi	27 C3
Georg	28 C3
Mõnus Margarita	29 B3
Si-si	30 C5
Steffani Pizzeria	31 C4
Steffani Pizzeria	32 B6
Supermarket	33 D3
Trahter Postipoiss	34 C4
Villa Wesset	(see 24)

DRINKING	
Kuursaal	35 B5
Picadilly	36 C3
Romantic Bar	(see 22)
Veerev Õlu	37 C3

ENTERTAINMENT	
Club Tallinn	(see 35)
Endla Theatre	38 C3
Pärnu Concert Hall	39 C3
Sugar	40 C3
Sunset Club	41 C6

TRANSPORT	
Avis	42 C4
Bus Station	43 D3
Bus Station Ticket Office	44 D3
Eurolines Ticket Office	(see 43)
Ferry to Kihnu	45 B2
Pärnu Yacht Club	46 A3
Sixt	47 C3
Taxi Stand	48 D3
Tõruke Rattarent	49 B5

Parts of the 17th-century Swedish moat and ramparts remain at the western end of Rüütli; where the rampart meets the western end of Kuninga it's pierced by the tunnel-like **Tallinn Gate** (Tallinna Värav), which once marked the main road to Tallinn. Across Nikolai from the late 18th-century **town hall** (cnr Nikolai & Uus) there's a half-timbered house dating from 1740, and a block down the street on the corner of Nikolai and Kuninga is the baroque Lutheran **Elisabeth Church**, also from the 1740s, named after the Russian empress of the time. The Russian Orthodox **Catherine Church** (Ekatarina Kirik; cnr Uus & Vee), from the 1760s, is named after another Russian empress, Catherine the Great.

The **Pärnu New Art Museum** (☎ 443 0772; www .chaplin.ee; Esplanaadi 10; adult/concession 25/15Kr; ☯ 9am-9pm), in the former Communist Party headquarters southwest of the centre, is among Estonia's cultural highlights with its cafe, bookshop and exhibitions which always push the cultural envelope. Founded by film - maker Mark Soosaar, it also hosts an annual film festival (below).

The **Lydia Koidula Memorial Museum** (☎ 443 3313; Jannseni 37; adult/concession 15/10Kr; ☯ 10am-6pm Tue-Sat) stands north of the river. Here you can learn about one of Estonia's great poets in the former school she attended.

Despite its modest size, the **Pärnu Museum** (☎ 443 3231; www.pernau.ee; Aia 4; adult/concession 30/15Kr; ☯ 10am-6pm Tue-Sat) covers 11,000 years of regional history. Archaeological findings along with relics from the country's German, Livonian, Russian and even Soviet periods are on display.

And on a completely different (and infinitely more creepy) note, an eclectic collection of snakes, spiders, geckos and passive pythons await you at the **Mini Zoo** (☎ 551 6033; Akadeemia tee 1; adult/concession/family 50/25/110Kr; ☯ 10am-6pm Mon-Fri, 11am-4pm Sat & Sun).

Festivals & Events

The biggest annual event is the **Pärnu International Film Festival** (early July), showcasing documentary and anthropology films since 1987. It's held at the Pärnu New Art Museum and other venues in town (and around Estonia). See www.chaplin.ee for details.

The tourist office distributes the annual *Pärnu This Week*, which lists events happening around town.

Sleeping

There's loads of accommodation here, from hostels to apartments with everything in between. In summer, however, it's well worth booking ahead; outside of high season you should be able to snare yourself a good deal. Prices listed below are for high season (websites will list low-season rates, which can be up to 40% lower).

BUDGET

Camping Konse (☎ 5343 5092; www.konse.ee; Suur-Jõe 44a; tent sites 60Kr plus 60Kr per person, r with shared/private bathroom 550/700Kr) Perched on a spot by the river only 1km from the Old Town, Konse offers tent and camp sites and a variety of rooms (half with private bathroom, half with shared facilities, all with kitchen access). There's sauna, rowboat and bike rental. It can get crowded, but that makes it easier to meet people. Open year-round.

Lõuna Hostel (☎ 443 0943; www.eliisabet.ee/hostel; Lõuna 2; dm 300-360Kr, tw with shared/private bathroom 720/1100Kr) Overlooking a park, this spotless hostel in a grand 1909 *Jugendstil* building offers quality budget digs in spacious, two- to seven-bed rooms with high ceilings (those on the renovated 1st floor have private bathroom; on the 2nd floor they share bathrooms). The shared kitchen doubles as social room, where people compare suntans and travel tales. Entrance is on Akadeemia

MIDRANGE

Hommiku Hostel (☎ 445 1122; www.hommikuhostel .ee; Hommiku 17; dm/s/d/tr/q 300/600/900/1200/1400Kr) You'll do well to snare a room at Hommiku, far more like a hotel than a hostel (except for its prices). This modern place has handsome rooms with private bathrooms, TV and kitchenettes, and some with old beamed ceilings. It's in a prime in-town position with good eateries as its neighbours.

Villa Johanna (☎ 443 8370; www.villa-johanna.ee; Suvituse 6; s/d 680/1180Kr) On a street lined with family-run guesthouses, this pretty place stands out thanks to its hanging flowerpots and planter boxes. Many pine trees died in the making of the interior fit-out and furnishings, and the place is spotless. Low-season rates are a steal (single/double 250/600Kr). Not much English is spoken.

Koidula Park Hotel (☎ 447 7030; www.koidulapark hotell.ee; Kuninga 38; s/d 990/1350Kr; ☯ Apr-Dec) Serenely facing leafy Koidula Park in the town's centre is this humble, full-service hotel which boasts the Green Key (a title given to Estonian hotels fulfilling environmentally friendly criteria). Rooms are snug and on the small side, but the old-world elegance makes up for that.

Inge Villa (☎ 443 8510; www.ingevilla.ee; Kaarli 20; s/d/ste 1000/1250/1450Kr) In a prime patch of real estate not far back from the beach you'll find the low-key and lovely Inge Villa, a 'Swedish-Estonian villa hotel'. Its 11 rooms are simply decorated in muted tones with Nordic minimalism at the fore. The garden, lounge and sauna seal the deal.

Villa Wesset (☎ 697 2500; www.wesset.ee; Supeluse 26; s/d 1150/1590Kr) This elegant new boutique hotel is kitted out in warm chocolate and vanilla tones (appropriately enough, given the 1928 villa was built by a candyman). It's in a great location just a stone's throw from the beach, and with an acclaimed restaurant downstairs.

Netti (☎ 516 7958; www.nettihotel.ee; Hospidali 11-1; ste 1200-1600Kr) Anni, your host at Netti, is a ray of sunshine, and her three-storey guesthouse, comprising four two-room suites (all with kitchenette), positively gleams under her care. The suites sleep three, are bright and breezy (reminiscent of the '80s), and the downstairs sauna area is a lovely place to unwind after a hard day at the beach.

TOP END

Tervise Paradiis (☎ 445 1600; www.terviseparadiis.ee; Side 14; s/d/ste from 1650/2150/3030Kr) Big (120-odd rooms) and *busy* in summer, this smartly designed hotel near the water has slick, shiny rooms, all with balconies and beach views (ask for a room on a higher floor). Here, happy-holiday facilities are laid on thick: bowling alley, kids' playroom, spa, fitness club, waterpark, restaurants, bar. It's very popular with Swedish and Finnish guests, so book ahead in high season. It's capped off by polished service and a complex schedule of rates – prices peak in summer, and with altitude (ie you'll pay a premium for the better views).

Ammende Villa (☎ 447 3888; www.ammende.ee; Mere pst 7; r/ste from 3500/4800Kr) If money's no object, this is where to spend it. Class and luxury abound in this exquisitely refurbished 1904 Art Nouveau mansion, which lords over handsomely manicured grounds. The gorgeous exterior is matched by an elegant lobby, individually antique-furnished rooms and top-notch service. Blow the budget on the luxuriously appointed Ammende Suite and enjoy breakfast on your balcony; rooms in the gardener's house are more affordable but lack a little of the wow factor. If you're staying elsewhere, enjoy the ambience by stopping in at the restaurant (left).

Eating & Drinking

Georg (☎ 443 1110; Rüütli 43; meals 30-60Kr; ☺ 7.30am-7.30pm Mon-Fri, 9am-7.30pm Sat & Sun) This cafeteria-style corner cafe has the cheapest eats in town. Soups, salads and daily specials for a quick, budget-friendly fill-up.

Mõnus Margarita (☎ 443 0929; www.monusmargarita.ee; Akadeemia 5; mains 69-310Kr; ☺ 11am-midnight) Huge, colourful and decidedly upbeat, as all good Tex-Mex places should be – but if you're looking for heavy-duty spice, you won't find it here. Fajitas, burritos and quesadillas all score goals, and there are margaritas and tequilas for the grown-ups; a play area for the kids.

Steffani Pizzeria (☎ 443 1170; www.steffani.ee; Nikolai 24; pizzas 75-105Kr; ☺ 11am-midnight Sun-Thu, 11am-2am Fri & Sat) The queue out front should alert you – this is a top choice for thin-crust and pan pizzas, particularly in summer when you can dine alfresco on the big, flower-filled terrace. In a smart business move, a second summertime branch opens near the beach at Ranna pst 1.

Citi (☎ 444 1847; Hommiku 8; mains 75-145Kr; ☺ 10am-midnight) When the sun's shining the outdoor tables at this lively cafe-pub are jam-packed with a diverse crowd, while the rustic interior matches the simple menu of beery snacks and inexpensive meaty mains (salmon fillet, grilled chicken, pork roast). It's popular with visitors and locals, and the owner's a definite local character.

Si-si (☎ 447 5612; www.si-si.ee; Supeluse 21; mains 75-220Kr; ☺ noon-midnight) Beachside dining is disappointingly bland, but a walk up Supeluse presents some good options, including this brand-spanking-new Italian restaurant-lounge. Inside is smart white-linen dining, outside is a stylishly relaxed terrace peopled by equally stylish holidaymakers. There's a good selection of pizzas (topped by parma ham, gorgonzola and the like), plus mains including wild boar stew and *osso buco*.

Kuursaal (☎ 442 0367; Mere pst 22; mains 80-220Kr; ☺ noon-2am Wed-Thu, noon-4am Fri & Sat) This late-19th-century dance hall has been transformed into a spacious countrified beer hall with a large terrace at the back. An older mix of tourists and locals come for draft beer and occasional rock shows, and a menu that takes its meat and beer snacks seriously.

Villa Wesset (☎ 697 2500; www.wesset.ee; Supeluse 26; mains 80-250Kr; ☻ noon-11pm) Opposite Si-si, the summer terrace at Villa Wesset holds big appeal, as does the fresh, modern menu – most interesting are the creative salads and soups (ie, bloody Mary cold soup with crabmeat). In cooler weather the indoor dining room is a more formal place to chow down.

Trahter Postipoiss (☎ 446 4864; www.trahterposti poiss.ee; Vee 12; mains 98-320Kr; ☻ noon-11pm Sun-Thu, noon-2am Fri & Sat) One of Pärnu's highlights, this converted 17th-century postal building houses a rustic Russian tavern, with excellent Russian cuisine, a convivial crowd (especially after a few vodka shots) and imperial portraits watching over the proceedings. The spacious patio opens during the summer, and there's live music on weekends to further boost the atmosphere.

Ammende Villa (☎ 447 3888; www.ammende.ee; Mere pst 7; breakfast buffet 150Kr, mains 120-350Kr; ☻ breakfast 7-10am Mon-Fri, 8-11am Sat & Sun, restaurant noon-11pm) Nonguests of the hotel can get a taste of life at this Art Nouveau gem by joining in the morning breakfast buffet – a splendid spread of salmon, fresh fruit and champagne. Otherwise, various salons and the beautiful garden terrace are great spots to dine on roulade of lamb, steamed Greenland flatfish and a range of French and Mediterranean dishes – or simply stop by for a glass of bubbles and a cheese platter. To help unleash your inner sophisticate, weekly classical concerts are held on the lawn in summer.

Café Grand (☎ 444 3412; www.victoriahotel.ee; Kuninga 25; mains 200-300Kr; ☻ noon-midnight) Inside Hotel Victoria, Pärnu's most stately dining room serves up delicately prepared Chateaubriand, rack of lamb and other French-leaning favourites amid 1920s grandeur. The two-course weekday 'business lunch' (150Kr) is a good offer, while the cafe corner makes a cosy spot for afternoon coffee and *crème brûlée*.

Picadilly (☎ 442 0085; Pühavaimu 15; ☻ 11am-midnight) The city's only wine bar-cafe offers down-tempo bliss in plush surroundings, plus a top wine selection alongside extensive coffee, tea and hot choc. Savoury food begins and ends with quiche – here it's all about the sweeties, including moreish cheesecake (25Kr) and handmade chocolates.

Romantic Bar (☎ 445 1600; Tervise Paradiis, 8th fl, Side 14; ☻ noon-midnight) Cheesy name but superb water views and a modern Scandi-chic interior make this the perfect setting for a sundowner cocktail or a nightcap, either inside on the white, pod-like leather chairs, or on the small outdoor terrace. Don't come here looking to sate any hunger though, just thirst (food selections are almost nonexistent).

Veerev Õlu (☎ 442 9848; www.rollingbeer.com; Uus 3a; ☻ 11am-11pm Sun-Thu, 11am-1am Fri & Sat) The 'Rolling Beer' (after the Rolling Stones) wins the award for friendliest and cosiest pub by a long shot – a tiny rustic space with lots of good vibes, cheap beer and the occasional live rock-folk band (with compulsory dancing on tables, it would seem).

SELF-CATERING

Provisions abound at the **central market** (Suur-Sepa 18; ☻ 7am-4.30pm Tue-Sat, 7am-3pm Sun), southeast of the centre. The most central **supermarket** (☻ 9am-10pm) is inside the Port Artur 2 complex, off Pikk (opposite the bus station).

Entertainment

In summer there are various concerts, held at traditional venues such as the Concert Hall and Kuursaal, as well as in parks, the town hall, churches, and the grounds of the beautiful Ammende Villa.

Pärnu Concert Hall (Konserdimaja; ☎ 445 5800; www .concert.ee; Aida 4) A stunning riverside glass-and-steel auditorium considered the best concert venue in Estonia. Its acoustics are first-rate – check the website to see if your visit coincides with a performance.

Endla Theatre (☎ 442 0666; www.endla.ee; in Estonian; Keskväljak 1) Pärnu's best theatre, staging a wide range of performances (usually in Estonian). It also houses an art gallery and an open-air cafe.

NIGHTCLUBS

Club Tallinn (www.clubtallinn.ee; Mere pst 22; ☻ Wed-Sat Jun-Aug) This summertime-only club is held in one section of Kuursaal (opposite). It's the city's hottest spot, with excellent DJs and an eager young crowd.

Sunset Club (☎ 443 0670; www.sunset.ee; Ranna pst 3; ☻ 11pm-4am Fri & Sat) In a grandiose seafront building dating from 1939, Pärnu's biggest and most famous nightclub has an outdoor beach terrace and a sleek multifloor interior with plenty of cosy nooks when the dance floor gets crowded. Imported DJs and bands plus a wild young crowd keep things cranked until the early hours.

Sugar (☎ 442 1100; www.sugarclub.ee; Vee 10; ☻ 11pm-4am Wed-Sat) Shiny new Sugar offers you temptation in the form of the 'sweetest nightlife' and is building a solid reputation for its themed nights (particularly Wednesday's retro night); Friday and Saturday see big-name DJs play.

Getting There & Away

Pärnu lies 130km south of Tallinn on the main road to Rīga.

AIR

Pärnu's **airport** (☎ 447 5001; www.eepu.ee) lies on the northern edge of town, west off the Tallinn road, 4km from the town centre. Bus 23 runs from the bus station to the airport (20 minutes). In winter flights connect Pärnu with the islands of Kihnu (right) and Ruhnu (opposite).

BOAT

It's possible to take a ferry or private boat trip from Pärnu to Kihnu (see opposite). **Pärnu Yacht Club** (Pärnu Jahtklubi; ☎ 447 1750; www.jahtklubi .ee; Lootsi 6) has a harbour with a customs point and passport control.

BUS

The **bus station** (Ringi 3) is at the north end of Ringi, just off Pikk. **Eurolines** (☎ 12550; www .eurolines.ee) tickets to Rīga, Vilnius and beyond are sold by Cargobus, near platform 8, though you can usually purchase tickets from the driver. For destinations throughout Estonia, the **ticket office** (☎ 12012; ☻ 6.15am-7.30pm), a red-brick building, is 100m south on the opposite side of Ringi.

About 30 daily buses connect Pärnu with Tallinn. Buses depart two or three times daily (one hour) for Munalaiu Port, the departure point for ferries to Kihnu. Other direct buses to/from Pärnu:

Kuressaare (200Kr, 3½ hours, three daily)
Rīga (110Kr to 190Kr, three hours, seven daily)
Tallinn (115Kr to 125Kr, two hours, about 30 buses daily)
Tartu (135Kr to 150Kr, 2½ to three hours, 10 buses daily)
Viljandi (90Kr, 1½ to two hours, eight to 11 buses daily)
Vilnius (360Kr to 435Kr, 7½ hours, two daily)
Virtsu (75Kr, 1¼ hours, three daily)

TRAIN

Two daily trains run between Tallinn and Pärnu (75Kr, 2¾ hours), but this isn't a great option given that **Pärnu station** (Riia mnt 116) is an inconvenient 5km east of the town centre along the Rīga road. There's no station office; buy tickets on the train.

Getting Around

A main local bus stop in the town centre is on Akadeemia tee in front of the main post office; there's another by the main bus station. Tickets for local journeys are 8Kr if pre-purchased (or 10Kr from the driver).

Taxis line up near the bus station on Ringi. You'll get better rates by calling **E-Takso** (☎ 443 1111) or **Pärnu Takso** (☎ 443 9222).

From June to August you can rent bicycles from **Tõruke Rattarent** (☎ 502 8269; www .torukebicycles.ee; cnr Ranna pst & Supeluse; bike per hr/day/ week 40/150/650Kr), a bike stand near the beach. For 15Kr you can expect a bike delivered to you, year-round.

There are numerous car-hire agencies in town; options include **Sixt** (☎ 605 8148; www.sixt .ee; Aida 5) and **Avis** (☎ 5671 1310; www.avis.ee; Kuninga 34), just behind Hotel Victoria.

KIHNU
pop 600

Kihnu island, 40km southwest of Pärnu in the Gulf of Rīga, is almost a living museum of Estonian culture. Many of the island's women still wear the traditional, colourful striped skirts nearly every day. There are four villages on the 7km-long island, plus a school, church, lighthouse (shipped over from Britain), museum and combined village hall and bar in the centre of the island. Long, quiet beaches line the western coast. Kihnuans are among the few non-Setu Estonians who follow the Russian Orthodox religion. After WWII a fishery collective was established. Fishing and cattle herding continue to be the mainstay of employment for Kihnu's inhabitants.

In December 2003 Unesco declared the Kihnu Cultural Space a masterpiece of the Oral and Intangible Heritage of Humanity. This honour is a tribute to the rich cultural traditions that are still practised, in song, dance, the celebration of traditional spiritual festivals and the making of handicrafts. In part, the customs of Kihnu have remained intact for so many centuries thanks to the island's isolation.

Many of the island's first inhabitants, centuries ago, were criminals and exiles from the mainland. Kihnu men made a living from fishing and seal hunting, while women effectively governed the island in their absence. The most famous Kihnuan was the sea captain Enn Uuetoa (better known as Kihnu Jõnn), who became a symbol of lost freedom for Estonians during the Soviet period when they were virtually banned from the sea. Kihnu Jõnn, said to have sailed on all the world's oceans, drowned in 1913 when his ship sank off Denmark on what was to have been his last voyage before retirement. He was buried in the Danish town of Oksby but in 1992 his remains were brought home to Kihnu and reburied in the island's church.

You can learn more about him and life on Kihnu at the **Kihnu Museum** (☎ 446 9983; adult/child 15/6Kr; ☽ 10.30am-3pm Jun-Sep, other times by arrangement), across the street from the picturesque Orthodox church. Tourist information and internet access is available 50m up the road at the **civic centre** (☽ 1-4pm Tue-Fri, noon-3pm Sat). **Kihnurand Travel Agency** (☎ 446 9924; kihnurand @kihnu.ee) on Kihnu is the best agency for arranging full-day or longer excursions there. Transport to and from the island is easy and the number of tourists is increasing every year. Find out more at www.ki hnu.ee.

Sleeping & Eating

Tolli Tourist Farm (☎ 446 9908; www.kihnutalu.ee; sites/r per person 60/250Kr) This farm offers accommodation in the main house or in a more rustic log cabin; you can also pitch a tent. Tolli offers bike rental, boating excursions, and guests can order meals. The farm is located about 2km north of the port; it can even arrange to sail you over from the mainland. Sauna available.

Rock City (☎ 446 9956, 5340 2408; rockcity@kihnu.ee; d/tr 460/660Kr; ☽ May-Sep) Near Tolli, this place offers simple, wood-floored rooms with shared bathroom. The restaurant serves hearty country fare.

Kurase Pood Kohvik (☎ 446 9938; ☽ shop 9am-7pm) Near the church and museum in the island centre, this food shop has a pleasant restaurant with a patio out the back. It's Kihnu's best place to pop in for a meal, and in summer is open until 1am daily (hot meals served until 9pm); the shop keeps shorter hours.

Getting There & Away

As long as ice conditions allow (usually from around late March to late December),

there are regular ferries to Kihnu operated by **Veeteed** (☎ 443 1069; www.veeteed.com) from both the port of Pärnu (adult/child/car/bike 70/35/190/25Kr, journey time 2¼ hours) and from the Munalaiu port (adult/child/car/bike 40/20/160/15Kr, 50 minutes) in the village of Pootsi, 40km southwest of Pärnu (buses from Pärnu are theoretically timed to meet the ferries). Tickets can be purchased at both ports. The Pärnu tourist office (p129) keeps updated ferry departure times.

In winter **Avies** (☎ 605 8022; www.avies.ee) operates a small-aircraft service connecting Pärnu and Kihnu a couple of times daily. The journey takes all of 15 minutes.

Getting Around

Bicycle is the best way to get around the island. You can rent bikes and pick up a map at **Jalgrattaläe nutus** (bikes per hr/day from 25/125Kr), in a brick building 150m from the port.

RUHNU

pop 65

Ruhnu, smaller than Kihnu at just 11 sq km and harder to reach, is 100km southwest of Pärnu and nearer to Latvia than the Estonian mainland. For several centuries Ruhnu had a mainly Swedish population of about 300, but they all fled in August 1944, abandoning homes and livestock, to avoid the advancing Red Army. Ruhnu has some sandy beaches, but the highlight is a very impressive **wooden church** (dating back to 1644), making it the oldest surviving wooden structure in Estonia. It has a wooden altar and pulpit dating from 1755 in its atmospheric interior. The island is flat but there's a forest of 200- to 300-year-old pines on its eastern dunes.

If you're thinking about visiting, the website www.ruhnu.ee has plenty of useful information, including links to the summertime ferry timetable (from Roomassaare on Saaremaa) – there are a handful of services weekly; contact **SLK Ferries** (Saaremaa Laevakompanii; ☎ 452 4444; www.laevakompanii.ee) for details. In the cooler months (October to April), a light aircraft does a triangular run connecting Pärnu, Ruhnu and Kuressaare on Saaremaa – call ☎ 447 5001 for more information, or go to www.ruhnulend.ee and click on Liinigraafik for the schedule, in Estonian but easy enough to make sense of if you know the days of the week (see p421).

VILJANDI

pop 20,300

One of Estonia's most charming towns, Viljandi overlooks a picturesque valley with the lovely Lake Viljandi at its centre. The town is relaxed and peaceful, with some evocative castle ruins, historic buildings and abundant surrounding greenery. It makes a good base for exploring the natural wonders of Soomaa National Park, or for just unwinding in a pretty country town. If you visit in late July, make sure your accommodation is sorted – the four-day Viljandi Folk Music Festival is the biggest music festival in Estonia.

The Knights of the Sword founded a castle at Viljandi in the 13th century. The town around it later joined the Hanseatic League, then was subject to the usual comings and goings of Swedes, Poles and Russians. Today its tiny centre, with an eclectic mix of 19th-century architecture, makes for lovely strolls, and it's easy to feel like you've stepped back in time.

Orientation & Information

The centre of town is about 500m back from Lake Viljandi, with steps leading down to the shoreline. The central square is Keskväljak, where Tartu meets Lossi. Lossi leads south to the castle park. The bus station is on Tallinna, 500m north of the centre, past the **main post office** (Tallinna 22; 8am-6pm Mon-Fri, 8am-3pm Sat); the train station is 2km west of the centre along Vaksali.

The **tourist office** (433 0442; www.viljandi.ee; Vabaduse plats 6; 9am-6pm Mon-Fri, 10am-3pm Sat & Sun mid-May–mid-Sep, 10am-5pm Mon-Fri, 10am-2pm Sat mid-Sep–mid-May) is one of Estonia's finest, with local maps and information in loads of languages (catering to the huge festival crowd); it also has information on Soomaa National Park. For free internet access, head to the **library** (Tallinna 11; 10am-8pm Mon-Fri, 9am-4pm Sat).

Sights & Activities

A highlight is visiting **Castle Park** (Lossimäed), a lush area containing the ruins of the 13th-century **Viljandi Order castle**, founded by the German Knights of the Sword and open for all to muck about in. The park sprawls out

from behind the tourist office, and has sweeping views over the primeval valley and the lake directly below. Also in the park are the medieval **St John's Church** (Jaani Kirik) and a **suspension footbridge** built in 1931. The ravines surrounding the castle ruins are what remain of the castle moat; trenches from WWII came later. A small cemetery to the rear of the castle area is the final resting place of the Germans killed in the fighting.

Close to the park is the excellent **Kondase Keskus** (433 3968; www.kondase.ee; Pikk 8; adult/concession 15/5Kr; 10am-5pm Wed-Sun), housing vibrantly colourful works by local painter Paul Kondas and other self-taught artists working outside the mainstream. It's the country's only gallery dedicated to native art.

The old part of town is lined with brick streets and handsome wooden buildings with finely wrought details. Facing the old market square stands the modest two-storey **Viljandi Museum** (433 3316; Laidoneri plats 10; adult/concession 20/10Kr; 10am-5pm Wed-Sun), which has displays tracing Viljandi's history from the Stone Age to the mid-20th century. There are folk costumes, black-and-white photos of the city, and a mock-up of what the original castle probably looked like. Nearby, the **old water tower** (Vana Veetorn; Kauba; adult/concession 10/5Kr; 11am-6pm May-Sep) offers fine views over the countryside.

The **lake** (Viljandi järv) is a lovely place for a swim on warm summer days. There's a pleasant cafe near the water and a swim platform just offshore, while you can rent boats from a shack by the water. Access the steps to the lake by heading east along Kauba.

From June to August a bargain-priced one-hour guided **walking tour** (20Kr) of the town departs from outside the tourist office. Tickets and information are from the tourist office; commentary is in English and Estonian.

Festivals & Events

Viljandi's festivals happen in summer; June's **Hanseatic Days** celebrates the town's past, while the **Old Music Festival** (mid-July) is staged in and around the 15th-century St John's Church. Easily the biggest event on the calendar is the hugely popular, four-day **Viljandi Folk Music Festival** (www.folk.ee/festival) in late July and renowned for its friendly relaxed vibe and impressive international line-up. It's the country's biggest music festival and sees Viljandi's population double in size, with over 20,000 attendees. Check the website or visit

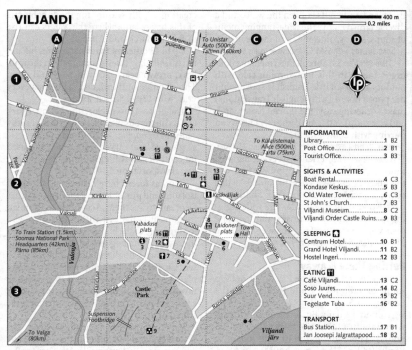

VILJANDI

0 ———— 400 m
0 ———— 0.2 miles

the tourist office for venue and ticket details; there are festival and day passes, or tickets to individual performances.

Sleeping

Hostel Ingeri (☎ 433 4414; www.hostelingeri.ee; Pikk 2c; s 350Kr, d 500-600Kr) On one of Viljandi's loveliest streets, this small six-room guesthouse offers seriously good value with its bright, comfortable rooms, all with TV and bathroom. Plant-life and a kitchen for guest use make it a good home-from-home, while the park-side location couldn't be better.

Külalistemaja Alice (☎ 434 7616; www.matti.ee /~alice; Jakobsoni 55; s 400Kr, d 600-700Kr; 🖳) In a peaceful neighbourhood 10 minutes' walk east of the centre, this small, friendly guesthouse is another excellent choice, with its bright, neat rooms all featuring bathroom and TV. Guests can use the kitchen, and there's wi-fi and a large garden. Breakfast included.

Centrum Hotel (☎ 435 1100; www.centrum.ee; Tallinna 24; s/d 780/980Kr) On the 3rd floor above a supermarket (close to the bus station) and geared to businessfolk, Centrum has spacious rooms that have recently benefited from a lick of paint and new curtains and bedcovers. There's a sauna and a restaurant on-site. It's a decent, albeit uninspiring, choice.

Grand Hotel Viljandi (☎ 435 5800; www.ghv.ee; Tartu 11; s/d/ste 1100/1400/2600Kr) The town's most chichi choice, in the heart of the old-town area, has art deco–styled rooms with dark-wood trim, satiny chairs, large windows and wildly patterned carpets. There's a pleasant summertime cafe in front, as well as a smart à la carte restaurant. Look for the sign for 'EVE', the name of the 1938 building housing the hotel.

Eating & Drinking

Café Viljandi (☎ 433 3021; Lossi 31; mains 40-125Kr; 🕑 8am-9pm Mon-Fri, 9am-9pm Sat & Sun) This cosy cafe has lots of old-world charm; the full menu offers basic meals, or you can come for coffee and pastries (seductively displayed in the front counter). The weekday lunchtime dish of the day is a bargain 37Kr.

Tegelaste Tuba (☎ 433 3944; Pikk 2b; mains 45-80Kr; 🕑 11am-midnight Sun-Thu, 11am-2am Fri & Sat) The terrace overlooking the park is the big drawcard of this tavern-style restaurant – as are the comfy interiors on cold, rainy days.

Estonian handicrafts enliven the walls, and a diverse crowd enjoys the wide-ranging menu of soups, salads, omelettes and meaty mains.

Soso Juures (☎ 5566 5295; Posti 6; mains 50-125Kr; ☒ 11am-9pm Mon-Sat) Succulent Armenian cooking is found in this unassuming cafe with outdoor terrace. Little English is spoken, but the photo board (with English translations) makes ordering easy; the *harcho* (spicy lamb and rice soup) and lamb dishes will have you purring with contentment.

Suur Vend (☎ 433 3644; Turu 4; mains 70-190Kr; ☒ noon-10pm or later) Friendly service, big portions, a pool table and boppy music from the jukebox create a cheerful mood at this cosy pub, with an outdoor deck and lots of dark-wood ambience inside. The wide-ranging menu offers few surprises, and there are plenty of snacks perfect for beer-drinking ('beer sandwich', anyone?).

Getting There & Away

Viljandi is 90km east of Pärnu, or 160km south of Tallinn en route to Valga on the Latvian border.

Around 12 daily buses connect Viljandi with Tallinn (140Kr to 150Kr, two to 2½ hours). There are about 10 daily buses to Pärnu (90Kr, 1½ to two hours), up to 16 to Tartu (70Kr to 85Kr, 1½ hours), seven to Valga (75Kr, 1¾ hours) and three to Kuressaare, Saaremaa (250Kr, 4¾ to five hours). The **bus station** (Tallinna) is 500m north of the centre; for bus schedules, call ☎ 433 3680.

The **train station** (Vaksali 44) is 2km west of the centre. Two to three trains run daily to/from Tallinn (85Kr to 95Kr, 2½ hours); for train schedules, call ☎ 434 9425.

Unistar Auto (☎ 435 5921; unistar@unistar-auto.ee; Tallinna 86) has cars for rent from around 600Kr a day (cheaper for longer hires) – a convenient way to reach Soomaa National Park. Hire bikes from **Jan Joosepi Jalgrattapood** (☎ 434 5757; Turu 6; per day 150Kr).

SOOMAA NATIONAL PARK

Embracing Estonia's largest area of swamps, flat meadows and waterside forests, Soomaa National Park (Soomaa: literally 'land of wetlands') is primarily made up of four bogs (no laughing!) – Valgeraba, Öördi, Kikepera and Kuresoo – the peat layer of which measures 7m in places. The bogs are split by tributaries of the Pärnu River, the spring flooding creating a 'fifth season' for the inhabitants of this boggy land, where the waters can rise to 5m in March and April.

Up to 43 different mammal species inhabit the surrounding forests, among them the wolf, lynx, brown bear, elk, wild boar and otter. Thousands of birds migrate to Soomaa every year, with 180 observed species.

The best way to explore the national park and its numerous meandering waterways is by canoe or by *haabja*, a traditional Finno-Ugric single-tree boat carved from aspen and used for centuries for fishing, hunting, hauling hay and transportation.

Bogs, as forest, have historically provided isolation and protection to Estonians. Witches were said to live there. According to Estonian folklore, it is the evil will-o'-the-wisp who leads people to the bog, where they are forced to stay until the bog gas catches fire, driving the grotesque bog inhabitants out for all to see. Closer to reality, bogs were also hiding places for partisans escaping from outside invaders who couldn't penetrate the bogs as easily as forests (probably because they were scared of the witches).

Park information is available from the **Soomaa National Park visitor centre** (☎ 435 7164; www.soomaa.ee; ☒ 10am-6pm May-Sep, 10am-4pm Oct-Apr) in Kõrtsi-Tõramaal. It distributes hiking maps and can arrange accommodation and guide service (best to contact the centre in advance). There's free, basic camping at the centre, plus the worthwhile 2km Beaver Trail starts here and leads past beavers' dams. Other walking trails in the park get you acquainted with forest, bog or wooded meadow, ranging from 4km to a two-night 30km trail.

The best way to get up close and personal with the park is with **Soomaa.com** (☎ 506 1896; www.soomaa.com), a local company promoting ecotourism and sustainable development within Soomaa, working in cooperation with local accommodation and service providers. The company has a fabulous range of activities on offer year-round (with transfers available from Pärnu). The 'Discover Soomaa National Park' day trip includes walking on peat bog and river-canoeing (782Kr from Soomaa, 1095Kr from Pärnu; runs from May to September). There are also guided and self-guided canoe trips, beaver-watching by canoe, bog-shoeing and mushroom-picking experiences, and in winter, kick-sledding, cross-country skiing and snowshoe excursions. For independent adventures, you can rent gear such as tents and sleeping bags, as well as canoes. Accommodation in an old farmhouse can be arranged (from 156Kr per night), as can the rental of our favourite Soomaa treat, the floating sauna atop the Raudna River. A maximum of 15 people can steam up here, and it costs 1050Kr to hire it for the afternoon, or 2080Kr for an evening. For more traditional experiences, you can rent a smoke sauna, or learn to build a traditional *haabjas*. You'll need to contact Soomaa.com in advance to arrange your itinerary; check the website for all the options.

There is no public transport to Soomaa National Park, but by car the visitor centre is 22km west of the village of Kõpu, itself 20km west of Viljandi. Before you set off, call into the Viljandi tourist office (p136) to pick up maps and brochures.

WESTERN ESTONIA & THE ISLANDS

One of the Baltic's most alluring regions, the west coast of Estonia is the gateway to forest-covered islands, idyllic countryside, and seaside villages slumbering beneath the shadows of picturesque medieval castles.

Pine forests and juniper groves cover Saaremaa and Hiiumaa, Estonia's largest islands. Dusty roads loop around them, passing desolate stretches of coastline, with few signs of development aside from 19th-century lighthouses and old wooden windmills – both iconic symbols of the islands. Here you'll find peaceful settings for hiking, horse riding or simply rambling through the countryside in search of hidden stone churches and crumbling fortresses – ruins left behind by both 14th-century German knights and 20th-century Soviet military planners.

Saaremaa, the largest and most visited of the islands, boasts spa resorts, a magnificent castle and a pretty 'capital' that comes to life during the summer months. It's also the departure point for the wildlife-rich islands in Vilsandi National Park. Vormsi is another peaceful island of tiny villages and pristine coastline, as is Muhu.

On the mainland, Haapsalu is an enchanting but ragged town that was once a resort for 19th-century Russian aristocrats. The jewel of its Old Town is a 14th-century bishop's castle, today the setting for open-air festivals and summer concerts.

The birdlife in this region is the best in the country. Birdwatchers should head to the Matsalu National Park, where some 280 bird species can be found.

HAAPSALU
pop 12,000
Set on a fork-shaped peninsula that stretches into Haapsalu Bay, this quaint, peaceful resort town (100km from Tallinn) makes a fine stopover en route to the islands. Haapsalu has a handful of museums and galleries, and a few rather modest spa hotels, but the town's biggest attraction is its striking castle. A bit rough around the edges, Haapsalu's Old Town is more rustic than urban, with old wooden houses set back from the narrow streets, a slender promenade skirting the bay, and plenty of secret spots for watching the sunset.

Those seeking mud or spa treatments might opt for Haapsalu over Pärnu or Kuressaare, though the centres here are a bit more proletarian. Nevertheless, Haapsalu lays claim to superior mud, which is used by health centres throughout Estonia.

Additional appeal? Haapsalu makes a good base for visiting Vormsi island or Matsalu National Park.

History
Like other Estonian towns, Haapsalu has changed hands many times since its founding centuries ago. The German Knights of the Sword conquered this region in 1224, and Haapsalu became the bishop's residence, with a fortress and cathedral built soon afterwards. The Danes took control during the Livonian War (around 1559), then the Swedish had their turn in the 17th century, but they lost it to the Russians during the Great (but brutal) Northern War in the 18th century.

The city flourished under the tsars, mostly because of mud. Once the curative properties of its shoreline were discovered in the 19th century, Haapsalu transformed into a spa centre. The Russian composer Tchaikovsky and members of the Russian imperial family visited the city for mud baths. A railway that went all the way to St Petersburg was completed in 1907 with a 214m-long covered platform, then said to be the longest in the Russian empire. Visitors can still admire the colourfully designed station with its wooden lace ornamentation and grand colonnade, though now only buses run from this station.

Orientation

The castle, which is the centre of Old Town, is just over 1km northeast of the bus station. About halfway between the two is the tour-ist office. Väike viik, a tranquil lake, is just north of the castle. The nicest beach in town is 1km west of the bus station (on foot; if you're driving it's just under 2km).

Information

Haapsalu tourist office (☎ 473 3248; www.haapsalu .ee; Posti 37; ☒ 9am-6pm Mon-Fri, 10am-3pm Sat & Sun mid-May–mid-Sep, 9am-5pm Mon-Fri mid-Sep–mid-May) This friendly, well-staffed office has loads of info about Haapsalu and the surrounding area.

THE FOREST BROTHERS' RESISTANCE AND THE UNDERGROUND WAR

Today the sleepy marshes and quiet woodlands of Estonia are a haven only for wildlife, but between 1944 and 1956 much of what is now national park and nature reserve was a stronghold of the Metsavennad (or Metsavendlus, Forest Brothers) proindependence movement. The Forest Brothers fiercely resisted the Soviet occupation. Many resorted to an underground existence in the woods and some remained there for years. They knew their terrain well and used this knowledge to their advantage both for their own survival and in the fight to restore the republic.

The Soviets claimed Estonia in the Molotov-Ribbentrop Pact of 1939 and, after the Germans retreated from a difficult three-year occupation, secured this claim by advancing on Tallinn in 1944. The early resistance, believing this latest occupation would not be recognised in accordance with the British-US Atlantic treaty of 1941 (which states that sovereignty and self-governance should be restored when forcibly removed), rallied support for what some thought would be a new war. As international assistance did not eventuate, the independence cause remained Estonia's own.

Resistance action began with isolated attacks on Red Army units that claimed the lives of around 3000 soldiers. Tactical expertise and secure intelligence networks resulted in damaging offensives on Soviet targets. At the height of the resistance there were over 30,000 Forest Brothers and their supporters, which included women, the elderly, young people and a network of 'Urban Brothers'. The impact of resistance activity is found in Soviet records from the time, which detail incidents of sabotage on infrastructure such as railways and roads that hindered early attempts at moulding Estonia into a new Soviet state.

In the years that followed the Metsavennad suffered high casualties, with varied and increasing opposition. The NKVD (Soviet secret police) provided incentives to some of the local population who were able to infiltrate the resistance. The Soviets coordinated mass deportations of those suspected to be sympathetic to the resistance cause and some Metsavennad supporters were coerced into acting against the resistance. By 1947 15,000 resistance fighters had been arrested or killed. The greatest blow to the Metsavennad came in 1949 with the deportation of 20,000 people – mainly women, children and the elderly – many of whom had provided the support base and cover for resistance activities.

The movement continued for some years but was greatly impeded by the strength of the Soviets and loss of local support due to ongoing deportations and the clearing of farmhouses for collectivisation. Some of the Forest Brothers who were not killed or imprisoned escaped to Scandinavia and Canada.

There are many heroes of the Metsavennad; most came to a tragic end. Kalev Arro and Ants Kaljurand (hirmus, or 'Ants the Terrible' to the Soviets) were famous for their deft disguises and the humour and tact with which they persistently eluded the Soviets. It was only in 1980 that the final active Forest Brother, Oskar Lillenurm, was found – shot dead in Lääne county.

Much work has been done to compile a history of the movement by recording accounts of local witnesses. Enemies of the Forest Brothers are still finding themselves in court, while surviving members are regarded as national heroes and are awarded some of the country's highest honours. For more detail on the resistance, a good reference is former Estonian prime minister (and historian) Mart Laar's War in the Woods: Estonia's Struggle for Survival, 1944–1956.

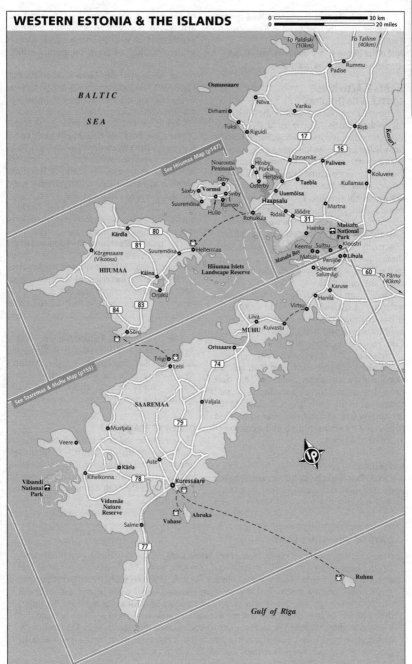

WESTERN ESTONIA & THE ISLANDS

0 ———— 30 km
0 ———— 20 miles

BALTIC

SEA

To Paldiski (10km)
To Tallinn (40km)

Rummu
Padise

Osmussaare

Nõva
Variku

Dirhami

Tuksi
Riguldi
17
Risti

16

Linnamäe
Palivere

See Hiiumaa Map (p147)
Noarootsi
Peninsula
Hõsby
Pürksi
Koluvere

Diby
Herjava
Taebla
Kullamaa

Saxby **Vormsi**
Sviby
Österby
Uuemõisa

Suuremõisa
Rumpo
Haapsalu

Hullo
Martna

Ridala
Jõõdre **31**

Rohuküla
Haeska
Matsalu National Park

Kärdla
80
Keemu Suitsu Kloostri

81
Suuremõisa
Heltermaa
Matsalu **Lihula**

Matsalu Bay
Penijõe

Körgessaare (Vikoosa)
Salevere
Salumägi
60
To Pärnu (40km)

HIIUMAA
Käina
Hiiumaa Islets Landscape Reserve
Karuse

Orjaku
Hanila

84
83
Virtsu

Sõru
Liiva
MUHU Kuivastu

Orissaare

Triigi
Leisi
74

SAAREMAA
Valjala

Mustjala
79

Veere

Aste
Kärla
78
Kuressaare

Vilsandi National Park
Kihelkonna

Vidumäe Nature Reserve
Vahase
Abruka

Salme
77

Ruhnu

Gulf of Rīga

See Saaremaa & Muhu Map (p155)

Library (Posti 3; ☺ 10am-7pm Mon-Fri, 10am-3pm Sat) Free internet access. The town art gallery (Linnagalerii) is next door.

Post office (Nurme 2; ☺ 7.30am-6pm Mon-Fri, 8am-2pm Sat) A block east of the tourist office.

Sights & Activities
CASTLE & CATHEDRAL

Haapsalu's unpolished gem is the 13th-century **Bishop's Castle** (Piiskopilinnus; ☎ 472 5346; www .haapsalulinnus.ee; adult/concession 30/20Kr; ☺ grounds 7am-midnight daily, interiors 10am-6pm Jun-Aug, 10am-4pm May & early–mid-Sep). Today the fortress stands in partial but very picturesque ruins. A turreted tower, most of the outer wall and some of the moat still remain. To find out about the castle's history and see some dramatically displayed cassocks and medieval weaponry, don't miss the **museum** and **Dome Church**. The church is actually a Roman-Gothic cathedral, with three inner domes – the largest such structure in the Baltic – and its acoustics are phenomenal. The cathedral was not strictly Roman Catholic from the start, due to the lukewarm welcome Christianity received in these parts. It was assimilated into the Episcopal stronghold in the second half of the 13th century. Concerts are regularly held here. Inside the church keep your eyes peeled for the ghost of the White Lady (see the boxed text, below). For fine views, you can climb the 38m **clock tower**. In summer there's a medieval-themed restaurant in the castle grounds. Entry to the grounds is free and possible year-round, but to visit the museum, church and clock tower you'll need a ticket.

MUSEUMS

The **Evald Okas Museum** (☎ 508 9105; www.evaldokase muusem.ee; Karja 24; adult/concession 20/10Kr; ☺ noon-6pm Jun-Aug) features the colourful works of one of Haapsalu's oldest and best-known local artists. His portraits are excellent, while his preoccupation with the nude female form is evident on the 2nd floor. Temporary exhibitions are also staged.

The somewhat dry **Lääne Regional Museum** (☎ 473 7665; Kooli 2; adult/concession 25/10Kr; ☺ 10am-6pm Wed-Sun mid-May–mid-Sep, 11am-4pm Wed-Sun mid-Sep–mid-May) offers a glimpse of the region's history. It's set in an 18th-century building that was at one time the town hall. Much more fun is the nearby **Ilon's Wonderland** (Iloni Imedemaa; ☎ 473 7065; Kooli 5; adult/concession 25/10Kr; ☺ 11am-6pm Wed-Sun), which showcases the works of Estonian-Swedish illustrator Ilon Wikland, who spent her childhood in Haapsalu. She is best known for her illustrations of Pippi Longstocking books. The gallery is fabulously set up for kids, with many artworks hung at kid levels.

The quaint **Museum of the Estonian Swedes** (Rannarootsi Muuseum; ☎ 473 7165; Sadama 32; adult/concession 20/10Kr; ☺ 10am-6pm Tue-Sat May-Aug, 11am-4pm Tue-Sat Sep-Apr) has relics, photos, old fishing nets and a marvellous tapestry tracing the history of Swedes in Estonia from the 1200s to their flight back to Sweden on the *Triina* in 1944.

The boxcar-sized **Railway Museum** (Raudteemuuseum; ☎ 473 4574; Raudtee 2; adult/concession 25/10Kr; ☺ 10am-6pm Wed-Sun) on the station's west side records the golden years of train travel. You're free to check out the old locomotives nearby.

OTHER ATTRACTIONS

The streets in the area around the castle are the hub of the historic centre – an idyllic setting for a stroll past old wooden houses along leafy streets. Between Kooli and Jaani, east off Lossi plats, is the 16th-century **St John's Church** (Jaani Kirik).

DAYS OF THE WHITE LADY

Haapsalu's biggest annual event, **Days of the White Lady**, coincides with the August full moon. The day begins with merriment – storytelling for the kids, theatre for the adults – and culminates with a ghastly apparition. During the full moon every August and February, moonlight at a precise angle casts a ghostly shadow across a cathedral window. According to legend, the shadow is cast by a young girl who in the 14th century was bricked up alive inside the walls. Back then, the castle was an all-male enclave, and the archbishop got pretty worked up when he heard that a young woman, disguised in monastic vestments, sneaked in to be close to her lover-monk. In August excited young crowds stay out late to see a play recounting the story in the castle grounds, after which everyone gathers around the wall to await the shadow.

Just north of the church is a **birdwatching tower** that you can climb and a small park overlooking the pint-sized **Africa Beach** (Aafrikarand), which earned its name from the statues of wild animals that used to grace the shoreline (and which were sadly used as firewood by Soviet soldiers in the 1940s). The **promenade** begins here and passes by the magnificent pale-green-and-white **Haapsalu Kuursaal** (Spa Hall), which functions as a restaurant in summer (see p145). Sculptures dating from Haapsalu's fashionable era are scattered along the promenade, including a sundial commemorating mud-cure pioneer Dr Carl Abraham Hunnius and the symphony-playing **Tchaikovsky Bench**, erected in 1940.

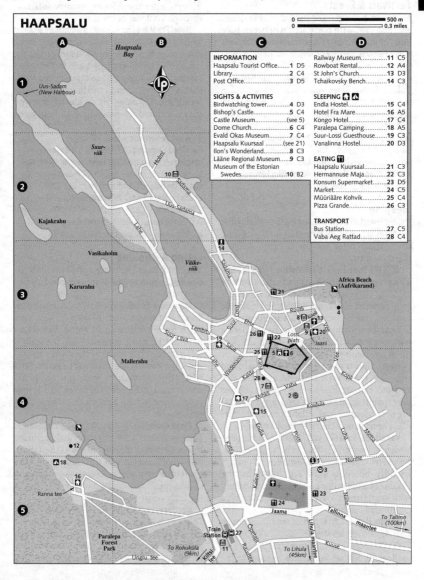

HAAPSALU

0 — 500 m
0 — 0.3 miles

INFORMATION
Haapsalu Tourist Office.......1 D5
Library...................2 C4
Post Office.................3 D5

SIGHTS & ACTIVITIES
Birdwatching tower............4 D3
Bishop's Castle................5 C4
Castle Museum..............(see 5)
Dome Church.................6 C4
Evald Okas Museum..........7 C4
Haapsalu Kuursaal ....(see 21)
Ilon's Wonderland..............8 C3
Lääne Regional Museum....9 C3
Museum of the Estonian
    Swedes...................10 B2

Railway Museum..............11 C5
Rowboat Rental..............12 A4
St John's Church.............13 D3
Tchaikovsky Bench..........14 C3

SLEEPING
Endla Hostel.................15 C4
Hotel Fra Mare................16 A5
Kongo Hotel..................17 C4
Paralepa Camping............18 A5
Suur-Lossi Guesthouse......19 C3
Vanalinna Hostel.............20 D3

EATING
Haapsalu Kuursaal..........21 C3
Hermannuse Maja...........22 C3
Konsum Supermarket........23 D5
Market......................24 C5
Müüriääre Kohvik............25 C4
Pizza Grande................26 C3

TRANSPORT
Bus Station..................27 C5
Vaba Aeg Rattad..............28 C4

On the western edge of town, beyond the train station, is the **Paralepa Forest Park** with a serene beachfront. It attracts plenty of sunseekers in the summer, with **rowboat rental** (per hr 100Kr; ☺ 10am-8pm) nearby. The spa treatments of Hotel Fra Mare (right) are open to nonguests.

Festivals & Events

Haapsalu has a packed calendar of concerts and festivals, with party action between June and August. Among the attractions is the **Early Music Festival** (www.concertogrosso.ee), held in early July and making full use of the magnificent acoustics of the Dome Church at the Bishop's Palace. **August Blues** (Augustibluus; www.augustibluus.ee), over two days in early August, is Estonia's biggest blues festival. The biggest annual event is **Days of the White Lady** (Valge Daami Päevad); see the boxed text, p142, for more information. And finally, don't be deterred from a wintertime visit – coincide it with the creepy, kooky **Haapsalu Horror & Fantasy Film Festival** (www.hoff.ee), held in late March.

Sleeping

Prices listed are for the summer period (June to August); all but Suur-Lossi Guesthouse drop their rates by up to 25% outside these months.

our pick **Suur-Lossi Guesthouse** (☎ 510 7011; www.suurlossi.net; Suur-Lossi 6; s/d with shared bathroom 350/500Kr) There's loads of history in this rustically restored old home, full of quirky, artistic touches and blessed with a superb garden. Downstairs, a single and twin room share a bathroom; upstairs is a large room sleeping up to five (with private bathroom; 200Kr per person). Guests share a lovely living space and sunroom; breakfast is available, as is massage, and you can arrange a variety of art courses here (painting, drawing, ceramics, glass painting or blacksmithing). A fabulous, character-filled option, and cheap to boot.

Vanalinna Hostel (☎ 473 4900; www.vanalinna bowling.ee; Janni 4; d/tr with shared bathroom 495/700Kr, d/tr with private bathroom 650/800Kr) Above a family-friendly bowling alley and right by the Bishop's Castle is this good-value new option, with neat, trim, TV-free rooms on offer, plus communal kitchen.

Kongo Hotel (☎ 472 4800; www.kongohotel.ee; Kalda 19; s/d/apt Sep-May 850/1000/1200Kr, Jun-Aug 1100/1300/1550Kr) The unassuming exterior and the legend behind the hotel's name give little indication of Kongo's stylish, Scandi-chic decor, all caramel-coloured walls, neutral linens and pale wooden floors. Rooms are on the small side – the double apartments, with kitchenette, are a good choice for claustrophobes. And the name? A rough drinking den once stood on this spot, and was known for its brawling. The place was nicknamed 'Kongo' after the African country suffering through civil war at the time.

Hotel Fra Mare (☎ 472 4600; www.framare.ee; Ranna tee 2; s/d from 1100/1500Kr) Haapsalu's biggest spa hotel has a beachside location away from the town (bike rental available) and facilities laid on thick, including a huge range of spa treatments (go for the mud treatments for a local indulgence). Rooms are lacklustre, but you may not spend too much time in them given all the activities and services on offer.

Also recommended:

Paralepa Camping (☎ 5564 1674; info@paralepa camping.ee; Ranna tee 4; dm 160Kr, caravan 160Kr, sites per person 50Kr; ☺ Jun-Aug) No-frills summertime option on the beach. No kitchen; showers cost 20Kr.

Endla Hostel (☎ 473 7999; www.endlahostel.ee; Endla 5; tw/tr/q with shared bathroom 450/630/800Kr; ☺ Apr-Oct) Decent budget option on a quiet street, with small, bright quarters and a guest kitchen. No dorms.

Eating & Drinking

The hotel restaurants aren't bad options; the beachside one at Fra Mare is a good choice on a sunny day.

Müüriääre Kohvik (☎ 473 7527; www.muuriaare.ee; Karja 7; light meals & snacks 35-100Kr; ☺ 10am-10pm) With more umlauts in its name than seems natural (the name means 'beside the walls'), this gorgeous cafe is clearly the town's favourite, if the crowds are anything to go by. And what's not to love in the warm interior, pretty rear terrace, cabinet full of cakes, and simple menu of fresh, tasty light meals such as salads and quiche.

Pizza Grande (☎ 473 7200; www.pizzagrande.ee; Karja 6; small pizzas 39-69Kr; ☺ 11am-11pm) Featuring the same crowd-pleasing menu as the Tallinn branch of Pizza Grande, this casual spot offers a raft of decent, well-priced pizzas, pastas and salads, preferably enjoyed on a mild night in the leafy courtyard out back.

Hermannuse Maja (☎ 473 7199; www.hermannus.ee; Karja 1a; meals 50-280Kr; ☺ 11am-11pm Sun-Thu, 11am-2am Fri & Sat) With eclectic furnishings and a warm and inviting atmosphere, this pub-cafe serves hearty meals, though it's a cosy spot just for a drink. The traditional menu runs the gamut from herring salad to grilled lamb.

ourpick Haapsalu Kuursaal (☎ 473 5587; www.haap salukuursaal.ee; Promenaadi 1; mains 125-160Kr; ☼ 11am-midnight May-Aug) This fairy-tale confection sits plumb on the waterfront, surrounded by rose gardens. The restaurant inside is staffed by students from the local vocational college, and the menu is one of the best we've seen in Estonia. Creative, complex dishes (eg tomato and orange soup with vegetable ravioli; filet mignon with chanterelle quiche and caramelised carrot chips) are carefully prepared and presented with panache. And at astoundingly reasonable prices too (pasta and risotto dishes cost a bargain 50Kr to 65Kr). It's a brilliant package, with a top-quality meal costing a fraction of what it would cost in Tallinn. Cultural events are also staged here.

For fresh fruits and vegetables visit the **market** (turg; Jaama; ☼ 7am-2pm Tue-Sun), a few blocks east of the bus station. Don't miss fresh strawberries in summer. There's **Konsum supermarket** (cnr Tallinna mnt & Posti; ☼ 9am-10pm) at the southern end of town.

Getting There & Away

The **bus station** (☎ 473 4791; Jaama 1) is inside the pretty but defunct train station. Around 18 daily buses connect Haapsalu and Tallinn (85Kr to 105Kr, two hours). There's also one daily bus to/from Tartu (180Kr, 4½ hours), and two daily buses to Kärdla, Hiiumaa (2½ to three hours). Unfortunately, the fastest way to reach Pärnu, Virtsu or Kuressaare, Saaremaa, is to go to Tallinn first.

Ferries to Hiiumaa and Vormsi leave from Rohuküla, 9km west of Haapsalu. See p148 and right for ferry details.

Getting Around

You can rent bicycles at **Vaba Aeg Rattad** (☎ 521 2796; Karja 22; bikes per hr/day 30/175Kr). Bus 1 runs almost hourly between Lossi plats, the train station and Rohuküla (the ferry terminal); timetables are posted at Lossi plats and the bus station. For taxi service, call **EsraTaxi** (☎ 473 4555).

VORMSI

pop 340

Vormsi, Estonia's fourth-biggest island (93 sq km), lies covered in pine and spruce forests and juniper shrubs, mixed with coastal pastures and wooded meadows. It has re-

mained largely undisturbed owing to sparse human settlements, largely Swedes until 1944. Information about the wildlife and landscape, including the 30 protected islets in Hullo Bay, is available through **Vormsi Landscape Reserve** (☎ 472 9430; http://vormsi.silma.ee; Rumpo Village).

The island, 16km from east to west and averaging 6km from north to south, is a good place to tour by bicycle; there is about 10km of paved road. The cheerfully named **Hullo**, Vormsi's largest village, lies about 3km west of Sviby. A further 7km by paved and dirt road will bring you to Saxby, the westernmost village, where it's a short walk to a **lighthouse**. Rumpo is due south of the stretch between Sviby and Hullo.

Other highlights include the **14th-century church** at Hullo, which has a fine baroque pulpit and a collection of old Swedish-style, wheel-shaped crosses in the graveyard; the southern **Rumpo Peninsula**, dotted with juniper stands; and the 5.8m-high boulder, **Church Rock** (Kirikukivi), near Diby in the northeast.

Sleeping

You can find more options online (www .vormsi.ee) or at the tourist office in Haapsalu. Both places listed here rent out bicycles and boats, have saunas, and include breakfast in the price.

Rumpo Mäe Talu (☎ 472 9932; www.hot.ee/streng; sites per person 45Kr, d 680Kr; ☼ Apr-Nov) Near Rumpo, and just a few steps from the coast, this handsome thatched-roof farmhouse offers Vormsi's best accommodation. Rooms in the main house have an authentic, old-style feel, and guests have access to kitchen and grill.

Elle-Malle Külalistemaja (☎ 473 2072; www.vormsi .ee/ellemall, in Estonian; r per person from 275Kr) Another good option is this cosy spot in Hullo. There's a romantic double room inside a windmill or rooms inside a separate wooden cottage.

Getting There & Around

Vormsi lies 3km off the Noarootsi Peninsula. Ferries make the 10km-crossing to Sviby on Vormsi's south coast from Rohuküla, 9km west of Haapsalu. **Veeteed** (☎ 443 1069; www .veeteed.com) runs a ferry (adult/concession/car 40/20/100Kr, 45 minutes) between Rohuküla and Sviby two to three times daily. If you're taking a vehicle in the summer, reserve a place in advance.

Haapsalu town bus 1 runs regularly (eight times daily) to Rohuküla from Lossi plats and the bus station, where timetables are posted. All the Vormsi ferries wait for this bus except on Sunday morning. There are also daily buses to/from Tallinn.

On the island, bike and boat rental can be arranged through **Sviby Bike & Boat Rental** (☎ 517 8722; www.vormsi.ee/sviby; ☼ May-Sep), in Sviby. It can also arrange guided cycling tours and speedboat tours around the island. Accommodation providers generally offer these services too.

MATSALU NATIONAL PARK

A twitcher's paradise about 30km south of Haapsalu, Matsalu National Park (Matsalu Rahvuspark) is a prime bird-migration and breeding ground, both in the Baltic and in Europe. Some 280 different bird species have been counted here. The reserve was founded in 1957 and was renamed a national park in 2004; it encompasses Matsalu Bay, which is over 20km long and is also the deepest inlet along the west Estonian coast.

Spring migration peaks in April/May, but some species arrive as early as March. Autumn migration begins in July and can last until November.

Birdwatching towers, with extensive views of resting sites over various terrain, have been built at Penijõe, Kloostri, Haeska, Suitsu and Keemu. There are two marked **nature trails**, one at Penijõe (5km), another at Salevere Salumägi (1.5km). Bring reliable footwear, as the ground is wet and muddy. The reserve's headquarters is 3km north of the Tallinn–Virtsu road at Penijõe, near Lihula. There you'll find a small **nature centre** (☎ 472 4236; ☼ 8am-5pm Wed, Thu, Sat & Sun, 8am-3.45pm Fri) and a permanent exhibition with slide show. The centre can hook you up with guides offering tours of the reserve, from two-hour canoe trips around the reed banks to several days of birdwatching. It can also recommend lodging in the area. It's best to contact the centre in advance. If you're planning an extensive birdwatching trip, consider contacting **Estonian Nature Tours** (☎ 477 8214; www.naturetours.ee), based in nearby Lihula, before you head out. This outfit employs naturalist guides who have a wealth of knowledge on Matsalu's avian riches.

HIIUMAA
pop 11,100

Hiiumaa, Estonia's second-biggest island, is a peaceful and sparsely populated place with some delightful stretches of coastline and a forest-covered interior. Though there's plenty to do on the island, most visitors come here to breathe in the fresh sea air and simply relax amid pastoral splendour. The island is less developed than Saaremaa, with considerably fewer options for lodging and dining – most places to stay are small guesthouses, holiday homes or tourist farms.

Scattered about Hiiumaa you'll find picturesque lighthouses, eerie old Soviet bunkers, empty beaches and a nature reserve with over 100 different bird species. Those seeking a bit more activity can hike, horse ride or indulge in a raft of watersports. Get great information about the island from http://turism.moonsund.ee, or www.hii umaa.ee.

Given their relative isolation from mainland Estonia, it's not surprising that the islanders have a unique take on things, and a rich folklore full of legendary heroes, such as Leiger, who had nothing to do with Kalevipoeg (the hero over on the mainland). People who move onto the island must carry the name *isehakanud hiidlane* (would-be islanders) for 10 years before being considered true residents. Hiiumaa is also said to be a haven for fairies and elves, ancestors of those born on the island. Modern-day Hiiumites rarely discuss this unique aspect of their family tree, however, as this can anger their elusive relatives.

Hiiumaa (1000 sq km) is not quite visible from the mainland, 22km away.

GETTING THERE & AWAY
If you don't want to waste time, you can fly directly from Tallinn to Kärdla. A passenger and vehicle ferry runs between Rohuküla on the mainland (south of Haapsalu) and Heltermaa at Hiiumaa's eastern end. Buses from Tallinn via Haapsalu run all the way to Hiiumaa; the ferry crossing is included in the trip. Other buses will drop you off or pick you up at either ferry terminal. It's also common to hitch or ask for lifts off the ferries at either end. A ferry also connects Hiiumaa and Saaremaa, just 5.5km away.

Air
Avies Air (☎ 605 8002; www.avies.ee) flies once or twice daily between Tallinn and Kärdla (adult/child under 12 one way 300/180Kr, 30 minutes).

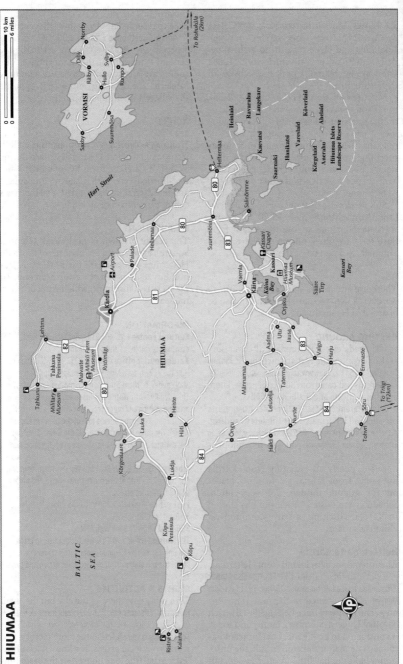

HIIUMAA

VORMSI

Norrby
Diby
Rälby
Hullo
Sviby
Rumpo
Saxby
Suuremõisa

Hari Strait

To Rohuküla (2km)

Heltermaa

80

Heinlaid
Ravarahu
Langekare

Kaevatsi
Hanikatsi
Saarnaki
Varelaid
Köverlaid
Ahelaid

Kõrgelaid
Aneraha
Hiiumaa Islets
Landscape Reserve

Salinõmme

80

Heltermaa

Heltermaa

80

Hellamaa

83

Suuremõisa

Kassari Chapel
Kassari
Hiiumaa Museum

Kassari Bay

Palade
Airport
Kärdla

Vaemla

Käina
Käina Bay
Orjaku
Siiare Tirp

81

Lehtma

Tahkuna Peninsula
Malvaste
Mihkli Farm Museum
Ristimägi

Aadma
Utu
Jausa

83

Valgu
Hagju

Emmaste

Tahkuna
Military Museum

82

80

HIIUMAA

Mänmaa
Taterma
Leluselja
Nurste

84

Sõru
To Triigi (12km)

Tohvri

Heiste
Lauka
Hüti
Õngu
Haldi

Kõrgessaare

Luidja

Köpu Peninsula
Köpu

84

BALTIC SEA

Ristna
Kalana

0 ____ 10 km
0 ____ 6 miles

Boat

SLK Ferries (Saaremaa Laevakompanii; ☎ 452 4444; www.laevakompanii.ee) runs ferries between Rohuküla and Heltermaa up to eight times daily (adult/concession/vehicle 40/22/120Kr one way, 1½ hours). Check the website for departure times.

Most people don't bother calling ahead, but if you're taking a car and you want to be on the safe side, book ahead – this is a good idea if you're travelling at popular times (ie onto the island on Friday evening or Saturday morning; to the mainland on Sunday afternoon). You'll need your vehicle registration. You can purchase tickets at either port, online or by phone.

SLK Ferries also operates a year-round ferry (adult/concession/vehicle 35/20/100Kr one way, one hour) one to four times daily from Sõru ferry terminal, on the southern tip of Hiiumaa, to Triigi on Saaremaa.

Bus

There are two buses daily from Tallinn to Kärdla (185Kr, 4½ hours), which can also be boarded in Haapsalu and Rohuküla.

GETTING AROUND

Paved roads circle Hiiumaa and cover several side routes; the rest are dirt roads. **Jaanus Jesmin** (☎ 511 2225; www.carrent.hiiumaa.ee; Põllu 2a, Kärdla) rents out cars from 300Kr per day. There are fuel stations at Kärdla and Käina.

Jalgrattarent (☎ 5660 6377; per day 100Kr) rents bicycles in Heltermaa, near the ferry landing. At the **Priiankru pub** (☎ 5344 4759; www.rollu.ee, in Estonian; Sadama 13, Kärdla) you can rent mopeds for 450Kr per day.

Buses, nearly all radiating from Kärdla but some from Käina, get to most places on the island, though not very often. Schedules are posted inside the bus station in Kärdla. Hitching is fairly common on Hiiumaa's roads.

Heltermaa to Kärdla

At Suuremõisa, 6km inland from Heltermaa, you can visit the chateau-like **Suuremõisa Manor** (Suuremõisa loss; adult/concession 15/7Kr; ☒ 10am-6pm Mon-Sat Jul-Aug), created in the mid-18th century. The property once belonged to the rich baronial Ungern-Sternberg family and today is considered to be the most magnificent baroque-style manor in Estonia. Still, the unrestored building has little to offer inside, but

the grounds are nice for a stroll. The nearby **Pühalepa Church** dates from the 13th century.

Allika Guesthouse (☎ 462 9026; www.allika.com; Suuremõisa; s/d/tr 500/700/800Kr) was originally the servant's quarters of the manorhouse. The rooms are airy, country-style but vibrantly modern. The driveway entrance is opposite the village's small supermarket.

Kärdla
pop 3700

Hiiumaa's 'capital' grew up around a cloth factory founded in 1829 and destroyed during WWII. It's a green town full of gardens and tree-lined streets, with a sleepy atmosphere and few diversions except that it's Hiiumaa's centre for services of all kinds.

ORIENTATION

The centre of town is Keskväljak (Central Square), a long plaza 500m north of the main Heltermaa–Kõrgessaare road. The bus station lies 200m north of its northern end. To the west is Rannapark, which runs down to the sea.

INFORMATION

Cultural Centre (☎ 463 2182; Rookopli 18) Hosts occasional exhibitions and performances.

Kärdla tourist office (☎ 462 2232; www.hiiumaa.ee; Hiiu 1; ☒ 9am-6pm Mon-Fri, 10am-3pm Sat & Sun mid-May–mid-Sep, 10am-5pm Mon-Fri mid-Sep–mid-May) This friendly centre distributes maps and can help arrange accommodation and guide service. It also sells the *Lighthouse Tour*, a 40-page driving tour of the island in English (25Kr). The office is housed in an old fire tower. Climb up the steps for a great view over the area (adult/concession 5/2Kr).

Library (☎ 463 2182; Rookopli 18; ☒ 10am-6pm Mon-Fri, 10am-2pm Sat) Above the cultural centre, the library provides internet access.

Post office (Keskväljak 3; ☒ 8am-5.30pm Mon-Fri, 8.30am-1pm Sat)

SEB (Keskväljak 7) Bank with ATM.

Tiit Reisid (☎ 463 2077; www.tiitreisid.ee, in Estonian; Sadama 13) Run by Hiiumaa experts, this travel agency inside the bus station arranges accommodation and tours.

SIGHTS & ACTIVITIES

On a rainy day, there's little else but the small **Hiiumaa Museum** (☎ 463 2091; Vabrikuväljak 8; adult/concession 15/10Kr; ☒ 10am-5pm Mon-Sat), which has so-so displays related to the cloth factory, and work from local artists. It's known locally as 'Pikk Maja' (the long house). At the **beach** (follow Lubjaahju) there's a clean, sandy shore, Rannapaargu restaurant-cafe, and minigolf.

SLEEPING

KiviJüri Külalistemaja (☎ 469 1002; www.hot.ee/kivijuri; Kõrgessaare mnt 1; s/d incl breakfast 400/600Kr; 🖳) This cosy, bright-red country house has only four pleasant rooms, each with TV and bathroom. There's a backyard patio and lots of greenery nearby. Tent campers are welcome, and the hospitable owner can help arrange bike and car rental. A fine choice.

Padu Hotell (☎ 463 3037; www.paduhotell.ee; Heltermaa mnt 22; s/d/apt incl breakfast 600/750/900Kr; 🖳 🖳) If you're staying here you may feel like you're sleeping inside a sauna, with the pine motif taken to extremes: walls, floors, ceilings, doors, furniture. Still, rooms are cosy and decently equipped, all with balconies. There's a sauna with a small pool, and an on-site cafe.

Nordtooder (☎ 509 2054; www.nordtooder.ee; Rookopli 20; s/d incl breakfast 800/1000Kr) Very smart rooms are on offer at this central guesthouse, above a sadly nonfunctioning restaurant. Wood-floored rooms are stylishly elegant, with antique furnishings, plasma-screen TVs, and back-and-white tiled bathrooms.

EATING & DRINKING

Linnumäe Puhkekeskus (☎ 462 9244; Heltermaa mnt; mains 40-95Kr; 🕙 11.30am-9pm Sun-Thu, 11.30am-11pm Fri & Sat) The outdoor deck at this restaurant-bar holds plenty of appeal for an afternoon beer, or you can opt to enjoy a meal in the handsome interior. The menu holds few surprises but it's well priced and well executed, with big portions the name of the game. Try the tasty trout with béarnaise sauce. It's on the outskirts of town (500m past Padu Hotell).

Rannapaargu (☎ 463 2053; www.rannapaargu.ee; Lubjaahju 3; mains 75-110Kr; 🕙 noon-11pm) The liveliest place in Kärdla, this pyramid-shaped restaurant has huge windows overlooking the beach, plus an outdoor terrace. The well-priced menu has some decent offerings, including pasta with trout sauce or pork fillet in gin marinade. A kids' menu and playground make it a popular spot for locals and holidaymakers; DJ-hosted dance parties are held here from 11pm Friday and Saturday (entrance 50Kr).

Gahwa Café (☎ 520 3789; Põllu 2a; 🕙 9am-8pm Mon-Fri, 9am-6pm Sat & Sun) A pretty pit stop, this cafe offers light meals such as soup or quiche, but is better for cake and a coffee.

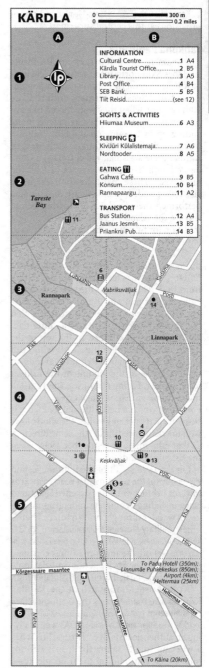

KÄRDLA

0 ____ 300 m
0 ____ 0.2 miles

INFORMATION	
Cultural Centre	1 A4
Kärdla Tourist Office	2 B5
Library	3 A5
Post Office	4 B4
SEB Bank	5 B5
Tiit Reisid	(see 12)

SIGHTS & ACTIVITIES	
Hiiumaa Museum	6 A3

SLEEPING 🏠	
KiviJüri Külalistemaja	7 A6
Nordtooder	8 A5

EATING 🍽	
Gahwa Café	9 B5
Konsum	10 B4
Rannapaargu	11 A2

TRANSPORT	
Bus Station	12 A4
Jaanus Jesmin	13 B5
Priiankru Pub	14 B3

Konsum (Keskväljak; 9am-10pm) Load up on provisions at this central supermarket.

Tahkuna Peninsula

The sparsely populated Tahkuna Peninsula stretches 8km north into the Baltic Sea, west of Kärdla. Northern Hiiumaa had a population of free Swedish farmers until the late 18th century, when they were forced to leave on orders of Catherine the Great, with many ending up in Ukraine on the false promise of a better life. At Ristimägi, 7km west of Kärdla, there's a small **Hill of Crosses**, a dune decked with handmade crosses just off the main road. These mark the spot where the last 1000 Swedish people living on Hiiumaa performed their final act of worship before leaving the island in 1781. It has become a tradition for first-time visitors to Hiiumaa to lay a cross here.

At Tahkuna, on the peninsula's northwest tip, there's a **lighthouse** (527 7454; adult/concession 20/10Kr; 10am-7pm Tue-Sun May–mid-Sep) dating from 1875. This area was the scene of a battle between German and Russian troops during WWII; the official Soviet story was that the Soviets bravely fought to the bitter end, and the last man climbed to the top of the lighthouse and flung himself off while still firing at the Germans. Behind it stands an eerie **memorial** to the victims of the *Estonia* ferry disaster. Facing out to sea, the 12m-tall metal frame encases a huge cross, from the bottom of which a bell with sculpted faces is suspended; it only rings when the wind blows with the same speed and in the same direction as that fatal night in September 1994, when the *Estonia* went down.

On the road south of the lighthouse, and especially on the winding dirt road eastwards towards Lehtma, you'll see deserted **Soviet army bases**, including a complete underground bunker to wander through; bring a torch. There's a new **Military Museum** (Militaarmuuseum; 5347 9819; adult/concession 30/15Kr; 10am-6pm Tue-Sun mid-May–mid-Sep) off the main road that can shed some light on the Soviet period, but alas, only for Estonian-speakers (no English labelling).

At Malvaste, 2km north of the Kärdla–Kõrgessaare road, there's the open-air **Mihkli Farm Museum** (523 2225; adult/concession 15/10Kr; 9.30am-5.30pm mid-May–mid-Sep). As well as giving an authentic taste of early rural life, it has a working smoke sauna (built in 1915) for hire, which can hold up to 10 people. It's a

unique, old-fashioned experience – but not recommended for sensitive eyes.

SLEEPING

If you're looking for a dose of nature, there are good tourist-farm options on Tahkuna Peninsula.

Randmäe Puhketalu (5691 3883; www.hot.ee /puhketalu; sites per person 50Kr, barn rooms per person 150Kr, house 800Kr) Just south of Kalda Puhketalu and also close to the beach, this friendly, family-run place offers loads of space and rustic accommodation in its barn rooms – low on frills but rich in character. A small house (sleeps four) is also available.

Kalda Puhketalu (462 2122; www.kaldapuhke talu.ee; cabins per person 225Kr, holiday houses 1900-3200Kr) Less than 1km north of Malvaste you can rent simple wooden cabins (with separate shared bathrooms and communal kitchen) and larger holiday houses, with kitchen and bathroom (the largest sleeping up to eight people). It's an excellent location 200m from a sandy beach. Sauna, bike and boat hire are available.

Western Hiiumaa

The village of **Kõrgessaare**, 20km west of Kärdla, offers little by way of distractions except a quaint restaurant and guesthouse on your way westward. Set in a photogenic 1880s stone building (once a distillery), **Viinaköök** (469 3337; www.viinakook.com; Sadama 2; s/d 629/939Kr; Jun-Aug) offers reasonable rooms – the set-up has two bedrooms sharing a bathroom and lounge (perfect for families). The rates include breakfast, dinner buffet and evening sauna; there's a two-night minimum stay. The restaurant-pub here has a reasonable all-you-can-eat buffet (150Kr) between noon and 9pm.

The best-known landmark on Hiiumaa is the inland **Kõpu lighthouse** (469 3474; adult/concession 20/10Kr; 10am-8pm May–mid-Sep), the third-oldest, continuously operational lighthouse in the world. A lighthouse has stood on this raised bit of land since 1531, though the present white limestone tower was built in 1845. At 37m high, it can be seen 55km away. East of here, near the 61km highway mark, is the 1.5km Rebastemäe **nature trail**, which takes in forest paths along the highest (therefore oldest) parts of the island. You can get more info at the small information booth next door to the restaurant near the lighthouse base; also here you can arrange **camping** (469 3476; sites per person 20Kr) in the vicinity, or grab a meal or

M/S ESTONIA: CONSIGNED TO MYSTERY

About 30 nautical miles northwest of Hiiumaa's Tahkuna Peninsula lies the wreck of the ferry *Estonia*, which sank during a storm just after midnight on 28 September 1994, en route from Tallinn to Stockholm. Only 137 people survived the tragedy, which claimed 852 lives in one of Europe's worst maritime disasters.

In 1993 the Swedish-Estonian joint venture Estline launched the *Estonia* to service the increasingly popular route between Tallinn and Stockholm. The 15,000-tonne roll-on/roll-off ferry was already a veteran of Scandinavian seas, having sailed between Sweden and Finland for 14 years. The ferry was a source of pride and a symbol of freedom to the newly independent Estonians.

The cause of the tragedy remains the subject of contention and burgeoning conspiracy theory. In 1997 the final report of the Joint Accident Investigation Commission (JAIC), an official inquiry by the Estonian, Swedish and Finnish governments, concluded that the ferry's design was at fault and the crew were probably underskilled in safety and emergency procedures. The report claimed the bow gate, or visor, was engineered inadequately for rough sailing conditions and that during the storm the visor was torn from the bow and in the process breached the watertight seal of the loading ramp. This exposed the car deck to tonnes of seawater that sank the *Estonia* completely within one hour. Escape time for the 989 people on board was estimated at only 15 minutes and they were denied access to lifeboats due to the sudden list and sinking of the ferry. For those who did escape, the freezing conditions of the water that night reduced survival time to only minutes.

The integrity of the report was questioned after dissent within the JAIC became public. Allegations followed that vital information had been withheld and that the Commission did not act impartially. The report also met with criticism from relatives of the victims, the majority of whom were Swedes. In 2000 a Swedish newspaper survey claimed over 70% of victims' families were still calling for a new investigation. Subsequent reports from Sweden and an inquiry commissioned by the ferry's German manufacturers argued that, contrary to the JAIC findings, the *Estonia* was not seaworthy, it had been poorly serviced and the visor-securing mechanisms were in need of repair.

In 2000 a joint US-German diving expedition and new analyses of the *Estonia*'s recovered visor prompted theories of an explosion on board, which explosive experts believe would be the most feasible explanation for the damage sustained and the ferry's rapid sinking. Estline suspected an underwater mine, while it has also been suggested that the ferry collided with another vessel. Conspiracy theorists claim that the *Estonia* was transporting unregistered munitions cargo, as an illicit trade in weapons was to be curtailed with new export laws about to come into effect. Claims of a cover-up have been bolstered by the alleged disappearance of eight crew members, initially listed as survivors.

Unexplained interference with the wreck, along with the Swedish government's dumping of sand to stabilise it in 2000, further fuelled conspiracy claims and calls for a new inquiry. The governments of Estonia, Finland and Sweden are resolute that the ferry will remain where it sank as a memorial to the dead; an estimated 700 people are thought to be inside. To date no one has been found liable and no compensation has been paid to the victims or their families.

snack from the cafe. On Friday nights in July and August popular concerts are staged in the lighthouse grounds.

A second **lighthouse** (☎ 524 3824; adult/concession 20/10Kr; ☺ 10am-7pm Tue-Sun May–mid-Sep) stands at the western end of the peninsula near **Ristna** (Stockholm is just over 200km west of here). It was brought to Hiiumaa by freighter from Paris, where it was made, together with the lighthouse at Tahkuna. There's a small bar here serving drinks and snacks.

About 1km on a rough unmade road from Ristna (the turn-off is just before you reach the lighthouse) is an unexpected treat – the very laid-back, very cool **our pick** **Surf Paradiis** (☎ 5625 1015; www.paap.ee/eng/suvi; ☺ mid-late May–Sep), set on a stretch of sandy beach. Here, you can undertake any number of activities: windsurfing, kitesurfing, parasailing, sea kayaking, jet-skiing, scuba diving, ATV (all-terrain vehicle) safaris, waterskiing etc etc. Everything's offered, from beginners to advanced level, plus there are kid-friendly options such as banana boats and huge trampolines on the water. If the weather's good, there's no better place on the island to hang out – but it's a good idea to call ahead, as all activities are weather-dependent, and the place is sometimes booked solid by groups. A day pass for the 'waterpark' costs 600Kr and includes use of boogie boards, water trampoline, kayaks, skimboards, zip lines (from the roof of the sauna into the sea), snorkelling, sauna and sun lounges.

You can also overnight here in one of a number of kooky options: from hammocks to tepees, bungalows or even in a surfboard bag (or on the sand, under an upturned boat). There are also traditional rooms, for those after more creature comforts. Camping costs 25Kr per person; beachfront bungalows cost 500Kr and sleep up to four; a bed under an upturned boat is 100Kr. The new log-built Paradise Villa sleeps up to 15 and is fully self-contained – prices here depend on season, the number of people and the length of your stay. You'll need to bring your own food, however you decide to sleep, although the nearby lighthouse has a bar selling drinks and snacks.

Käina & Käina Bay Bird Reserve
pop 2390

Hiiumaa's second-largest settlement is a nondescript place, apart from the ruins of a fine **15th-century stone church**, which was wrecked by a WWII bomb, near the main road. On the western edge of Käina is the **Tobias Museum** (☎ 469 7121; Hiiu mnt; adult/concession 15/10Kr; ☼ 10am-6pm Wed-Sun mid-May–mid-Sep), former home of Rudolf Tobias (1873–1918), composer of some of Estonia's first orchestral works.

The main appeal of the town is its proximity to the shore of **Käina Bay**, an important bird reserve that is virtually cut off from the open sea by the twin causeways to **Kassari Island**. You can get a good view over the action from the birdwatching tower north of Orjaku on Kassari, where you'll also find a short walking trail. During the hot summer months a large part of the bay dries up and becomes nothing more than a mud field. About 70 different species breed at Käina Bay.

At Vaemla on the road to Kassari, 4km east of Käina, is a small **wool factory** (Hiiu Vill; ☎ 463 6121; www.hiiuvill.ee; admission free; ☼ closed Sun mid-Sep–mid-May), which still uses original 19th-century weaving and spinning machines to produce some fine traditional knitwear. You can rug up in the sweaters and mittens for sale, or stock up on wool to knit your own. There's a sweet summer cafe on-site.

SLEEPING & EATING
Tondilossi (☎ 463 6337; www.tondilossi.ee; Hiiu mnt 11; s/d with shared bathroom 300/600Kr) This is a comfortable wooden lodge behind the supermarket car park offering comfy, no-frills rooms. There's also a spacious garden, sauna and small cafe on-site. Bike rental is available for guests.

Hotell Liilia (☎ 463 6146; www.liiliahotell.ee; Hiiu mnt 22; s/d 750/850Kr) Set in a central two-storey building across from the church ruins, Liilia offers small and uninspiring rooms (breakfast costs extra), but there's little else in town by way of choice. There's also a popular restaurant and bar here – the menu's decent, even if the decor's super-bland.

GETTING THERE & AWAY
A good paved road runs 20km across the island from Käina to Kärdla. Five or six buses daily go between Kärdla and Käina, with fewer runs on weekends.

Kassari
pop 90

This 8km-long island (linked to Hiiumaa by two causeways) is thickly covered with mixed woodland and boasts some striking coastal scenery. Southern Kassari narrows to a promontory with some unusual vegetation and ends in a thin 3km spit of land, the tip of which, **Sääre Tirp**, juts out into the sea. It's a beautiful place for a walk. On the way towards Sääre Tirp you'll pass by a small but popular **swimming beach** (1.2km past the fork to Orjaku). In summertime the snack stand at the beach rents bikes and kayaks.

At the Sääre Tirp fork you'll notice a **statue** of the local hero, Leiger, carrying a boulder on his shoulder. He was a relative of Suur Tõll, Saaremaa's hero. Legend has it that the Sääre Tirp is the result of an aborted bridge he started to build to Saaremaa, to make it easier for Suur Tõll to visit and join in various heroic acts.

Just inland of the main road, a short distance west of the Sääre Tirp fork, is the single-storey **Hiiumaa Museum** (☎ 463 2091; adult/concession 15/10Kr; ☼ 10am-5.30pm, closed winter weekends), with its small collection of artefacts and exhibits on Hiiumaa's history and biodiversity. Among the curiosities: a 1955 Russian-made TV, the jewel-like prism of the 1874 Tahkuna lighthouse, and the stuffed body of the wolf that allegedly terrorised the island in the 1960s.

Another enjoyable walk, ride or drive is to a pretty, whitewashed, 18th-century **chapel** at the east end of Kassari. A sign 'Kassari Kabel' directs you down a dirt road from the easternmost point of the island's paved road. A path continues nearly 2km to a small bay in Kassari's northeastern corner.

Along the way to the chapel you'll pass Hiiumaa's largest horse farm, **Kassari Ratsamatkad** (☎ 508 3642; www.kassari.ee; 5hr trek 600Kr), which offers a range of horse-riding excursions through forests and along untouched coastline, right up to weeklong treks. The roadsign points to 'Ristitee Talu'.

Moored at Orjaku harbour is a fabulous **floating sauna** (☎ 5666 6622, 504 0039; www.tynni saun.ee; per hr 400Kr), which it's possible to rent for you and up to 10 of your closest sweaty mates. Swim off the deck, or crank up the barbecue and enjoy a long summer night on the water.

SLEEPING & EATING

Camping (☎ 5625 3535; sites 50Kr) is available near the swimming beach on the way to Sääre Tirp. Stop in at the snack stand by the side of the road.

Vetsi Tall (☎ 462 2550; www.vetsitall.ee; sites per person 50Kr, cabins with shared bathroom s/d 280/560Kr, apt 1800Kr) On the main road between Orjaku and the fork to Sääre Tirp, Vetsi Tall is a camping ground with a sense of humour; its tiny wooden cabins set amid apple trees are barrel shaped! It also rents a comfortable three-room apartment above the tavern (three-night minimum). You can camp, use the sauna or have a meal at the dark and atmospheric tavern (meals 80Kr to 140Kr; restaurant open 10am to 10pm). The food is basic but among Hiiumaa's better options.

our pick **Dagen Haus Külalistemaja** (☎ 518 2555; www.dagen.ee; Orjaku; d 790-1490Kr) At the western end of Orjaku is one of Hiiumaa's most attractive options – an environmentally restored former granary with rough-hewn walls and timber beams, and five stylish modern bedrooms and bathrooms, all set in big green grounds. The gorgeous communal lounge and kitchen will have you plotting to move in permanently. The owners have appealing holiday houses on offer too, with reasonable prices (250Kr to 350Kr per adult) – see the website.

GETTING THERE & AWAY

There are only two buses a day between Kärdla and Kassari. Check with the tourist office in Kärdla for the latest times. It's also possible to hitch.

SAAREMAA

pop 35,600

Saaremaa (literally 'island land') is synonymous to Estonians with space, spruce, peace and fresh air – and killer beer. Estonia's largest island (roughly the size of Luxembourg) still lies covered in thick pine and spruce forests and juniper groves, while old windmills, slender lighthouses and tiny villages still appear as if unchanged by the passage of time. Saaremaa, more than any other place in Estonia, offers a glimpse of 'old Estonia'. There are long empty stretches of sparkling coastline, juniper bushes slumbering beneath the ruins of a 15th-century church, and stray sheep staring out from old stone walls.

This unique old-time setting goes hand-in-hand with inextinguishable Saaremaan pride. Saaremaa has always had an independent streak and was usually the last part of Estonia to fall to invaders. Its people have their own customs, songs and costumes. They don't revere mainland Estonia's Kalevipoeg legend, for Saaremaa has its own hero, Suur Tõll, who fought many battles around the island against devils and fiends.

Yet this vision of the idyllic clashes somewhat with the modernity that Kuressaare has thrust upon it. With its magnificent castle, numerous spa hotels, charming Old Town and picturesque bayside setting, Saaremaa's capital has established itself as a premier summer destination. When the long days arrive so do the crowds of Finns and Swedes, jostling for beach space beside urban Estonians arriving from the city. Meanwhile, it's easy to beat the tourist trail by heading out of town, where it's still possible to find gorgeous sandy beaches, mystifying old ruins and windswept peninsulas, with no other soul in sight.

During the Soviet era the entire island was off limits (due to an early-radar system and rocket base stationed there), even to 'mainland' Estonians who needed a permit to visit. This resulted in a minimum of industrial build-up and the unwitting protection of the island's rural charm.

To reach Saaremaa you must first cross Muhu, the small island where the ferry from the mainland docks and which is connected to Saaremaa by a 2.5km causeway. Kuressaare, on the south coast, is a natural base for visitors.

More information is online at www.saar emaa.ee.

HISTORY

Saaremaa's earliest coastal settlements (dating from the 4th millennium BC) now lie inland because the land has risen about 15m over the last 5000 years. In the 10th to 13th centuries Saaremaa and Muhu were the most densely populated parts of Estonia. Denmark tried to conquer Saaremaa in the early 13th century; however, in 1227 the German Knights of the Sword subjugated it. The island was then carved up between the knights, who took Muhu and eastern and northwestern parts of Saaremaa, and the Haapsalu-based bishop of Ösel-Wiek, who made Kuressaare his stronghold.

Saaremaa rebelled against German rule numerous times between 1236 and 1343 (when the knights' castle was destroyed and the Germans were expelled from the island), though their efforts were always short-lived (in 1345 the Germans reconquered the island).

In the 16th century Saaremaa became a Danish possession during the Livonian War, but by 1645 the Swedes had their turn compliments of the Treaty of Brömsebro. Russia took over in 1710 during the Great Northern War and Saaremaa became part of the Russian province of Livonia, governed from Rīga.

GETTING THERE & AWAY
Air
Estonian Air (☎ 640 1163; www.estonian-air.ee) flies once a week in either direction between Stockholm and Kuressaare (in summer), and up to eight times a week year-round between Tallinn and Kuressaare (one way adult/concession 484/425Kr, 45 minutes).

Kuressaare airport (Lennujaam; ☎ 453 0313; www .eeke.ee) is at Roomassaare, 3km southeast of the town centre. Buses 2 and 3 connect it with the bus station at Kuressaare.

Boat
SLK Ferries (Saaremaa Laevakompanii; ☎ 452 4444; www .laevakompanii.ee) operates frequent services between Virtsu on the mainland and Kuivastu on Muhu. The ferries make the 30-minute crossing hourly between about 6am and 11pm (adult/concession/vehicle 35/20/100Kr). You

can reserve a place for your car online, or by calling SLK Ferries (you should certainly do this to avoid the queues that form getting onto the island on Fridays, and off on Sundays).

Year-round ferries run from Sõru on Hiiumaa to Triigi on the north coast of Saaremaa at varying frequencies. For further details, see p148. For details on the Saaremaa ferry to Ventspils in Latvia, see p410.

Saaremaa is very popular with visiting yachties. The best harbour facilities are at the **Kuressaare City Harbour** (☎ 453 3450, 503 1953), within a stone's throw of three spa hotels. Visit http://marinas.nautilus.ee for details of it and other harbours on Saaremaa.

Bus
Around 12 direct buses travel daily between Tallinn and Kuressaare (205Kr to 250Kr, four to 4½ hours, 220km). There are three buses daily to/from Tartu (250Kr, six to 6½ hours) and three buses daily to/from Pärnu (200Kr, 3¼ hours). Most of these you can board at Virstu or Kuivastu (Muhu).

GETTING AROUND
There are over 400km of paved road on Saaremaa and many more dirt roads. Hitching is not uncommon on the main routes (but you'll need time on your hands, and there's not much traffic on minor roads). Buses do get around the island, but not very frequently; it's usually possible to put a bike or two in the baggage compartments. Before you head out, call **Kuressaare bus station** (☎ 453 1661; Pihtla tee 2) for help in route planning.

For more practical information on getting around the island, see p160.

Eastern Saaremaa
After you've crossed Muhu (the 'doormat of Saaremaa'), the first place you reach on the island is sleepy, nondescript **Orissaare**, the island's second-largest town. The small **tourist office** (☎ 454 5051; Sadama 1; ☥ 9am-5pm Mon-Fri, 9am-3pm Sat & Sun Jun-Aug) can provide maps and general information. There's a tiny handicrafts shop, **Uku** (Rana pst 9; ☥ 9am-4pm), where you can watch Orissaare's old weavers in action. The German knights built **Maasilinn Castle**, 4km north of Orissaare, during the 14th to 16th centuries. It was badly damaged in 1576 but you can still see the ruins, and wander through a restored underground chamber.

ESTONIA

SAAREMAA & MUHU

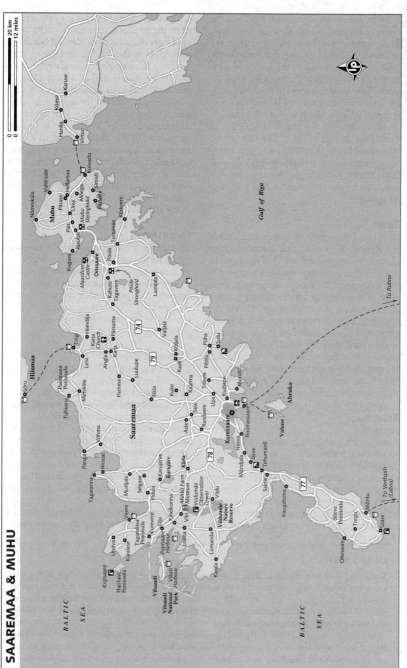

ESTONIA

Põide, 3km south of the main road, was the German knights' headquarters on Saaremaa. Their fortress was destroyed in 1343 in the St George's Night Uprising, but **Põide Church**, built by the Germans in the 13th and 14th centuries a short distance east of the road, remains an imposing symbol of their influence. Its dark, crumbling exterior is offset by a perfect stained-glass window above the altar.

Also south of the main road, east of Tornimäe at Kõrkvere, is **Tika Talu** (☎ 452 8169; www.tikatalu.ee; 5hr trek 500Kr), a farm offering simple accommodation plus plenty of horseback action – coastal sightseeing treks for adults and kids. Overnight riding treks can be arranged.

Kaali

At Kaali, 18km north of Kuressaare, stands a 100m-wide, water-filled **meteorite crater** blasted into existence about 2700 years ago. In Scandinavian mythology, the site was known as 'the sun's grave'. It's Europe's largest and most accessible meteorite crater, though it looks small up close. A tourist village of sorts has sprung up here – there's a museum, handicrafts stores and a hotel, as well as an old-style tavern, the **Kaali Trahter** (☎ 459 1210; www.kaalitrahter.ee; mains 65-180Kr), offering Estonian fare and locally brewed beer. To get there, take Rd 10 north from Kuressaare, and keep your eyes peeled for the well-marked turn-off on the left.

Kuressaare
pop 14,900

Things are motoring along nicely in Kuressaare, Saaremaa's star attraction. It's a picturesque town with peaceful leafy streets, charming guesthouses and cafes, and a magnificent castle rising up in its midst. There are plenty of new eating options, and every second hotel appears to be undergoing refurbishment and adding a spa. The town built a reputation

as a health centre as early as the 19th century, when the ameliorative properties of its coastal mud were discovered and the first health spas opened. Now they're a dime a dozen, ranging from Eastern-bloc sanatoriums to sleek and stylish resorts, and giving the island the inevitable nickname of 'Sparemaa'.

Kuressaare's reason for being is its castle, which was founded in the 13th century as the Haapsalu-based Bishop of Ösel-Wiek's stronghold in the island part of his diocese. Kuressaare became Saaremaa's main trading centre, developing quickly after passing into Swedish hands in 1645. In the Soviet era Kuressaare was named Kingisseppa, after Viktor Kingissepp, an Estonian communist of the 1920s.

ORIENTATION

The road from Kuivastu and the mainland enters Kuressaare as Tallinna, passing southwest through modern suburbs to the central square, Keskväljak. Kuressaare Castle and its surrounding park, which reaches down to the coast, are 750m beyond Keskväljak, along Lossi. The **bus station** (Pihtla tee 2) is northeast of Keskväljak.

INFORMATION

There are several banks, ATMs and exchange bureaus on Keskväljak.

Kalev (☎ 453 3088; Tallinna 19a; per hr 20Kr; ⌚ 8.30am-7pm Mon-Fri, 9am-4pm Sat) Cheap internet inside a chocolate shop – what could be better?

Kuressaare tourist office (☎ 453 3120; www.kuressaare.ee; Tallinna 2; ⌚ 9am-7pm Mon-Fri, 9am-5pm Sat, 9am-3pm Sun May-Sep, 9am-5pm Mon-Fri Oct-Apr) Inside the old town hall. It sells maps and guides, arranges accommodation, and books boat trips and island tours.

Library (Tallinna 6; ⌚ 10am-7pm Mon-Fri, 10am-4pm Sat) Free internet access.

Mere travel agency (☎ 453 3610; www.rbmere.ee; Tallinna 27) Extremely knowledgeable about the islands

---

ISLAND BREW

Saaremaa has a long history of beer home-brewing, and even its factory-produced brew has a great reputation. Tuulik and Tehumardi are the most popular (but don't mention that they're now brewed in Tartu). The country's second-biggest beer festival, **Õlletoober** (www.olletoober.ee), takes place in Leisi (northern Saaremaa) in mid-July, showcasing both sophisticated and feral brews and with plenty of live music and festivities.

Beer-lovers should be sure to try any homemade beer where it's offered. A long-time island tradition, the brew features the traditional malt, yeast and hops, but comes off a bit sour on the palate. It's light and refreshing, best quaffed from a wooden tankard on a warm summer day.

(Saaremaa, Hiiumaa, Muhu, Vormsi, Vilsandi) and offers arranged boat trips to Vilsandi. Also offers a once-weekly bus tour around the main sights of Saaremaa (400Kr).

Pärimusmatkad Heritage Tours (☎ 526 9974; www.parimusmatkad.ee) A recommended company that arranges a raft of year-round Saaremaa excursions and activities, including berry- and mushroom-picking, horse riding, birdwatching, bog walks and jeep safaris. Lots of Vilsandi options too.

Post office (Torni 1; ☷ 8am-6pm Mon-Fri, 8.30am-3pm Sat)

SIGHTS & ACTIVITIES
Kuressaare Castle
The majestic Kuressaare Castle stands at the southern end of the town, on an artificial island ringed by a partly filled moat. It's the best-preserved castle in the Baltic and the region's only medieval stone castle that has remained intact.

A castle was founded in the 1260s, but the mighty dolomite fortress that stands today was not built until the 14th century, with some protective walls added between the 15th and 18th centuries. It was designed as an administrative centre as well as a stronghold. The more slender of its two tall corner towers, Pikk Hermann to the east, is separated from the rest of the castle by a shaft crossed only by a drawbridge, so it could function as a last refuge in time of attack.

Inside the castle is a warren of chambers, halls, passages and stairways to fuel anyone's fantasies about Gothic fortresses. It also

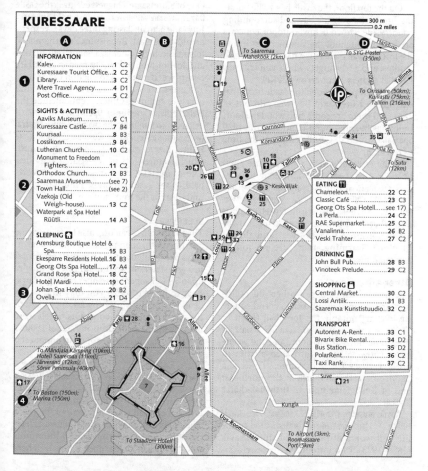

KURESSAARE

0 ——————— 300 m
0 ——————— 0.2 miles

INFORMATION	
Kalev	**1** C2
Kuressaare Tourist Office	**2** C2
Library	**3** C2
Mere Travel Agency	**4** D1
Post Office	**5** C2

SIGHTS & ACTIVITIES	
Aaviks Museum	**6** C1
Kuressaare Castle	**7** B4
Kuursaal	**8** B3
Lossikonn	**9** B4
Lutheran Church	**10** C2
Monument to Freedom Fighters	**11** C2
Orthodox Church	**12** B3
Saaremaa Museum	(see 7)
Town Hall	(see 2)
Vaekoja (Old Weigh-house)	**13** C2
Waterpark at Spa Hotel Rüütli	**14** A3

SLEEPING	
Arensburg Boutique Hotel & Spa	**15** B3
Ekesparre Residents Hotell	**16** B3
Georg Ots Spa Hotell	**17** A4
Grand Rose Spa Hotel	**18** C2
Hotel Mardi	**19** C1
Johan Spa Hotel	**20** B2
Ovelia	**21** D4

EATING	
Chameleon	**22** C2
Classic Café	**23** C3
Georg Ots Spa Hotell	(see 17)
La Perla	**24** C2
RAE Supermarket	**25** C2
Vanalinna	**26** B2
Veski Trahter	**27** C2

DRINKING	
John Bull Pub	**28** B3
Vinoteek Prelude	**29** C2

SHOPPING	
Central Market	**30** C2
Lossi Antiik	**31** B3
Saaremaa Kunstistuudio	**32** C2

TRANSPORT	
Autorent A-Rent	**33** C1
Bivarix Bike Rental	**34** D2
Bus Station	**35** D2
PolarRent	**36** C2
Taxi Rank	**37** C2

houses the **Saaremaa Museum** (☎ 455 7542; www .saaremaamuuseum.ee; adult/concession/family 50/25/100Kr; 🕑 10am-6pm May-Aug, 11am-6pm Wed-Sun Sep-Apr). A self-guided audio tour costs 80Kr (including admission), with comprehensive coverage of the island's history – particularly interesting is the section detailing the effects of WWII on Saaremaa.

According to legend, condemned prisoners were dispatched through a small floorless room near the bishop's chamber, to be received by hungry lions. Legends also tell of a knight's body found when a sealed room was opened in the 18th century. It's said that, upon discovery, the knight's body dissolved into dust, which has given rise to varying accounts of how he met his tragic fate.

On the top floor, the castle has a cafe boasting fine views over the bay and surrounding countryside. Down below, outdoor concerts are held throughout the summer just inside the fortress walls. There is a handful of artisan studios, and a few targets where you try your hand at archery (four arrows 20Kr).

The shady park around the castle moat that extends to Kuressaare Bay was laid out in 1861 and there are some fine wooden resort buildings in and around it, notably the 1889 **Spa Hall** (Kuursaal) – sadly empty at the time of research.

If the weather's nice, you can hire rowboats or canoes and float idly along the castle's moat. Boat hire is available at **Lossikonn** (☎ 452 9838; Allee 8; per hr 120Kr; 🕑 noon-7pm Mon-Thu, 11am-8pm Fri-Sun May-Sep); this pretty cafe is also where you can hire ice skates in winter if the moat freezes over (and thanks to global warming, there are no longer any guarantees).

Other Attractions

The best of Kuressaare's other old buildings are grouped around the central square Keskväljak, notably the **town hall** (built in 1670), on the eastern side, with a pair of fine stone lions at the door, and the **weighhouse** (now Vaekoja pub) across from it, both 17th-century baroque. There's a handsome **Lutheran church** at the northeast end of Keskväljak and an **Orthodox church** (Lossi 8).

Aaviks Museum (☎ 455 7583; Vallimaa 7; adult/child 10/5Kr; 🕑 11am-6pm Wed-Sun) is dedicated to the life and works of linguist Johannes Aavik (1880–1973), who introduced major reforms

to the Estonian language, and his musically talented cousin, Joosep Aavik (1899–1989).

Beaches & Waterparks

The best beach in the Kuressaare area is **Järverand** at Järve, about 14km west, some 2km past Mändjala. There's also a beach at **Sutu**, 12km east. Salme, Torgu or Sääre buses from Kuressaare go to Järverand.

In Kuressaare, there's a small sandy beach behind the castle, or if the weather means an indoor splash is best, head along to the **waterpark** (☎ 454 8147; Pargi 12; admission 80-100Kr; 🕑 noon-10pm Mon-Fri, 10am-10pm Sat & Sun) attached to the Spa Hotel Rüütli.

FESTIVALS & EVENTS

One of Kuressaare's biggest events is the **Castle Day** (www.saaremaamuuseum.ee) fest held in early July (and actually lasting three days). Vespers, an old-time feast, Renaissance tournaments, folk music, night cinema, a handicrafts market and lots of family-friendly medieval fanfare take place. If you're in town, don't miss it.

Kuressaare's dance card is certainly full over the summer. Other events include the **Waltz Festival** (late June), **Opera Days** (www.concert .ee), mid- to late July, the **chamber-music festival** (www.kammerfest.ee), early August, and **Maritime Festival** (www.merepaevad.ee) also in early August, which features lots of sea-related activities. There are also regular summer concerts held in the castle grounds. Find out what's underway at the tourist office.

SLEEPING

The tourist office can organise beds in private apartments throughout the region, and farmstays are available across the island. Hotel prices listed here are for summer – they're up to 50% cheaper September through April. Bear in mind too that you may find better deals in summer simply by asking – eg both the Arensburg and George Ots hotels were offering high-season drop-in rates of 1000Kr when we visited. Spas are open to nonguests.

Town Centre

SYG Hostel (☎ 455 4388; www.syg.edu.ee; Kingu 6; s/d/q with shared bathroom 300/420/640Kr; 🖳) A comfy and well-priced hostel about 600m from the city centre; being attached to a school, there's a small gym and internet room, plus a cafeteria doling out cheap meals. On the minus side, there hasn't been much renovation here in ages, there's no kitchen, and the place is not exactly overflowing with backpacker cheer. Prices drop a little from Sunday to Wednesday. Campervans welcome.

Ovelia (☎ 455 5732; www.ovelia.ee; Suve 8; d incl breakfast 500Kr; 🖳) One of the cheapest places in town, friendly Ovelia is a budget guesthouse with small, basic rooms plus a pleasant garden area. Some rooms have private bathroom, some have TV – it's worth having a look before committing.

Staadioni Hotell (☎ 453 3556; www.staadionihotell .ee; Staadioni 4; s/d 625/790Kr; 🌣 May-Sep; 🖳) Some of the best-value rooms (spacious and bright) are available at this pleasant, secluded spot, 1km south of the centre and surrounded by parkland and sports facilities. The only downside is that it's a ways from the town centre, but bikes can be hired here.

Arensburg Boutique Hotel & Spa (☎ 452 4700; www .arensburg.eu; Lossi 15; s/d/ste from 1250/1550/3950Kr; 🍸) Arensburg is almost two hotels in one, with a split personality and severe case of old versus new. Our vote goes to the bold and sexy charcoal-painted rooms in the slick 2007 extension to the historic hotel (standard rooms in the old wing are OK but unremarkable). A new spa and two restaurants round things out nicely.

Grand Rose Spa Hotel (☎ 666 7000; www.grandrose .ee; Tallinna 15; s/d/ste 1575/1750/3990Kr; 🍸) The floral-themed decor of this newish hotel is every little girl's fantasy, and the execution comes close to overkill, from the high-backed black velvet chairs, chandeliers and water feature in the rose-filled lobby, to the rose carpet throughout. Still, it's impressively done and certainly romantic. The spa and restaurant have both garnered a reputation as among the town's best.

Georg Ots Spa Hotell (☎ 455 0000; www.gospa.ee; Tori 2; s/d 1903/2123Kr; 🍸) Kuressaare's funkiest hotel, the Georg Ots (named after a renowned Estonian singer) has modern rooms with wildly striped carpet, enormous king-sized beds, CD-player and a warm but minimalist design. Most rooms have balconies, and there's a lovely pool, fitness centre and spa services just down the hall, as well as top nosh (see p160).

Ekesparre Residents Hotell (☎ 453 3633; www .ekesparre.ee; Lossi 27; r Sun-Thu 2900Kr, Fri & Sat 3900Kr) This elegant 10-room hotel stands in pole position on the castle grounds. The 1908 building is newly refurbished and returned to its Art Nouveau glory – exquisite period

wallpaper, Tiffany lamps and a smattering of orchid plants add to the refined, clubby atmosphere, while the 3rd-floor guests lounge is a gem. As you'd expect from the price, it's a polished operator.

Also recommended:

Hotel Mardi (☎ 452 4633; www.hotelmardi.eu; Vallimaa 5a; hostel dm/s/d/tr with shared bathroom 200/300/400/600Kr, hotel s/d incl breakfast 580/830Kr; 🖳) Summer hostel and year-round hotel attached to a college. Simple, fuss-free rooms at good prices.

Johan Spa Hotel (☎ 454 0000; www.johan.ee; Kauba 13; s/d from 950/1200Kr; 🍸) Another hotel smartening up its act with a new spa. Older rooms are cheaper, new rooms slick and minimalist.

Out of Town

Owing to infrequent bus service, these places are mainly geared towards people with their own wheels. In summer, half-a-dozen buses from Kuressaare to Salme, Torgu or Sääre stop at the Mändjala bus stop.

Mändjala Kämping (☎ 454 4193; www.mandjala.ee; sites/cabins per person 60/220Kr, cabins with private bathroom 850Kr; 🌣 May-Sep; 🖳) Heaving in high summer (with a capacity for 1000 people), this camping ground 10km west of Kuressaare offers rustic wooden cabins and camp sites amid lots of pine-filled greenery. It's a short walk to the beach, and watersports are available, as are sauna, bike rental, bar, restaurant etc.

Hotell Saaremaa (☎ 454 4100; www.saarehotell.ee; d/ste 1260/2310Kr) About 600m past Mändjala Kämping, this low-key whitewashed hotel has trim, modern rooms and a pleasant outdoor terrace, plus a new Thalasso spa. Best of all, it's right on the beach (request a sea-facing room with balcony).

EATING & DRINKING

Vanalinna (☎ 455 5309; Kauba 8; pastries & cakes 5-20Kr; 🌣 7.30am-9pm Mon-Fri, 8am-9pm Sat & Sun) With its timber-and-stone interior and black-and-white photos hanging from orange walls, this cafeteria-style bakery is a more appealing spot than the cheap prices would lead you to believe.

Classic Café (☎ 455 4786; Lossi 9; light meals & mains 25-135Kr; 🌣 8.30am-10pm) A cruisy menu (all-day breakfasts – a real rarity in Estonia!) and relaxed, stylish decor are the hallmarks of this, um, classic cafe. You can order meaty dishes from the grill, but better value are the fresh salads, soups and pasta dishes. The lunchtime hot dish of the day is a steal at 40Kr.

ESTONIA

ourpick **Saaremaa Maheköök** (☎ 5198 2598; www
.mahekook.ee; Kihelkonna mnt; mains 45-110Kr; ☿ noon-
7pm Tue-Sun) Well worth a trip out of town
(about 2km northwest, by the Kihelkonna
roundabout) is Saaremaa Organic Kitchen,
the first of its kind in Estonia and owned and
operated by a group of local organic farmers.
The majority of produce is local and seasonal
(with a short, daily-changing menu), so meals
like spinach soup, grilled flounder, lamb burgers and veal meatballs are guaranteed to have
low 'food miles' and be bursting with fresh
flavours. Sorbets, mousses and cheesecakes
made from island fruits are divine. And you
certainly can't quibble at the price. Hours
seem variable – it's a good idea to call first.

Chameleon (☎ 668 2212; Kauba 2; meals 50-140Kr;
☿ 11am-midnight Sun-Thu, 11am-2am Fri & Sat) Newly
opened Chameleon is indeed a changing creature, effortlessly morphing from daytime cafe
to night-time restaurant, then to late-night
cocktail bar. The sleek black and grey decor
(with pink lighting) adds an air of city-slick,
but it's not too cool to offer a kids' menu
and playroom. The menu is classic cafe fare,
from pastas and nachos to mains of salmon
or lamb.

La Perla (☎ 453 6910; www.laperla.ee; Lossi 3; mains
65-245Kr; ☿ noon-11pm) A pearl of a menu makes
dining at this popular Italian restaurant a
warming Mediterranean treat. Swing from
bruschetta to *tiramisu* via all manner of pizza,
pasta and grilled meats, preferably with a glass
of cheeky Italian red to accompany.

Boston (☎ 455 5059; Tori 4; mains 75-195Kr; ☿ 11am-
11pm) Down by the town's small marina (just
past the Georg Ots hotel) is this two-storey
pub-restaurant, named after the owner's
hometown. As befits the location, there's a
laid-back nautical feel, and the menu highlights seafood (though not exclusively so). The
outdoor tables are great for indulging sailing
fantasies on a sunny afternoon.

Georg Ots Spa Hotell (☎ 455 0000; Tori 2; mains
80-290Kr; ☿ noon-11pm) Some nominate the
restaurant at the Grand Rose hotel as
Kuressaare's finest, but for our money you
can't beat this bright and shiny dining
room, with its suede booths peopled by a
mixed crowd enjoying the views from the
huge windows. The food is light, fresh and
creative, making good use of local produce.
Try the delicious smoked trout salad or the
fresh mushroom ravioli, and top it off with
blackcurrant cheesecake.

Veski Trahter (☎ 453 3776; www.veskitrahter.eu;
Pärna 19; mains 105-250Kr; ☿ noon-10pm Sun-Thu, noon-
1am Fri & Sat) How often can you say you've
dined inside a windmill from 1899? Without
being too touristy, this place keeps quality and
ambience at a premium, with plenty of hearty
local fare – wild boar hotpot, cabbage soup,
Saaremaa cheeses.

John Bull Pub (☎ 453 9988; Pargi 4; ☿ 11am-
midnight) In the park surrounding the castle,
this pub (not particularly English, despite its
name) has a great moat-side outdoor deck,
a meal of cheap-n-cheerful pub classics, and
our favourite feature, a bar made from an old
Russian bus.

Vinoteek Prelude (☎ 453 3407; www.prelude.ee; Lossi
4; ☿ noon-2am or later May-Aug, 4pm-midnight or later Sep-
Apr) A cute bunch of grapes heralds the entrance
to this cosy, dimly lit wine bar. Climb the
staircase to sofas under the eaves, and choose
from a menu of international wines (plenty by
the glass) and antipasti-style snacks.

RAE Supermarket (☎ 453 3776; Raekoja 10; ☿ 9am-
10pm) The best grocery store in Saaremaa (behind the tourist office too).

SHOPPING

Central market (Tallinna) Next to Vaekoja pub
you'll find dolomite vases, wool sweaters,
honey, strawberries and other Saaremaa treats
(and plenty of tat too).

Lossi Antiik (☎ 455 4818; Lossi 19) Towards the
castle, Lossi Antiik sells all sorts of antiques,
from 19th-century farm tools to Soviet memorabilia. It's a fun place to browse. A handicrafts market sets up next door, at Lossi 17.

Saaremaa Kunstistuudio (☎ 453 3748; Lossi 5) This
bright gallery contains a variety of works by
Estonian artists, including the fantasy works
of Navitrolla and winning prints by artist-
illustrator Kadi Kurema. You'll find covetable
textiles, ceramics, sculptures and paintings.

GETTING THERE & AROUND

For direct bus/ferry connections between
Kuressaare, the mainland and Hiiumaa,
see p154. Kuressaare's **bus station** (☎ 453
1661; Pihtla tee 2; ☿ 7am-7.30pm) is the terminus
for most buses on the island; schedules
are posted inside. There's a left luggage
office downstairs.

For taxis, call **Kuressaare Takso** (☎ 453 0000)
or **Saare Takso** (☎ 453 3333). There are ranks
at the bus station, and opposite the Grand
Rose Hotel.

GOOD CLEAN FUN

A lovely outing on the island is to visit **GoodKaarma** (☎ 5348 4006; www.goodkaarma.com; Kuke; ⓥ 10am-6pm Jun-Aug, other times by arrangement), a cottage industry run by Steve and Ea, an English-Estonian couple, from their farm outside the village of Kaarma, about 15km north of Kuressaare (we suggest you take a good map along to avoid getting lost! Download one from the website.) Here, the couple lovingly craft organic soaps that make the perfect island souvenir, especially as many are made with local ingredients – the 'Saaremaa' soap is fragrant with juniper and pine, while 'Rise & Shine' is made from local sea-buckthorn berries together with orange and geranium. If you're interested in learning more, you can book into a one-hour soap-making workshop (100Kr; minimum six people – advance booking required). Also on-site is a pretty garden terrace and cafe-bar, with homemade snacks, organic teas, local beers etc. Besides GoodKaarma soaps, the farm shop sells local arts and crafts.

For car hire, try **Autorent A-rent** (☎ 453 6620; Vallimaa 5) or **PolarRent** (☎ 453 3660; www.polarrent.ee; Tallinna mnt 9). It's wise to book ahead in summer (and note that A-rent shares its location with a strip club!). PolarRent also has mopeds for hire. You can rent bicycles (and touring gear such as trailers for kids or luggage) at **Bivarix** (☎ /fax 455 7118; Tallinna mnt 26; bike per day/week 150/700Kr; ⓥ 10am-6pm Mon-Fri, 10am-2pm Sat). It's not well signposted – look for the 'Rattapood' sign near the bus station.

Sõrve Peninsula

Small cliffs, such as the Kaugatoma pank (bank) and Ohessaare pank, rear up along the west coast of the 32km-long southwestern Sõrve Peninsula. Legend has it that the cliffs were formed when the Devil tried in vain to wrench this spit of land from the mainland to separate Suur Tõll, who was vacationing on Sõrve, from Saaremaa. This is where the island's magic can really be felt. A bike or car trip along the coastline will reveal fabulous views. A summertime ferry runs from Mõntu to Ventspils in Latvia (p410).

This sparsely populated strip of land saw heavy fighting during WWII, and the battle scars remain; by the lighthouse at Sääre, on the southern tip, you can walk around the ruins of an old Soviet army base. Other bases and the remnants of the Lõme-Kaimri antitank defence lines still stand. There's a large monument at Tehumardi, south of the beach at Järve, which was the site of a gruesome night battle in October 1944 between retreating German troops and an Estonian-Russian Rifle Division. The horror defies belief: both armies fought blindly, firing on intuition or finding the enemy by touch.

Russian-Estonian dead lie buried in double graves in the cemetery nearby.

Near the village of Torgu on the Sõrve Peninsula in rugged windswept surrounds, **Sõrve Turismitalu** (☎ 452 3061; www.saaremaa.ee/sorve; cabins per person 125Kr, d 500-650Kr, cottages from 1300Kr) is a 20-minute walk to the coast. Here you'll find rustic cabins, rooms, comfy cottages with kitchens and a range of excursions on offer (boating, hiking, birdwatching).

Viidumäe Nature Reserve

Founded in 1957, Viidumäe Nature Reserve covers an area of 19 sq km, with a 22m observation tower on Saaremaa's highest point (54m), about 25km west of Kuressaare. The tower, about 2km along a dirt road off the Kuressaare–Lümanda road at Viidu, offers a panoramic view of the reserve and the wonders of the island itself. The view is particularly memorable at sunset. There are two nature trails (2.2km and 1.5km), marked to highlight the different habitats of the area. Viidumäe is a botanical reserve, its favourable climate and conditions making it home to rare plant species.

At the reserve's **headquarters** (☎ 457 6442; ⓥ 10am-6pm Jun-Aug) in Viidu, you can see a small exhibition and book guided tours.

The West & North Coasts

At Viki on the road to Kihelkonna, about 30km from Kuressaare, a 19th-century farm has been preserved as the **Mihkli Farm Museum** (Talumuuseum; ☎ 454 6613; www.saaremaamuuseum .ee; adult/concession 20/10Kr; ⓥ 10am-6pm mid-Apr–Sep, closed Mon-Tue in Apr & Sep). In a pretty setting you can tour the old wooden farmhouses, play on the village swing, rent out the sauna (250Kr per hour; prebooking advised) or pitch a tent (camp site 25Kr). Kihelkonna, 3km beyond, has a tall, austere, early-German church.

On the western side of the Tagamõisa Peninsula, north of Kihelkonna, there's an old **watchtower** and the ruins of a port where Saaremaans were shipped to Siberia. Further up the peninsula stretches a beautiful and rarely visited coastline. At its northwestern tip, on the Harilaid Peninsula (accessible only on foot), is the striking **Kiipsaare lighthouse**, which began leaning at a steep angle towards the sea from the early 1990s. In a fascinating twist, in recent times the lighthouse has righted itself again, largely thanks to beach erosion (the same thing that led it to lean in the first place).

East of the peninsula and 1km west of Pidula is the idyllic **Pidula Fish Farm** (Pidula Kalakasvatus; ☎ 454 6513; www.pidulakalakasvatus.ee; trout per kg 175Kr), where you can 'fish' for trout in stocked ponds. They'll even clean it and cook/smoke/grill it for you if you wish. It's a lovely spot for a DIY meal on a sunny summer evening, but it's not well signed so be on the lookout. Camping and accommodation are also available (see right).

Some 7km north of Mustjala at Ninase (on the Ninase Peninsula) are two of Saaremaa's kitschier icons. You can't miss the clunky wooden **folk windmills**, built to resemble a giant man in traditional costume, and his counterpart, a giant female.

Panga pank, Saaremaa's highest cliffs, run along the northern coast near Panga and offer some panoramic views from the top. There's a sandy beach at Tuhkana, 3km north of Metsküla.

Leisi is the venue for Õlletoober, a popular annual beer festival held in mid-July (see p156). From Leisi it's 3.5km to the harbour of Triigi, with views across to Hiiumaa. If you're arriving from Hiiumaa via the Sõru–Triigi ferry (p148), pick up maps and get general Saaremaa information at the tiny **Leisi tourist office** (☎ 457 3073; ⏱ noon-8pm Jun-Aug), inside the pretty, vine-covered restaurant, Sassimaja.

About 5km south of Leisi (on the main road to Kuressaare) at Angla is the site of the biggest and most photogenic grouping of Saaremaa's old **windmills** – five of them of various sizes and ages lined up together on the roadside. Opposite the windmills is the turn-off to the 14th-century **Karja Church**, 2km east, which has a fortress-like facade.

SLEEPING & EATING

Värava Talu (☎ 5645 1606; www.varava.fie.ee; sites per person 25Kr, cabins & barns 400-500Kr; 🖵) In a forested area along the idyllic northern coast, this pretty tourist farm offers rustic accommodation in wooden cabins and old barn houses. Camping is possible, and the owners rent bicycles and offer hiking tours. It's located near Selgase, just off the Kihelkonna–Mustjala road.

Pidula Fish Farm (Pidula Kalakasvatus; ☎ 454 6513; www.pidulakalakasvatus.ee; sites per person 30Kr, cabins 450Kr, d/tr 500/650Kr) At the laid-back, bucolic fish farm (left), accommodation is available for campers, in simple cabins, or in rooms in the 'big house'. We particularly love the tiny hut on the island in the river.

Kämping Karujärve (☎ 454 2181; www.karujarve .ee, in Estonian; sites/cabins 45/320Kr; ⏱ mid-May–mid-Sep) Among the trees on the east side of Lake Karujärv, some 9km east of Kihelkonna (5.5km north from Kärla), this camping ground offers basic tepee huts, sauna and boat rental in a pretty locale.

Loona Manor (☎ 454 6510; www.loona.ee; sites per person 50Kr, s/d/ste 640/800/1300Kr) This handsome 16th-century manor house south of Kihelkonna offers simple, modern rooms in a historic setting (the suites are a roomy option). There's a pleasant restaurant and sauna on-site. The manor is home to the Vilsandi National Park headquarters, so stop in if you're planning a trip and load up on local information.

Lümanda Söögimaja (☎ 457 6493; Lümanda; mains 30-130Kr; ⏱ 10am-10pm) This rustic farmhouse eatery is on the main road in Lümanda, right next door to the village church and providing an idyllic snapshot of island life. The menu features the kind of food eaten by the island's forefathers, largely organic – fish soup, boiled pork with turnips and carrots, cabbage rolls. The friendly owner also has two small cabins in the garden (180Kr per person).

VILSANDI & VILSANDI NATIONAL PARK

Vilsandi, west of Kihelkonna, is the largest of 161 islands and islets off Saaremaa's western coast protected under the Vilsandi National Park (which also includes parts of Saaremaa itself, including the Harilaid Peninsula). The park covers an area of 238 sq km (163 sq km of sea, 75 sq km of land) and is an area of extensive ecological study. The breeding patterns of the common eider and the migration of the barnacle goose have been monitored very closely here. Ringed seals can also be seen in their breeding season and 32 species of orchid thrive in the park.

Vilsandi, 6km long and in places up to 3km wide, is a low, wooded island. The small islets surrounding it are abundant with currant and juniper bushes. Around 250 bird species are observed here, and in spring and autumn there is a remarkable migration of waterfowl: up to 10,000 barnacle geese stop over on Vilsandi in mid-May, and the white-tailed eagle and osprey have even been known to drop by.

The **Vilsandi National Park headquarters** (☎ 454 6510), at Loona Manor (opposite), can arrange accommodation and wildlife-watching tours given advance notice, as can the Mere travel agency in Kuressaare and Pärimusmatkad Heritage Tours (p156).

One of few places to stay on the island is **Tolli Turismitalu** (☎ 5342 5318; www.tolli.vilsandi.info; d 600-880Kr), a tourist farm offering an idyllic setting amid the island's beauty. Its homestead is the oldest on the island, and accommodation is available here, or inside a summer house or a windmill. Camping is possible, as is sauna rental, bike and boat hire, and nature trips.

Sülla Eco-Farm (☎ 5649 0505; aivar.kallas@gmail .com) offers boating excursions to Vilsandi or around the Tagamõisa Peninsula. It's located in Oju, a tiny village 4km northwest of Kihelkonna. It also offers coastal horse-riding excursions (on Saaremaa).

In summer a **private boat** (☎ 520 2656; harri61@ hot.ee; adult/concession one way 50/30Kr) makes semi-regular trips between Papisaare and Vikati (five times a week); reservations are required. You can also book the boat at nonscheduled times for 1500Kr (return trip).

MUHU
pop 1900

Muhu, unfortunately, has a reputation for being the 'doormat' for Saaremaa – lots of people passing through, but no one stopping. In fact, Estonia's third-biggest island has plenty of reasons to hang around, from a traditional old village, now functioning as a living museum, to Teutonic ruins, a charming cooking school, plus one of Estonia's finest boutique hotels. Good information is online at www.muh u.info.

Koguva, on the western tip of Muhu, 6km off the main road, is an exceptionally well preserved, fairy-tale fishing village, now protected as an **open-air museum** (☎ 454 8872; www .muhumuuseum.ee; adult/concession 25/15Kr; ☽ 10am-7pm

mid-May–mid-Sep, 10am-5pm Wed-Sun mid-Sep–mid-May). One ticket allows you to wander through a number of interesting houses: an old schoolhouse, and a museum containing beautiful traditional textiles from the area, including the painstakingly detailed folk costumes once worn by the locals in the area. You can also peer into author Juhan Smuul's ancestral home. Also on the grounds of the village is the handsome modern-art gallery and cafe **Koguva Kunstitall** (☎ 454 8873; www.koguva-art.ee; ☽ 11am-6pm Jun-Aug), a civilised spot for a glass of wine or coffee and cake.

Back on the main road at Nautse, the **Eemu Tuulik** (windmill; ☎ 452 8130; adult/concession 10/5Kr; ☽ 10am-6pm Wed-Sun mid-Apr–Sep) has a small exhibit and sells bread baked with its milled flour. Southwest of here is the **Muhu stronghold**, which is where the islanders surrendered to the Knights of the Sword in 1227, marking the end of Estonian resistance.

The turn-off to the **Muhu Ostrich Farm** (☎ 452 8148; www.jaanalind.ee; adult/concession 30/20Kr; ☽ 10am-6pm mid-May–mid-Sep) is 200m east of the windmill. The quirky owners will give you an earful about these strange creatures and let you feed them (mind your fingers); also here are kangaroos, emus and ponies (for pony rides for kids). A small shop sells feathers, eggs, purses and shoes made from a certain leather.

Also worth investigating if you'd like your travels to take a culinary bent is **Nami Namaste** (☎ 454 8890; www.naminamaste.com; Simiste; ☽ Apr-Oct), a rustic-chic farmhouse lodge in Muhu's south owned by Finnish TV personality Sikke Sumari. Sikke offers bespoke cooking classes (2033Kr per person for a three-hour workshop and three-course meal) or group dinners, plus B&B accommodation for course participants. Most ingredients are seasonal and local (many are homegrown); classes can be given in a number of languages, including English.

Sleeping & Eating

Vanatoa Turismitalu (☎ 454 8884; www.vanatoa.ee; sites per person 80Kr, s/d/tr with shared bathroom 500/900/1350Kr) In an idyllic setting right by the open-air museum, family-run Vanatoa has homey, down-to-earth (but overpriced) rooms in various outbuildings, plus a large, barnlike restaurant that's popular with tour groups. It's open for lunch and dinner, serving up Estonian staples like stewed pork fillet and herring with potatoes and sour cream (mains 75Kr to 185Kr).

PRACTICALITIES

■ For news, the best English-language weekly is the *Baltic Times* (www.baltictimes.com).

■ The monthly *City Paper* (www.citypaper.ee) is a glossy magazine with some excellent in-depth articles and sometimes quirky features.

■ For events listings pick up the invaluable *In Your Pocket* series (www.inyourpocket.com), published bimonthly for Tallinn and twice yearly for Tartu and Pärnu (also available as free pdf downloads from the website).

■ PAL is the main video system used in Estonia.

■ Electrical current is 220V, 50Hz AC. Sockets require a European plug with two round pins.

■ Estonia uses the metric system for weights and measures. Food and drink occasionally appears on menus listed by the gram (200g of wine, 500g of schnitzel etc).

---

ourpick **Pädaste Manor** (☎ 454 8800; www.padaste .ee; r low/high season from 2280/2850Kr) Pädaste wins our vote as Estonia's finest place to bed down. In a manicured bayside estate in the island's south, the boutique resort encompasses the exquisitely restored manor house (opened in mid-2008, housing 14 rooms and suites and a fine-dining restaurant), a stone carriagehouse that's home to nine rooms and suites and a wellness spa, and a separate stone cottage housing a brasserie and terrace. The attention to detail is second-to-none, from the carriagehouse's private cinema, and the antique furnishings and Muhu embroidery, to the island's herbs, mud and honey used in the spa treatments. Even if you're not staying at Pädaste, you can stop by for a teaser. The exclusive Restaurant Alexander (three/four/ five/six-course meal 690/750/875/985Kr), inside the manor, serves table d'hôte dinner nightly year-round. Lunch is also served here September to May. In summer the Sea House Terrace & Brasserie (lunch mains 155Kr to 295Kr) is open for lunch from noon to 4pm, and for drinks and snacks until 7pm. Here you can enjoy watery views over Muhu lamb or ostrich, or fresh catch of the day. The home-made blueberry ice cream is a treat.

The town of Liiva, about midway across the island, is home to a supermarket, handicrafts stores and **Muhu Restaurant** (☎ 459 8160; meals 50-150Kr; ☺ 11am-11pm May–mid-Sep), a cheerful restaurant decorated with Muhu embroidery and serving up wholesome traditional food.

Getting There & Away

Use the Kuivastu-Kuressaare bus to reach Liiva and Piiri, and ask the driver if they'll stop at other points along the island's main road. Plenty of people thumb rides.

ESTONIA DIRECTORY

The following contains practical information related to travelling in Estonia. For regional information pertaining to all three countries, see the Regional Directory (p389).

ACTIVITIES

Estonia offers plenty of adventure and relaxation amid pastoral splendour or along lengthy coastline. Whatever you do, don't leave Estonia without a trip to the sauna. You'll find them on lakesides, tucked away in forests and in most hotels. It's the true Estonian experience.

For a complete rundown of activities in the Baltic, see the Great Outdoors chapter, p201.

CUSTOMS REGULATIONS

If arriving from another EU country, the limits for alcohol and tobacco are generous (far less generous if you're arriving from outside the EU); see www.emta.ee for full details and restrictions.

EMBASSIES & CONSULATES

For up-to-date contact details of Estonian diplomatic organisations as well as foreign embassies and consulates in Estonia, check the website of the **Estonian Foreign Ministry** (Map pp66-7; ☎ 637 7000; www.vm.ee; Islandi Väljak 1, Tallinn).

Estonian Embassies & Consulates

Estonia has diplomatic representation in a number of overseas countries, including the following:

Latvia (☎ 6781 2020; www.estemb.lv; Skolas iela 13, Rīga LV 1010)

Lithuania (☎ 5-278 0200; www.estemb.lt; Mickevičiaus gatvė 4a, Vilnius)

Embassies & Consulates in Estonia

Most of the following embassies or consulates are in or near Tallinn's Old Town.

Australia (Map pp62-3; ☎ 650 9308; mati@standard.ee; Marja 9)

Canada (Map p70; ☎ 627 3311; tallinn@canada.ee; Toom-Kooli 13, 2nd fl)

Finland (Map p70; ☎ 610 3200; www.finland.ee; Kohtu 4)

France (Map pp62-3; ☎ 631 1492; www.ambafrance-ee .org; Toom-Kuninga 20)

Germany (Map pp62-3; ☎ 627 5300; www.tallinn.diplo .ee; Toom-Kuninga 11)

Ireland (Map p70; ☎ 681 1888; tallinnembassy @dfa.ie; 2nd fl, Vene 2)

Japan (Map p70; ☎ 631 0531; www.japemb.ee; Harju 6)

Latvia (Map pp66-7; ☎ 627 7860; embassy.estonia @mfa.gov.lv; Tõnismägi 10)

Lithuania (Map p70; ☎ 616 4991; http://ee.mfa.lt; Uus 15)

Netherlands (Map p70; ☎ 680 5500; www.nether landsembassy.ee; Rahukohtu 4-I)

New Zealand (Map pp62-3; ☎ 627 2020; toomas.luman @nordecon.ee; Liivalaia 13/15)

Russia Narva (☎ 646 4166; narvacon@narvacon.neti.ee; Lai 18, Narva) Tallinn (Map p70; ☎ 646 4175; www .rusemb.ee; Pikk 19)

Sweden (Map p70; ☎ 640 5600; www.sweden.ee; Pikk 28)

UK (Map pp66-7; ☎ 667 4700; www.britishembassy.ee; Wismari 6)

EMERGENCY NUMBERS

■ 24-hour roadside assistance for drivers ☎ 1888

■ Fire, ambulance and urgent medical advice ☎ 112

■ Police ☎ 110

■ Tallinn's First Aid hotline (☎ 697 1145) can advise you in English about the nearest treatment centres.

USA (Map pp66-7; ☎ 668 8100; www.usemb.ee; Kentmanni 20)

FESTIVALS & EVENTS

Like its neighbours, Estonia has an impressive list of festivals and cultural events, especially during the summer months. A good source of online information is at www.cul ture.ee.

For more on what party to join, and when and where to do so, see the Events Calendar on p18.

HOLIDAYS

New Year's Day 1 January

Independence Day 24 February; anniversary of 1918 declaration

Good Friday March/April

Spring Day 1 May

Whitsunday May/June; seventh Sunday after Easter

Victory Day 23 June; commemorating the anniversary of the Battle of Võnnu (1919)

St John's Day (Jaanipäev; Midsummer's Night) 24 June; taken together, Victory Day and St John's Day are the excuse for a week-long midsummer break for many people

Day of Restoration of Independence 20 August; marking the country's return to independence in 1991;

Christmas Eve 24 December

Christmas Day (Jõulud) 25 December

Boxing Day 26 December

INTERNET ACCESS

Wireless internet access (wi-fi) is marvellously widespread in 'E-stonia' (you may find yourself wondering why your own country lags so far behind this tech-savvy wizard). You'll find over 1170 hotspots throughout the county, and at last count 370-plus hotspots in Tallinn (we're talking in hotels, hostels, restaurants, cafes, pubs, shopping centres, ports, petrol stations, even on long-distance buses!). See www.wifi.ee for a complete list (and keep your eyes peeled for orange-and-black stickers and signs indicating wi-fi availability). In many places connection is free (the website indicates this). If you can't find a free connection, prices are around 35 senti per minute. The only adjustment you may have to make is to set your outgoing mail server (SMTP) to a local host such as mail.hot.ee.

If you're not packing a laptop, options for getting online are not as numerous as they once were (thanks to all that wi-fi and the abundance of laptop-toting locals, there is considerably less demand for internet cafes). Many accommodation providers will offer a computer for guest use. There are a few internet cafes (charging around 40Kr to 60Kr per hour) with speedy connections, plus public libraries have web-connected computers that anyone can use free of charge.

INTERNET RESOURCES

For more information about Estonia, check out the following websites:

Estonia Directory (www.ee) This Estonia-wide directory has links to national parks, car-hire agencies, guesthouses and hundreds of other businesses in Estonia. Start your search on 'tourism'.

Estonica (www.estonica.org) Nicely designed website with information on Estonian history, culture, the economy and nature.

Estonian Institute (www.einst.ee) This site has 'publications' that you can click on, which provide colourful info on Estonian cuisine, art, song traditions and more.

Tallinn Tourism (www.tourism.tallinn.ee) The portal to Tallinn's events and attractions.

MAPS

EO Map (www.eomap.ee) has fold-out maps for every Estonian county, and city- and town-centre maps. If you're driving, pick up EO's excellent road atlas or its *Estonia in Your Pocket*, featuring detailed street maps for several dozen cities. **Regio** (www.regio.ee) produces excellent road atlases and maps for professional reference, and digital maps on CD-ROM. Maps are available at most bookstores.

MONEY

See the inside front cover for exchange rates.

Estonia's currency is the kroon (pronounced krohn), which is pegged to the euro at 15.65Kr. The kroon comes in 2, 5, 10, 25, 50, 100 and 500Kr notes. One kroon is divided into 100 senti (cents), and there are coins of 5, 10, 20 and 50 senti, as well as 1Kr (and rare 5Kr coins).

The government's original target for adopting the euro as the national currency was 2007, but a fast-growing economy and inflation rate above 3% meant that Estonia was unable to meet the criteria necessary for joining the euro zone. The country now intends to adopt the euro sometime between 2011 and 2013. Stay tuned – and note that in the meantime, all in-country purchases are made in kroon.

POST

Mail service in and out of Estonia is highly efficient. Most letters or postcards take one or two days within Estonia, three or four days to Western Europe and about a week to North America and other destinations outside Europe. There is a poste-restante bureau, where mail is kept for up to one month, in Tallinn's **central post office** (Narva mnt 1, Tallinn 10101).

To post a letter up to 50g anywhere in the world costs 9Kr (8Kr to Latvia, Lithuania or Scandinavia).

TELEPHONE

There are no area codes in Estonia; if you're calling anywhere within the country, just dial the number as it's listed in this book. All landline phone numbers have seven digits; mobile (cell) numbers have seven or eight digits, and begin with ☎ 5. Estonia's country code is ☎ 372. To make a collect call dial ☎ 16116, followed by the desired number. To make an international call, dial 00-country code-area code-subscriber number.

Close to 100% of Estonia is covered with digital mobile-phone networks, and every man and his dog has a mobile. To avoid the high roaming charges, you can get a starter kit (around 50Kr), which will give you an Estonian number, a SIM card that you pop into your phone and around 50Kr of talk time (incoming calls are free with most providers). You can buy scratch-off cards for more minutes as you need them. SIM cards and starter kits are available from mobile-phone stores, post offices, supermarkets and kiosks.

Public telephones accept chip cards (50Kr or 100Kr), available at post offices, hotels and most kiosks. For placing calls outside Estonia, an international telephone card with PIN, such as Voicenet (www.voicenet .ee), available at many kiosks and supermarkets, is better value. Note that these cards can only be used from landlines, not mobile phones.

TOURIST INFORMATION

In addition to the info-laden, multilingual website of the **Estonian Tourist Board** (www.visitestonia.com), there are tourist offices in many of the towns and national parks throughout the country. At nearly every one you'll find English-speaking staff. See the Information sections in each destination for individual phone numbers, addresses and opening hours.

Helsinki Excursion

Often called the Daughter of the Baltic, Helsinki has had a long love affair with the Estonian Prince, Tallinn. Historically the two had a tension borne out by centuries of trade rivalry as Helsinki was wooed into the Russian and Swedish empires. Today the two cities have a stable relationship with ferries plying the waters so regularly that Finns almost think of Tallinn as a suburb of Helsinki.

Helsinki has plenty of culture and activities to easily extend that day trip into a week. The fortress of Suomenlinna makes for a historic afternoon's excursion while the bleeding-edge art of Kiasma will let you don a beret and embrace your inner art critic. There's the architectural heritage that stretches beyond Alvar Aalto to include magnificent churches and one of northern Europe's most stunning public squares. And when it's time to rest your weary feet, summer terraces are the best way to take advantage of the long days; or, in winter, cosy up in the famous club scene or gobble some of the best food in the Nordic countries. Or you can keep your hip pocket happy by grazing the Kauppatori (Market square) for Finnish pastries and other local delicacies.

Not that the Finns will be blowing their capital's trumpet. These northern folk are renowned for being quiet – there's an old joke that they invented text messaging so they wouldn't have to speak to one another – but they certainly loosen up after a few drinks. You might have to go easy on shouting drinks, though, as Helsinki prices are the reason those ferry boats are so busy: Finns think of Tallinn as their 'pub suburb'.

FAST FACTS

- **Area** 227,420 sq km
- **Birthplace of** Tove Jansson (Moomin author); Linus Torvalds (Linux creator); Jari Kurri (hockey hall-of-famer)
- **Country** Finland
- **Country code** ☎ 358
- **Departure tax** none
- **Famous for** innovative design, 1952 Olympics, Suomenlinna, saunas
- **Money** euro; US$1= €0.76; UK£1 = €1.10
- **Population** 564,521
- **Official language** Finnish, Swedish
- **Visas** not needed for most visitors for stays of up to 90 days

HELSINKI

Pop 564,521 / ☎ 09

Swedish King Gustav Vasa founded Helsinki in 1550 as a rival to the Hansa trading town of Tallinn. He shanghaied merchants and artisans from across Finland for his newly founded Helsingfors (Swedish for Helsinki). During the war of 1808 the Russians captured Helsinki and its theoretically impenetrable fortress, Suomenlinna. They decided that they wanted a capital closer to St Petersburg, so in 1812 they anointed Helsinki; the Finnish city's status survived independence in the 20th century.

Today you'll hear Russian tourists and see Swedish on most signage: Swedish is officially the country's second language (and is often easier to figure out than the vowel-mangling Finnish). Luckily most people working in the city will speak even just a little English. Much of the city's charms are around its port, though frequent cruise-boat arrivals mean it's a buzzing spot. The main sights are all within walking (or cycling if you want to explore further out) distance.

ORIENTATION

Built on a peninsula surrounded by an archipelago of islets, Helsinki is linked together by bridges and ferries. The city itself has two centres around which its transport is based: Rautatientori (Railway square) and Kauppatori (Market square) at the city's port. From Kauppatori, Esplanadi Park runs west with popular strolling streets Eteläesplanadi and Pohjoisesplanadi on either side. Several ferries depart to the islands and Estonia from the port.

INFORMATION

If you're seeing a few sights and want to use the city's public transport, the **Helsinki Card** (☎ 2288 1200; www.helsinkicard.fi; 24/48/72hr adult €33/43/53, child €11/14/17) is the ideal option, available at the city tourist office or at hotels and transport terminals.

Forex (www.forex.fi; 🕑 8am-9pm Jun-Aug, 8am-7pm Mon-Sat Sep-May) Mannerheimintie (Mannerheimintie 10); Pohjoisesplanadi (Pohjoisesplanadi 23) Has good exchange rates, with a flat €2 fee on travellers cheques and no commission. There are other offices at the train station and along Pohjoisesplanadi.

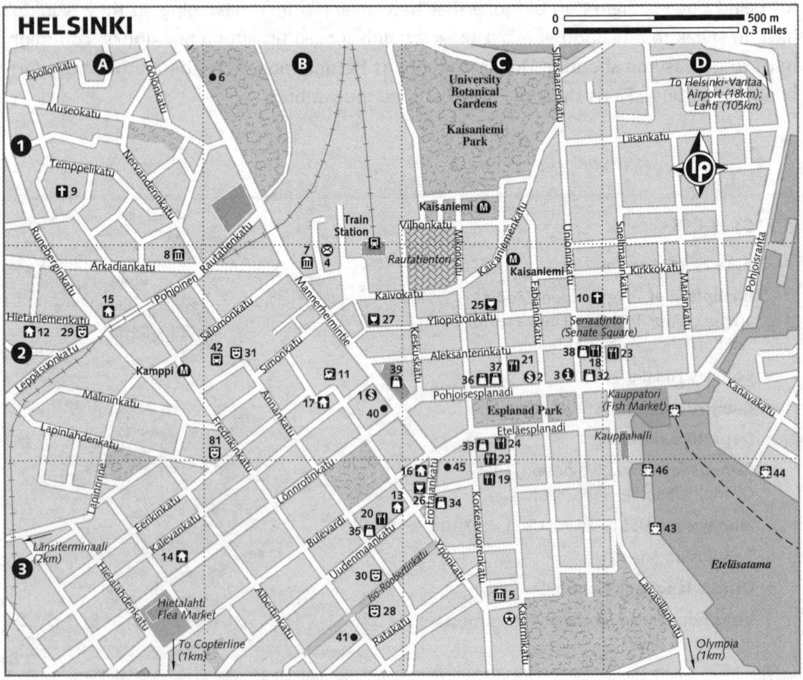

Helsinki City Tourist Office (☎ 169 3757; www.hel
.fi/tourism; Pohjoisesplanadi 19; ⏰ 9am-8pm Mon-Fri,
9am-6pm Sat & Sun May-Sep, 9am-6pm Mon-Fri, 10am-
4pm Sat & Sun Oct-Apr) Busy multilingual office with a
great quantity of information on the city.

Helsinki Expert (www.helsinkiexpert.fi) Book hotel
rooms and purchase tickets for train, bus and ferry travel
around Finland and for travel to Tallinn and St Petersburg.
Also sells Helsinki Card and is located in the tourist office.

Main post office (☎ 020-451 4400; Mannerheimin
aukio 1; ⏰ 7am-9pm Mon-Fri, 10am-6pm Sat & Sun) The
post office is in the large building between the bus and
train stations with the poste restante office adjacent.

SIGHTS & ACTIVITIES

Just a 15-minute ferry ride from Kauppatori,
Suomenlinna ('fortress of Finland') is the
must-do half-day trip from the city. Set on
a tight cluster of islands, this Unesco World
Heritage site has been hotly contested real
estate ever since the Swedes built here in 1748
to stave off Russian attacks, naming their bastion Sveaborg (Swedish fortress). Of course
the Russians took the fort in 1808 and it remained in Russian hands until independence.
Ironically, during the Finnish Civil War it
served as a prison for communist prisoners.

Suomenlinna actually spans two islands:
Iso Mustaari in the north and Susisaari in
the south, which are connected by a small
bridge. Most visits to the island begin at the
bridge with the **Inventory Chamber Visitor Centre**
(☎ 668 800; www.suomenlinna.fi; ⏰ 10am-6pm May-Sep,
walking tours 11am & 2pm Jun-Aug), which has tourist
information, maps and guided walking tours

HELSINKI ON A HANDSET

Packed your mobile or cell phone? Helsinki
Tourism has a cut-down version of its tourism site designed to be delivered to your
mobile at www.helsinki.mobi.

(€6.50; free with a Helsinki Card) in summer.
You can also hop off at the King's Gate Quay
on Suisaari, if you want to explore for yourself. There's a blue-signposted walking path
that takes in the islands' several museums
and cafes.

For a more modern take, in the city centre you'll find the quirky curves of **Kiasma**
(Museum of Contemporary Art; ☎ 1733 6501; www.kiasma
.fi; Mannerheiminaukio 2; adult/under 18yr €7/free; ⏰ 10am-
8.30pm Wed-Sun, 9am-5pm Tue), a contemporary art
space that still surprises with exciting new
exhibits. Focusing on the left of field, it has
a permanent collection on the 3rd floor and
an experimental theatre with a changing
program (tickets usually cost extra) on the
ground floor, which is known for the handwritten clock outside the artsy museum shop.
The building has become a meeting point for
artists as well as drinkers on its popular terrace, who look out on the horseback figure of
the **Mannerheim statue**.

The **Design Museum** (☎ 622 05421; www.design
museum.fi; Korkeavuorenkatu 23; adult/child €7/free;
⏰ 11am-6pm Tue-Sun, plus Mon Jun-Aug, 11am-8pm
Tue Sep-May) has a permanent collection that
looks at the uniqueness of Finnish design,

HELSINKI EXCURSION

HELSINKI EXCURSION

particularly the recent Fennofolk movement. Changing exhibitions focus on contemporary design – everything from clothing to household furniture.

Recently renovated, the **Natural History Museum** (Luonnontieteellinen Museo; ☎ 1912 8800; www.fmnh.helsinki.fi; Pohjoinen Rautatienkatu 13; adult/child €5/2.50; ◷ 9am-5pm Tue-Fri, 11am-4pm Sat & Sun) is known for its controversial weather vane of a sperm impregnating an ovum. New exhibitions like the Story of the Bones, which puts skeletons in an evolutionary context, bring new life to the University of Helsinki's extensive collection of mammals, birds and other creatures, including all Finnish species. The dinosaur skeletons and the saggy African elephant in the foyer are hits with kids.

One of the finest creations of German architect CL Engel is the **Senaatintori** (Senate Square), a magnificent city square. It's dominated by the chalk-white neoclassical **Tuomiokirkko** (Lutheran cathedral; ☎ 709 2455; Unioninkatu 29; ◷ 9am-6pm Mon-Sat, noon-6pm Sun Sep-May, 9am-midnight Jun-Aug); as it was not completed until 1852, Engel himself never saw its majesty as he died in 1840. Given the Lutheran sensibilities, it was created to serve as a reminder of God's supremacy over the square. Its high flight of stairs, however, is a popular meeting place for canoodling couples and a setting for New Year's revelry. The interior features statues of the Reformation heroes Luther, Melanchthon and Michael Agricola and, true to their ideals, there is little other ornamentation under the lofty dome.

Hewn into solid rock, **Temppeliaukio Church** (☎ 494 698; Lutherinkatu 3; ◷ 10am-8pm Mon-Fri, 10am-6pm Sat, noon-1.45pm & 3.30-6pm Sun) was designed by Timo and Tuomo Suomalainen in 1969 and remains one of Helsinki's foremost attractions. The church symbolises the modern innovativeness of Finnish religious architecture and features a stunning 24m-diameter roof covered in 22km of copper stripping. There are regular concerts, with great acoustics. The entrance is at the northern end of Fredrikinkatu.

A little further out on Mannerheimintie is one of Alvar Aalto's most famous works, the angular **Finlandia Talo** (☎ visiting info 40241, box office 402 4400; Mannerheimintie 13; guided tours €6), a concert hall built in 1971. Opening hours depend on events; ring for information.

Everyone will tell you that you haven't been to Finland unless you've had a sauna. The

Yrjönkadun Uimahalli (☎ 3108 7401; Yrjönkatu 21; admission €4-11; ◷ men 6.30am-9pm Tue, Thu & Sat, women noon-9pm Sun & Mon, 6.30am-9pm Wed & Fri) is one of the more historic options in a sleek Art Deco complex first opened in 1928.

SLEEPING

Budget options are rare in Helsinki, but fortunately there are some excellent *kesahotellis* (summer hostels) that are available from June to August.

Academica Summer Hostel (☎ 1311 4334; www.hostelacademica.fi; Hietaniemenkatu 14; dm €23, standard s/tw up to €42/59, modern s/tw up to €55/69; ◷ Jun-Aug; ✗ ▣ ☂ P) One of the best hostels, this definitely doesn't feel like a student sharehouse. It's super-clean and packed with features (pool, sauna and wi-fi). Traditional rooms are older, but still have great additions like bar fridges and en-suite bathrooms. Dorms are limited to four bunks to a room so even the cheapest feel uncrowded. Management is also environmentally aware, with a carbon offset program and a WWF-certified green office.

Hostel Erottajanpuisto (☎ 642 169; www.erottajanpuisto.com; Uudenmaankatu 9; dm/s/d/tr €23.50/49/68/81; ✗ ▣) An excellent central option if you're on a tight budget. In the thick of the happening Punavuori area, it's a social spot with a large drawing room that doubles as a basic kitchen where free coffee is always brewing. Dorms are limited to eight bunks to a room though singles are a good chance to escape the party people.

our pick **Hotelli Helka** (☎ 613 580; www.helka.fi; Pohjoinen Rautatiekatu 23a; s/d €136/171, weekends & summer €90/112; ✗ ▣ P) If you're into Finnish design, you'll love this hip hotel with renovated rooms decked out in chocolate browns and wheaty tones. Every room has a print of an autumn forest hanging over it that's backlit to give rooms a moody glow – daunting but delicious. Keitto (kitchen) is the restaurant which serves a generous buffet breakfast. Bikes can be hired (€15).

Hotel Linna (☎ 010-344 4100; www.palace.fi; Lönnrotinkatu 29; s/d up to €130/119, weekends up to €130/250; P ✗ ▣) For your own castle, this fits the bill: Linna is Finnish for 'castle'. The turreted facade and courtly service give you the royal treatment, although this place was only built in 1903 as the student clubhouse for the technical university opposite. The castle decor never feels cheesy: rooms are tastefully kitted out with extra-long beds, minibars and, in some rooms, bathtubs. There's a choice of three saunas; wi-fi is available (€12 per day).

Klaus K (☎ 020-770 4700; www.klauskhotel.com; Bulevardi 2; s/d from €140/180; ▣) The swankiest option in town is definitely this designer hotel. It's easily the slickest of the new generation of Helsinki hotels, with *Kalevala* (Finland's national epic) quotes woven into the gold walls of the lobby and the thread running onto a framed verse in every room. It's distinctly Finnish, from luxurious birch-scented toiletries to space-conscious architecture to the corrugated sauna-style roofs of bathrooms. But there are worldly comforts like high-speed wi-fi and DVDs in all rooms, plus two good restaurants and a frostily cool bar.

Sokos Hotel Torni (☎ 020-1234 604; www.sokoshotels .fi; Yrjönkatu 26; s/d €220/250, weekends €105/115; ✖ ▣) In 1931 'Finland's Empire State Building' was built as the tallest structure in Helsinki and has become Sokos Hotel Torni. Although no longer the country's tallest building, it still boasts excellent views, especially from Ateljee Bar (see p172). Now rooms have been stylishly renovated in keeping with the historic feel, in art deco and Art Nouveau style, though modern rooms in rich red and black have hip decor. Each room has its own guestbook filled with glowing comments.

EATING

Fazer (☎ 6159 2959; Kluuvikatu 3; sandwiches €7-8, pies €9-10; ☽ 7.30am-10pm Sun-Fri, 9am-10pm Sat) This classic cafe can feel a little cavernous, but it's the flagship for Finland's mighty chocolate empire of the same name. There are sandwiches galore, but it's one of the better places to buy Fazer confectionery or to enjoy towering sundaes or slabs of cake.

our pick **Cafe Engel** (☎ 652 776; Senaatintori; meals €10-18; ☽ 8am-10pm Mon-Fri, 9am-10pm Sat, 10am-10pm Sun) This heavenly spot in the Senaatintori hums with both tourists and university students alike. There's always a good selection of cakes and enticing meals often of a vegetarian bent (such as a beetroot lasagne). It's a cultural hub with films shown in the courtyard during summer, irregular piano recitals and a plump English-language magazine selection.

Savotta (☎ 7425 5588; Aleksanterinkatu 22; mains €16-25; ☽ 11am-11pm Mon-Fri, 1-11pm Sat & Sun) This representation of a logger's mess hall offers traditional Finnish working food. Waitresses

in peasant tops bring *karjalanpiirakka* (Karelian pies) as starters before moving on to meaty fare like elk, bear stew or the Forest Foreman's Plate which is a carnivore's sampler served in a skillet. If you enter into the spirit of things, it can be a top night out.

Demo (☎ 228 90840; www.restaurantdemo.fi; Uuden-maankatu 9-11; mains €19-25, set menu €48-52; ☽ 4-11pm Tue-Sat) A favourite with Helsinki's chefs, this fashionable spot does modern European food such as artichoke ravioli or roasted goose breast at affordable prices. The location means it attracts bright young things who delight in the liquorice ice cream or rhubarb sorbets.

Savoy (☎ 6128 5300; Eteläesplanadi 14; mains €36-58; ☽ lunch & dinner Mon-Fri) Originally designed by Alvar and Aino Aalto, this is definitely a stand-out dining room with blondewood and Artek furniture throughout. Dishes source the best in local ingredients with an eye on sustainability and conserving your food miles, with highlights such as roasted partridge with duck liver. It's proof that green grub doesn't have to be all alfalfa sprouts and mashed yeast.

Chez Dominique (☎ 612 7393; www.chezdominique.fi; Rikhardinkatu 4; mains €45-50, set menus €99-139; ☽ lunch & dinner Tue-Fri, dinner Sat, closed Jul) Helsinki's best French restaurant has moved to a larger location but has maintained its pair of Michelin stars. The menu sticks to French classics such as Dover sole and Anjou pigeon with Finnish flourishes (set menus from four to nine courses) include a divine *pulla*, a Finnish pastry.

Olo (☎ 665 565; www.olo-restaurant.com; Kasarmikatu 44; mains €75-38; ☽ lunch Mon-Fri, dinner Tue-Sat) A relative newcomer on the fine-dining scene, Olo is refreshingly unpretentious with a dining room of muted greys and whites. The menu is playful Finnish with a saddle of lamb sauced with Madeira and forest mushrooms or tender piglet. All meals come with house-baked breads (try the fruity malt) and a wine list broad enough to appeal to all palates.

The **Kauppahalli** (covered market; Eteläranta; ☽ 8am-6pm Mon-Fri, 8am-4pm Sat) was built in 1889 and remains one of the country's best markets, with good snacks and produce to graze on. The always-busy Kauppatori is good for grilled salmon, cheap snacks and fresh produce such as berries in summer. Most food stalls set up plastic chairs and tables on summer afternoons – which are besieged by seagulls.

DRINKING

Finns like a drink and there's no shortage of places to slake your thirst. Look out for summer terraces that spill out onto the pavements and rooftops of Helsinki when the weather's good. In autumn terrace bars will often bring out blankets and heaters to stretch the outdoor season.

Zetor (☎ 010-766 4450; www.ravintolazetor.fi; Mannerheimintie 3-5; 🕑 11am-4am Sat, 3pm-1am Sun & Mon, 3pm-3am Tue, 3pm-4am Wed & Thu) Ever wondered where the Leningrad Cowboys would park their pointy shoes? This kooky restaurant and pub (mains €10 to €22) has a kitschy Czech tractor theme from the mind of Finnish film-maker Aki Kaurismäki. Food like cabbage rolls, salmon soup and other traditional dishes compliment the Finnish booze (including *sahti, a* traditional ale flavoured with juniper berries), but ease off if you're finishing the night with a tractor ride.

Arctic Icebar (☎ 278 1855; Yliopistonkatu 5; admission €10; 🕑 10pm-4am Wed-Sat) Not cold enough outside? Then try this bar that's literally carved out of ice (that includes tables and the bar). It's -5°C so you'll need the furry cape you're offered on entry and the complimentary warming drink included in the price. There's a minimum age of 24. It's above La Bodega.

Cuba! Cafe (☎ 050-505 0425; www.cubacafe.fi; Erottajankatu 4; 🕑 5pm-2am Sun-Thu, 5pm-4am Fri & Sat) Certainly one of Helsinki's brighter bars, this place is done out in peach and mojito limes with a small stage that features a Havana-style taxi and DJs or salsa bands. Beers, cocktails and dancing are the order of the night in this party place.

Ateljee Bar (Sokos Hotel Torni, Yrjönkatu 26; 🕑 2pm-2am Mon-Thu, noon-2am Fri & Sat, 2pm-1am Sun) It's worth the climb up to this tiny perch on the roof of the Sokos Hotel Torni for the city panorama. Taking the lift to the 12th floor is the best option, then there's a narrow winding staircase to the top.

ENTERTAINMENT

Helsinki has a buzzing club culture with new places popping up all the time. Nightclubs have varying minimum-age restrictions (some as high as 24 years old) so check websites before hitting the town.

LUX (☎ 020-775 9350; www.luxnightclub.fi; Urho Kekkosen katu 1a; door charge €5-10; 🕑 10pm-4am Wed-Sat) Ascend into clubbing heaven at this super-slick club with stellar lighting. Its position on top of Kamppi (one of the biggest shopping complexes) means brilliant views and high-altitude cocktails. Music runs from sexy lounge to sweaty funk with local DJs and international visitors. Enter via Kamppi Sq.

DTM (Don't Tell Mama; ☎ 676 315; www.dtm.fi; Iso Roobertinkatu 28; door charge €2-10; 🕑 9am-4am Mon-Sat, noon-4am Sun; 💻) Scandinavia's biggest gay club is a multilevel complex with an early-opening cafe-bar (admission free). A couple of club areas open at 9pm (minimum age 22) and there are regular club nights as well as drag shows or women-only sessions.

Lost & Found (☎ 680 1010; www.lostandfound.fi; Annankatu 6; 🕑 evening only) You can skip the bar upstairs and head to the dark grotto-like dance floor downstairs that's decked out in luminescent designs. Still a gay venue (it styles itself as a 'hetero-friendly gay club'), the tunes are often chart-based with a sign near the DJ booth, 'Don't request. I'll play it eventually.' It's often the spot for after-parties following big gigs.

Heavy Corner (☎ 458 4309; www.heavycorner.com; Hietaniemenkatu 2; 🕑 6pm-late Wed-Sat) Metal is huge in Finland and this club is the place to hear the rockingest tunes and often metal karaoke, featuring super-serious patrons who believe they are auditioning for Metallica. Wear anything other than black here and they'll know you're a tourist.

SHOPPING

Helsinki is known for design, from fashion to the latest furniture and homewares. By wandering along Pohjoisesplanadi, the main tourist street in town, you'll find most of the big name places, though the Punavuori has hipper designers and boutiques. Look out for the black-and-white sticker of **Design District Helsinki** (www.designd istrict.fi).

Design Forum Finland (☎ 6220 810; www.designforum.fi; Erottajankatu 7; 🕑 10am-7pm Mon-Fri, 10am-6pm Sat, noon-6pm Sun) A good place to start tracking down innovative craft, this place operates a shop that hosts many designers' works.

Aarikka (☎ 652 277; www.aarikka.fi; Pohjoisesplanadi 27; 🕑 10am-7pm Mon-Fri, 10am-5pm Fri) Specialising in wood, Aarika is known for its distinctly Finnish jewellery.

Artek (☎ 6132 5277; www.artek.fi; Eteläesplanadi 18) Originally founded by Alvar Aalto and his wife Aino, this homewares, glassware and furniture store maintains the simple design principle of its founders.

Marimekko (☎ 686 0240; www.marimekko.fi; Pohjoisesplanadi 31) Finland's most celebrated designer fabrics, including warm florals and hipper new designs, are available here as shirts, dresses, bags, sheets and almost every other possible application.

IvanaHelsinki (☎ 622 4422; www.ivanhelsinki.fi; Uudenmaankatu 15; ☺ 11am-7pm Mon-Fri, 11am-4pm Sat) Currently the coolest label with its own Fennofolk style, it has to-die-for dresses and T-shirts that deftly play with Finnish icons.

Moomin Shop (☎ 622 2206; Kämp Galleria, Pohjoisesplanadi 33; ☺ 10am-8pm Mon-Fri, 10am-6pm Sat) Stock up on all things related to Finland's most-loved children's characters, the Moomins, including books in English and Finnish.

Sauna Market (☎ 278 5051; Aleksanterinkatu 26-28; ☺ 10am-6pm) Gather sauna oils, back-scrubbers, water ladles and hundreds of other accoutrements for your own sauna.

Stockmann (☎ 1211; Aleksanterinkatu 52) Helsinki's 'everything store' does a good line of Finnish souvenirs and Sámi handicrafts, as well as Finnish textiles, Kalevala Koru jewellery, Lapponia jewellery, Moomintroll souvenirs and lots more.

GETTING THERE & AWAY
Air
There are flights to Helsinki from the USA, Europe and Asia on many airlines. **Finnair** (☎ reservations 0600 140 140; www.finnair.fi; Asema-aukio 1; ☺ 9am-6pm Mon-Sat) and its subsidiaries offer international as well as domestic services, with flights to 20 Finnish cities – generally at least once a day. Budget carriers **Blue1** (☎ 0600 25831; www.blue1.com) and **Finncomm** (☎ 4243 2003; www.fc.fi) have budget flights to some Finnish and international destinations. The airport is in the satellite city of Vantaa, 19km north of Helsinki.

Until Copterline suspended services in late 2008 (a victim of the global financial crisis), the quickest way to Tallinn was by helicopter. **Copterline** (☎ 0200 18181; www.copterline.com; Hernesaari helicopter terminal, Hernematalankatu 2b) flew from Helsinki to Tallinn (one way €98, hourly 7am to 8pm Monday to Friday, 9am to 5pm Saturday, 10am to 4pm Sunday) in a zippy 18 minutes. There is a chance that services will resume in the future – check the website.

Boat
International ferries travel to Tallinn and on to Stockholm. There is also a regular catamaran and hydrofoil service to Tallinn.

Four of the five ferry terminals are just off Kauppatori: Kanava and Katajanokka terminals are served by bus 13 and trams 2, 2V and 4; and Olympia and Makasiini terminals by trams 3B and 3T. The last terminal, Länsiterminaali (West Terminal), is served by bus 15.

Ferry tickets may be purchased at the terminal, from a ferry company's office (and often its website) or, in some cases, from the city tourist office. Book in advance during the high season (late June to mid-August).

Some ferry company offices in Helsinki:

Eckerö Line (☎ 228 8544; www.eckeroline.fi; Mannerheimintie 10, Länsiterminaali) Runs *Nordlandia* car ferry, which sails daily to Tallinn (adult/car from €19/21, three to 3½ hours) year-round.

Linda Line (☎ 668 9700; www.lindaliini.ee; Makasiini terminal) Small passenger-only hydrofoil company plying the waters to Tallinn (adult from €19, 1½ hours). with up to seven trips daily (when waters are ice-free).

Nordic Jet Line (☎ 681 770; www.njl.info; Kanava terminal) Runs two catamarans, *Nordic Jet* and *Baltic Jet*, to Tallinn (adult/car from €28/35, 1¾ hours) sailing from May to September or later (depending on the weather) with seven daily crossings.

Tallink (☎ 2282 1222; www.tallinksilja.com; Erottajankatu 19) Runs at least five services from Kanava terminal to Tallinn (adult/vehicle one way from €23/20, two to 3½ hours) on high-speed *Star* and *Superstar* or the slower *Baltic Princess*. Also serves Rostock (Germany) and Stockholm (Sweden).

Viking Line (☎ 123 577; www.vikingline.fi; Mannerheimintie 14) Operates car ferry *Rosella* to Tallinn(adult/car from €19/18, 2½ hours) from Katajanokka and Makasiini terminals.

Bus
Purchase long-distance and express bus tickets at **Kamppi Station** (Frederikinkatu; ☺ 7am-7pm Mon-Fri, 7am-5pm Sat, 9am-6pm Sun) or on the bus itself. Buses run to destinations throughout Finland and internationally to Russia.

Train
The **train station** (rautatieasema) is in the city centre and is linked by pedestrian subway with Helsinki's metro. Helsinki is the terminus for Finland's three main railway lines so you can get to anywhere in Finland from here.

There is a separate ticket counter for international trains, including the ones that go to St Petersburg (€62, 6½ hours), Moscow (€92, 13 hours) and Vyborg (€42, four hours). In 2010 a new high-speed train is scheduled to St Petersburg, but at the time of research no ticketing information was available.

GETTING AROUND

Bicycle

With a flat inner city and well-marked cycling paths, Helsinki is ideal for cycling. Get hold of a copy of the Helsinki cycling map at the tourist office. The city provides 300 distinctive green 'City Bikes' at stands within a radius of 2km from Kauppatori. The bikes are free: you deposit a €2 coin into the lockable stand, then reclaim it when you return it to any stand.

For something more sophisticated, **Greenbike** (☎ 8502 2850; www.greenbike.fi; Fredrikinkatu 31; bikes per day/24hr/week from €15/20/60; ⊙ 10am-6pm Mon-Fri, 10am-3pm Sat, 10am-2pm Sun) rents out quality bikes including 24-speed hybrid mountain bikes.

Car & Motorcycle

Parking in Helsinki is strictly regulated and can be a big headache. Metered areas in the city centre cost €3 per hour during the week, but are free on weekends. There are undercover car parks in Kampii and Forum; for other locations consult the *Parking Guide for the Inner City of Helsinki*, a free map available at the city tourist office.

Public Transport

Central Helsinki is easy to get around on foot or by bicycle but there's also a metro line and a reasonably comprehensive transport network. The city's public transport system, **Helsingin Kaupungin Liikennelaitos** (HKL; ☎ 310 1071; www .hkl.fi), operates buses, metro and local trains, trams and a ferry to Suomenlinna. A one-hour flat-fare ticket for any HKL transport costs €2.20 when purchased on board, €2 when purchased in advance. A single tram ticket is €2 full fare. Tourist tickets (one/three/five days €6/12/18) are the best option if you're in town for a short time. Alternatively, the Helsinki Card (see p168) gives you free travel anywhere within Helsinki.

HKL ferries to Suomenlinna (see p169) depart from the passenger quay at Kauppatori (return €3.80, 15 minutes, three times hourly, 6.20am to 2.20am). Tickets are available at the pier. **JT-Lines** (☎ 534 806; www.jt-line.fi) runs an hourly waterbus from Kauppatori to Suomenlinna (return €5.50, 30 minutes), 8am to 7pm from mid-May to August.

HKL offices (⊙ 7.30am-7pm Mon-Thu, 7.30am-5pm Fri, 10am-3pm Sat) at the Kamppi bus station and the Rautatientori and Hakaniemi metro stations sell tickets and passes, as do many of the city's R-kioskis. Metro services run daily from about 6am to 11.30pm. The metro line extends to Ruoholahti in the western part of the city and northeast to Mellunmäki and Vuosaari.

Taxi

You can hail cabs on the street or join a queue at one of the taxi stands located at the train station, bus station or Senaatintori. Alternatively, phone for a cab on ☎ 0100 0700.

Latvia

Latvia

Tucked between Estonia to the north and Lithuania to the south, Latvia is the meat of the Baltic sandwich. We're not implying that the neighbouring nations are slices of white bread, but Latvia is the savoury middle, loaded with colourful fixings. Thick greens take the form of Gauja Valley pine forests peppered with castle ruins. Onion-domed Orthodox cathedrals cross the land from salty Liepāja to sweet Cēsis. Cheesy Russian pop blares along the beach in Jūrmala. And spicy Rīga adds an extra zing as the country's cosmopolitan nexus, and unofficial capital of the entire Baltic region.

Latvians often wax poetic about their country, calling it 'the land that sings'. It seems to be in the genes; locals are blessed with unusually pleasant voices, and their canon of traditional tunes is the power source for their indomitable spirit. Latvians (along with their Baltic brothers) literally sang for their freedom from the USSR in a series of dramatic protests known as the 'Singing Revolution', and today the nation holds the Song and Dance Festival every five years, which unites thousands upon thousands of singers from across the land in splendid harmony.

Travellers who manage to tear themselves away from enchanting Rīga will discover a second spin on the singing metaphor – the land itself provides a feast of sounds. Frigid waves pound the desolate coasts like a drum, choirs of cicadas cut the muggy midsummer air with melodic chirping, and soft seagull coos accent the rhythmic clopping of roving horses.

The next few years will prove to be quite interesting as this hearty hinterland approaches its 20th birthday. No more are the days of teenage growing pains – big things are in store for this little country…

LATVIA

FAST FACTS

- **Area** 64,589 sq km (half the size of England)
- **Birthplace of** ballet dancer Mikhail Baryshnikov and artist Mark Rothko
- **Capital** Rīga
- **Country code** ☎ 371
- **Departure tax** none
- **Famous for** the jaw-dropping Song and Dance Festival held every five years
- **Money** Latvian lats; 1€ = 0.70Ls; US$1 = 0.52Ls; UK£1 = 0.75Ls
- **Population** 2.25 million
- **Visa** not needed for most nationalities. See p399 for details.

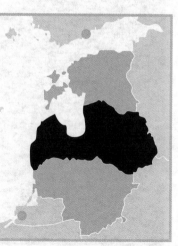

HOW MUCH?

- **Small bottle of Black Balzām** 2.89Ls
- **Big bowl of pelmeņi** 2Ls
- **Public sauna session** 7Ls
- **Dorm bed in Rīga** from 7Ls
- **Public-transport ticket** 0.40Ls

LONELY PLANET INDEX

- **Litre of petrol** 0.64Ls
- **Litre of Vichy bottled water** 0.34Ls
- **Pint of beer in a store/bar** 0.50/2Ls
- **Souvenir T-shirt** 5-15Ls
- **Pancake blintz** 0.65Ls

HIGHLIGHTS

- **Rīga** (p186) Click your camera at the capital's shimmering church spires, devilish Art Nouveau gargoyles, and cobbled lanes secreted behind gingerbread trim.
- **Gauja National Park** (p253) Trek through this Never-Never Land by bike, chronicling its vivid history with stops at rambling Livonian castles and top-secret Soviet bunkers.
- **Kurzeme Coast** (p233 to p243) Close your eyes and listen to the pounding waves along this stunning stretch of coastline studded with surfer towns such as Pāvilosta and Liepāja, and crowned by the awesomely remote Cape Kolka.
- **Jūrmala** (p226) Hobnob with Russian jetsetters in the land of the three 'B's: beaches, bikinis and bad haircuts.
- **Latgale Lakelands** (p269) Uncover endless emerald lakes and wispy blueberry fields steeped in 1000 years of Latgallian traditions.

ITINERARIES

- **Three days** Fill your first two days with a feast of Rīga's architectural eye candy, and spend your third day hiking betwixt Sigulda's castles, sunbathing in scintillating Jūrmala, or snapping photos of Rundāle's opulent palace. Check out the boxed text on p200 for other excursion ideas.
- **One week** After a couple of days in the capital, swing through Jūrmala on your way up the horn of Cape Kolka for saunas, sunsets and solitude. Alternatively,

blaze a trail through Gauja National Park for a rousing trip back in time, spiced with adrenalin sports. Either way, try to squeeze an afternoon at Rundāle Palace into the mix.

- **Two weeks** After absorbing Rīga's cosmopolitan vibe, head deep into the countryside, stopping first in the castle-clad Gauja National Park. Glide through the Vidzeme Uplands and compare the ultra-bucolic Latgale Lakelands to Rundāle's majestic grounds. Continue west into the Kurzeme region following the Baltic coastline from gritty Liepāja all the way up to the desolate tip of Cape Kolka.

CURRENT EVENTS

Latvia is looking ahead. The country is almost as old as it was when it was subjected to Soviet Occupation at the tender age of 20 back in 1940. After retracing its steps upon achieving a second taste of liberty, Latvia is ready to propel itself beyond its past achievements and take a position among the global community. Even with a freshly minted EU membership card, the country is still experiencing the typical growing pains of a pubescent nation. In the last three years, as personal vehicles have become more prevalent, the number of car-related fatalities have spiked, making Latvia one of the most dangerous nations in the EU to drive a car. EU funding, which pushed the fledging economy forward by leaps and bounds, is starting to slow down, and the country is learning how to fill in the gaps and grapple with its seemingly uncontrollable inflation. In 2006 Latvia was the poorest country in the EU, but today the nation is experiencing continued economic growth despite the depressed global climate. Economists are focused on better controlling the currency so as to make the eventual switch over to the euro. Original estimates pegged the switchover in 2009, but realistic calculations suggest 2012 or even 2015. And there are some who are against the switch altogether.

Although both genders are well represented in Latvian politics and business, and gender discrimination feels like a dated topic, dealing with sexual orientation is still a tempestuous issue compared with the EU's Western European nations. Former prime minister Aigars Kalvītis publicly condemned the first gay march, held in 2005, and legislation has been ratified to ban same-sex marriage.

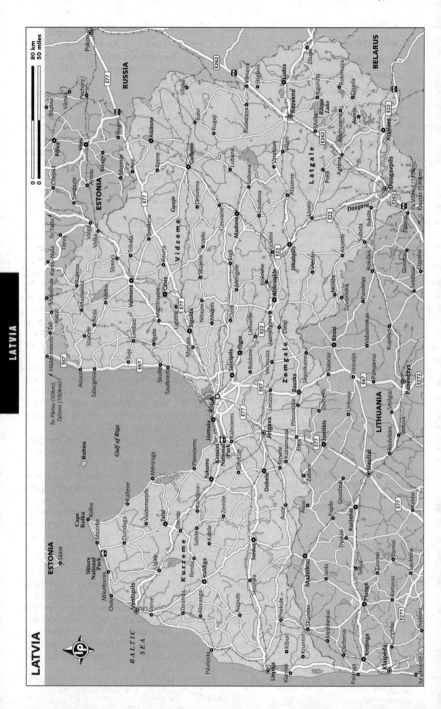

Annual pride parades have continued since, although supporters continue to be jeered by protesters at large, and organised antigay committees such as No Pride still graffiti hate messages around Rīga.

HISTORY
The Beginning
The first signs of modern man in the region date back to the Stone Age, although Latvians descended from tribes that migrated north from around Belarus and settled on the territory of modern Latvia around 2000 BC. These tribes settled in coastal areas to fish and take advantage of rich deposits of amber, which was more precious than gold in many places until the Middle Ages.

Eventually, four main Baltic tribes evolved: the Selonians, the Letts (or Latgals), the Semigallians and the Cours. From the latter three derived the names of three of Latvia's four principal regions: Latgale, Zemgale and Kurzeme. The fourth region, Vidzeme (Livland), derived its name from the Livs, a Finno-Ugric people unrelated to the Balts (p235).

During succeeding centuries of foreign rule these tribes merged into one Latvian identity. They were pagan until the first Christian missionaries arrived in the late 12th century.

Christianity
The first Christian missionaries arrived in Latvia in 1190 and tried to persuade the pagan population to convert. It was an uphill battle: as soon as the missionaries left, the new converts jumped into the river to wash off their baptism. In subsequent years more missionaries would arrive, and more Latvians would submit and then renounce Christianity.

In 1201, at the behest of the pope, German crusaders, led by Bishop von Buxhoevden of Bremen, conquered Latvia and founded

A PRESIDENTIAL SEAL OF APPROVAL

President Vaira Vīķe-Freiberga made quite a name for herself in the European community as a much-needed female political presence. She was the first female Latvian president and held the position for two terms (from 1999 to 2007). The strong leader (and Canadian émigré) was applauded for returning to her motherland to pull Latvia out of economic uncertainty and catapult the little nation towards EU membership. We had a chance to sit down with the former president to talk about her life beyond the political spotlight. She offered her impressions of Latvia from a visitor's perspective since she had a chance to view her country with fresh eyes after spending most of her life abroad.

'There are three things in Rīga that everyone should see: the amazing *Jugendstil* (Art Nouveau) architecture (p209), the Blackheads' House (p190), where I used to hold my state dinners, and finally, the Opera House (p223), which, in my opinion, features one of the finest opera companies in the world. If you have the time, try to catch a performance by Kamer, a prize-winning choir made up of local musicians. They sing mostly modern music and are currently performing a repertoire of sun-themed songs written specifically for the choir by 17 composers from 16 different lands.'

'Beyond Rīga, which was, by the way, at one time a bigger port than Stockholm, I would encourage visitors to seek out the many festivals around the country, particularly during the summer. Sigulda, Bauska and Rundāle host some of my favourite music festivals. Rundāle Palace is undoubtedly the most famous castle in Latvia, but I personally enjoy the castle in Stāmeriena (p264) for its elegant architecture and interesting history. The country's wooden architecture is also of note, particularly in Kurzeme.'

'Those who enjoy nature should spend some time in Jūrmala along the Bay of Rīga (p226). I have fond memories of entertaining foreign dignitaries at the presidential estate in Jūrmala – I remember watching a beautiful sunset on my lawn during a barbecue I hosted for Boris Yeltsin. The bay is quite shallow, so it is perfect for families, and sometimes in the summer it can even be warmer than the Mediterranean Sea.'

'In the more rural parts of the country, you will discover unique flora (a new type of mushroom was just discovered), wild herds of bison and horses in Kurzeme, hundreds of bird species all over the country, and interesting swampy ecosystems near the coast.'

Rīga. Von Buxhoevden also founded the Knights of the Sword, who made Rīga their base for subjugating Livonia. Colonists from northern Germany followed, and during the first period of German rule, Rīga became the major city in the German Baltic, thriving from trade between Russia and the West and joining the Hanseatic League (a medieval merchant guild) in 1282. Furs, hides, honey and wax were among the products sold westward from Russia through Rīga.

Power struggles between the church, knights and city authorities dominated the country's history between 1253 and 1420. Rīga's bishop, elevated to archbishop in 1252, became the leader of the church in the German conquered lands, ruling a good slice of Livonia directly and further areas of Livonia and Estonia indirectly through his bishops. The church clashed constantly with knights, who controlled most of the remainder of Livonia and Estonia, and with German merchant-dominated city authorities who managed to maintain a degree of independence during this period.

Sweden, Poland & Russia

The 15th, 16th and 17th centuries were marked with battles and disputes about how to divvy up what would one day become Latvia. The land was at the crossroads of several encroaching empires and everyone wanted to secure the area as a means of gaining a strategic upper hand. It was at this time that Martin Luther posted his theses and Lutheran ideals flooded east. Rīga quickly became a centre for the Reformation and merchant elites adopted the doctrine. Fervent religious movements spawned the emergence of written Latvian.

Western Latvia grew in influence and power under the Duchy of Courland, a semi-autonomous kingdom governed by the capable Duke Kettler, who established far-flung colonies in the Gambia and on Tobago. At this time, southeastern Latvia was grabbed by Poland and Sweden took Rīga and the northeast. The Russians barged in at the end of the 1620s and gobbled everything up during the Great Northern War (1700–21).

National Awakening

The idea of a cohesive national identity began around the 17th century when the peasant descendants of the original tribes started to unite under the name 'Latvia'. By the mid-19th century, the sentiment grew stronger as the first newspapers printed their issues in Latvian and the first Song and Dance Festival started up. Farmers flocked to the big city and demanded equal rights. Political parties emerged to organise worker strikes to oust the remaining German aristocracy. Democratic leaders would later call this push for freedom the 'Lativan Revolution'.

A Taste of Freedom

Out of the post-WWI confusion and turmoil arose an independent Latvian state, declared on 18 November 1918. By the 1930s Latvia had achieved one of the highest standards of living in all of Europe. In 1934 a bloodless coup, led by Kārlis Ulmanis, Latvia's first president, ended the power of parliament.

Initially, the Soviets were the first to recognise Latvia's independence, but the honeymoon didn't last long. Soviet occupation began in 1939 with the Molotov-Ribbentrop Pact. Nationalisation, killings and mass deportations to Siberia followed (see the boxed text, p216). Latvia was occupied partly or wholly by Nazi Germany from 1941 to 1945, when an estimated 175,000 Latvians, mostly Jews, were killed or deported. See p190 for more information.

Soviet Rule

When WWII ended, the Soviets marched back in claiming to 'save' Latvia from the Nazis. A series of deportations began anew as the nation was forced to adapt to communist ideologies. Smoke-spewing factories were swiftly erected and everyone went to work like bees in a hive. Notions of individuality were stripped away as lovely country cottages and state cosmopolitan buildings were 'nationalised', forcing everyone into drab apartment blocks.

The first public protest against Soviet occupation was on 14 June 1987, when 5000 people rallied at Rīga's Freedom Monument to commemorate the 1941 Siberia deportations. New political organisations emerged in the summer of 1988. The Popular Front of Latvia (PLF) quickly rose to the forefront of the Latvian political scene. Less than two months later, on 23 August 1989, two million Latvians, Lithuanians and Estonians formed a 650km human chain from Vilnius, through

Rīga, to Tallinn, to mark the 50th anniversary of the Molotov-Ribbentrop Pact.

Looking Towards Today

Although an all-important Moscow coup failed in 1991, the attempt rocked the Soviet Union just enough so that Latvia could break free. The country declared independence on 21 August 1991 and on 17 September 1991, Latvia, along with Estonia and Lithuania, joined the UN and began taking steps to consolidate its newfound nationhood. Democratic elections were held in 1993 and the new government, headed by Guntis Ulmanis (a farmer and descendant of Kārlis Ulmanis), lurched from crisis to crisis, while a game of prime minister roulette followed the devastating crash of the country's largest commercial bank.

In 1999 Vaira Vīķe-Freiberga, a Latvian by birth but who spent most of her life in Canada, won the presidential election with her promise of propelling the country towards EU membership. It was a tough uphill battle as the nation shook off its antiquated Soviet fetters, and on 1 May 2004 the EU opened its doors to the fledgling nation. Long the Baltic laggard (and the poorest country in the EU), Latvia registered the highest economic growth in the EU in 2004, 2005, 2006 and 2007, even though thousands of Latvians left for jobs in Ireland and elsewhere.

The nation's current president is Valdis Zatlers, a surgeon and a former member of the Popular Front of Latvia in the late 1980s. Zatlers has been accused of corruption, although the high court has cleared him of any suspicions of wrongdoing.

THE CULTURE
Lifestyle

Casual hellos on the street aren't common, but Latvians are a friendly and welcoming bunch. Some will find that there is a bit of guardedness in the culture, but this caution, most likely a response to centuries of foreign rule, has helped preserve the unique language and culture through changing times. As Latvia opens up to the world, this slight xenophobia is quickly melting away. Citizens are growing secure with their nation's freedom and the younger generations have access to a more cosmopolitan culture (especially since youths are almost always trilingual and speak Latvian, Russian and English).

Latvian women were traditionally responsible for preserving the hearth and home by passing on traditional songs, recipes, legends and tales. The men, enriched by these closely kept customs, would guard the land. The women in the households are a strong presence and while gender equality is still a bit of a slippery slope, women have prominent positions in politics and business. Over 33% of the nation's CEOs are women, and Latvia's most noted president was Vaira Vīķe-Freiberga.

Latvians generally adore nature and continue to incorporate their ancient pagan traditions and customs into everyday life. Superstitious beliefs are quite common and often linked to the wildlife that shares the land. In rural Latvia, families will place high wooden beams in their yard to attract storks, which are believed to bring children. Latvians also love flowers; if you go to a birthday party or are invited to someone's home, always bring a bouquet (but make sure it's an odd number of flowers – even numbers are reserved for funerals).

Population

Of Latvia's population of 2,250,000, just 58.8% are ethnically Latvian. Russians account for 28.7% of the total population, and Belarusians (3.8%), Ukrainians (2.6%), Poles (2.5%) and a small Jewish community (0.4%) round out the rest of the demographics. Latvians make up less than 50% of the population in Daugavpils, Jūrmala, Liepāja, Rēzekne, Ventspils and the capital, Rīga, where 43% are Russian and 41% Latvian.

The country's declining population, which continues to drop with each passing year and has decreased by 14% since 1989, is of particular concern. The population in rural Latvia is decreasing at an alarming rate as locals move to the capital, but the national population continues to drop as young Latvians leave for England, Ireland and other nations to earn higher wages and find a better standard of living.

In addition to the extremely low birth rate, the divorce rate in Latvia remains among the highest in Europe: more than 60% of marriages end in divorce and almost 40% of children are born into one-parent families.

As a result of the 20th-century Soviet and Nazi oppression, a diaspora of over 250,000 Latvians can be found in Canada, the USA, Australia, Germany, Sweden and Great Britain.

Multiculturalism

Ethnic consciousness and identity is very pronounced in Latvia, which many attribute to a history of oppression. Centuries ago, Germans ruled the area and employed the local Latvians (who then made up 90% of the populace) as serfs and servants. During the Soviet rule, the colourful Latvian culture clashed with the ideals of the USSR, further exacerbating civil differences. Latvians used their distinctiveness (namely language) to avoid assimilation and Russification even when over 1.5 million Russians moved in, causing Latvians to become the ethnic minority in their own land.

When Latvia regained its independence, displaced Latvians from before WWII were given back their citizenship. Ethnic minorities living in Latvia before the war were granted citizenship as well, but those who returned in more recent times had to pass a citizenship test (consisting of a Latvian language exam requiring about two months' worth of coursework) or else they could remain in the nation as noncitizen residents. Many people chose to leave, restoring Latvians as the ethnic majority at around 58%. Over the last 12 years, non-citizen percentages have dropped from 30% to 19% and it's expected to reach 10% (the mean in the EU) by 2010 as more noncitizens pass the citizenship test.

SPORT

Though it has exported its top talent to the USA-based National Hockey League, Latvia's sporting forte remains ice hockey. On big game nights devoted fans pack Rīga's sports pubs, their eyes locked on the giant-screen TVs broadcasting the match. If you're interested in the sport, stop by a pub on a night when the Latvian national team is playing and join the chaotic party: Latvians may be a reserved bunch, but after a few pints they'll cut loose and cheer their home team on with some seriously raw enthusiasm.

Latvia hosted the IIHF World Ice Hockey Championships in 2006. To prepare for the event, the country constructed a state-of-the-art arena. One of the largest construction projects launched in Latvia since independence, the 12,500-seat Arena Rīga is now used for both concerts and sporting events.

Basketball also draws crowds, though its following is not quite as large as in Lithuania. Latvian basketball player Uljana Semonova ranks among the best female players of all time. Of Russian origin, Semonova was born in Daugavpils in 1952 and won over 45 medals (including two Olympic golds for the USSR in 1976 and 1980) in an 18-year career. At 2.1m tall, she is the tallest female player in Olympic history.

RELIGION

Today, most Latvians are members of the Lutheran church (Russian citizens are mostly Roman Catholics, Orthodox and Old Believers), although ancient pagan traditions still influence daily life and are readily embraced around the nation. These pre-Christian beliefs are centred on nature-related superstition and although they seem incongruous when juxtaposed with Christian ideals, Latvians have done a good job of seamlessly uniting the two. Midsummer's Day, or Jāņi as it's commonly known, is the most popular holiday in Latvia. The solstice was once a sun-lit night of magic and sorcery, and today everyone flocks to the countryside for an evening of revelry come late June each year.

ARTS
Cinema

The Fisherman's Son (*Zvejnieka dēls*), made in 1940, marked both the beginning and the end of an era in Latvian filmmaking. It was the nation's first full-length sound film, but it was one of the last major works before WWII and the subsequent years of oppression. At the beginning of the USSR period, the state-owned Rīga Documentary Film Studio created heaps of movies, but most were laden with propaganda. Other films had to meet ideological standards laid out by the communist government, which stifled creativity for obvious reasons. After Stalin's death in 1953, directors earned slightly more freedom, but it wasn't until the 1980s that pastiche and parody became commonplace. Most of the films up until then were adaptations of famous Latvian legends and modern novels.

Latvian director Jānis Streičs has produced a number of films pertinent to Latvia's turbulent past. *Limousine in the Colour of Summer Solstice Night* (1981) and *The Child of Man*

(1991) remain popular for their blend of irony and comedy. The latter, about a boy growing up and falling in love in Soviet-occupied Latvia, won the Grand Prix at San Remo in 1992 and was nominated for an Academy Award for best foreign film in 1994. Streičs' more recent film, *The Mystery of the Old Parish Church* (2000), addresses the prickly issue of locals collaborating with Nazi and Soviet occupiers during WWII.

Other filmmakers of note include Laila Pakalnina, whose 1998 feature film *The Shoe*, about occupied Latvia, was an official selection at the Cannes 1998 film festival. Pakalnina's film *The Mail* shows the isolation of Latvia, as symbolised by the lonely delivery of the morning mail.

Rural towns such as Kuldīga (p236) are often used to stage period pieces, while other directors prefer to use the synthetic town of Cinevilla (p233), now a major tourist attraction, for shooting.

Check out www.latfilma.lv, the official website for the National Film Centre in Latvia, which offers detailed information about directors, festivals, production houses and more.

Music & Dance

Traditional folk songs have always played an integral role in Latvian culture, although the recognition of music as an established art form did not come about until the mid-19th century. In 1869 Jānis Cimze started cataloguing folk tunes, some dating back 1000 years, and his collection of 20,000 melodies became the basis for Latvia's first song festival, where thousands of singers joined together in huge choirs to celebrate traditional folk music. During the Soviet occupation the song festivals were pivotal in forging a strong sense of national identity and pride, and became part of the battle cry that rallied Latvians to fight for independence. The Song and Dance Festival is held every five years (the most recent one being in July 2008) and continues to unite myriad voices in a jaw-dropping display of patriotism.

The National Opera House, reopened in 1996 after renovation, is the home of the Rīga Ballet, which produced Mikhail Baryshnikov and Aleksander Godunov during the Soviet years. The opera itself is considered to be one of the finest in Europe and cheap seats have made it accessible to the public, who regard the theatre with the utmost respect.

Latvia struck it big when Patra Vetra, also known as Brainstorm, finished third at the Eurovision contest in 2000, and then the wee nation hit the jackpot when Marie N (Marija Naumova) took home the grand prize in 2002.

Visual Arts

Of Latvia's spectrum of visual arts, visitors will be most awestruck by the collection of Art Nouveau architecture in Rīga. The capital has more *Jugendstil* buildings than any other European city – 750 buildings and counting (as renovations continue). See p209 for more information and an interactive walking tour.

Jānis Rozentāls, Latvia's first major painter, lived in Rīga's Art Nouveau district and his former home has since been transformed into a museum (p198). Mark Rothko, born in Daugavpils, is arguably the most famous Latvian artist around the world. Although he grew up in the USA, a recent interest in the artist and his oeuvre have inspired the construction of a new modern art space (p268), which will hopefully stimulate tourism in the otherwise quiet region of Latgale.

ENVIRONMENT
The Land

Latvia is 64,589 sq km in area – a little smaller than Ireland. Unlike its relatively compact Baltic neighbours, Latvia is a lot wider from east to west than from north to south. A good half of its sweeping 494km coast faces the Gulf of Rīga, a deep inlet of the Baltic Sea shielded by the Estonian island of Saaremaa.

Latvia's borders include Estonia to the north, Russia and Belarus to the east and Lithuania to the south. Rīga lies on the Daugava River, just inland from the Gulf of Rīga. The country has four regions beyond the capital: Vidzeme, the northeast; Latgale, the southeast; Zemgale, the south; and Kurzeme, the west.

The Vidzeme Uplands in eastern Latvia is topped by Latvia's highest point, Gaiziņkalns, at 312m; p265.

Wildlife

Latvia has over 27,700 species of flora and fauna spread across a mostly rural landscape dominated by forests (45%) and mires (10%). Main characters in the animal kingdom include bird species such as the black stork,

LATVIA

white stork, lesser-spotted eagle and corncrake. Large creatures include the Eurasian beaver, European wolf, European lynx, red deer, roe deer, elk, wild boar and Eurasian otter. Herds of wild bison and horses can be spotted by lucky travellers along the desolate tracts of land in the Kurzeme region.

Mushrooms and lichen abound throughout the country in various shapes and sizes, including the miatake mushroom, which can grow to more than 5kg. Plant life is also rich and diverse, with over 30 species of rare orchids and myriad berry-bearing trees and shrubs.

National Parks & Reserves

Latvians love nature, and it's no surprise because almost half of the nation is covered with thick patches of forest. Much of this leafy terrain falls under protected jurisdiction, which continues to grow as Soviet industrial relics are eradicated. **WWF Latvia** (☎ 6750 5640; www.pdf.lv; Elizabetes iela 8-4, Rīga) is involved in several projects around the country, aimed at rural development, forest conservation, freshwater management and species protection.

Environmental Issues

Over the last two decades, Latvia's environmental climate has improved by leaps and bounds, largely due to tax reforms and an infusion of EU and private money. When the little country gained its independence, the damages to the ecosystem inflicted during the Soviet era were promptly addressed. Since 1990 the amount of factory pollution has decreased by 46%, and wastewater has dropped by 44%. Latvia has over 1300 wastewater treatment plants, which have increased the purity of river waters – the Daugava and Lielupe Rivers are now deemed 'good-quality cyprinid waters'. Pesticides and chemical farming, widely used during Soviet times, have also been monitored and addressed. Today, over 2750 hectares of farming land (around 200 farms) refrain from using any type of artificial fertilisers, which has helped reduce the number of airborne pesticides by 1000%.

Latvia's water and sewage reforms are restoring the Baltic Sea and Gulf of Rīga to their former swimmable state. The European Blue Flag water safety and purity ranking (with its rigorous criteria) has been awarded to beaches in Jūrmala, Ventspils and Liepāja.

The Latvian Sustainable Development Strategy, a broad-reaching scheme uniting environmental, social and economic structures to increase the longevity and viability of the Latvian land, was conceived in 2002.

For additional information about environmental issues and targeted programs, check out the website for Latvia's Ministry of the Environment (www.vidm.gov.lv).

NATIONAL PARKS & RESERVES

National park or reserve	Area	Features	Activities	Best time to visit
Abava River Valley (p235)	149 sq km	the small towns of Kandava and Sabile; Pedvāle Open-Air Art Museum	hiking	Jun-Aug
Gauja National Park (p253)	917 sq km	virgin pine forests sprinkled with castle ruins	cycling, hiking	Jun-Aug
Ķemeri National Park (p230)	428 sq km	Latvia's oldest forest, wetlands, many bird species, nature trails and sulphur springs	birdwatching, hiking, boardwalks across bogs	Jun-Aug
Krustkalni Nature Reserve (p265)	30 sq km	9 lakes and 48 protected species of flora	hiking	Jun-Aug
Razna National Park (p270)	593 sq km	forested lakeland featuring deep lakes and shrubby plains	swimming, canoeing, hiking, horseback riding	Jun-Aug
Slītere National Park (p233)	164 sq km	coastal and hinterland nature reserve	hiking	Jun-Aug
Teiči Nature Reserve (p265)	190 sq km	an important feeding and nesting ground for many bird species	bog walking, birdwatching	Jun-Aug

BLUE MOOER

It sounds like your classic old wives' tale: blue cows delivered from the sea by mermaids. Yet at least part of this Liv legend is true – Latvia does indeed have blue cows. About 100 of them, to be exact, making it the world's rarest breed of cow.

These curious ruminants originated in Latvia's Kurzeme region. The first ones appeared in the early 1900s. No one is sure why or how they appeared, which is why the bit about mermaids can't be completely ruled out, but their star quickly waxed as they proved remarkably resistant to cold, rain and wind – three things that Latvia has in great supply.

The blue-cow population dwindled to less than 50 in Soviet times, but began to rebound in the 1990s as geneticists realised the value in cross-breeding with these hearty beasts. Your best bet for seeing one is to ask at the Information Centre of Ķemeri National Park (p230), where several of them roam.

FOOD & DRINK

Attention foodies: pack a sandwich if you don't want to pack an artery – food in Latvia is (to put it nicely) very hearty. For centuries, eating has been but a utilitarian task rather than an art and a pleasure, and although things are starting to change (namely in Rīga; p215), one should still expect greasy menus governed by the almighty pig and ubiquitous potato.

Staples & Specialities

A walk through a Latvian market, such as Rīga's Central Market (p195), will quickly reveal the local faves: roasted meats (including heaps of sausage), smoked fish (herring, pike, trout or salmon), fried potatoes, boiled veggies and loads of pork grease. Dairy products are also a big hit, and *biezpiens* (cottage cheese), *siers* (cheese) and *rūgušpiens* (curdled milk) are main ingredients in many dishes.

During the summer months berry picking is a national obsession. During autumn, fresh-picked mushrooms, cranberries and nuts replace strawberries and raspberries at the little stalls. Honey is another popular delicacy. Latvians are intrepid beekeepers and many farms have beehives and honey-production facilities.

Sweet tooths won't be left disappointed; berries turn into scrumptious fruit pies and *kūka* (tarts). Ancient Cour Viking dessert recipes made from sweet creams and dark breads can still be found in Western Latvia. Try *rupjmaizes kārojums/kārtojums,* which tastes like black-forest cake.

Drinks

Not to be missed is Latvia's famous Black Balzām, which Goethe called 'the elixir of life'.

This insidious jet-black, 45% proof concoction is a secret recipe created by Rīga druggist Abraham Kunze in the 18th century. Orange peel, oak bark, wormwood and linden blossoms are among some 14 fairy-tale ingredients known to stew in the wicked witch's cooking pot. A shot a day keeps the doctor away, so say most of Latvia's pensioners. Its name originates from *balsamon,* the ancient Greek word for a sweet-smelling medicinal balm or ointment. Its opaque ceramic bottle, labelled with a black and gold Rīga skyline, is reminiscent of the clay jars the potent liquid used to be stored in during the 18th and 19th centuries to keep it safe from sunlight. Check out p221 for Black Balzām cocktail ideas.

Alus (beer) has long been a traditional favourite, and for such a small country Latvia has more than its share of breweries. Figure around 0.50Ls for a pint from a kiosk (every kiosk stocks beer) and around 1Ls to 2Ls in a bar. Try Aldaris or Cēsu brands and keep an eye out for regional Bauskas, Piebalgas, Tērvetes and Užavas, each with a distinct taste.

Wine choices are often found on restaurant and bar menus, and tend to be a selection from the usual gamut of celebrated wine-producing nations, as well as lesser regions like the Caucasus.

Where to Eat & Drink

Restorāns (restaurants) in Latvia are generally slower, sit-down affairs, while *kafejnīca* (cafes; pronounced ka-fay-*neet*-za) are multipurpose facilities where patrons enjoy a coffee, a faster meal, or drinks in the evening. Bars, especially in Rīga and other major cities, often serve a full range of food. For quick, self-service choices, keep an eye out for *pelmeņi* (dumpling) and pancake shops, cafeteria-style venues

EAT YOUR WORDS

These days, most restaurants have English menus, but why not impress your waiter and order your pork gristle in Latvian. We've listed a few of the more useful eating phrases here.

Useful Phrases

A table for ... people, please.	*loo-*dzu *gahl-*du ... *per-*so-nahm	*Lūdzu galdu ... personām.*
Do you have a menu?	vai yums ir *eh-*dean-kar te	*Vai jums ir ēdienkarte?*
I'm a vegetarian.	es es-mu ve-gye-tah-reah-tis/te	*Es esmu veģetārietis/te.* (m/f)
What do you recommend?	kwo yoos *eah-*sah-kut	*Ko jūs iesakat?*
I'd like ...	es *vaa-*lwos ...	*Es vēlos ...*
The bill, please.	*loo-*dzu *reh-*kyi-nu	*Lūdzu rēķinu.*

Food Glossary

biešu zupa	beetroot soup (similar to borscht)
cepts lasis ar piedevām	fried salmon with potatoes, pickled and fresh vegetables
dārzeņu salāti	diced vegetable salad in sour cream and mayonnaise
desa	sausage (usually smoked)
kāpostu salāti	fresh grated cabbage
karbonāde ar piedevām	fried pork chop with potatoes, pickled and fresh vegetables
kotletes	meatballs
lasis krējuma mērcē	salmon in cream sauce
lasis sēņu un diļļu mērcē	salmon in mushroom and dill sauce
mednieku desiņas	Hunter's sausages (pork)
pelēkie zirņi ar speķi	grey peas with pork fat and onions
pelmeņi	dumplings
siļķe kažokā	pickled herring with sour cream, egg and beetroot
sīpolu sitenis	beefsteak with fried onions
zivju zupa	fish soup

such as the LIDO restaurants, and supermarkets, namely Rimi, which sell to-go snacks and meals. Small towns have Latvian restaurants that often offer the occasional international dish (usually pizza); see p215 for information on Rīga's international dining scene.

A Latvian *brokastis* (breakfast), available from sunrise to around 11am, usually consists of bread and cheese, cold meat and smoked fish. *Pusidienās* (lunch) and *vakariņas* (dinner) are more substantial affairs, with heartier Baltic staples. Restaurants serve lunch at midday and daylight patterns often influence dinner times, which can vary from 5pm to midnight.

See p215 for more information about dining venues and tipping in Latvia's ever-changing eating scene.

RĪGA

pop 717,371

'The Paris of the North', 'The Second City That Never Sleeps' – everyone's so keen to tack on qualifying superlatives to Latvia's capital, but regal Rīga does a hell of a job of holding its own. For starters, the city has the largest and most impressive showing of Art Nouveau architecture in Europe. Nightmarish gargoyles and praying goddesses adorn over 750 buildings along the stately boulevards radiating out from Rīga's castle core. The heart of the city – Old Town – is a fairy-tale kingdom of winding wobbly lanes and gingerbread trim that beats to the sound of a bumpin' discotheque.

Although some Latvians may lament the fact that they are an ethnic minority in their own capital, others will be quick to point out that Rīga was never a 'Latvian' city. Founded in 1201 by the German Bishop Albert von Buxhoevden (say that three times fast) as a bridgehead for the crusade against the northern 'heathens', Rīga became a stronghold for the Knights of the Sword and the newest trading junction between Russia and the West. When Sweden snagged the city in 1621, it grew into the largest holding of the Swedish Empire (even bigger than Stockholm!). Then the Russians snatched Latvia from Sweden's grip and added an industrial element to the bustling burg. By the mid-1860s Rīga was the world's biggest timber port and Russia's third city after Moscow and St Petersburg. The 20th century also saw the birth of cafes, salons, dance clubs and a thriving intellectual culture, which was all bombed to high hell in WWI, and subsequently captured by the Nazis during WWII. Somehow, Rīga's indelible international flavour managed to rise up from the rubble, and even as a part of the USSR, Rīga was known for its forward thinking and thriving cultural life.

Today, Rīga's cosmopolitan past has enabled the city to effortlessly adjust to a global climate, making it more than just the capital of Latvia – it's the cornerstone of the Baltic.

ORIENTATION

Rīga quietly sits along the Daugava River, which flows another 15km north before dumping into the Gulf of Rīga. Old Rīga (Vecrīga), the historic heart of the city, stretches 1km along the river's eastern side and 600m back from its banks. This medieval section of town is mostly pedestrian, containing a flurry of curving cobbled streets and alleys. Kaļķu iela (Kalku street) carves a straight path through the centre of Old Rīga, splitting the area into two equal halves.

As Kaļķu iela continues away from the river, it turns into Brīvības bulvāris (Freedom Boulevard) when it hits the thin, picturesque ring of parkland that protects the medieval centre from the gridiron of grand boulevards just beyond. The copper-topped Freedom Monument, in the middle of Brīvības bulvāris, is the unofficial gateway into Central Rīga. This part of the city, constructed in the 19th and 20th centuries, sports wide avenues, luxurious apartment blocks and plenty of Art Nouveau architecture. At outer edges of the city centre, the European grandeur begins to fade into Soviet block housing and *microrajons* (microregions, or suburbs).

The 'left' side of the Daugava River is connected to the city by three main bridges that zip across the river like guitar strings. The train and bus stations border the central market and are a five-minute walk apart on the southeastern edge of old Rīga. The ferry terminal is 900m north of Old Rīga, and the airport is approximately 13km southwest of the city centre.

INFORMATION

Bookshops

Globuss (Map p190; ☎ 6722 6957; Valņu iela 26) Generous selection of classic English-language books and lots of newspapers.

Jāņa Sēta (Map pp196-7; ☎ 6724 0894; Elizabetes iela 83-85; ☺ 10am-7pm Mon-Sat, to 5pm Sun) The largest travel bookstore in the Baltic overflows with a bounty of maps, souvenir photo books and plenty of Lonely Planet guides to plan your next adventure.

Emergency

Latvia's general emergency number is ☎ 112, which can be dialled for free from any payphone or from any Latvian mobile phone. Also, a special English-speaking telephone hotline offering information and assistance for tourists operates 24 hours a day: ☎ 2203 3000. For more emergency details see Quick Reference on the inside front cover.

Internet Access

Every hostel and hotel has some form of internet connection available. Most accommodations offer wi-fi and at least one computer terminal for those without their own laptop. See the boxed text on p189 for information on wi-fi access throughout the city. Internet cafes are a dying breed in Rīga and they're usually filled with kids blasting cyber monsters.

Elik Kafe (Map pp196-7; ☎ 6722 7079; www.elikkafe .lv; Merķela iela 1; 30 min 0.35Ls; ☺ 24hr) Located near the train station above the McDonald's. Prices increase by 0.05Ls per 30 minutes in the late evening.

net.café (Map p190; ☎ 6781 4440; Peldu iela 17; per hr 1Ls; ☺ 24hr) A chill-out spot to update your blog. Full-service bar.

Internet Resources

www.1188.lv Lists virtually every establishment in Rīga and the rest of Latvia. The Latvian language setting yields the most search results. The search engine also provides up-to-date information on nightlife and traffic.

www.riga-life.com Features loads of information on sleeping, eating, drinking and partying in the capital.

www.rigaoutthere.com A site managed by a locally run tour operator and featuring a handy travel planner on the right-hand column.

www.zl.lv Another excellent Latvian database offering detailed information about businesses in Rīga and the entire country.

Laundry

Several hostels offer do-it-yourself laundry services for 2Ls washing and 2Ls drying. Most midrange and top-end hotels have laundry

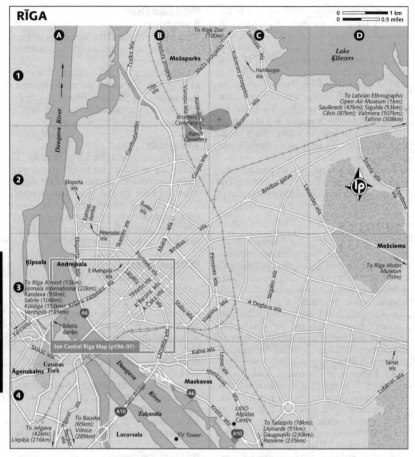

RĪGA

services, although they are so overpriced you might as well go to the mall and buy new clothes. Laundrettes cost around 2.40Ls per load.
Nivāla (Map pp196-7; ☎ 6728 1346; Akas iela 4; ⏱ 24hr) Self-service washing machines, dry cleaning available between 6.30am and 10pm.
Vienmēr Tīrs (Map pp196-7; ☎ 6727 6108; K Barona iela 52, entrance from Ģertrūdes iela; ⏱ 8am-8pm Mon-Fri, 10am-5pm Sat) Self-service laundrette.

Left Luggage
Bus station (per piece 1Ls; ⏱ 5.30am-11pm)
Train station (per piece 1Ls; ⏱ 4.30am-midnight) In the basement.

Media & Maps
City Spy (www.cityspy.info) Pocket-sized *City Spy* was the best map we found in town. The backside lists a bunch of

quality places to sleep, eat and drink. Pick up a copy at most budget digs.
Rīga in Your Pocket (www.inyourpocket.com/latvia/city /riga.html; per issue 2Ls) Handy city guide published every other month. Check the website for a PDF version or pick up a copy at most hotels, tourist offices and newspaper kiosks. Is that *In Your Pocket* or are you just happy to see me?
Rīga This Week (www.rigathisweek.lv) An excellent (and free!) city guide available at virtually every sleeping option in town. Published every other month.

Medical Services
ARS Clinic (Map pp196-7; ☎ 6720 1001, emergency 6720 1003; Skolas iela 5; ⏱ 24hr) English-speaking service and an emergency home service.
Pauls Stradiņš Clinical Hospital (☎ 6706 9600; Pilsoņu iela 13; ⏱ 24hr) A university medical centre with diverse facilities across the Daugava River.

Money

There are scores of ATMs scattered around the capital. If for some reason you are having trouble locating a bank, walk down Kaļķu iela (which turns into Brīvības Bulvāris) and within seconds you will find a bank or ATM. Withdrawing cash is easier than trying to exchange travellers cheques or foreign currencies; exchange bureaus often have lousy rates and most do not take travellers cheques. For detailed information about Latvian currency and exchange rates visit www.bank.lv.

Marika (Map pp196-7; ☎ 6728 0875; Brīvības iela 30; ☻ 24hr) Offers currency-exchange services with reasonable rates.

Post

Those blue storefronts with 'Pasta' written on them aren't Italian restaurants – they're post offices. See www.post.lv for additional information.

Central post office (Map pp196-7; ☎ 6707 3900; Stacijas laukums 1; ☻ 7am-9pm Mon-Fri, 9am-8pm Sat, 10am-8pm Sun) Convenient location next to the train station in the Origo complex. International calling and faxing services also available.

Post office (Map pp196-7; ☎ 6733 1609; Elizabetes iela 41/43; ☻ 7.30am-9pm Mon-Fri, 8am-4pm Sat)

Post office (Map pp196-7; ☎ 6728 5446; Marijas iela 20; ☻ 7.30am-8pm Mon-Fri, 8am-4pm Sat)

Tourist Information

Rīga Tourist Office (www.rigatourism.lv) main office (Map p190; ☎ 6703 7900; Rātslaukums 6; ☻ 10am-7pm); bus station (Map pp196-7; ☎ 6722 0555; ☻ 9am-7pm); train station (Map p190; ☎ 6730 7900; ☻ 10am-6.30pm) Gives out free maps and has loads of information. It can arrange accommodation and book

walking, bus or boat tours from a variety of operators. The website has great Old Town walking-tour suggestions. The useful Rīga Card (see the boxed text, p191) is available for purchase at all of the tourist offices.

DANGERS & ANNOYANCES

Over the last few years, Rīga has been struggling with a stag swell, and although you may encounter a gaggle of loud foreigners engaged in tomfoolery, there are plenty of bars, restaurants and hotels that strictly forbid this type of behaviour. It's not out of the ordinary to be discreetly offered drugs or prostitutes around Old Rīga (especially in Līvu Laukums). A simple 'no thanks' will do the trick. Of course, dangerous actions beget dangerous consequences, so use common sense when making decisions, especially when it's late in the hour.

Taxi drivers who run scams can be a minor irritation as well. It is best to have the meter running *and* ask the driver for a sense of how much the journey will cost (some drivers have managed to rig their meters). Avoid taxis into Old Rīga, which cost an extra 5Ls, and a ride within Central Rīga should never set you back more than 5Ls.

SIGHTS
Old Rīga (Vecrīga)

The curving cobbled streets of Rīga's medieval core are best explored at random. Once you're sufficiently lost amid the tangle of gingerbread trim and crooked alleyways, you will begin to uncover a stunning, World Heritage–listed realm of sky-scraping cathedrals, gaping city squares and crumbling castle walls. Amid the chaos of thin, rambling roads, Kaļķu iela perfectly slices Old Rīga into two equal sections, each with their own collection of historical goodies.

LATVIA

WI-FI ACCESS

Rīga is covered in a virtual blanket of wireless internet access. Lattelecom, the main service provider, has set up wi-fi beacons at every payphone around the city. Users can access the internet from within a 100m radius of these phone booths (although not all of them work). Almost every hotel and hostel has wireless access (usually free of charge), as do a large percentage of restaurants (including the dozens of Double Coffee cafes peppered around the city centre).

To register for a Lattelecom password and username, call ☎ 9000 4111, or send a text message with the word 'WiFi' to ☎ 1188. One hour of internet costs 0.94Ls. Prepaid user cards are also available for purchase at most of the establishments with a wireless connection. Visit www.wifi.lv for more information (although at the time of research the site was predominantly in Latvian and Russian).

EAST OF KAĻĶU IELA
Rātslaukums

Touristy Rātslaukums is a great place to start one's exploration of the old city. The square is home to Old Rīga's most picture-worthy building, the **Blackheads' House** (Melngalvju nams; Map p190; Rātslaukums 6; admission 1.50Ls; 10am-5pm Tue-Sun). The uber-ornate edifice was originally built in 1344 as a veritable fraternity house for the Blackheads guild of unmarried German merchants. The society's black patron saint, St Mauritius, is depicted with a flag and shield on the building's facade. The house was destroyed in 1941, and flattened by the Soviets seven years later. Somehow the original blueprints survived and an exact replica was constructed in 2001 for Rīga's 800th birthday.

Once the home of a wealthy tradesman, the 17th-century **Mentzendorff's House** (Mencendorfa nams; Map p190; 6721 2951; www.mencendorfanams .com; Grēcinieku iela 18; admission 1.50Ls; 10am-5pm Wed-Sun), right behind the Blackheads' House, continues Rīga's history of mercantile excess.

Facing the Blackheads' House across the square is the **town hall**, also rebuilt from scratch in recent years. A statue of Rīga's patron saint, **St Roland**, stands between the two buildings. It's a replica of the original, erected in 1897, which now sits in St Peter's Lutheran Church.

The Latvian government has done an admirable job of razing all traces of Soviet oppression (ie ugly utilitarian structures), but they left one hideous reminder behind to purposefully contrast the rest of Rātslaukums' ornate

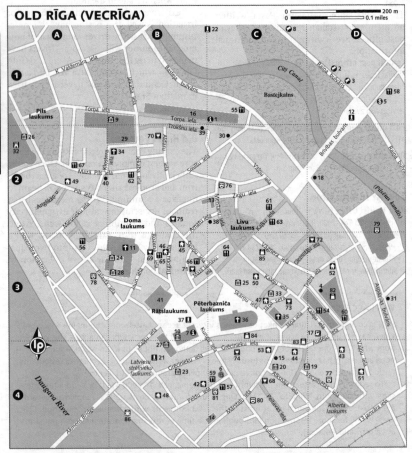

architecture. The **Museum of Occupation in Latvia** (Latvijas okupācijas muzejs; Map p190; ☎ 6721 2715; www .occupationmuseum.lv; Latviešu Strēlnieku Laukums 1; admission free; ☉ 11am-6pm daily May-Sep, 11am-5pm Tue-Sun Oct-Apr) ironically inhabits this Soviet bunker, and carefully details Latvia's Soviet and Nazi occupations between 1940 and 1991. Some of the exhibits have been curated to shock visitors – dozens of gruesome photographs depict murdered and mangled Latvians. Captions are in a variety of languages, although they can sometimes be difficult to follow without a basic knowledge of Latvia's recent history. Audio guides are available for supplemental information. Allow a couple of hours to take it all in.

The square on the other side of the Occupation Museum is known as **Latviešu strēlnieku laukums** (Latvian Riflemen Sq; Map p190), once home to Rīga's central market. Today the square is dominated by the imposing, dark-red **Latvian Riflemen Monument**, a controversial statue honouring Latvia's Red Riflemen, some of whom served as Lenin's personal bodyguards.

Pēterbaznīca Laukums

Rīga's skyline centrepiece is Gothic **St Peter's Lutheran Church** (Sv Pētera baznīca; Map p190; ☎ 6722

9426; www.peterbaznica.lv; Skārņu iela 19; admission 2Ls; ☉ 10am-5pm, Tue-Sun), thought to be around 800 years old. Don't miss the view from the spire, which has been rebuilt three times in the same baroque form. Legend has it that in 1667 the builders threw glass from the top to see how long the spire would last. A greater number of shards meant a very long life. The glass ended up landing on a pile of straw and didn't break – a year later the tower was incinerated. When the spire was resurrected after a bombing during WWII,

LATVIA

RĪGA IN...

Two Days

Start your adventure in the heart of the city at the **Blackheads' House** in Rātslaukums (p190). Pick up some handy brochures and maps, and spend the rest of the morning getting lost among the twisting cobbled alleys that snake through medieval **Old Rīga** (p189). For lunch, clog your arteries with some traditional **Latvian cuisine** (p217), and walk off the calories in the afternoon with a stroll through the eye-popping **Art Nouveau district** (p209). Indulge in the city's colourful **cafe culture** (p217) with a light dinner at an artsy eatery along the grand boulevards in Central Rīga. After sunset, bar-hop your way through Old Rīga (don't forget to try some Black Balzām!) and end the evening with a well-deserved cocktail at the **Skyline Bar** (p221) overlooking the twinkling urban lights below.

On day two, fine-tune your bargaining skills (and your Russian) with a visit to the **Central Market** (p195) and snag some snacks for a picnic lunch in up-and-coming **Andrejsala** (p199) along the banks for the Daugava River. Grab tickets for an evening at the **opera** (p223) and treat yourself to some of the finest classical music in Europe.

Four Days

After completing the two-day itinerary above, spend day three in your speedos along the silky sands in **Jūrmala** (p226), Latvia's uber-resort town. Rent a bike in the afternoon and roam around the stunning wooden cottages near the sea. End the day with a relaxing spa treatment, then binge on **pelmeņi** (Russian dumplings; p216) when you get back to the capital.

Stretch your legs with another **day trip** (p200) on day four, be it castle hunting, art ogling or hiking among the towering pines along the Gauja River. If you decide to stay in town, visit the **Latvian Ethnographic Open-Air Museum** (p200), saunter through leafy **Mežaparks** (p199), Europe's first planned suburb, and, for something truly offbeat, try firing a round with an AK-47 in a former **Soviet fallout shelter** (p209).

the ceremonial glass chucking was repeated, and this time it was a smash hit. The spire is 123.25m, but the lift only whisks you up to 72m.

Behind St Peter's sits another impressive religious structure – the former **St George's Church** – which is now the **Museum of Decorative & Applied Arts** (Dekoratīvi lietišķās mākslas muzejs; Map p190; ☎ 6722 7833; www.dlmm.lv; Skārņu iela 10/20; admission 0.70Ls; ☺ 11am-5pm Tue-Sun, to 7pm Wed) ,highlighting Latvia's impressive collection of woodcuts, tapestries and ceramics. The building's foundations date back to 1207 when the Livonian Brothers of the Sword erected their castle here.

Yet more ceramics can be viewed in the **Rīga Porcelain Museum** (Map p190; ☎ 6750 3769; Kalēju iela 9/11; admission 0.50Ls; ☺ 11am-6pm Tue-Sun), which is tucked away in **Jāņa Sēta** (John's Yard; Map p190; Skārņu iela 22), the restored courtyard of a former convent and original residence of Bishop Albert, the founder of Rīga.

Located next door, **St John's Church** (Jāņa baznīca; Map p190; Skārņu iela 24) is a 13th- to 19th-century amalgam of Gothic, Renaissance and baroque styles.

Kalēju iela & Mārstaļu iela

Zigzagging Kalēju iela and Mārstaļu iela are both dotted with poignant reminders of the city's legacy as a wealthy Northern Europe trading centre. The **House of Johannes Reitern** (Map p190; Mārstaļu iela 2-4), built by a rich German merchant, boasts elaborate stone carvings. The baroque **House of Dannenstern** (Map p190; Mārstaļu iela 21) was also home to a wealthy 17th-century businessman. Don't forget to look up at the curling vines and barking gargoyles adorning several **Art Nouveau facades** (see Walking Tour, p209). A third merchant's manor has been transformed into the **Latvian Photography Museum** (Latvijas fotogrāfijas muzejs; Map p190; ☎ 722 7231; Mārstaļu iela 8; admission 1.40Ls; ☺ 10am-5pm Wed, Fri & Sat, noon-7pm Thu), displaying unique photographs of 1920s Rīga.

Nearby, the one-room **Latvian People's Front Museum** (Latvijas tautas frontes muzejs; Map p190; ☎ 6722 4502; Vecpilsētas iela 13-15; admission free; ☺ 2-7pm Tue, noon-5pm Wed-Fri, noon-4pm Sat) remains furnished exactly as it was when it served as the office of the Latvian People's Front prior to 1990.

WEST OF KAĻĶU IELA
Livu Laukums
Lively Livu Laukums, near the busiest entrance to Old Rīga along Kaļķu iela, features several beer gardens during summer and an outdoor **ice rink** (admission free; skate rental per hr 0.50Ls; 10am-1am Nov-Mar) in the colder months.

A colourful row of 18th-century buildings lines the square – most of which have been turned into restaurants. The 19th-century Gothic exterior of the **Great Guild** (Lielā gilde; Map p190; Amatu iela 6) encloses a sumptuous merchants' meeting hall, built during the height of German power in the 1330s. Today, the Great Guild houses the Latvian Philharmonic Orchestra. The fairy-tale castle next door is the **Small Guild** (Mazā gilde; Map p190; Amatu iela 5), founded in the 14th century as the meeting place for local artisans.

Don't miss the **Cat House** (see Walking Tour, p209) nearby on Mieataru iela.

Doma Laukums
The centrepiece of expansive Doma Laukums is Rīga's enormous **Dome Cathedral** (Doma baznīca; Map p190; 6721 3498; admission 0.50Ls; 11am-6pm Tue-Fri, 10am-2pm Sat). Founded in 1211 as the seat of the Rīga diocese, it is still the largest church in the Baltic. The behemoth's architecture is an amalgam of styles from the 13th to the 18th centuries: the eastern end, the oldest portion, has Romanesque features; the tower is 18th-century baroque; and much of the rest dates from a 15th-century Gothic rebuilding. The floor and walls of the huge interior are dotted with old stone tombs – note the carved symbols denoting the rank or post of the occupant. Eminent citizens would pay to be buried as close to the altar as possible. In 1709 the cholera and typhoid outbreak that killed a third of Rīga's population was blamed on a flood that inundated the tombs. The cathedral's pulpit dates from 1641 and the huge 6768-pipe organ was the world's largest when it was completed in 1884 (it's now the fourth largest). During Soviet times, services were strictly forbidden and much of the cathedral's ornate interior decor was stripped away. Today, mass is held at noon on Sundays, and at 8am every other day of the week.

The **Museum of the History of Rīga & Navigation** (Rīgas vēstures un kuģniecības muzejs; Map p190; 6721 1358; www.rigamuz.lv; Palasta iela 4; admission 2.50Ls;

11am-5pm Wed-Sun), the Baltic's oldest museum, is situated in the monastery's cloister at the back of the Dome Cathedral complex. Founded in 1773, the exhibition space features a permanent collection of artefacts from the Bronze Age all the way up to WWII. The three-room **Museum of Barricades of 1991** (1991 gada barikāžu muzejs; Map p190; 6721 3525; www.barikades.lv; admission free; 10am-5pm Mon-Fri, 11am-5pm Sat), also at the back of the Dome Cathedral, details the events that took place in Rīga in January 1991 through models, replicas and photographs.

Located behind Doma Laukums, away from the cathedral, three architectural gems neatly line up in a photogenic row. Known as the **Three Brothers** (Trīs brāļi; Map p190; Mazā Pils iela 17, 19 & 21), these three stone houses exemplify Old Rīga's diverse collection of architectural styles (and echo Tallinn's 'Three Sisters'). No 17 is over 600 years old, making it the oldest stone dwelling in town, and No 19 (built in the 17th century) is now the **Rīga Museum of Architecture** (Latvijas arhitektūras muzejs; Map p190; 6722 0779; www.archmuseum.lv; Mazā Pils iela 19; admission free; 10am-6pm Mon-Fri). Note the tiny windows on the upper levels – Rīga's property taxes during the Middle Ages were based on the size of one's windows.

Latvia's first Lutheran services were held in nearby **St Jacob's Cathedral** (Sv Jēkaba katedrāle; Map p190; Klostera iela), which has an interior dating back to 1225. Today it is the seat of Rīga's Roman Catholic archbishopric.

Pils Laukums
In the far corner of Old Rīga near the Vanšu Bridge, verdant Pils Laukums sits at the doorstep of **Rīga Castle** (Rīgas pils; Map p190; Pils laukums 3). Originally built as the headquarters for the Livonian Order, the foundation dates to 1330 and served as the residence of the order's grand master. The canary yellow bastion (which doesn't feel very castle'y when viewed from Pils Laukums) is now home to Latvia's president.

There are also two museums within the castle's confines: the **Museum of Foreign Art** (Ārzemju mākslas muzejs; Map p190; 6722 6467; www.amm.lv; Pils laukums 3; adult/child 1.20/0.70Ls; 11am-5pm Tue-Sun), exhibiting Latvia's largest treasury of international artwork dating back to the 14th century; and the **History Museum of Latvia** (Latvijas vēstures muzejs; Map p190; 6722 3004; www.history-museum.lv; admission 1Ls, free Wed;

○ 11am-5pm Wed-Sun), which traces the history of Latvia and its people from the Stone Age to present day. Displays are only captioned in Latvian, although English brochures can be purchased at the ticket counter.

The **Arsenāls Museum of Art** (Mākslas muzejs Arsenāls; Map p190; ☎ 6721 3695; Torņa iela 1; adult/child 0.70/0.40Ls; ○ 11am-5pm Tue, Wed & Fri-Sun, to 7pm Thu) sits just east of Pils Laukums and shares a block with Latvia's **Parliament** (Saeima; Map p190; Jēkaba iela 11), a Florentine Renaissance structure originally commissioned as the Knights' House of the German landlords.

Torņa iela

From Pils Laukums, photogenic Torņa iela makes a beeline for Pilsētas kanāls (City Canals) at the other end of Old Rīga. Almost the entire north side of the street is flanked by the custard-coloured **Jacob's Barracks** (Jēkaba Kazarmas; Torņa iela 4), built as an enormous warehouse in the 16th century. Tourist-friendly cafes and boutiques now inhabit the refurbished building.

On the other side of the street, find Trokšņu iela, Old Rīga's narrowest iela, and snap a photo of the **Swedish Gate** (Zviedru vārti; Map p190; Torņu iela 11), which was built onto the city's medieval walls in 1698 while the Swedes were in power. It is the only remaining gate to Old Rīga. The cylindrical **Powder Tower** (Pulvera Tower; Map p190; Smilšu iela 20) dates back to the 14th century, and is the only survivor of the 18 original towers that punctuated the old city wall. Nine Russian cannonballs from 17th- and 18th-century assaults are embedded in the tower's walls. In the past it has

served as a gunpowder warehouse, prison, torture chamber and frat house. Today it is the **Museum of War** (Kara muzejs; Map p190; ☎ 6722 8147; www.karamuzejs.gov.lv; Smilšu iela 20; admission free; ○ 10am-6pm Wed-Sun May-Sep, 10am-5pm Wed-Sun Oct-Apr), which details the political and military history of Latvia from medieval times to present day (with a special focus on the World Wars).

Central Rīga (Centrs)

As Kaļķu iela breaks free from the urban jumble of turrets and towers, it turns into Brīvības iela (Freedom St), and continues to neatly cut the city centre into two equal parts. An emerald necklace of lush parks acts as a buffer between the medieval walls and the large-scale gridiron of stately boulevards. Central Rīga's hodgepodge of memorable sights includes the flamboyant Art Nouveau district, a sprawling Central Market housed in mammoth zeppelin hangars, and the iconic Freedom Monument.

FREEDOM MONUMENT

Affectionately known as 'Milda', Rīga's **Freedom Monument** (Brīvības bulvāris; Map pp196-7) towers above the city between Old and Central Rīga. Paid for by public donations, the monument was designed by Kārlis Zāle and erected in 1935 where a statue of Russian ruler Peter the Great once stood. At the base of the monument there is an inscription which reads 'Tēvzemei un Brīvībai' (For Fatherland and Freedom), accompanied by granite friezes of Latvians singing and fighting for their freedom. A copper female Liberty tops the soaring monument, holding three gold

---

A ROOM WITH A VIEW

Check out the top five places around town to score postcard-perfect views of Rīga's diverse skyline.

■ **Skyline Bar** (p221) Enjoy a sweeping panorama from this glitzy lounge on the top of Central Rīga's tallest building, Reval Hotel Latvija.

■ **Academy of Science** (p196) Not many tourists know that you can climb this Soviet birthday cake to watch Central Rīga's grand boulevards collide with the snaking streets of Old Rīga.

■ **Fabrikas Restorāns** (p219) A hot spot for Russian jetsetters, this posh address in Ķīpsala faces Rīga's jungle of twisting church spires from a privileged spot across the river.

■ **St Peter's Church** (p191) Ascend 72m up this veritable lightning rod for an eagle's perspective of Old Rīga below.

■ **Gutenbergs** (p219) Go one better than dining with a view – dine in the view. This rooftop terrace in the heart of Old Rīga squats between sky-scraping spires and gingerbread rooftops.

stars in her hands. The three stars represent the three original cultural regions of Latvia: Kurzeme, Vidzeme and Latgale (Latvia's fourth cultural region, Zemgale, was initially part of Kurzeme).

Surprisingly, during the Soviet years the Freedom Monument was never demolished. The communist government reinterpreted the star-toting Liberty as 'Mother Russia' caring for its three newest members (the three stars) of the union: Estonia, Latvia and Lithuania. Milda was strictly off limits, and anyone seen placing flowers at the base was promptly arrested and deported to Siberia. To further decrease the monument's significance, a large statue of Lenin was erected up the street, facing the other way down Brīvības. It was removed when Latvia regained its independence.

Today, two soldiers stand guard at the monument through the day and perform a modest changing of the guards every hour on the hour from 9am to 6pm.

A second spire, the **Laima Clock**, sits between Milda and the entrance to Old Rīga. Built in the 1920s as a gentle way to encourage Rīgans not to be late for work, the clock is now used as a meeting place for young Latvians.

EAST OF BRĪVĪBAS

If you're not game to leave the cosy confines of Rīga's city centre, then the Russified area east of Brīvības is the best part of town to get a taste of everyday life.

Vērmanes Garden (Vērmanes dārzs)

From Brīvības, pass the swirls of colour at the 24-hour **Flower Market** (see the boxed text, p220) along Tērbatas iela to find the inviting Vērmanes dārzs (garden) frequented by locals. During the summer months, local bands perform in the small **outdoor amphitheatre**, and artisans set up shop along the brick walkways.

The **Natural History Museum** (Dabas muzejs; Map pp196-7; ☎ 6735 6024; www.dabasmuzejs.gov.lv; K Barona iela 4; admission 1Ls; ☉ 10am-5pm Wed, Fri & Sat, noon-6pm Thu, 10am-4pm Sun) sits cater-corner to the garden across K Barona iela. The museum features a permanent collection that includes stuffed birds, dinosaur fossils, details about Latvia's ecosystem and information on the region's ethnic origins.

Central Market (Centrāltirgus)

Visiting Rīga without seeing the **Central Market** (Centrāltirgus; Map pp196-7; www.centraltirgus.lv; Nēģu iela 7; ☉ 7am-5pm Sun & Mon, 7am-6pm Tue-Sat) is like

---

OH CHRISTMAS TREE

Rīga's Blackheads' House was known for its wild parties; it was, after all, a clubhouse for unmarried merchants. On a cold Christmas Eve in 1510, the squad of bachelors, full of holiday spirit (and other spirits, so to speak), hauled a great pine tree up to their clubhouse and smothered it with flowers. At the end of the evening, they burned the tree to the ground in an impressive blaze. From then on, decorating the 'Christmas Tree' became an annual tradition, which eventually spread across the globe (as you probably know, the burning part never really caught on).

An octagonal commemorative plaque, inlaid in cobbled Rātslaukums, marks the spot where the original tree once stood.

---

going to Paris and not stopping by the Louvre. Although, rather than stuffy still lifes of fruit, Rīga's bustling centrepiece bursts with life as vendors peddle crates stuffed with freshly picked fruit.

A 1330 manuscript makes reference to a small market in Doma Laukums being moved to what is now called Latviešu strēlnieku laukums (Latvian Riflemen Square). Rīga's market moved once again in 1570, this time to the banks of the Daugava to facilitate trading directly along the river. The market flourished during the mid-1600s when the city outgrew Stockholm to become the largest stronghold of the Swedish empire.

In 1930 the market moved to its current location on the border of Central Rīga and the Russified Maskavas neighbourhood ('Little Moscow') to make use of the railway, which replaced the river as the principal trade route. Confronted with the market's ever-growing size, the city of Rīga decided to bring in five enormous zeppelin hangars from the town of Vainode in Western Latvia. At a cost of five million lats, these hangars – each 35m high – added 57,000 sq metres of vending space, allowing an additional 1250 vendors to peddle their goods.

Parts of the market are closed for maintenance on the mornings of each month's first and last Monday. Check the website for additional information. For more information about Rīga's markets, see the boxed text, p220.

LATVIA

Akadēmijas Laukums

The most interesting building adorning Rīga's eccentric skyline sits in the heart of Akadēmijas Laukums. Known to most as 'Stalin's birthday cake', the **Academy of Science** (Zinātņu Akadēmija; Map pp196-7; ☎ 2649 1237; www .lza.lv; Turgeņeva iela; ⊙ 9am-8pm) is Rīga's own Russified 'Empire State Building'. Those

with keen eagle eyes will spot hammers and sickles hidden in the convoluted façade. A mere 1.50Ls grants you admission to the sprawling observation deck on the 17th floor.

Don't miss the moving **Holocaust Memorial**, aptly sitting a block behind the square in a quiet garden. A large synagogue once oc-

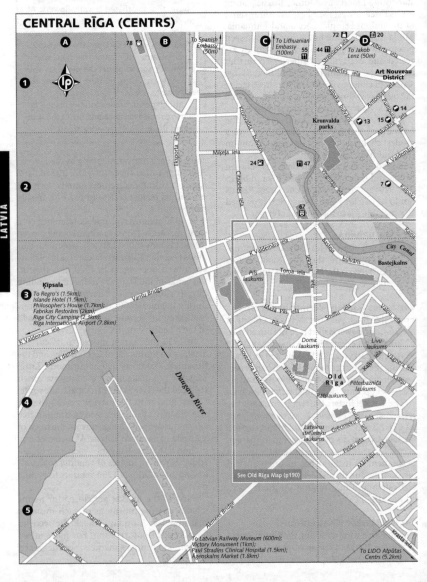

CENTRAL RĪGA (CENTRS)

cupied this street corner until it was burned to the ground during WWII, tragically, with the entire congregation trapped inside. No one survived. Today the concrete monument standing in its place is dedicated to the brave Latvians who risked their lives to help hide Jews during the war. The inspiring memorial, made out of sheets of concrete, is also an al-

legorical reminder that, ultimately, we are all one and the same.

WEST OF BRĪVĪBAS

Rīga's wealthier neighbourhood sprawls west of Brīvības, and features scores of ornate Art Nouveau facades, rolling park greens, and most of the city's embassies and diplomatic estates.

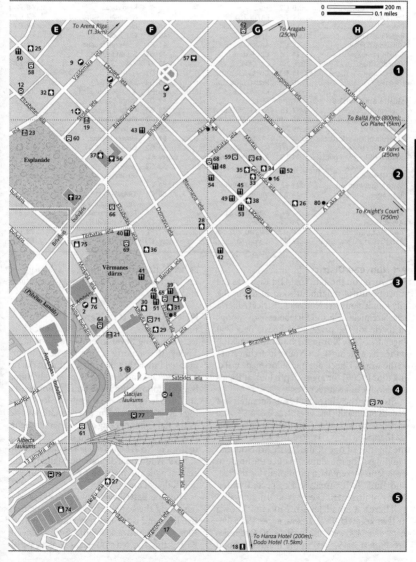

Art Nouveau District

Just when you thought that Old Rīga was the most beautiful neighbourhood in town, the city's audacious Art Nouveau district (Alberta iela, Strēlnieku iela and Elizabetes iela) swoops in to vie for the prize. Rīga boasts over 750 *Jugendstil* (Art Nouveau) buildings, making it the city with most Art Nouveau architecture in the world. Check out our tailor-made walking tour (p209) for an in-depth look at Rīga's Art Nouveau architecture.

Stop by the **Museum of Janis Rozentāls and Rūdolfs Blaumanis** (Jaņa Rozentāla un Rūdolfa Blaumaņa muzejs; Map pp196-7; ☎ 6733 1641; www.rtmm.lv; Alberta iela 12; admission 1Ls; ☽ 11am-6pm Wed-Sun) to explore the interior of one of the lavish Art Nouveau buildings. The museum was once the home of both Janis Rozentāls, a prominent local artist, and Rūdolfs Blaumanis, a respected writer. Many of Rozentāls' sketches adorn the walls.

There's a small Jewish Museum known as **Jews in Latvia** (Ebreju Kopienas muzejs; Map pp196-7; ☎ 6728 3484; www.rtmm.lv; Skolas iela 6; admission free; ☽ noon-5pm Sun-Thu) in the neighbourhood

as well. Its recounts the city's history of Jewish life until 1945 through artefacts and photography.

Pilsētas Kanāls (City Canal)

Pilsētas kanāls, the city's old moat, once protected the medieval interior from invaders. Today, the snaking ravine has been incorporated into a thin belt of stunning parkland splitting Old and Central Rīga. Stately Raina bulvāris follows the rivulet on the north side, and used to be known as 'Embassy Row' during Latvia's independence between the World Wars. Raina has once again assumed its dignified status, with the stars and stripes fluttering in front of No 7, and *bleu blanc rouge* installed at No 9. Additional diplomatic estates face the central park and moat on Kronvalda bulvāris and Kalpaka bulvāris.

Humble **Bastejkalns** (Bastion Hill; Map pp196-7) lies along the banks of Pilsētas kanāls near Brīvības, and is the last remnant of medieval Rīga's sand bulwark fortifications. Beneath Bastejkalns, five red stone slabs lie as **memorials** to the victims of 20 January 1991 (they were killed here when Soviet troops stormed the nearby Interior Ministry).

On 18 November 1918, Latvia declared its independence at the baroque **National Theatre** (Nacionālais teātris; Map pp196-7; K Valdemāra iela), at the junction of the canal and K Valdemāra iela. The beloved **Latvia National Opera** (Map pp196-7; ☎ 6707 3777; www.opera.lv; Aspazijas bulvāris 3; ⏱ box office 10am-7pm), which resembles Moscow's Bolshoi Theatre, sits at the other end of the park near K Barona iela.

Esplanāde

An echo of Vērmanes Garden across bustling Brīvības, the expansive Esplanāde is a large park dotted with imposing trees, wooden benches, historic statues and a couple of cafes. The **State Museum of Art** (Valsts mākslas muzejs; Map pp196-7; ☎ 732 4461; K Valdemāra iela 10a; admission adult/child 3/1.50Ls; ⏱ 11am-5pm Wed-Mon) sits within the leafy grounds along K Valdemāra iela, and features pre-WWII Russian and Latvian art displayed amongst the Soviet grandeur of ruched net curtains, marble columns and red carpets.

At the other end of the park, the stunning 19th-century **Russian Orthodox Cathedral** (Pareizticīgo katedrāle; Map pp196-7; Brīvības bulvāris), with its rolling gilded cupolas, majestically rises off Brīvības. During the Soviet era, the church was used as a planetarium.

Outlying Neighbourhoods

Those who venture beyond Rīga's inner sphere of cobbled alleyways and over-the-top Art Nouveau will uncover a burgeoning artists' colony, a couple of excellent museums, and a handful of other neighbourhoods that help paint a full picture of this cosmopolitan capital.

ANDREJSALA

At first glance, **Andrejsala** (Map p188; www.andrejsala .lv), northwest of Old Rīga, looks like an abandoned port littered with outmoded Soviet parts. A closer glimpse reveals a sprouting artists' colony amid the grungy warehouses. The development company that owns Andrejsala is letting the former industrial zone develop slowly and organically by renting out studios to creative locals and allowing them to morph the landscape. Leases are renewed on a yearly basis, and at the time of research, 'co-

op' members included local installation artists, a media agency, a Russian drama troupe and a kick-ass hostel. Check out the website for regularly updated information on social activities and exhibitions.

Follow Kronvalda bulvāris 1.5km north of Old Rīga, or take tram 7 from the Freedom Monument to the end of the line.

MEŽAPARKS

Woodsy Mežaparks (literally 'Forest Park' in Latvian), along Lake Ķīšezers, 7km north of the centre, is Europe's oldest planned suburb. Built by the Germans in the 20th century, this 'garden city', originally called Kaiserwald, was the go-to neighbourhood for wealthy merchants looking to escape the city's grimy industrial core. The atmosphere hasn't changed all that much over the last 100 years – tourists will find prim country homes, hiking trails, bike paths and lazy sailboats gliding along the lake.

Mežaparks is home to the **Rīga National Zoo** (Zooloģiskais dārzs; ☎ 6751 8669; www.rigazoo.lv; Meža prospekts 1; adult/child 4/3Ls; ⏱ 10am-6pm). Set in a hilly pine forest, the zoo has a motley collection of animals, including a new assortment of tropical fauna, as well as the usual cast of Noah's ark.

There are also a handful of picturesque cemeteries nearby including **Brothers' Cemetery** (Brāļu kapi; Map p188), which features a monument by Kārlis Zāle (the designer of the Freedom Monument) dedicated to the Latvian soldiers who died defending their country between 1915 and 1920. The **Rainis Cemetery** (Raiņa kapi; Map p188) is the final resting place of Jānis Rainis, his wife (feminist poet Aspazija) and several other influential Latvians.

To reach Mežaparks, take tram 11 from K Barona iela to the 'Mežaparks' stop; get off at the 'Brāļu Kapi' stop for the Brothers' Cemetery.

ĶĪPSALA

Just a quick, 10-minute walk west over the Vanšu Bridge, quiet Ķīpsala is Rīga's veritable Left Bank. Over the last few years, the island has seen quite a bit of gentrification – wooden houses have been completely restored, and abandoned factories turned into trendy loft apartments. Rīga Technical University and the Ķīpsala Exhibition Hall complex are also located on the island. The tree-lined riverside is a great spot for taking photos of the city centre across the Daugava River.

LATVIA

TOP 5 DAY TRIPS FROM RĪGA

Leave Rīga's mess of Art Nouveau goblins and swirling church spires behind, and explore Latvia's other gems: flaxen shorelines, rambling palaces, quaint provincial villages, and forests full of shady trees.

- **Jūrmala** (p226) The Soviet Union's ultimate beach destination still teems with the Russian elite sporting bikinis and bad haircuts. Take Rīga's suburban train bound for Skola or Tukums, get off at Majōri station, and you'll be smack in the middle of spa-land in 30 minutes flat. If you're looking for a quieter stretch of sand undisturbed by the tan-hungry glitterati, try quaint **Saulkrasti** (p252), only an hour by train up the Vidzeme Coast.

- **Sigulda** (p253) It's hard not to be enchanted by Turaida Castle, hidden deep within the pine forests of Gauja National Park. Adrenalin junkies will get their fix with an endless array of activities such as bobsledding and bungee jumping from a moving cable car. Sigulda is only 1¼ hours away by bus or train.

- **Rundāle Palace** (p248) Latvia's miniature version of Versailles (but without the crowds) is a stunning, 138-room homage to aristocratic ostentatiousness. Try a tour or a rental car to navigate the 75km trek; buses only run to Bauska, where you must switch to a local route to complete the last 12km.

- **Abava River Valley** (p235) The quiet valley along the murmuring Abava River starkly contrasts Rīga's bustling urban core. Wander through charming three-street villages, an organic farmstead, and picnic under looming sculptures at the awesome Pedvāle Open-Air Art Museum. A rental car is the best mode of transport.

- **Liepāja** (p243) What? An excursion to the other side of the country? Everything's possible now that flights on airBaltic have opened up Latvia's rockin' west coast to day trippers. The government has subsidised most of the ticket price, making it cheaper to travel by plane than by bus. Flights are also available to prim-and-proper **Ventspils** (p239).

LATVIA

ĀGENSKALNS

Rīga's gritty working-class neighbourhood across the Daugava River is a serious throwback to earlier times, especially at Uzvaras Park. This sprawling green space (now mostly used as a soccer field) is home to the so-called **Victory Monument** (Uzvaras Piemineklis), which was built by the Soviets to commemorate the communist 'victory' over fascism. The monument has five stars commemorating the five years of WWII. Don't miss the **Āgenskalns Market** (see the boxed text, p220) sitting among the stacks of wooden houses, and the informative **Latvian Railway Museum** (☎ 6723 2849; www.railwaymuseum.lv; Uzvaras iela 2/4; admission 1Ls; ☒ 10am-5pm Tue-Sat), located in a renovated engine warehouse.

Take tram 2 or 8 over the Akmens Bridge, and disembark at the 'Āgenskalna Tirgus' stop, or take tram 5 and get off at the second stop on the other side of the bridge.

LATVIAN ETHNOGRAPHIC OPEN-AIR MUSEUM

If you don't have time to visit the heart of the Latvian countryside, then a stop at the **Latvian Ethnographic Open-Air Museum** (Latvijas etnogrāfiskais

brīvdabas muzejs; ☎ 6799 4510; www.muzejs.lv; Brīvības gatve 440; adult/child 1/0.50Ls; ☒ 10am-5pm mid-May–mid-Oct) is a must. Sitting along the shores of Lake Jugla just northeast of the city limits, this vast stretch of forest contains over 100 wooden buildings from each of Latvia's four cultural regions. These churches, windmills and farmhouses contain myriad artefacts, which tell the story of a bygone bucolic lifestyle.

Take bus 1 from the corner of Merķeļa iela and Tērbatas iela to the 'Brīvdabas muzejs' stop.

MOTOR MUSEUM

The stars of the collection at the fantastic **Riga Motor Museum** (Rīgas motormuzejs; Map p188; ☎ 6709 7170; www.ltg.lv/motormuzejs; Eizenšteina iela 6; adult/child 1/0.50Ls; ☒ 10am-6pm) are cars that once belonged to Soviet luminaries such as Gorky, Stalin, Khrushchev and Brezhnev, complete with irreverent life-sized figures of the men themselves. Stalin, pockmarked cheeks and all, sits regally in the back of his 7-tonne, 6005cc-armoured limousine. The car has 1.5cm-thick iron plating everywhere

(Continued on page 209)

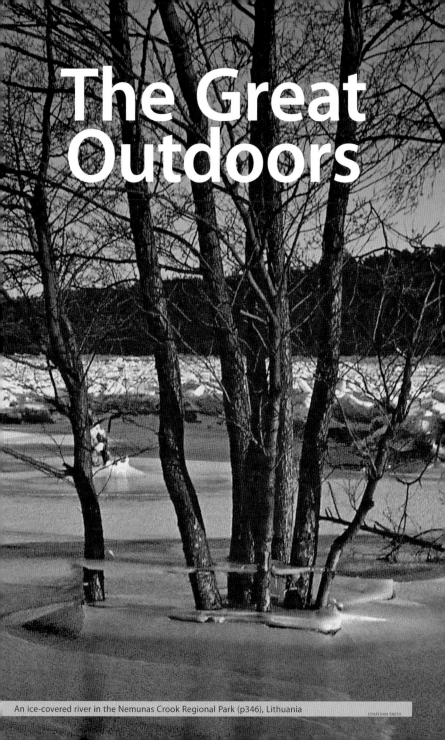

The Great Outdoors

An ice-covered river in the Nemunas Crook Regional Park (p346), Lithuania

JONATHAN SMITH

Jūrmala's Blue Flag beach (p226), Latvia
WAYNE WALTON

The Baltic countries offer visitors plenty of up-close-and-personal encounters with Mother Nature at her most gentle – paddling on a sparkling lake, rambling or cycling through pretty birch or pine forest. Instead of craning your neck at sky-reaching peaks, here you can marvel over accessible nature – tame and neat – and superbly pretty scenery. Still, while the region lacks the drama of mountains and cliffs, there are places where you're left in no doubt that it's Mother Nature calling the shots, and she can sometimes be tempestuous – witness the shifting sands of the awesome Curonian Spit, or windswept, desolate Cape Kolka.

There's plenty of breathing space in Estonia, Latvia and Lithuania, too. Check those population figures and you'll be in little doubt that open space abounds here. Factor in the relatively low tourist numbers (compared with southern European destinations, for example) and you'll understand the appeal of some of the continent's best opportunities to ditch the crowds and simply frolic in the wilderness.

A smorgasbord of active endeavours awaits anyone with an appetite for the great outdoors. You can whet your appetite with berry picking before feeding on an alfresco meal of brisk, salty air, pristine white-sand beaches and icy-blue Baltic Sea vistas. Want seconds? Try cycling through dense, pine-scented forests, canoeing down a lazy river, or checking out the flora and fauna in a quiet nature reserve. Those craving an adrenalin fix can find some surprising options too; from bobsledding to bungee jumping. If you still have room for dessert, try baby-gentle downhill or cross-country skiing, or just get hot-and-sweaty in a sauna. In fact, whatever you're craving, the Baltic countries can usually deliver.

CYCLING

The Baltic offers superb cycling territory. The region's flatness makes tooling around the countryside on a bicycle an option for anyone: casual cyclists can get the hang of things on

Cyclists' heaven in Curonian Spit National Park (p362), Lithuania
CHRISTIAN KLEIN/

BALTIC BIKING

We met Englishman Malcolm Russell in Narva, on the Estonia–Russia border, on the last leg of his seven-week marathon bike ride from Amsterdam to St Petersburg. Madness or inspiration? We can't really tell! Over a couple of well-earned beers, he happily shared his insider information from a two-wheeled journey that had taken him across the Baltic countries and Kaliningrad.

What are your tips for anyone planning a cycling trip across the Baltic? You can do this sort of journey on any kind of bike, including a road bike. The most important thing is to get a decent map showing road surfaces. It's tricky and slow going on a road bike tackling gravel surfaces, so plot your itinerary accordingly. You can usually get perfectly adequate maps for free from the tourist offices; Lithuania has an amazing free cycling map for the country, available at any tourist office.

A normal touring distance of 45km to 60km a day is reasonable, although wind on somewhere like the Curonian Spit can slow you down. It seems there are plenty of guesthouses and hotels, about every 30km to 50km, so you can be spontaneous about where you want to spend the night.

Even the main roads are cyclable – there's not too much traffic (with the exception of Kaliningrad) and the roads are generally nice and wide.

If you are on a road bike, bring spares! Everyone in this part of the world rides cheap shitty bikes bought from the supermarkets, so good-quality spares aren't readily available. You should be OK if you're riding a mountain bike.

What are the highlights? The Curonian Spit is one of the great cycling trips of Europe. Without a Russian visa (ie if you're not heading north from Kaliningrad, but west from Vilnius), hire a boat to take you and your bike from Rusnė to the bottom of the Lithuanian part of the Spit, then cycle north to Klaipėda. (In 2007 Malcolm spent seven days cycling from Vilnius to Klaipėda via the Curonian Spit; this time around he accessed it from Kaliningrad. The Lithuanian side of the Spit has a bike path; the Russian side doesn't.)

The underground Soviet missile base in Lithuania's Žemaitija National Park is also incredible.

What are the biggest problems when cycling the Baltic? Dogs and drunks. In that order. Large guard dogs are often unleashed. At night, if you're doing some remote camping, drunks will think nothing of paying you a visit and causing a ruckus. Or they'll stand in the middle of the road swinging a carrier bag that you'll have to dodge.

Hazards include fissures and potholes in Kaliningrad – the biggest potholes this side of Phnom Penh!

gentle paved paths, while hard-core fanatics can rack up the kilometres on more challenging multiday treks. Although there's not much along the lines of steep single-track trails, dirt tracks through forests and (mini)hills abound, and the varied but always peaceful scenery ensures you'll never tire of the view.

Among the most popular places to cycle are Lithuania's spectacular Curonian Spit (p362), Muhu (p163), Saaremaa (p153) and Hiiumaa (p146) islands of Estonia, and the Kurzeme coastline (p231) and 'Baltic Riviera', Jūrmala (p226), in Latvia. The forested surrounds of the region's national parks offer superb two-wheeled adventures – top picks include lake-studded Dzūkija National Park (p334) in Lithuania, the bay-fringed Lahemaa National Park (p94) in Estonia, or castle-clad Gauja National Park (p253) in Latvia.

If you want someone to help with planning, a growing band of cycling operators offer everything from itinerary-planning services to fully guided treks. In Estonia, try **City Bike** (www.citybike.ee), in Latvia, **Bikerent.lv** (www.bikerent.lv) and in Lithuania, look for **BaltiCCycle** (www.bicycle.lt). Also, some tour operators (p415) offer guided cycling treks. For DIY planning, check out the info-laden sites www.bicycle.ee and www.bicycle.lt.

SOMETHING DIFFERENT?

The Baltic countries certainly have a way to go to rival New Zealand in the crazy-activities stakes, but here's our list of activities to take you off the usual tourist trails and outside your comfort zone while you amble round the region. See our Top 10 Activities list on p16 for other favourites.

- bog-shoe-walking expeditions in the wetlands of Soomaa National Park, Estonia (p138)
- hot-air ballooning over Vilnius, Lithuania (p309)
- hiring a floating sauna, for the ultimate chill-out experience, at either Soomaa National Park (p138) or Hiiumaa (p152), both in Estonia
- bungee jumping from a moving cable car, Sigulda, Latvia (p256)
- kiiking (p51), a kooky swinging sport invented in Estonia
- bobsledding down a 16-bend track at 80km/h in Sigulda, Latvia (p256)
- braving the winter to go ice fishing on the Curonian Spit, Lithuania (p362)
- going on a beaver-spotting canoe safari in Soomaa National Park, Estonia (p138)
- getting high at the aerodium wind tunnel in Sigulda, Latvia (p256)

HIKING & WALKING

While the Baltic countries lack the craggy grandeur or wild expanses of some of their neighbours, a day or two hiking in one of the forested national parks is rewarding all the same. All that forest (it covers 51% of Estonia, 45% of Latvia and 33% of Lithuania) just begs to be explored, especially if there are beavers to spot, berries to pick, or resident witches and fairies to hear tales of along the way.

Grab your hiking boots, breathe deeply of the pine-fresh air, and hit the trails in the likes of Žemaitija National Park (p377) in Lithuania, Gauja National Park (p253) in Latvia, and Lahemaa National Park (p94) in Estonia. Pretty villages that make good bases for exploration include Estonia's Otepää (p116) and Rõuge (p122); Valmiera (p262) and Cēsis (p260) in Latvia; and Nida (p365) in Lithuania. If regular walking doesn't float your boat, make a beeline for Estonia's Soomaa National Park (p138), where you can go on a guided walk through the park's wetlands using special bog shoes (don't laugh), which give you access to otherwise hard-to-reach areas.

Hikers walking through the 3.5km Viru Bog Nature Trail (p98), Lahemaa National Park, Estonia
IMAGEBROKER/AI

Rowing boats on the Danė River (p357), Klaipėda, Lithuania
JONATHAN SMITH

WATERSPORTS

Having been cooped up for most of the winter, the region comes alive in summer, with locals and visitors taking any opportunity to soak up some vitamin D during the gloriously long days. You're never far from the sea or a lake offering fishing, sailing, windsurfing and swimming. And when the weather's not favourable towards outdoor frolicking, there's no shortage of wet 'n' wild waterparks (with indoor pools, slides, saunas etc) in big cities and holiday areas (these guys know from experience that a Baltic summer is no guarantee for beachgoing weather).

Great Baltic beachy spots are Pärnu, Narva-Jõesuu, Pirita (Tallinn) and Saaremaa in Estonia; Jūrmala, Ventspils, Pāvilosta and Liepāja in Latvia; and Palanga, Klaipėda and Nida in Lithuania. Myriad watersports can be attempted at the western end of Hiiumaa island in Estonia, and Pāvilosta in Latvia.

CANOEING & RAFTING

Watching the landscape slide slowly by while paddling down a lazy river is a fabulous way to experience the natural world from a different angle. As the region's rivers are not known for their wild rapids, this is a great place for beginners to hone their skills or for families to entertain the kids. Even if you're usually more into wild than mild, the region's scenic beauty and tranquillity create such a Zen experience you'll quickly forget you haven't hit a single rapid.

In Latvia, the Gauja (p256) and Abava Rivers (p235) offer uninterrupted routes stretching for several days, and you can join an organised tour or rent gear and run the routes on your own – the best places to start are Sigulda, Valmiera and Kandava. In Lithuania, Labanoros Regional Park (p329), Dzūkija National Park (p334), Trakai (p322) and Nemunas Crook Regional Park (p346) all offer the opportunity for great canoeing. Canoes or traditional *haabjas* (Finno-Ugric boats carved from a single log) serve as the primary vehicles for exploring Soomaa National Park (p138) in southwest Estonia – you can even learn to build your own *haabjas*. Otepää (p118) is another good Estonian spot to organise and access canoe trips, including ones that combine canoeing with hiking and cycling.

Ice-fishing outside Trakai's Island Castle (p323), Lithuania

FISHING

Abundant lakes and miles of rivers and streams provide ample fishing opportunities in all three countries. Visit a regional tourist office for the scoop on the best angling spots and information pertaining to permits.

In the dark depths of the Baltic winter there is no finer experience than dabbling in a touch of ice-fishing with vodka-warmed local fishermen on the frozen Curonian Lagoon (p362), off the west coast of Lithuania, or at Trakai (p323). The Nemunas Delta Regional Park (p370) is another good western Lithuanian fishing spot. In Latvia, the Latgale Lakelands (p269) is packed with hundreds of deep-blue lakes offering fishing opportunities galore. In northern Kurzeme, Lake Engure (p234) is another favourite angling spot. Huge Lake Peipsi (p105) is popular in Estonia.

BERRYING & MUSHROOMING

The Balts' deep-rooted attachment to the land is reflected in their obsession with berrying and mushrooming – national pastimes in all three countries. Accompanying a local friend into the forest on a summer berrying trip or autumn mushrooming expedition is an enchanting way to appreciate this traditional rural pastime.

If you're keen on picking but lack a local invitation, join an organised tour (locals closely guard the location of their favourite spots, so just asking around probably won't reap any useful information). For info on berrying and mushrooming tours, check out www.countryside.lt (Lithuania), www.maaturism.ee (Estonia) and www.traveller.lv (Latvia), and ask at local tourist offices. You can't go wrong at Lithuania's Dzūkija (p330) or Aukštaitija National Parks (p326). Failing that, head to any market and check out the freshly picked produce, or peruse menus for in-season treasures from local forests, and pat yourself on the back for the low food miles your meal has travelled.

HORSE RIDING

The gentle pace of horseback exploration is definitely in keeping with the yesteryear feel of parts of the Baltic countries. Some of the best and most bucolic places to get saddlesore include Lahemaa National Park (p98) and the islands of Hiiumaa (p146) and Saaremaa (p153) in Estonia – operators here will usually combine rural and coastal rides, and can arrange multiday treks. In Latvia, head to Plosti (p235), between Kandava and Sabile in the picturesque Andava River Valley; Untumi country ranch (p269), 7km northwest of Rēzekne; or the well-established Klajumi stables (p271), outside Kraslava in the Latgale Lakelands. Lithuanian visitors hankering for some four-legged fun can head to Trakai (p323); the stud farm (p349), 12km northeast of Šiauliai; or the horse museum (p352), in the village of Niūronys, outside Anykščiai.

BIRDWATCHING

Thanks to a key position on north–south migration routes, the Baltic countries are a twitcher's paradise. Each year, hundreds of bird species descend upon the region, attracted by fish-packed wetlands and wide-open spaces relatively devoid of people. White storks arrive by the thousands each spring, nesting on rooftops and telegraph poles throughout the region. Other annual visitors include corncrakes, bitterns, cranes, mute swans, black storks and all types of geese.

In Estonia, some of the best birdwatching in the Baltic is found in the Matsalu National Park (p146), where 280 different species (many migratory) can be spotted, and where regular tours are run. Spring migration peaks in April/May, but some species arrive as early as March. Autumn migration begins in July and can last until November. Vilsandi National Park (p162), off Saaremaa, is another prime spot for feathery friends, and the park's headquarters can help arrange birdwatching tours.

Some 270 of the 330 bird species found in Lithuania frequent the Nemunas Delta Regional Park (p371), making it a must visit for serious birders. Park authorities can help organise birdwatching expeditions during the peak migratory seasons. The nearby Curonian Spit National Park (p362) offers opportunities for spotting up to 200 different species of birds amid dramatic coastal scenery.

Storks' nests dot the countryside in Latvia
BRANDON PRESSER

In Latvia, keep an eye out for some of Europe's rarest birds in splendid Gauja National Park (p253). With thick forests and numerous wetlands, Ķemeri National Park (p230), in northern Kurzeme, is another great birdwatching spot. The boggy Teiči Nature Reserve (p265), in the Vidzeme Uplands, is an important feeding and nesting ground for many bird species. Lake Engure (p234), in northern Kurzeme, is a major bird reservation with 186 species (44 endangered) nesting around the lake and its seven islets.

208

SWEAT IT OUT

Given that it's cold, dark and snowy for many months of the year in the Baltic, it's little surprise that the sauna is an integral part of local culture. Most hotels have one, and some cities have public bathhouses with saunas. But it's the ones that silently smoulder next to a lake or river, by the sea or deep in the forest that provide the most authentic experience.

There are three main types of sauna in the Baltic:

- the Finnish-style sauna, where an electric stove keeps the air-temperature high (between 70°C and 95°C), and humidity is kept low. These are found in plenty of private homes, most hotels, all spas and waterparks etc. Some hotel suites have a private sauna attached to the bathroom. Public or hotel saunas charge an hourly fee, and there are plenty of small, private saunas that can be rented by the hour.

- the smoke sauna – the most archaic type of sauna, whereby a fire is lit directly under rocks in the chimney-less sauna (generally a one-room wooden hut), and heating can take up to five hours. After the fire is put out in the hearth, the heat comes from the heated rocks. The smoke is let out just before participants enter, and the soot-blackened walls are part of the experience. Smoke saunas are rare but have become more popular in recent times.

- the 'Russian sauna' or steam sauna/steam bath – not as popular in the Baltic region as the Finnish style of sauna, but found mainly in spas or waterparks. In these, the air temperature is medium (about 50°C) and air humidity is high.

Locals use a bunch of birch twigs to lightly slap or flick the body, stimulating circulation, irrespective of which sauna type they're sweating in. Cooling down is an equally integral part of the experience: most Finnish-style saunas have showers or pools attached, while the more authentic smoke saunas are usually next to a lake or river. In the depths of winter, rolling in snow or cutting out a square metre of ice from a frozen lake in order to take a quick dip in is not unheard of.

SKIING & SNOWBOARDING

They might not have anything closely resembling a mountain, but Estonia and Latvia haven't let this geographic hurdle hinder their ski-resort efforts. Instead these countries have become masters at working with what they've got – and that means constructing lifts and runs on the tiniest of hills, and using rooftops and dirt mounds to create vertical drops. At least they've got the climate working for them, with cold temperatures ensuring snow cover for at least four months of the year. Don't expect much in the way of technical terrain or long powder runs – but you've got to admit that saying you've skied or snowboarded the Baltic is pretty damn cool!

Otepää (p119), in southeast Estonia, is probably the best of the Baltic winter resorts. It offers a variety of downhill-skiing and snowboarding areas, myriad cross-country trails, a ski jump and plenty of outlets from which to hire gear. Lively nightlife and a ski-town vibe heighten the appeal for skiers and boarders. Kicksledding, cross-country skiing and snowshoe excursions are available at Soomaa National Park (p138).

The Gauja Valley is the centre of Latvia's winter-sports scene. Sigulda (p256), Cēsis (p261) and Valmiera (p262) all offer short-but-sweet downhill runs as well as loads of cross-country trails. Adrenalin junkies disappointed by Sigulda's gentle slopes can get their fix swishing down the town's 1200m-long artificial bobsled run – the five-person contraptions reach speeds of 80km/h! The Vidzeme Uplands (p265), centred on the whopping 312m Gaiziņkalns, is adored as the country's top spot for skiers and snowboarders.

Lithuania hasn't really joined the downhill game, but you can cross-country ski amid deep, whispering forests and frozen blue lakes in beautiful Aukštaitija National Park (p326).

(Continued from page 200)

except on the 8cm-thick windows. It drank a litre of petrol every 2.5km.

The museum is 8km outside the city centre along Brīvības iela, then 2km south to the Mežciems suburb. Take bus 21 from the Russian Orthodox Cathedral to the Pansionāts stop on Šmerļa iela.

RĪGA AVIATION MUSEUM
If you have a long layover at the airport, check out the **Riga Aviation Museum** (☎ 2686 2707; www.aviamuseum.lv; admission 5Ls; ☽ 10am-6pm Mon-Fri, Sat & Sun by request) right next door. Over 40 Soviet planes are permanently on display, from camouflaged utility copters to stealth military bombers.

ACTIVITIES
For an intense adrenalin fix, like bungee jumping, bobsledding, mountain biking and skydiving, head to the town of Sigulda (p253) in Gauja National Park. Water-sports enthusiasts should spend the day in Jūrmala (p226).

Arcades & Entertainment Centres
All your gaming desires will be fulfilled at **Go Planet** (☎ 6714 6346; Astras iela 2b; ☽ 2pm-midnight Mon-Fri, 11am-midnight Sat, 11am-11pm Sun), a 15,000-sq-metre funhouse featuring laser tag, go-carts, a racing simulator and billiards. From Brīvības, take trolleybus 17 northeast to the 'Mēbeļu nams' stop.

Saunas & Spas
You don't have to run all the way to Jūrmala to see some serious spa action. Rīga has a few standout places to get pampered in traditional Latvian style: getting whipped by dried birch branches while sweating it out in temperatures beyond 40°C. Sounds relaxing…

High-end **Taka Spa** (Map pp196-7; ☎ 6732 3150; www.takaspa.lv; Kronvalda bulvāris 3a; cleansing 'rituals' from 29Ls; ☽ 11am-9pm Mon-Wed, 9am-9pm Thu & Fri, 10am-7pm Sat, 10am-5pm Sun) offers massages, wraps, scrubs and sauna treatments. Try the signature 'opening ritual' in which clients move between saunas and plunge pools while drinking herbal teas. Yoga classes, pilates courses and exercise facilities are also available.

Frequented mostly by locals rather than tourists, **Baltā Pirts** (☎ 6727 1733; www.baltapirts.lv; Tallinas iela 71; sauna 7Ls; ☽ 8am-8pm Wed-Sun) combines traditional Latvian relaxation techniques (the name means 'white birch') with a subtle, oriental design scheme. Take a tram heading north along A Čaka until you reach Tallinas iela.

Kolonna Spa (Map p190; ☎ 6701 8034; www.kolonna.lv; Audeju iela 16, Galerija Centrs; classic massage 30Ls; ☽ 8am-10pm Mon-Fri, 9am-8pm Sat & Sun), part of the Kolonna hospitality chain, offers a full menu of international treatments in the heart of Old Rīga.

Shooting Range
The ambience at **Regro's** (☎ 6760 1705; Daugavgrīvas iela 31; per bullet 0.80-2Ls; ☽ 10am-5pm Mon-Sat, Sun by appointment) is reason enough to visit: a dingy Soviet fallout shelter adorned with posters of rifle-toting models wearing fur bikinis. Choose from a large selection of retro firearms (including Kalashnikovs) to aim at your paper cut-out of James Bond. You pay by the bullet, and don't forget your passport.

Take the Vanšu Bridge across the river, pass Ķīpsala, and take your first right until you hit a petrol station. Trams 13 and 13A will take you directly to Regro's – get off at Kiņģeru iela; if you pass two petrol stations you've gone too far.

WALKING TOUR: ART NOUVEAU IN RĪGA
If you ask any Rīgan where to find the city's world-famous Art Nouveau architecture, you will always get the same answer: 'Look up!' Over 750 buildings in Rīga (more than any other city in Europe) boast this flamboyant and haunting style of decor; and the number continues to grow as myriad restoration projects get under way. Art Nouveau is also known as *Jugendstil*, meaning 'youth style', named after a Munich-based magazine called *Die Jugend*, which popularised the design in its pages.

Art Nouveau's early influence was Japanese print art disseminated throughout Western Europe, but as the movement gained momentum, the style became more ostentatious and freeform – design schemes started to feature mythical beasts, screaming masks, twisting flora, goddesses and goblins. The turn of the 20th century marked the height of the Art Nouveau movement as it swept through every major European city from Porto to Petersburg.

In Rīga, the most noted *Jugendstil* architect was Mikhail Eisenstein (father of Sergei Eisenstein, a noted Soviet film director) who

LATVIA

WALK FACTS

Start Alberta iela
Finish Meistaru iela 10
Distance 3km
Duration two hours (leisurely pace)

ART NOUVEAU WALKING TOUR

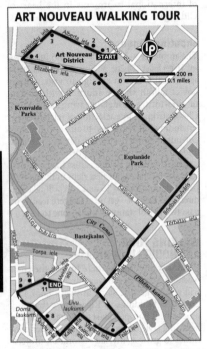

flexed his artistic muscles on Alberta iela. At **Alberta iela 2a (1)**, constructed in 1906, serene faces with chevalier helmets stand guard atop the facade, which noticeably extends far beyond the actual roof of the structure. Screaming masks and horrible goblins adorn the lower sections amid clean lines and surprising robot-like shapes. The three heads on **Alberta iela 4 (2)** next door will surely capture your attention. If you look carefully, you'll see a nest of snakes slithering around their heads, evoking Medusa. All six eyes seem transfixed on some unseen horror, but only two of the faces are screaming in shock and fear. Two elaborate reliefs near the entrance feature majestic griffins, and ferocious lions with erect, fist-like tails keep watch on the roof. Further down the street, the Rīga Graduate School of

Law at **Alberta iela 13 (3)** epitomises *Jugendstil's* attention to detail. Peacocks, tangled shrubs and bare-breasted heroines abound while cheery pastoral scenes are depicted in relief on Erykah Badu–like turbans atop the giant yawning masks. The triangular summit is a mishmash of nightmarish imagery; lion heads taper off into snake tails (like Chimera), sobbing faces weep in agony, and a strange futuristic mask stoically stares out over the city from the apex. Turn the corner to find the Stockholm School of Economics at **Strēlnieku iela 4a (4)**, filled in with sumptuous blue brick, and framed by garland-wielding goddesses. More eye candy awaits at **Elizabetes iela 33 (5)**, with muscular men balancing stacks of Corinthian columns on their shoulders. The blue-and-white facade at **Elizabetes iela 10b (6)**, also designed by Eisenstein, is one of the city's earliest examples of Art Nouveau and a clear fan favourite. The enormous sullen heads squished at the top of the facade are the subjects of myriad postcards. Continue down Elizabetes iela in the direction of the towering Reval Hotel Latvija and make a right on Brīvības iela. Follow Brīvības past the Freedom Monument and make your way into medieval Old Rīga.

Most visitors don't realise that Old Rīga also offers wonderfully ornate gargoyle heads, mythical beasts and ancient gods hidden amongst its patchwork of gabled roofs and church spires. Enter the city's medieval core on Teātra iela and pause at **Teātra iela 9 (7)**, the Italian Embassy, to admire the facade's pantheon of Greek figures – two ragged older men (Prometheus perhaps) frantically clutch their neck while supporting the convoluted wrought-iron balcony above. Further up, reliefs of Athena and Hermes stand proud. Look way up high to spot Atlas with the world on his shoulders (literally). The stunning zinc and glass globe sparkles in the evening. If you look closely at **Šķūņu iela 10/12 (8)** you'll spot a variety of 'D's hidden in the front design – the initials of the original owner. A watchdog stands guard at the top. The building at **Smilšu iela 2 (9)** is considered to be one of the finest examples of *Jugendstil* in Old Rīga. The exterior features a variety of hybrid creatures including intertwining vines that morph, like a mermaid's tail, into the torso of two caryatids. On the same street, at **Smilšu iela 8 (10)**, two women stand atop a protruding bay carrying an elaborate crown of leaves.

A large mask of a melancholic woman with her eyes shut hovers over the entrance – a common theme early on in the Art Nouveau movement. The building's lobby continues a similar ornamental theme to the exterior. Veer right along Maza Smilšu iela to find **Meistaru iela 10 (11)**, known to most as the 'Cat House' for the spooked black cat sitting on the roof. According to legend, the owner was rejected from the local Merchant's Guild across the street, and exacted revenge by placing a black cat on the top of his turret with its tail raised towards the esteemed Great Guild Hall. The members of the guild were outraged, and after a lengthy court battle the merchant was admitted into the club on the condition that the cat be turned in the opposite direction.

RĪGA FOR CHILDREN

The Unesco-protected streets of Old Rīga can feel like a magical time warp for the 12-and-under bunch. For a trip into the future, try laser tag and a racing simulator at **Go Planet** (p209). During the summer months, take the tykes to the zoo in forested **Mežaparks** (p199) or let the little ones cool off on the beach in nearby **Jūrmala** (p226). Between spirited sessions of wave jumping and sand-castle building try **Līvu Akvaparks** (☎ 6775 5636; www .akvaparks.lv; Viestura iela 24; 1-day adult/child/family/under 6yr 14.85/10.90/36.20Ls/free; ☻ 11am-10pm Mon-Fri, 10am-10pm Sat & Sun), Latvia's largest indoor water park, which features a wave pool and a tangle of waterslides.

TOURS

Swarms of operators offer tours around Rīga as well as day trips to popular sights nearby. For more information on day trips, see the boxed text on p200.

Amber Way (☎ 6727 1915; www.sightseeing.lv; tour 10Ls) A smorgasbord of city tours, either on a bus or walking. Tours depart at 11am, noon, 1pm and 3pm. Ask about a walking-bus-lunch combo for 20Ls. Day trips depart at 11am from the Opera House: to Rundāle Palace (every Saturday), to Sigulda (every Friday) and to Jūrmala (every Sunday). Most midrange and top-end hotels can book these tours.

Baltic Info Centre (Map pp196-7; ☎ 2202 2924; www.balticinfocentre.com; Torņu iela 4; tours from 4Ls) Organises walking tours of the Art Nouveau district, which depart from the office.

Eat Riga (☎ 2246 9888; www.eatriga.com; tour 5Ls) No, it's not a foodie's tour; three-hour walks stop at less-

touristy attractions around town. Tours depart in front of St Peter's Church every day at noon.

Retro Tram (☎ 6730 7900; adult/child 6/3Ls; ☻ 10am-5pm) Two routes, aboard a restored tram, meander through the Art Nouveau district and on to Mežaparks. Free guided walking tours of the Art Nouveau district available on weekends departing 11.40am, 1.40pm and 3.40pm from the Ausekļa tram stop.

Rīga City Tour (☎ 2665 5405; www.citytour.lv; adult/child 10/9Ls) A hop-on, hop-off double-decker bus that wends its way through Rīga stopping at 15 spots on both sides of the Daugava River. Buses leave from Rātslaukums on the hour between 10am and 3pm.

Riga Mobile Guide (☎ English 9000 6102, German 9000 6104, Russian 9000 6103, Latvian 9000 6101; call 0.84Ls) A savvy, self-guided tour using your mobile phone. Dial the code for your desired attraction (21 stops in total) and learn about its history and significance.

Riga Out There (Map pp196-7; ☎ 2938 9450; www .rigaoutthere.com; tours from 10Ls) Organises loads of tours and activities for tourists including day trips to adrenalin-packed Sigulda, AK-47 shooting excursions, Soviet walking tours, spas bookings and late-night pub crawls. It also runs a hostel on the same premises (see p204).

FESTIVALS & EVENTS

Rīgans will find any excuse to celebrate, especially when the sun comes out during the summer months. Check out www.km.gov.lv for a complete listing of events.

International Baltic Ballet Festival (www.ballet -festival.lv) This three-week festival starts in late April; performances by Latvian and international companies.

Rīga Opera Festival (www.music.lv/opera) The Latvian National Opera's showcase event takes place over 10 days in June and includes performances by world-renowned talents.

Rīgas Ritmi (www.rigasritmi.lv) 'Rīga's Rhythms' is the capital's international music festival held at the beginning of July.

Baltā Nakts (www.baltanakts.lv) Held at the end of August, this 'white night' event, sponsored by the Contemporary Art Forum, mirrors Paris' night-long showcase of artists and culture around the city.

Arsenāls International Film Forum (www.arsenals.lv) An annual film festival held in September showcasing over 100 movies relating to experiential and interactive themes.

Arēna New Music Festival (www.arenafest.lv) Contemporary music festival held at venues throughout Rīga during the last two weeks of October.

SLEEPING

If you're only in town for a short period of time, go for a room in the heart of Old Rīga. Those who are more concerned with getting

LATVIA

the biggest bang for their buck will find the best deals along Central Rīga's grand boulevards. Expect wireless internet access no matter where you are staying, and complimentary breakfast (of varying sizes) is included at most midrange and top-end digs.

The summer months are quite busy, so it's best to book in advance. Check out www.hotels.lv for more hotel and booking information in Rīga and the rest of Latvia.

Budget

Hostels dominate the budget accommodation scene in Rīga, and the competition is fierce. There are now almost 30 hostels in the capital, and that number is set to rise over the next few years. Soaring real-estate prices means that the mainstream backpacker scene is always in flux – it's best to book ahead as some places close their doors for the winter and never reopen when high season rolls around. Hostelworld (www.hostelworld.com) has become Rīga's unofficial go-to website for choosing budget digs; managers encourage their guests to post comments on the site before checking out. Virtually every hostel has free internet and wi-fi, and count on price hikes (1 or 2 lats) for weekend rates.

OLD RĪGA (VECRĪGA)

Argonaut Backpackers Hostel (Map p190; ☎ 2614 7214; www.argonauthostel.com; Kaļēju iela 50; dm/d from 7/28Ls; 🖳) Five years ago Argonauts was undoubtedly the coolest spot to hang your hat. Today, the rooms feel a bit worn-out, but the staff is superfriendly and the couch-strewn common room is still a great spot to chill with new friends. Search 'Argonaut Hostel Riga' on YouTube for a video tour of the hostel. Wi-fi available.

Friendly Fun Franks (Map p190; ☎ 6722 0040; www.franks.lv; Novembra Krastmala iela 29; dm/d from 6.90/40Ls; 🖳) If you want to party, look no further than this bright orange stag-magnet, where every backpacker is greeted with a hearty hello and a complimentary pint of beer. The staff offers guided tours of Old Rīga and frequent trips to the beach (5Ls). Bus 22 from the airport conveniently stops in front of the hostel. Wi-fi available.

Old Town Hostel (Map p190; ☎ 6722 3406; www.rigaoldtownhostel.lv; Vaļņu iela 43; dm/d 7/35Ls; 🖳) The brick-lined pub on the ground floor doubles as the hostel's hang-out space, and if you can manage to lug your suitcase up

the narrow, twisting staircase, you'll find spacious dorms with chandeliers and plenty of sunlight. Private rooms are located in another building near the train station. Wi-fi available.

The following hostels offer beds in prim and proper rooms with little atmosphere. They're a bit uninspiring, but situated in the heart of the action.

Dome Pearl Hostel (Map p190; ☎ 6721 2161; www.hostelwlcome.com.lv; Tirgonu iela 4; dm/s/d 7/20/30Ls; 🖳) Four-person rooms are spacious and bright. The entrance is tucked in-between a row of cafes.

Doma Hostel (Map p190; ☎ 6721 3101; www.domahostel.com; Skunu iela 16; dm/d from 8/35Ls; 🖳) Great views of Doma Laukums from the white, orphanage-like rooms. Reception open from 8am to 11pm.

Profitcamp (Map p190; ☎ 6721 6361; www.profitcamp.lv; Teātra iela 12; dm/s/d incl breakfast 8/39/53Ls; 🖳) The name says it all – the owners turn a profit with their camp of sterile, no-frills accommodation.

CENTRAL RĪGA (CENTRS)

Riga Out There House (Map pp196-7; ☎ 2649 1235; www.rigaouttherehouse.com; K Barona iela 44, entrance on Lāčplēša iela; dm/d from 7/28Ls; 🖳) Warning: if you stay at 'The House', you probably won't see any of Rīga's sights – the ultrachill common space is both effortlessly stylish and a veritable black hole for backpackers. The hostel doubles as the office for Riga Out There, a reputable tour operator, so you can pick ask them about things to do and get discounts on their tours.

Knight's Court (☎ 6784 6400; www.knightscourt.lv; Bruņinieku iela 75b; dm/s/d incl breakfast from 7/25/32Ls; 🖳) Enter under a bright orange sign saying 'Double Sun' to find the courtyard access for this quiet hostel. The furnishings are a bit outdated (especially the patterned carpets), but everything is squeaky clean. Wi-fi available.

Barons (Map pp196-7; ☎ 2910 5939; www.baronshostel.com; K Barona iela 25; dm/s/d 11/30/35Ls; 🖳) Perched high on the top floor (sorry, no elevator), Barons has a bit more personality than the other low-key hostels in Central Rīga. Guests can save a lat or two and cook in the spacious kitchen, or relax in front of the plasma TV with a DVD. Room 5 is the quietest, although rooms 1 and 4 have great views of the cool Art Nouveau buildings across the street. Search 'Barons Hostel Riga' on YouTube for a flashy guided tour.

our pick **City Lounge** (Map pp196-7; ☎ 2935 8958; www
.citylounge.lv; Alfrēda Kalniņa iela 4; dm/d from 11/36Ls; 🖳)
Rumour has it that they're building an eleva-
tor, but until then guests should hire a sherpa
to climb the 128 stairs. Once you get to the top,
however, you'll find a fantastic hostel that's both
hip and spotless. The lounge area feels a bit 'ori-
ent-meets-Ikea' with its smooth red-and-black
design scheme. Guests staying in the London
room can store their luggage in the iconic red
telephone booth, and in the Rīga room there's
a giant city map on the ceiling so you can plan
tomorrow's itinerary while lying in bed. Book
nooks and electrical outlets are conveniently
found beside every pillow.

Backpackers Planet (Map pp196-7; ☎ 6722 6232;
www.backpackersplanet.lv; Neģu iela 17; dm/d 12/32Ls; 🖳)
Smack in the heart of the Central Market, this
quiet hostel, built in a remodelled warehouse,
is a much better option than the dismal Posh
Backpackers across the street. Faux exposed
brick adorns the hallways, and the tidy rooms
have en-suite toilets.

KB (Map pp196-7; ☎ 6731 2323; www.kbhotel.lv;
K Barona iela 37; s/d/tr from 27/32/38Ls; 🖳) One of
the only nonhostels in the budget category,
this great B&B is located in a rather opulent
building with bucolic frescos on the ground
floor, and a sweeping marble staircase taking
travellers up to the hotel. The rooms are simple but well appointed, and there's a modern
communal kitchen.

Multilux (Map pp196-7; ☎ 6731 1602; www.multilux.lv; K
Barona iela 37; s/d/tr 35/40/50Ls, with shared bathroom
29/34/41Ls; 🖳) Multilux isn't brimming with
character, but the spartan rooms are good
second choice if KB is full. Wi-fi available but
it doesn't work in every bedroom. Breakfast
included.

If the aforementioned spots are booked
solid, there are three passable hostels crammed
into the apartment buildings at Elizabetes iela
101 and 103.

OUTLYING NEIGHBOURHOODS

Riga City Camping (☎ 6706 5000; www.bt1.lv/camping;
Ķīpsalas iela 8; sites per adult/child/tent 1.50/1/5Ls; 🕑 mid-
May–mid-Sep; 🖳) Located on Ķīpsala across the
river from Old Rīga, this large camp site is
surprisingly close to the city centre and offers
plenty of rooms for campers and campervan-
ners. Tents (5Ls) and sleeping bags (1.50Ls)
can be rented if you don't have your own gear.
Discounts are available for those staying more
than a couple nights.

Dodo Hotel (☎ 6724 0220; www.dodohotel.com;
Jersikas iela 1; r from 27Ls; 🖳) Hidden deep in
the Maskavas neighbourhood (east of the
Central Market), this new cheapie is a fantastic find if you don't mind being slightly
removed from the action. Savvy designers
have feng shui-ed the small rooms with stylish details such as a scarlet-accent wall, a
mini plasma TV, and teeny bucket sink in
the bathroom.

Midrange

Rīga's selection of midrange hotels is a
diverse assortment of quaint B&B-style
digs and large-scale lodging behemoths.
Breakfast is almost always included in the
price, and the best deals can be scouted in
Central Rīga.

OLD RĪGA (VECRĪGA)

Radi un Draugi (Map p190; ☎ 6782 0200; www.draugi
.lv; Mārstaļu iela 1; s/d/ste 42/52/58Ls; 🖳) Despite
recent renovation attempts, this old-timer
is starting to show its age. We're not a huge
fan of puke-green shag carpeting, but if you
can turn your expectations down a notch,
then Radi un Draugi offers a great bang for
your buck if you want to stay in the heart
of Old Rīga.

Ekes Konventas (Map p190; ☎ 6735 8393; www
.ekeskonvents.lv; Skarnu iela 22; s/d 55/60Ls; 🖳) Not to
be confused with Konventa Sēta next door,
Ekes Konventas, housed in a 600-year-old
building, oozes wobbly medieval charm
from every crooked nook and cranny. Curl
up with a book in the adorable stone alcoves
on the landing of each floor.

Konventa Sēta (Map p190; ☎ 2708 7501; www
.konventa.lv; Kalēju iela 9/11; s/d/ste 63/67/95Ls; 🅿 🖳)
Beyond its location in a 15th-century convent,
there's nothing particularly special about this
Old Rīga behemoth. Rooms are prim with
white linen drapes (ask for a nonsmoking
room), but they feel small like a nun's cell.
Parking is 8Ls per night.

Centra (Map p190; ☎ 6722 6441; www.centra.lv;
Audēju iela 1; s/d 77/84Ls; 🖳 ❌) Centra is a great
choice for comfort in the heart of Old Rīga.
Recently renovated rooms are spacious and
sport loads of designer details such as swish
LCD TVs, porcelain basin sinks, and minimalist art on the walls. Rooms on the 5th
and 6th floors have lower ceilings but better
views of the medieval streets below. The
hotel is completely nonsmoking.

CENTRAL RĪGA (CENTRS)

Krišjānis & Ģertrūde (Map pp196-7; ☎ 6750 6604; www
.kg.lv; K Barona iela 39, entrance on Ģertrūdes iela; s/d/tr from
30/40/60Ls; ☐) Step off the bustling intersec-
tion into this quaint, family-run B&B adorned
with still-life paintings of fruit and flowers.
It's best to book ahead since there are only six
cosy rooms tucked around the sociable dining
room with its crooked upright piano.

Jakob Lenz (Map pp196-7; ☎ 6733 3343; www
.guesthouselenz.lv; Lenču iela 2; s/d from 35/45Ls, with
shared bathroom 30/35Ls; ☐) Tucked away along
a random side street on the fringes of the
Art Nouveau district, this great find offers 25
adorable rooms and a gut-busting breakfast
in the morning.

B&B Rīga (Map pp196-7; ☎ 2652 6400; www.bb-riga.lv;
Ģertrūdes iela 43; s/d from 35/46Ls; ☐) Snug, apart-
ment-style accommodation comes in different
configurations (suites with lofted bedrooms
are particularly charming), and are scattered
throughout the otherwise residential building.
Street-side rooms can be a bit noisy. Take a
sharp left after entering the flower-filled
courtyard to find the reception.

Albert Hotel (Map pp196-7; ☎ 6733 1717; www
.alberthotel.lv; Dzirnavu iela 33; s/d 51/56Ls; ☒ ☐) The
boxy, metallic facade starkly contrasts with
the surrounding Art Nouveau gargoyles, but
the interior design is undeniably hip and
pays tribute to the hotel's namesake, Albert
Einstein. The patterned carpeting features
rows of atomic-energy symbols, the clocks in
the lobby are set to 'imaginary time' and 'lin-
ear time', and the 'do not disturb' doorknob
danglers have been replaced with red tags
that say 'I'm thinking'. The complimentary
buffet breakfast is a bit of a bloodbath as 200
rooms' worth of guests battle it out for the
last strip of bacon.

Reval Hotel Latvija (Map pp196-7; ☎ 6777 2222; www
.revalhotels.com; Elizabetes iela 55; d incl breakfast from 69Ls;
☒ ☐) During the height of the Soviet regime,
this hotel was a drab monstrosity in which several floors were devoted to monitoring the various goings-on of the hotel's guests. The room
keys weighed several kilos because they were
outfitted with listening devices. Today, after a
much-needed facelift, the days of espionage are
long gone; it's all swipe-card access and every
level offers comfortable accommodation with
wi-fi. Don't miss the views from the Skyline
Bar on the 26th floor (p221).

Hotel Valdemārs (Map pp196-7; ☎ 6733 4462; www
.valdemars.lv; Valdemāra iela 23; s/d from 63/88Ls; ☒ ☐)
Modern Hotel Valdemārs is a great find geared
towards the Scandinavian market – rooms feel
efficient yet homey, in an upscale Ikea kind of
way. Check out the Turkish spa and whirlpool
in the basement, and don't forget to give away
the flower adorning the bureau in your room –
it's a Latvian tradition! Online bookings yield
cheaper rates.

OUTLYING NEIGHBORHOODS

Philosopher's House (☎ 6760 7150; www.mg.lv; Balasta
dambis 68b; house for 12/24hrs 35/65Ls; ☐) Once used
as a fish smokehouse, this stunning wooden
lodge on the banks of the Daugava River is the
ultimate secret sleeping spot in Rīga.

Islande Hotel (☎ 6760 8000; www.islandehotel.lv;
Ķīpsalas iela 20; s/d 55/64Ls; ☐) The international
clocks hung above the front desk display the
local time in the all-important global centres
of Reykjavik and Tobago (we're as confused
as you are). Upstairs, guests will find modern
rooms with great views of downtown Rīga
across the river. Strike out at the six-lane
bowling alley in the basement.

Hanza Hotel (☎ 6779 6040; www.hanzahotel.lv; Elijas
iela 7; s/d/ste incl breakfast 62/75/90Ls; ☐) Just beyond
the Central Market, this newer addition to
Rīga's lodging scene is a former apartment
building transformed into six floors of tidy
rooms, some with great views of Stalin's
Birthday Cake (p196).

Top End

There are two distinct classes of hotels
among the city's crème de la crème: flamboyant throwbacks to Rīga's aristocratic
days (think sumptuous antiques and gushing drapery) and avant-garde gems ripped
straight from the latest Scandinavian
architectural magazine.

OLD RĪGA (VECRĪGA)

Ainavas Boutique Hotel (Map p190; ☎ 6781 4316;
www.ainavas.lv; Peldu iela 23; s/d/ste 84/109/168Ls;
☒ ☐) Located near Rātslaukums, Ainavas'
original structure dates back to the 15th century, although the interior reeks of boutique
modernity with shiny concrete floors, fuchsia
accent walls and recessed lighting. Breakfast
is served under the charming brick arches of
the building's restored storage cellar.

Grand Palace Hotel (Map p190; ☎ 6704 4000; www
.grandpalaceriga.com; Pils iela 12; s/d/ste incl breakfast from
158/190/316Ls; ☒ ☐) If you don't mind small-
ish rooms, you'll find no better place to be

pampered than the lavish Grand Palace. The staff wax nostalgic about the various luminaries who have stayed here, including Catherine Deneuve and REM, but it's actually more fit for royalty than rock stars.

CENTRAL RĪGA (CENTRS)

Reval Hotel Elizabete (Map pp196-7; ☎ 6778 5555; www.revalhotels.com; Elizabetes iela 73; r incl breakfast from 84Ls; ✗ ▣) The newest link in the Reval chain is a flash address designed by an up-and-coming London architectural firm. The facade is an eye-catching mix of chrome, steel and giant sheets of glass, and interior sports stylish furnishings that feel both minimal and futuristic. Wi-fi available.

our pick **Europa Royale** (Map pp196-7; ☎ 6707 9444; www.europaroyale.com; K Barona iela 12; s/d/ste incl breakfast from 83/94/105Ls; ✗ ▣) Once the home of media mogul Emilija Benjamiņa (see the boxed text, p216), this ornate manse retains much of its original opulence with sweeping staircases and stately bedrooms. In fact, when Latvia regained its independence, the house was initially chosen to be the president's digs but government didn't have enough funds for the restoration. Swig an afternoon cocktail in the hunting-lodge-style lounge, or under the Murano glass chandelier, and try the hotel's signature gold foil chocolate cake made with sheets of edible 24 carat gold. There are 60 large rooms, yet guests will feel like they're staying at their posh aunt's estate.

our pick **Hotel Bergs** (Map pp196-7; ☎ 6777 0900; www.hotelbergs.lv; Elizabetes iela 83/85; r/ste incl breakfast from 123/173Ls; ✗ ▣) Hotel Bergs: the name even rings with a certain sexiness, and the manor house-meets-spaceship exterior will grab you before you walk in the door. The lobby's mix of sharp lines, rococo portraits and tribal imagery all seems to click, while spacious suites are lavished with monochromatic furnishings that feel avant-garde yet remarkably comfortable. Countless other treats await, including our favourite – the 'pillow service' – which allows guests to choose from an array of different bed pillows based on material and texture.

EATING

For centuries in Latvia, food equalled fuel, energising peasants as they worked the fields, and warming their bellies during bone-chilling Baltic winters. Today, the era of boiled potatoes and pork gristle has begun to fade as food becomes a sensorial experience rather than a necessary evil. Although it will be a while before globetrotters stop qualifying local restaurants as being 'good by Rīga's (mediocre) standards', the cuisine scene has improved by leaps and bounds over the last decade. The city's diverse dining options currently include flavours from France, Italy, Japan, America, India, Egypt, Spain, Mexico and, of course, Russia and Latvia.

Lately the 'slow food' movement has taken the city's high-end dining scene by storm. Seasonal menus feature carefully prepared, environmentally conscious dishes using organic produce grown across Latvia's ample farmland. Beyond the sphere of upmarket eats, most local joints embrace the literal sense of the term 'slow food' with turtle-speed service.

As Rīga's dining scene continues to draw its influence from a clash of other cultures, tipping (*apkalpošana*) is evolving from customary to obligatory. A 10% gratuity is common in the capital, and many restaurants are now tacking the tip onto the bill.

For information on the self-catering options around town, see the boxed text on p220.

Budget

Despite the never-ending inflation, cheap chow can be easily scouted around town. In general, as the price drops, the calories go up, so the cheapest grub around are quick eats such as delicious *pelmeņi* (Russian dumplings; fried, boiled or bobbing in soup) and *pankukas* (fried, blintz-like pancakes stuffed with meat or veggies). There are a couple of restaurants that have managed to sneak into the budget category, but the rest of the frugal options are light meals at one of Rīga's trendy cafes. The city's vibrant cafe culture is exploding around the city – the gems are peppered among the grand boulevards of Central Rīga.

OLD RĪGA (VECRĪGA)

Šefpavārs Vilhelms (Chef William; Map p190; ☎ 2949 5409; Šķūņu iela 6; pancake rolls 0.65Ls; ✓ 9am-10pm Mon-Fri, 10am-10pm Sat & Sun) Every time we visited, customers of every ilk were eagerly queuing for a quick nosh. Three blintz-like pancakes

FROM RAGS TO RICHES TO RAGS

At the beginning of WWII, after 22 years of independence, the Soviet regime forced Latvia into the USSR, setting up a puppet government in Rīga. In order to avoid dissent, the Soviets rounded up those deemed a potential threat to safeguarding the newly instated ideals. Politicians, writers, professors, bankers and many others were carted off to Siberia and forced to work in lumber camps. No one could escape the communist clutches, not even the city's wealthiest citizens – not even Emilija Benjamiņa, Latvia's unofficial First Lady.

During the 1920s and '30s, Emilija was the pinnacle of Rīga's social elite. The daughter of a widowed peasant, Emilija rose from obscurity to become the country's media queen and beloved socialite. The following details about Emilija's inspirational rags-to-riches life were recounted to us during an interview with Laima Muktupāvela, one of Latvia's most prominent writers, who chronicled the famed Rīgan's story in a popular biography entitled *Mila Benjamiņa*.

At a young age, the future media mogul escaped a bucolic lifestyle to sell ads for a newspaper in Rīga. She quickly realised that she had a knack for sales and began her own journal with her soon-to-be-husband Antons Benjamiņš. Her recipe for success was simple: since most Latvians were literate but poor, she sold her newspapers for one cent. Soon after she was selling 900,000 copies per day. In the office, Emilija rewarded intelligence, offering high salaries to her staff and attracting the nation's top writers, including Vilis Lācis, a peasant who enjoyed writing about the 'common man'. Under the guidance of Emilija, Vilis quickly became one of Latvia's best-known figures.

At the height of her career, Ms Benjamiņa was a full-fledged cosmopolitan woman who travelled across Europe and dabbled in fashion and plastic surgery. She grew beyond the status of 'media queen' – her power and influence were absolute, and she would often accompany the president to formal affairs since he was a bachelor. She opened the floodgates for cultural life in Latvia, making her salon the epicentre of the intellectual avant-garde. Dozens of intriguing personalities would pass through, including foreign dignitaries, poets, opera singers and even a clairvoyant – a man by the name of Eižens Finks, who was laughed out the door when he told Emilija that she would meet her end in rags rather than surrounded by riches.

When the Soviets seized power in 1940, her sumptuous mansion, the site of so many world-class affairs, was 'nationalised'. Friends and family encouraged Emilija to leave the country after hearing rumours that she might be deported, but she could not fathom that a shift in power could mean serious trouble. After all, five of her former employees were granted the top positions in the new local Soviet government, including Vilis Lācis, who became Minister of the Interior.

On a humid June evening in 1941, armed soldiers surprised Emilija in her pink nightie while she was preparing for bed. They carried orders for her arrest, signed by none other than Vilis Lācis. She was allowed to change into an elegant black gown before being loaded onto a cattle-car bound for the Siberian Gulag. She brought nothing else.

Emilija, dressed in rags, died of dysentery and starvation in her Siberian work camp on 23 September 1941…exactly as the clairvoyant Eižens Finks had predicted.

smothered in sour cream and jam equals the perfect backpacker's breakfast.

Pelmeņi XL (Map p190; ☎ 6722 2728; Kaļķu iela 7; dumpling bowls 0.90-2.50Ls; ☺ 9am-4am) A Rīga institution for backpackers and undiscerning drunkards, this extralarge cafeteria stays open serving up huge bowls of *pelmeņi* to hungry mobs. There are two other locations nearby, although this one is open the latest.

Frenču Maiznīca (Cadets de Gascogne; Map p190; ☎ 6732 0103; Basteja bulvāris 8; baguette sandwich 2.20Ls; ☺ 7am-10am Mon-Sat) Got a tummy ache from

one too many *pelmeņi*? Nurse your digestive system at this French-run bakery, and pick up a mug of hot chocolate and a baguette sandwich stuffed with ham and *cornichons* (gherkins). Additional seating available on the roof promenade.

John Lemon (Map p190; ☎ 6722 6647; Peldu iela 21; mains 2.50-5Ls; ☺ 10am-midnight Sun-Mon, to 2am Tue-Thu, to 5am Fri & Sat) This trendy spot attracts bleary-eyed partiers from Pulkvedis (across the street) for cheap, late-night munchies. Take your pick of three stylish rooms: an orange realm with '60s space station sofa seating, the trellis-lined courtyard, or a small nook drenched in hot, lipstick reds and disco lights.

Vecmeita ar kaki (The Spinster & Her Cat; Map p190; ☎ 6732 5077; Mazā Pils iela 1; mains 3-7.50Ls; ☯ 11am-11pm) This cosy spot across from the president's palace specialises in cheap Latvian cuisine. Menus have been crafted from old-school newspaper clippings and patrons dine on converted sewing machine tables – you can play footsy with the iron pedals while waiting for your pork and potatoes.

CENTRAL RĪGA (CENTRS)

Pīrādziņi (Map pp196-7; ☎ 6728 7824; K Barona iela 14, entrance on Elizabetes iela; pancake rolls 0.40-0.60Ls; ☯ 9am-11pm) This no-nonsense chow spot parades tasty meat- and vegetable-filled pancake rolls in a glass display case. Most customers grab their blintzes to go, since the beige-tiled floors and walls feel a bit like a public bathroom.

Index (Map pp196-7; ☎ 6728 7718; Brīvības iela 32; sandwiches/salads from 1.85/2.19Ls; ☯ 7am-10pm Mon-Fri, 10am-10pm Sat, 10am-8pm Sun) Latvia's trendy version of Subway is a giant step up from the ready-made sandwiches at the grocery store. Black and yellow stencil art rocks the walls and large picture windows open up onto busy Brīvības – the perfect spot for some serious people watching.

Rāma (Map pp196-7; ☎ 6727 2490; K Barona iela 56; mains 2-5Ls; ☯ 10am-7pm Mon-Fri, 11am-5pm Sat) The cheapest veggie spot in town, this Indian joint, run by the local Hare Krishna chapter, throws together mostly rice and bean dishes accented by chilli and curry flavours. The food gets mixed reviews, but all proceeds go to charity, so you can't help but leave happy.

Meta Kafe (Map pp196-7; ☎ 6777 4334; Kronvalda bulvāris 2b; soups & salads 3Ls; ☯ 10am-11pm Mon-Thu, to 5am Fri & Sat) Safely tucked away from those who are not in the know, this hipster hang-out is an inconspicuous prefab at the tennis club in Kronvalda parks. The staff serves light, mostly veggie options on concrete tables as loiterers mess around on their laptops (wi-fi available) and listen to lounge beats. Weekend poetry slams and DJ dance parties usually last until sunrise.

Osiriss (Map pp196-7; ☎ 6724 3002; K Barona iela 31; soups & omelettes 3-4Ls, mains 5-7Ls; ☯ 8am-midnight Mon-Fri, 10am-midnight Sat & Sun) Although Rīga's wishy-washy cafe culture sees establishments come and go like the seasons, Osiriss continues to be a local mainstay. The green faux-marble tabletops haven't changed since the mid-'90s

and neither has the clientele: angsty artsy-types scribbling in their moleskines over a glass of red wine. Wi-fi available.

Istaba (Map p196-7; ☎ 6728 1141; K Barona iela 31a; mains 3-8Ls; ☯ noon-midnight, Mon-Sat) A cafe and art space all rolled into one, Istaba has a cluster of rickety tables perched over the turquoise gallery below. The friendly chef scrapes together whatever the heart desires, and even though the food is nothing to write home about, the knick-knack-clad atmosphere can't be beat.

OUTLYING NEIGHBOURHOODS

LIDO Atpūtas Centrs (LIDO Recreation Centre; ☎ 6750 4420; Krasta iela 76; mains 3-7Ls; ☯ bistro 10am-11pm, amusement park 11am-9pm) If Latvia and Disney World had a lovechild it would be the LIDO Atpūtas Centrs – an enormous wooden palace dedicated to the country's coronary-inducing cuisine. Servers dressed like Baltic milkmaids bounce around as patrons hit the rows of buffets for classics such as pork tongue, potato pancakes and cold beet soup. Take tram 3, 7 or 9, or bus 17E from the junction of Akems tilts and Novembra krastmala, and get off at the 'LIDO' stop. There are a handful of miniature LIDO restaurants dotted around the city centre for those who don't have time to make it out to the mothership.

Midrange

After *pelmeņi* and pub grub, the city's second tier of restaurants is a diverse mix of international and local options, each with a certain *je ne sais quoi* (or a clever gimmick), which keeps them afloat amid Rīga's capricious dining scene.

OLD RĪGA (VECRĪGA)

Ķiploka krogs (Garlic Bar; Map p190; ☎ 6721 1451; Jēkaba iela 3/5, entrance on Mazā Pils; mains 4-11Ls; ☯ 11am-11pm Mon-Sat, 1-11pm Sun) Vampires beware – *everything* at this joint contains garlic, even the ice cream. The menu is pretty hit or miss (though you can't go wrong with the pasta), but no matter what, it's best to avoid the garlic pesto spread – it'll taint your breath for days (trust us).

Habibi (Map p190; ☎ 6722 8551; Peldu iela 24; mains 5-7Ls; ☯ 2pm-midnight) This totally cool Egyptian-run hookah joint serves up Middle Eastern food in a rich, cushiony interior oft-visited by gyrating belly dancers. Fruit-flavoured tobacco costs 6Ls per pipe.

Kaļķu Vārti (Map p190; ☎ 6722 4576; 11 Kaļķu iela 11; mains 5-11Ls; ☯ noon-3am) Kaļķu Vārti has been a

LATVIA

heavy hitter in Rīga's upscale dining scene for many years. Locals usually skip the flash dining room in favour of the bistro hidden next door (open 10am to 6pm) for fried fare at half the price. On summer evenings, tables spill out across Livu Laukums, and the outdoor bar serves up 1Ls beers.

Nostalģija (Map p190; ☎ 6722 2338; Kaļķu iela 22; mains 6-11Ls; ☼ 10am-2am) If you are *da*-ing for Russian grub, try this gaudy, gilded monument to all things Soviet in Livu Laukums. Nibble on anything from *pelmeņi* to caviar or go for a Western classic while admiring the baroque chandeliers and overornate stemware.

Kabuki (Map p190; ☎ 6728 2052; Audēju iela 14; mains 6-12Ls; ☼ 11am-11pm) Kabuki is top dog amongst the city's sushi chains. Sleek, minimalist lines and well-priced maki will have you convinced that you've left Rīga for some trendy spot on the Pacific Rim. There's another location at K Barona iela 14 where the sashimi spins on a mesmerising conveyor belt (entrance on Elizabetes iela).

Dada (Map p190; ☎ 6710 4433; Kalēju iela 30; noodle bowl 6.90Ls; ☼ 10am-10am Sun-Wed, 10am-midnight Thu-Sat) Only at Dada could Mongolian BBQ mix with antibourgeoisie zeitgeist from the early 20th century. The theme is utter chaos: waiters don mismatched clothing, table legs have been replaced with precarious stacks of books, and the bill is inexplicably delivered in a baby's running shoe.

CENTRAL RĪGA (CENTRS)

Paparazzi (Map p196-7; ☎ 6750 5710; Antonijas iela 12; pizza 4-6Ls; ☼ 11am-11pm) Paparazzi whips up thin-crust pizza in an airy space festooned with geometric shapes. The waitresses are like a veritable who's who of Scandinavian runway models…oh, and the food is pretty good too. Go for a table on the outside patio along chic Antonijas iela in the centre of the sumptuous Art Nouveau district.

Citi Laiki (Different Times; Map pp196-7; ☎ 6724 0590; Brīvības iela 41; mains 4-6Ls; ☼ 11am-midnight Mon-Thu, 11am-2am Fri, noon-midnight Sat, noon-11pm Sun) This bitty blue wooden abode is one of the top spots to load up on classic Latvian dishes such as grilled mushrooms, herring, and hearty pork platters. Folk music further enhances the bucolic atmosphere on Friday evenings.

Andalūzijas Suns (A. Suns; Map pp196-7; ☎ 6728 8418; Elizabetes iela 83/85 3, Berga Bazārs; mains 4-8Ls; ☼ 10am-1am Mon-Thu, 10am-3am Fri, 11am-3am Sat, 11am-1am Sun) Thanks to some seriously devoted patrons, the Dali-inspired 'A. Suns' in the Berga Bazārs is a perennial expat fave. You'll dig the red-tinted walls, chill vibe and menu of international pub grub: juicy burgers, tangy chilli soups and endless glasses of wheat ale.

…AND TWO FOR TEA

Let's face it; despite the dozens of cafes around town, coffee isn't Rīga's strongest suit. Why not stain your teeth with delicious, locally grown teas instead?

our pick Goija (Map pp196-7; ☎ 6733 3370; Strēlnieku iela 1a; tea 2-6Ls; ☼ 2pm-2am) Sneak by the graffiti-ed 'Goija' on the entrance to find velvet couches, shelves decked with dusty novels and trippy tile patterns on the floor. Pass through an inviting Moroccan pillow room before stepping into the stone cloister at the back. Then, pick a comfy spot amid tattered sofas, slap-shut chairs and wobbly tables decorated with teeny Oriental scenes. The tea menus look like an eight-year-old's art project of magazine cut-outs and cursive doodles. Goija might just be the coolest teahouse ever, and the best part: they're not even trying.

Apsara (Map pp196-7; ☎ 6722 3160; Vērmanes Garden; tea 2-8Ls; ☼ noon-10pm Jun-Aug) During the summer, Apsara opens a charming wooden pagoda in the heart of Vērmanes Garden. Daintily sip your imported teas from the East while relaxing on the floor amid a sea of pastel pillows. A second (and equally charming) tea pavilion lives on a grassy knoll along the city channel near K Barona iela.

Teātra Bāra Restorāns (Map pp196-7; ☎ 6728 5051; Lāčplēša iela 25; mains 5-9Ls; ⏰ 11am-midnight) This hip spot, associated with the progressive theatre next door, lures artsy types with affordable prices and trendy decor that spills out into a spacious courtyard. After dinner, head to the like-named bar across the street for a round of evening cocktails while eavesdropping on local gossip.

Charlestons (Čarlstons; Map pp196-7; ☎ 6777 0572; Blaumaņa iela 38/40; mains 5-11Ls; ⏰ noon-midnight) If you're up to your elbows in pork tongue, Charlestons is a sure bet to get rid of the meat sweats. Lounge around the terraced courtyard in the heart of a residential block and feast on delicious platters of Norwegian salmon, sautéed duck and the best Caesar salad in the Baltic.

our pick Aragats (Map pp196-7; ☎ 6737 3445; Miera iela 15; mains 6-9Ls; ⏰ 1-10pm Tue-Sun) Ignore the plastic shrubbery, this place is all about sampling some killer cuisine from the Caucasus. Start with an appetiser of pickled vegetables – the perfect chaser for your home-brewed *chacha* (Georgian vodka). Then, make nice with the matronly owner as she dices up fresh herbs at your table to mix with the savoury lamb stew. She'll scold you if you don't finish everything on your plate (and why wouldn't you – it's delish). At the end of the meal be a gentleman and pay for the ladies at the table, especially since the women's menus don't have any of the prices listed!

Hospitālis (Map p190; ☎ 6731 3530; 4 Tirgoņu iela; mains 7-15Ls; ⏰ 11am-11pm) We're not sure how appealing it is to eat at a place whose logo is a syringe, but Hospitālis was all the buzz when it opened during the summer of 2008 with flyers depicting customers in straitjackets being fed by nurses in knickers. In reality the restaurant is much more playful than tawdry; patrons are served perfectly normal meals on gurneys and other medical contraptions.

Top End

When foreign dignitaries come to town, they choose from a select group of restaurants known for their world-class cuisine and wallet-busting prices.

OLD RĪGA (VECRĪGA)

Rozengrāls (Map p190; ☎ 6722 0356; Rozena iela 1; mains 9-15Ls; ⏰ noon-midnight) Hey, remember 500 years ago when potatoes weren't the heart and soul of Latvian cuisine? We sure don't, but Rozengrāls does – this candle-lit haunt takes diners back a few centuries, offering medieval game served by costume-clad waiters. Even though the traditional dinner is sans spuds, it's a fairly pricey time warp.

Gutenbergs (Map pp196-7; ☎ 6781 4090; Doma laukums 1; mains 9.90-19.90Ls; ⏰ 7-10pm) At the Hotel Gutenbergs' rooftop restaurant you don't look down on the spires of Old Rīga, you sit among them. Potted plants, cherubic statues and trickling fountains contribute to a decidedly Florentine vibe, although the menu focuses on local favourites.

CENTRAL RĪGA (CENTRS)

Restaurant Bergs (Map pp196-7; ☎ 6777 0957; Elizabetes iela 83/85; mains 8.50-16.50Ls; ⏰ 7am-midnight) The short-but-sweet menu reads like a poem: spring salmon fillet with an orange and fennel salad, rack of lamb with whole-grain mustard and minted aubergine stew. Bergs' ever-changing menu of international eats is Vincents' biggest competitor.

Vincents (Map pp196-7; ☎ 6733 2634; Elizabetes iela 19; mains 16-22Ls; ⏰ 12.30-11pm Mon-Fri, 6-11pm Sat) Ask any Rīgan – they'll all tell you that Vincents is the best restaurant in town. So, it's no surprise that it's also the most expensive. Apparently when Queen Elizabeth spent a day in town, she ate both her lunch and dinner here, and other world figures have followed suit. The head chef is a stalwart of the 'slow food' movement, and crafts his ever-changing menu amid eye-catching van Gogh–inspired decor (hence the name). The 'business lunch' is a great deal if you're looking for gourmet eats without draining your bank account.

OUTLYING NEIGHBOURHOODS

Fabrikas Restorāns (☎ 6787 3704; Balasta dambis 70; meals 8-18Ls; ⏰ 11am-midnight) Once a crumbling gypsum factory (*fabrikas* means factory), this chic dining option is now the preferred address for switched-on Russian jetsetters. Located on the banks of the Daugava River across from the city centre, Fabrikas serves up some of the best views in town, not to mention a tasty assortment of international cuisine. Live music on Friday evenings. Reservations recommended.

DRINKING

If you want to party like a Latvian, assemble a gang of friends and pub crawl your way through the city, stopping at colourful haunts for rounds of beers, belly laughter and, of course, Black Balzām (see the boxed text, opposite). On summer evenings, nab a spot at one of the beer gardens in rowdy Livu Laukums. All of the pint-peddling establishments have dozens of tables sprawled out across the cobbled square – the perfect spot to sit back with a stein of local brew and watch the storm of revellers roll through.

Old Rīga (Vecrīga)

Cuba Cafe (Map p190; ☎ 6722 4362; Jaun iela 15; drinks from 2Ls; ☼ 2pm-6am) An authentic mojito and a table overlooking Doma laukums are just what the doctor ordered after a long day of sightseeing. On colder days, swig your caipirinha inside amid dangling Cuban flags, wobbly stained-glass lamps and the subtle murmur of trumpet jazz. Happy hour (buy one get one free) is from 5pm to 8pm.

Lounge Eight (Map p190; ☎ 6735 9595; Vaļņu iela 19, entrance on Gleznotāju iela; cocktails 4.20Ls; ☼ noon-midnight Sun-Wed, to 1am Thu, to 3am Fri & Sat) Take a cigar from a swish humidor on the ground floor and follow the stairs up to the cosy dark-wood lounge with burgundy leather couches. The vaulted space at the back feels like an Art Deco metro station with its arcing ceiling and long bar stretched lengthwise down the middle. Cocktails are on the pricier side since this is more of a see-and-be-seen type of place.

Orange Bar (Map p190; ☎ 6722 8423; Jāņa sēta 5; drinks from 2Ls; ☼ noon-midnight Sun-Thu, to 2am Fri & Sat) An alternative spot slathered in jet-black paint and splashes of neon orange light, this edgy alternative joint attracts hipsters of every ilk for some late-night carousing on the bar top.

La Belle Epoque (French Bar; Map p190; ☎ 6721 2280; Mazā Jaunavu iela 8; ☼ 5pm-3am Mon-Sat) Students flock to this basement bar to power down its trademark 'apple pie' shots (go for the '10 shots for 9 lats' deal if you're with friends.) The Renoir mural and kitsch *Moulin Rouge* posters seem to successfully ward off stag parties.

I Love You (Map p190; ☎ 6722 5304; Aldaru iela 9; beer 2.50Ls; ☼ 10am-midnight Mon-Thu, to 1am Fri, noon to 1am Sat, to 10pm Sun) The three words everyone loves to hear is a chill joint tucked away down one of Old Rīga's wobbly streets. Sneak downstairs

---

TO MARKET TO MARKET

A visit to one of Rīga's local markets is a great way to tap into the daily goings-on around town and escape the tourism bubble. And the best part is that these local haunts haven't been yuppiefied, and the organic products plucked from nearby farms are often cheaper than the chilled produce found in the grocery stores.

If you only have time to hit one market, make it Rīga's bounteous **Central Market** (p195) housed in a series of mammoth zeppelin hangars. Additional vendors peddling anything from sunglasses to berries spill out onto the surrounding streets. It's a fantastic spot to assemble a picnic lunch and ogle some seriously outdated hairdos (more like hair-don'ts).

For an even bigger Soviet throwback, try the **Āgenskalns Market** (☎ 6761 1564; Bāriņu iela) in the Russian suburb of the same name located across the Daugava River. Housed in and around a large brick building along Nometnu iela, the market has been a mainstay in the neighbourhood since before WWI. You won't hear a drop of English. Take tram 2 or 8 over the Akmens Bridge, and disembark at the 'Āgenskalna Tirgus' stop, or take tram 5 and get off at the second stop on the other side of the bridge.

On Tērbatas iela along the Vērmanes Garden (p195), you'll find one of Rīga's 24-hour **Flower Markets** offering a truly magnificent assortment of blossoms from the countryside. A 24-hour flower market may seem a bit odd at first, but apparently the venders make a killing in the wee hours of the night when drunken locals buy up all the petals to ease the wrath of their loved ones when they stumble home with the sunrise.

Every second and fourth Saturday, **Berga Bāzars** (Bergs Bazaar; Map pp196-7; www.bergabazars.lv; Dzirnavu iela 84; ☼ 9am to 3pm) hosts an upmarket market featuring a variety of products including organic produce, handicrafts, exotic antiques and 'slow food' lunch stands.

If you don't have the time to heckle for your huckleberries, there are plenty of high-quality grocery stores around town. **Rimi** (☎ 6704 5409; www.rimi.lv; ☼ 9am-10pm) has two central locations: Audēju iela 16 in Old Rīga's Galerija Centrs shopping mall (Map p190), and K Barona iela 46 in Central Rīga's Barona Centrs shopping mall (Map pp196-7).

DO IT YOURSELF: BLACK BALZĀM COCKTAILS

A jug of Black Balzām is the perfect souvenir to bring home to your loved ones. The slender bottle has an attractive antique design, and its contents – a secret concoction of herbs and berries – are delicious. For more information about the legendary Black Balzām, see p185. Give your family and friends a little taste of Rīga by mixing them one of the following popular Black Balzām cocktails:

■ **Black Mojito**: mix one part Black Balzām with four parts Sprite, add a half of lime smashed and a drizzle of fruit syrup. Serve over crushed ice.

■ **Innocent Balzām**: blend one part Black Balzām, 0.5 parts peach liqueur, three parts peach juice, three parts vanilla ice cream, and 1 canned peach.

■ **Lazybones**: add a shot of Black Balzām to a cold glass of Coke (our favourite).

---

for a sea of comfy couches. DJs spin alternative beats on Thursday nights.

Radio Bar (Map p190; ☎ 6722 4457; Šķūņu iela 17, entrance on Zirgu iela; drinks from 2.50Ls; ☺ 3pm-midnight Mon-Wed, to 3am Thu, to 5am Fri & Sat) A stone's throw from Doma Laukums, this happenin' bar/nightclub, decked out in radio dials and doodads, blasts mostly house and hip-hop.

Bon Vivant (Belgian Beer Cafe; Map p190; ☎ 6722 6585; Mārstaļu iela 8; beer 2Ls; ☺ 11am-midnight Mon-Thu, to 1am Fri, noon-1am Sat, to 11pm Sun) Skip the *moules frites* (mussels with fries) and go for Bon Vivant's huge selection of imported beers.

Paddy Whelan's (Map p190; ☎ 6721 0150; Grēcinieku iela 4; drinks from 2Ls; ☺ 11am-1am) Rīga's first Irish pub (which now feels more like a generic sports bar) has been an expat institution for years; however, these days most people stop by for the ridiculously delicious Indian curry.

Central Rīga (Centrs)

our pick Skyline Bar (Map pp196-7; ☎ 6777 2222; Elizabetes iela 55; cocktails from 3.40Ls; ☺ 3pm-2am Sun-Thu, to 3am Fri & Sat) A must for anyone visiting Rīga, glitzy Skyline Bar sits on the 26th floor of the Reval Hotel Latvija. The sweeping views are the city's best, and the mix of glam spirit-sippers make for great people watching under the retro purple lighting. Go buy a lottery ticket if you can nab a window seat – no matter what time of day you stop by, only the luckiest visitors will score a table near the floor-to-ceiling panes.

Sarkans (Red; Map pp196-7; ☎ 6727 2286; Stabu iela 10; drinks from 3.50Ls; ☺ 10am-midnight Mon-Thu, to 4am Fri, noon-4am Sat, noon-midnight Sun) Safely removed from Old Rīga's mix of backpackers and stag fests, 'Red' lures party animals of all ages with three fantastic levels of lounges and dance floors.

D'vine (Map pp196-7; ☎ 6777 2217; Elizabetes iela 55; mixed drinks from 4Ls; ☺ noon-midnight Mon-Thu, to 1am Fri & Sat) This cleverly named wine bar in the Reval Hotel Latvija could easily be mistaken for a Scandinavian space station (even the toilets look futuristic). Spanish tapas accompanies the laundry list of imported wines and champagnes.

ENTERTAINMENT

Rīga in Your Pocket and *Rīga This Week* have the most up-to-date listings for opera, ballet, guest DJs, live music and other events around town. Several trip operators (p211) offer bar and club tours if you'd rather have someone else arrange your big night out. Backpackers staying at sociable digs might find hostel-organised pub crawls and parties.

Nightclubs

Rīga's nightclubs are always brimming with bouncing bodies; however Latvians, tend to prefer pub-crawling across town and tossing back vodka shots with friends. Check the drinking and eating sections – after dark, a lot of establishments in Rīga transform, like a superhero, into a grittier venue with pumping beats.

Some of the city's nightspots have a bit of an edge and cater to an unsavoury clientele. Check the 'Culture & Events' chapter of *Rīga in Your Pocket* for a list of businesses black-listed by the American Embassy.

Club Essential (Map pp196-7; ☎ 6724 2289; www .essential.lv; Skolas iela 2; admission free-5Ls; ☺ 10pm-6am Thu, to 8am Fri & Sat, to 5am Sun) Rīga's hottest club is a spectacle of beautiful people boogying to some of Europe's top DJ talent. Overzealous security aside, there's no safer bet if partying till dawn is your mission.

LATVIA

Pulkvedim Neviens Neraksta (No One Writes to the Colonel; Map p190; ☎ 6721 3886; www.pulkevis.lv; Peldu iela 26/28; cover weekend/weekday 3Ls/free; ☽ 8pm-3am Mon-Thu, to 5am Fri & Sat) The atmosphere at Pulkvedim is 'warehouse chic', with pumping '80s tunes on the ground floor and trance beats down below. There's no such thing as a dull night at this old favourite.

Nautilus (Map p190; ☎ 6781 4455; Kungu iela 8; cover 4-10Ls; ☽ 10.30pm-8am Wed-Sat) Nautilus is a throbbing hot spot inside a faux submarine. There's a chill-out room with plush red couches, a frantic dance floor and a tad too much uniformed security. It's not worth showing up before midnight.

Coyote Fly (Map p190; ☎ 6724 2289; Palasta iela 3; cover 3-8Ls; ☽ 11am-10am Wed, to 3am Thu, to 6am Fri, 4pm-6am Sat) An evening at Coyote Fly is more of an anthropological experiment than a night out on the town. The bouncers are notorious for only letting Latvians in – try your luck at the door and see if you can fool security.

Jazz, Blues & Rock

Latvians love their music, and live concerts are always popping up around town. Fabrikas Restorāns (p219) has piano on Fridays. The following spots are among the top places in town for live blues, jazz and rock.

Bites Blues Club (Map pp196-7; ☎ 6733 3123; www.bluesclub.lv; Dzirnavu iela 34a; cover 3-5Ls; ☽ 11am-11pm Mon-Wed, to 2am Thu-Sat) Try stopping for some grub (mostly French or Italian) an hour or two before the show – you'll skip the cover charge and catch some preconcert riffing. Friday nights see most of the live-music action during the summer; in winter expect tunes on Thursday and Saturday as well.

City Jazz Club (Map pp196-7; ☎ 2612 9191; www.cityjazzclub.lv; Ģertrūdes iela 34; cover 10Ls; ☽ 6pm-midnight Mon-Thu, to 1am Fri & Sat) Rīga's newest live-music lounge is a swank affair with claret-coloured tablecloths, a lengthy wine list and an international menu. The cover charge is steep, but worth it.

Četri Balti Krekli (Four White Shirts; Map p190; ☎ 2721 3885; www.krekli.lv; Vecpilsētas iela 12; cover 1-5Ls) This is the spot to see live Latvian rock bands any night of the week. The bouncers will turn you away if you aren't wearing nice shoes.

Carpe Diem (Map p190; ☎ 6722 8488; Meistaru iela 10/12; mains from 10Ls; ☽ 10pm-midnight, live music 7.30-10.30pm) Jazz is the main dish at this upmarket restaurant in the infamous Cat House.

Gay & Lesbian Venues

If you're looking for a thriving gay scene, pick another city. Rīga has been struggling with accepting its homosexual population for quite some time. Hate crimes are very rare, but an antigay organisation, ironically named No Pride, often hangs homophobic posters around town and was successful in having authorities ban pride parades on public streets.

Despite the antigay sentiment, the city's liberal population enjoys a small selection of gay and lesbian venues without disturbance:

Golden (Map pp196-7; ☎ 2550 5050; www.goldenbar.lv; Ģertrūdes iela 33/35; admission free-5Ls; ☽ 7pm-2am Sun-Thu, to 5am Fri & Sat) Wind your way up the dark staircase to find slick lounge beats and trendy tribal decor under a glass roof. Expect 'face control' at the door.

Purvs (☎ 6731 1717; Matīsa iela 60/62; cover free-5Ls; ☽ 10pm-6am) Believe it or not *purvs* isn't short for 'pervert'; it's Latvian for 'swamp'. Behind the unmarked entrance lies pumping club music, go-go dancers and the occasional tranny show.

XXL (Map pp196-7; ☎ 6728 2276; Alfrēda kalniņa iela 1; cover 1-10Ls; ☽ 6pm-7am) 'Tom of Finland' porno adorns the walls and disco music blares on weekends. A dark labyrinth and video screening room are also available. Sunday is men only.

Concert Venues

The following venues around town offer frequent musical concerts, mostly of the classical variety.

Arena Rīga (☎ 6738 8200; www.arenariga.com; Skantes iela 21) Rīga's new 10,000-seat venue hosts dance revues and pop concerts when it is not being used for sporting events.

Dome Cathedral (Map p190; ☎ 6721 3213; www.hbf.lv; Doma laukums; ☽ box office noon-6pm Tue-Sat) The acoustics and massive organ make this venue a must for music lovers. Twice-weekly evening organ concerts (Wednesday and Friday) are well worth attending.

Great Guild (Map p190; ☎ 6722 7105; www.hbf.lv; Amatu iela 6; ☽ box office noon-6pm Tue-Sat) Home to the acclaimed Latvian National Symphonic Orchestra. Classical music and jazz scats are often heard from the window.

Jāzeps Vītols Latvian Academy of Music (Map pp196-7; ☎ 6722 8684; K Barona iela 1) Latvia's best-known music school hosts frequent classical music performances.

Sapņu Fabrika (Map pp196-7; ☎ 6728 1222; www.sapnufabrika.lv; Lāčplēša iela 101) Housed in a former industrial plant, the 'Dream Factory' hosts live bands, hip hop and elecronica.

Cinemas

Catching a movie is a great way to spend a rainy day in Rīga (trust us, there are many). Films are generally shown in their original language – usually English – with Latvian or Russian subtitles. Tickets cost between 2Ls and 4Ls depending on the day of the week and venue. Check the cinemas' websites for show time details. All theatres (except K. Suns) have assigned seating.

Coca-Cola Plaza (Map pp196-7; ☎ 1189; www.forum cinemas.lv; Janvāra iela 13) Rīga's multiplex has stadium seating, 14 screens and a cafe on the top floor. Expect the usual Hollywood fare and the occasional Latvian film.

Daile (Map pp196-7; ☎ 1189; K Barona iela 31) Shows hand-me-down films from Rīga's main Cineplex at Coca-Cola Plaza.

Kino Rīga (Map pp196-7; ☎ 6728 9755; Elizabetes iela 61) The Baltic's first theatre to feature movies with sound now specialises in European films and hosts several film festivals including the international Future Shorts (www.futureshorts.lv).

K. Suns (Map pp196-7; ☎ 6728 5411; www.kinogalerija .lv; Elizabetes iela 83/85, Bergs Bazārs) An artsy cinema that projects mostly indy films on its one screen. Popcorn and soda available.

Opera, Ballet & Theatre

Rīga's ballet, opera and theatre season breaks for summer holidays (between June and September).

The **Latvia–National Opera** (Map pp196-7; ☎ 6707 3777; www.opera.lv; Aspazijas bulvāris 3; tickets 5-30Ls; ☾ box office 10am-7pm) is the pride of Latvia, boasting some of the finest opera in all of Europe (and for the fraction of the price in other countries). Mikhail Baryshnikov got his start here.

Theatre venues include:

Daile Theatre (Dailes teātris; Map pp196-7; ☎ 6729 4444; Brīvības iela 75) Stages classical favourites in Latvian.

Latvian National Theatre (Nacionālais teātris; Map pp196-7; www.teatris.lv; ☎ 6700 6337; Kronvalda bulvāris 2) Entry via K Valdemāra iela.

New Rīga Theatre (Jaunais Rīgas Teātris; Map pp196-7; ☎ 6728 0765; www.jrt.lv; Lāčplēsa iela 25) Rīga's venue for avant-garde productions (mostly in Latvian).

Russian Drama Theatre (Krievu Drāmas Teātris; Map p190; ☎ 6722 4660; Kaļķu iela 16) Stages plays in Russian.

SHOPPING

The shopping mall has boomed in the last decade with scores of plazas around Old and Central Rīga. Street sellers peddle their wares – amber trinkets, knitwear, paintings and Russian dolls – outside St Peter's Church on Skarnu iela and along the southern end of Vaļņu iela. Rīga's large crafts fair, the Gadatirgus, is held in Vērmanes dārzs on the first weekend in June. Keep an eye out for the beautiful Namēju rings worn by Latvians around the world as a way to recognize one another.

Art Nouveau Riga (Map pp196-7; ☎ 6733 3030; Strēlnieku iela 9; ☾ 9am-7pm) Here, you can purchase a variety of Art Nouveau – related souvenirs from guidebooks, postcards and even stone gargoyles.

Latvijas Balzams (Map p190; ☎ 6722 8714; Audēju iela 8) A chain of liquor stores selling the trademark Latvian Black Balzām. Try mixing the liquor with coffee, Coke, or blackcurrant juice.

Upe (Map p190; ☎ 6772 6119; Vāgnera iela 5; ☾ 11am-7pm Mon-Fri, to 4pm Sat) Classical Latvian music wafts through the air as customers peruse traditional instruments and CDs of local folk, rock and experimental artists.

Tornis (Map p190; ☎ 6722 0270; Grēcinieku iela 11-2, entrance from Pēterbaznīcas Laukums; ☾ 11am-6pm Mon-Sat) A fine assortment of jewellery depicting intriguing pagan symbols.

Istaba (Map pp196-7; ☎ 6728 1141; K Barona iela 31a; ☾ noon-8pm Mon-Sat) A wee gallery displaying the works of local artisans as well as kitsch trinkets and souvenirs. The 2nd floor doubles as a trendy cafe.

Senā Klēts (Map pp196-7; ☎ 6724 2398; Merķeļa iela 13; ☾ 10am-6pm Mon-Fri, 11am-5pm Sat) Dress-up enthusiasts can find ready-to-wear Latvian traditional costumes or they can be made to measure. Linens are available as well.

The following shops are located in **Berga Bazārs** (Bergs Bazaar; Map pp196-7; www.bergabazars .lv; Dzirnavu iela 84), a veritable maze of sleek, upmarket boutiques orbiting the five-star Hotel Bergs between Elizabetes iela and Dzirnavu iela:

Emihla Gustava Šhokolahde (☎ 6728 7510; ☾ 9am-10pm Mon-Sat, 11am-8pm Sun) Latvia's finest chocolate shop doubles as a chic cafe. The fruit-stuffed truffles are divine.

Garage (☎ 6728 8308; www.garage.lv; ☾ 10am-8pm Mon-Fri, to 7pm Sat, 11am-7pm Sun) A gallery and souvenir shop featuring upscale handicrafts designed by Latvian artists.

Stenders (☎ 6728 3959; www.stenders.lv; ☾ 10am-8pm Mon-Fri, to 6pm Sat, noon-6pm Sun) Latvia's version of the Body Shop offers handmade organic soaps and cosmetics.

GETTING THERE & AWAY

See p401 for additional information regarding travel between Latvia and countries beyond the Baltic.

Air

Rīga International Airport (Lidosta Rīga; ☎ 6720 7009; www.riga-airport.com) is in the suburb of Skulte, about 13km southwest of the city centre. Most major European airlines have an office here, including Latvia's national carrier, **airBaltic** (☎ 6720 7886; www.airbaltic.com; Rīga International Airport, Marupes pagast).

AirBaltic flies six times daily (less on weekends) to/from Tallinn and five times daily (three times on Saturdays) to/from Vilnius. Return fares to Tallinn/Vilnius start at 7Ls/2Ls when booking online. Yes, that's 1Ls each way!

AirBaltic also offers government-subsidised domestic flights twice daily (Monday to Friday) to/from Ventspils and five daily (all week) to/from Liepāja. One-way tickets start at 1Ls if purchased in advance, or 4Ls if booked in the same month as the flight.

Boat

Rīga's outdated passenger **ferry terminal** (Map pp196-7; ☎ 6703 0800; www.rop.lv; Eksporta iela 3a), located about 900m downstream (north) of Akmens Bridge, offers service to Stockholm aboard **Tallink** (☎ 6709 9700; www.tallink.lv). **DFDS Tor Line** (☎ 2735 3523; www.dfdstorline.lv; Zivju iela 1), 10km outside of town, goes to/from Lübeck, Germany (from 45Ls, 34 hours, two weekly).

Bus

Buses to/from other towns and cities use Rīga's **international bus station** (Rīgas starptautiskā autoosta; Map pp196-7; www.autoosta.lv; Prāgas iela 1), behind the railway embankment just beyond the southeastern edge of Old Rīga. Up-to-date timetables and fares (with final destination and departure platforms) are displayed in the station, on the bus station's well-organised website, and at the ultrahandy website: www.1188.lv.

Ecolines (☎ 6721 4512; www.ecolines.lv; ☷ 7am-9.30pm) has an office at the bus station, another called **Norma-A** (Map pp196-7; ☎ 6727 4444; A Čaka iela 45; ☷ 9am-7pm) in town, and additional offices in Daugavpils and Liepāja. **Eurolines Baltic** (☎ 6721 4080; www.eurolines.lv) is also based at the bus station. These all offer bus services out of Latvia to various destinations.

International destinations include Warsaw, Berlin, Brussels, Kyiv, London, Moscow, St Petersburg, Paris and Prague (for details, see p404).

Bus services within Latvia and the neighbouring Baltic countries include:

Aglona (5.35Ls, 4¼ hours, three per week at 4pm)

Bauska (1.90Ls, 1¼ hours, three or four per hour between 6.15am and 11.20pm)

Cēsis (2.50Ls, around two hours, two or three per hour between 6.15am and 10.20pm)

Daugavpils (4–5.50Ls, 3½– 4¼ hours, 40 daily between 4am and 1.30am)

Dobele (2–2.30Ls, 1½ hours, twice hourly between 6.45am and 9pm)

Jelgava (0.95–1.50Ls, 45 minutes to one hour, every 10 minutes between 6am and midnight)

Kandava (2.55Ls, 1½–2¼ hours, one per hour between 7am and 8pm)

Kaunas (9.30Ls, 2¾–5¾ hours, four daily between 7.45am and 10.10pm)

Kolka (3.85–4.85Ls, 3½–4½ hours, five daily between 7.20am and 5.15pm)

Kuldīga (2.50Ls, 2½–3¼ hours, 15 daily between 7am and 8pm)

Liepāja (4.50–5.40Ls, 3½–4½ hours, two or three per hour between 6.45am and 8.30pm)

Pärnu (5–5.40Ls, 2¾ hours, 12 daily between 6.20am and 9pm)

Pāvilosta (5.35Ls, 4½ hours, one per day at 4pm)

Tallinn (9–10Ls, 4½ hours, 15 daily between 6.20am and 10.50pm)

Sigulda (1Ls, one hour and 10 minutes, twice hourly between 8.10am and 10.15pm)

Valmiera (3–3.20Ls, two to 2½ hours, twice hourly between 6.20am and 10.50pm)

Ventspils (4.55Ls, 2¾ to four hours, hourly between 7am and 10.30pm)

Vilnius (9Ls, four hours, 12 daily between 7.45am and 11.20pm)

Please note that due to inflation, the aforementioned prices are subject to quite a bit of change.

Car & Motorcycle

An article in the *Baltic Times* newspaper in 2008 stated that Latvia was the country with the second-highest percentage of car accident-related fatalities in the entire EU (Lithuania took first place). If you are planning to rent a car to explore Rīga and beyond, keep in mind that local drivers tend to be aggressive.

It is best to avoid driving through Old Rīga as there is a 5Ls fee to access the medieval streets.

If you decide to rent a car, start your search by asking at your hotel's reception desk. Several small businesses around town offer rental cars, usually at a much cheaper price than the international companies (expect cash-only transactions). Rentals range from 20Ls to 50Ls per day depending on the type of car and time of year. The number of automatic cars in Latvia is limited.

Be sure to ask for 'Benzene' when looking for a petrol station – *gāze* means 'air'.

Car-hire firms:

Avis Airport (☎ 6720 7353; rix@avislv); Lačplēša iela 92 (☎ 6722 5876; avis@avis.lv; Lačplēša iela 92)

DH (☎ 2885 5553; www.dhauto.lv; Brīvības iela 217)

Elite Rent (☎ 2555 5777; www.eliterent.lv; K Barona iela 108-11)

Hertz Airport (☎ 6720 7980; airport@hertz.lv); Ernestīnes iela (☎ 6722 4223; hertz@hertz.lv; Ernestīnes iela 24)

Noma (☎ 6718 6266; www.noma.lv; Lielgabalu iela 4)

Train

Rīga's **Central Train Station** (Centrālā stacija; Map pp196-7; ☎ 6723 1181, 1188; Stacijas laukums) is located near the Central Market in a large, glass-encased complex. Purchase your ticket in the main departure hall: windows 1 to 6 sell tickets for *starptautiskie vilcieni* (international trains); windows 7 to 9 sell tickets for long-distance *dīzeļvilcieni* (diesel trains); and windows 10 to 13 sell tickets for slower *elektrovilcieni* (electric suburban trains).

Most Latvians live in the large suburban and rural ring around Rīga, and commute into the city for work and out again every day. The city's network of ultrahandy suburban train lines help facilitate commuting, and thus makes day tripping to nearby towns a whole lot easier for tourists too. Rīga has six suburban lines: the oft-used Sigulda–Cēsis–Valmiera Line (regularly stopping in all three towns), the Dubulti–Sloka–Ķemeri–Tukums Line (the track to take for Jūrmala), the Orge–Krustpils Line (headed for Salaspils and Daugavpils), the Jelgava Line and the Ērgļi–Suntaži Line.

Beyond the sphere of suburban rails, Latvia's further destinations are easier to access by bus or by plane. Usually, only one train per day connects Rīga to towns such as Liepāja and Daugavpils. It is also much more convenient (and faster) to get to Tallinn and Vilnius by bus. See p406 for information on trains to non-Baltic destinations.

Amid the jumble of trains and schedules, the following services are available:

Cēsis (1.72Ls, 1¾ hours, five daily between 6.35am and 9pm)

Jūrmala (Majori) (0.65Ls, 30 minutes, two per hour between 5.50am and 11.40pm)

Jelgava (0.95Ls, 45 minutes, two per hour between 5.40am and 11.20pm)

Kandava (2.88Ls, 1½ hours, one daily at 6.15pm)

Ķemeri (0.97Ls, one hour, one per hour between 5.50am and 11.40pm)

Salaspils (0.50Ls, 25 minutes, two or three per hour between 5am and 11pm)

Saulkrasti (1.03Ls, one hour, one or two per hour between 5.45am and 11pm)

Sigulda (1.11Ls, one to 1¼ hours, hourly between 6am and 9pm)

Valmiera (2.13Ls, 2¼ hours, five daily between 6.35am and 9pm)

High inflation rates mean that prices are constantly in flux. All train schedule queries can be answered at www.1188.lv.

GETTING AROUND
To/From the Airport

There are three means of transport connecting the city centre to the airport. The cheapest option is bus 22, which runs every 15 minutes and stops at several points around town. Tickets (0.40Ls) are sold by the bus drivers, and exact change is highly preferred. AirBaltic runs lime green vans from the airport to the hotel of your choice (so long as it's in Central Rīga – those staying in Old Rīga will be dropped off on the outskirts of the medieval neighbourhood and will have to walk the last five to 10 minutes to their hotel). Taxis are the final option and should not cost more than 7Ls.

Car & Motorcycle

Latvians joke that the traffic is so bad in Rīga that it takes longer to drive across the city than it does to drive across the entirety of Latvia. For more information on car rentals, see opposite.

Bus, Tram & Trolleybus

If you weren't born in Rīga, you won't have the gene that innately enables you to understand the city's horribly convoluted network of buses, trams and trolleybuses. Fortunately, most of the main tourist attractions are within walking distance of one another, so you might never have to use any of Rīga's 11 tram lines, 23 trolleybus paths or 39 bus routes. Tickets cost 0.40Ls (0.50Ls if you buy your tram or trolleybus ticket from the driver – exact change is required). Tram and trolley-bus tickets can also be purchased at Narvesen superettes (Latvia's version of 7-Eleven). City transport runs daily from 5.30am to midnight. Some routes have an hourly night service. For Rīga public transport routes and schedules visit www.rigassatiksme.lv.

Taxi

Officially, taxis charge 0.30Ls per kilometre (0.40Ls between 10pm and 6am), but don't be surprised if you get ripped off. Insist on the meter running before you set off; see p189 for more information. Meters usually start running at 0.50Ls to 1.50Ls. Don't pay more than 3Ls for short journeys. There are taxi ranks outside the bus and train stations, at the airport and in front of major hotels like Reval Hotel Latvija (p214) and Albert Hotel (p214).

AROUND RĪGA

It's hard to believe that long stretches of flaxen beaches and shady pine forests lie just 20km from Rīga's metropolitan core. Both Jūrmala and Ķemeri National Park make excellent day trips from Rīga. For other excursion ideas, check out the boxed text on p200 and p231.

The highway connecting Rīga to Jūrmala (Latvia's only six-lane road) was known as '10 minutes in America' during Soviet times, because locally produced films set in the USA were always filmed on this busy asphalt strip.

Jūrmala

pop 55,580

The Baltic's version of the French Riviera, Jūrmala (pronounced *yoor*-muh-lah) is a long string of townships with stately wooden beach estates belonging to Russian oil tycoons and their trophy wives. Even during the height of communism, Jūrmala was always a place to *sea* and be seen. Wealthy fashionistas would flaunt their couture beachwear while worshipping the sun between spa treatments. On summer weekends, vehicles clog the roads when jetsetters and day tripping Rīgans flock to the resort town for some serious fun in the sun.

ORIENTATION

Jūrmala is actually a giant 32km strip of land consisting of 14 townships. If you don't have a car or bicycle, you'll want to head straight to the heart of the action – the townships of Majori and Dzintari. A 1km-long pedestrian street, Jomas iela, connects these two districts and is considered to be Jūrmala's main drag, with loads of tourist-centric venues. Unlike many European resort towns, most of Jūrmala's restaurants and hotels are several blocks away from the beach, which keeps the seashore (somewhat) pristine.

INFORMATION

Free internet access is available at the tourism office. The Jūrmala City Museum has free wi-fi access. Public toilets are located in Concert Garden behind the information centre.

Bulduri Hospital (☎ 6775 2254; Vienības prospekts 19/21) Hospital service.

Latvijas Krājbanka (☎ 6709 2661; Jomas iela 37; ⏲ 9am-5pm) On-site 24-hour ATM available.

Majori post office (☎ 6776 2430; Strēlnieku prospekts 16; ⏲ 7.30am-7pm Mon-Fri, 8am-4pm Sat) Located in Dubulti township, a 2km walk west from Majori.

Tourist office (☎ 6714 7902; www.jurmala.lv; Lienes iela 5; ⏲ 9am-7pm Mon-Fri, 10am-5pm Sat, 10am-3pm Sun) Located across from Majori train station, this helpful office has scores of brochures outlining walks, bike routes and attractions. Staff can assist with accommodation bookings. A giant map outside helps orient visitors when the centre is closed.

SIGHTS

Besides its 'Blue Flag' beach, Jūrmala's main attraction is its colourful Art Nouveau **wooden houses**, distinguishable by frilly awnings, detailed facades and elaborate towers. There are over 4000 wooden structures (most are lavish summer cottages) found throughout Jūrmala, but you can get your fill of wood by taking a leisurely stroll along Jūras iela, which parallels Jomas iela between Majori and Dzintari. The houses are in various states of repair; some are dilapidated and abandoned, others are beautifully renovated, and some are brand-new constructions. The tourist office has a handy booklet called *The Resort Architecture of Jūrmala City*, which features several self-guided architectural walking tours – page eight highlights Majori neighbourhood.

At the other end of the architectural spectrum are several particularly gaudy beach-

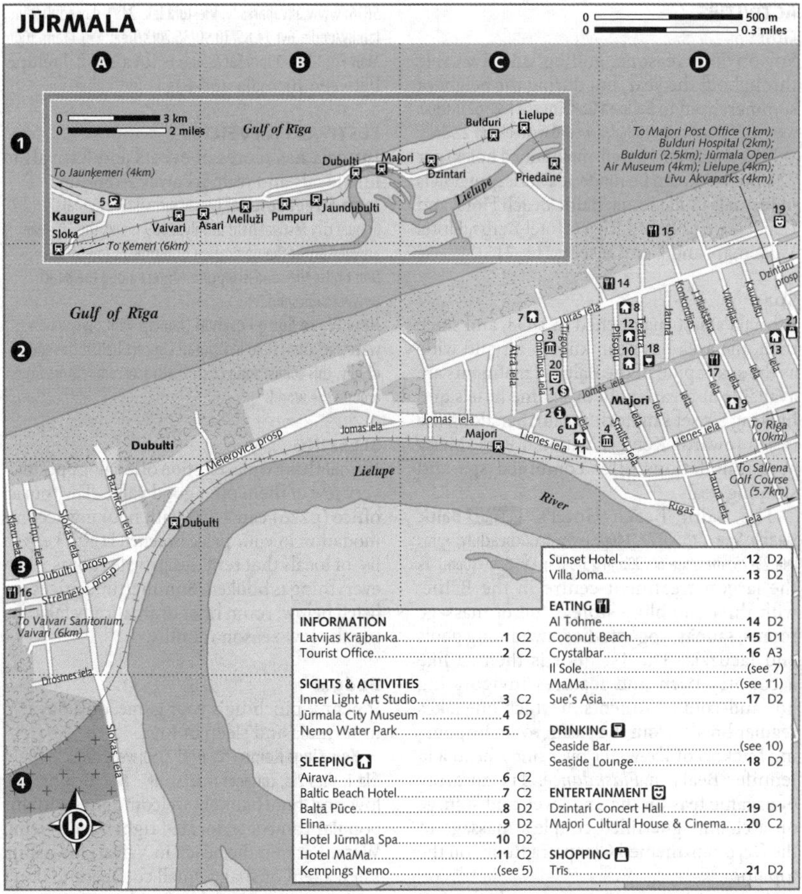
JŪRMALA
0 500 m
0 0.3 miles
A
B
C
D
1
2
3
4
0 3 km
0 2 miles
Gulf of Rīga
To Jaunķemeri (4km)
Kauguri
Sloka
To Ķemeri (6km)
Vaivari
Asari
Melluži
Pumpuri
Jaundubulti
Dubulti
Majori
Dzintari
Bulduri
Lielupe
Priedaine
To Majori Post Office (1km); Bulduri Hospital (2km); Bulduri (2.5km); Jūrmala Open Air Museum (4km); Lielupe (4km); Līvu Akvaparks (4km);
Gulf of Rīga
Dubulti
Jūras iela
Jomas iela
Majori
Z Meierovica prosp
Lienes iela
Lielupe
River
Rigas iela
To Rīga (10km)
To Saliena Golf Course (5.7km)
Dzintaru prosp
Ātrā iela
Omnibusa iela
Tirgoņu
Pilsoņu
Teātra
Smilšu iela
Konkordijas
J Pliekšāna
Jaunā
Vikonijas
Kaudzīšu
Jaunā iela
Baznīcas iela
Slokas iela
Ceriņu iela
Kļavu iela
Dubultu prosp
Strēlnieku prosp
To Vaivari Sanitorium, Vaivari (6km)
Drošmes iela
Slokas iela
INFORMATION
Latvijas Krājbanka....1 C2
Tourist Office....2 C2
SIGHTS & ACTIVITIES
Inner Light Art Studio....3 C2
Jūrmala City Museum....4 D2
Nemo Water Park....5...
SLEEPING
Airava....6 C2
Baltic Beach Hotel....7 C2
Baltā Pūce....8 D2
Elina....9 D2
Hotel Jūrmala Spa....10 D2
Hotel MaMa....11 C2
Kempings Nemo....(see 5)
Sunset Hotel....12 D2
Villa Joma....13 D2
EATING
Al Tohme....14 D2
Coconut Beach....15 D1
Crystalbar....16 A3
Il Sole....(see 7)
MaMa....(see 11)
Sue's Asia....17 D2
DRINKING
Seaside Bar....(see 10)
Seaside Lounge....18 D2
ENTERTAINMENT
Dzintari Concert Hall....19 D1
Majori Cultural House & Cinema....20 C2
SHOPPING
Trīs....21 D2

front Soviet-era sanatoriums. No specimen glorifies the genre quite like the **Vaivari sanatorium** (Asaru prospekts 61), on the main road 5km west of Majori. It resembles a giant, beached cruise ship that's been mothballed since the Brezhnev era. Surprisingly it still functions, catering to an elderly clientele who have been visiting regularly since, well, the Brezhnev era.

A visit to **Inner Light Art Studio** (☎ 6787 1937; www.jermolajev.lv; Omnibusa iela 19; adult/child 0.50Ls; 🕑 11am-6pm Jun-Aug, noon-5pm Sat & Sun Sep-May) will surely cure any rainy-day blues. A local Russian artist runs the studio out of his home, and dabbles with a secret recipe for glow-in-the-dark paint by creating portraits that morph when different amounts of light strike the painting. Ethereal Enya music further enhances the trippy experience as the paintings shine brilliantly in the pulsing darkness.

After a pricey renovation, the **Jūrmala City Museum** (☎ 6776 4746; Tirgoņu iela 29; adult/child 0.40/0.20Ls, free Fri; 🕑 11am-6pm Wed-Sun) now features a beautiful permanent exhibit detailing Jūrmala's colourful history as *the* go-to resort town in the former USSR.

The **Jūrmala Open Air Museum** (☎ 6775 4909; Tīklu iela 1a; admission 0.50Ls, free Tue; 🕑 10am-6pm Tue-Sun), further afield in Lielupe, preserves 19th-century fishers' houses and a collection of nautical equipment. If you're lucky, you'll get to try smoked fish prepared in a traditional Latvian manner.

LATVIA

ACTIVITIES
Golf

For obvious reasons, golfing isn't available throughout the year, but during the height of summer, head to **Saliena Golf Course** (☎ 6716 0300; www.salienagolf.com; 18 holes weekday/weekend 22/28Ls; ☑ 8.20am-6pm) for 18 well-maintained holes (par 72). Bookings can be made at a variety of hotels in Jūrmala (Villa Joma, Baltic Beach Hotel and Elina; see p229) and Rīga (Hotel Bergs, Hotel Valdemars and Centra; see p213, 215).

Spas

Jūrmala's first spa opened in 1838, and since then, the area has been known far and wide as the spa capital of the Baltic. Treatments are available at a variety of big-name hotels and hulking Soviet sanatoriums further along the beach towards Ķemeri National Park. Many accommodations offer combined spa and sleeping deals.

The Baltic Beach Hotel's our pick **Baltic Beach Spa** (☎ 6777 1400; www.balticbeach.lv; Jūras iela 23-25; massage 60/90min 25/35Ls; ☑ 8am-10pm) is the largest treatment centre in the Baltic, with three rambling storeys full of massage rooms, saunas, yoga studios, swimming pools and Jacuzzis. The 1st floor is themed like a country barn and features invigorating hot-and-cold treatments in which one takes regular breaks from the steam room by pouring buckets of ice water over one's head à la Jennifer Beals in *Flashdance*. Try an array of organic teas on the 2nd level, and splurge on a champagne-filled couple's massage in the Egyptian-themed Cleopatra Room on the top floor.

Another large spa centre with the full spread of treatments is located on the 2nd and 3rd floors of the **Hotel Jūrmala Spa** (☎ 6778 4436; www.hoteljurmala.com; Jomas iela 47/49; massage 20/60min 10/30Ls; ☑ 7am-11pm Mon-Fri, 8am-11pm Sat, 8am-10pm Sun). A one-day pass to the sauna, pool and gym costs 10Ls (12Ls on weekends).

Watersports

Vaivari township, about 5km west of central Majori, is home to the wet and wonderful **Nemo Water Park** (☎ 6773 2350; www.nemo.lv; Atbalss iela 1; admission 5/2.50Ls; ☑ 11am-5pm Wed-Sun May-Sep), with shoelace-like waterslides, a sauna and two heated pools right on the beach. The centre also rents bicycles for 5Ls per hour. A second waterpark, **Līvu Akvaparks** (☎ 6775 5636; www.akvaparks.lv; Viestura iela 24; 1-day adult/child/family/under 6yr 14.85/10.90/36.20Ls/free; ☑ 11am-10pm Mon-Fri, 10am-10pm Sat & Sun) is located in Lielupe, between Jūrmala and Rīga.

FESTIVALS & EVENTS

Jūrmala has scores of events and festivals to lure locals and tourists away from Rīga.

Joma Street Festival (www.jurmala.lv) Jūrmala's annual city festival held in July; 2009 marks the 50-year anniversary of the unification of Jūrmala's townships. Don't miss the sand-sculpture contest along the beach (www.magicsand.lv).

New Wave Song Festival (Jaunais Vilnis; www.new wavestars.com) Held in Dzintari Concert Hall at the end of July, this soloist song contest attracts competitors from around the world.

SLEEPING

Jūrmala has a wide selection of lodging options – very few of them offer good value. The tourist office (p226) can assist with booking accommodation in your price bracket. It also keeps a list of locals that rent out private rooms when everything is booked. Summertime prices are listed below; room rates dramatically fall during the low-season months.

Budget

If penny-pinching's your game, do a day trip to Jūrmala and sleep in Rīga.

Kempings Nemo (☎ 6773 2350; www.nemo.lv; Atbalss iela 1; sites 2Ls; cottages 8-32Ls; ℗ ⚲) Bright yellow-and-blue banners welcome guests to this popular camp site, located right beside Nemo Water Park on the beach in Vaivari township. Pitch a tent or snag a small cottage, and don't miss home-cooked Latvian breakfast every morning (3.90Ls). Parking is 2 LS.

Airava (☎ 2923 7659; www.airava.rk.lv; Jomas iela 42/3; dm 15Ls) Ramshackle Airava is best described as 'utilitarian'. The hallways are a bit rundown but the dorm bedrooms are an acceptable place to crash for a night. Kitchen facilities are available. Prices drop 50% in low season.

Midrange

Jūrmala's midrange options are small inns located a block or two from the beach.

Sunset Hotel (☎ 6775 5311; www.sunsethotel.lv; Pilsoņu iela 7/9; s 40-50Ls, d 55-95Ls; ☐) Set in a summery, pistachio-coloured beach house, Sunset's refurbished rooms sport antique hardwood floors and hi-tech showers covered with tonnes of nozzles and buttons. Wi-fi available.

Elina (☎ 6776 1665; www.elinahotel.lv; Lienes iela 43; d 45Ls) This mom-and-pop operation offers cheery, no-frills accommodation in a wobbly wooden house. There's a small convenience store on the ground floor and the kitchen staff whips up ubercheap eats (3Ls).

Villa Joma (☎ 6777 1999; www.villajoma.lv; Jomas iela 90; s 52-97Ls, d 55-100Ls) This inviting boutique hotel sports 15 immaculate rooms that come in quirky configurations. Try for a room with a skylight. Although Villa Joma is several blocks from the beach, there's a lovely garden terrace in the back to catch some rays. Don't miss out on the fantastic food (lunch mains 6Ls to 8Ls, dinner mains 9Ls to 17Ls) served at the airy ground-floor restaurant.

Baltā Pūce (☎ 6751 2722; www.baltapuce.lv; Pilsoņu iela 7/9; s 65-110Ls, d 70-115Ls) Literally 'the White Owl', this charming inn, set in a 100-year-old house, has quaint rooms and a lobby littered with toy hooters. The rooms are a smidgen nicer at Sunset Hotel next door, but Baltā Pūce has a much more sociable vibe. Wi-fi available.

Top End

Beach views are an elusive breed and can only be found at top-end accommodation.

Hotel Jūrmala Spa (☎ 6778 4415; www.hoteljurmala .com; Jomas iela 47/49; s 90-150Ls, d 100-150Ls; 🖳 🖳) The rooms in this towering black behemoth are on the small side, but you'll hardly notice – everything sparkles after a recent renovation. Breakfast is included. Rooms on the 8th and 9th floor have sweeping views of both the inland river and sea. Check out the swinging cocktail lounge on the top floor (right).

ourpick Hotel MaMa (☎ 6776 1271; www.hotel mama.lv; Tirgonu iela 22; d from 90Ls) The bedroom doors have thick, mattress-like padding on the interior (psycho-chic?) and the suites themselves are a veritable blizzard of white drapery. A mix of silver paint and pixie dust accents the ultramodern furnishings and amenities (plasma TVs, kitchenettes, California-king-sized beds, and suspiciously erotic floral imagery framed on the ceiling). If heaven had a bordello, it would probably look something like this. Sneak up to the widow's walk on the roof for breezy views of beach town.

Baltic Beach Hotel (☎ 6777 1400; www.balticbeach .lv; Jūras iela 23-25; s/d incl breakfast 120/135Ls; 🖳 🖳)

Concrete Soviet monstrosities look especially ugly along the sea, and Baltic Beach Hotel is no exception. However, the hotel's interior ain't so shabby – the lobby sparkles with polished marble after a recent renovation, and rooms upstairs all have excellent ocean views. The top-notch spa – the Baltic's biggest – is the hotel's best feature (opposite). Wi-fi available.

EATING & DRINKING

In summer, stroll down Jomas iela and take your pick from beer tents, cafe terraces and trendy restaurants. If you're not feeling adventurous, almost all of Rīga's popular chain restaurants have a franchise in Jūrmala. Most places are open year-round, catering to beach bums in the summer and spa junkies who pass through for treatments during the winter months. Most hotels also have on-site restaurants.

Coconut Beach (Majoru pludmale; pizzas 4-5Ls; 🕑 Jun-Aug) This beach hut dishes out dirt-cheap chow smack in the middle of Jūrmala's silky sands. Check out the DJ beach discos every Friday and Saturday nights.

Crystalbar (☎ 2780 8222; Klavu iela 14; mains 5-10Ls; 🕑 noon-2am) Located well off the tourist track, this slick hang-out is a popular pick amongst young locals who come for cocktails on the patio and fresh homemade pasta. It's across the street from a hard-to-miss bright blue Orthodox church.

Al Tohme (☎ 6775 5755; Pilsoņu iela 2; mains 5-14Ls; 🕑 11am-11pm Tue-Sun) One of the only restaurants with beach views, this Middle Eastern spot specialises in kebabs and cold mezze. Live music mixes with shisha smoke and ocean breezes on Friday and Saturday nights.

MaMa (☎ 6776 1271; Tirgonu iela 22; mains 5.50-16.50Ls; 🕑 11am-midnight) At MaMa, Italian and Latvian fusion cuisine is served on crisp white-clothed tables surrounded by a mish-mash of throne-like chairs. You may notice that some of the seats are particularly tiny – these are reserved for pets (the chef even created a gourmet menu for Fido). Don't miss the technicoloured bathroom with a fun surprise on the ceiling.

Sue's Asia (☎ 6775 5900; Jomas iela 74; mains 6-15Ls; 🕑 noon-midnight) Although it's a bit odd seeing bleach-blonde Baltic women serving pan-Asian platters in saris, Sue's is worshipped by locals for its almost-authentic cuisine. Enjoy spicy curries or tender butter chicken amid statues of praying deities.

LATVIA

Il Sole (☎ 6777 1428; Jūras iela 23/25; mains 8-25Ls; ⊙ 11am-11pm) A romantic restaurant, Il Sole has fantastic ocean-side seating and a long list of delicious Italian dishes matched with imported wines.

Seaside Lounge (☎ 2862 9458; www.seasidelounge.lv; Jomas iela 57; ⊙ 10pm-6am Fri, 11pm-5am Sat) This 2nd-storey nightclub, above the popular Slāvu restaurant, rocks late into the night with a spacious dance floor and a host of local DJs. Friday nights bump with electronica and house, Saturdays slow down with a bit of R&B. Check the website for a complete list of upcoming themed parties.

Seaside Bar (☎ 6778 4400; Jomas iela 47/49; ⊙ 3pm-3am) This hot dancing spot sits high above the trees on the 11th floor of Hotel Jūrmala Spa. Nurse your cocktail in a space-age bucket seat or get jiggy with it under the disco ball.

ENTERTAINMENT
Majori Culture House & Cinema (Majori Kultūras nams; ☎ 6776 2403; Jomas iela 35) Hosts films, music concerts and various arts and craft exhibitions.

Dzintari Concert Hall (Dzintari Koncertzāle; ☎ 6776 2092; Turaidas iela 1) At the northern beach end of Turaidas iela and features a season of summer concerts from June to August.

SHOPPING
Of all the souvenir shops dotting the streets of Jūrmala, **Tris** (☎ 2631 4949; Jomas iela 92; ⊙ noon-6pm) is your best bet to find authentic handmade amber jewellery created by a local artist.

GETTING THERE & AROUND
Two to three trains per hour link the sandy shores of Jūrmala to Central Rīga. Take a suburban train bound for Sloka, Tukums or Dubulti and disembark at Majori station (0.65Ls, 30 to 35 minutes). The first train departs Rīga around 5.50am and the last train leaves Majori around 12.10am. Jūrmala-bound trains usually depart from tracks 3 and 4, and stop six or seven times within the resort's 'city limits' if you wish to get off in another neighbourhood. Visit www.1188.lv for the most up-to-date information.

Minibuses are also a common mode of transport between Rīga and Jūrmala. Take the minibus (1Ls, 30 minutes) in the direction of Sloka, Jaunķemeri or Dubulti and ask the driver to let you off at Majori. If you go further, the ride will cost 1.40Ls. These vans depart every five to 15 minutes between 6am and midnight and

leave opposite Rīga's Central Train Station. Catch the bus at Majori train station for a lift back. These regularly running minibuses can also be used to access other townships within Jūrmala's long sandy stretch. From 9am to midnight, minibuses also connect Jūrmala to Rīga International Airport (2Ls).

A **slow boat** (Map p190; ☎ 2923 7123; Lielais Kristaps; adult/child 5/3Ls; ⊙ 11am, 2.30pm, 4pm, 5.30pm & 7pm) departs from Rīga Riflemen Square and docks in Majori near the train station. The journey takes one hour.

Motorists driving the 15km into Jūrmala must pay a 1Ls toll per day, even if you are just passing through. Keep an eye out for the self-service toll stations sitting at both ends of the resort town. Drivers caught without proof of payment will be fined 50Ls. All parking around Jūrmala is free.

Bicycle rentals are available at Kempings Nemo (p228) or arrangements can be made at the tourist office (p226).

Ķemeri National Park
After Jūrmala's chic stretch of celebrity homes and seaside bar huts lies a verdant hinterland called **Ķemeri National Park** (☎ 6714 6819; www.kemeri.gov.lv; ⊙ Jun-Aug). Today, the park features sleepy fishing villages tucked between protected bogs, lakes and forests, but at the end of the 1800s, Ķemeri was known for its curative mud and spring water, attracting visitors from as far away as Moscow.

Ķemeri's **park information centre** (☎ 6714 6819; www.kemeri.gov.lv; ⊙ 10am-6pm Jun-Aug) is located in an old barn-like hotel and restaurant called the 'Funny Mosquito'. Although most of the info is in Latvian, you can rent bikes (4Ls for two hours) and sign up for lectures and programs such as bat- and birdwatching. A scenic 600m **trail** starts at the info centre and circles through a slice of flat plain forest.

The mosquito theme continues at the **Ķemeri Motel** (☎ 6751 2622; www.kemerimotel.lv; Tukuma iela 2; d/ste 40/70Ls), with its large cartoon blood-sucking mascot sitting on the roof. A two-minute walk west of the Ķemeri train station, the motel has brand-new rooms, a restaurant, and a small spa centre with a Jacuzzi and tanning bed.

The pungent smell of rotten eggs wafts through the air at the national park's spa resort, also called Ķemeri (pronounced kyeh-meh-ree or tyeh-meh-ree, depending on who you ask), known for its sulphurous springs. Ķemeri's first mud bath opened in the late

---

THE EARTH GROANS AT SALASPILS CONCENTRATION CAMP

Between 1941 and 1944 about 45,000 Jews from Rīga and about 55,000 other people, including Jews from other Nazi-occupied countries and prisoners of war, were murdered in the Nazi concentration camp 'Kurtenhof' at Salaspils, 20km southeast of Rīga. Giant, gaunt sculptures stand as a memorial on the site, which stretches over 40 hectares. The inscription on the huge concrete bunker, which forms the memorial's centrepiece, reads 'Behind this gate the earth groans' – a line from a poem by the Latvian writer Eizens Veveris, who was imprisoned in the camp. Inside the bunker a small exhibition recounts the horrors of the camp. In its shadow lies a 6m-long block of polished stone with a metronome inside, ticking a haunting heartbeat, which never stops.

To get there from Rīga, take a suburban train on the Ogre–Krustpils line to Dārziņi (not Salaspils) station. The path from the station to the *piemineklis* (memorial) starts on the barracks side. It's about a 15-minute walk. If you're driving from Rīga on the A6 highway, the hard-to-spot turn-off is on the left 300m before the A5 junction.

1800s, and until WWII the resort had a widespread reputation as a healing oasis. The area's spring water is perfectly potable and apparently quite healthy. Try filling your Nalgene at **The Lizard**, a stone sculpture at the mouth of a spring that trickles into the river. Sip your pungent brew while meandering past faded mint-green gazebos and small wrought iron bridges with romantic names like The Bridge of Sighs or the Bridge of Caprices – everything remains exactly as it was during the height of the resort's popularity in the 1930s.

It's hard to miss **Hotel Ķemeri**. Known as the 'White Ship', it was built during Latvia's brief period of independence in the 1930s, and has one of the most impressive facades outside of Rīga. At the moment, only the exterior can be appreciated due to a lack of renovation money. Have a wander across the park and take a look at the **St Peter-Paul Orthodox Church**. Built in 1893, it is the oldest place of worship in Ķemeri, and if you look closely, you'll notice that this large wooden structure was constructed entirely without nails.

Fish smoking and canning remain traditional occupations in the villages further afield along the coastal road (Rte P128) leading north towards Cape Kolka. Nowhere smells fishier than **Lapmežciems**, overlooking Lake Kaņieris, 3km west of Jūrmala. Sprats are canned in the factory on the right at the village's eastern entrance. The village market sells freshly smoked eel, sprat, salmon and tuna, as does the market in **Ragaciems**, 2km north.

Ķemeri National Park is easily accessible from Rīga, as it sits just beyond Jūrmala along the capital's west-bound suburban rail line. Trains to/from Rīga (0.97Ls, one hour) and Jūrmala's Majori station (0.55Ls,

30 minutes) run 15 times per day. The park can also be accessed by bus 11 from Majori station, or directly from Rīga (1.40Ls, one hour, 15 daily).

WESTERN LATVIA (KURZEME)

Just when you thought that Rīga was the only star of the show, in comes Western Latvia from stage left, dazzling audiences with a whole different set of talents. While the capital wows the crowd with intricate architecture and metropolitan majesty, Kurzeme (Courland in English) takes things in the other direction: miles and miles of jaw-dropping natural beauty. The region's sandy strands of desolate coastline are tailor-made for an off-the-beaten-track adventure. A constellation of coastal towns – Kolka, Ventspils, Pāvilosta and Liepāja – provide pleasant breaks between the large stretches of awesome nothingness.

Kurzeme wasn't always so quiet; the region used to be occupied by the namesake Cours, a rebellious tribe known for teaming up with the Vikings for raids and battles. During the 13th century, German crusaders ploughed through, subjugating the Cours, alongside the other tribes living in Latvia. When the Livonian Order collapsed under assault from Russia's Ivan the Terrible in 1561, the Order's last master, Gotthard Kettler, salvaged Courland and neighbouring Zemgale as his own personal fiefdom.

Duke Jakob, Courland's ruler from 1640 to 1682, really put the region on the map

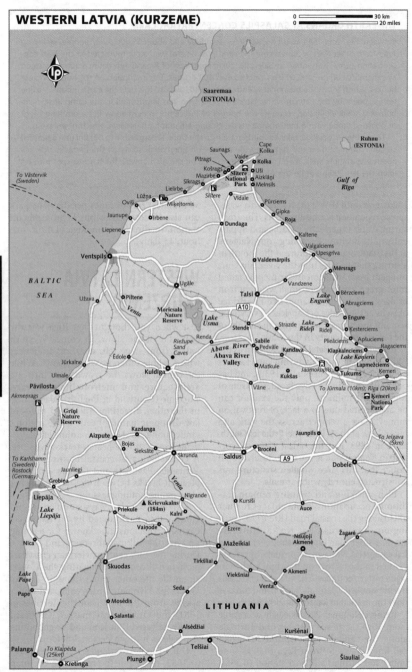

WESTERN LATVIA (KURZEME)

LATVIA

when he developed a fleet of navy and merchant ships, and purchased two far-flung (and totally random) colonies: Tobago, in the Caribbean, and an island in the mouth of Africa's Gambia River. He even had plans to colonise Australia! His son continued the delusions of grandeur with plans to turn Jelgava (Mitau) into a 'northern Paris' (needless to say, this didn't quite work out…).

TUKUMS
pop 19,830

If you're heading west from Rīga, Tukums is Kurzeme's welcome mat, and the home of Western Latvia's most-visited tourist attraction, **Cinevilla** (Kinopilsēta Cinevilla; ☎ 6774 4647; www.cinevilla.lv; adult/child 2/1Ls; ☺ 10am-7pm). After an unsuccessful search across the country for an appropriate place to shoot *Rīgas sargi*, a film set in 1919, director Aigars Grauba decided to construct an entire city from scratch in 2004. When the movie was complete, savvy entrepreneurs turned the lot into a small theme park consisting of a faux 'city' and bogus 'small town'. In 2008 noted Latvian director Jānis Streičs began filming his comedy *Rudolf's Gold* on a third part of the lot – a simulated Kurzeme farmstead.

Tourists can follow guided tours (3Ls), play with movie props, try on costumes and even shoot their own movie. There's an on-site restaurant, the **Backlot Pub** (mains 2-5Ls; ☺ 10am-6pm Tue-Sun) run by LIDO, and a makeshift **hotel** (d 30Ls; ☺ May-Oct) set up in several movie trailers originally assembled for the film crews.

Tukums is the terminus for the suburban rail line that passes through the townships of Jūrmala. Fourteen daily trains from Rīga ply the route (1.30Ls, 1¼ hours). There are two stations in town – Tukums-1 and Tukums-2 – the former is closer to the centre and information centre. The bus station (across from Tukums-1) links Rīga (1.95Ls, 1¼ hours, one hourly), Kuldīga (2.50Ls, 1½ to two hours, five daily) and Talsi (1.75Ls, 1¼ hours, five daily).

TALSI
pop 11,400

Once a medieval war zone, peaceful Talsi, 115km from Rīga, is the commercial centre of northern Kurzeme and the gateway to Western Latvia's desolate Cape Kolka. Locals are ferociously proud of the nine small hills that guard the city's cobbled lanes and nearby

lakes, but there's very little that would appeal to a tourist.

Talsi is the unofficial transfer junction for those taking the bus between Latvia's western coast and Cape Kolka. If you want to break up the journey, the staff at the **tourist office** (☎ 6322 4165; www.talsi.lv; Lielā iela 19/21; ☺ 10am-5pm Mon-Fri), located in the **Talsi Folk House**, can recommend a couple of countryside gems such as **Lake Usma**, 30km west – a puddle of water polka-dotted with seven islands and backed by leafy forests. Spend a night on the lake at **Usma Spa Hotel & Camping** (☎ 6367 3710; www.usma.lv; Priežkalni; sites per person 6Ls, cabins from 24Ls, s/d incl breakfast 27/45Ls; ☺ May-Oct), the perfect get-away-from-it-all option for those who seek peace. You can fish, sail, row, swim and enjoy a full array of spa treatments at this lakeside site, 1km south of Rte A10 on the road to Usma village.

From the **bus station** (☎ 6322 2105; Dundagas iela 15) there are buses to/from Rīga (2.90Ls to 3.25Ls, 1¾ to 2½ hours, hourly), Kolka (1.85Ls to 2.35Ls, 1¼ to two hours, three daily), Ventspils (2.10Ls to 2.30Ls, 1½ to two hours, eight daily) and Liepāja (3.95Ls to 4.20Ls, 3¼ to four hours, three daily).

CAPE KOLKA (KOLKASRAGS)

Enchantingly desolate and hauntingly beautiful, a journey to Cape Kolka (Kolkasrags) feels like a trip to the end of the earth. During Soviet times the entire peninsula was zoned off as a high-security military base, strictly out of bounds to civilians. The region's development was subsequently stunted, and today the string of desolate coastal villages has a distinctly anachronistic feel – as though they've been locked away in a time capsule.

Slītere National Park (☎ 6329 1066; www.slitere.gov .lv) guards the last 25km of the cape, right up until Dižjūra (the Great Sea, or Baltic Sea) meets Mazjūra (the Little Sea – the Gulf of Rīga) in a great clash full of sound and fury. The park's administrative offices are in the nearby town of **Dundaga** (the purported birthplace of the man who inspired the film *Crocodile Dundee*), although information is also available at the Slītere Lighthouse (p234). This towering spire acts as the gatekeeper to the park's rugged, often tundra-like expanse, home to wild deer, elk, buzzards and beaver. In mid-April, during spring migration, the Kolka peninsula sings with the calls of 60,000-odd birds, and during the summer, the park's meagre human population (1245)

LATVIA

doubles when high-profile Rīgans escape to their holiday retreats.

The easiest way to reach Cape Kolka is by private vehicle, but buses are also available. To reach the town of Kolka, buses either follow the Gulf Coast Rd through Roja, or they ply the route through Talsi and Dundaga (inland). Either way, there are five buses that link Rīga and Kolka town per day between 4.30am and 5.15pm (3.85Ls to 4.85Ls, 3½ to 4¾ hours). The first and last bus of the day continues on to Vaide and Mazirbe (for an extra 0.45Ls). Note that there are two stops in the town of Kolka: 'Delfini' and 'Ūši' (in that order). The first three daily buses departing Cape Kolka for Rīga all leave before 7am. Those travelling to/from Kuldīga, Ventspils or Liepāja must switch buses in Talsi.

Gulf Coast Road

Those with a need for speed will prefer taking the inland road through Talsi and Dundaga to reach the tip of the cape, but if you have a little extra time on your hands, try taking this slower scenic coastal road (Rte P131) that wanders through dozens of lazy fishing villages along the Gulf of Rīga.

Break up the journey to the horn of the cape with a stop at **Lake Engure Nature Park** (☎ 2947 4420; www.eedp.lv), tucked away on the isthmus between Lake Engure and the sea. Bird-buffs can spy on over 180 types of avian, and lucky visitors might spot a wild horse or an elusive blue cow (see the boxed text, p185).

Roja, 36km further north, is an angler's haven, and the last real 'town' (and we use that term lightly) before the quiet ride to Kolka. If you need to spend the night in town (there's that word again), the **Roja Hotel** (☎ 6323 2227; Jūras iela 6; s/d 20/25Ls), just past the harbour, is a comfortable place with run-of-the-mill motel furnishings.

Kolka

The village of Kolka is nothing to write home about, but the windswept moonscape at the waning edge of the cape (just 500m away) could have you daydreaming for days. It's here that the Gulf of Rīga meets the Baltic Sea in a very dramatic fashion. The raw, powerful effect of this desolate point was amplified by a biblical winter storm in 2005, which uprooted dozens of trees and tossed them like matchsticks onto the sandy beach, where they remain hideously entombed, roots in the air.

A **monument** to those claimed by treacherous waters marks the entrance to the beach near a small **information centre** (☎ 2914 9105). The poignant stone slab, with its haunting anthropomorphic silhouette, was erected in 2002 after three Swedes drowned in the cape's shallow but turbulent waters. One side reads, 'For people, ships and Livian earth'; the other, 'For those the sea took away'. Locals claim the cape's waters are littered with more shipwrecks than anywhere else in the Baltic. For obvious reasons, Cape Kolka's beauty is best appreciated from the safety of the sand.

Centuries ago, bonfires were lit at the cape's tip to guide sailors around the protruding sandbar. Today, the solar-powered **Kolka Lighthouse** guides vessels to safety. The shimmering scarlet tower, built in 1884, sits on an artificial island 6km offshore.

If you plan to stay the night, **Ūši** (☎ 2947 5692; www.kolka.info; s/d incl breakfast 26/38Ls) has simple but prim rooms, and a spot to pitch tents in the garden. Look for the brick guesthouse, opposite the onion-domed Orthodox church near the 'Ūši' bus stop. Daily bike rentals are available for 7.50Ls per day. **Hotel Zitari** (☎ 6327 7145; Rutas iela; d incl breakfast 40Ls), further south along the main road, is Kolka's only hotel. Both accommodation options have in-house restaurants, although try to track down a local fisherman for some authentic smoked fish.

See p233 for information about reaching Kolka by bus.

Baltic Coast Road

The dusty, unpaved path stretching south from Kolka towards Ventspils used to be a secret runway for Soviet aircrafts. Today, it's the widest road in Latvia, connecting a quiet row of one-street villages like a string of pearls. Time moves especially slowly here, as very little has changed over many decades. Rusty Soviet remnants occasionally dot the landscape, but they feel more like abstract art installations than reminders of harder times. The beaches' west-facing position offers unforgettable sunsets over the churning sea and stark, sandy terrain.

Elk antlers dangle from a signpost in **Vaide**, 10km southwest of Kolka, where there is little to see or do except wonder at the simple wooden houses. If the antlers spark your curiosity, there are 518 more in the **Museum of Horns & Antlers** (Ragu kolekcija; ☎ 6324 4217; admission 0.50Ls; ⏰ 9am-8pm May-Oct). The collection, cre-

THE LAST OF THE LIVS

Kurzeme is home to some of the last remaining Livs, a Finno-Ugric peoples who first migrated to northern Latvia 5000 years ago. Although many Latvians descended from this fishing tribe, less than 200 Livs remain in Latvia today, clustered in 14 fishing villages along the Baltic coast south of Cape Kolka. Hungary, Finland and Estonia also have small Liv populations, but they consider this area their homeland and return every August for the **Liv Festival** in Mazirbe, 18km southwest of Kolka.

While the Liv language is still taught in local elementary schools and at Tartu University in Estonia, there are fewer than 20 native speakers remaining in the world. You can learn about the Livonians at the small **Livonian Centre** (☎ 2327 7267; ☼ 9am-6pm Mon-Fri) behind the library on the main street in Kolka, and in a few other Kurzeme towns.

atively arranged in an attic, is the result of one man's lifetime of work as a forest warden in the region (none are hunting trophies). In summer you can **camp** (sites per person 1Ls) in the field behind the museum (there are toilets and picnic tables), although the temperature markedly drops to sweater weather in the evenings, even during the height of summer.

Eighteenth-century wooden buildings line the sand-paved streets in pleasant **Košrags**, 6km further along. Spend the night at **Pitagi** (☎ 2937 2728; www.pitagi.lv; sites per person 1.50Ls, d/tr 25/30Ls), a quaint guesthouse with newly furnished rooms, an on-site sauna, and hearty breakfasts in the morning. Rent a bike for the day (5Ls) and peddle up to the cape's tip.

The gorgeous strip of dune-backed beach in neighbouring **Mazirbe**, another 4km down the coast, is home to the **Livonian People's House** (Lībiešu tautas nams; Livlist rovkuoda in Livonian), which hosts gatherings of Liv descendants and has exhibitions on their culture. Liv ethnographical and household treasures, including a small costume display, are found at the **Rundāli Museum** (Muzejs Rundāli; ☎ 6324 8371; ☼ by appointment), located inside a squat, barn-like building on your right when entering the village.

About 5km south of Mazirbe you will see a sign for **Slītere Lighthouse** (Slīteres bāka; ☎ 6329 1066; www.slitere.gov.lv; ☼ 10am-6pm Tue-Sun Jun-Aug), 1.4km down an even rougher track. Built in 1849, the lighthouse now functions as an information booth and lookout tower for the park. If the lighthouse is closed, have a wander down the neighbouring nature trail.

ABAVA RIVER VALLEY

When the glaciers receded at the end of the last Ice Age, the crescent-shaped Abava Valley was born. Gnarled oaks and idyllic villages dot the gushing stream, luring city slickers away for a day of unhurried scenery. This area is best explored by private vehicle.

Kandava

Bucolic Kandava, 30km west of Tukums, is a good example of a typical town in rural Latvia. There's a charming collection of stone and wooden houses, a soaring church spire, and traces of a fallen empire in the form of **Livonian Order castle ruins**. From the top of the castle mound, there is an excellent view of the fine **stone bridge** (1875) – one of Latvia's oldest – across the Abava River.

Kandava's **tourist office** (☎ 6318 1150; www.kandava.lv; Kūrortu iela 1b; ☼ 9am-6pm Mon-Fri, 10am-5pm Sat May-Sep, 9am-5pm Mon-Fri, 10am-2pm Sat Oct-Apr) is located directly on Rte P130, which connects Rīga to Kuldīga. The affable staff can help you sort out a bike rental, or you can stop at **Plosti** (☎ 2613 0303; www.plosti.lv; Rēdnieki; canoes per day 7Ls), further along the Abava River towards Sabile. Plosti also offers canoe hire, horse rides, and guided paddles down the Abava.

Near the village of Kukšas, 10km south of Kandava, foodies can pamper their tastebuds at **Kukšu Muiža** (☎ 2920 5188; www.kuksumuiza.lv; meals from 10Ls), a large peach-coloured mansion serenely sitting along the banks of the Vēdzele River. The owner has poured his heart and soul into turning the once-derelict estate into one of the top rural inns in Latvia – even former President Vaira Vīķe-Freiberga has spent the evening here. The rooms (single/double from 60/80Ls) and salons are stuffed with gilded aristocratic heirlooms and flamboyant chandeliers, but the true *pièce de rèsistance* is the owner's made-to-order dinner menu, which caters to every guest's whim and only features locally grown organic produce.

LATVIA

Sabile

The sleepy, cobbled-street village of Sabile (pronounced *sah*-bee-leh), 14km downstream from Kandava, is famed for its vineyard – listed in the *Guinness Book of Records* as the world's most northern open-air grape grower. **Vīnakalns** (Wine Hill), located on a tiny mound, just 200m from the **tourist office** (☎ 6325 2344; www.sabile.lv; Pilskalna iela 6; 10am-5.30pm Mon-Fri, to 3pm Sat & Sun), started operating during the 13th century and was resurrected in the 17th century by Duke Jakob of Courland. The duke's vineyard was never very productive and fell into disuse. Although operations resumed in 1936, the vineyard's focus lay in researching hardy strains of vines rather than producing high-quality wines. The only chance to taste local wine (it's impossible to buy) is at Sabile's **wine festival** during the last weekend in July.

Across the river from Sabile the road climbs to the not-to-be-missed **Pedvāle Open-Air Art Museum** (Pedvāles brīvdabas mākslas muzejs; ☎ 6325 2249; www.pedvale.lv; adult/child 2Ls/free, group guide 25Ls; 10am-6pm May–mid-Oct, to 4pm mid-Oct–Apr), located about 1.5km south of the tourist office. Founded in 1991 by Ojars Feldbergs, a Latvian sculptor, the museum showcases over 100 jaw-dropping installations on 100 hectares of rolling hills. Many of the sculptures were created by Feldbergs himself, who often collaborates with other artists from all over the globe. Every year the pieces rotate, reflecting a prevalent theme that permeates the museum's works. Past themes have included meditations on the Earth's prime elements and time. Standout works include **Muna Muna**, a swirling sphere of TV parts, **Chair**, an enormous seat made from bright blue oil drums, and the iconic **Petriflora Pedvalensis**, a bouquet of flowers whose petals have been replaced with spiral stones. The handy orange *Pedvāle Walk* booklet plots all of the sculptures on a neatly drawn map, and provides simple captions with the artists' names. Additional pieces are on display at Sabile's former **synagogue** (☎ 6325 2249; Strauta iela 4), which Mr Feldbergs transformed into a contemporary art space.

Spend the night at the on-site inn, **Firkspedvāle Muiža** (☎ 6325 2248; www.pedvale.lv; r per person 10Ls), an atmospheric guesthouse with a handful of simply furnished rooms featuring wooden floors and rustic beams. Next door, **Dāre** (☎ 6325 2273; mains from 4Ls) dishes up satisfying food, from simple salads to hearty plates of freshly caught trout. Sit outside on the wooden terrace in summer.

For a truly unique experience, you can **our pick** **camp** (sites per person 1Ls; May–mid-Oct) anywhere within the open-air museum. Uncurl your sleeping bag and watch the midnight shadows dance along the larger-than-life sculptures – we can't think of a better place in Latvia to pitch a tent.

Other Sabile highlights include a 17th-century **Lutheran church**, at the western edge of town. The blazing white chapel features an arresting baroque pulpit held up by four griffon-headed snakes. Follow the trail behind the church to the summit of **Castle Hill**, where there's an ancient fort and excellent views of the valley.

KULDĪGA

pop 13,010

If adorable Kuldīga (kool-*dee*-ga) were a tad closer to Rīga it would be crowded with legions of day-tripping camera-clickers. Fortunately, the town is located deep in the heart of rural Kurzeme, making it just far enough to be the perfect reward for more intrepid travellers. In its heyday, Kuldīga served as the capital of the Duchy of Courland (1596–1616) and was known throughout the region as the 'city where salmon fly'. Kuldīga earned its puzzling moniker due to its strategic location along Ventas Rumba – the widest waterfall in Europe. During spawning season, the salmon would swim upstream, and when they reached the waterfall they would jump through the air attempting to surpass it.

Kuldīga was badly damaged during the Great Northern War, and was never quite able to regain its former lustre. Today, this blast from the past is a favourite spot to shoot Latvian period-piece films – 29 movies and counting…

Orientation

Kuldīga is oriented around three town squares on the west side of the Venta River. Pedestrian Liepājas iela, with its 19th-century lanterns, links Rātslaukums (home of the tourist office) to Pilsētas laukums, the town's 'new square', complete with a couple of hotels, banks and a grocery store. Kuldīga's unremarkable medieval square was the first place in all of Latvia to trade potatoes.

TURNING RED TO GREEN

Renda is one of those blink-and-you'll-miss-it towns nestled along the muddy banks of the Abava River. There's a two-by-four grocery store, a wobbly church and the occasional barking dog, so it's hard to initially imagine why Prince Charles would make a special trip from England to check out this seemingly unremarkable dot on the map. But at the far end of town, a dusty trail leads deeper into the valley revealing the purpose of the Prince's visit – beautiful Upmaļi, a hidden Eden overflowing with lush organic produce.

This sprawling acreage, secreted behind a forest of gnarled oaks, was once a favourite farming plot of Duke Jakob, the ruler of the Duchy of Courland, and for the last century, Upmaļi has been lovingly tended to by the Bergmaņi family.

The grass wasn't always so green at Upmaļi; during WWI the Bergmaņi family was forced to flee and seek refugee status in Russia. After the war, several relatives returned to the farm only to lose the property once more during the Soviet regime. In 1949, the communist military ploughed through and shipped half of Renda's farming community to Siberia. The remaining farmers were forced to participate in a 'collective' infrastructure, which left the locals impoverished and hungry. Although practically destitute, the Bergmaņi family desperately clung to their land, and in 1989 the newly emerging Latvian government officially handed them the deeds.

Armed with a copy of *The Secret Life of Plants* by ethnobotanist Stephen Buhner, Mara, the Bergmaņi matriarch, revitalised her farm, paying careful attention to natural products. Far ahead of her time, she began blazing a trail for organic farmers in the Baltic. Over the last few years, Mara's eco efforts have been noticed around the globe. After Prince Charles stopped through, the farm received special recognition by the Ashoka Foundation (www.ashoka.org/node/2926). Mara is the founder and president of Latvia's Eco-Health Farms club, and she was a finalist at the global Geotourism Challenge Competition held in 2008 in Washington DC.

For more information about the Bergmaņi family and their farm, visit www.anna-bergmans.eu (the website is in Latvian; click 'kontakti' to enquire about details in English). Travellers who cannot make it out to Upmaļi can sample Mara's signature teas in restaurants all over Latvia. Small sacs (made from recycled paper, of course) of organic tea leaves can also be purchased throughout the country for a modest 1.50Ls. These bagged blends are inspired by Native American recipes, and fuse a variety of local and foreign flavours; 'Pūķa Spēks' is our favourite.

Information

Public toilets are located in '1905 Park'.

Hansabanka (Liepājas iela 15) Offers currency exchange and has an ATM outside.

Post office (Liepājas iela 34) Near Pilsētas Laukums.

Tourist office (☎ 6332 2259; www.kuldiga.lv; Baznīcas iela 5; ☻ 9am-6pm Mon-Sat, 10am-2pm Sun mid-May–mid-Sep, 9am-5pm Mon-Fri mid-Sep–mid-May) Has tons of informative brochures about the town and two charming souvenir shops on either side.

Sights & Activities

OLD TOWN

Kuldīga's Old Town orbits three town squares: the medieval square, town hall square and 'new' square. The town hall square, known as **Rātslaukums**, is the most attractive and makes a good place to start your trip. The square gets its name from the 17th-century **town hall** (Rātslaukums 5), now home to an information centre, some souvenir shops and a charming cafe. The new town hall, built in 1860 in Italian Renaissance style, is at the southern end of the square, and Kurzeme's **oldest wooden house** – built in 1670, reconstructed in 1742 and renovated in 1982 – stands here on the northern corner of Pasta iela.

The Lutheran **St Katrina's Church**, on Baznīcas iela, isn't particularly beautiful, but it's the most important house of worship in town, since Katrina (St Catherine) is Kuldīga's patron saint and protector (she's even featured on the town's coat of arms). The first church on the site was built in the 1200s, and the current incarnation dates back to Duke Jacob's rule in the mid-1600s. During the Soviet era, the church was used as a barn for horses and cows, and today it is once again a place for prayer, with a large organ and fresh flowers adorning the pews.

Cross the teeny Aleksupīte ravine to reach the site of the **Livonian Order castle**, built from 1242 to 1245, but ruined during the Great Northern War. The **castle watchman's house** (Pils

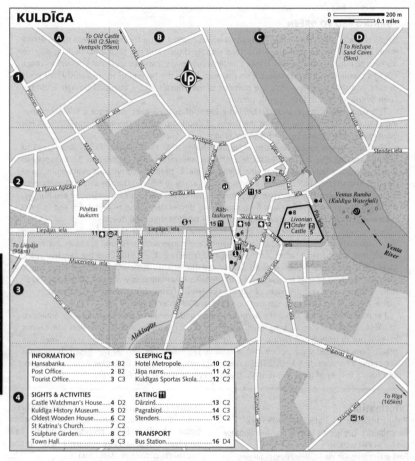

KULDĪGA

0 ────────── 200 m
0 ────────── 0.1 miles

iela 4) was built in 1735 to protect the ruins. Legend has it that the house was the site of executions and beheadings and the stream behind the house ran red with the victims' blood. Today a lovely **sculpture garden** has been set up around the subtle ruins. On the grounds you'll find the mildly interesting **Kuldīga Historic Museum** (Kuldīgas novada muzejs; ☎ 6332 2364; Pils iela; adult/child 0.50/0.30Ls; ☼ 10am-5pm), located inside a home built in Paris in 1900 to house the Russian pavilion at the World Exhibition. The museum features an exhibit on international playing cards, Viking history, and an art gallery on the top floor. A cluster of Duke Jakob's cannons sit on the front lawn.

From the old castle grounds, you'll have a great view of **Ventas Rumba** (Kuldīga Waterfall),

the widest waterfall in Europe stretching 275m across the river. The chute is only about 2–3m high and is a popular spot for a quick (and frigid) swim.

AROUND TOWN

The large **old castle hill** (pilskalns), 2.5km north of town on the western bank of the Venta, was the fortress of Lamekins, the Cour who ruled much of Kurzeme before the 13th-century German invasion. Legend has it that the castle was so staggeringly beautiful (glistening copper pendants hung from the roof) that invaders were reluctant to sack the structure. To get to the hill, follow Ventspils iela then Virkas iela north from the centre, and take a right at the fork in the road.

Located 5km outside of town along the uppaved Krasta iela, **Riežupe Sand Caves** (Smilšu alas; ☎ 6332 6236; adult/child 2/1Ls; ⊙ 11am-5pm May-Oct) feature 460m of the labyrinthine tunnels that can be visited by candlelight. They're a chilly 8°C, so bring a warm sweater. The cave is accessible by personal vehicle – staff at the tourist office can give directions (like most places in rural Latvia, private transport is a must if you don't want to wait five or more hours for a bus).

Several attractive **bike routes** wind their way through the dense forests around town (one of them also leads to the caves). Stop by the information centre to rent a bicycle (6Ls) and pick up one of the six brochures detailing these cycle trails.

Festivals & Events

During the third week of July, Kuldīga hosts an enormous handicrafts show with hundreds of artisan booths lined up along Liepājas iela.

Sleeping

Kuldīgas Sporta Skola (☎ 6332 2465; kuldiga.sp.skola @inbox.lv; Kalna iela 6; dm from 4Ls) A great spot for those tight on cash, this sports school's dorm rooms have fastidiously clean linoleums floors and matching pastel walls. Toilets are at the end of the long hallways, and the common showers are inconveniently located in the basement.

Jāņa Nams (☎ 6332 3456; www.jananams.lv; Liepājas iela 36; s/d incl breakfast 27/29Ls) Jāna's rooms, while slightly on the spartan side, are accented with a couple of crafts by local artisans (including the batik curtains). The hotel's sulphuric well water is particularly pungent in the bathroom. The funky in-house cafe has bright-yellow walls and a varied Latvian menu (mains 2Ls to 5Ls).

Hotel Metropole (☎ 6335 0588; Baznīcas iela 11; d/ste incl breakfast from 40/100Ls; ⌨) Kuldīga's best hotel rolls out the red carpet (literally) up its mod concrete stairwell to charming double-decker bedrooms overlooking pedestrian Liepājas iela and Rātslaukums Square. Black-and-white photos of old Kuldīga are sprinkled throughout, even in the trendy cafe. Wi-fi available.

Eating

Kuldīga's hotels also offer decent places to grab grub. Several restaurants in town serve *rupjmaizes kārojums/kārtojums*, which translates to 'black bread mix'. The recipe for the popular dessert is over 1000 years old: Vikings would blend crumbled bread, cream and honey for an after-dinner treat. It tastes a bit like black-forest cake.

Dārziņš (☎ 6332 5554; Baznīcas iela; snacks 0.10-2Ls; ⊙ 8am-6pm Mon-Fri, to 3pm Sat) This traditional bakery is such a wonderful throwback to earlier days – the cashier tallies your bill with an amber abacus. Try the *sklandu rausis* (0.12Ls), an ancient Cour Viking carrot cake made from carrot, potato, rye bread and sweet cream purée.

Stender's (☎ 6332 2703; Liepājas iela 3; mains 3Ls; ⊙ 11am-11pm) Not to be confused with Stenders soap shop across the street, this popular joint, housed on the 2nd storey of an 18th-century storage house, specialises in warm potato pancakes and cool pints of Užavas.

Pagrabiņš (☎ 6332 0034; Baznīcas iela 5; mains 4Ls; ⊙ 9am-11pm) Pagrabiņš lurks in the cellar beneath the information centre in what used to be the town's prison. Today, scrumptious homemade chocolates are served with your Italian coffee under low-slung alcoves lined with honey-coloured bricks. In warmer weather, enjoy your snacks on the small veranda,which sits atop the trickling Alekšupīte River, out the back.

Getting There & Away

From the **bus station** (☎ 6332 2061; Stacijas iela 2), buses run to/from Rīga (3.90Ls to 4.45Ls, 2½ to 3½ hours, 12 daily), Liepāja (2Ls to 2.40Ls, 1¾ hours, eight daily), Ventspils (1.75Ls to 1.90Ls, 1¼ hours, seven daily) and Talsi (2Ls to 2.25Ls, 1½ to 2¼ hours, four daily).

VENTSPILS

pop 43,300

Fabulous amounts of oil and shipping money have turned Ventspils into one of Latvia's most beautiful and dynamic cities. The air is brisk and clean, and the well-kept buildings are done up in an assortment of cheery colours – even the towering industrial machinery is coated in bright paint. Latvia's biggest and busiest port wasn't always smiles and rainbows though – Ventspils' strategic ice-free location served as the naval and industrial workhorse for the original settlement of Cours in the 12th century, the Livonian Order in the 13th century, the Hanseatic League through the 16th century, and finally the USSR in recent times. Although

LATVIA

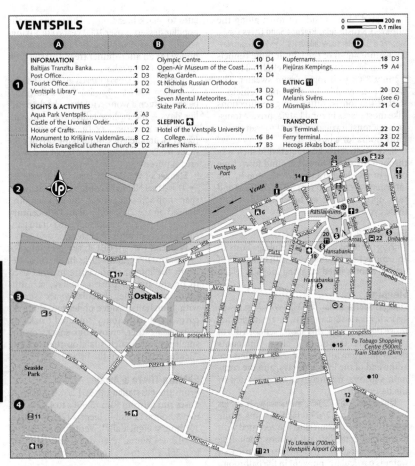

VENTSPILS

0 ——————— 200 m
0 ——————— 0.1 miles

INFORMATION	
Baltijas Tranzītu Banka.....................1	D2
Post Office.....................................2	D3
Tourist Office.................................3	D2
Ventspils Library 4	D2

SIGHTS & ACTIVITIES	
Aqua Park Ventspils.......................5	A3
Castle of the Livonian Order.........6	C2
House of Crafts.............................7	D2
Monument to Krišjānis Valdemārs..8	C2
Nicholas Evangelical Lutheran Church.9	D2

Olympic Centre............................10	D4
Open-Air Museum of the Coast.....11	A4
Reņķa Garden.............................12	D4
St Nicholas Russian Orthodox	
Church...................................13	D2
Seven Mental Meteorites.............14	C2
Skate Park..................................15	D3

SLEEPING 🏠	
Hotel of the Ventspils University	
College...................................16	B4
Karlīnes Nams............................17	B3

Kupfernams................................18	D3
Piejūras Kempings.......................19	A4

EATING 🍴	
Buginš......................................20	D2
Melanis Sivēns...........................(see 6)
Mūsmājas..................................21	C4

TRANSPORT	
Bus Terminal...............................22	D2
Ferry terminal.............................23	D2
Hecogs Jēkabs boat.....................24	D2

locals coddle their Užavas beer and claim that there's not much to do, tourists will find a weekend's worth of fun in the form of brilliant beaches, interactive museums, and winding Old Town streets dotted with the odd boutique and cafe.

Orientation

The Venta River flows up the eastern side of the town then turns west for its final 2.5km to the sea. Old Town, south of the river, was the real town centre until the Soviet navy took over the riverside area, and a new centre was created around Ganību iela and Kuldīgas iela, 750m or so further south. Most of the notable tourist attractions, hotels and restaurants are located around Old Town.

Information

Baltijas Tranzītu Banka (cnr Liela & Kuldīgas iela)
Currency exchange and ATM.

Post office (Platā iela)

Tourist office (☎ 6362 2263; www.tourism.ventspils.lv; Dārza iela 6; ☯ 8am-7pm Mon-Fri, 10am-5pm Sat, 10am-3pm Sun May-Sep, 8am-5pm Mon-Fri, 10am-3pm Sat & Sun Oct-Apr) Reams of tourist info; accommodation bookings.

Ventspils Library (☎ 6362 4333; Akmeņu iela 2; ☯ 10am-7pm Mon-Fri, to 4pm Sat) Free internet and wi-fi.

Sights & Activities

Ventspils' prime attraction is its coastline, which is laced with a sandy, dune-backed **beach** stretching south from the Venta River mouth. During the warmer months, beach bums of every ilk – from nudist to kiteboarder –

line the sands to absorb the sun's rays. A lush patch of forest south of the town centre contains an amusement park called **Aqua Park Ventspils** (Ūdens atrakciju parks; ☎ 6366 5853; Mednu iela 19; per hr adult/child 1/0.50Ls, per day adult/child 2/1Ls; ☼ 10am-10pm Jun-Sep), and the **Open-Air Museum of the Coast** (Ventspils jūras zvejniecības brīvdabas muzejs; ☎ 6322 4467; Riņķu iela 2; adult/child 0.60/0.30Ls; ☼ 11am-6pm May-Oct, 11am-5pm Wed-Sun Nov-Apr), with a collection of fishing craft, anchors and other seafaring items. On weekends between May and October you can ride around the museum's extensive grounds on a narrow-gauge railway (adult/child 0.50/0.25Ls) dating back to 1916.

The city's 13th-century **Castle of the Livonian Order** (☎ 6362 2031; Jāņa iela 17; adult/child 1/0.50Ls; ☼ 9am-6pm May-Oct, 10am-5pm Tue-Sun Nov-Apr) looks rather drab and modern from the outside, but the ancient interior hosts a cutting-edge interactive museum on the region's trade and feudal history, with digital displays and two panoramic telescopes for visitors to enjoy an eagle's-eye view of the port and city. The museum also showcases fine pieces of amber discovered on archaeological digs in the region. During Soviet rule, the castle was used as a prison and a frightening exhibit in the stables next door recounts the horrors of the jail. An adjacent Zen rock garden will sooth your soul after looking at the nightmarish photographs and frantic claw marks on the prison doors.

The Venta River, across from the castle, separates the Old Town from the colourful port on the opposite riverbank. From April to November the **Hecogs Jēkabs boat** (☎ 2635 3344; cnr Ostas iela & Tirgus iela; adult/child 0.50/0.20Ls) sails around the mouth of the Venta River. The 45-minute excursions depart six times daily from dock 18. Keep an eye out for Feldbergs' **Seven Mental Meteorites** and the **monument to Krišjānis Valdemārs**, founder of Latvian shipping. Take a walk through the **Ostgals neighbourhood** for a glimpse at simpler days when the town was merely a humble fishing village dotted with wooden abodes.

At the **House of Crafts** (☎ 6362 0174; Skolas iela 3; adult/child 0.60/0.30Ls; ☼ 11am-7pm Tue-Fri, 10am-7pm Sat, 11am-3pm Sun), visitors can learn about the handicrafts of Kurzeme and watch local artisans weave together colourful knits. Housed in a wooden structure constructed during the reign of the dukes of Courland, the building was used as a boys' school during Soviet times before being converted into an exhibi-

tion hall. English is pretty scarce, so call ahead if you are interested in watching ceramics demonstrations, or if you would like a guided explanation about the history of the building (a classroom still remains intact with desks and chalk slates) and the town.

Two churches soar above the clutter of prim wooden architecture: the onion-domed **St Nicholas Russian Orthodox Church** (Sv Nivolaja pareizticīgo baznīca; Plosu iela 10), built near the modern ferry pier in 1901, and the **Nicholas Evangelical Lutheran Church** (Nikolaja luterāņu baznīca; Tirgus iela 2), built in 1835 on stately Rātslaukums. Note that the church actually isn't 'St Nicholas', because the house of worship was named for Tsar Nicholas II (who was never canonised) when he donated loads of cash to the local Lutherans in a random act of guilt-induced kindness (keep in mind that he was Russian Orthodox).

Amid the mix of historical structures, markets and shipping relics, tourists will delight in Ventspils' most light-hearted attraction, the omnipresent **cow sculptures**. In 2002, the town benefited from the International Art and Patronage Project, known locally as the Ventspils Cow Parade. Around seven of the original 26 cows remain around town including the 'Travelling Cow', which looks like a weathered leather suitcase dotted with stamps. More quirky sculptures can be found in the **Reņka Garden**, which features dream-inducing novelty items like a giant set of keys. During the summer months, **flower sculptures** also cheer the city centre.

Boarders, bladers and BMX bikers can leap around in the region's only **skate park** (Skeitparks; ☎ 6362 2172; Sporta iela 7-9; admission free; ☼ 24hr), with 18 jumps. Ice-skaters can twirl around the city's ice-skating rink inside the modern **Olympic Centre** (☎ 6362 1996; Sporta iela 7-9; per hr 1Ls; ice-skate rental adult/child 0.50/0.20Ls).

Sleeping

Piejūras Kempings (☎ 6362 7925; www.camping.vent spils.lv; Vasarnicu iela 56; sites per person 2Ls, 4-person cottage 18-45Ls; 💻) This charming campus of grassy tent grounds and pine cottages is a full-service operation with an on-site laundrette, bicycle rental (1Ls per hour), and tennis, volleyball and basketball courts. Wi-fi available.

Hotel of the Ventspils University College (☎ 6362 9202; studentu.viesnica@ventspils.gov.lv; Inženieru iela 101; s/d with shared bathroom from 10/14Ls; ☼ Jul-Aug; 💻) Drab rooms and hallways from *The Shining* confirm

LATVIA

I-SPY

The Soviets designed a mammoth 32m-diameter radio telescope in Irbene to eavesdrop on Western satellite communications. Today scientists use it to gaze at the stars, moon and sun.

Hidden in the forest 24km north of Ventspils, Irbene's superpowerful antenna was one of three used to spy on the world by the Soviet army at the USSR Space Communication Centre. When the last Russian troops left in 1994, they took one antenna with them but left the remaining two behind (they were too large to move).

The R-32, a 600-tonne dish mounted on a 25m-tall concrete base, was built by the USSR in the 1980s and is the world's eighth-largest parabolic antenna. Since 1994 the former military installation has belonged to the **Ventspils International Radio Astronomy Centre** (VIRAC; Ventspils starptautiskais radioastronomijas centrs; ☎ 2923 0818; virac@venta.lv), which is part of the **Latvian Academy of Sciences** (☎ 6755 8662; www.lza.lv; Institute of Physical Energetics, Akadēmijas laukums 1, Rīga). Essentially a research centre, the antennae can be visited by guided tour (2Ls), arranged in advance by calling ☎ 6368 2541.

the old adage 'you get what you pay for', but alas, these are the cheapest beds in town.

Karlines Nams (☎ 2927 7050; www.karlinesnams.lv; Karlines iela 28; r 28Ls) Located off scenic Livu iela in the quaint Ostgals Fisherman's Village, Karlīnes Nams is a newer establishment set up in a former butchery. Rooms are decorated with simple slats of wood, and come with fridges and TVs. Wi-fi available.

Kupfernams (☎ 6362 6999; Kārļa iela 5; s/d 25/35Ls) Our favourite spot to spend the night, this charming sleeping spot sits in an inviting wooden house at the centre of Old Town. The cheery rooms with slanted ceilings sit above a fantastic restaurant and a trendy hair salon (which doubles as the reception desk during the day). Wi-fi available.

Eating & Drinking

The **Tobago shopping centre** (Lielais prospekts 3/5; 9am-9pm) has a **Rimi supermarket** (9am-10pm).

Mūsmājas (☎ 6362 6806; Puķu iela 33; snacks 1-4Ls; 8am-7pm Mon-Sat, 9am-6pm Sun) Mūsmājas, which means 'our house', is a very fitting name for this homey pastry shop and cafe covered with generous swatches of floral-printed wallpaper. On warmer days, enjoy your espresso and tasty confection in the quaint garden out back.

Ukraina (☎ 6362 2677; Ganibu iela 95a; mains 2-4Ls; 9am-11pm Mon-Sat, 11am-11pm Sun) Known only to locals, this hidden Ukrainian joint sits inside a car-repair shop on the way to the airport. Although housed in a metal-plated warehouse, the interior has a jolly country vibe with wooden furnishings and an adorable pastoral mural. There's one English menu for those who can't decipher tasty dish names in Russian or Ukrainian.

Buginš (☎ 6368 0151; Lielā iela 1/3; mains 3-5.50Ls; 11am-11pm) The decor is absolutely idiotic – creepy taxidermic owls, neon yellow picnic tables, checkerboard ristorante tablecloths, and rusty wheels that double as chandeliers – but Buginš remains a local fave due to the equally eclectic and nonsensical menu featuring decent Latvian and international dishes.

our pick Melanis Sivēns (☎ 6362 2396; Jāņa iela 17; meals 4-12Ls; 11am-11pm Mon-Wed, to midnight Thu-Sun) When archaeologists restored Ventspils' Livonian Castle, they unearthed the perfectly preserved skeletal remains of a black pig (melanis sivēns means 'black pig'). This was quite the conundrum as ham was a favourite dish in medieval times – in other words, no one would have ever let the pig die of natural causes. Historians believe that the castle's cook was just about to roast the poor porker when invaders suddenly attacked. The restaurant is located in the castle's dungeon and specialises in dishes that would have been served on the night of that fateful ambush.

Getting There & Away

During the week, two government-subsidised flights per day (1Ls; at 8am and 8pm) connect Ventspils' **airport** (☎ 6362 4262; www.airport.ventspils .lv; Ganibu iela 103) with Rīga.

Ventspils' **bus terminal** (☎ 6362 4262; Kuldiga iela 5) is served by buses to/from Rīga (4.55Ls, 2¾ to four hours, hourly), Liepāja (3.30Ls, 2¼ to three hours, seven daily), Pāvilosta (2Ls, 1¼ hours, four daily), Kuldīga (1.85Ls, 1¼ hours, seven daily) and Jelgava (3Ls, 4¾ to 5½ hours, four daily) via Kandava and Tukums.

Scandlines (☎ 6360 0173; www.scandlines.lt) runs seasonal ferries five times weekly from the **ferry terminal** (Dārza iela 6) to Nynashamn, Sweden (60km from Stockholm), and Rostock, Germany. **SSC Ferries** (☎ 6360 7184; www.sscf.lv) runs a ferry service four to five times per week to Montu harbour on Saaremaa in Estonia.

PĀVILOSTA

If we awarded 'our pick' symbols to entire towns, Pāvilosta would easily win the prize. This sleepy beach burg, located halfway between Ventspils and Liepāja, casually pulls off a chilled-out California surfer vibe despite its location on the black Baltic Sea. Summer days are filled with kiteboarding and windsurfing interspersed with beach naps and beers. Make sure to notify the weather gods when you plan on passing through – dreary weather in Pāvilosta means there's really nothing to do.

Information

There is a 24-hour ATM right beside the tourist office.

Post office (☎ 6349 8149; Tirgus iela 1; ⏰ 9am-5pm Mon-Fri)

Tourist office (☎ 6349 8229; www.pavilosta.lv; Dzintaru iela 2; ⏰ 7.30am-9pm Jun-Aug, 7.30am-7.30pm Sep-May) Friendly, English-speaking staff can help arrange accommodation and activities.

Sights & Activities

Pāvilosta's one and only worthwhile sight is its **beach** – a stretch of thick sand with a small pier at the south end. Great gusts of wind kick up close to shore, making the beach town a great spot for **windsurfing**, **kiteboarding**, **surfing** and **sailing**. Learn how to get involved at the friendly tourist office – the staff can also set you up with fishing equipment, and if you're lucky, you might get a tutorial on how to smoke fish.

Sleeping & Eating

Beyond the following sleeping options, Pāvilosta has scores of quaint guesthouses (6Ls to 12Ls) – the information centre can assist with bookings. Almost none of the accommodation in town is situated along the beach (although everything is within walking distance).

Veju Paradize (☎ 2644 6644; www.veju-paradize.lv; Smilšu iela 14; s/d/ste incl breakfast 28/32/42Ls) 'Wind Paradise' is Pāvilosta's largest sleeping spot, with 17 tidy rooms that are simple yet feel

distinctly beach-y. The aloe plants are a clever touch, especially after spending one too many hours splashing around in the sea. Veju's on-site restaurant is open during the summer months from 9am to 10pm and specialises in light, international dishes (4Ls to 6Ls).

Das Crocodill (☎ 2615 1333; www.crocodill.lv; Kalna iela 6; s/d/ste incl breakfast 40/45/55Ls; 🖭) Crocodill oozes personality from every mosaic tile and light fixture. The decoration is a delightful mishmash of styles from all over the world: Aboriginal Australia, tribal Africa, and a hint of Polynesia as well. Splurge for one of the suites in the back overlooking the inviting blue swimming pool.

Teātra Bičbārs (cnr Kalna & Smilšu iela, Vējdēlu Noma; coffee 1Ls, cocktails 3.50Ls; ⏰ 11am-11pm Sat & Sun Jun-Aug) This modified tiki hut sells coffee and cocktails along the dirt path leading to the beach. Take your beverage to go, or chill-out on the trendy wicker furniture and thumb through a weathered copy of the latest fashion mag.

Āķagals (☎ 2916 1533; Dzintaru iela; mains 4.20-6Ls; ⏰ noon-10pm Sun-Fri, to midnight Sat) Even if you aren't staying in Pāvilosta, a stop at Āķagals is a great way to break up the trek between Liepāja, Kuldīga and Ventspils. Enjoy stacks of delicious Latvian cuisine on varnished picnic tables made from thick logs. There's a large swing set, windswept dunes and a rusty lookout tower out the back to keep you busy while you wait for your nosh (the menu inexplicably refers to its dishes as 'noshes').

Getting There & Away

Intercity buses link Pāvilosta to Liepāja (1.60Ls, 70 minutes, five daily between 6.30am and 9pm), to Kuldīga (1.85Ls, 65 minutes, once daily with continued service to Rīga), and to Ventspils (2Ls, 1¼ hours, four daily between 8am and 9pm). Buses usually stop in front of the tourist office.

LIEPĀJA
pop 85,050

Founded by the Livonian Order in the 13th century, Latvia's third-largest city wasn't a big hit until Tsar Alexander III deepened the harbour and built a gargantuan naval port at the end of the 1800s. For years the industrial town earned its spot on the map as the home to the first Baltic fleet of Russian submarines, but after WWII the Soviets occupied what was left of the bombed-out burg and turned it into a strategic military base.

LATVIA

For the last decade, Liepāja (pronounced lee-ah-*pa*-yah) has been going about searching for its identity like an angsty teenager. The city's growing pains are evident in the visual clash of gritty warehouses stacked next to swish hipster bars and tricked-out nightclubs. The local tourist office markets Liepāja as 'the place where wind is born', but we think the city's rough-around-the-edges garage-band scene is undoubtedly the city's biggest draw.

Orientation

Liepāja occupies a slim neck of land (about 2km to 3km wide) between Lake Liepāja and the sea, connected by the man-made Tirdzniecības Canal. The train and bus stations both sit north of the canal, while the city centre lies to the south. Crumbling Karosta, a must-see, is 4km north of the city centre. At the time of writing, the Karosta Bridge, connecting the two touristy parts of town, was under reconstruction, so traffic was flowing around Korstas kanāls instead.

Information

Banks with ATMs can be found along Lielā iela and Kungu iela.

Sapņu sala (☎ 6348 5333; Lielā iela 12; per hr 0.60Ls; 🕑 9am-9pm) Internet access.

Tourist office (☎ 6348 0808; www.liepaja.lv/turisms; Rožu laukums 3/5; 🕑 9am-7pm Mon-Fri, to 4pm Sat, 10am-3pm Sun Jun-Aug, 9am-5pm Mon-Sat Sep-May) Loads of information and services available to tourists. Hertz rental car located in the coffee shop next door.

Sights

Liepāja is light on sights, so why not head to the **beach** for some R&R. A thin greenbelt known as **Jūrmala Park** acts as a buffer between the soft dunes and tatty urban core.

KAROSTA

Off limits to everyone during the Soviet occupation, Karosta is a former Russian naval base encompassing about one-third of Liepāja's city limits. From ageing army barracks to ugly Soviet-style, concrete apartment blocks (many abandoned), evidence of the occupation still remains.

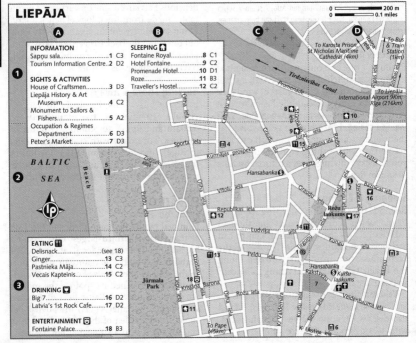

A detention facility until 1997, today grungy **Karosta Prison** (Karostas cietums; ☎ 2636 9470; www.karostascietums.lv; Invalīdu 4; tour 2Ls, 2hr reality show 5Ls, sleepover reality show 10Ls; ☺ 10am-6pm May-Sep, by appointment only Oct-Apr) is a must-see for tourists. Originally designed as an infirmary in 1900, the Soviets quickly turned it into a military prison even before the building was completed.

Daily tours from noon to 5pm, given in a mix of Latvian, Russian and English, detail the history of the prison, which was strictly used to punish disobedient soldiers in the Russian army. Prisoners sat in their decrepit cells for six hours per day, spending the rest of time engaged in gruelling exercises and their training.

If you're craving some serious punishment, or just want to brag that you've spent the night in a Latvian jail, sign up to become a prisoner for the night. You'll be subjected to regular bed checks, verbal abuse by guards in period garb and forced to relieve yourself in the world's most disgusting latrine (seriously). Try booking the night in cell 26 – solitary confinement – you won't be bothered, but the pitch-blackness will undoubtedly drive you off the edge.

For those wanting a pinch of masochism without having to spend the night, there are two-hour 'reality shows' available for those who book ahead. Note that all shows require a quorum of participants.

The stunning **St Nicholas Maritime Cathedral**, with its bulbous cupolas, starkly contrasts the rest of Karosta's bleak architecture. Built in 1901, its stunningly ornate architecture resembles the Russian Orthodox churches from the 17th century, although the gilded domes are supported by four crossed arch vaults rather than columns. During WWI, the church was stripped of its ornate interior decorations, and after years as a cinema and sports complex, the cathedral was restored in the 1990s.

CITY CENTRE

After tackling Karosta, Liepāja's city centre has a couple of touristy treats as well. Make your first stop the **House of Craftsmen** (☎ 6348 0808; Cnr Kungu & Bāriņu iela; admission free; ☺ 10am-5pm) to check out the largest piece of amber in the world (an enormous dangling tapestry) and legions of adorable old women knitting scarves, mittens and blankets available for purchase.

Vendors have touted their wares at **Peter's Market** on Kuršu laukums since the mid-17th century. The market expanded in 1910, when a pavilion was constructed adjacent to the square. Today you'll find stalls inside and out at this bustling complex, selling everything from second-hand clothes and pirated DVDs to fresh fruits and veggies.

The **Liepāja History & Art Museum** (Liepājas vēstures un mākslas muzejs; ☎ 6342 2327; Kūrmājas prospekts 16/18; adult/child 0.50/0.30Ls; ☺ 10am-5pm Wed-Sun Sep-May, 11am-6pm Wed-Sun Jun-Aug) features a variety of impressive displays such as Stone and Bronze Age artefacts unearthed on local archaeological digs, and an interesting collection of old jewellery and weapons and vintage memorabilia from both World Wars. In a second building, visitors will find the **Occupation and Regimes Department** (☎ 6342 0274; K Ukstiņa iela 79; admission free; ☺ 10am-5pm Wed-Sun), which traces the bloody history of the Soviet and Nazi occupations in Latvia, with an emphasis on Liepāja. Captions are in Latvian, but no words are needed to explain the powerful images of the 1939–40 deportations to Siberia (an estimated 2000 people from Liepāja were deported), the genocide committed against Latvian Jews, and the 1991 fight for independence.

Festivals & Events

Every July, Latvia's 1st Rock Cafe (see p246) helps throw the **Baltic Beach Party** (www.baltic beachparty.lv), fast becoming a must-stop on the Eastern Europe party circuit. In August it puts on the **Amber of Liepāja** (www.liepajas dzintars.lv) rock festival.

Sleeping

There are a gaggle of budget digs out in Karosta, including a former Soviet military prison (opposite).

Traveller's Hostel (☎ 2869 0106; www.liepajahostel .com; Republikas iela 25; dm 10Ls; ☐) The top choice in town for penny-pinchers, this friendly spot in an old brick house, has five bright rooms and oodles of common space. Prices drop to 5Ls per night for backpackers staying three nights or more. Wash/dry laundry costs 6Ls. Search 'Liepaja Hostel' on YouTube to watch a couple of short clips about the hostel. Wi-fi available.

Hotel Fontaine (☎ 6342 0956; www.fontaine.lv; Jūras iela 24; r from 20Ls; ☐) You'll either adore or abhor this funky hostel set in a charming 18th-century wooden house with lime-green trim. The whole place feels like a second-hand

LATVIA

store, from the kitschy knick-knack shop used as the reception, to the 20-plus rooms stuffed to the brim with rock memorabilia, dusty oriental rugs, bright tile mosaics, Soviet propaganda, and anything else deemed appropriately offbeat. There's a communal kitchen and chill-out space in the basement. Some rooms are located in a second wooden house out the back.

Fontaine Royal (☎ 6343 2005; www.fontaineroyal .lv; Stūrmaņu iela 1; d 30-45Ls, d with shared bathroom 23Ls,) Everything is gaudy and gilded here at Hotel Fontaine's flashy fraternal twin. The amount of gold trimming and sparkly spray paint is blinding – it's sorta like sleeping in a framed Renaissance painting – although we much prefer staying here than at one of the drab cookie-cutter motels around town. Wi-fi available.

Roze (☎ 6342 1155; www.parkhotel-roze.lv; Rožu iela 37; s/d from 39/47Ls) Stylish and comfortable, this pale-blue wooden guesthouse near the sea was once a summer home for the elite, and still has a certain Art Nouveau styling. Rooms are spacious, and each is uniquely decorated with antique wallpaper and sheer drapery. Extras include satellite TVs, a sauna, and a gazebo-ed garden in the yard.

Promenade Hotel (☎ 6348 8288; www.promenade hotel.lv; Vecā Ostmala 40; s/d/ste from 55/65/90Ls; 🖳) The poshest hotel in Kurzeme lives in an enormous harbour warehouse that was once used to store grain. Wi-fi available.

Eating

The city's drinking and entertainment venues also have menus with Latvian and international favourites.

Delisnack (☎ 6348 8523; Dzintaru iela 4; mains 1.40-7.50Ls; 🕒 24hr) Attached to Fontaine Palace, Liepāja's cheapest chow joint was designed with the inebriated partier in mind: the American-style burgers are a fool proof way to sop up some of those vodka shots downed earlier in the evening.

Vecais Kapteinis (Old Captain; ☎ 6342 5522; Dubelsteina iela 14; mains 3-8Ls) Housed in a timber-framed building dating to 1773, the 'Old Captain' generates a romantic nautical theme with maritime curios and a lengthy seafood menu. The separate Italian menu is slightly cheaper and not half bad.

Ginger (cnr Peldu & Uliha iela; mains from 6Ls; 🕒 11am-11pm Mon-Sat, noon-11pm Sun) A new spot on the edge of Jūrmala Park, Ginger's colourful sushi menu is an instant hit with the locals.

Pastnieka Māja (☎ 6340 7521; Brīvzemnieka iela 53; mains 6-12Ls; 🕒 11am-midnight) This ultraslick two-level restaurant is housed in the city's old post office (*pastnieka māja* means 'post-office house'). The menu features traditional Latvian favourites, as well as a few very exotic offerings: chase your 'bulls' balls' (you'll see) with a pint of Līvu alsu, Liepāja's local beer.

Drinking & Entertainment

Liepāja has a reputation throughout Latvia as the centre of the country's rock-music scene, and taking in a concert is a real treat. Even if you can't understand the lyrics, just being a part of the screaming, pulsating masses is a cultural experience you won't soon forget.

Latvia's 1st Rock Cafe (☎ 6348 1555; Stendera iela 18/20; www.pablo.lv; cover free-5Ls; 🕒 8am-6pm) There's no way you'll miss this massive three-storey structure with loads of shiny windows and a pseudo-industrial look. Restaurants, bars, dance floors, billiards and a rooftop beer garden are all rolled into one mega-complex. The walls are plastered with old concert posters, and Pablo, the roaring basement club, features live music every night and rave parties on the weekends. Don't forget to buy your Hard Rock Café T-shirt…er…we mean…1st Rock Cafe…

Fontaine Palace (☎ 6348 8510; Dzirnavu iela 4; 🕒 24hr) Yet another establishment of the Fontaine name fame, this never-closing rock house lures loads of live acts that jam over the crowd of sweaty fanatics.

Big 7 (☎ 6342 7318; Baznīcas iela 14/16; 🕒 noon-7am Fri & Sat) This giant complex offers a little bit of everything. Divided into multiple sections for dancing, drinking, eating and chilling, it also offers stripteases, pool and slot machines. Head upstairs to King 7 if you want to zone out on couches and pillows or fill your lungs with hookah smoke (6Ls per hookah).

Getting There & Away

Liepāja's **bus & train stations** (☎ 6342 7552; Rīgas iela) are rolled into one, linked by tram 1 with Lielā iela in the downtown. There are convenient daily bus services to/from Rīga (4.50Ls to 5.40Ls, 3½ to 4½ hours, two or three hourly), Kuldīga (2Ls to 2.40Ls, 1¾ to three hours, eight daily), Pāvilosta (1.60Ls, 70 minutes, five daily) and Ventspils (3.30Ls, 2¼ to three hours, seven daily).

The city's **airport** (☎ 6340 7592; www.liepaja-airport.lv; Lidostas iela 8) offers five daily airBaltic flights to/from Liepāja. One-way tickets start at 1Ls if purchased in advance, or 4Ls if booked in the same month as the flight.

At the time of research, ferries were no longer operating in and out of Liepāja.

SOUTHERN LATVIA (ZEMGALE)

A long snake-like strip of land between Rīga and the Lithuanian border, Southern Latvia has been dubbed the 'bread basket' of Latvia for its plethora of arable lands and mythical forests. The region is known locally as Zemgale, named after the defiant Baltic Semigallian (or Zemgallian) tribe who inhabited the region before the German conquest at the end of the 1200s. The Semigallians were a valiant bunch, warding off the impending crusaders longer than any other tribe. Before retreating to Lithuania, they burned down all of their strongholds rather than surrendering them to the invaders.

From the 16th to the 18th centuries, the region (along with Kurzeme) formed part of the semi-independent Duchy of Courland, whose rulers set up shop with two mind-boggling palaces in the town of Jelgava (called Mitau) and in Rundāle, just outside of Bauska. Today, the summer palace at Rundāle is Zemgale's star attraction, and a must-see for art and architecture buffs.

BAUSKA
pop 10,210

Wish Bauska a happy birthday – the rural township turned 400 years old in 2009, but we don't think it looks a day over 380. Centuries ago, little Bauska was an important seat in the Duchy of Courland, but today it's best known as the jumping-off point for the splendid Rundāle Palace (p248). Before leaving town, swing by the **tourist office** (☎ 6392 3797; www.bauska.lv; Rātslaukums 1; ☯ 9am-6pm Mon-Fri, to 3pm Sat). Staff will point you in the direction of a couple of interesting sights around town, including the **Bauska Castle Ruins** (Bauskas pilsdrupas; ☎ 6392 3793; admission 0.50Ls; ☯ 9am-7pm May-Sep, to 6pm Oct). Sitting on an artificial hillock between the snak-

ing Mēmele and Mūsa Rivers, the stone ruins were once a stronghold for Livonian knights in the 15th century, while the more modern half, known as the New Castle, was constructed as the residence for the Duke of Courland in the 16th century. Take a good look at the grey blocks along the facade of the New Castle – they appear to be bulging out of the wall, but it's actually an optical illusion – the lower left corner of each brick has been scraped with a chisel to trick the viewer into thinking that they are seeing a shadow.

The **Bauska Castle Museum**, located within the castle grounds, will open sometime during 2009 and display various archaeological finds and a collection of 16th- and 17th-century art.

During the 18th century, an Italian by the name of Magno Cavala moved to Bauska in search of a new business venture. He was something of a casanova (and a conman), and started collecting the water at the junction of the two rivers near the castle. He claimed that the water was a pungent love potion and made a fortune scamming the poor townspeople.

To find the castle ruins from the bus station, walk towards the central roundabout along Zaļā iela then branch left along Uzvaras iela for another 800m.

Sleeping & Eating

Bauska's one-stop shopping mall at the roundabout along Route A7 has a Rimi supermarket and a couple of decent spots to grab a meal.

Rozmalas (☎ 6779 1178; www.rozmalas.lv; Ceraukste; s/d from 25/40Ls) Rozmalas can be spotted from miles down the road with its signature wooden windmill. The 'farming chic' theme continues on the inside – keys are strung to teeny sacs of grain, and barn-like accoutrements adorn the rooms and spa. The modern restaurant spins a variety of upmarket fare, not to mention a colourful assortment of Emihls Gustavs chocolates (which you'll find on your pillow if you're staying the night). Rozmalas is located 7km east of Bauska at the Ceraukste bus stop.

Day & Night (☎ 6399 1000; www.hoteldayandnight.lv; Slimnīcas iela 7; s/d from 40/55Ls) If you somehow get stuck in Bauska for the night, try this newly renovated orange-and-grey monster near the bus station.

LATVIA

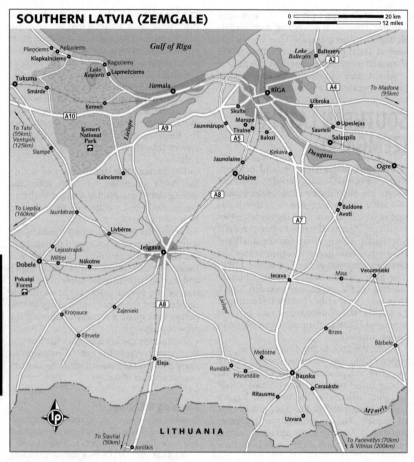

SOUTHERN LATVIA (ZEMGALE)

Getting There & Away

Bauska's **bus station** (☎ 6392 2477; Slimnīcas iela 11) offers at least three buses per hour between 7am and 10pm to/from Rīga (1.90Ls, 70 minutes to 1½ hours). For transport details to Rundāle Palace, see below.

RUNDĀLE PALACE

Built for Baron Ernst Johann Biron (1690–1772), Duke of Courland, between 1736 and 1740, **Rundāle Palace** (Rundāles pils; ☎ 6396 2197; www.rundale.net; garden 1Ls, palace adult/child 2.50/2Ls, combined ticket adult/child 5/4.30Ls, guided group tour 32Ls; ⏱ 10am-7pm Jun-Aug, to 6pm Sep-Oct, to 5pm Nov-Apr) is a monument to 18th-century aristocratic ostentatiousness, and rural Latvia's primo architectural highlight.

Ernst Johann had a tumultuous time as the Duke of Courland. After the death of Empress Anna Ioannovna, he was named Regent of Russia, but vying aristocratic houses quickly became threatened by his power and they banished the duke to Siberia. After he'd spent 22 years in exile, Catherine the Great restored his title and gave him back his duchy. During the greater part of his reign, Ernst Johann lived at his main palace in Jelgava (p250), now used as a university, and summered here in Rundāle.

During court times the castle was divided into two halves; the **East Wing** was devoted to formal occasions, while the **West Wing** was the private royal residence. The **Royal Gardens**, inspired by the gardens at Versailles, were also used for public affairs. Of the palace's 138 rooms, around 40 are open to visitors. The rooms were heated by a network of 80 porcelain stoves (only six authentic stoves remain) as the castle was mostly used during the warmer months. Only three rooms in the West Wing are completely restored: the duchess' bedroom, boudoir and toilette. The **Toilette Room** is adorned with a playful colour scheme – even the chamber pot has a delightful painting of swimming salmon. The room is quite quaint compared with the rest of the castle, largely because the ceiling is noticeably low. Maid's quarters were cleverly lofted about the bathroom, which were accessed through the hidden door in the **Duchess' Bedroom** (note the slit in the wall next to the duchess' bed).

Rundāle was used in several different capacities between being a royal residence and a museum. During WWI the castle's **White Room** (the main ballroom) was turned into a hospital for wounded soldiers. If you aren't too distracted by the ornate ceiling (depicting the four seasons), look closely at the milky white walls (especially along the far wall opposite the entrance); you may notice small engravings and initials made by bored soldiers during their rehabilitation. Similarly, if you take a good look in some of the other restored rooms, you'll find the monogram 'EJ' (for Ernst Johann) incorporated into the Baroque decor. After the war, the **Gold Room** (the throne room) was used as a granary, and later on, parts of the castle were turned into a makeshift school. The **Marble Room** was the basketball court, and reliefs of Romanesque busts mark the spots where the nets used to hang.

The palace became a museum in the 1970s when a team of historians dug out the detailed plans of the original palace layout and began the lengthy restoration process. Carefully detailed notes were left by the palace's Italian architect, Bartolomeo Rastrelli, who supposedly designed his first palace at 21 years old! After studying architecture in Paris, Rastrelli quickly earned his reputation as a baroque genius and was appointed court architect to the Russian royal family. He would later design the palace in Jelgava, and mostly notably, the awe-inspiring Winter Palace in St Petersburg.

Like any good castle, Rundāle has loads of eerie ghost tales, but the most famous spectre that haunts the palace grounds is the 'White Lady'. In the 19th century, the royal doctor had a young daughter who was courted by many men, but on her 18th birthday she suddenly grew ill and died. Obsessed with her untimely demise, the doctor kept her corpse in his laboratory to study her and tried to figure out why she was ravaged by illness (or was she poisoned by a lovelorn suitor?). Unable to rest eternally, the daughter's spirit began haunting the castle and cackling wildly in the middle of the night. During Rundāle's restorations, several art historians and masons heard her wicked laughter and brought in a special priest to exorcise the grounds.

Sleeping & Eating

Balta Māja (☎ 6396 2140; www.kalpumaja.lv; Rundāle; dm/d 10/14Ls) The 'White House' is a quaint B&B and cafe sitting in the palace's Tudor-style servants' quarters near the entrance to the grounds. Salads and meat platters are prepped in the kitchen, and the handful of bedrooms are cluttered with wool duvets and agrarian antiques.

our pick Mežotne Palace (☎ 6396 0711; www.mezo tnespils.lv; Mežotne; s/d/ste 50/75/125Ls) Live like Duke Ernst Johann and check into Mežotne Palace, about 2km from Rundāle. The palace was built in a classical style from 1797 to 1802 for Charlotte von Lieven, the governess of Russian Empress Catherine II's grandchildren. After many years in disrepair, it was restored in 2001 and transformed into a hotel and restaurant. A handful of rooms are open to the public for a small fee, although a visit to Mežotne isn't worth the trek if you aren't sleeping over or eating at the popular restaurant. Rooms are stocked with aristocratic collectibles – think cast-iron bed frames, swinging chandeliers and carefully chosen antiques.

Rundāle Palace Restaurant (☎ 6396 2116; salads from 1.20Ls, mains from 4Ls) Located in the palace basement, it's a convenient spot for a quick bite. Most of the food is of the Latvian persuasion.

Getting There & Away

Rundāle Palace is about 12km west of Bauska along Rte P103. Reaching the palace will require some planning and patience if you are not on a guided tour or have your own set of wheels. Those taking public transport will arrive in Bauska (p247), and must switch to a Rundāle-bound bus. Make sure you get off at Pilsrundāle, the village before Rundāle. From Bauska there are nine Pilsrundāle buses daily (0.35Ls) between 8am and 4.30pm.

LATVIA

JELGAVA

pop 65,635

Jelgava was once known as the most beautiful city in Latvia – even more stunning than Rīga. Duke Ernst Johann, who summered in Rundāle (p248), built his main castle here, and for 200 years (between the 16th and 18th centuries) it was the capital of the Duchy of Courland. During the World Wars, Jelgava was bombed to high hell, and today the city is nothing more than Zemgale's biggest town and commercial centre.

Even though most of the city's aristocratic flavour was incinerated, Jelgava is a pleasant pit stop if you're travelling between Rīga and the Hill of Crosses (p347) in Lithuania. The duke's castle, the aptly named **Jelgava Palace** (Jelgavas pils; ☎ 6300 5617; www.llu.lv; Leilā iela 2), miraculously still stands, and is currently the home of the Latvian Agricultural University.

If you decide to spend the night, stop by the **tourist office** (☎ 6302 2751; www.jelgava.lv; Pasta iela 37; ☺ 9am-5pm Mon-Fri) for accommodation details.

Buses run every 15 minutes to/from Rīga and Jelgava (0.95Ls to 1.50Ls, 55 minutes) between 5am and 9pm. One or two suburban trains per hour link Rīga and Jelgava (0.95Ls, 50 minutes).

DOBELE & AROUND

pop 11,130

Provincial Dobele, in the far western corner of Zemgale, is the gateway to a vast acreage of mythical forests and meandering rivers. The only attraction of note in the town of Dobele is the impressive **Livonian Order castle ruins**, which date back to the mid-1330s. This brick bastion was built over the original site of an earlier Zemgallian stronghold. In 1289, the Zemgallians incinerated their own castle and fled to Lithuania rather than surrender the structure to the invading crusaders. A **monument** in town commemorates their departure.

Dobele is easily accessible by bus to/from Rīga (2.30Ls, 1½ hours), which stops in Jelgava along the way. The nearby forest reserves are best reached by car.

Pokaiņi Forest

Located 13km southwest of Dobele, the **Pokaiņi Forest Reserve** (☎ 6372 6212, 6376 2334; www .mammadaba.lv; adult/child 1.20/0.60Ls, car 1Ls, camping per day 1Ls; ☺ toll booth 10am-7pm) is one of Latvia's biggest unsolved mysteries. In the mid-'90s, a local historian discovered subtle stone cairns throughout the park and realised that the rocks had been transported to the forest from faraway destinations. Historians have theorised that Pokaiņi was an ancient sacred ground used in protopagan rituals over 2000 years ago. Recent volunteer efforts have helped create walking trails through the reserve, which is often visited by healers and New Age-y types. Ask at the toll booth for available tour guides.

Tērvete

The town of Tērvete, 18km south of Dobele, sits amongst scores of ancient Zemgallian castle mounds. **Tērvete Nature Park** (☎ 6372 6212; www.tervete.lv; adult/child 2/1.20Ls, car 10Ls) protects three of these ancient mounds, including the impressive **Tērvete Castle Mound**, which was abandoned by the Zemgallians after several battles with the Livonian Order. Nearby **Klosterhill** was first inhabited over 3000 years ago by Zemgallian ancestors, and **Swedish Hill** was constructed by the Livonian Order in the 13th century.

In recent years, the nature park has built a variety of family attractions such as the **Fairy Tale Forest**, filled with whimsical woodcarvings. A witch lives in the park during the summer entertaining the little ones with games and potions. At the park's **History Museum** (☺ May-Oct), visitors can learn about the history of Zemgallia through artefacts and costumes.

NORTHEASTERN LATVIA (VIDZEME)

When Rīga's urban hustle fades into a pulsing hum of chirping crickets, you've entered Northeastern Latvia. Known as Vidzeme, or 'the Middle Land', to locals, the country's largest region is an excellent sampler of what Latvia has to offer. Forest folks can hike, bike or paddle through the thicketed terrain of Gauja National Park, ski bums can tackle bunny slopes in the Uplands, and history buffs will be sated with a generous sprinkling of castles throughout.

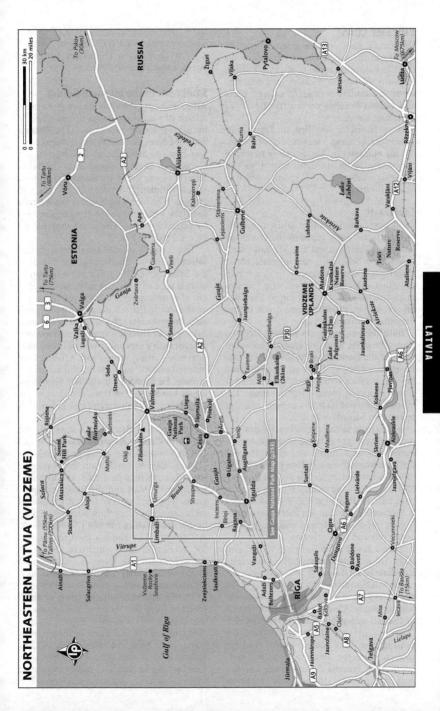

VIDZEME COAST

Vidzeme's stone-strewn coast is usually seen from the car window by travellers on the Via Baltica en route to Rīga or Tallinn. Those who stop for a closer look will uncover a desolate strand of craggy cliffs and pebble beaches carved from eons of pounding waves.

Buses north from Rīga to Pärnu and Tallinn travel along Vidzeme's coastal road, usually stopping in Ainaži before touching the border. Suburban trains from Rīga run as far as Saulkrasti (1.03Ls, one hour, one or two hourly).

Saulkrasti

Saulkrasti, a quick 44km jaunt from the capital, is a closely guarded secret among Latvians. While tourists and Russian jetsetters make a beeline for ritzy Jūrmala, locals gingerly tiptoe up the coast for a day trip in the other direction. The lack of a tourism infrastructure is as refreshing as the salty breeze, so you'd better come quick before the other tourists catch on.

Both the bus and train stations (located across the street from one another) are 900m north of the **tourist office** (☎ 6795 2641; Ainažu iela 10; ⏰ 9am-5pm Mon-Fri). There are plans to move the tourist office across the street to the two-storey shopping plaza. After the move, the office will extend its hours to 6pm, and will operate on Saturdays as well.

It's a cinch to turn your beachy day trip into an overnight extravaganza – scores of bungalows, guesthouses and camp sites dot the pine-fronted sea. Try **Jūras Priede** (☎ 2958 8010; www.juraspriede.lv; Ūpes iela 56a; sites 2Ls, cabins 10Ls) for a teeny log cabin or a spot to pitch your tent. **Pie Maijas** (☎ 6795 1372; www.hotelmaja .lv; Murjāņu iela 3; r from 25Ls) is a friendly cluster of seaside guesthouses within walking distance of the bus and train stations.

Take a break from jumping waves, and head 16km north to visit the bodacious **Munchausen's Estate** (☎ 6406 5633; www.min hauzens.lv; Duntes Estate; ⏰ 10am-5pm Mon-Tue, to 7pm Wed-Sun mid-May–mid-Sep, 10am-5pm mid-Sep–mid-May) in Dunte. Once the retirement home of the tall-tale-teller Baron Karl Friedrich Hieronymus von Munchausen (imagine putting *that* on a business card), and his wife Jacobine, the house is now a wax museum with famous figures from Latvia's past and present (though you might be

hard pressed to recognise any of them). The adjacent forest trail (5.3km) features dozens of wooden characters from the Baron's stories.

Saulkrasti to the Estonian Border

After Saulkrasti, the Vidzeme Coast is a silent stretch of windswept dunes dotted with the occasional lonely guesthouse. The **Vidzeme Rocky Seashore** (☎ 2946 4686; www.lambazi.lv), half-way between Saulkrasti and Salacgrīva, is a scenic spot to stretch your legs. The 14km stretch of protected parkland has rippled sands undulating between tiny capes and caverns. The park's highlight is the **Veczemju Red Cliffs**, a sandstone outcropping crinkled by jagged grottoes. The entire crag has an ethereal reddish hue.

The coast's most substantial town, **Salacgrīva** sits on a harbour at the mouth of the Salaca River. It's still a blink-or-you'll-miss-it type of place, not really worth going out of your way to visit, but if you're hungry on the way to Estonia it makes a good lunch stop. **Zvejnieku Sēta** (☎ 2962 4153; Rīgas iela 1; mains 2-6Ls; ⏰ 11am-11pm) is a friendly seafood restaurant with a pleasing, rustic old-time nautical vibe – creaky wood floors, a fishing boat moored outside and nets draped across the terrace. **Pie Bocmaņa** (☎ 6407 1455; Pērmavas iela 6; mains from 2Ls; ⏰ 11am-11pm), supposedly 'the most legendary fisherman's pub in town', is another option.

Salacgrīva is also the headquarters for the **North Vidzeme Biosphere Reserve** (☎ 6407 1408; www.biosfera.lv; Rīgas iela 10a; ⏰ 8.30am-5pm) a pristine, 4500-sq-km domain that is roughly 6% of Latvia's total land share and inscribed in Unesco's 'Man and the Biosphere' program. The vast reserve is best uncovered on a canoeing or cycling adventure. Stop by the **tourist office** (☎ 6404 1254; Rīgas iela 10a; ⏰ 9am-5pm Mon-Fri) and ask the friendly staff for details on local outfitters, or search for a tour on the internet (free access) at the local **library** (☎ 6407 1995; Silas iela 2; ⏰ 10am-6pm Mon-Fri).

The former shipbuilding town of **Ainaži** (derived from the Liv word *annagi*, meaning 'lonely') is 1km south of Estonia. Its only attraction is the old naval academy, now home to the **Naval School Museum** (☎ 6404 3349; Valdemāra iela 45; admission 0.50Ls; ⏰ 10am-4pm Jun-Aug, closed Sun & Mon Sep-May). This mildly interesting museum exhibits the naval academy's history and the history of shipbuilding along the Vidzeme Coast.

GAUJA NATIONAL PARK

A stunning stretch of virgin pines, **Gauja National Park** (Gaujas nacionālais parks; www.gnp .gov.lv), extends from castle-strewn Sigulda to quiet Valmiera, passing picture-perfect Cēsis and industrial Ligatne along the way. Founded in 1973, Latvia's first national park protects a very leafy hinterland popular for hiking, biking, backcountry camping, canoeing and slew of offbeat adrenalin sports.

The park's main office is located in Sigulda (right). There is no entrance fee for Gauja National Park.

Sigulda
pop 10,700
With a name that sounds like a mythical ogress, it comes as no surprise that the gateway to the Gauja (gow-yah) is an enchanting spot with delightful surprises tucked behind every dappled tree. Locals proudly call their pine-peppered town the 'Switzerland of Latvia', but if you're expecting the majesty of a mountainous snow-capped realm, you'll be rather disappointed. Instead, Sigulda mixes its own brew of scenic trails, extreme sports and 800-year-old castles steeped in legends.

ORIENTATION

Sigulda sprawls between its three castles with most of the action occurring on the east side

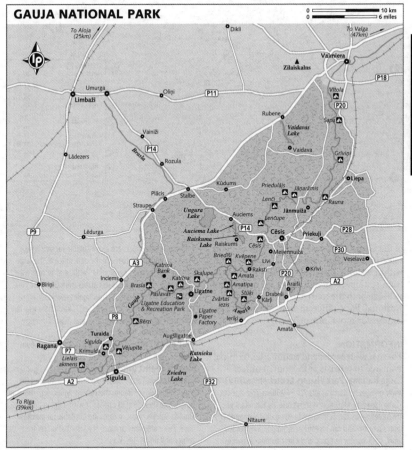

GAUJA NATIONAL PARK

LATVIA

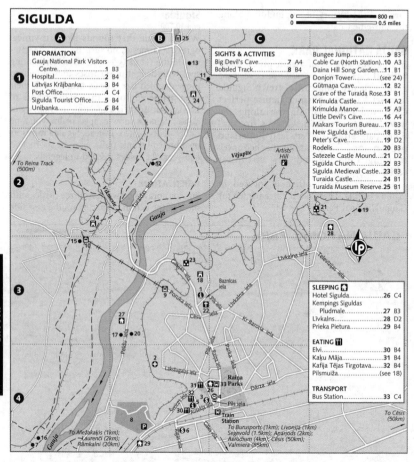

SIGULDA

0 _____ 800 m
0 _____ 0.5 miles

INFORMATION
Gauja National Park Visitors
  Centre........................1 B3
Hospital.........................2 B4
Latvijas Krājbanka............3 B4
Post Office......................4 C4
Sigulda Tourist Office.......5 B4
Unibanka........................6 B4

SIGHTS & ACTIVITIES
Big Devil's Cave................7 A4
Bobsled Track..................8 B4

Bungee Jump....................9 B3
Cable Car (North Station)..10 A3
Daina Hill Song Garden.....11 B1
Donjon Tower..............(see 24)
Gūtmaņa Cave................12 B2
Grave of the Turaida Rose.13 B1
Krimulda Castle..............14 A2
Krimulda Manor...............15 A3
Little Devil's Cave............16 A4
Makars Tourism Bureau.....17 B3
New Sigulda Castle..........18 B3
Peter's Cave...................19 D2
Rodelis..........................20 B3
Satezele Castle Mound....21 D2
Sigulda Church................22 B3
Sigulda Medieval Castle...23 B3
Turaida Castle.................24 B1
Turaida Museum Reserve.25 B1

SLEEPING
Hotel Sigulda.................26 C4
Kempings Siguldas
  Pludmale....................27 B3
Līvkalns........................28 D2
Prieka Pietura.................29 B4

EATING
Elvi..............................30 B4
Kaķu Māja......................31 B4
Kafija Tējas Tirgotava.......32 B4
Pilsmuiža..................(see 18)

TRANSPORT
Bus Station.....................33 C4

---

of the Gauja River near Sigulda castle. A good selection of eating and sleeping options are within walking distance of both the bus and train station. Note that plans are under way to move both the tourist office and the Gauja National Park office to new locations (see listings for more information).

INFORMATION
There is wi-fi access and a computer terminal available to tourists at the tourist office.
Gauja National Park Visitors Centre (☎ 6780 0388; www.gnp.gov.lv; Baznīcas iela 7; 9.30am-7pm Apr-Oct, 10am-4pm Nov-Mar) Access the centre via Pils iela if you are travelling by car. Sells maps to the park, town and cycle routes nearby, and can arrange accommodation, guided tours, backcountry camping and other outdoor activities.

Cold drinks and snacks are also available for purchase. Plans are under way to move the park office to the large white house beside new Sigulda Castle, and to create a visitors centre on Turaidas iela across from Gūtmaņa Cave.
Hospital (☎ 6797 3003; Lakstugalas iela 13)
Latvijas Krājbanka (☎ 6797 2427; Valdemāra iela 1a; 9am-5pm Mon-Fri) One of several ATMs. Currently located next door to the tourist office.
Post office (☎ 6787 1740; Pils iela 2; 8am-6pm Mon, to 5pm Tue-Fri, to 2pm Sat)
Sigulda Tourist Office (☎ 6797 1335; www.sigulda.lv; Valdemāra iela 1a; 10am-7pm Jun-Sep, to 5pm Oct-May) Mountains of information about sights, activities and hotels. The friendly staff can assist with lodging bookings. Sigulda Spiekis discount cards are available for purchase here. There are plans to move the information centre to the corner of Raina & Ausekla iela.

Unibanka (☎ 6797 0172; Rīgas iela 1; ◷ 9am-5pm Mon-Fri) Has a currency-exchange facility.

SIGHTS
Follow our **walking tour** (p257) for an abridged version of Sigulda's greatest hits, and don't forget to take a ride on the **cable car** (☎ 6797 2531; www.lgk.lv; Poruka iela 14; one-way ride 1Ls; ◷ 10am-7.30pm Jun-Aug, 10am-5pm Sat & Sun May-Sep) across the valley for an awesome, aerial perspective.

Turaida Museum Reserve
The centrepiece of Sigulda's **Turaida Museum Reserve** (Turaidas muzejrezervats; ☎ 6797 1402; www.turai da-muzejs.lv; Turaidas iela 10; admission 3Ls; ◷ 10am-9pm May-Oct, 10am-5pm Nov-Apr) is the stunning **Turaida Castle** (Turaidas pils; ◷ 10am-6pm May-Oct, to 5pm Nov-Apr), a red-brick archbishop's castle founded in 1214 on the site of a Liv stronghold. It's no surprise that Turaida means 'God's Garden' in ancient Livonian; the castle's position on an enviable knoll is nothing short of a fairy tale. A **museum** inside the castle's 15th-century granary offers a rather interesting account of the Livonian state from 1319 to 1561, and additional exhibitions can be viewed in the 42m-high **Donjon Tower**, and the castle's western and southern towers.

The rest of the reserve features a variety of houses that have been transformed into small galleries and exhibits. As you make your way to the castle, don't forget to pay your respects to ill-fated Maija Roze (see the boxed text, below) at her onyx headstone, which bears the inscription 'Turaidas Roze 1601–1620'. The hillside behind her tombstone is known as Daina Hill (Dainu kalns) and shelters the **Daina Hill Song Garden**. The *daina* (poetic folk song) is a major Latvian tradition, and the hillside is dotted with sculptures dedicated to epic Latvian heroes immortalised in the *dainas*.

Krimulda Castle & Manor
On the northern side of the valley, a track leads up from near the bridge to ruined **Krimulda Castle** (Krimuldas pilsdrupas), built between 1255 and 1273 and once used as a guesthouse for visiting dignitaries. Only one original wall remains. The big white building just west of the northern cable-car station is **Krimulda Manor** (Krimuldas muižas pils; Mednieku iela 3), built in 1897, confiscated by the government in 1922 and later turned into a tuberculosis hospital. Today it is a sanatorium.

Sigulda Castles
Little remains of **Sigulda Medieval Castle** (Siguldas pilsdrupas), a **knights' stronghold**, built between 1207 and 1226 among woods on the northeastern edge of Sigulda. The castle hasn't been repaired since the Great Northern War, but its ruins are perhaps more evocative as a result. There's a great view through the trees to the archbishop's reconstructed Turaida Castle, on the far side of the valley.

On the way to the ruins from town, you'll pass **Sigulda Church** (Siguldas baznīca; 2 Baznīcas iela), built in 1225 and rebuilt in the 17th and 18th centuries, and also the 19th-century **New Sigulda Castle** (Siguldas jaunā pils), a

---

THE ROSE OF TURAIDA

Sigulda's local beauty, Maija Roze (May Rose), was taken into Turaida Castle as a little girl when she was found among the wounded after a battle in the early 1600s. She grew into a famous beauty and was courted by men from far and wide, but her heart belonged to Viktors, a humble gardener at nearby Sigulda Medieval Castle. They would meet in secret at Gūtmaņa Cave halfway between the two castles.

One day, a particularly desperate soldier among Maija Roze's suitors lured her to the cave with a letter forged in Viktors' handwriting. When Maija Roze arrived, the soldier set his kidnapping plan in motion. Maija Roze pleaded with the soldier and offered to give him the scarf from around her neck in return for her freedom. She claimed it had magical protective powers, and to prove it, she told him to swing at her with his sword. It isn't clear whether or not she was bluffing or if she really believed in the scarf – either way, the soldier duly took his swing and killed the beauty.

The soldier was captured, convicted and hanged for his crime. Court documents have been uncovered, proving that the tale was in fact true. Today, a small stone memorial commemorates poor Maija Roze, the Rose of Turaida.

SIGULDA SPIEĶIS

While roaming around Sigulda, you'll probably spot several candy cane–shaped walking sticks – these are known as *spieķis*, the symbol of Sigulda. The town's brand new discount card goes by the same name, and offers great deals (even freebies) at museums, restaurants and hotels. The card (adult/child 11/5.50Ls) lasts for 24 hours after 'activation' and can be purchased at the Sigulda Tourist Office.

---

sanatorium and former residence of the Russian Prince Kropotkin.

Gūtmaņa Cave

The largest erosion cave in the Baltic is most famous for its role in the tragic legend of the Rose of Turaida (see boxed text, p255). Most tourists visit to peruse the inordinate amount of graffiti spread along the walls – some of it dates back to the 16th century – apparently eagle eyes have found the coats of arms of long-gone hunters. Some believe that the stream water flowing out of the cave has a magical blend of minerals that remove facial wrinkles (it didn't work for us).

ACTIVITIES

If you're looking to test your limits with a bevy of adrenalin-pumping activities, then you've come to the right place. Those looking for something more subdued will enjoy hiking and cycling trails through the national park's shady pines, or canoeing down the lazy Gauja River.

High-Adrenalin Sports

Sigulda's 1200m artificial **bobsled track** (☎ 6797 3813; Sveices iela 13) was built for the former Soviet bobsleigh team. Today, the track hosts a portion of the European luge championships every January. In winter you can fly down the 16-bend track at 80km/h in a five-person **Vučko tourist bob** (ride per person 6Ls; ☺ noon-7pm Sat & Sun Oct-Mar), or contact Karīna at the **Makars Tourism Bureau** (☎ 924 4948; www.makars.lv; Peldu iela 1) for the real Olympian experience on the hair-raising **winter bob** (ride per person 35Ls). Summer speed fiends can ride a wheeled **summer sled** (ride per person 6Ls; ☺ 11am-6pm Sat & Sun May-Sep) without booking in advance.

If the bobsled wasn't enough to make you toss your cookies, take your daredevil shenanigans to the next level and try a 43m **bungee jump** (☎ 2644 0660; www.bungee.lv; Poruka iela 14; Friday/weekend jump 20/25Ls; ☺ 7.30pm to last jump Fri-Sun May-Sep) from the bright orange cable car that glides over the Gauja River high up in the clouds. Weekday jumps can sometimes be arranged with an advance booking.

The one-of-a-kind **aerodium** (☎ 2838 4400; www.aerodium.lv; Hwy A2; 2min ride weekday/weekend 15/18Ls, additional min weekday/weekend 5/6Ls; ☺ 4-10pm Mon-Fri, noon-8pm Sat & Sun May-Sep) is a giant wind tunnel that propels participants up into the sky as though they were flying. Instructors can get about 15m high, while first-timers usual rock out at about 3m. Even though you will only be airborne for a couple of minutes, there is a brief introductory course before going skyward, so give yourself a full hour to participate and call in advance. To find the wind tunnel, look for the sign along the highway and follow a dirt road down a small hill past Sigulda Bloks warehouse.

For something a bit tamer, head to **Rodelis** (☎ 2700 1187; www.rodelis.lv; Peldu iela; toboggan track 1/6 rides 2/10Ls ropes course adult/child 9/5Ls; ☺ 10am-9pm May-Oct), across the street from the Makars Tourism Bureau, to swish down a **toboggan track** or monkey around on the 'Tarzan' ropes course. There's a ropes course at **Mežakaķis** (☎ 6797 1624; www.kakiskalns.lv; Senču iela 1; adult/child 12/6.50Ls; ☺ 10am-7pm May-Oct) as well.

Hiking & Cycling

Sigulda is prime hiking territory so bring your walking shoes. A popular (and easy) route is the 40-minute walk from Krimulda Castle to Turaida Museum Reserve via Gūtmaņa Cave and Viktors' Cave. Or you can head south from Krimulda and descend to **Little Devil's Cave** and **Big Devil's Cave**, cross the river via footbridge, and return to Sigulda (about two hours). Note the black walls in Big Devil's Cave, which are believed to be from the fiery breath of a travelling demon that took shelter here to avoid the sunlight. Check out the handy brochure at the Sigulda Tourist Office detailing a half-day walking route linking all three castles in the region.

East of Sigulda, try the well-marked loop that joins **Peter's Cave**, **Satezele Castle Mound** and **Artists' Hill**; it starts from behind the Līvkalns hotel and takes about 1½ hours. The panoramic view of Turaida Castle and the Gauja River valley from Artists' Hill is spectacular.

The Gauja National Park Visitors Centre (p254) has details of plenty more walks in the national park. Particularly interesting are its day- and night-time birdwatching and bird-song discovery walks. The park office also sells a variety of biking route maps throughout the park and beyond.

Many outfitters around Sigulda offer daily bicycle and mountain bike rentals for around 7Ls to 10Ls per day. Try **Burusports** (☎ 6797 2051; www.burusports.lv; Mazā Gāles iela 1; ☺ noon-8pm Mon, 10am-8pm Tue-Sat), **Rāmkalni** (☎ 6797 7277; www .ramkalni.lv; Inčukalna pagasts; ☺ 9am-10pm), **Reiņa Track** (☎ 2927 2255; www.reinatrase.lv; Krimulda pagasts; ☺ 2pm-midnight Mon-Thu, to 1am Fri, 10am-1am Sat, 9am-11pm Sun) or **Makars Tourism Bureau** (☎ 924 4948; www.makars.lv; Peldu iela 1).

Canoeing & Boating

Floating down the peaceful Gauja River is a great way to observe this pristine area and have a couple of wildlife encounters (if you're lucky). There are camping grounds all along the stretch of river from Cēsis to Sigulda. Team up with one of the outfitters within the national park that organises boat trips along the Gauja, or you can just head upstream, stick your arse in an innertube, and float back to town.

On the banks of the river in Sigulda, inside the Gauja National Park, **Makars Tourism Bureau** (☎ 924 4948; www.makars.lv; Peldu iela 1) arranges one- to three-day water tours in two- to four-person boats from Sigulda, Līgatne, Cēsis and Valmiera, ranging in length from 3km to 85km. Tours cost between 10Ls and 60Ls per boat including equipment, transport between Sigulda and the tour's starting point, and camp-site fees for up to four people. Tents, sleeping bags and life jackets can also be rented for a nominal fee. For the less intrepid paddler, Makars rents out canoes and rubber boats seating between two and six people starting at 10Ls per day.

Reāmkalni (☎ 6797 7277; www.ramkalni.lv; Inčukalna pagasts; ☺ 9am-10pm) and **Reiņa Track** (☎ 2927 2255; www.reinatrase.lv; Krimulda pagasts; ☺ 2pm-midnight Mon-Thu, to 1am Fri, 10am-1am Sat, 9am-11pm Sun) also rent out boating equipment.

WALKING TOUR: CASTLES DAY TRIP

If you're short on time, or visiting Sigulda on a day trip, the town's three main castle reserves and one legendary cave can be easily tackled in an afternoon.

If you just arrived from the train or bus station, walk down Raiņa iela to linden-lined Pils iela until you reach **Sigulda New Castle (1)**, built in the 18th century during the reign of German aristocrats. Check out the ruins of **Sigulda Medieval Castle (2)** around the back, which was constructed in 1207 by the Order

---

WALK FACTS

Start Sigulda Train Station
Finish Turaida Museum Reserve
Distance 6km
Duration 4½ hours (leisurely pace)

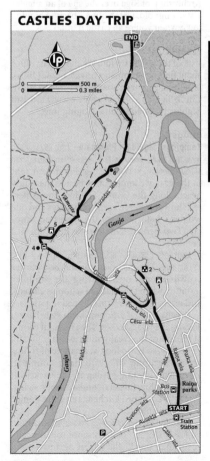

CASTLES DAY TRIP

of the Brethren of the Sword, but now lies mostly in ruins after being severely damaged in the 18th century during the Great Northern War. Follow Ainas iela to the rocky precipice and take the **cable car (3)** over the scenic river valley to **Krimulda Manor (4)**, an elegant estate currently used as a rehabilitation clinic. After exploring the grounds, check out the crumbling ruins of **Krimulda Medieval Castle (5)** nearby, then follow the serpentine road down to **Gūtmaņa Cave (6)**. Immortalised by the legend of the Rose of Turaida (see the boxed text, p255), it's the largest erosion cave in the Baltic. Take some time to read the myriad inscriptions carved into the walls then head up to the **Turaida Museum Reserve (7)**. The medieval castle was erected in the 13th century for the Archbishop of Rīga over the site of an ancient Liv stronghold. Catch bus 12 back to Sigulda town when you're all castle'd out.

SLEEPING

If all of the hotels are full, ask the tourist office about finding a room in a private home (10Ls), or renting your own apartment (25Ls to 50Ls). Check Sigulda's official website www.tourism .sigulda.lv for additional lodging info.

Budget

Kempings Siguldas Pludmale (☎ 2924 4948; www.makars.lv; Peldu iela 2; person/tent/car/caravan 3/1.50/1.50/6Ls; ⏳ 15 May-15 Sep) Pitch your tent in the grassy camping area beside the sandy beach along the Gauja. The location is perfect; however, there's only one men's and one women's bathroom for the scores of campers. Two-person tents can be hired for 4Ls per day.

Laurenči (☎ 6797 1852; Laurenču iela; dm 7-10Ls; ⏳ Jun-Aug) The best deal for the backpacker crowd is only open during the summer months (when the attached school is closed), and offers spartan rooms dipped in pastels.

Livonija (☎ 6797 0916; www.livonija.viss.lv; Pulkveža Brieža iela 55; s/tw/d 25/26/30Ls; 🖳) The eight rooms at the top of the creaky staircase vary greatly in quality, so try to look at a couple of rooms before deciding where to hang your hat. There's an inviting garden in the back with bursts of colourful petals and a droopy swing. The fully equipped kitchen is an extra bonus. Wi-fi available.

Livkalns (☎ 6797 0916; www.livkalns.lv; Pēteralas iela; s/d from 25/30Ls) No place is more romantically rustic than this idyllic retreat next to a pond

on the forest's edge. The rooms are pine-fresh and sit among a campus of adorable thatch-roof manors. The cabin-in-the-woods-style restaurant is fantastic. Wi-fi available.

Midrange & Top End

Prieka Pietura (☎ 2921 1630; www.priekapietura.lv; Stacijas iela 6; s/d from 38/45Ls) The three fully equipped apartments in this modern home are outfitted with a mix of natural materials and sleek, monochrome furnishings. As you channel surf on the LCD monitor, you'll think you're in the heart of some cosmopolitan capital rather than in the middle of the sticks. Longer stays can get discounted rates. Wi-fi available.

Hotel Sigulda (☎ 6797 2263; www.hotelsigulda.lv; Pils iela 6; s/d 38/48Ls; 🖳 🖳) A hop, skip and jump from the bus station, this comfortable and modern spot has spacious rooms and standard-issue furniture – rooms on the top floor have sloping ceilings. The steam room and sauna are only open weekends. Wi-fi available.

Segevold (☎ 2647 6652; www.hotelsegevold.lv; Mālpils iela 4b; s/d 40/55Ls; 🖳) After entering the swankified lobby, you'll immediately forget that Segevold is bizarrely located in the heart of an industrial park – the futuristic lighting and giant tentacle-like reliefs starkly contrast the grungy Soviet tractors around the corner. Upstairs, the rooms are noticeably less glam, but they're in mint condition and kept pathologically clean. Wi-fi available.

Aparjods (☎ 6797 2230; www.aparjods.lv; Ventas iela 1; s/d 40/55Ls; 🖳) Now that Aparjods is part of the Best Western conglomerate, most of the inn's country charm feels synthetic. The complex of barn-like structures with reed-and-shingle roofs contains 33 rooms that are cosy but lack any defining character save the subtle pagan symbols carved into the wooden shutters. The hotel is located 1.5km southwest of town. Wi-fi avilable.

EATING & DRINKING

Most of Sigulda's hotels and guesthouses have a small restaurant attached.

Kaķu Māja (☎ 2915 0104; Pils iela 8; mains from 2Ls; ⏳ 8am-11pm, club 10pm-4am) The 'Cat House' is the top spot around town for a cheap bite. In the bistro, point to the ready-made dishes that tickle your fancy, and hunker down on one of the inviting picnic tables outside. For dessert, visit the attached bakery to try out-of-this-world pastries, pies and cakes. On Friday and Saturday nights, the restaurant in the back turns into a nightclub that busts out the disco ball until the wee hours of the morning.

Elvi (☎ 6797 3322; Vidus iela 1; mains from 2Ls; ☺ 9am-10pm Mon-Sat, to 9pm Sun) Elvi is a multiservice supermarket with aisles upon aisles of groceries, a small cafeteria-style restaurant (the meats tend to be undercooked), and a bowling alley upstairs (open until midnight) that serves up some decent grub.

Kafija Tējas Tirgotava (☎ 6797 4032; Valdemāra iela 3; salads 2-5Ls, mains from 5Ls; ☺ 10am-8pm Mon-Thu, to 9pm Fri & Sat, 11am-8pm Sun) The cashier's booth has been fashioned out of an antique apothecary's table stuffed full of dried tea, and the menu looks like a grandmother's photo album with collages of grainy black-and-white snapshots. Portions are on the small side. Enjoy them with an organic beverage or a glass of fine wine.

Pilsmuiža (☎ 6797 1425; Pils iela 16; mains 4-10Ls; ☺ noon-2am) Inside New Sigulda Castle, this eatery overlooks the ruins of the medieval bastion and has panoramic views of the Gauja Valley. The food is typical Latvian fare.

Aparjods (☎ 6797 2230; Ventas iela 1; mains 6-15Ls; ☺ noon-midnight) Aparjods' elegant restaurant gets a special mention for its delectable assortment of cuisine served amongst charming clutters of household heirlooms and gold-embroidered seating. A roaring fire warms the dark-wood dining room in winter, while tables spill out onto the patio during summer. The upmarket atmosphere tends to attract an older clientele.

GETTING THERE & AWAY

Buses trundle the 50-odd km between Sigulda's bus station and Rīga (1Ls, 1¼ hours, two per hour between 8am and 10.30pm).

One train per hour (between 6am and 9pm) travels the Rīga–Sigulda–Cēsis–Valmiera Line and stops in Sigulda. Fares from Sigulda include Rīga (1.11Ls, one or 1¼ hours), Valmiera (1.34Ls, 1¼ hours), Līgatne (0.40Ls, 10 minutes) and Cēsis (0.90Ls, 40 minutes).

GETTING AROUND

Sigulda's attractions are quite spread out and after a long day of walking, bus 12 will become your new best friend. It plies the route to/from Sigulda New Castle, Turaida Castle and Krimulda Manor seven times daily (more on weekends) between 6.30am and 8.30pm.

Bus times are posted at the station and on the info centre's official website.

Līgatne

Deep in the heart of the Gauja National Park, little Līgatne is a twilight zone of opposite extremes. The town's collection of hideous industrial relics sprouts up from a patchwork of picturesque pine forests and cool blue rivulets. Despite the unsightly Soviet reminders, it's worth stopping by for a wildlife photo shoot and a Cold War history lesson.

After entering Līgatne, the road forks in three different directions. If you follow the road as it curves to the right, you will wind your way up a small hill until you reach a dreary Rehabilitation Centre. This is no ordinary rehab hospital; hidden underneath the bland '60s architecture lies a top-secret Soviet bunker, known by its code name, **The Pension** (☎ 6416 1915, 2646 7747; www.rehcentrsligatne.lv; Skaļupes; admission per person 2Ls). When Latvia was part of the USSR, 'The Pension' was one of the most important strategic hideouts during a time of nuclear threat. In fact, the bunker's location was so tightly guarded that it remained classified information until 2003. Almost all of the bunker's 2000 sq metres still look as they did when it was in operation. Tours last up to 1½ hours and can be translated into English and German. All tours must be booked in advance and require a minimum of 10 people. If your group is smaller than 10, ask if you can tag along with a group that has already made a reservation.

Should you decide to follow Līgatne's main road straight on, rather than forking, you will reach a collection of charred crimson brick and soaring smoke stacks known as **Papirfabrika** (Paper Factory; ☎ 2943 4104; Pilsoņu iela 1), Latvia's oldest industrial enterprise. In the not-so-distant past, the plant was used to print maps for the Russian army, and it also minted Estonia's paper currency. Today, the factory is still in operation and continues to use traditional paper-production machinery.

Those who decide to head left will find the **Līgatne Nature Footpath** (☎ 6415 3313; adult/child 2/1Ls; ☺ 9.30am-5pm Mon, to 6.30pm Tue-Sun May-Oct), a nature park where elks, beaver, deer, bison, lynx and wild boar roam in sizable open-air enclosures in the forest. A 5.1km motor circuit and a network of footpaths link a series of observation points, and there's a 22m lookout tower with a fine panorama.

LATVIA

Marked footpaths include a 5.5km nature trail with wild animals, a botanical trail (1.1km), a wild nature trail (1.3km) and a fun fairy-tale trail (900m), which winds its way through a fantastical path of 90-odd wooden sculptures. The nature trails were closed for renovations when we visited, but they are rumoured to be open by the time this guide makes it to the bookstore.

Those who decide to stay the night should check out the adorable **Lāču Miga** (☎ 6415 3481; www.lacumiga.lv; Gaujas iela 22; s/d from 30/40Ls) near the nature trails. Built in a large log chalet, the 'Bears' Den' stays true to its moniker with a gargantuan plush teddy bear positioned at the front entrance. Slews of stuffed bears welcome guests in their rooms – there are even ursine pillows that look like a teddy bear swallowed a giant Rubik's cube. The attached **restaurant** (mains from 3.50Ls; ☉ noon-9pm Mon-Thu, to 10pm Fri, 10am-10pm Sat, to 9pm Sun) offers pleasant outdoor seating overlooking the scenic nature trails nearby.

Before returning to Rte A2, stop by **Vienkoču Parks** (☎ 2932 9065; www.vienkoci.lv; adult/child 2/1Ls; ☉ 10am-6pm). Richards, a local wood carver, has filled a 10-hectare park with his unique creations. Small trails snake past bold modern art installations, a classical garden, sundials and a collection of torture instruments. Rent out the park's rustic cabin (25Ls), lit by candles in the evenings, for a 'back to nature' experience.

Public transport to Līgatne requires a bit of patience. Two buses per hour trundle along the Cēsis–Sigulda route, stopping in Līgatne along the way (1Ls). If you have your own transport, it's a quick 20-minute drive from either Sigulda or Cēsis.

Cēsis
pop 18,260

Cēsis' unofficial moniker, 'Latvia's most Latvian town', is a bit of a chicken-and-the-egg mystery: was Cēsis (pronounced *tsay-sis*) always known by this superlative, or did it only earn the title after the government poured loads of cash into renovating the Old Town? Either way, the nickname pretty much holds true, and day trippers will be treated to a mosaic of quintessential country life – a stunning Livonian castle, soaring church spires, cobbled roads and a lazy lagoon – all wrapped up in a bow like an adorable adult Disneyland.

ORIENTATION
Buses and trains to Cēsis stop in the same place – a five-minute walk from the tourist office. Take Raunas iela to the town's main square Vienības laukums, punctuated by a granite Freedom Monument. A ring road orbits Cēsis medieval core.

INFORMATION
There are two banks with ATMs on Raunas iela between the bus/train station and the main square (Vienības laukums). An internet kiosk is also available at the tourist office (0.30Ls per 10 minutes).

Capital Rīga Datoru Salons (☎ 6410 7111; Rīgas iela 7; per hr 0.60Ls; ☉ 9am-6pm Mon-Fri, to 4pm Sat) Located on the 2nd floor. Twenty computer terminals; wi-fi available.

Cēsis Tourist Office (☎ 6412 1815; www.tourism .cesis.lv; Pils laukums 2; ☉ 9am-7pm Jun-Aug, 9am-6pm Sep-May) Note that there are plans to move the tourist office across the square to Pils laukums 5. Staff can arrange bike rentals (6Ls per day), and accommodation bookings in Cēsis and rural Vidzeme.

DnB Nord (Rigas iela 23; ☉ 7.30am-6.30pm Mon-Fri, to 4.30pm Sat) Bank with 24-hour outdoor ATM.

SIGHTS
Cēsis Castle (Cēsu pils) was founded in 1209 by the Knights of the Sword. Its dominant feature is two stout towers at the western end. To enter, visit **Cēsis History & Art Museum** (Cēsu Vēstures un mākslas muzejs; Pils laukums 9; adult/child 2/1Ls; ☉ 10am-5pm Tue-Sun), in the adjoining 18th-century 'new castle', painted salmon pink. The castle's western tower has a viewpoint overlooking **Castle Park**, which sits along a scenic lake with lily pads. Temporary art exhibitions and chamber-music concerts are held in **Cēsis Exhibition House** (Cēsu Izstāžu nams; ☎ 6412 3557; Pils laukums 9; ☉ 10am-5pm Tue-Sun), next to the tourist office on the same square. The yellow-and-white building housed stables and a coach house (1781) in the 18th and 19th centuries.

Cēsis' Old Town, surrounding Cēsis Castle, is a delightful collection of **wooden houses** (along Rīgas iela), and colourful town squares orbiting the commanding **St John's Church** (Svēta Jāņa baznīca; Skolas iela), built in 1287. During the time of research a lot of construction was under way around the Old Town and will result in altered facades and several refurbished cobbled squares, all in-

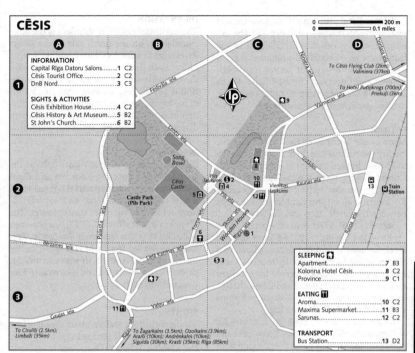

CĒSIS

0 — 200 m
0 — 0.1 miles

INFORMATION
Capital Rīga Datoru Salons........**1** C2
Cēsis Tourist Office..................**2** C2
DnB Nord..............................**3** C3

SIGHTS & ACTIVITIES
Cēsis Exhibition House.............**4** C2
Cēsis History & Art Museum.....**5** B2
St John's Church......................**6** B2

To Cēsis Flying Club (2km);
Valmiera (37km)

To Hotel Putiņkrogs (700m);
Priekuļi (3km)

Song Bowl

Pils laukums

Castle Park
(Pils Park)

Cēsis Castle

Vienibas laukums

Train Station

Wooden Houses

SLEEPING 🏠
Apartment...............................**7** B3
Kolonna Hotel Cēsis................**8** C2
Province.................................**9** C1

EATING 🍴
Aroma....................................**10** C2
Maxima Supermarket...............**11** B3
Sarunas..................................**12** C2

TRANSPORT
Bus Station.............................**13** D2

To Cīruļi (2.5km);
Limbaži (35km)

To Žagarkalns (3.5km); Ozolkalns (3.9km);
Araiši (10km); Andrēnkalni (10km);
Sigulda (30km); Krasti (35km); Rīga (85km)

creasing the town's old-school charm. Keep an eye out for new sights and museums as the renovations wrap up over 2009.

ACTIVITIES

In winter, skiers and snowboarders poodle down the gentle slopes and cross-country trails at **Žagarkalns** (☎ 2626 6266; www.zagarkalns .lv; 3hr lift hire weekday/weekend 5.50/8Ls) and **Ozolkalns** (☎ 2640 0200; www.ozolkalns.lv; 3hr lift hire weekday/ weekend 7/9Ls), the two largest skiing areas in Vidzeme. In summer, they offer bicycle and canoe rentals, and Ozolkalns has a ropes course. Ask at the tourist office to set up a bike rental if you can't make it out to one of the hills.

FESTIVALS & EVENTS

There are concerts and festivals almost every weekend during the summer.

From mid-July to mid-August, Cēsis comes alive on the weekends with performances ranging from symphonies to storytelling held at a variety of venues around town as part of the **Mākslas Festivāls** (www.cesufestivals.com).

SLEEPING

Cēsis has loads of respectable accommodation several kilometres outside of the town centre. Check out www.tourism.cesis.lv for more information and photos. If everything in town seems full, there is a lovely two-room **apartment** (☎ 2914 4339; Rīgas iela 43; ste 60Ls) available above Makss un Morics cafe.

Hostel Putiņkrogs (☎ 6412 0290; www.cdzp.lv; Saules iela 23; s/d with shared bathroom 9/18Ls) Find the sign with a symbol of a fork and knife, and you've just about reached this grubby Soviet-style building. Pass the doors for the convenient store and cafe to find shockingly cheery (and tidy) rooms – even the once-sterile lobby is warmed with a mural of technicolour flowers. The hostel is located 900m from the bus/train station. Wi-fi available.

Province (☎ 6412 0849; www.provincecesis.viss.lv; Niniera iela 6; s/d 30/38Ls) This cute celery-green guesthouse pops out from the dreary Soviet block housing nearby. The five rooms are simple, spotless and sport funky bedspreads. The popular inhouse restaurant in a glass solarium serves up a variety of tasty dishes including a few veggie options (mains start from 2.50Ls).

LATVIA

Kolonna Hotel Cēsis (☎ 6412 0122; www.hotelkol onna.com; Vienības laukums 1; s/d 35/45Ls; 🖳) The exterior is vaguely neoclassical while the inside features rows of standard upmarket rooms. The in-house restaurant serves top-notch Latvian and European cuisine (mains 4Ls to 10Ls) in a formal setting or outdoors in the pristine garden. Wi-fi available.

EATING

Most of the accommodation in Cēsis have quality restaurants attached. Beyond that, the town has a limited amount of worthwhile eats. Consider swinging by **Maxima Supermarket** (Livu Laukums; ⏲ 9am-10pm) to pick up some groceries for a picnic along the rambling stone steps between the castle ruins and the lake.

Sarunas (☎ 6410 7173; Rīgas iela 4; pizzas 2.50-4Ls; ⏲ 10am-11pm Mon-Thu, to 4am Fri & Sat, to 10pm Sun) Sleek Sarunas dishes out decent pizzas to a mix of young locals and older tourists. Grab a booth on the outdoor terrace for excellent views of the central square and Cēsis' charming wooden architecture. A disco ball spins stars on the walls in the evening.

Aroma (☎ 6412 7575; Lencū iela 4; mains 4-8Ls; ⏲ 8am-8pm Mon-Sat, 10am-8pm Sun) Enjoy cake and coffee on the shaded patio overflowing with colourful flowers. At night the back opens into a slick club with an industrial vibe – red walls and silver piping.

GETTING THERE & AWAY

Cēsis's bus and train station can be found in the same location at the roundabout connecting Raunas iela to Raina iela. There are up to five trains per day between 6.35am and 9pm linking Cēsis and Rīga (1.72Ls, 2¾ hours). Bikes are allowed onboard. Two or three buses per hour between 6.15am and 10.20pm ply the route from Rīga to Cēsis (2.50Ls, around two hours). Trains also run to Valmiera (0.71Ls, 30 minutes) and Sigulda (0.90Ls, 40 minutes).

Valmiera
pop 27,465

Although less historic than Sigulda or Cēsis, as most of its Old Town burnt down in 1944, Valmiera (formerly Wolmar) dishes out its own brand of easy small-town charm. About 30km north of Cēsis, it sits at the northeastern tip of the Gauja National Park, and is the only place in Latvia where you can board a canoe in the heart of downtown.

ORIENTATION

The unofficial centre of Valmiera is the large roundabout on the north side of the Gauja River near St Simon's Church and the tourist office. Both the bus and train station are on the opposite side of the river. The bus station is within easy walking distance (500m) of the town centre, but the train station is further afield (1.8km) along Stacijas iela (which diverges from Cēsu iela at the bus station).

INFORMATION

Pilsetas Galerija, the giant glass cube at the roundabout connecting Cēsu iela and Rīgas iela, contains an **Iki supermarket** (⏲ 8am-10pm), a **post office** (⏲ 10am-10pm) and several 24-hour ATMs among other conveniences. The Valmiera **tourist office** (☎ 6420 7177; www.valmiera .lv; Rīgas iela 10; ⏲ 9am-6pm Mon-Fri, 10am-5pm Sat, 10am-3pm Sun Jun-Aug, 9am-6pm Mon-Fri, 10am-3pm Sat Sep-May) has maps and friendly staff who can arrange private accommodation and bike rentals. Free internet and wi-fi available.

SIGHTS

Valmiera's historic area stands on a point of land between the Gauja River ansd a tributary called the Ažkalna. **St Simon's Church** (Svētā Sīmaņa Baznīca; Bruņinieku iela 2) dates to 1283 and shelters a fine 19th-century organ. You can climb its church tower for a donation. Along the same street, you'll find the ruins of **Valmiera Castle**, founded by the Livonian Order in the 13th century.

The **Valmiera Regional Museum** (Valmieras Novadpētniecības muzejs; ☎ 6423 2733; Bruņinieku iela 3; adult/child 0.50/0.30Ls; ⏲ 10am-5pm Mon-Fri, to 3pm Sat) is of limited interest, but it's a good source of information on the district…if you read Latvian. English guides are available for 15Ls.

ACTIVITIES

In town, **Eži** (☎ 6420 7263; www.ezi.lv; Valdemāra iela; ⏲ 9am-7pm Mon-Sat, to 1pm Sun), once a popular hostel, now concentrates solely on outdoor adventures. It organises all sorts of active pursuits from themed one- or two-day hiking and biking excursions to river rafting to zip-wires through the trees (trips start at 20Ls per day). It also rents out mountain bikes (6Ls per day), helmets (2Ls per day), saddlebags and seats for kids (each 2Ls per day) along with canoes (10Ls per day). In winter the company does cross-country skiing tours across lakes and through snow-covered forests complete with picnic lunch cooked over a bonfire in the woods.

SECRETS OF THE GAUJA

Beyond the park's four main towns, there are plenty of hidden treasures tucked deep within the Gauja National Park. If you have a little extra time, try checking out these three gems.

Āraiši

Plopped on an islet in the middle of Āraiši Lake, about 10km south of Cēsis, **Āraiši Lake Fortress** (Āraišu ezerpils; ☎ 6419 7288; adult/child 0.60/0.20Ls; ☼ 10am–6pm May–mid-Oct) is a reconstruction of a settlement inhabited by ancient Latgallians in the 9th and 10th centuries. A wooden walkway leads across the water to the unusual village, which was discovered by archaeologists in 1965. Peering across the lake are the ruins of **Āraiši Stone Castle** (Āraišu mūra pils), built by Livonians in the 14th century and destroyed by Ivan IV's troops in 1577. From here, a path leads to a reconstructed Stone Age settlement – there's a couple of reed dwellings and earth ovens for roasting meat and fish. The fortress and castle, together with the iconic 18th-century **Āraiši windmill** (Āraišu vējdzirnavas), are signposted 1km along a dirt track from the main road and form the **Āraiši Museum Park** (Āraišu muzejparks).

Bīriņi Castle

Like a big pink birthday cake sitting on a verdant lawn, **Bīriņi Castle** (Bīriņu pils; ☎ 6402 4033; www.birinupils.lv; admission 2Ls) governs a scenic tract of land overlooking a tranquil lake. Located on the outer western edges of the Gauja towards Saulkrasti, the baronial estate has been transformed into an opulent hotel (doubles/suites from 48/95Ls) swathed in a Renaissance style focused around the grand foyer staircase. For those without the time (or cash) to spend the night, daytime visitors can still reap the benefits on a guided tour (8Ls), spa session (from 15Ls), or just taking in the lovely scenery with a picnic or a boat ride (2.50Ls). Operating hours can be erratic (especially in the summer when there's a wedding every week). Call first and make a reservation to avoid difficulties.

Dikli Castle

Stately **Dikli Castle** (Diķu pils; ☎ 6402 7480; www.diklupils.lv; d/ste from 45/100Ls) completes the trifecta of tucked-away castles. Dikli has an important place in the nation's history, as it was here, in 1864, that a priest organised Latvia's first Song Festival. Like at Bīriņi, this aristocratic manor has been transformed into a luxurious retreat with hotel rooms and spa services. Visitors can also enjoy strolls in the 20-hectare park, boat rides (3Ls) and tours detailing the history and restoration of the palace are also available (1Ls).

The tourist office can assist with bike rentals. It also has pamphlets detailing biking routes throughout the region. The most popular route is the ride between Valmiera and Cēsis (42km), which is flagged by orange labels along the way. You'll need a mountain bike to properly tackle the trek. A shorter route from Valmiera to Brenguli, just 10km east, is more about the scenic journey than the destination. Once you arrive, treat yourself to a 'live beer' (unfiltered beer) at **Alus Sēta** (☎ 6423 0272; Brenguli; ☼ 9am–10pm Jun–Aug) – you'll see the beer garden right when you pull into the village.

SLEEPING

Mēnesnīca (☎ 6423 2556; menesnica@4id.lv; Vadu iela 3; dm/s/d with shared bathroom 5/8/16Ls) The upside: Mēnesnīca has ridiculously low prices and it's walking distance to the train station. The downside: no English is spoken here. Climb this Tower of Babel to find sun-filled rooms sprouting off rather derelict hallways. The dorm rooms are cramped, but hey, it's only 5Ls.

Elēna Guest House (☎ 2929 9287; www.elena.viss.lv; Garā iela 8; r 15Ls) If you ignore the particleboard floors, Elēna is great value for your money – the eight rooms above the cafe have TVs, sparkling bathrooms and comfy beds with plenty of squishy pillows. Cash only. Wi-fi available.

Wolmar (☎ 6420 7301; www.hotelwolmar.lv; Tērbatas iela 16a; s/d/ste 32/40/42Ls; ▣) The town's modern, upmarket choice features 30 comfortable rooms in a yellow-and-black striped hotel. Wi-fi available.

EATING & DRINKING

Those who visit little Valmiera are limited to the following dining options (in addition to

LATVIA

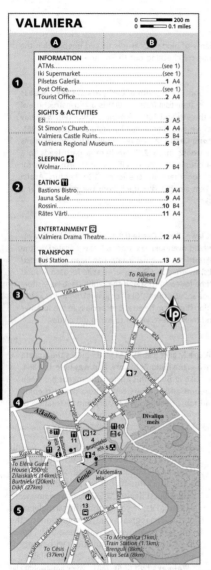

standard array of hearty Latvian dishes, as well as a couple of happy surprises like a salad bar, ice cream and lemon-spritzed salmon. Outdoor seating overlooking the water is available during the summer months.

Jauna Saule (☎ 6423 3812; Rīgas iela 10; mains from 3Ls; ☺ noon-10pm Sun-Tue, to midnight Wed-Thu, to 2am Fri & Sat) This bar and cafe dishes out a vast array of Latvian fare. There's an attached nightclub and a plastic jungle gym to keep the tykes busy while you have a relaxing lunch on the inviting summer terrace overlooking busy Rīgas iela.

Rātes Vārti (☎ 6428 1942; Lāčplēša iela 1; salads 1.50-4Ls, mains 3-9Ls; ☺ noon-11pm Sun-Thu, to midnight Fri & Sat) The decor leaves something to be desired – napkins are fanned out like peacocks, and the walls are blotted with sponge paint – but locals flock to this joint across from the theatre for their excellent assortment of delicious meat dishes.

Rossini (☎ 6422 6622; Bruņinieku iela 3; pasta 4-6.50Ls, mains 4-15Ls; ☺ 11am-midnight Sun-Thu, to 1am Fri & Sat) This trendy Italian spot, Valmiera's most expensive, lies hidden behind the crumbling Hanseatic Castle. Pass the ruins and make a right when directly in front of 'Muzejs'; you'll find white tablecloths and faux exposed brick as you stroll down the small hill. The pasta is reasonably priced, and in summer there are views of a picturesque canal from the wicker-filled veranda.

ENTERTAINMENT

The **Valmiera Drama Theatre** (☎ 6420 7335; www .vdt.lv; Lāčplēša iela 4; ☺ box office 10am-6.30pm Mon-Fri, 11am-2pm Sat & Sun) began in 1919, and has garnered a lot of respect around the nation as one of the top repertory theatres. Check the website for show times and production details.

GETTING THERE & AWAY

From Valmiera **bus station** (Mazā Stacijas iela 1) buses run twice hourly between 6.20am and 10.30pm to/from Rīga (3Ls to 3.20Ls, around 2¼ hours). Other services include 15 buses per day to/from Cēsis (1.10Ls, 45 minutes).

The **train station** (☎ 6429 6203; Stacijas laukums) is served by five trains daily to/from Rīga (2.13Ls, 2¼ hours) via Cēsis (0.71Ls, 30 minutes) and Sigulda (0.90Ls, 40 minutes).

ALŪKSNE & GULBENE

Located in the far northeastern corner of the country, the regions of Alūksne and Gulbene are far removed from the well-trodden tourist trail. Most visitors come to the area to take a

the restaurants at their lodging), which are all surprisingly decent.

Bastions Bistro (☎ 2925 8168; Bastiona iela 24; mains 1-4Ls; ☺ 8am-9pm Sun-Thu, to 10pm Fri & Sat) Housed in a stately yellow manor house high on a hill overlooking the river, Bastions is Valmiera's cheapest spot to grab a bite. Locals line up at the entrance to the basement cafeteria for the

ride on 'Marisa', the **Gulbene–Alūksne Narrow-Gauge Railway** (☎ 6447 3037; www.banitis.lv; one-way ticket 1.70Ls), one of two narrow-gauge railways still operating in Latvia. There are three departures per day in either direction. The full ride takes one hour and 25 minutes.

The town of Gulbene is rundown and holds little interest for tourists. By contrast, sleepy Alūksne, the town with the largest percentage of ethnic Latvians, is a charming little village with clusters of quaint wooden houses. Ernest Glueck (1654–1705), the Lutheran clergyman who translated the Bible into Latvian, was from Alūksne, and his home has been converted into the **Ernest Glueck Bible Museum** (Ernsta Glika Bībeles muzejs; ☎ 6432 3164; Pils iela 25a; adult/child 0.40/0.20Ls; ☉ 10am-5pm Tue-Thu, 8am-5pm Fri, 10am-2pm Sat).

Stop by the **Alūksne Tourist Office** (☎ 6432 2804; www.aluksne.lv; Dārza iela 8a; ☉ 8am-6pm Jun-Aug, to 5pm Sep-May) or the **Gulbene Tourist Office** (☎ 6449 7729; www.gulbene.lv; Ābelu iela 2-44; ☉ 8am-6pm Jun-Aug, to 5pm Sep-May) for more info on the area's activities and accommodations.

If you are riding the narrow-gauge rail, consider getting off in the village of Stāmeriena to find the **Stāmeriena Castle** (☎ 6449 2054; www.stamerienaspils.lv; Stāmeriena; adult/child 0.70/0.20Ls; ☉ 10am-5pm Mon-Sat). Owned by the affluent von Wolff family, the rambling manorhouse was passed down through many generations. In the 1920s, Alexandra von Wolff inherited the castle and had a largely publicised affair with noted Italian writer Giuseppe di Lampedusa, author of *The Leopard*. She later divorced her husband to marry the writer in Rīga.

Alūksne can be reached by bus from Rīga (4.90Ls to 5.25Ls, four to 4½ hours, seven daily) and Madona (2.75Ls, two to 2½ hours, two daily). Gulbene can also be reached from Rīga via a different bus route (4Ls to 4.65Ls, 3½ to 4½ hours, seven daily). There is one daily bus that connects Alūksne and Gulbene (1.35Ls, 1¼ hours).

VIDZEME UPLANDS

Did you know that there is no word for 'mountain' in Latvian? It's true. The word never evolved in the Latvian language for one very simple reason: there are no mountains in Latvia. The word *kalns* (hill) is used instead to describe scrubby bumps in the terrain. Latvia's biggest *kalns* is **Gaiziņkalns**, gradually rising to a whopping 312m (about 70m shorter than the Empire State Building). But Latvians are a resourceful bunch who appreciate the fruits of their land – even if it's vertically challenged – so little Gaiziņkalns is adored as the country's top spot for skiers and snowboarders.

Rīga's LIDO chain (see p217) is on the verge of opening its newest Latvian-themed **LIDO Complex** (☎ 2633 9869; Kalnadzisli) at the base of the hill, serving pints and pork tongue in a wonderfully synthetic country inn. Plans for ski-season accommodation are also in the works (call for up-to-date details).

The Uplands' economic centre is located 10km east of Gaiziņkalns in the town of **Madona** (pronounced *mah*-dwoh-nah – the emphasis is on the first syllable, unlike the pop diva). The friendly staff at the town's **tourist office** (☎ 6486 0573; Saieta laukums 1; ☉ 8am-6pm Mon-Sat Jun-Aug, 8am-5pm Mon-Fri Sep-May) can help get you sorted with a variety of accommodation and activities, including tours of (Teiču reservāts; 190 sq km), the Baltic's biggest swamp, and **Krustkalni Nature Reserve** (Krustkalni rezervāts; 30 sq km), a leafy realm of indigenous vegetarian. Both parks are located south of Madona, and their fragile ecosystems require visitors to always be accompanied by a guide.

For a dose of culture, head to the former home of Latvian writer Rūdolfs Blaumanis (1863–1908) at **Braki** (☎ 2640 6289; adult/child 0.80/0.30Ls; ☉ 10am-6pm mid-May–Nov). The Jurjāni brothers, noted Latvian musicians, lived at **Meņģeļi** (☎ 2943 1659; adult/child 0.50/0.20Ls; ☉ 10am-6pm mid-May–Nov), now a picturesque open-air museum and farmstead by Lake Pulgosnis.

Spa junkies should look no further than the luxurious **Marciena Manor** (☎ 6480 7300; www.marciena.com; s/d 35/60Ls; ☐ ☒), a renovated country estate dedicated to the art of relaxation. The manor is located just outside of Sauleskalns, 11km south of Madona.

Like every other region in Latvia, the Vidzeme Uplands are best explored by private vehicle. Buses link Madona to Rīga (4.20Ls, 3½ hours, 10 daily), Cēsis (2.45Ls, three daily, 1¾ to two hours), Jēkabpils (1.70Ls, 1¾ hours, three daily) and Alūksne (2.75Ls, 2½ to three hours, two daily).

SOUTHEASTERN LATVIA (LATGALE)

Toto, I don't think we're in Rīga any more. Latvia's poorest region (and one of the poorest regions in the entire EU), Southeastern

Latvia sits at the far end of the mighty Daugava River along the Russian border. The area gets its name from the Latgal (Lettish) tribes who lived near the myriad lakes when German crusaders invaded in the 12th and 13th century. Evidence of great medieval battles remains in the form of haunting castle ruins that starkly contrast the hideous Soviet fossils from a much more recent era of oppression. The hushed Latgale Lakelands is the region's pearl (tucked deep within a crusty oyster), offering visitors a chance to push 'pause' on life's problems while idling through friendly lakeside villages topped with glittering steeples.

DAUGAVA RIVER VALLEY

Latvia's serpentine Daugava River, known as the 'river of fate', winds its way through Latgale, Zemgale and Vidzeme before passing Rīga and emptying out in the Gulf of Rīga. For centuries the river was Latvia's most important transport and trade corridor for clans and kingdoms further east, and today, goods travel via road (Rte A6) and railway following the northern bank of the river.

For those travelling to the scenic Latgale Lakelands (or gritty Daugavpils), navigating the Daugava River Valley could feel like a necessary evil if not for the handful of conveniently placed attractions, which help recount the route's rich history.

From Rīga, the first worthy stopping place is **Salaspils**, just 20km southeast of the city. During WWII this town on the outskirts of the capital was the site of a Nazi **concentration camp** known as Kurtenhof to the Germans. See the boxed text on p231 for more information.

Lielvārde (leel-*var*-deh), 10km further east, is the hometown of Andrejs Pumpurs, a 19th-century poet best known for weaving an epic poem around the myth of Lāčplēsis, Latvia's national hero. The **Andrejs Pumpurs Museum** (Andreja Pumpura muzejs; ☎ 6505 3759; adult/child 0.50/0.20Ls; ☀ 10am-5pm Tue-Sun) has a mildly interesting collection of materials that honour the author and his epic tale. The whopping stone next to the museum was once, legend has it, the mighty Lāčplēsis' bed.

The photogenic ruins of a 13th-century **knights' castle** lie at the confluence of the Daugava and Perse Rivers in **Koknese**, 95km east of Rīga. Built by German crusaders in 1209, the castle ruins lost some of their dramatic cliff-top position after a hydroelectric dam increased the river's water level. Today the twisting ruins appear to be practically sitting in the river, and the sight is enchanting.

Pause in **Jēkabpils**, another 43km down the river; the midsized town is split in two by the roaring river. The northern half was once a separate village called **Krustpils** – today the towns are united and both are riddled with creaky wooden houses and a number of old churches with rusty spires. If you are travelling by train along the Daugava, get off at Krustpils station to visit Jēkabpils. Only a smidgen of English is spoken at the **tourist office** (☎ 6523 3822; Brīvības iela 140/142; ☀ 2-6pm Mon, 10am-6pm Tue-Fri, 10am-2pm Sat) but you'll find loads of brochures detailing activities and accommodation in the region. The small square just beyond has a couple of cafes, and down the street lies the town's best restaurant and lodging option, **Hercogs Jēkabs** (☎ 6523 3433; www.jnami.lv; Brīvības iela 182; s/d 18/25Ls).

The rest of the way from Jēkabpils to Daugavpils is a rather boring drive through flat lands with gnarled trees interrupted by the occasional wooden barn or crooked steeple. Those in search of Latgale's myriad lakes can veer off at **Līvāni**, an industrial town famous for its traditional glass blowing, before moving on.

DAUGAVPILS
pop 105,958

Okay, so sometimes it's hard to smile when the grey sky matches the grey tic-tac-toes of crumbling Soviet block housing – especially in a city with as many prisons as churches – but Latvia's second-largest city really isn't as scary as its reputation. Yes, Rīgans will snicker when the words 'visit' and 'Daugavpils' appear in the same sentence, so bear in mind that most of them have never even stopped through. Those who have travelled to the heart of Latgale sing a much different tune. A trip to Daugavpils will reveal a funky, friendly, energetic vibe that starkly contrasts with the drab architecture.

Information

City Center (☎ 6545 4540; Viestura iela 8; ☀ 10am-6am) Internet, wi-fi access and ATMs available.

Post office (☎ 6542 8755; Stacijas iela 42) Next to the train station.

Tourist office (☎ 6542 2818; Rīgas iela 22a; ☀ 9am-5pm Mon-Sat)

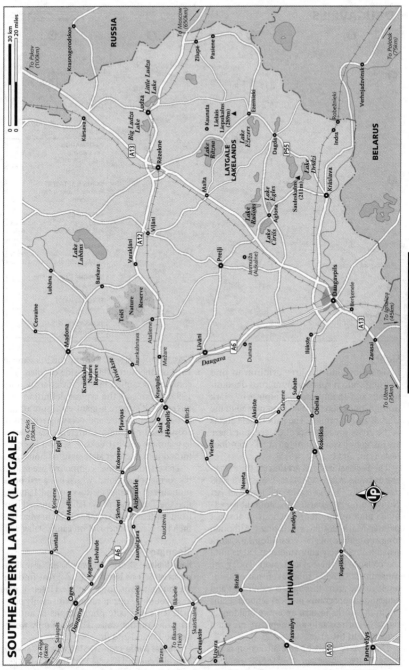

SOUTHEASTERN LATVIA (LATGALE)

LATVIA

0 — 30 km
0 — 20 miles

RUSSIA

To Pskov (100km)
To Moscow (650km)
To Polotsk (75km)

Krasnogorodskoe

Kārsava

Little Ludza Lake
Ludza
Big Ludza Lake

Zilupe
Pasiene

Vehņladzvinski

LATGALE LAKELANDS

Rēzekne
A13

Kaunata
Lielais Liepukalns (289m)
Lake Rāzna
Lake Ežezers
Ezernieki
Robežnieki
Indra
BELARUS

Malta

P55
Dagda
Lake Dridzi
Krāslava

Viļāni
A12

Lake Egles
Lake Rušoni
Lake Cirīšs
Aglona
Sauleskalns (211m)

Varakļāni

Lake Lubāns

Preiļi
Jasmuiža (Aizkalne)

Barkava

Lubāna

Cesvaine

Madona

Teiči Nature Reserve

Atašiene
Jaunkalsnava

Līvāni
Daugava
Dunava

Daugavpils
Berķenele
A13
To Līksna (45km)

Krustpils Nature Reserve

Aiviekste

Mežāre

Krustpils
Sala
Jēkabpils

Birži

Ilūkste
Subate
Garsene

Zarasaj
To Utena (35km)

Pļaviņas

Koknese

Viesīte
Aknīste
Nereta
Obeļiai
Rokiškis

Kokneese

Aizkraukle

Daudzeva

To Cēsis (30km)

Ērgļi

Madliena
Keipene

Skrīveri
Jaunjelgava

Pandėlys

Kupiškis

Suntaži

Kegums
A6

Ogre
Daugava
To Riga (6km)
Salaspils

Vecumnieki

Bārbele
Skaistkalne
Ceraukste
Užvara
Bizes

Biržai

Pasvalys
LITHUANIA
A10
Panevėžys

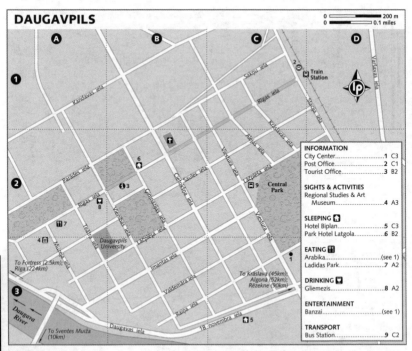

DAUGAVPILS

INFORMATION
City Center....................1 C3
Post Office.....................2 C1
Tourist Office.................3 B2

SIGHTS & ACTIVITIES
Regional Studies & Art
Museum....................4 A3

SLEEPING
Hotel Biplan.................5 C3
Park Hotel Latgola........6 B2

EATING
Arabika.....................(see 1)
Ladidas Park.................7 A2

DRINKING
Gliemezis.....................8 A2

ENTERTAINMENT
Banzai........................(see 1)

TRANSPORT
Bus Station...................9 C2

Sights

Look up beyond the grey gridiron to find swirling church spires of numerous denominations and an impressive sculpture by Mark Rothko, born here in 1903 (and moved to the USA as a young child). The Park Hotel Latgola is the city's unsightly centrepiece, but there are intriguing views from the hotel's top-floor restaurant and bar.

The **Regional Studies & Art Museum** (Novadpētnie-cības un mākslas muzejs; ☎ 6542 4073; Rīgas iela 8; adult/child 0.40/0.20Ls; ⏰ 11am-6pm Tue-Sat), inside an Art Nouveau house guarded by stone lions, exhibits high-quality reproductions of abstract painter Mark Rothko's paintings. Although long recognised in the West, Rothko's work remained relatively anonymous in Latvia until the collapse of the Soviet Union. Today the museum is striving to awaken national interest in the artist through its exhibition and educational programs in local schools. Plans are in the works to turn an entire building at the city's fortress into an interactive museum dedicated to the artist.

Daugavpils' most bizarre attraction is the huge **fortress** (cietoksnis; ☎ 6542 6398; adult/child 0.20/0.10Ls; ⏰ 8am-6pm), built by the Russians in 1810 on the northwestern side of town. The complex, occupied by the Soviet army until 1993, doesn't fit the typical definition of a fortress – it's more a giant enclosure of uninspired architecture and decaying remains of abandoned hospitals, conference halls, artillery storage and barracks. A section has been turned into decrepit state-assisted housing.

Tickets to the inner compound are sold at the former checkpoint, which has a red-brick monument stating (in Russian and Latvian) that the Tatar poet Musa Jalil languished here from September to October 1942, in what was then the Nazi concentration camp Stalag 340.

Sleeping

Hotel Biplan (☎ 6544 0596; www.hotelbiplan.lv; 18 novembra iela 50; r incl breakfast 22Ls) A great find for the budget conscious, simple Hotel Biplan has a couple of dozen rooms with comfy beds, little TVs and cute photographs of antique airplanes on the walls. The wi-fi only works on the 1st and 2nd floor.

Sventes Muiža (☎ 6542 5108; www.sventehotel.lv; Alejas iela 7, Svente; d 40Ls; 🖥) Sitting in a thicket,

10km from the city centre, this attractive country estate is a welcome retreat from the drab Soviet gridiron. Rooms are designed with a pinch of aristocratic class, and culinary treats are served up amid flamboyantly framed still lifes.

Park Hotel Latgola (☎ 6540 4900; www.hotellatgola.lv; Ģimnāzijas iela 46; r 45-66Ls; 🖳) The city's centrepiece and largest building, this Soviet monster sports modern (but overpriced) rooms behind its freshly renovated facade. Check out the views from the hotel's top-storey restaurant and bar.

Eating, Drinking & Entertainment

Daugavpils' new City Center complex (www.citycenter.lv) sees most of the local action. During the warmer months, local youngsters sometimes throw parties inside the crumbling walls of Daugavpils' fortress.

Arabika (☎ 6545 4540; Viestura iela 8; mains 1-4Ls; 🕑 11am-11pm Sun-Thu, to 6am Fri & Sat) A social spot with mod furnishings, Arabika sits on the ground level of the popular City Center. Try the mushroom soup, with locally picked fungi, or go for one of the international dishes; there's sushi, Greek salad and even spicy Indian curry.

Ladidas Park (☎ 6547 6660; Rīgas iela 14; mains 3-5Ls; 🕑 11am-11pm) Ladidas' lonely chandelier casts soft rays on patrons at this decidedly classier spot that's one taxidermic elk away from being a dimly lit dark-wood hunting lodge.

Gliemezis (☎ 6547 1002; Rīgas iela 22; 🕑 3pm-1am) A top chill-out spot around town, 'The Snail' feels like a college dorm with tattered sofas, sticky floors and amateur art strung up on the walls. Friday nights are the most happenin'.

Banzai (☎ 6545 4540; Viestura iela 8; 🕑 10pm-5am Fri & Sat) The grind-worthy beats at Banzai blast so loud you can feel the base tremors back in Rīga. In fact, this joint's hardcore party rep is so widespread that Rīgans are often lured down for a weekend of revelry.

Getting There & Away

There are four rail routes radiating out from Daugavpils' **train station** (☎ 6548 7261, Stacijas iela), which head to/from Rīga (3.57Ls to 4.57Ls, 2¾ to 3¾ hours, four daily), Vilnius (2½, one daily), Rēzekne (1¼ hours, one daily) and Indra. For more information, see p401.

From the **bus station** (☎ 6542 3000; www.buspark.lv; Viestura iela 10) buses run to/from

Rīga (4Ls to 5.50Ls, 3¾ hours, one hourly) and Rēzekne (2.40Ls, 1½ to two hours, eight daily).

LATGALE LAKELANDS

A secret realm of greens and blues, Latvia's land of enchanting lakes has stolen the hearts of many. Hidden runes suggest that the region was first settled at the end of the Stone Age when wandering hunters, captivated by the area's serene beauty, paused along **Lake Lubāns**, Latvia's largest, covering 82 sq km. Thousands of years later, vital trade routes zigzagged between the languid lagoons connecting faraway capitals like Warsaw and St Petersburg. Today, the hushed forests and lakeside villages attract those seeking simpler times and pleasures.

Rēzekne
pop 35,883

Rēzekne furtively pokes its head up from a giant muddle of derelict factories and generic block housing. The town took a heavy beating during WWII when most of its historic buildings were pulverised by artillery fire. Today, there isn't much to keep a tourist in town (even the castle ruins aren't that impressive); however, frequent trains and buses make it a convenient jumping-off point to explore the quiet Lakeland further south.

The main street, Atbrīvošanas alejā, runs from Rēzekne II train station (north) to the bus station (south), and crosses the central square en route. In the square's middle stands **Māra**, a statue twice destroyed by the Soviet authorities in the 1940s and only re-erected in 1992. Its inscription 'Vienoti Latvijai' means 'United Latvia'.

Across from Māra, you'll find the town's **tourist office** (☎ 6460 5005; Atbrīvosanas alejā 98; 🕑 9am-5pm Mon-Fri) tucked inside **Hotel Latgale** (☎ 6462 2180; www.hotellatgale.lv; Atbrīvosanas alejā 98; s/d from 27/38Ls), a passable sleeping option in town.

Continue along Atbrīvošanas alejā and take a walk down **Latgales iela**, the town's oldest street, which is lined with dozens of charming brick facades constructed by wealthy Yiddish merchants several hundred years ago.

If you've noticed the enormous stork nests dotting the Latvian countryside, then head to **Untumi** (☎ 6463 1255; www.untumi.lv), a country ranch 7km northwest of town signposted off Rte A12. Here you'll find cameras and binoculars set up around a couple of stork nests allowing tourists to watch the mothers feeding their young. Horseback riding is available as well (9Ls for one hour).

Follow Rte P55 south of Rēzekne to find **Ezerkrasti Resort** (☎ 2645 0437; www.raznaslicis.lv; Dukstigals, Čornajas pagasts; s from 8Ls, cottage 45Ls) along the banks of Lake Rāzna, Latvia's largest lake by volume. The lake is located within Razna National Park, a quiet preserve protecting roughly 600 sq km of Latgale's Lakeland. The lush green property, dotted with charming wooden cottages, offers volleyball, paddleboats, a lake for swimming, and an indoor pool and sauna. On the other side of the lake, along Rte P56, is **Rāznas Gulbis** (☎ 2999 4444; www.razna.lv; d from 28Ls, townhouse from 120Ls), a spacious resort with paddleboats, an on-site **restaurant** (noon-11pm) and a small 'aquarium' of corralled fish in the lake.

The **bus station** (Latgales iela 17) has services to/from Daugavpils (2.40Ls, 1¾ to 2¼ hours, nine daily), Ludza (1Ls to 1.10Ls, 30 minutes to one hour, one hourly), Preiļi (1.65Ls to 1.90Ls, one to 1¾ hours, seven daily) and Rīga (5.90Ls to 6.40Ls, four to 5½ hours, 10 daily), among other destinations.

Rēzekne 2 train station (Stacijas iela) has one train daily each way between Rīga and St Petersburg, and Moscow–Rīga. In all, there are six trains daily to/from Rīga (3.66Ls, three to 3¾ hours). Only the St Petersburg–Vilnius train (every second day) stops at the Rēzekne I train station.

LATVIA

Ludza

pop 9,875

Little Ludza, just a hop from the Russian border, was founded in 1177, making it the oldest town in all of Latvia. Located at the junction of two lakes (known as Big Ludza Lake and Little Ludza Lake), the small village and trading post grew around **Ludza Castle**, built by German crusaders in 1399 to protect the eastern front of the Livonian Order. The castle has been in ruins since 1775, and today the melange of crumbling crimson brick and smoky grey boulders is both haunting and beautiful, and makes a great place for a picnic overlooking the church spires and rivulets down the hill.

The **Ludza Craftsmen Centre** (☎ 2946 7925; www.ludzasamatnieki.lv; Tālavijas iela 27a; 9am-5pm Tue-Sat) features an excellent selection of locally made handicrafts. The centre has three attached workshops in which local artisans perfect their trade. If you ring ahead, you too can try your hand at time-honoured methods of wool spinning, pottery making and sewing. There's a collection of old tools to peruse and a traditional Latgalian costume to try on for picture taking.

Ludza is located 26km east of Rēzekne along Rte A12 as it makes its way into Russia. Traffic can often be an issue along the A12 as vehicles line up to cross the border (note the abundance of porta-potties along the side of the road for the truck drivers waiting hours on end to pass through the red tape at customs). An hourly bus connects Luzda to Rēzekne (1Ls, 40 minutes), and there's one bus per day linking the little town to Rīga (6.85Ls, 4½ hours).

Krāslava

pop 10,640

Sleepy Krāslava sits 6km north of Belarus at the southern tip of the triangular Latgale Lakelands region. Founded by a Polish nobleman in the 18th century, Krāslava was established as a trade centre along the Daugava River. Many craftsmen moved to the town from Poland to trade with wealthy Jewish and Russian merchants from down the river. Due to the heavy Polish influence, Krāslava is predominantly Catholic, and has several whitewashed houses of worship, including **St Donath Catholic Church**, along the town's main drag.

For a view of the town head to **Karņička Hill**, which is marked with a large cross – the tomb of a lovelorn soldier. According to legend, a young Polish officer was invited to Krāslava Castle for a party and fell in love with the lord's daughter. She too was struck by Cupid's arrow, but her father wouldn't allow them to get married. Crestfallen, the lovers decided that they couldn't live without each other and planned a suicide pact. At the stroke of midnight the lord's daughter would light a candle from her bedroom, meaning that she was ready to jump out the window and plummet to her death. The officer, once having seen the candle, would shoot himself. When the young soldier saw the flickering light, he followed through with his promise, but the maiden was caught by her nurse before she had a chance to jump.

From the top of Karņička Hill, one quickly understands why Krāslava has been dubbed the 'Cucumber City' of Latvia – tonnes of small cucumber farms are peppered among the collection of humble wooden homes below.

Stop by the **pottery studio** (☎ 2912 8695; valdispaulins@inbox.lv; Dūmu iela 8; group demonstration 5Ls, clay 0.50Ls;

9am-7.30pm) run by Valdis and Olga Paulins, a husband-and-wife team who preserve the traditional Latgalian method of creating and decorating ceramics. There's a bit of a language barrier if you don't speak Latvian, Russian or German, but the friendly couple offers spirited demonstrations with big smiles and even bigger hand gestures. If you contact them in advance, they can recruit a local to swing by and translate. Although it takes quite a bit of time and talent to sculpt a vase or pot, you can learn in a matter of minutes how to make a clay duck whistle (and we guarantee you'll have a chuckle when you find out where you have to blow).

Take Rte P61 towards the village of Dagda to reach two quality lakeside resorts. Follow the signs for Konstantanova to reach **Dridži** (☎ 2944 1221; www.dridzi.lv; tent 4Ls, camper-van parking 7Ls, d weekday/weekend 20/25Ls, cottage weekday/weekend 50/60Ls), the perfect spot for families, featuring volleyball nets, tugboats, rafts and a lovely hillside dotted with wooden gazebos. Each cottage comes with a fully equipped kitchen. Also on Lake Dridži, **Sauleskalns** (☎ 2619 0186; info@skalns.lv) is popular in the winter for its gentle ski slope – the longest in Latvia. Rent a boat during the summer months and paddle around the deepest lake in the region. New motel units overlooking the water were being completed when we stopped by to have a look. Both recreation destinations are open year-round.

For those interested in horseback riding, head to **Klajumi Stables** (☎ 2947 2638; www.klajumi.lv; 2-/4-/ 7-day tours 75/189/359L, 1 hr trot 10Ls), 11km southwest of town near Kaplava. Ilze, the owner, comes from a long line of horse keepers and offers a variety of activities from overnight riding trips to simple countryside afternoon gallops. The adorable guest cottage (weekday/weekend 30/50Ls) looks like a gingerbread house, and comes with a sauna (that doubles as a shower), kitchenette and lofted bedroom with satellite TV. The toilet is located in an outhouse nearby.

To reach Krāslava, take Rte A6 east from Daugavpils, or follow Rte P62 from Aglona. There is one daily bus (1.55Ls, 1½ hours) at 12.25pm that plies the route from Krāslava to Aglona and on to Preiļi.

Aglona

Believe it or not, teeny Aglona (*a*-glwo-nuh) is one of the most visited towns in all of Latvia, primarily due to the **Aglona Basilica** (☎ 6538 1109; Cirisu iela 8; ☺ gift shop/info booth 10am-3pm & 4-7pm Mon-Fri,

9am-3pm & 4-7pm Sat & Sun), founded over 300 years ago when a group of wandering Dominican monks discovered a healing source hidden among a thicket of spruce trees (Aglona means spruce tree in an old dialect). Although the sulphur fount lost its apparent power a century later, pilgrims still visit the site, and incorporate the spring water in their religious rituals, especially on Ascension Day (15 August).

The 18th-century church lies along the shores of Lake Egles in a vast grass courtyard, created for Pope John Paul II's visit in 1993 to bestow the title of 'Basilica Minoris' (small basilica) upon the holy grounds. One of the basilica's 10 altars guards a miraculous icon of the Virgin Mary, said to have saved Aglona from the plague in 1708. Mass is held at 7am and 7pm on weekdays, and at 10am, noon and 7pm on Sundays. Rosary is held at noon on weekdays, and at 9.30am on Sundays.

While you're in town, consider stopping by the **Bread Museum** (Aglonas maizes muzejs; ☎ 2928 7044; Daugavpils iela 7; group admission 25Ls; ☺ 9am-6pm Mon-Sat) to learn about the history and traditions surrounding traditional Latgalian dark bread, a local staple. Very little English is spoken so it is best to call ahead to arrange a complimentary translator for the one-hour presentation. Even if you don't have time for the presentation, you can still stop by for fresher-than-fresh loaves of bread baked minutes before you walked in the door. Peep through the small window into the kitchen to watch the bakers hard at work.

A small **guesthouse** (☎ 2928 7044; Daugavpils iela 7; dm 10Ls) can be found above the Bread Museum with several cheery dorm rooms swathed in pastels. **Aglonas Cakuli** (☎ 6537 5465; http://aglonas cakuli.lv; Ezera iela 4; s/d from 15/25Ls), another adequate sleeping option, sits one block away along Lake Cirišs.

Around 10km south of Aglona lurks **Devil's Lake** (☎ 6564 1332; www.lvm.lv), also called Čertoks ('little devil'). For centuries, locals have passed down the tale of a malicious demon that lives at the bottom of the oddly tranquil lagoon. Compasses and sensory equipment never seem to work when activated within the lake's vicinity, which has led scientists to speculate that a magnetic meteor sits below the crystalline surface. Some believe that a little devil never existed and that the name Čertoks is a bastardisation of the Russian word Čertog, which means 'beautiful place'. To reach Devil's Lake, take rte P62 towards Krāslava; however, the turn off to the lake is not marked (to avoid a deluge of tourists), so you will have to get directions from the friendly staff at the **Aglona Tourist Office** (☎ 6532 2100; www.latgaletourism.lv; Somersētas iela 34; ⊙ 10am-6pm Mon-Fri, to 3pm Sat Jun-Aug, 9am-5pm Mon-Fri Sep-May). To check email, head to the town's **library** (Daugavpils iela 37; ⊙ 10am-6pm Mon-Fri, to 3pm Sat), which has free internet access and wi-fi.

Aglona village, wedged between Lake Egles (east) and Lake Ciriss (west), is 31km north of Krāslava along Rte P62, and 9km off the main road between Daugavpils and Rēzekne (Rte A13), which crosses the western part of the Latgale Lakelands. Six daily buses connect Aglona and Preiļi (0.50 to 1Ls, 30 minutes).

Preiļi
pop 8,270

There isn't a lot to do in provincial Preiļi (*pray-lee*), but a stop at the **tourist office** (☎ 2910 0689, 2911 6431; tic@preili.lv; Kārsavas iela 4; ⊙ 8.30am-5pm Mon-Sat Jun-Aug, closed Sat Sep-May) is helpful if you are just arriving in the Latgale Lakelands region. The English-speaking staff can offer activities suggestions and help arrange accommodation at a countryside guesthouse. The attached **library** (⊙ 10am-8pm Mon-Fri, to 5pm Sat & Sun) has free internet and wi-fi access. Note that the info office is usually closed for lunch between noon and 12.30pm.

Jānis Rainis (1865–1929), known as the Shakespeare of Lativa, wrote some of his earliest works in **Aizkalne** (also called Jasmuiža), 12km south of town. There, the small **Rainis Museum** (☎ 6535 4677; admission 0.30-0.70Ls; ⊙ 10am-5pm Tue-Sat mid-May–Nov) showcases traditional Latgalian pottery as well as changing literary exhibitions devoted to the poet.

Preiļi is halfway between Daugavpils and Rēzekne, about 16km north of the junction of Rte A13 and Rte P62. There is one daily bus (1.55Ls, 1½ hours) at 12.25pm that plies the route from Preiļi to Aglona and on to Krāslava.

LATVIA DIRECTORY

The following directory contains practical information pertinent to travel in Latvia. For regional information pertaining to all three Baltic countries, see the Regional Directory p389.

ACTIVITIES

Latvia's miles of forested acreage are great for hiking, cycling, camping, birdwatching, berry picking, mushrooming and canoeing during the summer months. In winter, skiing and snowshoeing are but some of the uplifting pursuits Latvia has to offer active visitors. In the last couple of years, visitors have been dabbling with day trips from Rīga (see the boxed text, p200).

For more information and a listing of national parks, check out the boxed text on p184, and don't forget to have a look at our colour activities chapter, p201.

CUSTOMS

The **Latvian Tourism Development Agency** (www.latviatourism.lv) posts the latest customs rules on its website.

There are no customs controls at the borders with other EU countries. When travelling within Schengen, tourists (18 years and up) are only allowed to move 800 cigarettes, 200 cigars or 1kg of tobacco across the border. For alcohol, the maximum is 110L of beer, 90L of wine (not more than 60L of sparkling wine) and 10L of other alcohol products. When travelling beyond the EU, quantities of cigarettes and alcohol are reduced to 200 cigarettes, 50 cigars, 250g of smoking tobacco and 1L of distilled beverages.

Special permits are needed for exporting game, furs and hunting trophies, and permits can be obtained at the **State Forests Office** (www.vmd.gov.lv). Exporting documents or copies from the state archive also require permits; see www.mantojums.lv.

EMBASSIES & CONSULATES

The following embassies are in Rīga:

Australia (Map pp196-7; ☎ 6722 4251; australia@apollo.lv; Arhitektu iela 1-305)

Canada (Map pp196-7; ☎ 6781 3945; www.dfait-maeci.gc.ca/canada-europa/baltics; Baznicas laukums 4)

Estonia (Map pp196-7; ☎ 6781 2020; www.estemb.lv; Skolas iela 13)

Finland (Map pp196-7; ☎ 6707 8800; www.finland.lv; Kalpaka bulvāris 1)

France (Map p190; ☎ 6703 6600; www.ambafrance-lv.org; Raiņa bulvāris 9)

Germany (Map p190; ☎ 6708 5100; www.riga.diplo.de; Raiņa bulvāris 13)

Japan (Map pp196-7; ☎ 6781 2001; www.eoj@latnet.lv; Valdemāra iela 21)

Lithuania (☎ 6732 1519; lt@apollo.lv; Rūpniecības iela 24)

Netherlands (Map p190; ☎ 6732 6147; www.netherlandsembassy.lv; Torņa iela 4)

PRACTICALITIES

- The only pan-Baltic English-language paper *Baltic Times* (www.baltictimes.com) is published every Thursday in Rīga and has an entertainment guide that includes cinema listings.

- *Rīga in Your Pocket* (www.inyourpocket.com) and *Rīga This Week* (www.rigathisweek.lv) are bimonthly English-language guides with hotel, restaurant and nightlife reviews.

- On air, tune into *Latvian State Radio* (www.radio.org.lv), which transmits daily short-wave broadcasts on four channels: Latvian Radio 1 (news and talk), Radio 2 (songs in Latvian), Radio 3 (classical music) and Radio 4 (news and music in Russian). Radio NABA is the popular alternative university station. European Hit Radio and Radio Nord are popular stations with Top 40 playlists.

- **Latvian State TV** (Latvijas Televizija; www.ltv.lv) broadcasts three TV channels: LTV, LTV1 and LTV7 (sports). TV5 (www.tv5.lv) is Rīga's city channel, broadcasting programs about the capital and its inhabitants. The country's most popular private TV broadcast station is **Latvian Independent TV** (Latvijas NeatkaRīga Televizija; www.lnt.lv).

- PAL-625 and SECAM-625 are the main video systems used in Latvia.

- Electrical current is 220V, 50Hz AC. Sockets require a European plug with two round pins.

- The metric system is used for weights and measures.

Russia (Map pp196-7; ☎ 6733 2151; www.latvia.mid.ru; Antonijas iela 2)

Spain (Map pp196-7; ☎ 6732 0281; Elizabetes iela 11)

Sweden (Map pp196-7; ☎ 6768 6600; www.sweden abroad.com/riga; Pumpura iela 8)

UK (Map pp196-7; ☎ 6777 4700; www.britain.lv; Alunāna iela 5)

USA (Map p190; ☎ 6703 6200; www.usembassy.lv; Raiņa bulvāris 7)

FESTIVALS & EVENTS

Latvians find any and every excuse to throw a party. Check out the events calendar (p18) for a comprehensive list of activities around Latvia and the other Baltic nations next door.

HOLIDAYS

The **Latvia Institute website** (www.li.lv) has a page devoted to special Latvian Remembrance Days under the 'About Latvia' link:

New Year's Day 1 January

Easter In accordance with the Western Church calendar

Labour Day 1 May

Restoration of Independence of the Republic of Latvia 4 May

Mothers' Day Second Sunday in May

Whitsunday A Sunday in May or June in accordance with the Western Church

Līgo Eve (Midsummer festival) 23 June

Jāņi (St John's Day and Summer Solstice) 24 June

National Day 18 November; anniversary of proclamation of Latvian Republic, 1918

Christmas (Ziemsvētki) 25 December

Second Holiday 26 December

New Year's Eve 31 December

INTERNET ACCESS

Almost every hotel and hostel in Rīga offers some form of internet access, whether it's wi-fi or a computer terminal located in a communal area. Lately, hotels and hostels in small cities and towns have been doing a good job of following suit. Internet cafes are a dying breed as many restaurants, cafes, bars and even clubs are installing wireless connections.

For detailed information about wireless access in Rīga and around Latvia, see the boxed text on p189.

In provincial Latvia an internet cafe tends to translate as a *datorsalons*, crammed with square-eyed kids playing computer games. Make it clear you want to access the internet (rather than tangle with Lara Croft) and a kid will be kicked off to make way for you.

INTERNET RESOURCES

Dear intrepid travel, meet **www.1188.lv**, your new best friend. Latvia's top search engine is like a genie that grants three wishes…and then 1000 more, answering any questions you might have about bus/train transport, postal services, business listings, traffic reports and taxis. You can even send an SMS to the website service to get listings sent to your phone.

The **Latvian Tourism Development Agency** (www .latviatourism.lv) and the **Latvia Institute** (www.li.lv)

LATVIA

both have fantastic websites providing information targeted at foreign visitors.

MAPS

Country, city and town maps of Latvia are available from Rīga-based **Jāņa sēta** (Map pp196-7; ☎ 6724 0894; Elizebetes iela 83-85; ☺ 10am-7pm Mon-Sat, to 5pm Sun). Its town-plan series covers practically every town in Latvia; individual maps range in scale from 1:15,000 to 1:20,000 and cost 0.70Ls to 3Ls.

The Latvian Tourism Development Agency has a very detailed map covering each of Latvia's five regions (which correspond to the five sections of this chapter).

MONEY

Latvia's currency, the lats, was introduced in March 1993. The lats (Ls) is divided into 100 santīms. Lats come in coin denominations of 1Ls and 2Ls and notes of 5Ls, 10Ls, 20Ls, 50Ls, 100Ls and 500Ls; and santīms come in coins of 1, 2, 5, 10, 20 and 50.

The national bank **Latvijas Bankas** (Latvian Bank; www.bank.lv) posts the lats' daily exchange rate on its website. For exchange rates, see the inside front cover of this guide.

POST

Latvia's **postal service** (www.post.lv) website can answer any mail-related questions, including post-office sites and shipping prices. Stamps for postcards to international addresses cost between 0.36Ls and 0.58Ls depending on the destination. Standard letters (20g) to international destinations cost 0.50Ls to 0.55Ls, and increase with weight. Mail to North America takes about 10 days, and to Europe about a week.

TELEPHONE

Latvian telephone numbers have eight digits; all landlines start with '6' and all mobile phone numbers start with '2', each with seven numbers following. The first two digits after the mobile or landline designation indicate the town or region within the country. To make any call within Latvia, simply dial the eight-digit number. To make an international call, dial the international access code (00), followed by the appropriate country code, area code (if applicable), and the subscriber's number. To call a Latvian telephone number from abroad, dial the international access code, then the country code for Latvia (371), followed by the subscriber's eight-digit number. Telephone

rates are posted on the website of the partly state-owned **Lattelecom** (www.lattelecom.lv), which enjoys a monopoly on fixed-line telephone communications in Latvia.

Two -, three -, or four-digit numbers, such as ☎ 02, ☎ 112 or ☎ 1188, are directory and emergency number where English, Latvian and Russian are spoken. Eight-digit numbers starting with '80' are toll free, and numbers starting with '90' incur fees.

Calls on a public phone are made using cardphones called *telekarte*, which come in different denominations, and are sold at post offices, newspaper stands and superettes.

Mobile Phones

Mobile phone have eight numbers and always start with the digit '2'. Mobile phones are available for purchase at most shopping malls around Rīga and other major Latvian cities. If your own phone is GSM900/1800-compatible, you can purchase a SIM-card package from one of Latvia's mobile-telephone operators, available at any Narvesen superette or Rimi store.

Okarte (www.lmt.lv), Latvijas Mobilais Telfons's prepaid plan, provides reliable service throughout the country. A starter kit costs 3Ls, and comes with 3Ls worth of credit. To add credit to your prepaid plan, simply stop by a Narvesen superette or Rimi and purchase a recharge card for 1, 3 or 5Ls. Dial ☎ 2920 2010 and follow the English prompts to type in the number listed on the card and the password under a scratch-away sheath. **Tele2** (www.tele2.lv), pronounced 'tele-divi', has a comparable plan as well.

TOURIST INFORMATION

In recent years, the **Latvian Tourism Development Agency** (☎ 6722 9945; www.latviatourism.lv; Pils laukums 4) has been streamlining tourist information throughout the country. In general, you can email tic@*cityname*.lv and insert the town name for pertinent information pertaining to that destination. Try www.tourism.*city name*.lv, or simply www.*cityname*.lv for official city websites (English translations are often limited for small destinations). Every city and town in Latvia worth visiting has a tourist office, open during normal business hours (at the very least), with extended hours during the summer. Almost all of the tourist offices have English-speaking staff and oodles of pamphlets and maps.

Check out the **Latvia Institute**'s website (www .li.lv) for additional information about Latvia.

Lithuania

Lithuania

Lithuania (Lietuva) is an enigma. Once boasting an empire stretching from the Baltic to the Black Sea, the biggest of the Baltic states has been reduced to an underling by neighbouring countries more than once in its long history, and disappeared completely off world maps for centuries. Its strong Catholic ties – spilling out onto the streets in the form of one house of worship after the next – are plain to see in every town and city, as are its unbreakable pagan roots, which appear at every turn. Politically and culturally Lithuania faces west and embraces all that the EU has to offer – all the while struggling to shake off ingrained and unwanted Soviet ideals.

And yet, none of this matters when you consider what lies within its borders. Obviously Mother Nature didn't think height was appropriate for this flat land, but she used her immense skills to bless it in other ways. White sandy beaches edge the unique slither that is Curonian Spit; lush forests, home to witches, fairies and tall tales of mysterious happenings, guard lakes that twinkle between a wall of pine trees; and lonely coastal wetlands lure migrating birds by their hundreds of thousands.

The country's capital, Vilnius, is a beguiling artists' enclave, with mysterious courtyards, worn cobbled streets and crumbling corners overshadowed by baroque beauty beyond belief. Further afield, remnants of the Soviet occupation – a nuclear power plant, disused nuclear missile site and Soviet sculpture park – fascinate and shock. The Hill of Crosses and Orvydas stone garden are but two more oddities that could only occur in this perplexing land.

LITHUANIA

FAST FACTS

- **Area** 65,303 sq km
- **Birthplace of** composer and painter Čiurlionis; Baltic Gold
- **Capital** Vilnius
- **Country code** ☎ 370
- **Departure tax** none
- **Famous for** causing the USSR to collapse, Europe's largest baroque old town
- **Money** Lithuanian litas; €1 = 3.45Lt; US$1 = 2.84Lt; UK£1 = 5.04
- **Population** 3.4 million
- **Visa** not needed for most nationalities. See p399 for details.

HIGHLIGHTS

- **Vilnius** (p292) Wander the backstreets of this beautiful baroque capital looking for that perfect bar or bistro.
- **Curonian Spit** (p362) Spend time cycling, swimming in the Baltic Sea, or exploring hardy human settlements on this thin spit of sand and spruce.
- **Hill of Crosses** (p348) Stand in awe in front of thousands upon thousands of crosses – some tiny, others gigantic – that grace a small hillock outside Šiauliai.
- **Žemaitija National Park** (p377) Stare down the barrel of a disused nuclear missile silo, before taking a peaceful stroll through bewitching woods.
- **Aukštaitija National Park** (p326) Take time out for fishing, boating, bathing and berrying in Lithuania's beloved Lakeland.

ITINERARIES

- **Three days** Devote two days to Vilnius (see p296) and spend the third day in Trakai exploring lake and castle.
- **One week** Combine a few days in Vilnius with a day trip to Trakai, and spend the rest bathing in the Baltic and gliding through the greenery on Curonian Spit.
- **Two weeks** Start with the One Week itinerary above, then catch a boat across the lagoon to explore the backwaters of the Nemunas Delta, before zipping up to Žemaitija National Park for its Soviet missile base and forest-ringed lake. Move on to the poignant Hill of Crosses and, if time remains, travel back to Vilnius via Kaunas.

CURRENT EVENTS

Forever rebellious and feisty, Lithuania has recently resurrected its role as David to Russia's Goliath after years of serviceable relations. It was one of the first countries to actively support Georgia after its invasion by Russia, and, along with its Baltic neighbours, it threatened to pull out of the 2009 Eurovision song contest in Moscow in protest against its former rulers' actions. The country is also seeking around €19 million in compensation for damages it says it endured during the Soviet occupation.

The country's wrangle with Russia could have major consequences for its future energy security. The EU is forcing Lithuania

HOW MUCH?
- **Cup of coffee** 3-7Lt
- **Taxi fare** 3Lt/km
- **Local bus/trolleybus ticket** 1.40-2Lt
- **Bicycle hire** 5/35Lt per hour/day
- **One-hour private sauna session** 100-200Lt

LONELY PLANET INDEX
- **Litre of petrol** 3.10Lt
- **1½L bottled water** 2-2.50Lt
- **50cl bottle of Švyturys beer** 2.40Lt
- **Souvenir T-shirt** 20-50Lt
- **Pancake** 5-10Lt

to close its Ignalina nuclear power plant (see p331), which supplies 70% of the country's energy. Lithuania's government is fighting Brussels, refusing to close the plant until 2012 if the EU rejects Lithuania's claim for compensation for loss of its energy-producing capabilities.

Despite plans to build a new nuclear power plant, which could be online as early as 2015, Lithuania faces a major energy deficit in the interim years. It is thought that the country's gas-powered energy stations will take up the slack; Lithuania is currently completely dependent on Russia for all its natural gas supply, however, and demand for gas could increase by 75% in 2010. There could be light at the end of the natural-gas pipeline though. Plans are afoot to connect the Lithuanian and Polish power grids, thus connecting the country with the rest of the EU. The project is estimated to cost €434 million and could be complete by 2011.

Lithuania's enthusiasm for the EU continues unabated. In a mid-2008 poll, 70% of the population still viewed EU membership optimistically. Many are gagging for the euro, but the EU currency won't be introduced until at least 2010. As with everything, EU membership has its downside: the country's younger generation is leaving in droves for the greener pastures of the UK and Ireland.

Politically, Lithuania is the land of the comeback kid. In October 2008 the country went to the polls and handed the right-wing Homeland Union party, headed by Andrius Kubilius, a slight majority over its closest rival,

LITHUANIA

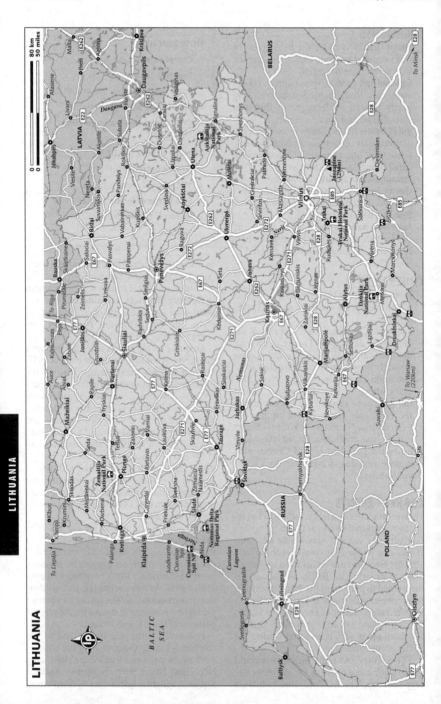

the Social Democrats Party. Kubilius quickly formed a coalition with two minor parties, the National Revival Party and the Liberals' Movement of the Republic of Lithuania, and after a break of eight years, began his second term as prime minister. Kubilius and his coalition face a tough few years ahead, battling to rein in the country's budget deficit and tackling a slowing economy hit hard by the global financial crisis.

HISTORY

A powerful state in its own right at its peak in the 14th to 16th centuries, Lithuania subsequently disappeared from the map in the 18th century, only to reappear briefly during the interwar period. Lithuania regained its independence in 1991 after decades of Soviet rule. Kaunas' Military Museum of Vytautas the Great (p341) and Vilnius' National Museum (p297) cover the whole span of Lithuania's history.

Tribal Testosterone

Human habitation in the wedge of land that makes up present-day Lithuania goes back to at least 9000 BC. Trade in amber started during the Neolithic period (6000 to 4500 years ago), providing the Balts – the ancestors of modern Lithuanians – with a ready-made source of wealth when they arrived on the scene from the southeast some time around 2000 BC.

Two millennia on, it was this fossilised pine resin and the far-flung routes across the globe its trade had forged – all brilliantly explained in Palanga's Amber Museum (p373) – that prompted a mention of the amber-gathering *aesti* on the shores of the Baltic Sea in *Germania,* a beast of a book about Germanic tribes outside the Roman Empire written in AD 98. It wasn't until AD 1009 that Litae (Latin for Lithuania) was mentioned for the first time in written sources (the *Kvedlinburgh Chronicle*) as the place where an archbishop called Brunonus was struck on the head by pagans.

By the 12th century Lithuania's peoples had split into two tribal groups: the Samogitians (lowlanders) in the west and the Aukštaitija (highlanders) in the east and southeast. Around this time a wooden castle was built on the top of Gediminas Hill in Vilnius.

Medieval Mayhem

In the mid-13th century Aukštaitija leader Mindaugas unified Lithuanian tribes to create the Grand Duchy of Lithuania, of which he was crowned king in 1253 at Kernavė. Mindaugas accepted Catholicism in a bid to defuse the threat from the Teutonic Order – Germanic crusaders who conquered various Prussian territories, including Memel (present-day Klaipėda). Unfortunately, neither conversion nor unity lasted very long: Mindaugas was assassinated in 1263 by nobles keen to keep Lithuania pagan and reject Christianity. Vilnius did reap its first cathedral, though, from this sacred decade of peace.

In 1290 Lithuania was reunified and under Grand Duke Gediminas (1316–41) its borders extended south and east into modern-day Belarus. After Gediminas' death two of his sons shared the realm: in Vilnius, Algirdas pushed the southern borders of Lithuania past Kyiv, while Kęstutis – who plumped for a pretty lake island in Trakai as a site for his castle – fought off the Teutonic Order.

Algirdas' son Jogaila took control of the country in 1382, but the rising Teutonic threat forced him to make a watershed decision in the history of Europe. In 1386 he wed Jadwiga, crown princess of Poland, to become Władysław II Jagiełło of Poland and forge a Lithuanian–Polish alliance that would last 400 years. The Aukštaitija were baptised in 1387 and the Samogitians in 1413, making Lithuania the last European country to accept Christianity.

Glory Days

Jogaila spent most of his time in Kraków, but trouble was brewing at home. In 1390 his cousin Vytautas revolted, forcing Jogaila's hand – in 1392 he named Vytautas Grand Duke of Lithuania, on condition that he and Jogaila share a common policy. The decisive defeat of the Teutonic Order by their combined armies at Grünwald (in modern-day Poland) in 1410 ushered in a golden period of prosperity, particularly for the Lithuanian capital Vilnius, which saw its legendary Old Town born.

Vytautas ('the Great') extended Lithuanian control further south and east. By 1430 when he died, Lithuania stretched beyond Kursk in the east and almost to the Black Sea in the south, creating one of Europe's largest empires. Nowhere was its grandeur and clout better reflected than in 16th-century Vilnius, which, with a population of 25,000-odd, was one of eastern Europe's biggest cities. Fine late-Gothic and Renaissance buildings sprung up, and Lithuanians such as Žygimantas I and II occupied the Polish-Lithuanian throne inside the sumptuous Royal Palace. In 1579 Polish Jesuits founded Vilnius University and made the city a bastion of the Catholic Counter Reformation. Under Jesuit influence, baroque architecture also arrived.

Polonisation & Partitions

Lithuania gradually sank into a junior role in its partnership with Poland, climaxing with the formal union of the two states (instead of just their crowns) at the Union of Lublin in 1569 during the Livonian War with Muscovy. Under the so-called Rzeczpospolita (Commonwealth), Lithuania played second fiddle to Poland. Its gentry adopted Polish culture and language, its peasants became serfs and Warsaw usurped Vilnius as political and social hub.

A century on it was Russia's turn to play tough. In 1654 Russia invaded the Rzeczpospolita and snatched significant territory from it. By 1772 the Rzeczpospolita was so weakened that the Prussia-Brandenburg state of Russia, Austria and Prussia simply carved it up in the Partitions of Poland (1772, 1793 and 1795). Most of Lithuania went to Russia, while a small chunk around Klaipėda in the west went to Prussia.

Russification & Nationalism

While neighbouring Estonia and Latvia were governed as separate provinces, Russian rule took a different stance with rebellious Lithuania.

Vilnius had quickly become a refuge for Polish and Lithuanian gentry dispossessed by the region's new Russian rulers and a focus of the Polish national revival, in which Vilnius-bred poet Adam Mickiewicz was a leading inspiration. When Lithuanians joined a failed Polish rebellion against Russian rule in 1830, Tsarist authorities clamped down extra hard. They shut Vilnius University, closed Catholic churches and monasteries and imposed Russian Orthodoxy. Russian law was introduced in 1840 and the Russian language was used for teaching. A year after a second rebellion in 1863, books could only be published in Lithuanian if they used the Cyrillic alphabet, while publications in Polish (spoken by the Lithuanian gentry) were banned altogether.

National revival became a hot trend in the 19th and early 20th century, the rapid industrialisation of Vilnius and other towns simply lending nationalist drives more clout. Vilnius became an important Jewish centre during this period, Jews making up around 75,000 of its 160,000-strong population in the early 20th century to earn it the nickname 'Jerusalem of the North'.

Independence

Ideas of Baltic national autonomy and independence had been voiced during the 1905 Russian revolution, but it was not until 1918 that the restoration of the Independent State of Lithuania was declared. During WWI Lithuania was occupied by Germany and it was still under German occupation on 16 February 1918 when a Lithuanian national council, the Taryba, declared independence in Vilnius in the House of Signatories. In November Germany surrendered to the Western Allies, and the same day a Lithuanian republican government was set up.

With the re-emergence of an independent Poland eager to see Lithuania reunited with it or to cede the Vilnius area, which had a heavily Polish and/or Polonised population, things turned nasty. On 31 December 1918 the Lithuanian government fled to Kaunas, and days later the Red Army installed a communist government in Vilnius. Over the next two years the Poles and Bolsheviks played a game of tug-of-war with the city, until the Poles annexed Vilnius once and for all on 10 October 1920. Thus from 1920 until 1939 Vilnius and its surrounds was an isolated corner of Poland while the rest of Lithuania was ruled from Kaunas, for the most part under the iron-fist rule (1926–40) of Lithuania's first president, Antanas Smetona (1874–1944).

In 1923 Lithuania annexed Memel (present-day Klaipėda), much to the displeasure of Germany.

WWII & Soviet Rule

With the fatal signing of the Molotov-Ribbentrop nonaggression pact, Lithuania soon fell into Soviet hands. The 'mutual-assistance pact' the USSR insisted on signing with Lithuania regained it Vilnius in October 1939 (the Red Army had taken the city in its invasion of eastern Poland at the same time as Germany had invaded western Poland). But this was little consolation for the terror Lithuania experienced as a USSR republic – Soviet purges saw thousands upon thousands of Balts killed or deported.

Following Hitler's invasion of the USSR and the Nazi occupation of the region in 1941, nearly all of Lithuania's Jewish population – between 135,000 and 300,000 people according to varying estimates – were killed; most Vilnius Jews died in its ghetto or in Paneriai Forest. In all some 475,000 Lithuanians perished during WWII, and 80,000 Lithuanians escaped to the West between 1944 and 1945 to avoid the Red Army's reconquest of the Baltic countries.

Immediate resistance to the reoccupation of Lithuania by the USSR, in the form of the partisan movement 'Forest Brothers', began in 1944. Discover their story in museums across the country, including the Museum of Deportation & Resistance (p342) in Kaunas. Between 1944 and 1952 under Soviet rule, a further 250,000 Lithuanians were killed or deported, suppression of spirit and free thought being the order of the day. Nowhere is this dark period explained more powerfully than at the Museum of Genocide Victims (p307) in the old KGB headquarters in Vilnius.

1989–91

A yearning for independence had simmered during the glasnost years, but it was with the storming success of Lithuania's popular front, Sajūdis, in the March 1989 elections for the USSR Congress of People's Deputies (Sajūdis won 30 of the 42 Lithuanian seats) that Lithuania surged ahead in the Baltic push for independence. The pan-Baltic human chain, which was formed to mark the 50th anniversary of the Molotov-Ribbentrop Pact a few months later, confirmed public opinion and, in December that year, the Lithuanian Communist Party left the Communist Party of the Soviet Union – a landmark in the break-up of the USSR.

Vast pro-independence crowds met Gorbachev when he visited Vilnius in January 1990. Sajūdis won a majority in the elections to Lithuania's supreme soviet in February, and on 11 March this assembly declared Lithuania an independent republic. In response, Moscow carried out weeks of troop manoeuvres around Vilnius and clamped an economic blockade on Lithuania, cutting off fuel supplies.

LITHUANIA

TOP FIVE HISTORICAL READS

■ *The Last Girl* (Stephan Collishaw) Absolutely spellbinding, this superb historical novel set in Vilnius flits between WWII and the 1990s.

■ *Lithuania Awakening* (Alfred Senn) From 'new winds' (the birth of the independence movement in the 1980s) to a 'new era' (independence), Senn's look at how the Lithuanians achieved independence remains the best in its field; read the entire thing free online at http://ark.cdlib.org/ark:/13030/ft3x0nb2m8.

■ *And Kovno Wept* (Waldemar Ginsburg) Life in the Kovno ghetto is powerfully retold by one of its survivors.

■ *Lithuania – Independent Again: The Autobiography of Vytautas Landsbergis* The scene outside parliament on 13 January 1991 is among the dramatic moments Landsbergis brings vividly to life in his autobiography.

■ *Forest of the Gods* (Balys Sruoga) The author's powerful account of his time spent in the Stutthof Nazi concentration camp in the early 1940s was censored, hence not published until 1957. Transferred onto celluloid by Algimantas Puipa in 2005.

Soviet hardliners gained the ascendancy in Moscow in winter 1990–91, and in January 1991 Soviet troops and paramilitary police occupied and stormed Vilnius' TV tower and TV centre, killing 14 people. Some of the barricades put up around the parliament remain. On 6 September 1991 the USSR recognised the independence of Lithuania.

Towards Europe

Lithuanians have a sense of irony: they led the Baltic push for independence then, at their first democratic parliamentary elections in 1992, raised eyebrows by voting in the ex-communist Lithuanian Democratic Labour Party (LDDP). Presidential elections followed in 1993, the year the last Soviet soldier left the country, with former Communist Party first secretary Algirdas Brazauskas landing 60% of the vote. Corruption scandals dogged his term in office – a painful time as inflation ran at 1000% and thousands of jobs were lost from inefficient heavy industry. The collapse of the country's banking system in 1995–96 did little to aid economic performance.

But change was under way: the litas replaced the talonas (coupon), the transitional currency used during the phasing out of the Soviet rouble in Lithuania; a stock exchange opened, the death penalty was abolished and Lithuanian became the official language.

Presidential elections in 1998 ushered in wild card Valdas Adamkus (b 1926), a Lithuanian émigré and US citizen, resident in the US since his parents fled the Soviets in 1944. Adamkus appointed a member of the ruling Conservative Party, 43-year-old Rolandas Paksas, prime minister in 1999. The popular Vilnius mayor and champion stunt pilot won instant approval as 'the people's choice' – so much so in fact that he ran against Adamkus in 2003 presidential elections and won.

Massive privatisation took place in 1997–98 but deep recession struck following the 1998 Russian economic crisis. However, Lithuania clawed its way back and by 2001 its economy was being praised by the International Monetary Fund as one of the world's fastest growing. It joined the World Trade Organization in 2000, and in 2002 – in a bid to make exports competitive and show determination to join Europe – pegged its currency to the euro instead of the US dollar.

True to his Lithuanian blood, Adamkus battled hard in the political ring and regained the country's presidency in June 2004 following the impeachment of Paksas for alleged dealings with the Russian mafia. In the same year Lithuania joined the EU and NATO, and has been a staunch supporter of both ever since – in November 2004 it became the first EU member to ratify the EU constitution, and the former USSR military base outside Šiauliai is now home to four NATO F-16 fighter jets.

THE CULTURE
Lifestyle

The contrast between life in Vilnius and elsewhere is stark. Citizens of the capital enjoy a lifestyle similar to those in Western Europe, living in stylish apartments, partying hard on weekends, working in professional jobs and often owning a car. Many have gained a cosmopolitan view of the world and consumerism has become a way of life. Church plays a lesser role in a town where casinos and strip joints rapidly threaten to outnumber churches.

In provincial towns and rural areas poverty is still prevalent – in 2007 urban dwellers had around a third more income at their disposal than their rural counterparts, and 34% of homes in farming communities were below the poverty line, compared to 19% in built-up areas. For many in the countryside it is simply a matter of working the land and that is about it, unemployment being far higher in rural areas than wealthier urban circles. Life expectancy for males is low compared to other European countries – 63 years for those on the land and 66 in the cities.

Until 1998 Vilnius was the only place in Lithuania to offer a university degree.

DOS & DON'TS

■ When visiting a Lithuanian bring an odd number of flowers: even-numbered bouquets are for dead-solemn occasions – and the dead!

■ Don't shake hands across the threshold; it brings bad luck.

■ Always maintain eye contact when toasting your host or they'll think you're shifty.

Since then, 21 universities and 28 colleges have sprung up. Almost 90% of Lithuanians complete secondary school, and more than 80% of pupils go on to further education; most students work full time alongside studying and live in university dorms or with friends rather than remaining in the parental nest. Family ties remain fiercely strong, however, and many married couples live with elderly parents who are no longer able to live alone. Despite increased career prospects, especially for women, Lithuanians marry young – almost 63% of women marry between the ages of 20 and 24. A high number of marriages – 49 of every 100 – end in divorce, but this figure is steadily dropping.

Population

The population is predominantly urban: two-thirds live in urban areas and 40% of people live in the country's five major cities – Vilnius, Kaunas, Šiauliai, Panevėžys and Klaipėda. Population density was 46.6 people per sq km before WWII, peaking at 56.6 people per sq km prior to independence in 1990 (when contraception was illegal) and shrinking to 51.8 people per sq km in 2007.

Easily the most ethnically homogeneous population of the three Baltic countries, indigenous Lithuanians count for almost 85% of the total population, making multiculturalism less of a hot potato than in Latvia or Estonia. Russians form 5.1% of the Lithuanian population, while Poles and Jews make up 6.3% and 0.1% respectively.

The country's smallest ethnic community, numbering just 280, are the Karaites. An early-19th-century prayer house and ethnographic museum in Trakai (p323) provide insight into the culture and beliefs of this tiny Turkic minority.

Lithuanian Roma officially number 2800. Vilnius' **Human Rights Monitoring Institute** (www.hrmi.lt) reckons some 46% are aged under 20 and many, unlike the Roma elders they live with, don't speak Lithuanian. Despite launching the Roma Rights Defense Legal Programme in April 2005, the Institute has made little headway in getting the government to put antidiscrimination legislation in place, and the community remains an impoverished and discriminated-against minority.

RANDOM FACTS

- In 1997 there were 835,000 cars on Lithuania's roads – by 2007 this had jumped to 1.45 million.

- The number of cinemas in the country is dropping, down from 51 in 2005 to 44 in 2007.

- Lithuanians are second only to Luxembourg in the EU's mobile phone usage stakes: in 2007 the country had 139 mobiles per 100 people, up from 29 mobiles in 2002.

- The computer age is slowly reaching the country's rural areas: 18% of homes have a computer and 16.4% have internet connection. In Lithuania's urban expanse, 43% of households have a PC and 40.2% internet access.

- Urban Lithuanians spend around a third more on alcoholic beverages than their rural counterparts.

Net migration has been negative for the past few years, peaking in 2004 at 9612. By 2007 this had almost halved to 5244. More than three million Lithuanians live abroad, including an estimated 800,000 in the USA. Other communities exist in Canada, South America, Britain and Australia.

SPORT

Basketball is akin to religion. The worshipped national team scooped bronze in three successive Olympic Games (1992, 1996 and 2000), only to be pipped at the post for bronze in both 2004 and 2008.

Basketball players of legendary status include retired Šarūnas Marčiulionis, the first Lithuanian to play in the NBA in 1989, and Arvydas Sabonis, one of basketball's greatest centres. Marčiulionis and Sabonis have since founded basketball schools – and luxury hotels – in Vilnius and Kaunas respectively.

Lithuania has a fine tradition in dancing, both on and off the ice. Ice-skaters Margarita Drobiazko and Povilas Vanagas are hugely popular in Lithuania and have raised the profile of the sport in the country, while Lithuanian dancesport duo Arūnas Bižokas and Edita Daniūtė gained major success at the 2005 Dance-sport World Games in Germany, landing gold.

LITHUANIA

World-champion cyclist Diana Žiliūtė won the Tour de France in 1999 and silver at the Sydney 2000 Olympics. Raimondas Rumšas surprised everyone by finishing third in the 2002 Tour de France, only for his wife to be stopped when driving home with a campervan full of drugs. The Bicycle Museum (p347) in Šiauliai is a fun spot to learn about lesser-known Lithuanian riders.

Lithuanian legends of lesser-known sports include Discus thrower Alekna Virgilijus who scooped Lithuania's only gold medals at the 2000 and 2004 Olympics, along with a bronze in 2008; Andrejus Zadneprovskis, a champion of the modern pentathlon who secured silver at the 2004 Olympics, bronze in 2008, and gold at the 2000 and 2004 world champs; and Austra Skujytė, winner of the 2004 Olympic silver medal in the decathlon and current world record holder.

RELIGION

Lithuania was the last pagan country in Europe, not baptised into Roman Catholicism until 1413. This explains why so much of its religious art, national culture and traditions have raw pagan roots. During the Soviet years, Catholicism was persecuted and hence became a symbol of nationalistic fervour. Churches were seized, closed and turned into 'museums of atheism' or used for other secular purposes (such as a radio station in the case of Christ's Resurrection Basilica in Kaunas, open for business as usual today) by the state.

Other minorities include Orthodox believers, Lutherans, Jews, Evangelical Christians and the pagan Romuva movement.

ARTS

Lithuania is Baltic queen of contemporary jazz, theatre and the avant-garde, while its arts scene is young, fresh and dynamic.

Literature

The Renaissance ushered in the first book to be published in Lithuanian – a catechism by Martynas Mažvydas, whose statue stands in Klaipėda – in 1547 and the creation of Vilnius University in 1579. But it wasn't until a couple of centuries later that a true Lithuanian literature emerged.

The land was the focus of the earliest fiction: *The Seasons (Metai)*, by Kristijonas Donelaitis, described serf life in the 18th cen-

tury in poetic form, and a century on Antanas Baranauskas' poem, *Anykščiai Pine Forest (Anykščių šilelis;* 1860–61), used the deep, dark forest around Anykščiai as a symbol of Lithuania, bemoaning its destruction by foreign landlords.

Russia's insistence on the Cyrillic alphabet for publishing from 1864 (until 1904) hindered literature's development – and inspired poet Jonas Mačiulis (1862–1932) to push for its national revival. A statue of the Kaunas priest, nicknamed Maironis, stands in Kaunas' Old Town. The city's Maironis Lithuania Literary Museum (p339), in Maironis' former home, tells his life story. Maironis' romantic *Voices of Spring (Pavasario balsai;* 1895) is deemed the start of modern Lithuanian poetry.

Several major Polish writers grew up in Lithuania and regarded themselves as partly Lithuanian, notably Adam Mickiewicz (1798–1855), the inspiration of 19th-century nationalists, whose great poem *Pan Tadeusz* begins 'Lithuania, my fatherland…'. The rooms in Vilnius' Old Town, where he stayed while studying at Vilnius University, form a museum (p302). Winner of the 1980 Nobel prize, Czesław Miłosz (1911–2004) translated Lithuanian folk songs into French and wrote about intellectuals and the Soviet occupation in *The Captive Mind*.

Novelists at the fore of contemporary Lithuanian literature include Antanas Škėma (1910–61), whose semiautobiographical novel *White Linen Shroud (Balta drobule;* 1954) recounts a childhood in Kaunas, then emigration to Germany and New York. It pioneered stream of consciousness in Lithuanian literature. Realist novelist and short-story writer Ričardas Gavelis (1950–2002) shocked the literary world with *Poker in Vilnius* (1989) and *Vilnius Jazz* (1993), which openly criticised the defunct Soviet system and mentality. Equally controversial was the story of a priest's love affair with a woman, *The Witch and the Rain (Ragana ir lietus)* by Jurga Ivanauskaitė (1961–2007), banned on publication in 1992. Her subsequent novel *Gone with Dreams* (2000) highlighted new issues and subjects, such as religion, travel and perceptions of others' religion and cultures, that couldn't be addressed in Lithuanian literature until after 1991.

TOP CONTEMPORARY READS

Online, visit **Books from Lithuania** (www.booksfromlithuania.lt), a comprehensive literary information centre reviewing the latest in Lithuanian poetry and prose, including English-language translations.

■ *Lithuanian Literature* (edited by Vytautas Kubilius) Read this to get the big picture.

■ *The Issa Valley* (Czesław Miłosz) Semiautobiographical account of boyhood life in a valley north of Kaunas.

■ *Tūla* (Jurgis Kunčinas) Spellbinding story of two lovers caught in the Soviet system, and battling it with every step.

■ *Bohin Manor* (Tadeusz Konwicki) Set in the aftermath of the 1863 uprising, this novel by a leading modern Polish writer born in the Vilnius area uses the past to comment on current events and evokes tensions between locals, their Russian rulers and a Jewish outsider, as well as the foreboding and mysterious nature of the Lithuanian backwoods.

■ *Raw Amber* (edited by Laima Sruoginis) Anthology of contemporary Lithuanian poetry.

Herkus Kunčius (b 1965) has gained a reputation for scandalous novels that tear at the fabric of cultural norms; his *The Tumulus of Cocks* (2004) has introduced gay and lesbian scenes to Lithuanian literature. Marius Ivaškevičius (b 1973), on the other hand, has distinguished himself by looking at historical themes through a modern lens. *The Green* (2002), detailing the partisan movement after WWII, has proven to be Ivaškevičius' best seller to date.

Cinema & TV

Lithuania has a long cinematic history – the first short films were shot way back in 1909 – but it wasn't until the late 1980s that independent film truly began to flourish.

The grim reality of the post-Soviet experience is the focus for talented film director Šarūnas Bartas (b 1964), whose silent B&W movie *Koridorius* (*The Corridor*; 1994) – set in a dilapidated apartment block in a Vilnius suburb – received international recognition. Bartas opened Lithuania's first independent film studio in 1987.

The 11 documentaries and one short film made by Audrius Stonys are acclaimed Europe-wide: *510 Seconds of Silence* (2000) – an angel's flight over Vilnius' Old Town, the lake-studded Aukštaitija National Park and Neringa – is awesome; watch it at www.stonys.lt.

Stonys codirected *Baltic Way* (1990) – which landed best European documentary in 1992 – with director-producer and European Film Academy member Arūnas Matelis (b 1961). Matelis won critical acclaim and a

heap of awards for *Before Flying Back to the Earth* (2005), a documentary on children with leukaemia. Find him and his film crew at www.nominum.lt.

Algimantas Puipa became prominent with *Vilko dantu karoliai* (The Necklace of Wolf's Teeth; 1998) and *Elze is Gilijos* (Elsie from Gilija; 1999), and hit the headlines again with both *Forest of the Gods* (2005) and *Whisper of Sin* (2007).

Lithuania has been the location for a number of big-budget TV series, including *The New Adventures of Robin Hood* (1995–96) and *Elizabeth I* (filmed 2005) starring Jeremy Irons and Helen Mirren, due to its reputation as a cheap film location.

The **Lithuanian Film Studios** (www.lfs.lt), founded in Kaunas in 1948 and now located in Vilnius, has had a hand in all major foreign productions in the country.

More information on Lithuania's cinema and TV heritage can be gleaned at the Theatre, Music & Cinema Museum (p305) in Vilnius.

Music

Dianos – the Lithuanian name for songs – form the basis of the country's folk music. Their lyrics deal with every aspect of life, from birth to death, and more often than not they are sung by women, alone or in a group. Instruments include the Kanklė, a Baltic version of the zither, a variety of flutes, and reed instruments. Kaunas' Folk Music & Instruments Museum (p339) has a fine collection to peer at.

LITHUANIA

FOLK ART

The carved wooden crosses (*Rupintojėlis*) placed at crossroads, cemeteries, village squares and at the sites of extraordinary events across Lithuania are a beautiful expression of religious fervour – and a striking nationalistic statement. Pagan symbols of suns, moons and planets are intertwined, making the totems a unique cultural contradiction. Vincas Svirskis (1835–1916) was the master; see his carvings in Vilnius' Museum of Applied Arts (p297). In the Soviet period, such work was banned, although it has survived to amazing effect at the Hill of Crosses (p348) near Šiauliai. **Old Lithuanian Sculpture, Crosses and Shrines** (www.tradicija.lt) is an excellent online resource.

Several folk artists' workshops in Vilnius can be visited (see the boxed text, p303), while galleries and museums such as Vilnius' Contemporary Art Centre (p304), Aukso Avis (see the boxed text, p320), Vilnius' Potters Guild (p319) and Museum of Applied Arts (p297) and Kaunas' Čiurlionis Art Museum (p341) showcase contemporary creations. Ona Grigaitė and Dalia Laučkaitė-Jakimavičienė are big names in the ceramics world.

Romantic folk-influenced Mikalojus Konstantinas Čiurlionis (1875–1911) is Lithuania's leading composer from earlier periods. Two of his major works are the symphonic poems *Miske* (*In the Forest*) and *Jūra* (*The Sea*; 1900–07), but Čiurlionis also wrote many piano pieces.

Bronius Kutavičius (b 1932) is heralded as the harbinger of minimalism in Lithuanian music, while Rytis Mažulis (b 1961) represents a new generation of composers with his neo-avant-garde stance expressed in minimalist compositions for voice. Country-and-western icon Virgis Stakėnas is the larger-than-life force behind the country's cult country music festival, the Visagano Country (p329).

Lithuania is the Baltic jazz giant. Two noteworthy musicians are sparkling pianist Gintautas Abarius and cerebral saxophonist Petras Vysniauskas. As famed is the Ganelin Trio, whose avant-garde jazz stunned the West when discovered in the 1980s. Kurpiai (p360) in Klaipėda and Birštonas Jazz (p346) are *the* spots to catch Lithuanian jazz.

Lithuania has yet to break into the international rock and pop scene, but that doesn't mean there aren't any local heroes. Andrius Mamontovas has been a household name for almost two decades; Amberlife, Mango, and Auguestė dominate the boy and girl band genre; and Skamp is an interesting mix of hip-hop, R'n'B, and funk. The biggest bands to explode onto the scene in recent years are Inculto, an eclectic group whose creative output reflects diverse world influences, and Gravel, a Brit-pop four-piece with talent and attitude.

Electronic music is as big in Lithuania as it is in the rest of Europe. Top names to look for include Mamania, Bango Collective, Leon Somov, and Santi Touch. Gravity (p318), Cozy (p317), Woo (p318) and Pacha Vilnius (p318) in Vilnius are the places to catch the latest on the Lithuanian DJ scene. On air, tune into **Užupio Radijas** (www.uzupioradijas.lt; 94.9 FM).

Music Export Lithuania (www.mxl.lt) is a helpful online information source on Lithuania's various music genres.

Visual Arts

Lithuania's finest painter and musician is Varėna-born Mikalojus Konstantinas Čiurlionis, who spent his childhood in Druskininkai, where his home is now a museum (p332). He produced romantic masterpieces in gentle, lyrical tones, theatre backdrops and some exquisite stained glass. The best collection of these works is in the National Čiurlionis Art Museum (p341) in Kaunas. Depression dogged Čiurlionis, although when he died aged 35 it was of pneumonia.

Lithuania has a thriving contemporary art scene. Vilnius artists created the tongue-in-cheek Republic of Užupis (p304), which hosts alternative art festivals, fashion shows and exhibitions in its breakaway state. Some 19km north, Lithuanian sculptor Gintaras Karosas heads up a sculpture park, Europos parkas (p325).

From Lenin to rock legend, Konstantinas Bogdanas was famed for his bronzes of communist heroes (see some in Druskininkai's Grūtas Park; p336) and his bust of musician and composer Frank Zappa (p306).

Lithuanian photography has achieved international recognition. Vytautas Stanionis (b 1949) was the leading postwar figure, while artist Antanas Sutkus stunned the photographic world with his legendary shots of French philosopher Sartre and novelist Simone de Beauvoir cavorting in the sand on Curonian Spit. Vitalijus Butyrinas' (b 1947) famous series *Tales of the Sea* uses abstract expressionism to make powerful images. For more on these and other hot shots, visit the **Union of Lithuanian Art Photographers** (www.photography.lt).

Theatre

Lithuanian theatre is becoming an international force, with several young experimental directors turning European heads left, right and centre.

Theatres derive 15% of their income from box-office sales; 13 of Lithuania's 25-odd theatres are state funded.

Vilnius-based Oskaras Koršunovas (b 1969) has done Europe's theatre-festival circuit with *Old Woman, Shopping and Fucking, PS Files OK* and his 2003 adaptation of *Romeo and Juliet.*

In 1998 the controversial director established his own theatre company in Vilnius, the Oskaras Koršunovas Theatre (OKT; p318), albeit one with no fixed stage. His string of awards includes the Lithuanian National Prize and European New Reality Prize, both in 2002.

Other big names include Gintaras Varnas (b 1961), artistic director at the Kaunas Academic Drama Theatre (p345), voted Lithuania's best director of the year five times; and Rimas Tuminas (b 1952), who heads the Small Theatre of Vilnius (p318).

A key online information source on Lithuanian theatre is www.the atre.lt.

ENVIRONMENT
The Land

The largest of the Baltic countries, Lithuania is dotted with lush forests, 4000 lakes (covering 1.5% of the country) and a 100km-wide lowland centre. Latvia is its neighbour to the north, Belarus to the southeast, and Poland and the Kaliningrad Region (Russia) to the south. Juozapinės (294m), straddling the Belarusian border, is the country's highest point.

Half of Lithuania's short (99km) Baltic Coast lies along Curonian Spit – the region's most breathtaking natural feature. Split between Lithuania and Kaliningrad, the golden sand spit stretches for 98km and is just 4km at its widest point, with sand dunes majestically rising up to 60m high. Behind it spans the Curonian Lagoon, into which the Nemunas River – Lithuania's longest river – flows.

Wildlife

Lithuania is home to 70 species of mammal, including elks, wild boars and the very rare lynx, while the Nemunas Delta wetlands are an important breeding area for birds, including the stork (see the boxed text, below). The beaver, European bison and red deer have been reintroduced. Wolves breed in inland national parks and the Labanoras National Park; the Austrian grass snake slithers around in Dzūkija and large bat populations bat about everywhere. Occasionally, in a quiet spot in one of Lithuania's lovely lake lands, a rare freshwater turtle lays its eggs on an empty sandy shore.

Forest covers 33% of the country, pine, spruce and birch predominating. Predictably,

LITHUANIA

STORKS

Spring is marked by the arrival of the majestic stork, which jets in for the summer from Africa.

The height of sensibility, this bird of passage usually settles back into the same nest it has used for years. Large and flat, the nest is balanced in a tree or atop a disused chimney or telegraph pole. Some are splayed out across wooden cartwheels, fixed on tall poles by kindly farmers keen to have their farmstead blessed by the good fortune the stork brings. Lithuanians celebrate this traditional protector of the home with Stork Day (25 March), the day farmers traditionally stir their seeds, yet to be planted, to ensure a bigger and better crop.

Measuring 90cm in height, this beautiful long-legged, wide-winged creature is breathtaking in flight. Equally marvellous is the catwalk stance it adopts when strutting through meadows in search of frogs to feast on. It sleeps standing on one leg.

Lithuania, with approximately 13,000 pairs, enjoys Europe's highest density of storks. By contrast, it is estimated that only 500 black storks live in the country.

trees are a source of great pride for Lithuanians, who honour their oldest with names like Kapinių pušis (Cemetery Pine) and Ragaonos uosis (Witch's Ash). In pagan times trees were said to shelter souls of the dead, soldiers killed in battle turning into trees. A century ago people hollowed out beehives high up (so brown bears didn't steal the honey) in pine tree trunks; dozens still stud the Dzūkija National Park.

Dzūkija and Žemaitija are particularly rich in fauna, each protecting over 1000 species. Rare flowers found in the Aukštaitija National Park include the white water lily, ghost orchid, single-leafed bog orchid and hairy milk vetch. Sea holly is increasingly rare on the dunes of Curonian Spit thanks to walkers who pick it to take home.

National Parks & Reserves

Five national parks (one of which so spectacular and precious that Unesco declared it a World Heritage site in 2000), six nature reserves, 30 regional parks, 112 municipal reserves, 261 state reserves and one biosphere reservation protect 12% of Lithuanian land and plenty of rare and wonderful wildlife. Plenty more information on these parks and their wildlife habitats can be found in the regional chapters.

Environmental Issues

For years the hot potato has been Ignalina Nuclear Power Plant (p331), 120km north of Vilnius. One of two reactors similar in design to the Chernobyl plant in Ukraine was closed in December 2004 and, with the final shutdown of the plant scheduled for 2009, the big question now is how to decommission the grim Soviet monstrosity with the least cost to the environment. The financial cost will be at least €3.2 billion – paid, for the most part, by Brussels.

National Park or Reserve	Area	Features	Activities	Best time to visit
Aukštaitija National Park (p326)	405 sq km	69% forest, 15.5% river/lake; wolves and bears	walking, canoeing, kayaking, mushrooming and summer berrying, skiing	Mar-May
Čepkeliai Strict Nature Reserve (p334)	112 sq km	Lithuania's largest raised bog (54% of reserve), marsh, forest, cranes and woodgrouse	birdwatching (Jul-Mar), walking (Jul-Mar); walking season (Apr-Jun) forbidden during nesting	Jun-Nov
Curonian Spit National Park (p362)	265 sq km	high dunes, pine forests, beaches, lagoon and sea coast; rare species of mammals, birds and butterflies	cycling, swimming, walking, birdwatching, wild-boar spotting	Jun-Aug
Dzūkija National Park (p334)	550 sq km	forest, historic settlements	handicrafts, walking, canoeing, cycling, birdwatching, mushrooming and berrying	Mar-Nov
Labanoras Regional Park (p329)	528 sq km	Lithuania's largest regional park; rare flora and fauna, ancient burial mounds	canoeing, berrying and mushrooming	Jun-Nov
Nemunas Crook Regional Park (p346)	252 sq km	steep forested river banks, ravines and tallest pine trees (42m) in Lithuania	birdwatching, cycling, canoeing, self-pampering	Mar-May, Sep-Nov
Nemunas Delta Regional Park (p370)	289 sq km	unique delta of waterways, dikes, poldersand islands with varied birdlife	birdwatching, fishing, boating, cycling	Mar-May, Sep-Nov
Trakai Historical National Park (p322)	82 sq km	old town, castle museum, Kairates culture, 32 lakes including Lake Galvė with its 21 islands	swimming, sailing, fishing, canoeing	Jun-Aug
Žemaitija National Park (p377)	217 sq km	forest; Lake Plateliai, Žemaičių Kalvarija Catholic shrine centre, Polkštinė Soviet Missile base	boating, cycling, fishing, walking	Mar-Nov

GREEN LINKS

Lithuanian Fund for Nature (☎ 5-231 0700; www.glis.lt; Algirdo gatvė 22-3, Vilnius) **Lithuanian Green Movement** (☎ 37-324 241; www.zalieji.lt; Kanto gatvė 6, Kaunas)

Despite a slight dip in 2007, emissions of greenhouse gases have been on the rise since 2000. Among the main sources of air pollution are city transport and industrial sites. Of particular concern are the industrial centres of Vilnius, Kaunas and Jonava, where fertiliser and cement industries continue to contaminate both the air and water environment around them.

The delicate biodiversity of Lithuania's forests are under threat due to mismanagement and illegal logging. In recent years large swathes of forest have been divided up and given to small private owners with little or no knowledge of forest management, while illegal logging has resulted in unsustainable harvesting levels. Illegal construction and large corporate farming concerns have also begun to encroach on environmentally sensitive areas, which could soon cause havoc with their fragile ecology.

Oil extraction at the D-6 oil field in the Kaliningrad Region, 22km from the coast and 500m downstream from the Lithuania–Russia border, threatens Curonian Spit and Baltic Sea. In June 2004 Russian oil giant Lukoil began operations to extract 9.1 million tonnes of oil over a 30-year period; the oil is transferred to land by a 47km-long underwater pipeline. The Council of Europe recognised good operating practices at the rig but emphasised the huge risks its proximity to the spit posed and called for Lithuania and Russia to cooperate more fully in protecting its shared coastline.

FOOD & DRINK

Long, miserable winters are to blame for Lithuania's hearty, waist-widening diet based on potatoes, meat and dairy products. Cuisine between regions does not vary enormously, although certain traits become noticeable as you eat your way around: mushrooms, berries and game dishes dominate in heavily forested eastern and southern Lithuania; beer sneaks its way into northern cooking pots; while fish reigns on the coast and in lake districts like Trakai. Bread everywhere tends to be black and rye.

Staples & Specialities

Lithuanian food is epitomised in the formidable *cepelinai* (tse-pe-li-nai), parcels of thick potato dough stuffed with cheese, *mesa* (meat) or *grybai* (gree-bai; mushrooms), sometimes also known as a zeppelin. They come topped with a rich sauce made from onions, butter, sour cream and bacon bits. Another artery-furring favourite is sour cream-topped *kugelis* – a 'cannon ball' dish borrowed from German cuisine that bakes grated potatoes and carrots in the oven. *Koldūnai* (kol-doo-nai) are hearty ravioli stuffed with meat or mushrooms and *virtiniai* are stodgy dumplings.

Lithuanians like the less savoury bits of animals: *liežuvis* (lea-zhu-vis; cow's tongue) and *alionių skilandis* (a-lyo-nyoo ski-lan-dis; minced meat smoked in pork bladders) are delicacies, and Lithuanians pork out on *vėdarai* (fried pork innards). Hodgepodge or *šiupinys* (shyu-pi-nees) – often mistakenly assumed to be hedgehog – is pork snout stewed with pork tail, trotter, peas and beans (try it in Vilnius at Žemaičių Smuklė, p315). Smoked pigs' ears, trotters and tails are popular beer snacks alongside *kepta duona* (kep-ta dwa-na) – sticks of black rye bread heaped with garlic and deep-fried. Order them with or without a gooey cheese topping.

Wild boar, rabbit and venison are popular in the Aukštaitija National Park (p326), where hunted birds and animals were traditionally fried in a clay coating or on a spit over an open fire in the 18th century. When perpetually drifting sands on Curonian Spit (p352) in the 17th to 19th centuries made growing crops impossible, locals took to hunting and eating migrating crows in winter: one bite (followed by a generous slug of vodka) at the crow's neck killed the bird, after which its meat was eaten fresh, smoked or salted.

Blyneliai (blee-ne-lyai; pancakes) – a real favourite – are sweet or savoury and eaten any time of the day. *Varskečiai* (vars-ko-chyai) are stuffed with sweet curd, and *bulviniai blyneliai* are made with grated potato and stuffed with meat, *varske* (cheese curd) or fruit and chocolate.

Common starters include *silkė* (herring), *sprotai* (sprats), salads and soups. *Lietuviškos salotos* (lea-tu-vish-kos sa-lo-tos; Lithuanian

---

TASTY READING

Anyone wanting to build their own *cepelinai* (zeppelin), bake a rabbit or butter-braise a hen should invest in the excellent cookery book *Lithuanian Traditional Foods*, compiled by Birutė Imbrasienė.

---

salad) is a mayonnaise-coated mix of diced gherkins, boiled carrots, meat and anything else that happens to be in the fridge. *Šaltibarsčiai* (shal-ti-bars-chyai) – infamous for its fabulous shocking-pink colour – is a cold beetroot summer soup served with dill-sprinkled boiled potatoes and sour cream. Nettle, sorrel, cabbage and bread soup (not to mention blood soup, which does indeed have goose, duck or chicken blood in it) are other soups that have fed Lithuanians for centuries. Eel soup is specific to Curonian Spit, where eel also comes as a main course. In Aukštaitija, fish soup served in a loaf of brown bread is the dish to try.

Mushrooms are popular, especially in August and September when forests are studded with dozens of different varieties – some edible, some deadly. Mushrooms are particularly abundant in Aukštaitija and Dzūkija; see p330 for advice on picking mushrooms. In spring and early summer the same forests buzz with berry pickers; locals stand at roadsides in the region selling glass jamjars of wild strawberries, blueberries, blackberries and so on.

Drinks

Alus (beer) is the most widespread drink, local brands being Švyturys (p360), Utenos (p330) and Kalnapilis (p353). Brewing traditions are oldest in the northern part of Lithuania, where small family-run breweries treat lucky palates to natural beer free of preservatives.

Midus (mead) – honey boiled with water, berries and spices, then fermented with hops to produce an alcoholic drink of 10% to 15% proof – is Lithuania's oldest and most noble drink. It was popular until the decline of beekeeping in the 18th century, but made a comeback in 1959 when **Lietuviškas midus** (www.midus.lt) in Stakliškės in central Lithuania started making authentic mead; it produces seven varieties today.

Vynas (wine) has made inroads into the drinking habits of Vilnius locals (see p318) but provincial Lithuania is still in two minds about the fermented grape juice. *Degtinė* (vodka) is widely consumed and best enjoyed neat, chilled and with company.

The more sober-minded might enjoy the honey liqueur *stakliskes* or *starka*, made from apple-tree and pear-tree leaves. Herbal and fruit teas and brews made from linden, thyme, caraway, ginger, mint, rhubarb and a bounty of other sweet ingredients are age-old; Skonis ir Kvapas (p315) in Vilnius provides a unique opportunity to taste some.

Gira, another nonalcoholic drink, is a cloudy liquid made from bread. It's available across the country.

Celebrations

Christmas is the major culinary feast of the year. On 24 December families sit down to dinner in the evening around a candle-lit hay-covered table topped with a white linen cloth; the hay anticipates Jesus' birth and serves as a place for the souls of dead family members to rest. (Indeed, one place around the table is always laid for someone who died that year.) The Christmas Eve feast that unfolds comprises 12 dishes – one for each month of the coming year to ensure year-long happiness and plenty. Dishes are fish- and vegetarian-based and include festive *kūčiukai* (koo-chiu-kai) – small cubed poppy-seed biscuits served in a bowl of poppy-seed milk; others like herrings, pike, mushrooms and various soups are not necessarily seasonal.

Šakotis (sha-ko-tis) – 'egg cake' – is a large tree-shaped cake covered with long spikes (made from a rather dry, sponge-cake mixture of flour, margarine, sugar, sour cream and dozens and dozens of eggs), which is served at weddings and other special occasions.

Where to Eat & Drink

Dining Lithuanian-style can mean spending anything from 17Lt for a three-course meal in a self-service cafe in a provincial town well off the tourist trail to 345Lt in a swish up-market restaurant in the capital. In Vilnius, choice of cuisine and price range covers the whole gamut, and an English-language menu is usually available (likewise along the coast); elsewhere the choice is limited and menus are rarely translated. Service is at its best in the capital – and generally appalling everywhere else. It often pays to pick two main dishes

EAT YOUR WORDS

Don't know a pig's ear from its trotter? Here are a few useful phrases. For other words and phrases when ordering a meal see the Language chapter (p419).

Useful Phrases

A table for ..., please.	stah·lah ... prah·show	Stalą ..., prašau.
May I see the menu, please?	ahr gah·leh·chow gow·ti man·yew prah·show	Ar galėčiau gauti meniu prašau?
Do you have the menu in English?	ahr yoos tu·ri·ta man·yew ahn·glish·kai	Ar jūs turite meniu anglieškai?
I'd like to try that.	ahsh naw·reh·chow ish·bahn·dee·ti taw	Aš norėčiau išbandyti to.
I don't eat ...	ahsh na·vahl·gow	Aš nevalgau ...
meat	meh·sish·kaw	mėsiško

Food & Drink Glossary

alus	beer	kotlietai	rissoles
arbata	tea	mėlynės	bilberries
avietės	raspberries	menkė	cod
bifšteksas	beefsteak	midus	mead
blyneliai	pancakes	morkos	carrots
braškės	strawberries	pienas	milk
burokėliai	beetroot	plekšnė	plaice
cepelinai	boiled potato dumplings stuffed with meat and covered with bacon, cream and butter sauce	pupos	beans
		rūkytas ungurys	smoked eel
		silkė	herring
		šaltibarščiai	beetroot and sour-cream soup (cold)
duona	black rye bread	šernas	wild boar
ėriena	lamb	šilkmedžio uogos	mulberries
eršketas	sturgeon	skilandis	salami-style pork sausage
gervuogės	blackberries		
gira	sweet drink made from fermented grains or fuit and brown rye bread	stakliskes	honey liquer
		sterkas	perch
		sūris	cheese
grybai	mushrooms	sviestas	butter
jautiena	beef	ungurys	eel
karbonadas	breaded pork chop	upėtakis	trout
kava	coffee	varškė	curd; like cottage cheese
kiauliena	pork		
kiaušiniai	eggs	veršiena	veal
koldūnai	Lithuanian dim sims	vėžiukas	shrimp
		vištiena	chicken
kopūstai	cabbage	žirneliai	peas
kopūstų sriuba	cabbage soup	žuvies asorti	fish assortment

before ordering, as all too often the first choice isn't available.

Habits & Customs
A traditional dose of hospitality means loosening your belt several notches and skipping breakfast. Feasting is lengthy and plentiful, punctuated by many choruses of *Išgeriam!* (ish-ge-ryam; Let's drink!) and *Iki dugno!* (Bottoms up!). Starter dishes can be deceptively generous, leading unsuspecting guests to think they're the main meal. To decline further helpings may offend and be taken to mean that you don't like the food or the hospitality.

The family meal is a ceremonious affair and one that is taken very seriously, albeit one increasingly reserved for feast days, birthdays and other occasions in urban Lithuania's quicker-paced society. Each member of the family has a set place at the table – father at the head, mother opposite. If you arrive at someone's home while the family is seated, be sure to say *skanaus* (enjoy your meal); the response *prašom* (pra-shom; you're welcome) is an invitation to sit down and share the meal, while *ačiū* (a-choo) basically means 'thanks but go away'.

VILNIUS

☎ 5 / pop 542,800
Vilnius (vil-nyus), the baroque bombshell of the Baltic, is a city of immense allure. As beautiful as it is bizarre, it easily tops the country's best-attraction bill, drawing tourists to it like moths to a flame with an easy, confident charm and warm, golden glow that makes one wish for long midsummer evenings every day of the year.

The capital – not only of Lithuania but also Cultural Europe in 2009 (shared with Austria's Linz) – may be a long way north and east, but it is quintessentially continental. At its heart is Europe's largest baroque old town, so precious that Unesco added it to its World Heritage list. Viewed from the basket of an air balloon, the skyline pierced by (almost) countless Orthodox and Catholic church steeples looks like a giant bed of nails. Adding to the intoxicating mix is a combination of cobbled alleys, crumbling corners, majestic hilltop views, break-away states and traditional artists' workshops – all in

a city so small that sometimes you'd think it a village.

It has not always been good and grand here though. There are reminders of loss and pain too, from the horror of the KGB's torture cells to the ghetto in the centre of all this beauty where the Jewish community lived before their mass wartime slaughter. Yet the spirit of freedom and resistance has prevailed, and the city is forging a new identity, combining the past with a present and future that involves world cuisine, a burgeoning nightlife and shiny new skyscrapers. It's hard to ask for more from a European capital, now isn't it?

HISTORY
Legend says Vilnius was founded in the 1320s when Lithuanian grand duke Gediminas dreamt of an iron wolf that howled with the voices of 100 wolves – a sure sign to build a city as mighty as their cry. In fact, the site had already been settled for 1000 years.

A moat, wall and a tower on Gediminas Hill protected 14th- and 15th-century Vilnius from Teutonic attacks. Tatar attacks prompted inhabitants to build a 2.4km defensive wall (1503–22), and by the end of the 16th century Vilnius was among Eastern Europe's biggest cities. Three centuries on, industrialisation arrived: railways were laid and Vilnius became a key Jewish city. Occupied by Germany during WWI, it became an isolated pocket of Poland afterwards. WWII ushered in another German occupation and the death knoll for its Jewish population (p302). After the war, Vilnius' skyline was filled with new residential suburbs populated by Lithuanians from elsewhere alongside immigrant Russians and Belarusians. In the late 1980s the capital was the focus of Lithuania's push for independence from the USSR.

Vilnius has fast become a European city. In 1994 its Old Town became a Unesco World Heritage site and 15 years later shares the prestigious title of European Capital of Culture 2009 with Austrian city Linz. In between much of the Old Town has been restored and is now a tourist hot spot.

ORIENTATION
The city centre sits on the south bank of the Neris River. Its heart is cathedral-studded Katedros aikštė with Gediminas Hill rising behind it. Southward lies the cobbled Old Town, which has Pilies gatvė as the main pedestrian thoroughfare. East along the Vilnia River is

the self-proclaimed Užupis Republic. Heading out towards the west, Gedimino prospektas cuts straight across the newer part of the town centre to parliament.

Vilnius' main train and bus stations are about 1.5km from Katedros aikštė. Immediately north of the Neris River are the business district of Šnipiškės and Vilnius Beach.

Maps

The tourist offices have free maps of central Vilnius which will satisfy most visitors' needs. Otherwise they, along with bookshops, some hotels and supermarkets, sell maps of Vilnius published by **Briedis** (www.briedis.lt; Parodų gatvė 4) and Jāņa sēta. Jāņa sēta's *Vilnius* (1:25,000; 10Lt) covers the entire city and includes a 1:10,000 inset of the central city.

INFORMATION
Bookshops

Akademinė Knyga (Map pp298–9; ☎ 266 1680; www.humanitas.lt; Universiteto gatvė 4) Translated Lithuanian prose and fiction, Lonely Planet travel guides, maps.

Humanitas (Map pp298–9; ☎ 262 1153; www.humanitas.lt; Dominikonų gatvė 5) Lonely Planet guides and a staggering selection of art and design books.

Littera (Map pp298–9; ☎ 268 7258; Šv Jono gatvė 12) University bookshop.

Vaga (Map pp298–9; ☎ 249 8392; Gedimino prospektas 9 & 50) Great map selection and good coffee.

Emergency

For emergency telephone numbers, see the Quick Reference section on the inside cover of this book.

Internet Access

A growing number of cafes, restaurants and hotels have free wi-fi zones; check www.wifi.lt for more information.

Collegium (Map pp298–9; ☎ 261 8334; www.dora.lt; Pilies gatvė 22-1; per hr 5Lt; ⊙ 8am-midnight)

Interneto Kavinė (Map pp298–9; Pylimo gatvė 21; per hr 4Lt; ⊙ 9am-midnight)

Taškas (Map pp298–9; Jasinsko gatvė; per hr 5Lt; ⊙ 24hr)

Internet Resources

www.vilnius.lt Informative city municipality website.

www.vilnius-tourism.lt Tourist office website; brilliant up-to-the-minute capital guide.

www.vsaa.lt Vilnius Old Town Renewal Agency; the latest on the Old Town renovation.

Laundry

Most Vilnius hostels (p312) have a washing machine for guests, and upmarket hotels run a laundry service.

Skalbiu sau (Map pp294–5; ☎ 216 4689; www.skalbiusau.lt; Darbiniukų gatvė 21; ⊙ 9.30am-7.30pm) Service washes and self-service machines.

Left Luggage

Bus Station (Map pp294–5; Siuntos, Sodų gatvė 22; bag per 24hr 3Lt; ⊙ 5.30am-9.45pm Mon-Sat, 7am-8.45pm Sun)

Train Station (Map pp294–5; Geležinkelio gatvė; central hall basement; lockers per day 4-6Lt; ⊙ 24hr)

Libraries

American Centre (Map pp298–9; ☎ 266 5330; Akmenų gatvė 7; ⊙ 10am-4.30pm Mon-Fri) Housed in the US embassy.

Centre Culturel Français (Map pp298–9; ☎ 231 2985; www.centrefrancais.lt; Didžioji gatvė 1; ⊙ 1.30-6.30pm Mon-Fri, 10am-3pm Sat)

Media

Exploring Vilnius (www.exploringcity.com) Detailed guide, free in hotels and bookshops.

Vilnius in Your Pocket (www.inyourpocket.com) Quality city guide published every two months, available as PDF download or in bookshops, tourist offices and newspaper kiosks (5Lt).

Vilnius Visitor's Guide Produced by Vilnius Tourism; covers shopping, sightseeing, culture, eating out, accommodation and transport in the city. Available from tourist offices.

Medical Services

Baltic-American Medical & Surgical Clinic (off Map pp294–5; ☎ 234 2020; www.bak.lt; Nemenčinės gatvė 54a; ⊙ 24hr)

Euro vaistinė (Map pp298–9; ☎ 270 4704; Gedimino prospektas 8; ⊙ 8am-9pm Mon-Fri, 9am-8pm Sat, 10am-5pm Sun)

Gedimino vaistinė (Map pp298–9; ☎ 261 0135; Gedimino prospektas 27; ⊙ 24hr) Pharmacy handily located on Vilnius' main commercial street.

Gintarine vaistinė (Map pp294–5; Geležinkelio gatvė 16; ⊙ 7am-9pm Mon-Fri, 9am-6pm Sat & Sun) Pharmacy at the central hall of the train station.

Vilnius University Emergency Hospital (Map pp294–5; ☎ 216 9069; Šiltnamių gatvė 29; ⊙ 24hr)

Money

The following all have ATMs accepting Visa and MasterCard, but ATMs can be found throughout the city.

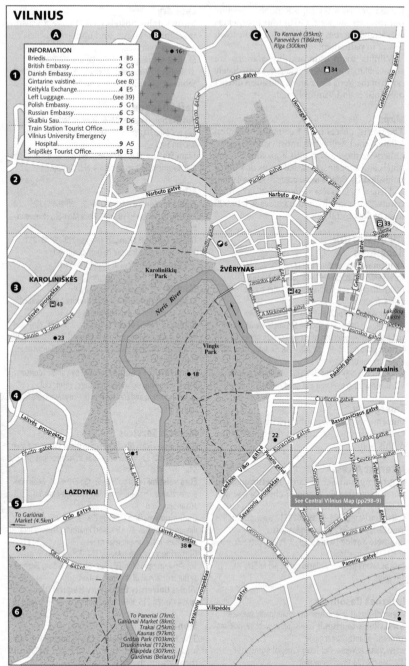

VILNIUS

INFORMATION
Briedis	1	B5
British Embassy	2	G3
Danish Embassy	3	G3
Gintarine vaistinė	(see 8)	
Keitykla Exchange	4	E5
Left Luggage	(see 39)	
Polish Embassy	5	G1
Russian Embassy	6	C3
Skalbiu Sau	7	D6
Train Station Tourist Office	8	E5
Vilnius University Emergency Hospital	9	A5
Šnipiškės Tourist Office	10	E3

To Kernavė (35km);
Panevėžys (186km);
Riga (300km)

Ožo gatvė

Paribio gatvė

Narbuto gatvė

Narbuto gatvė

KAROLINIŠKĖS

Karoliniškių Park

ŽVĖRYNAS

Neris River

Laisvės prospektas

Sausio 13-osios gatvė

Vingis Park

Tauraukalnis

Čiurlionio gatvė

Basanavičiaus gatvė

Laisvės prospektas

Efurto gatvė

LAZDYNAI

To Gariūnai
Market (4.5km)

Oslo gatvė

Laisvės prospektas

See Central Vilnius Map (pp298-9)

Kauno gatvė

Panerių gatvė

Vilkpėdės

To Paneriai (7km);
Gariūnai Market (8km);
Trakai (25km);
Kaunas (97km);
Grūtas Park (103km);
Druskininkai (112km);
Klaipėda (307km);
Gardinas (Belarus)

LITHUANIA

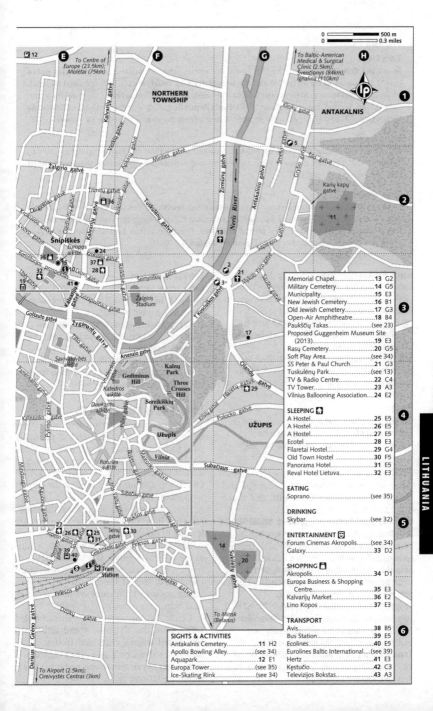

LITHUANIA

VILNIUS IN...

Two Days

Spend the first day exploring the Old Town, not missing the **cathedral** (opposite), **Pilies gatvė** (p301), the **Gates of Dawn** (p304) and the **university's 13 courtyards** (p302), followed by lunch on an Old Town terrace. At dusk hike (or ride the funicular) up **Gediminas Hill** (opposite) for a city-spire sunset. Second day, stroll around the **Užupis Republic** (p304), visit the **Museum of Genocide Victims**, (p307) and finish up with an aperitif and Vilnius panorama from the **TV Tower** (p308).

Four Days

Enjoy a couple of days exploring essential Vilnius and on the third day take a trip out of town to **Trakai** (p322). Last day, do some Vilnius museums and explore the city's **folk-artists' workshops** (see the boxed text, p303).

One Week

Depending on your interests, spend a day discovering **Jewish Vilnius** (p302), marvelling at religious jewels in the **Museum of Applied Arts** (opposite), wandering through the reconstructed **Royal Palace** (p301) or take your pick of churches. Finish up with a spot of **shopping** (p319): scour the city for linen, amber and Lithuanian **design** (p320).

Hansa Bankas (www.hansa.lt) Gedimino (Map pp298–9; Gedimino prospektas 56); Vilnius (Map pp298–9; Vilnius gatvė 16) Cashes Thomas Cook & Amex traveller's cheques.
Keitykla Exchange (Parex Bankas; Map pp294–5; ☎ 213 5454; www.keitykla.lt; Geležinkelio gatvė 6; ☽ 24hr) Currency exchange with ATM. Parex Bankas is Lithuania's Amex representative.
SEB Vilniaus Bankas Gedimino (Map pp298–9; Gedimino prospektas 12); Jogailos (Map pp298–9; Jogailos gatvė 9a); Vokiečių (Map pp298–9; Vokiečių gatvė 9)

Post
Branch post office (Map pp298–9; Vokiečių gatvė 7)
Central post office (Map pp298–9; Gedimino prospektas 7; ☽ 7am-7pm Mon-Fri, 9am-4pm Sat)

Tourist Information
All four tourist offices have free maps and handouts on self-guided strolls, and make accommodation bookings (6Lt).
Old Town tourist office (Map pp298–9; ☎ 262 9660; tic@vilnius.lt; Vilniaus gatvė 22; ☽ 9am-6pm Mon-Fri, 10am-4pm Sat & Sun) Organises city tours (p311), English-speaking guides (two hours 200Lt) and audio guides (35Lt).
Šnipiškės tourist office (Map pp294–5; ☎ 211 2031; turizmas@vilnius.lt; Konstitucijos prospektas 3; ☽ 9am-5pm Mon-Fri) In the municipality building.
Town hall tourist office (Map pp298–9; ☎ 262 6470; turizm.info@vilnius.lt; Didžioji gatvė 31; ☽ 9am-6pm Mon-Fri, 10am-4pm Sat & Sun) Organises city tours, English-speaking guides and audio guides (35Lt).
Train station tourist office (Map pp294–5; ☎ 269 2091; Geležinkelio gatvė 16; ☽ 9am-6pm Mon-Fri, 10am-4pm Sat & Sun) In the central hall.

Travel Agencies
Baltic Travel Service (Map pp298–9; ☎ 212 0220; www.bts.lt; Subačiaus gatvė 2) Reservations for country farm-stays, bus tickets and hotels.
West Express (Map pp298–9; ☎ 212 2500; www.westexpress.lt, in Lithuanian; Stulginskio gatvė 5) Large, nationwide travel agent.
Zigzag (Map pp298–9; ☎ 239 7397; www.zigzag.lt, in Lithuanian; Basanavičiaus gatvė 30) Cheap fares for International Student Identity Card holders.

DANGERS & ANNOYANCES

Vilnius is provincial compared with most other world capitals. That said, it definitely pays to be streetwise. Avoid walking alone on dark streets at night, stash your wallet in a front pocket, and watch for pickpockets in Old Town and on buses linking the airport with town.

Don't hop in a taxi direct from the street; ask your hotel or the restaurant/bar you are leaving to call one for you.

Resident beggars are sometimes a nuisance on Pilies gatvė. If someone asks for money, give them a green pocket-sized card (SPC card, free at the tourist office) with information in Lithuanian on how they can find help.

Unsavoury tap water (many drink bottled water; avoid the 'Vytautas' brand, unless you like salted water), crammed trolley buses, minibuses that don't stop when hailed and snail-slow service in some restaurants are minor irritations.

SIGHTS

Vilnius is a compact city, and most sights are easily reached on foot. Those visiting for a couple of days will scarcely move out of the Old Town, where souvenir stalls, folk-artist workshops and design boutiques jostle for attention with a treasure trove of architectural gems. Stay a couple more days and the New Town – with its museums, shops and riverside action – beckons.

Gediminas Hill

Vilnius was founded on 48m-high **Gediminas Hill** (Map pp298–9), topped since the 13th century by a red-brick tower. The original tower was a tier higher than the 20m edifice that marks the spot today. Its walls were ruined during the Russian occupation (1655–61), but it was restored in 1930 to house the **Upper Castle Museum** (Aukštutinės pilies muziejus; Map pp298–9; ☎ 261 7453; Arsenalo gatvė 5; adult/child 4/2Lt, guided tour 15Lt; 🕒 10am-7pm May-Oct, 10am-5pm Tue-Sun Nov-Apr), which contains shiny armour from the 16th to 18th centuries, models of the castle in former times, and panoramic views of the city. The museum can be reached by **funicular** (adult/child 2/1Lt; 🕒 10am-7pm May-Oct, 10am-5pm Nov-Apr) located at the rear of the Museum of Applied Arts.

The **Museum of Applied Arts** (Taikomosios dailės muziejus; Map pp298-9; ☎ 262 8080; www.ldm.lt; Arsenalo gatvė 3a; adult/child 6/3Lt; 🕒 11am-6pm Tue-Sat, to 4pm Sun), located in the old arsenal at the foot of Gediminas Hill, has temporary exhibitions alongside a permanent collection showcasing 15th- to 19th-century Lithuanian sacred art. Much of it was only discovered in Vilnius cathedral in 1985 after being hidden in the walls by Russian soldiers in 1655. Because of the fear that they'd be seized by the Soviets, the gems, valued at €11 million, remained a secret until 1998, when they were finally displayed to the world.

Sitting stoically nearby, the **National Museum of Lithuania** (Lietuvos nacionalinis muziejus; Map pp298-9) ☎ 262 9426; www.lnm.lt; Arsenalo gatvė 1; adult/child 4/2Lt, guided tour 15Lt; 🕒 10am-5pm Tue-Sat, to 3pm Sun) is guarded by a proud statue of Mindaugas, the first and only king of Lithuania. Inside are exhibits looking at everyday Lithuanian life from the 13th century till WWII. Of particular note are some of the country's earliest coins, dating from the 14th century, which feature the bust of Jogaila (p279).

Cathedral Square

Katedros aikštė – a square set to make your dreams come true (p301) – buzzes with local life. In the 19th century markets and fairs were held here and a moat ran around what is now the square's perimeter so ships could sail to the cathedral door. Within the moat were walls and towers, the only remaining part of which is the 57m-tall **belfry** (Map pp298–9) near the cathedral's western end.

In front of the Royal Palace at the square's eastern end is an **equestrian statue of Gediminas** (Map pp298–9), built on an ancient pagan site. Behind the grand old duke, **Sereikiškių Park** (Map pp298–9) leads to **Three Crosses Hill** (p306) and **Kalnų Park** (Map pp298–9).

CATHEDRAL

This national symbol was originally used for the worship of Perkūnas, the Lithuanian thunder god; later the Soviets turned **Vilnius Cathedral** (Arkikatedra bazilika; Map pp298-9; ☎ 261 1127; Katedros aikštė 1; admission free; 🕒 7am-7.30pm, Sun Mass 9am, 10am, 11am, 7pm) into a picture gallery. It was reconsecrated in 1989 and Mass has been celebrated daily ever since.

The first wooden cathedral was built here in 1387–88. A grander edifice was constructed under the auspices of Grand Duke Vytautas in the 15th century, which was in Gothic style, but has been rebuilt so often that its old form is unrecognisable. The most important restoration was completed from 1783 to 1801, when the outside was redone in today's classical style. The statues of Sts Helene, Stanislav and Casimir are replicas of wooden versions added in 1793 but destroyed under Stalin.

The statues on the cathedral's south side facing the square are Lithuanian dukes; those on the north side are apostles and saints. The bright and expansive interior retains more of its original aspect, though the entrances to

---

TOP FIVE PANORAMAS

For a breathtaking cityscape scale:

- **Upper Castle Museum** (left) while sightseeing
- **Europa** (p320) during a shopping spree
- **Tores** (p316) over lunch or dinner
- **Skybar** (p317) with aperitif in hand
- **TV Tower** (p308) for sunset vistas

LITHUANIA

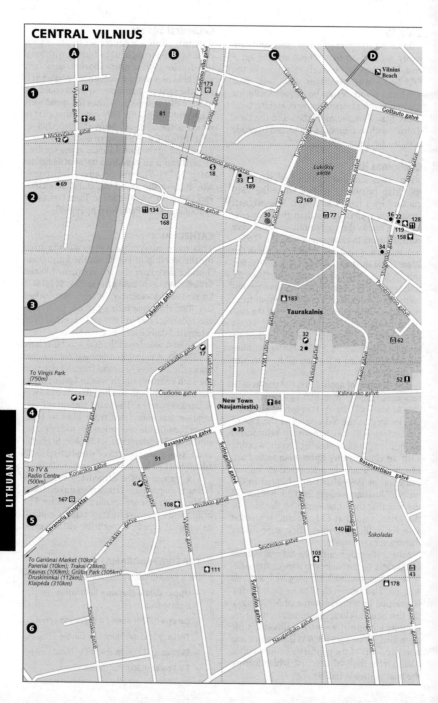

CENTRAL VILNIUS

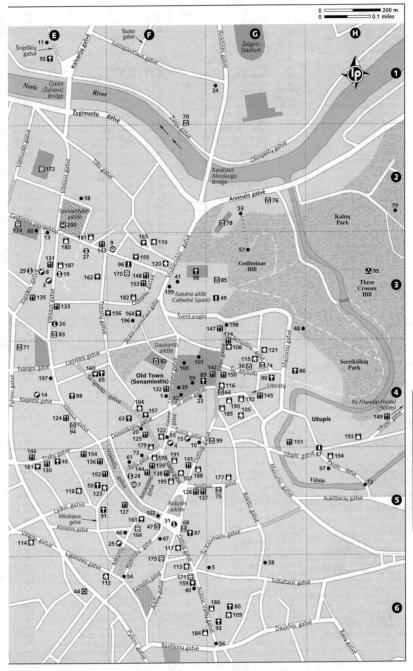

LITHUANIA

the side chapels were harmonised in the late 18th century.

St Casimir's Chapel (Map pp298–9) is the showpiece. It has a baroque cupola, coloured marble and granite on the walls, white stucco sculptures, and fresco scenes from the life of St Casimir (who was canonised in 1602 and is Lithuania's patron saint). Find it at the eastern end of the south aisle.

ROYAL PALACE

The Renaissance ushered in the **Royal Palace** (Valdovų rumai; Map pp298-9; www.lvr.lt, in Lithuanian). A quadrangle of four wings enclosing a vast courtyard measuring 10,000 sq metres, the palace buzzed with masked balls, gay banquets and tournaments during the 16th century. Between 1632 and 1648 the first Lithuanian operas were performed here. But in 1795, because of the Russian occupation of Lithuania, the palace – as well as the Lower Castle and the city defence wall – was demolished.

Currently being rebuilt red brick by red brick, this palace of incredible dimensions *should* rise from the ashes on 6 July 2009 to mark the millennial anniversary of the first mention of Lithuania in writing. Inside will be a museum with displays detailing the reconstruction project and a treasure trove of Gothic and baroque archaeological finds – ceramics, glassware and jewellery – discovered during the excavation work.

Old Town

Eastern Europe's largest old town deserves its Unesco status. The area, stretching 1.5km south from Katedros aikštė, was built up in the 15th and 16th centuries, and its narrow winding streets, hidden courtyards and lavish old churches retain the feel of bygone centuries. One of the purest pleasures the city has to offer is aimlessly wandering the Old Town backstreets in search of hidden gems. The main axis is along Pilies, Didžioji and Aušros Vartų gatvė. Its approximate boundary, starting from Katedros aikštė, runs along Stuokos-Gucevičiaus, Liejyklos, Vilniaus, Trakų, Pylimo, Bazilijonų, Šv Dvasios, Bokšto, Maironio, Radvilaitės and Sventaragio streets – an area of roughly 1 sq km.

PILIES GATVĖ

Cobbled Pilies Gatvė (Castle Street) – the hub of tourist action and the main entrance

---

WISH UPON A...

...star? No. Not in Vilnius. Rather, a tile bearing the word *stebuklas* (miracle). It marks the spot on Cathedral Sq where the human chain – formed between Tallinn and Vilnius by two million Lithuanians, Latvians and Estonians to protest Soviet occupation in 1989 – ended. To make a wish, do a clockwise 360-degree turn on the tile. Unfortunately, superstition forbids the location of Vilnius' elusive-but-lucky spot to be revealed, meaning you have to search for it yourself.

---

to Old Town from Katedros aikštė – buzzes with buskers, souvenir stalls, and the odd beggar. Until the 19th century the street was separated from the square by the lower castle wall, which ran across its northern end. Only a gate in the wall connected the two. Notice the 15th- to 17th-century brickwork of Nos 4, 12 and 16 towards the northern end of the street. The act granting Lithuania independence in 1918 was signed in No 26, the baroque **House of Signatories** (Lietuvos nepriklausomybės akto signatarų namai; Map pp298-9; ☎ 231 4442; Pilies gatvė 26; admission free; 10am-5pm Tue-Sat, to 3pm Sun May-Oct, 10am-5pm Tue-Sat Nov-Mar). The house, which can only be visited by guided tour, displays photos of the movers and shakers in Lithuania's push for independence and intriguing maps of Lithuania's place in Europe through the centuries.

VILNIUS UNIVERSITY

Founded in 1579 during the Counter-Reformation, **Vilnius University** (Map pp298-9; ☎ 268 7001; www.vu.lt; Universiteto gatvė 5), Eastern Europe's oldest, was run by Jesuits for two centuries and became one of the greatest centres of Polish learning. It produced many notable scholars, but was closed by the Russians in 1832 and didn't reopen until 1919. Today it has 23,000 students and Lithuania's oldest library, shelving five million books. The world's first **Centre for Stateless Cultures** (Map pp298-9; ☎ 268 7293; www.statelesscultures.lt; Universiteto gatvė 5) or those that don't have an army or navy, including Jewish, Roma and Karaimic cultures, is in the history faculty. The Tuesday evening seminars held at 6pm in room 29 of the faculty are open to everyone; see the website.

LITHUANIA

JERUSALEM OF THE NORTH

One of Europe's prominent Jewish communities flourished in prewar Vilnius (Vilne in Yiddish), but Nazi and Soviet brutality virtually wiped it out. Now the Jewish quarter is slowly being rebuilt – amid controversy in a country still haunted by the spectre of anti-Semitism.

The history of Vilnius is indebted to Jewish culture. Three thousand Jews settled in Vilnius eight centuries ago at the invitation of Grand Duke Gediminas (1316–41) and in the 19th century Vilnius became a centre for the European Jewish language, Yiddish. Famous Jews from the city's community include rabbi and scholar Gaon Elijahu ben Shlomo Zalman (1720–97), who led opposition to the widespread Jewish mystical movement Hassidism, and landscape artist Isaak Levitan (1860–1900).

The city's Jewish population peaked on the eve of WWI at almost 100,000 (out of 240,000 in Lithuania). However, plagued by discrimination and poverty, the Jewish community diminished in the interwar years when Vilnius was an outpost of Poland. Despite this, Vilnius blossomed into the Jewish cultural hub of Eastern Europe, and was chosen ahead of the other Yiddish centres, Warsaw and New York, as the headquarters of the Yiddish-language scientific research institute YIVO in 1925 (the institute stood on Vivulskio gatvė). Jewish schools, libraries, literature and theatre flourished. There were 100 synagogues and prayer houses, and six daily Jewish newspapers. By the end of WWII Lithuania's Jewish community was all but destroyed and during the *perestroika* years an estimated 6000 Jews left for Israel.

The hidden but linked **13 university courtyards** (Map pp298-9; Universiteto gatvė 3; adult/child 5/1Lt; 9am-6pm Mon-Sat) are accessed by passages and gates from surrounding streets. The south gate on Šv Jono gatvė brings you into the **Grand Courtyard**. Inside is St John's Church (Šv Jono bažnyčia; Map pp298-9; 10am-5pm Mon-Sat), founded in 1387 well before the university arrived. Its 17th-century bell tower, standing on the south side of the courtyard, is a distinctive feature in the Vilnius skyline. The arch through the 16th-century building opposite St John's leads to the **Astronomical Observatory Courtyard**, with an old two-domed **observatory**, the late 18th-century facade of which is adorned with reliefs of the zodiac.

DAUKANTO AIKŠTĖ

The exit from the university's **Sarbievijus Courtyard** to Universiteto gatvė brings you into the square opposite the former Bishops' Palace, now the **Presidential Palace** (Map pp298-9; 266 4011; www.president.lt; Daukanto gatvė 3; admission free; guided tours 9am-2.30pm Sat). It gained its current classical Russian Empire style early in the 19th century. The palace was used by Napoleon during his advance on Moscow, and by his Russian adversary General Mikhail Kutuzov when he was chasing Napoleon back to Paris. Military flag ceremonies take place outside the palace at 10am and 5.30pm daily, and visits by guided tour (in Lithuanian) must be booked in advance; bring your passport to get in.

MICKIEWICZ MEMORIAL APARTMENT & MUSEUM

'Lithuania, my fatherland…' is Poland's national romantic masterpiece. It's not surprising when you realise it was Polish poet Adam Mickiewicz (1798–1855) – muse to Polish nationalists in the 19th century – who wrote the infamous line in his poem *Pan Tadeusz*. He grew up near Vilnius and studied at the university (1815–19) before being exiled for anti-Russian activities in 1824. The rooms where he wrote the well-known poem *Gražia* in 1822 are now filled with a few of the poet's letters and appropriately named the **Mickiewicz Memorial Apartment Museum** (Mickevičiaus memorialinis butas-muziejus; Map pp298-9; 260 0148; Bernardinų gatvė 11; adult/child 4/2Lt; 10am-5pm Tue-Fri, to 2pm Sat & Sun).

ST MICHAEL'S & ST ANNE'S CHURCHES

Opposite the eastern end of Bernardinų gatvė, 17th-century **St Michael's Church** (Šv Mykolo bažnyčia; Map pp298-9; 261 6409; Šv Mykolo gatvė 9), which normally shelters a small museum focusing on 1918–90 architecture, was enjoying renovation at the time of writing.

Within sight of St Michael's spires is the **Amber Museum-Gallery** (Gintaro Muziejus-Galerija; Map pp298-9; 263 3092; Šv Mykolo gatvė 8; admission free; 10am-7pm). The usual array of amber trinkets and jewellery to buy are displayed on the ground floor, but it's the small but fine exhibition in the basement that warrants the most attention – not least for its archaeological excavations (the basement is set at 15th-century street level). Ceramics were fired in the two kilns in the 15th century.

Arguably the most beautiful church in Vilnius – at least for its exterior – is the 16th-century **St Anne's Church** (Šv Onos bažnyčia; Map pp298-9; ☎ 261 1236; Maironio gatvė 8). A graceful example of Gothic architecture, its sweeping curves and delicate pinnacles frame 33 different types of red brick. It is so fine that Napoleon reputedly wanted to take it back to Paris in the palm of his hand.

DIDŽIOJI GATVĖ

The Old Town's main artery continues south and passes from Pilies gatvė into Didžioji gatvė, home to the **Vilnius Picture Gallery** (Vilniaus Galerija Paveikslų; Map pp298-9; ☎ 212 4258; Didžioji gatvė 4; adult/child 6/3Lt; 🕑 noon-6pm Tue-Sat, to 5pm Sun), filled with 16th- to 20th-century Lithuanian art, and the city's oldest baroque church, **St Casimir's** (Šv Kazimiero bažnyčia; Map pp298-9; ☎ 212 1715; Didžioji gatvė 34; 🕑 10am-6.30pm Mon-Sat, 8am-6.30pm Sun). St Casimir's dome and cross-shaped ground plan defined a new style for 17th-century churches when the Jesuits built it between 1604 and 1615. Aside from the striking marble and gold-gilded high altar, its interior is a relatively plain example of baroque architecture.

Taking the side street Savičiaus gatvė brings you to the **MK Čiurkionis House** (Map pp298-9; ☎ 262 2451; Savičiaus gatvė 11; admission free; 🕑 10am-4pm Mon-Fri). Inside the former home of the great artist and composer are a handful of Čiurkionis reproductions, worth taking a peek at if you can't make it to the National Čiurkionis Art Museum (p339) in Kaunas.

Didžioji gatvė widens at its southern end into **Rotušės aikštė** (Town Hall Sq). The former town hall in the middle of the square has been here since the early 16th century, but its classical exterior dates from 1785 to 1799. Today it houses the tourist office.

Near the town hall is the **Kazys Varnelis Museum** (Map pp298-9; ☎ 279 1644; www.lnm.lt; Didžioji gatvė 26), home to the personal art collection of Kazys Varnelis. During his 50 years in the US, Varnelis, a Lithuanian artist who earned his fame and fortune State-side with optical and three-dimensional paintings, collected a vast and varied array of paintings, furniture, sculptures, maps and books, including works by Dürer, Goya and Matteo Di Givanni. Visits are by appointment only, so call or email beforehand.

AUŠROS VARTŲ GATVĖ

Vilnius' oldest street, which leads out of Didžioji gatvė, is laden with churches and souvenir shops. Walking south, it's hard to

CRAFTY VILNIUS

Lithuanian folk art is alive and well, as the clutch of enchanting folk-artists' workshops in and around the Old Town proves.

Aldona Mickuvienė's workshop (Map pp298–9; ☎ 216 5063; Žydų gatvė 2-10) and **Bronė Daškevičienė's workshop** (Map pp298–9; ☎ 275 9116; Žydų gatvė 2-9) Two elderly ladies have been weaving colourful wedding sashes in their neighbouring workshops for decades. Buy a ready-made sash (50Lt) or order one with your name on it (70Lt). Each sash takes a full day or more to weave.

Black Ceramics Centre (BCC; Map pp298–9; ☎ 8-699 42456; http://ceramics.w3.lt; Naugarduko gatvė 20) Ceramics as black as coal have been crafted since prehistoric times. See the end result at this innovative art centre.

Jonas Bugailiškis (Map pp298–9; ☎ 261 7667, 8-652 36613; Aušros Vartų gatvė 17-10) Angels, jumping horses, masks, bird houses, crosses and a menagerie of other wooden creations can be seen at this creative workshop. Making traditional folk-music instruments is the folk artist's other love.

Sauluva (Map pp298–9; ☎ 212 1227; Literatų gatvė 3; 🕑 10am-7pm) Learn how to make *verbos* (traditional woven dried flowers crafted to celebrate Palm Sunday) and paint traditional Lithuanian Easter eggs at this shop-cum-workshop.

Užupis Blacksmith Museum-Gallery (Užupio kalvystės muziejus galerija; Map pp298–9; Užupio gatvė 26) Forged-iron articles are sold at this traditional blacksmith's; demonstrations on Tuesday, Friday and Saturday.

Vilnius Potters' Guild (Vilniaus Puodžių Cechas; Map pp298-9; ☎ 8-659 99040; www.pottery.lt, in Lithuanian; Paupio gatvė 2-20; 🕑 11am-7pm Tue-Fri, noon-6pm Sat) Re-established in 2003, see p319.

Vitražo manufaktūra (Map pp298–9; ☎ 212 1202; www.stainedglass.lt; Stiklių gatvė 6-8; 🕑 10am-6pm Tue-Fri, to 4pm Sat) Exquisite stained-glass sculptures, wall murals and mobiles fill this creative stained-glass workshop; daily demonstrations noon to 4pm.

REBELS WITH A CAUSE

The cheeky streak of rebellion pervading Lithuania flourishes in Vilnius' bohemian heart, where artists, dreamers, drunks and squatters in Užupis have declared a breakaway state.

The Užupis Republic (Užupio Republika) was officially, in an unofficial sense, born in 1998. The state has its own tongue-in-cheek president, anthem, flags and a 41-point **constitution** (Map pp298–9), which, among other things, gives inhabitants: the right to hot water, heating in winter and a tiled roof; the right to be unique, to love, to be free, to be happy (or unhappy) and to be a dog. It ends 'Do not defeat. Do not fight back. Do not surrender'. Read the entire thing in English, French or Lithuanian on a wall on Paupio gatvė.

On April Fool's Day, citizens of the Republic of Užupis celebrate their wholly unofficial state. Border guards wearing comical outfits stamp passports at the main bridge and the Užupis president makes speeches in the quarter's small square – the intersection of Užupio, Maluno and Paupio gatvės where the republic's symbol, the **Angel of Užupis** (Map pp298–9), stands. Increasingly hip and trendy, the neighbourhood continues to fill with art galleries and folk artist workshops (see the boxed text, p303).

---

miss the late-baroque archway known as the **Basilian Gates** (Map pp298-9; Aušros Vartų gatvė 7) on the right. It forms the entrance to the crumbling Holy Trinity Basilian monastery, complete with decrepit Gothic church which is receiving some long-overdue attention. Almost opposite is the pink-domed 17th-century **Orthodox Church of the Holy Spirit** (Šv Dvasios cerkvė; Map pp298-9; Aušros Vartų gatvė 10), Lithuania's chief Russian Orthodox church. In a chamber at the foot of a flight of steps in front of the altar (you can even see their feet peeping out) lie the preserved bodies of three 14th-century martyrs – Sts Anthony, Ivan and Eustachius.

Continuing south brings you to the Catholic **St Teresa's Church** (Šv Teresės bažnyčia; Map pp298-9; Aušros Vartų gatvė 14), a church baroque through and through – early baroque outside and ornate late baroque inside. Underneath its entrance is a chamber for the dead, which contains some fine examples of baroque tombs, but unfortunately it is normally locked.

Marking the southern border of the Old Town is one of the city's resounding landmarks, the famous 16th-century **Gates of Dawn** (Aušros Vartai; Map pp298-9). They are the only gates of the original nine in the town wall still intact.

A door on the street's eastern side opens onto a staircase that leads to the 18th-century **Chapel of the Blessed Mary** (Map pp298-9; admission free; ☉ 6am-7pm, Mass 9am Mon-Sat, 9.30am Sun) above the gate arch. Inside, and visible from the street below, is a miracle-working icon of the Virgin, reputed to have been

souvenired from the Crimea by Grand Duke Algirdas in 1363, though more likely dating from the 16th century. It is revered by the deeply Catholic Polish community and is one of Eastern Europe's leading pilgrimage destinations.

ARTILLERY BASTION

From the Gates of Dawn, follow the old wall around on to Šv Dvasios gatvė, then continue north to reach the **Artillery Bastion** (Artilerijos bastėja; Map pp298-9; ☎ 261 2149; Bokšto gatvė 20/18). This 17th-century fortification houses a collection of old weaponry and armour and, like a number of historical buildings in Vilnius, was being spruced up for the 2009 Cultural Capital festivities when we visited; check the tourist offices for the latest opening times and prices.

VOKIEČIŲ GATVĖ AND AROUND

Vokiečių gatvė, the wide boulevard running northwest from Rotušės aikštė, is lined with restaurants that sprawl out on to the green parade at its centre. At its town hall end, changing exhibitions of excellent installation art and photography by Lithuanian and foreign avant-garde artists fills the **Contemporary Art Centre** (Šiuolaikinio meno centras; SMC; Map pp298-9; ☎ 262 3476; www.cac.lt; Vokiečių gatvė 2; adult/child 8/4Lt; ☉ noon-7.30pm Tue-Sun). About halfway up the street and hidden in a courtyard, the revamped **Evangelical Lutheran Church** (Evangelikų liuteronų bažnyčia; Map pp298-9; ☎ 262 6046; www .augustana.lt; Vokiečių gatvė 20; ☉ 11am-2pm Mon-Fri, English service 9.30am Sun) is home to Vilnius' tiny Protestant community. The church dates from 1555 but displays a mixture of Gothic, baroque and rococo elements in its architecture. Under the Soviets a concrete floor split the church into workshop and basketball court.

A little south of Vokiečių on quiet Mikalojaus gatvė is **St Nicholas' Church** (Šv Mikalojaus bažnyčia; Map pp298-9; Šv Mikalojaus gatvė 4), Lithuania's oldest Gothic church, founded by Germans around 1320. From 1901 to 1939 it was the only church in Vilnius where Mass was held in Lithuanian.

VILNIAUS GATVĖ & AROUND

At the confluence of Vokiečių gatvė, Vilniaus gatvė and Dominikonų gatvė stand four sizeable Catholic church and monastery complexes chiefly dating from the 17th- and 18th-century baroque era. **Holy Spirit Church** (Šv Dvasios bažnyčia; Map pp298-9; ☎ 262 9595; cnr Dominikonų & Šv Ignoto gatvė) is Vilnius' primary Polish church (1679). Once attached to a Dominican monastery, it has a splendid gold and white interior and is hugely popular with wedding parties. The two towers of peach and creamy-white **St Catherine's Church** (Šv Kotrynos bažnyčia; Map pp298-9; Vilniaus gatvė 30) nearby were once part

of a Benedictine monastery; these days the church often hosts classical concerts.

Take a short walk west of Vilniaus gatvė and you'll find the reconsecrated **Church of the Assumption** (Map pp298-9; Trakų gatvė 9/1). Dubbed 'Sands Church' after the quarter in which it stands, this 15th-century Franciscan church has a varied history – it was a hospital for the French army in 1812 and housed the state archives from 1864 to 1934 and 1949 to 1989. The building was returned to the Archbishopric of Vilnius in 1995 and to Franciscan friars three years later. The church is still in a sad state of disrepair but at least reconstruction has begun to return it to its original splendour.

Memorabilia from stage and screen is the star of the **Theatre, Music & Cinema Museum** (Teatro, muzikos ir kino muziejus; Map pp298-9; ☎ 262 2406; Vilniaus gatvė 41; adult/student 4/2Lt; ☉ noon-6pm Tue-Fri, 11am-4pm Sat). Of the three arts, the musical history section steals the show – the collection of traditional musical instruments, including a *pūslinė* (a primitive Baltic string instrument made from animal bladders) and several *kanklės* (plucked, fretted string instruments), will enchant anyone who has ever picked up an instrument.

JEWISH QUARTER & GHETTOS

The Jewish quarter lay in the streets west of Didžioji gatvė. Today the street names Žydų (Jews) and Gaono (Gaon) are among the few explicit reminders of this. The 1572 **Great Synagogue** (Map pp298–9) and its famous 1902 **Strashun Library** (Map pp298–9) stood at the western end of Žydų gatvė. For 80 years preceding 1941, the building at Gaono gatvė 6 (today the Austrian embassy) was a Jewish house of prayer. At Žydų gatvė 3, outside the **House of Gaon Elijahu Ben Shlomo Zalman** (Map pp298–9), is a **memorial bust** (Map pp298–9), erected in 1997 on the 200th anniversary of the death of the sage who recited the entire Talmud by heart at the age of six.

Virtually all of Vilnius' Jewish organisations, except communist ones, were dissolved when the Soviet Union took over eastern Poland in September 1939. Many Jewish leaders were deported. Meanwhile Polish Jews fleeing the Nazis arrived here as refugees. Vilnius fell to the Nazis two days after their invasion of the USSR on 22 June 1941. In the next three months some 35,000 Jews – almost half those in the city – were murdered in Paneriai Forest (p322), before a ghetto was established in a small area north of Vokiečių gatvė. This first ghetto – known as the **Small Ghetto** (Map pp298–9) – was liquidated after 46 days and its inhabitants killed at Paneriai; a memorial plaque outside Gaono gatvė 3 remembers the 11,000 Jews marched to their death from this ghetto between 6 September and 20 October 1941.

Vilnius' **Large Ghetto** (Map pp298–9), created on 6 September 1941 south of Vokiečių gatvė, lasted until the general liquidation of ghettos on Himmler's orders in September 1943, when 26,000 people were killed at Paneriai and a further 10,000 herded off to concentration camps. About 6000 Vilnius Jews escaped. The single gate of the main ghetto stood at what's now Rūdninkų gatvė 18, marked with a plaque bearing a detailed map of the former ghetto. The former **Judenrat** (ghetto administration building; Map pp298-9) was at Rūdninkų gatvė 8; its courtyard shelters a commemorative plaque to 1200 Jews selected to be sent to Paneriai.

LITHUANIA

A short stroll north along Vilniaus brings you to the entrance of **Radvilos' Palace** (Radvilų rūmai; Map pp298-9; ☎ 262 0981; Vilniaus gatvė 22; adult/student 6/3Lt; ☺ noon-6pm Tue-Sat, to 5pm Sun). This 17th-century residence houses the foreign fine-arts section of the Lithuanian Art Museum above ground and nightclub Woo (p318) below.

West of Vilniaus gatvė, rock 'n' roll legend **Frank Zappa** is immortalised in a **bronze bust** (Map pp298-9; Kalinausko gatvė 1) atop a 4.2m-high stainless-steel pole. It was the world's first memorial to the offbeat American who died from cancer in 1993.

East of Gediminas Hill

Crossing the Vilnia River brings you into foreign territory – the self-declared independent republic of Užupis (see the boxed text, p304). The district has a few quirky attractions, including **Lock Bridge** (Map pp298-9; Paupio gatvė), where newlyweds attach a padlock to the bridge railing to secure their marriage, but plenty more lies further east.

THREE CROSSES

East of Gediminas Hill, **Three Crosses** (Trys kryžiai; Map pp298-9) stand majestically atop Three Crosses Hill (Trijų kryžių kalnas). Crosses have stood here since the 17th century in

memory of three monks who were crucified on this spot. The remains of three crosses lie in the shadow of the erect ones. These are the original hill monuments, which the Soviets bulldozed after WWII. In the spirit of Lithuania the people rebuilt them but left the twisted remains of the originals as a historical reminder of oppression. Walk to them from Kosciuskos gatvė.

SS PETER & PAUL CHURCH

Don't be fooled by the uninspiring exterior of **SS Peter & Paul Church** (Šv Petro ir Povilo bažnyčia; Map pp294-5; ☎ 234 0229; Antakalnio gatvė 1). Its baroque interior – an orgy of thousands of ornate white sculptures created by Italian sculptors between 1675 and 1704 – is the finest icing on the cake of any church in the country. The church was founded by Lithuanian noble Mykolas Kazimieras Paca, whose tomb is on the right of the porch.

ANTAKALNIS

One of Eastern Europe's most peaceful graveyards lies in this leafy suburb, a short stroll east of the centre. Those killed by Soviet Special Forces outside the parliament on 13 January 1991 are buried in **Antakalnis Cemetery** (Map pp294-5; ☎ 234 0587; ☺ 9am-dusk), off Karių kapų gatvė. A sculpture of the Madonna cra-

---

JEWISH COMMUNITY TODAY

Today there are just 5000 Jews in Lithuania, 80% of whom live in Vilnius. Since independence, a number of notable events have revolved around this small community. In 1996 Germany agreed to pay €1 million to Lithuania to compensate Holocaust survivors and victims of Nazi persecution, and in 1999 the Holocaust Museum in Washington apologised for selling a satirical CD entitled *Songs of Kovno (Kaunas) Ghetto*. In 2001 the **Vilnius Yiddish Institute** (Map pp298-9; ☎ 268 7187; www.judaicvilnius.com; Universiteto gatvė 7) was established in the History faculty at Vilnius University, and in 2002 Lithuania handed hundreds of Torah scrolls that survived the Holocaust to Israelis in a ceremony in Vilnius.

Restoration of the Jewish ghetto – now lucrative property in the Old Town – is under way despite opposition. In 2000 parliament set aside €32 million for the project, which has been used to reconstruct the areas around the Great Synagogue, Žydų gatvė, and plots in Rūdninkų gatvė and near the French embassy between Švarco gatvė and Šv Jono gatvė. The city has also set up the **Jewish Centre of Culture and Information** (Map pp298-9; Mėsinių gatvė 3a/5) but to date it largely stands empty.

The **Centre for Tolerance** (Map pp298-9; ☎ 266 9666; www.jmuseum.lt; Naugarduko gatvė 10; adult/child 5/2Lt; ☺ 10am-6pm Mon-Thu, to 4pm Sun) is the rebuilding nerve centre. Along with hosting temporary exhibitions covering the life and times of Lithuanian Jews through the ages, it is also the place to go for information, as is the **Jewish Community of Lithuania** (Map pp298-9; ☎ 261 3003; www .litjews.org; Pylimo gatvė 4; admission free; ☺ 10am-5pm Mon-Fri), which publishes the country's only Jewish newspaper, *Jerusalem of Lithuania*.

dling her son memorialises them. Another memorial honours Napoleonic soldiers who died of starvation and injuries in Vilnius while retreating from the Russian army; the remains of 2000 of them were only found in 2002.

On All Saints' Day (1 November) thousands of people flock to the cemetery to light candles by the graves to respect the dead.

RASŲ & MILITARY CEMETERIES

Vilnius' **Rasų and Military Cemeteries** (Map pp294-5; Sukilėlių gatvė) sit side by side in the southeastern end of Old Town. Founded in 1801, Rasų Cemetery is the resting place for the Vilnius elite. More interesting, however, is the small military cemetery close by, where the heart of the Polish Marshal Jósef Piłsudki, responsible for Poland's annexation of Vilnius in 1921, is buried. His mother shares his heart's grave and his body is buried in Kraków.

New Town

The 19th-century New Town (Naujamiestis) stretches 2km west of the cathedral and Old Town. Here the medieval charm of the Old Town is replaced by wide boulevards and pockets of lush parkland.

GEDIMINO PROSPEKTAS

Sandwiched between the Roman Catholic cathedral's dramatic skyline and the silver domes of the Russian Orthodox **Church of the Saint Virgin's Apparition** (Map pp298-9), fashionable Gedimino is the main street of modern Vilnius. Its 1.75km length is dotted with shops, a theatre, banks, hotels, offices, a few park squares and the seat of various official bods, including that of the Lithuanian **Government Building** (Map pp298-9; www.lrv.lt; Gedimino prospektas 11) and Parliament House. Laid out in 1852, the sparkling street has had 11 name changes since: the tsarists named it after St George, the Poles after Mickiewicz, and the Soviet rulers first after Stalin, then Lenin.

Striking a theatrical pose at Gedimino prospektas 4 is the **Three Muses** (Map pp298-9) statue atop the Lithuanian National Drama Theatre. The unusual black-robed figures (representing drama, comedy and tragedy) hiding behind gold masks lean out towards an audience of tourists taking snap shots.

A handful of the street's historical buildings have been turned into shopping centres few Lithuanians can actually afford to

GUGGENHEIM TIME

Well, not yet, but soon-ish. By the end of 2013 Vilnius should be graced by a state-of-the-art Guggenheim Museum on the banks of the Neris River (Map pp294–5). The project, in conjunction with the State Hermitage Museum in Russia, will reputedly cost around €80 million, most of which will come from private sources. The winning design, by celebrated Iraqi architect **Zaha Hadid** (www.zahahadid.com), is a futuristic foray dominated by smooth surfaces and space-age windows – when complete, it will look as though a stainless-steel grey intergalactic cruiser has landed in the modern district of Šnipiškės.

shop in. Both **Gedimino 9** (Map pp298-9; ☎ 262 9764; www.gedimino9.lt; Gedimino prospektas 9) – the Harrods or Bloomingdale's of Vilnius – and the salmon-pink and cream **Grand Duke Palace** (Map pp298-9; Gedimino prospektas 20/1) are worth entering simply to admire the beautiful restoration work.

Lenin stood on **Lukiškių aikštė**, a square that used to bear the name of the levelled statue, now displayed in Druskininkai's Grūtas Park (p336). The KGB – and during the Nazi occupation, the Gestapo – was headquartered in the late-19th-century building facing the square. Part of it today houses the disturbing – and thought-provoking – **Museum of Genocide Victims** (Genocido aukų muziejus; Map pp298-9; ☎ 249 6264; www.genocid.lt; Aukų gatvė 2a; adult/child 4/1Lt; audioguide 8Lt; ☼ 10am-5pm Tue-Sat, to 3pm Sun), also known as the KGB Museum. Memorial plaques honouring those who perished in 1945 and 1946 tile the outside of the building. Inside, the floors above ground cover the harsh realities of Soviet occupation, including gripping personal accounts of life as a Lithuanian deportee in Siberia. The true horror hits home upon entering the basement, which contains inmate cells and the execution cell where, between 1944 and the 1960s, prisoners were shot or stabbed in the skull. In 1994 the remains of 766 victims killed here between 1944 and 1947 were found in a mass grave in **Tuskulėnai Park** (Map pp294-5), north of the Neris. In 2005 they were reburied in the park in a state-of-the-art cone-shaped

LITHUANIA

memorial chapel (Map pp294–5; Žirmūnų gatvė) built in memory of 20th-century terror victims. Disturbingly, the graveyard of those killed by the KGB in the 1950s, reckoned to be within a 30km radius of Vilnius, has not yet been found.

Outside **Parliament House** (Seimas; Map pp298–9; www.seimas.lt; Gedimino prospektas 53), concrete slabs with mangled barbed wire and daubed slogans are more poignant reminders of Lithuania's violent past. Barricades were erected here on 13 January 1991 to protect parliament from Soviet troops. The barricades to the north of the parliament building were left in place until December 1992, when the last Russian soldier left Vilnius.

SOUTH OF GEDIMINO PROSPEKTAS

A few blocks south of Gedimino prospektas is **Romanovs' Church** (Map pp298–9; Basanavičiaus gatvė 27), an eye-catching Russian Orthodox church with pea-green onion domes built in 1913. A little to the west of the church is Vilnius' fabulous **flower market** (Map pp298–9; Basanavičiaus gatvė 42; 24hr), a perfect place for those hit with a romantic streak at 3am.

West of Jasinskio gatvė across the Neris River is a **kenessa** (Map pp294–5; Liubarto gatvė 6), a traditional Karaites prayer house built in 1922.

VINGIS PARK

Just over 1km southwest of parliament, at the western end of Čiurlionio gatvė, is the wooded **Vingis Park** (Map pp294–5), surrounded on three sides by the Neris. The park has a large **open-air amphitheatre** (Map pp294–5) used for the Lithuanian Song and Dance Festival. Take trolleybus 7 from the train station or 3 from the Gedimino stop on Vilniaus gatvė to the Kęstučio stop (the second after the bridge over the river), then walk over the footbridge from the end of Treniotos gatvė.

Like the more distant TV Tower (right), the **TV & Radio Centre** (Map pp294–5; cnr Konarskio gatvė & Pietario gatvė), near the southeastern edge of the park, was stormed by Soviet tanks and troops in the early hours of 13 January 1991. Wooden crosses commemorate Lithuania's independence martyrs.

ŠNIPIŠKĖS

On the north bank of the Neris, the quarter of Šnipiškės has been transformed: the tatty Soviet concrete blocks have gone and in their place is a new skyline of skyscrapers, including the **Europa Tower** (Map pp294–5) on the **Europa Business & Shopping Centre** (p320), which – at 129m – is the Baltic's tallest skyscraper.

This new business district, dubbed 'Sunrise Valley', continues to grow apace, with high- rises and construction sites popping up like mushrooms after a rain. As part of the urban redevelopment project, two new bridges linking the Europa Tower with the centre have been built and the **municipality** (Map pp294–5; Konstitucijos prospektas 3) has moved here.

Thankfully it's not all glass and gleaming metal this side of the river. There are fine examples of Soviet architecture here, along with **St Raphael's Church** (Map pp298–9; Šv Rapolo bažnyčia; 6.30-9am & 5-7.30pm) near Žaliasis tiltas (Green Bridge) sporting a classic baroque interior behind a broken facade. The power-hungry can get along to the **Lithuanian Energy Museum** (Map pp298–9; 278 2085; Žvejų gatvė 14a; adult/child 4/2Lt; 10am-4pm Mon-Fri), which focuses on nuclear power and other Soviet (and subsequent) energy-making means. It's housed in the city's original power plant which ceased operation in 1998.

TV Tower

It's hard to miss the 326m **TV tower** (Televizijos Bokstas; Map pp294–5; 204 0300; www.lrtc.lt; Sausio 13-osios gatvė 10; adult/child 21/9Lt; observation deck 10am-10pm) on the city's western horizon. This tall needle symbolises Lithuania's strength of spirit; on 13 January 1991 Soviet special forces killed 12 people here. Lithuanian TV kept broadcasting until the troops came through the tower door. Wooden crosses commemorate the victims and on 13 January hundreds of people light candles here. At Christmas 6000-odd fairy lights are strung on the tower to create the world's largest Christmas tree!

From the observation deck (165m) all of Vilnius is spread out before you. Steel stomachs can eat while feasting on views at **Paukščių takas** (Milky Way; Map pp294–5; 252 5338; mains 20-30Lt; 10am-10pm), a revolving restaurant in the tower.

To get to the tower, take trolleybus 16 from the train station or 11 from Lukiškių aikštė to the Televizijos Bokstas stop on Laisvės prospektas. A trip here takes you to Vilnius' Soviet-era high-rise suburbs.

BEGINNING WITH A

'We want to show the world how a little nation fought for its independence; show how dear, how valuable, independence itself is.'

Juozas Aleksiejūnas, former inmate, KGB Prison

Juozas Aleksiejūnas, a tour guide at the Museum of Genocide Victims, was in his 80s when he died. Against all the odds, he survived Vilnius' KGB prison – an appalling house of horrors where blood still stains the walls of the cramped cells in which prisoners lived and died. His story, told before he died, is a proud but harrowing one.

Aleksiejūnas joined the partisan Resistance movement in 1944. As one of the country's estimated 50,000 to 100,000 'forest brothers', he roamed the forests around Molėtai, 75km north of Vilnius, with five other 'brothers'. His official task was to steal identity forms from the local passport office to pass on to fellow partisans.

On 26 March 1945 he was arrested by the KGB and tried for anti-Soviet activities. Within minutes he was found guilty and his ordeal in Vilnius' KGB prison, notorious for its high security and inhumane disciplinary measures, began.

Between 1944 and 1953, 200,000 Lithuanians passed through the Soviet prisons. The one in Vilnius was used for equally sinister purposes by the Gestapo during the Nazi occupation; its execution ward, various torture chambers and 9m-square cells, where up to 20 prisoners were kept at any one time, all remain today. Inmates were showered once a month and only allowed to go to the bathroom once a day; at other times, a bucket in the cell doubled as toilet pan.

Aleksiejūnas was interrogated and tortured for a week. 'How many of you are there?' and 'Who is your leader?' were the questions fired at him. Prisoners did not have names. They were called 'Beginning with A', 'Beginning with B' and so on to ensure prisoners knew as little about each other as possible. Inmates who attempted conversation were sent to an isolation cell, stripped to their underwear, rationed to 300g of bread and half a litre of water a day, and deprived of sleep.

Inmates who refused 'to talk' to KGB officers were sent to the 'soft cell'. Its walls were padded in 1973 to muffle the human cries and the sound of beatings. Prisoners were put in straitjackets and forced to sit in the pitch-black, silent cell until their spirit broke. Aleksiejūnas survived the soft-cell hell.

After three days in the 'wet room' he lost consciousness. This 8 x 10m punishment cell had a sunken floor covered with cold water, which turned to ice in winter. In the centre was a slippery metal pedestal, 30cm in diameter, which was the prisoners' only refuge from the wet floor.

Aleksiejūnas was later moved to another prison in Vilnius and on 29 June 1945 he was deported to Vorkuta, Siberia, where he spent five years in a hard-labour camp followed by another five years in a high-security prison. In 1955 he was released on parole. But he was not allowed to leave Vorkuta and had to report twice a month (which he did for nine years) to the prison's special commander. His Lithuanian wife, whom he married in 1943 (but had barely seen since), joined him in Vorkuta, where their first son was born. The Aleksiejūnas family returned home to Vilnius in 1963.

ACTIVITIES

Vilnius isn't blessed with an immensely wild array of outdoor pursuits, but it does however offer something you don't find everywhere – hot-air ballooning.

Take a gentle ride across the Old Town rooftops (as long as the wind is in the right direction) with the **Oreivystės Centras** (off Map pp294-5; ☎ 273 2703; www.oreivystescentras.lt; Motorų gatvė 6) around 3.5km south of the train and bus stations or **Vilnius Ballooning Association** (Map pp294-5; ☎ 8-676 00050; www.oreivis.lt; Krokuvos 11-29); both charge around 450Lt per person for a one-hour flight.

WALKING TOUR

Eastern Europe's largest old town and surrounds are made for meandering. This itinerary is a taster for those with just a few hours to spare.

Begin on Cathedral Sq, taking in its magical tile, **cathedral** (**1**; p297) and **Royal Palace** (**2**; p301) before climbing through the park to the **Upper Castle Museum** (**3**; p297) on Gediminas Hill. From the tower survey the city then hike down into the Old Town along Pilies gatvė. To shake off the crowd and get a feel for quaint old Vilnius, cut left onto Bernardinų gatvė and zigzag along Volano gatvė, Literatu gatvė, Rusu gatvė and Latako gatvė to Bokšto gatvė. Midway along Bokšto, turn right onto Savučiaus gatvė for the best of Lithuanian textiles at **Aukso Avis** (**4**; p320) and a taster of Lithuania's greatest artist at the **MK Čiurkionis House** (**5**; p303). Continue along Savučiaus to Didžioji gatvė, turn left and follow the street past the **former town hall** (**6**; Didžioji gatvė 31)

WALK FACTS
Start Cathedral Sq
Finish Skybar
Distance 3.5km (plus two 700m add-ons)
Duration one hour (brisk pace), half a day (meandering)

to its southern end. Continue along Aušros Vartų, past the **National Philharmonic** (**7**; p319), **Basilian Gates** (**8**; p304), **Orthodox Church of the Holy Spirit** (**9**; p303), **St Teresa's Church** (**10**; p304) and **artist workshops** (**11**; see p303) before stopping at the sacred **Gates of Dawn** (**12**; p304).

Duck through the Gates of Dawn and turn west on Bazilijonų gatvė before heading north along quiet Arklių gatvė to Rotušes aikštė where the **Contemporary Art Centre** (**13**; p304) awaits. Quench your thirst at a **cafe or restaurant terrace** (**14**) on Vokiečių gatvė, then cross the street and cut through the alleyway onto Žydų gatvė for a glimpse of Jewish Vilnius. Wander north along Jewish St, pausing to watch wedding sashes being woven at more **folk-artist workshops** (**15**). Take

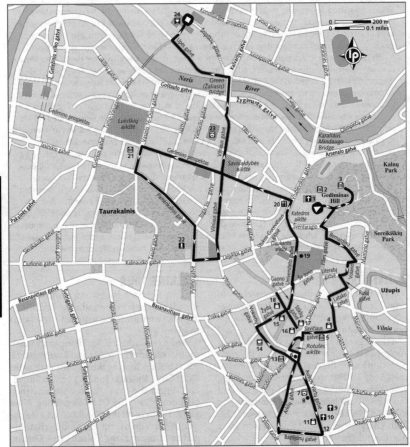

JEWISH MUSEUMS, SYNAGOGUES & CEMETERIES

With its temporary exhibitions and thought-provoking historical pieces, the Centre for Tolerance is a good place to begin a tour of Vilnius' Jewish community. The **Holocaust Museum** (Map pp298-9; ☎ 262 0730; Pamėnkalnio gatvė 12; adult/child 5/2Lt; ☼ 9am-5pm Mon-Thu, 10am-4pm Sun), in the so-called 'Green House', is very moving and not for the faint-hearted. The exhibition is a stark reminder of the true horror suffered by Lithuanian Jews in an 'unedited' display of horrific images and words. One of the few Vilnius ghetto survivors helped found the **Lithuanian State Jewish Museum of Vilna Gaon** (Lietuvos valstybinis Vilniaus Gaono žydų muziejus; Map pp298-9; ☎ 261 7907; www.jmuseum.lt; Pylimo gatvė 4), which was closed until further notice at the time of writing.

Vilnius' only remaining synagogue, the **Choral Synagogue** (Map pp298-9; ☎ 261 2523; Pylimo gatvė 39; entry by donation; ☼ 10am-2pm Sun-Fri), was built in 1894 for the wealthy and survived only because the Nazis used it as a medical store. Restored in 1995, it is used by a small Orthodox community (services 8.30am and 7.30pm).

The Soviets liquidated several Jewish cemeteries in the 1950s. The **old Jewish cemetery** (Map pp294-5; Krivių gatvė) where Rabbi Gaon Elijahu was originally buried was ripped up in 1957 and turned into a sports stadium (Žalgiris Stadium). The *maceivas* (tombstones) were recycled in the city as paving stones; the steps leading up Tauro Hill to the Trade Union Palace on Mykolaičio-Putino gatvė were originally built from Jewish gravestones. In 1991 the Jewish community retrieved many of these desecrated *maceivas*; a handful are now on display at the site of the old cemetery. Gaon Elijahu is now buried in the **new Jewish cemetery** (Map pp294–5), north of Vingis Park in the Virsuliškės district (entrance on Ažuolyno gatvė).

---

in the design boutiques, such as **Zoraza** (**16**; p320), **Sufle** (**17**; p320) and **Elementai** (**18**; p320), on Stiklių gatvė then continue south along Gaono gatvė to **Vilnius University** (**19**; p301) on Universiteto gatvė.

Exhausted? Cut back onto Cathedral Sq and flop on the terrace at **Zoe's Bar & Grill** or **Sue's Indian Raja** (**20**; p316). Still raring to go? Add on an amble west along Gedimino prospektas to the **Museum of Genocide Victims** (**21**; p307) and return to the Old Town via **Frank Zappa** (**22**; p306) or cut north along Vilniaus gatvė, past the **Opera & Ballet Theatre** (**23**; p318) to the river. Cross the bridge to Šnipiškės and its sky-high **Skybar** (**24**; p317), where grand views and inviting cocktails await.

VILNIUS FOR CHILDREN

Vilnius Beach (Map pp298-9), on the Neris' northern bank, used to be the place to keep kids cool on steaming summer days, but it's been upstaged by the Polynesian-themed **Aquapark** (Vandens Parkas; Map pp294-5; ☎ 211 1112; www .vandensparkas.lt; Ozo gatvė 14c; adult/child Mon-Fri 2hr 45/33Lt, 4hr from 49/41Lt, Sat & Sun 2hr 49/35Lt, 4hr 69/49Lt; ☼ noon-10pm Mon-Fri, 10am-10pm Sat & Sun). Little-uns can use up their energy on the adrenalin-pumping water rides and wave pool, while parents can recharge their batteries in the whirlpools, steam baths and massage salon.

Aquapark has both indoor and outdoor pools, making it a year-round attraction.

In town, the **electric cars** in Sereikiškių Park (Map pp298–9) are popular, as are pedal-powered taxis (p321) that loiter near the park entrance on Cathedral Sq. Otherwise, there's nothing like a **sky-high panorama** (p297) or ride on an **open-top bus** (p312) to impress.

In winter the best place for kidding around is Akropolis (p320), which has an **ice-skating rink** (Map pp298-9; ☎ 249 2878; ☼ 8am-midnight), the 20-lane **Apollo Bowling Alley** (Map pp298-9; ☎ 238 7777; ☼ 10am-2am Mon-Thu, 10am-3pm Fri, 9am-3am Sat, 9am-2am Sun) with eight automatic lanes for kids, and a **soft play area** (Map pp298-9; ☎ 238 7848; ☼ 10am-10pm) for under-12s.

TOURS

Two-hour walking tours of the Old Town in English (35Lt), starting at 2pm on Monday, Wednesday, Friday and Sunday from mid-May to mid-September, are organised by the tourist offices (p296). They also supply audio guides (35Lt) for self-guided tours and hand out free copies of thematic walking tours, including Jewish Vilnius, Musical Vilnius, and Castles and Palaces of Vilnius.

Other thematic tours with guide can be arranged through the tourist offices for 250Lt but they must be booked in advance.

LITHUANIA

GAY & LESBIAN VILNIUS

The scene is low-key and underground. For general information, chat rooms and guides, contact Vilnius-based **Lithuanian Gay League** (☎ 233 3031; www.gay.lt; PO Box 2862, Vilnius), which publishes a solid entertainment guide in English online. Gals can befriend the Lithuanian lesbian league **Sappho** (www.is.lt/sappho; PO Box 2204, Vilnius).

Buzz at the steely door of ravishingly popular gay club the **Men's Factory** (Map pp298-9; ☎ 8-699 85009; www.gayclub.lt; Švenkenkos gatvė 16/10; admission 5-40Lt; ☻ 10pm-4am Thu, to 7am Fri & Sat) to penetrate its hardcore underground scene. Door policy is strict but fair. Look for the line-up of flags outside.

Senamiesčio Gidas (Old Town Guides; Map pp298-9; ☎ 8-699 54064; www.vilniuscitytour.com; Aušros Vartų gatvė 7) Organises half-day minibus tours of Vilnius (75Lt, two hours) and Jewish Vilnius, as well as 'Trace your Family Roots' tours and day trips to Trakai (p322; 100Lt, 3¾ hours) and Kernavė (p325), Lithuania's Grūtas Park (Soviet sculpture park, p336) and Europe's geographical centre (p325). Prices – see its website – depend on numbers.

Yellow double-decker bus (☎ 273 8625; www .vap.lt, in Lithuanian; 1hr 40min tour adult/child 50/20Lt; ☻ departures 10am, noon, 2pm & 6pm Wed-Sun) For a whirl in an open-top bus, pitch up at the bus stop at either Katedros aikštė or Rotušės aikštė (Map pp298–9) and pay the driver. Tours depart half an hour later from the town hall.

FESTIVALS & EVENTS

Vilnius is blessed with year-round festivals, many of which are listed online at www.vil niusfestivals.lt and on www.vilnius-tour ism.lt. Following is a sample of sone of the bigger events:

Užgavėnės Pagan carnival (Mardi Gras) on Shrove Tuesday (usually February).

Kaziukas crafts fair Held in Old Town to celebrate St Casimir's Day on 4 March.

Lygiadienis Pagan carnival marking the spring equinox in March.

New Baltic Dance (www.dance.lt) Contemporary dance festival in early May.

Vilnius Festival Classical music, jazz and folk music concerts in Old Town courtyards during June.

Christopher Summer Festival (www.kristupofesti-valiai.lt) Music festival held in July and August.

Capital Days Music and performing arts festival from end of August to beginning of September.

Sirens (www.sirenos.lt) International theatre festival from mid-September to mid-October.

Gaida Showcases new music from Central and Eastern Europe in late October.

Mama Jazz Mid-November festival with big-name guests.

SLEEPING

For such a small capital, Vilnius has an extensive network of accommodation options. And while it's true that a large chunk of these resides in the top-end category, the range of budget choices is slowly increasing. Prices, however, are following suit, largely as a result of rising fuel and food prices, but partly due to Vilnius' status as Culture Capital in 2009. The following prices were correct when we went to press but are likely to rise rapidly in the lifetime of this book.

Summer season prices are quoted and include breakfast unless stated otherwise. Additionally, all hotels and guesthouses listed below include en suite bathrooms.

Budget

HOSTELS

Arts Academy Hostel (VDA Hostel; Map pp298-9; ☎ 212 0102; Latako gatvė 2; dm 20-22Lt, mid-Jul–mid-Sep bed in d/tr 30/26Lt, Apr-Sep s/d/tr 60/100/110Lt, Sep-Mar s/d/tr 50/90/100Lt; ℗) This cheap, basic and central option is fine for the budget-conscious, but anyone needing a smidgen of comfort may be disappointed overnighting here.

Filaretai Hostel (Map pp294-5; ☎ 215 4627; www .filaretaihostel.lt; Filaretų gatvė 17; dm 34Lt, s/d/tr without bathroom 70/100/120Lt; ℗ ☒ ▣) Affiliated with the Lithuanian Hostels Association, Filaretai occupies a quaint old villa 15 minutes' walk (uphill) from the Old Town. Dorms are five-to eight-bedded; bed linen is provided, but towels are an extra 1Lt, lockers 15Lt and laundry 15Lt. Breakfast isn't included but the hostel has satellite TV and a kitchen for guest to use. To get here take bus 34 from the bus and train stations to the seventh stop.

A Hostel (Map pp294-5; ☎ 8-680 18557; www.ahostel .lt; Šv Stepano gatvė 15; 8-bed/4-bed dm 34/48Lt; ☒ ▣) Squeakier than squeaky clean is the hallmark of this modern hostel where the interior decoration screams colour. The new Japanese-style sleeping pods are adequate but not for the claustrophobic, and there are good facilities, including laundry (1Lt per item), internet (first 15 minutes free) and lockers (3Lt). Two further hostels are located at Sodų gatvė 8 and 17; breakfast isn't included.

Old Town Hostel (Map pp294–5; ☎ 262 5357; oldtown hostel@lha.lt; Aušros Vartų gatvė 20-15a; dm 35Lt, d/tr without bathroom 110/144Lt, 4-person apt 176Lt; ☐) This small hostel tucked away in a private courtyard is handy to both the Old Town (it's located just *outside* the old walls) and the bus and train stations. Rooms are basic but accommodating, non–Hostelling International members pay 2Lt more, sheets/laundry are 3/15Lt and internet access is free on two computers in the noisy kitchen where guests slug free tea and coffee.

VB Sleep Inn (Map pp298-9; ☎ 8-638 32818; www .vb-sleep-inn.lt; Mikalojaus gatvė 3; dm 39-42Lt, tw 110Lt; ⓟ ⊠ ☐) It may have nothing to do with Melbourne beer, but the VB certainly has an Australian-hostel vibe. Staff are friendly and accommodating and not averse to guests having a shindig in the inner courtyard. The eight- to 12-bed dorms are big, basic and cool in summer. The hostel offers free internet access, tea, coffee and lockers, but no breakfast (there is a kitchen). Location couldn't be better, just off Vokiečių gatvė.

HOTELS & GUESTHOUSES

Šauni Vietelė (Map pp298-9; ☎ 212 4110; sauni .vietele@takas.lt; Pranciškonai gatvė 3/6; s/d 80/150Lt) This three-room guesthouse above a crumbling courtyard cafe is great value for money. Its rooms are old fashioned and filled with well-loved furniture, but they're all en suite, spacious and airy. Breakfast isn't included, but the cafe offers pancakes and such. The lovely old building was a Franciscan abbey in a previous life.

Litinterp (Map pp298-9; ☎ 212 3850; www.litinterp .lt; Bernardinų gatvė 7-2; s/d/tr 100/160/210Lt, with shared bathroom 80/140/180Lt, apt 210Lt; ☼ 8.30am-7pm Mon-Fri, 9am-3pm Sat; ⓟ ⊠) This bright, clean and friendly establishment has a wide range of options in the heart of the Old Town. Rooms

---

WHICH FLOOR?

Before you start traipsing up the stairs, note that in Lithuania the ground floor is referred to as the 1st floor.

---

with shared bathroom can be a little cramped, but those with en suite are generously large. Guests can check in after office hours providing they give advance notice.

our pick Domus Maria (Map pp298-9; ☎ 264 4880; www.domusmaria.lt; Aušros Vartų gatvė 12; s 100-289Lt, d 150-349Lt, tr/q 329/369Lt; ⓟ ⊠ ☐) No guesthouse better reflects the Vilnius soul than Domus Maria. With rooms sheltered in the cells of a Carmelite monastery that was attached to St Theresa's Church and the Gates of Dawn in the 17th century, the place oozes atmosphere and charm. It's architecturally faithful to its monastic origins, with rooms off long corridors arranged around an interior courtyard. Rooms 207 and 307 – the only hotel rooms in Vilnius with a Gates of Dawn view – are booked months in advance. Breakfast is served in the vaulted refectory, original 18th-century frescos decorate the conference room and one floor is kitted out for disabled access. Its cheapest rooms, with shared bathroom, are a bargain, but there aren't many to go around so book early.

Midrange

E-Guest House (Map pp298-9; ☎ 266 0730; www .e-guesthouse.lt; Ševčenkos gatvė 16; s/d/tr/q from 150/180/210/240Lt; ⓟ ⊠ ☐) This professional hotel with bold blue exterior and free internet connection throughout runs a handy rent-a-laptop service (50Lt per day). The quarter in which it stands is a building site as neighbours get spruced up, but it does share the same courtyard with the city's premier gay club (see opposite). Breakfast is an extra 5Lt, and guests receive a 20% discount at the restaurant next door.

Ecotel (Map pp294-5; ☎ 210 2700; www.ecotel .lt; Slucko gatvė 8; s/d/tr 179/199/255Lt; ⓟ ⊠ ⚒ ☐) Ecotel is a steal, with simple but smart furnishings filling its squeaky-clean rooms, in which bathrooms have heated towel rails. There is a computer with free internet access in the lobby, and some rooms are designed for both people with disabilities and those who are tall – beds are 2.10m long.

Senatoriai Hotel (Map pp298-9; ☎ 212 6491; www .senatoriai.lt; Tilto gatvė 2a; s 205Lt, d 300-350Lt; ⓟ ⊠) This small, homey hotel is so close to the cathedral you can almost hear Mass. Rooms are generally spacious and feature heavy leather furniture and clean wooden floors.

Panorama Hotel (Map pp294-5; ☎ 273 8011; www .hotelpanorama.lt; Sodų gatvė 14; s/d from 235/269Lt;

(P) (X) (🖳)) A Soviet-era hotel that surprises: dig beneath its kitsch, chocolate-brown tiled facade to find a bright, stylish and airy train-station hotel. Despite only being five storeys high, it has fabulous views of the Old Town and surrounding hills from its northern side.

Hotel Rinno (Map pp298-9; ☎ 262 2828; www.rinno .lt; Vingrių gatvė 25; s/d from 240/280Lt; (P) (X) (🖳) (🖳)) If you don't require a lift, you'll be hard pressed to find fault with Rinno. Its staff are exceptionally helpful and polite, its rooms first rate (more four-star than the three stars they're given), its location (between the Old Town and train and bus stations) handy, and its price a bargain. Breakfast is served in the pleasant and private back yard.

Algirdas Hotel (Map pp298-9; ☎ 232 6650; www.al gridashotel.lt; Algirdo gatvė 24; s/d from 260/310Lt; (P) (X)) Newer than new and not far from the Old Town, Algirdas pleases with simple, modern rooms, bathroom floors you could eat off (if you felt the urge), and little extras, such as heated towel rails and flat-screen TVs. Wi-fi is available in public areas.

Scandic Neringa (Map pp298-9; ☎ 268 1910; ner inga@scandic-hotels.com; Gedimino prospektas 23; s/d from 280/314Lt; (P) (X) (🖳)) It may be a preindependence old girl that has retained a few fabulous 1970s Soviet touches (take its restaurant with mosaic floor, frescoed wall and tinkling fountain), but everything else inside, from the reception to the warm, spacious rooms, has been refitted. Staff are professional and helpful, and bicycles are available for guest use.

Apia Hotel (Map pp298-9; ☎ 212 3426; www.apia .lt; Ignoto gatvė 12; s/d/tr 280/321/382Lt; (P) (X)) This smart, fresh and friendly hotel occupies some prime real estate in the heart of the Old Town. Choose from courtyard or cobble-street views, but if you're after a balcony, reserve room 3 or 4.

Grybas House (Map pp298-9; ☎ 216 9695; www .grybashouse.com; Aušros Vartų gatvė 3a; s 280-330Lt, d 370-420Lt, apt 400-490Lt; (P) (X)) Stase and Vladas run Grybas House – the first independent family-run hotel to crop up after independence – with grace, charm and bags of smiles. Rooms in this oasis of calm in the centre of the Old Town are old-fashioned but very comfortable and some peep at the private courtyard.

Atrium (Map pp298-9; ☎ 210 7777; www.atrium .lt; Pilies gatvė 10; s/d/ste 335/480/818Lt; (P) (X) (🖳) (🖳)) One floor inside this 16th-century town house is kitted out for travellers with disabilities,

and the cellar is equipped with a sauna and Jacuzzi. Rooms otherwise are standard midrange to top-end options in the tourist heart of Vilnius, and prices are substantially cheaper on weekends.

Reval Hotel Lietuva (Map pp294-5; ☎ 272 6272; www.revalhotels.com; Konstitucijos prospektas 20; s/d/ste from 380/449/794Lt; (P) (X) (🖳) (🖳)) Sky-rise Reval is the swankiest hotel in Vilnius' business sector and has views of the city that are hard to beat. Rooms are standard and businesslike, but there are plenty of extras such as a fitness and sauna centre, free wi-fi, bicycles for hire, and a signed portrait of Queen Elizabeth and Prince Philip. Reval is topped by the 22nd-floor Skybar (p317).

Top End

Vilnius boasts a divine selection of hotels for the well-heeled; most lounge in Old Town.

Shakespeare (Map pp298-9; ☎ 266 5885; www .shakespeare.lt; Bernardinų gatvė 8/8; s/d from 360/600Lt; (P) (X) (🖳) (🖳)) Striving to be the best of boutique hotels, Shakespeare is a refined Old Town gem that evokes a cultured, literary feel with its abundance of books, antiques and flowers. Each room pays homage to a different writer – in name and design.

Grotthaus (Map pp298-9; ☎ 266 0322; www.grot thusshotel.com; Ligoninės gatvė 7; r/ste from 442/863Lt; (P) (X) (🖳) (🖳)) Step through the red-canopied entrance of this buttercup-yellow town house to find Villeroy & Boch bathtubs, 19th-century *Titanic*-style fittings, Italian-made furniture, and curtains allegedly made with the same fabric as that used by the queen of England! Substantial discounts are available on weekends.

Narutis (Map pp298-9; ☎ 212 2894; www.narutis.com; Pilies gatvė 24; s/d/ste 587/725/1070Lt; (P) (X) (🖳) (🖳) (🖳)) Housed in red-brick town house built in 1581, this classy pad has been a hotel since the 16th century. Breakfast and dinner are served in a vaulted Gothic cellar, there's wi-fi access throughout, and free apples at reception add a tasty touch.

Radisson SAS Astorija (Map pp298-9; ☎ 212 0110; vilnius.radissonsas.com; Didžioji gatvė 35/2; s/d/ste 610/650/1380Lt; (P) (X) (🖳) (🖳) (🖳)) This mint-green classical wonder – a hotel since 1901 – overlooks St Casimir's Church. Its wintertime Sunday brunches (99Lt) are renowned, and trouser press, safe and self-regulating heating/air-con are standard. Business-class rooms boast added luxuries, such as king-sized bed, bathrobe, slippers, iron, tea- and coffee-making facilities and free internet access.

Stikliai (Map pp298-9; ☎ 264 9595; www.stikliaihotel.lt; Gaono gatvė 7; s/d/ste 655/828/1300Lt; P ⊠ ⊠ ⊒ ⊒) The cream of the crop is tucked down a picture-postcard cobbled street in the old Jewish quarter. Rooms are luxurious and the 17th-century digs are blessed with an abundance of charm.

Worth recommending:

Centrum UniqueStay Hotel (Map pp298-9; ☎ 268 3300; www.uniquestay.com; Vytenio gatvė 9/25; s/d 260/290Lt; P ⊠ ⊒ ⊒) Functional and businesslike, but good price and great add-ons such as a sauna and free tea and coffee in every room.

Centro Kubas (Map pp298-9; ☎ 266 0860; www .hotel.centrokubas.lt; Stiklių gatvė 3; s/d 320/360Lt; P ⊠ ⊒) A bizarre interior – complete with life-sized windmill in lobby – holds nothing back from the huge rooms, some with balcony. Parking is 34Lt a night.

Dvaras Hotel (Map pp298-9; ☎ 210 7370; www .dvaras.lt; Tilto gatvė 3; s/d 350/420Lt; P ⊠ ⊠ ⊒) Opposite Senatoriai; more like a plush country villa than a city hotel. Top restaurant on-site.

EATING

Whether it's *cepelinai* or *kepta duona* you want, Vilnius has it covered. That said, the Vilnius dining palate is now well used to cuisine from around the world, and the list of restaurants serving food from outside Lithuania's borders grows every month. Most restaurants can be found in the Old Town, but finding a meal after midnight is more challenging. In summer it's essential to reserve a table outside for evening dining.

Cafes

Skonis ir Kvapas (Map pp298-9; ☎ 212 2803; Trakų gatvė 8; ◷ 9.30am-11pm) Heaven for tea connoisseurs, this stylish courtyard cafe knows how to make a great cuppa. Choose from around 100 teas from across the globe (by the cup 2.50Lt, per pot 5Lt to 7Lt) and a sublime array of creamy and homemade cakes, cucumber sandwiches and breakfasts. The terrace is Old Town's most peaceful and shaded; there are rugs to wrap up in on chillier days; and the red-brick fireplace inside is a great wintertime toe-toaster.

Coffee Inn (Map pp298-9; ☎ 8-655 77764; Vilniaus gatvė 17) Coffee Inn, the first Lithuanian-owned cafe chain in the country, is all about freshness – its wraps (8Lt), sandwiches (6.50Lt), huge cookies (3.50Lt) and cheese-cake (arguably the best in town) are all made on the day and on- site, and the imported coffee beans are roasted in Vilnius. Eat in or pick up something to go; also found at Trakų gatvė 7 (Map pp298–9), Gedimino prospektas 9 (Map pp298–9) and Pilies gatvė 10 (Map pp298–9).

Pilies kepyklėlė (Map pp298-9; ☎ 260 8992; Pilies gatvė 19) A standout from the crowd on Vilnius' busiest tourist street, this relaxed tearoom mixes old-world charm with a fresh, upbeat vibe. Don't pass over the chance to sample the apple strudel and sweet and savoury pancakes (6Lt to 11Lt).

Užupio kavinė (Map pp298-9; ☎ 212 2138; Užupio gatvė 2; mains 15-40Lt) A legendary riverside cafe terrace in a legendary part of town. Take a pew with the bohemian crowd that frequents the place and watch folk brave the makeshift swing under the adjacent bridge. A plaque on the wall pays homage to its soulmate – Montmartre, Paris.

Other cafes to look out for while exploring Vilnius include the following:

Soprano Central Vilnius (Map pp298-9; ☎ 212 6042; Pilies gatvė 3); Šnipiškės (Map pp294-5; Konstitucijos prospektas 3) Ice cream, you scream, we all scream for ice cream! Get lickin' with fruit-topped *gelato Italiano* by the cone (3Lt).

Post Skriptum (Map pp298-9; ☎ 212 5271; Gedimino prospektas 7) Long, thin and often full; grand spot for people-watching on one of Vilnius' busiest streets. Post Skriptum serves simple, tasty Lithuanian dishes (mains 15Lt to 30Lt) and a variety of coffee.

Lithuanian

Čili Kaimas (Map pp298-9; ☎ 231 2536; Vokiečių gatvė 8; mains 12-25Lt; ◷ 10am-midnight Sun-Thu, to 2am Fri & Sat) Even if you don't eat here, stop in for a look. Fish swim in an indoor pond, hens cluck around in a glass enclosure, rustic farming tools cover every wall space, waitresses wear traditional dress, and – strangely – dozens of flat-screen TVs broadcast MTV. Oh, there's also food, such as mushroom soup served inside a brown-bread loaf.

Žemaičių Smuklė (Samogitian Tavern; Map pp298-9; ☎ 261 6573; Vokiečių gatvė 24; mains 20-60Lt) Who needs veges when you can feast on pig bits most people throw away (or throw up). Pig tongues, ears and trotters are all available here, alongside a pitchfork of assorted meat for 4 to 5 people (140Lt), 0.5m sausages, wild boar goulash and goose roast. Summertime seating is around wooden benches and cartwheels on cobbles or up top among Old Town church steeples and terracotta rooftops.

Tores (Map pp298-9; ☎ 262 9309; Užupio gatvė 40; mains 25-50Lt) Feast your tastebuds on a plentiful mix of Lithuanian and European dishes and your eyes on a stunning Old Town panorama at this well-placed eating and drinking hang-out, atop a hill in bohemian Užupis. Užupio Radijas (94.9FM) airs tunes in the basement.

Lokys (Bear; Map pp298-9; ☎ 262 9046; Stiklių gatvė 8; mains 30-60Lt) Hunt down the big wooden bear outside to find this Vilnius institution, a cellar maze going strong since 1972. Game is its mainstay, with delicacies like beaver-meat stew with plums or quail with blackberry sauce luring the culinarily curious. Folk musicians play here on summer evenings.

European

Guru (Map pp298-9; ☎ 212 0126; Vilniaus gatvė 22/1; salads 10-25Lt; ☽ 7am-9pm Mon-Fri, 9am-8pm Sat & Sun) Guru is a Zen salad lounge, decked out in a soothing and minimalist fashion. Floor-to-ceiling windows and crisp white linen set off a bold choice of soups and salads – a perfect and peaceful pad for lunch with the girls.

Les Amis (Map pp298-9; ☎ 212 3738; Savičiaus gatvė 7; mains 18-25Lt) This family restaurant dishes up the best value-for-money French cuisine in town. Whether it's the oil fish with mashed potato, veal medallions or salmon fillet, you'll be satisfied with your choice. The wine is also the right temperature (not always guaranteed in Lithuania) and the atmosphere relaxed and friendly. Simply pleasant dining.

our pick Bistro 18 (Map pp298-9; ☎ 8-677 72091; Stiklių gatvė 18; mains 20-40Lt) Bistro 18 is a breath of fresh air in Vilnius' restaurant scene. The service is friendly, polite and attentive, the decor minimalist yet comfortable, the food imaginative, international and flavoursome, and the wine list features bottles from as far away as the Antipodes. The lunch menu (around 20Lt for soup and main) is an absolute bargain; dine alone and your meal will be served with a couple of books so you won't feel lonely. Superb.

Fiorentino (Map pp298-9; ☎ 212 0925; Universiteto gatvė 4; mains 20-40Lt) This charming Italian newcomer is a winner on three accounts – staff who know how to serve, chefs who know their cuisine from the boot-shaped country, and an architect who knows his Renaissance period. Pick anything on the menu then sit

back to admire the colonnaded inner courtyard straight out of Rome (which backs onto the Presidential Palace, no less).

Saint Germain (Map pp298-9; ☎ 262 1210; Literatų gatvė; mains 30-50Lt) Paris is the inspiration behind this idyllic wine-bar-cum-restaurant inside a convivial century-old house on a quiet Old Town street. Of particular importance: the service is fit for the best restaurants on the continent, advance reservations for its street terrace are essential, and the resident cat is named 'The Grey'.

La Provence (Map pp298-9; ☎ 262 0257; Vokiečių gatvė 22; mains around 70Lt) La Provence is a silver-service restaurant that lives up to its '100% gourmet' motto. Expect to find such delicacies as boiled octopus or boneless pigeon stuffed with pheasant and goose *foie gras* filling the heavenly French menu.

Also tempting:

Čili Pica (Map pp298-9; ☎ 261 9071; Gedimino prospektas 23; pizzas 10-40Lt; ☽ 7.30am-3am Sun-Wed, 7.30am-6am Thu-Sat) Unremarkable pizza aside, serves nosh well into the wee hours in Old Town and near the train and bus station. Plus Lithuanians love it.

Trattoria Da Antonio (Map pp298-9; ☎ 261 8341; Pilies gatvė 20; mains 20-30Lt) Wins local votes for its Italian cuisine, and has a prime position on busy Pilies.

International

Balti Drambliai (Map pp298-9; ☎ 262 0875; Vilniaus gatvė 41; mains 10-17Lt) The 'White Elephant' whips up a vegan and vegie storm, offering pancakes, pizzas, Indian curries and tofu-based dishes to hungry non–meat-eaters. Its lively courtyard is also good for a drink, while winter dining is in its cavernous basement.

René (Map pp298-9; ☎ 212 6858; Antokolskio gatvė 13; mains 20-35Lt) René bases its cuisine on beer, Belgian beer no less. Everything on the menu, from pots of mussels to homemade oven-fried sausages and chilli con carne, features the amber brew. The overall theme is a nod to surrealist painter René Magritte – serving staff don bowler hats and pencils are provided to draw on paper tablecloths. And eating here won't break the bank, if you time it right – lunch menus and afternoon discounts are offered on weekdays.

Zoe's Bar & Grill (Map pp298-9; ☎ 212 3331; Odminių gatvė 3; mains 20-50Lt) Zoe's covers many culinary bases and manages to do it well, with the likes of fabulous homemade meatballs and sausages (26Lt), tender steaks (20Lt to 50Lt), and spicy Thai stir-fries and soups

(20Lt to 30Lt). Dine outdoors with cathedral views or indoors and receive an impromptu cooking lesson.

Pegasus (Map pp298-9; ☎ 260 9430; Didžioji gatvė 11; mains 20-50Lt) Everything from sushi to curry to pastas takes centre stage at Pegasus, a crisp white lounge with a strong design-led interior and one solitary but fabulous table on a balcony overlooking Didžioji gatvė. Its discreet entrance and live jazz attracts a moneyed local crowd.

Sue's Indian Raja (Map pp298-9; ☎ 266 1888; Odminių gatvė 3; mains 25-30Lt) The food served here is by no means the hottest Indian nosh you'll find on the planet, but expats in Vilnius swear by Sue's. It also has an enviable terrace location overlooking the cathedral.

Blusyne (Map pp298-9; ☎ 212 2012; Savičiaus gatvė 5; mains 25-45Lt) It may be tiny, but with offerings such as a pot of mussels (either Thai or French style), sea bass and pepper steak, Blusyne is big on gourmet food. If you're lucky you can secure a table in the wee garden, otherwise you might have to settle with someone's elbow in your soup.

Markus ir Ko (Map pp298-9; ☎ 262 3185; Antokolskio gatvė 11; mains around 50Lt) Markus is a long-time favourite that remains top-notch for sweet, succulent, melt-in-your-mouth steak. Enjoy your slab of meat inside under the sultry gaze of Marilyn Monroe or outside on the fabulous terrace occupying one half of a charming Old Town street.

Self-Catering

Self-catering is a doddle with a supermarket on every second street corner. **Iki** (www.iki .lt) Central Vilnius (Map pp298-9; ☎ 249 8340; Jasinskio gatvė 16); Bus station (Map pp294–5; ☎ 233 9162; Sodų gatvė 22) and **Maxima** (Map pp298-9; www.maxima. lt; Mindaugo gatvė 11; ⏰ 24hr) are leading chains. Both run smaller corner shops: **Ikiukas** (Map pp298-9; ☎ 231 3135; Jogailos gatvė 12) and **Mini Maxima** (Map pp298-9; Gedimino prospektas 64).

DRINKING

Nightlife is a laid-back affair: most places don't hum till late evening, and many double as restaurants. It's all quite Med Europe too, where punters sit at tables rather than stand around drinking. In summer Vokiečių gatvė, a street lined with wooden-decking terraces in summer, is an obvious starting point; as the night wears on, Totorių gatvė, with its ever-increasing number of bars, makes for a good target.

our pick Cozy (Map pp298-9; ☎ 261 1137; www.cozy .lt; Dominikonų gatvė 10; ⏰ 9am-2am Mon-Wed, to 4am Thu & Fri, 10am-4am Sat, to 2am Sun) Run by hip Bernie and his beaming smile from Holland, Cozy has been a hot address in Vilnius for years, and will probably continue to be so for years to come. It welcomes all comers and has something for everyone; street level is a lounge-style cafe-restaurant with attentive staff, convivial vibe and a chef who cooks until late, while local DJs spin tunes downstairs to a discerning crowd Thursday to Saturday.

Contemporary Art Centre (Map pp298-9; ☎ 261 7097; Vokiečių gatvė 2) The art centre has a smoky hide-out bar filled with arty Lithuanian luvvies and one of the most simple but hip summer terraces in town. At weekends roll up your jeans and hold your nose to enter the aeroplane-style loo.

Skybar (Map pp294-5; ☎ 272 6272; Konstitucijos prospektas 20; ⏰ 4pm-1am Sun-Thu, to 2.30am Fri & Sat) It may look – and feel – like an airport lounge, but nothing can beat the panoramas of this sky-blue bar on the 22nd floor of the Reval Hotel Lietuva. DJs spin tunes on Friday and Saturday.

Paparazzi (Map pp298-9; ☎ 212 0135; Totorių gatvė 3; ⏰ 4pm-3am Mon-Thu, to 6am Fri & Sat) Plop yourself down on a green, red or black sofa and look cool – someone could be watching you.

Also recommended:

Savas Kampas (Map pp298-9; ☎ 212 3203; Vokiečių gatvė 4; ⏰ 8.30am-midnight Mon-Wed, to 1am Thu, to 3am Fri, 10am-3am Sat, to midnight Sun) Average bar, but exceedingly popular, particularly its outdoor seating.

Būsi Terčias (Map pp298-9; ☎ 231 2698; Totorių gatvė 18) Simple all-wood interior and 12 varieties of locally brewed beer, including lime, raspberry and caramel. No garden; best enjoyed in winter.

Double Coffee (Map pp298-9; Gedimino prospektas 26; ⏰ 24hr) Starbucks-inspired chain with coffee in all shapes and sizes. Six locations in town.

LITHUANIA

DRINKING WITH DIONYSUS

Vilnius has suddenly discovered the joy of wine. Small wine bars have popped up across the Old Town, and local patronage is on the rise. Mingle with the crowd at the following:

In Vino (Map pp298-9; ☎ 212 1210; Aušros Vartų gatvė 7) Bar of the moment, with one of the loveliest courtyards in the city. Excellent wines, expensive tapas (20Lt to 30Lt) and a few mains. Arrive early in summer to secure a table, then watch the place fill to overflowing.

La Bohemé (Map pp298-9; ☎ 212 1087; Šv Ignoto gatvė 4/3) Choose between wooden tables below vaulted ceilings and chandeliers, or bypass the main room and grab a comfy couch out the back. Best enjoyed in winter, when the open fire is raging.

Tappo D'Oro (Map pp298-9; ☎ 8-686 16866; Stuokos-Gucevičiaus gatvė 7) Look for the giant corkscrew hanging out the front. Informal spot with inviting tree-shaded terrace; huge selection of Italian wines (not all are always available, though), best complimented by Italian cheeses, hams and olives.

Vintana (Map pp298-9; ☎ 212 2568; Tilto gatvė 6-8) Tiny wine bar with sunny terrace and partial views of the cathedral. International wine selection and never a problem securing a table.

ENTERTAINMENT

The tourist office publishes events listings, as does the *Baltic Times*.

Nightclubs

Vilnius has a small but lively clubbing scene that occasionally sees new venues open up. It doesn't get going till around midnight and is best experienced in winter, when everyone's around (in summer many go to the seashore to party). Cozy (p317) is also a popular night-owl haunt.

Pacha Vilnius (Map pp298-9; ☎ 241 3021; www.pacha vilnius.lt; Gyneju gatvė 14; admission 20-35Lt; ☾ 10pm-5am Thu-Sat) Part of the legendary Pacha club franchise, this massive club is arguably the best spot in town to shake it. Expect to find quality DJs and a happy crowd.

Gravity (Map pp298-9; ☎ 269 1880; www.clubgravity .lt; Jasinskio gatvė 16; admission 20-30Lt) Local and international DJs, exotic cocktails and thumping House make this stylish club hot – when the music is right.

Woo (Map pp298-9; ☎ 212 7740; www.woo.lt; Vilniaus gatvė 22; admission 10-30Lt; ☾ noon-midnight Mon-Wed, to 2am Thu, to 6am Fri, 5pm-6am Sat) Escape the mainstream at Woo, a basement club below Radvilos' Palace. Resident DJs spin D'n'B, Techno and House to a backdrop of VJ art, and jazz sessions occasionally fill the space.

Pablo Latino (Map pp298-9; ☎ 262 1045; Trakų gatvė 3; admission 15-30Lt) This sultry-red club specialises in sweet Latino tunes and strong cocktails. Put on your dancing shoes (Wednesday night for lessons), fortify your liver, and be prepared for a fun night out.

Also worth checking:

Galaxy (Map pp294-5; ☎ 210 3119; www.forumpal ace.lt; Konstitucijos gatvė 26; admission varies) Event-led club rather than a weekly haunt; DJ depending, draws a large crowd to its large amphitheatre-styled space.

Brodvéjus (Map pp298-9; ☎ 210 7208; www .brodvejus.lt; Mėsinių gatvė 4; admission 5-20Lt) Live bands and cheesy tunes nightly; hugely popular with expats, students, local lookers and travel-guide writers.

Cinemas

Find movie listings at www.cinema.lt (in Lithuanian only). Films are screened in English at **Coca-Cola Plaza** (Map pp298-9; ☎ 1567; www.forumcinemas.lt; Savanorių prospektas 7) and at the out-of-town **Forum Cinemas Akropolis** (Map pp294-5; ☎ 1567; www.forumcinemas.lt; Ozo gatvė 25) in the Akropolis multiplex.

Theatre & Classical Music

Oskaras Koršunovas Theatre (OKT; Oskaro Koršuno teatro; ☎ 212 2099; www.okt.lt) is Lithuania's most innovative, daring and controversial theatre company; check out the website for more details.

Resident companies perform opera and ballet at **Opera & Ballet Theatre** (Operos ir Baleto Teatras; Map pp298-9; ☎ 262 0727; www.opera.lt; Vienuolio gatvė 1).

Mainstream theatre – from both Lithuania and abroad – is performed several locations in town:

Lithuanian National Drama Theatre (Lietuvos nacionalinis dramos teatras; Map pp298-9; ☎ 262 9771; www.teatras.lt; Gedimino prospektas 4)

Small Theatre of Vilnius (Vilniaus Mažasis Teatras; Map pp298-9; ☎ 249 9869; www.vmt.lt; Gedimino prospektas 22)

Youth Theatre (Jaunimo teatras; Map pp298-9; ☎ 261 6126; www.jaunimoteatras.lt; Arklių gatvė 5).

The country's most renowned orchestras perform concerts at several locations:

National Philharmonic (Nacionalinė filharmonija; Map pp298-9; ☎ 266 5233; www.filharmonija.lt; Aušros Vartų gatvė 5) The country's foremost go-to location for classical music. Breaks for summer.

Lithuanian Music Academy (Lietuvos muzikos akademija; Map pp298-9; ☎ 261 3651; www.lma.lt; Gedimino prospektas 42) Stages concerts all year.

SHOPPING

The Old Town's main thoroughfare, running from Pilies gatvė to Aušros Vartų gatvė, is something of a bustling craft market or tourist trap, depending on your perspective. Traders' stalls are laden with cheap amber trinkets, clothing and small souvenirs; painters sell their wares; and amber and linen shops are a dime a dozen. The following are of particular note.

Lino ir Gintaro Studija (Linen & Amber Studio; www.lgstudija.lt) Aušros Vartų (Map pp298-9); Aušros Vartų gatvė 12); Pilies (Map pp298-9; Pilies gatvė 38) The Linen & Amber Studios stand out from the crowd of similar shops for its wide selection of quality goods at reasonable prices.

Lino Namai (Linen House; www.siulas.lt) Vilniaus (Map pp298-9; ☎ 212 2322; Vilniaus gatvė 12); Pilies (Map pp298-9; Pilies gatvė 38) These stores sell linen from Siulas, a company that has been producing above-par table and bed linen for 80 years.

Šokolado Namai (Map pp298-9; ☎ 212 1423; www.chocolade.lt; Gedimino prospektas 46) If you have a sweet tooth, you should stop by this place – although, with the quality of the handmade chocolate, you might never leave.

Kolekcininkų Klubas (Map pp298-9; VM Putino gatvė 5; ⊗ 8am-1pm Sat) The city's only flea market is a fine place to dig through mountains of Soviet relics for presents for the rellies.

Gedimino prospektas – the main shopping street – is lined with mainstream fashion shops and department stores. Of the latter, standouts include **Flagman** (Map pp298-9; Gedimino prospektas 16; ⊗ 10am-8pm Mon-Sat, 11am-6pm Sun), a big, bright and bold example, with plenty of

---

POTTY ABOUT POTTERY

Dainius Strazolas has been a potter almost all his adult life. In 2003 he re-established the **Vilnius Potters' Guild** (Vilniaus Puodžių Cechas; Map pp298-9; ☎ 8-659 99040; www.pottery.lt, in Lithuanian; Paupio gatvė 2-20; ⊗ 11am-7pm Tue-Fri, noon-6pm Sat), which today counts a total of six members.

You re-established the potters' guild? Yes. The first was founded in 1581. At the time Vilnius was quite famous in Europe for its pottery.

What is the idea behind the guild? To not only rejuvenate pottery in the country, but also the techniques once employed here. Ten years ago archaeologists discovered 15th- and 16th-century pottery close to our current workshop. It inspired us to give it a go ourselves.

What's with the techniques? We create our pottery on reconstructions of potters' wheels used in the 15th to 17th centuries. It's more labour-intensive but also very rewarding. And we often make leaven pottery.

Leaven pottery? It's a type of pottery once popular in Lithuania in the late Middle Ages that was pushed out by glazed pottery. Rolls of clay mixed with gravel are shaped into a pot, then fired in a red-hot oven. The hot pot is then taken out and dipped into a thin mixture of flour and leaven. The reason for this is twofold – to close the pores of the clay and give the surface a distinct streaked or spotted pattern.

Has the guild had much success rejuvenating pottery in Lithuania? During the Soviet time, about 90% of the old trades died out and nowadays the number of traditional potters can be counted on two hands. We do however get support from the municipality, but that can change with a change of local government. The reconstruction of the Royal Palace has been good for us though.

The Royal Palace? We were commissioned to make three 16th-century stoves for the palace, using 16th-century techniques. It's very rewarding to see our work on display for the public.

Can anyone have a go here? Yes, they can. We charge 15Lt for a lesson in 16th-century pottery, but if they want to fire something to take home, it costs a little bit more.

LITHUANIA

High St brands, while **Gedimino 9** (Map p298-9; ☎ 262 9764; www.gedimino9.lt; Gedimino prospektus 9) caters to an upmarket crowd with selective stores and an exclusive feel. For more details see also p307).

For clothes, consider a visit a local designer (below).

Away from the centre, **Europa** (Map pp294-5; www.europa.lt; Konstitucijos prospektas 3; ☼ 8am-midnight) and **Akropolis** (Map pp294-5; www.akropolis.lt; Ozo gatvė 25; ☼ 10am-10pm) are shopping and entertainment complexes.

Vilnius' main market is the oft disappointing **Gariūnai** (off Map pp294-5), to the west, off the Kaunas road. Minibuses marked 'Gariūnai' or 'Gariūnų Turgus' ferry shoppers from the train station road to the market every morning. By car it's 11km along Savanorių prospektas from Vilnius centre. Closer to town is the food-driven **Kalvarijų** (Map pp298-9; Kalvarijų gatvė 61). Both markets open sunrise to noon Tuesday to Sunday.

GETTING THERE & AWAY

See p401 for details on links with countries outside the region.

Air

For international flights to/from Vilnius, see p401; at the time of research there were no domestic flights. Between them, Air Lithuania, Air Baltic and Estonian Air connect Vilnius with Tallinn up to seven times daily, and Rīga up to eight times daily. Check up-to-date fares online.

Major airline offices at Vilnius airport:
Lithuanian Airlines (☎ 252 5001; www.f lylal.lt)
Lufthansa (☎ 232 9290; www.luf thansa.com)
SAS/Air Baltic (☎ 235 6000; www.flysas.lt, www.air baltic.com)

Bus

Vilnius **bus station** (Autobusų stotis; Map pp294-5; ☎ 216 2977; Sodų gatvė 22) is not far south of the Old Town. Inside its ticket hall, domestic tick-

---

LITHUANIAN FASHION DESIGN

A stroll in the Old Town reveals a band of Lithuanian designers, some well established on the international catwalk, others up and coming.

Crinkled linen designs with free-flowing feminine lines are the trademark of Rita Plioplienė, who named her small boutique for women near the Gates of Dawn after her two children, **Kristijonas ir Karolina** (Map pp298-9; ☎ 212 0398; Aušros Vartų gatvė 17). **Ramunė Piekautaitė** (Map pp298-9; ☎ 231 2270; www.ramunepiekautaite.com; Didžioji gatvė 20), a short strut away, is another well-known name to turn her hand to linen.

The Lithuanian master of linen is Giedrius Šarkauskas. Inspired by life's natural cycle, the designer lives out his wholly naturalist philosophy with collections sewn solely from linen. Accessories are made from amber, wood, leather and linen. **Lino Kopos** (Linen Dunes; Map pp294-5; ☎ 275 1200; www .linokopos.com; Krokuvos gatvė 6) is his design studio and shop.

Lithuania's other big name is the flamboyant **Juozas Statkrevičius** (Map pp298-9; ☎ 212 2029; Odminų gatvė 11), who is the country's best-known designer and has boutiques in Vilnius, Paris, Palm Beach and New York.

Daiva Urbonavičiūtė fronts the fun and funky fashion house **Zoraza** (Map pp298-9; ☎ 212 0084; www.zoraza.com; Stiklių gatvė 6), where a riot of colours and textures – suede, glitter, beads, felt, crystal, leather and so on – creates an urban, vintage feel. Hidden in a tiny courtyard opposite, **Sufle** (Map pp298–9; ☎ 243 0054; Stiklių 7) provides space for undiscovered Lithuanian designers to sell their urban clothes, shoes, bags and jewellery – at affordable prices. On the same street, **Elementai** (Map pp298-9; ☎ 260 8588; Stiklių gatvė 14) does much the same, and is crammed with designs by non-names. It sells a few pieces of sculpture, pottery, ceramic and glassware too. **Trinté** (Map pp298-9; ☎ 262 9518; Literatų gatvė 5) also gives a leg-up to local designers, and can offer the same outfit in various sizes.

Final stop on the fashion design trail is **Aukso Avis** (Golden Sheep; Map pp298-9; ☎ 261 0421; Savičiaus gatvė 10), a textile gallery established by Vilnius fashion designer Julija Žilėniene, which sells bags, T-shirts, wall murals and jewellery (think necklaces in felt or wool) made from a rich range of material. The gallery runs courses in knitting, embroidery, wool felting and weaving for those seeking some know-how (by appointment only).

Online, shop for Lithuanian design with Vilnius-based **Ona** (www.ona.com).

ets are sold at six windows from 5.30am to 7.30pm, and information is doled out at the **information office** (informacija; ☎ 1661; www.toks.lt, in Lithuanian; ⏱ 6am-9pm). Timetables are displayed on a board here and online. Passenger facilities include left luggage (p293), a pharmacy, ATM, Iki supermarket (p317), bistro and sandwich bar.

Tickets for international destinations, including Rīga and Tallinn, are sold at **Eurolines Baltic International** (Map pp294-5; ☎ 233 6666; www .eurolines.lt; Sodų gatvė 24d-1; ⏱ 8am-9pm Mon-Fri, 9am-9pm Sat & Sun) and **Ecolines** (Map pp294-5; ☎ 213 3300; www.ecolines.net; Sodų gatvė 24e; ⏱ 8am-7pm Mon-Fri, 9am-5pm Sat, 9am-3pm Sun).

Buses to destinations within the Baltic include the following:

Druskininkai (25Lt, two hours, 10 daily)
Ignalina (14Lt, 1¾ hours, up to 10 daily)
Kaunas (20Lt, 1¾ hours, at least every 30 minutes)
Klaipėda (59Lt, four to 5½ hours, up to 15 daily)
Molėtai (15Lt, 1¼ to two hours, hourly)
Palanga (63Lt, 4¼ to six hours, seven daily)
Panevėžys (28Lt, 1¾ to three hours, hourly)
Rīga (55Lt, five hours, four daily)
Šiauliai (41Lt, three to 4½ hours, six daily)
Tallinn (From 108Lt, 10½ hours, up to five daily)
Visaginas (22Lt, 2½ hours, 10 daily)

Car & Motorcycle

Numerous 24-hour petrol stations selling Western-grade unleaded fuel are dotted around Vilnius.

If you hire a car and intend to cross the border in a Lithuanian-registered car, check the car is insured for inter-Baltic travel. Hire companies:

Autobanga (☎ 212 7777; www.autobanga.lt) At the airport.
Avis Airport (☎ 232 9316); Town (Map pp294-5; ☎ 230 6820; www.avis.lt; Laisvės prospektas 3)
Budget (☎ 230 6708; www.budget.lt) At the airport.
Europcar Airport (☎ 216 3442); Town (Map pp298-9; ☎ 212 0207; www.europcar.lt; Stuokos-Gucevičiaus 9-1)
Hertz Airport (☎ 232 9301); Town (Map pp294-5; ☎ 272 6940; www.hertz.lt; Kalvarijų gatvė14)
Rimas Rent a Car (☎ 277 6213, 8-698 21662; rent-car-rimas.w3.lt) Charismatic Rimas offers the cheapest deal in town and offers self-drive cars or cars with English-speaking driver. There's no physical office so call or email for bookings.
Sixt (☎ 239 5636; www.sixt.lt) At the airport.
Unirent (☎ 700 55855; www.unirent.lt) At the airport.

Train

The **train station** (Geležinkelio stotis; Map pp294-5; ☎ 233 0088; Geležinkelio gatvė 16) is opposite the bus station and is equipped with ATMs, a supermarket and information desks. The domestic ticket hall is to the left as you face the central station building, and the international ticket hall to the right. Train information and timetables (in English) are available at the information office between the two halls and online at www.lit rail.lt.

There is no rail link between Vilnius and Rīga or Tallinn. For international trains, see p406. Direct daily services within the region to/from Vilnius:

Ignalina (14Lt, two hours, eight daily)
Kaunas (12Lt, 1¼ to 1¾ hours, up to 17 daily)
Klaipėda (42Lt, 4½ to five hours, three daily)
Šiauliai (29Lt, 2½ to three hours, three daily)
Trakai (3.40Lt, 40 minutes, up to 10 daily)

GETTING AROUND
To/from the Airport

Vilnius International Airport (☎ 273 9305; www.vno .lt; Rodūnė kelias 2) lies 5km south of the centre. Bus 1 runs between the airport and the train station; bus 2 runs between the airport and the northwestern suburb of Šeškinė via the Žaliasis bridge across the Neris and on to Lukiskių aikštė.

A taxi from the airport to the city centre should cost between 40Lt and 50Lt.

Bicycle

Hawaii Express (Map pp298-9; ☎ 261 1617; www.hawaii .lt, in Lithuanian; Vilniaus gatvė 37; ⏱ 10am-7pm Mon-Fri, to 5pm Sat, 11am-4pm Sun) hires out bicycles for 8/35Lt per hour/day plus 200Lt deposit. Otherwise, pick up a pedal-powered taxi (20Lt per 30 minutes) from Katedros aikštė or Pilies gatvė (Map pp298–9).

Car & Motorcycle

Vilnius is generally easy to navigate by car, but even though its traffic burden is light compared to other capitals, it is getting heavier each year. Street parking around the centre can sometimes be hard to find and costs 1Lt for 20/30/60 minutes in a red/yellow/green zone, payable by meter between 8am and 8pm. Avoid parking on unlit streets overnight; car break-ins are on the increase. Cars are not allowed in part of the pedestrian Old Town.

LITHUANIA

Public Transport

The city is efficiently served by buses and trolleybuses from 5.30am or 6am to midnight; Sunday services are less frequent. Tickets cost 1.10Lt at news kiosks and 1.40Lt direct from the driver; punch tickets on board in a ticket machine or risk a 20Lt on-the-spot fine.

Nippier minibuses shadow most routes. They pick up/drop off passengers anywhere en route (not just at official bus stops) and can be flagged down on the street. Tickets costs 2Lt from the driver (3Lt if they pass through the Old Town).

Bus 4 links the train station with Pylimo gatvė. Trolleybus 7 from the train station, or trolleybus 3 from the Gedimino stop on Vrublevskio gatvė near the cathedral, will take you along Jasinskio gatvė, a block south of Gedimino prospektas.

For route details see www.vilniustransport .lt or pick up a transport map from tourist offices.

Taxi

Taxis officially charge 3Lt per km and must have a meter. To avoid getting ripped off or robbed, ask your hotel or the bar/restaurant you are leaving to call you a taxi by telephone (☎ 261 6161, 240 0004, 239 5539). Hopping into a taxi on the street, especially if you are drunk and don't speak Lithuanian, is asking to be 'taken for a ride'.

Taxi ranks are numerous and include: outside the train station; in front of the old town hall on Didžioji gatvė; in front of the Contemporary Art Centre on Vokiečių gatvė; and outside the Radisson SAS Astorija hotel.

AROUND VILNIUS

The centre of Europe, a fairy-tale castle and ancient castle mounds lie within easy reach of the capital. Or there is the trip to Paneriai.

Paneriai

Here Lithuania's brutal history is starkly portrayed. Over 100,000 people were murdered by the Nazis between July 1941 and July 1944 at this site 10km southwest of central Vilnius. Around half the city's Jewish population – about 35,000 people – had been massacred here by the end of the first three months of the German occupation (June to September 1941) at the hands of Einsatzkommando 9, an SS killing unit of

elite Nazi troops. Lithuanian accomplices are accused of doing as much of the killing as their German overseers.

The forest entrance is marked by a memorial, the **Panerių memorialas**. The text in Russian, dating from the Soviet period, commemorates the 100,000 'Soviet citizens' killed here. The memorial plaques in Lithuanian and Hebrew – erected later – honour the 70,000 Jewish victims.

A path leads to the shocking **Paneriai Museum** (Panerių muziejus; ☎ 260 2001; Agrastų gatvė 15; ☒ 11am-6pm Wed-Sat Jun-Sep, by appointment Oct-May). There are two monuments here, one is Jewish (marked with the Star of David), the other is Soviet (an obelisk topped with a Soviet star). From here paths lead to a number of grassed-over pits where, from December 1943, the Nazis lined up 300 to 4000 victims at a time and shot them in the back of the head. The bodies were then covered with sand to await the next layer of bodies. The Nazis later burnt the exhumed corpses to hide the evidence of their crimes. One of the deeper pits, according to its sign, was where they kept those who were forced to dig up the corpses and pulverise the bones.

There are over two dozen trains daily (some terminating in Trakai or Kaunas) from Vilnius to Paneriai station (1.30Lt, 12 to 15 minutes). From Paneriai station (Agrastų gatvė) it's a 1km walk southwest along Agrastų gatvė straight to the site.

Trakai

☎ 528 / pop 5400

With its red-brick fairy-tale castle, Karaites culture, quaint wooden houses and pretty lakeside location, Trakai is a must-see within easy reach of the capital.

Gediminas probably made Trakai, 28km west of Vilnius, his capital in the 1320s and Kęstutis certainly based his 14th-century court here. Protected by the **Trakai Historical National Park** (www.seniejitrakai.lt), spanning 82 sq km since 1991, Trakai today is a quiet town (outside summer weekends) blessed with lake views in all directions and filled with song each July during the **Trakai Festival** which takes place on the Island Castle and features concerts and mock medieval battles.

Most of Trakai stands on a 2km-long, north-pointing tongue of land between Lake Luka (east) and Lake Totoriškių (west). Lake

Galvė opens out from the northern end of the peninsula and boasts 21 islands.

INFORMATION
Snoras Bankas (Vytauto gatvė 56) ATM and currency exchange opposite the tourist office. Two more ATMs are next door outside Iki.

Tourist Office (☎ 51 138; www.trakai.lt; Vytauto gatvė 69; ☻ 9am-5pm Mon, 8am-6pm Tue-Fri, 9am-3pm Sat & Sun May-Sep, 8am-5pm Oct-Apr) Sells maps and guides, books accommodation and proffers oodles of practical info.

SIGHTS
The centrepiece of Trakai is hard to miss. Occupying an island on Lake Galvė, the painstakingly restored red-brick Gothic **Island Castle** probably dates from around 1400, when Vytautas needed stronger defences than the peninsula castle afforded. A footbridge links it to the shore and a moat separates the triangular outer courtyard moat from the main tower with its cavernous central court and a range of galleries, halls and rooms. Some house the **Trakai History Museum** (Trakų istorijos muziejus; ☎ 53 946; www.trakaimuziejus.lt; adult/student & child 12/5Lt; ☻ 10am-7pm May-Sep, to 6pm Tue-Sun Oct, Mar & Apr, to 5pm Nov-Feb), which charts the history of the castle and features plenty of medieval weaponry and traditional Karaite costumes. In summer the castle courtyard is a magical stage for concerts and plays.

The peaceful ruins of Trakai's **Peninsula Castle**, built from 1362 to 1382 by Kęstutis and destroyed in the 17th century, are a little south of the Island Castle. Housed in a former Dominican chapel nearby is the **Sacral Art Exhibition** (☎ 53 941; Kestučio gatvė 4; adult/student & child 4/2Lt; ☻ 10am-6pm Wed-Sun). The collection is small but very fine and includes precious reliquaries and monstrances in its cellar. The peninsula itself is dotted with old wooden cottages, many built by the Karaites, a Judaic sect and Turkic minority originating in Baghdad, which adheres to the Law of Moses. Their descendants were brought to Trakai from the Crimea in around 1400 to serve as bodyguards. Only 12 families (60 Karaites) live in Trakai and their numbers – 280 in Lithuania – are dwindling, prompting fears that the country's smallest ethnic minority is dying out. The **Karaites Ethnographic Museum** (Karaimų etnografinė paroda; ☎ 55 286; Karaimų gatvė 22; adult/student & child 4/2Lt, camera 4Lt, guided tour 20Lt; ☻ 10am-6pm Wed-Sun) traces their ancestry.

Their beautifully restored early-19th-century **Kenessa** (Karaite prayer ☻ ouse; Karaimų gatvė 30; admission by donation) can be visited but there are no set opening times.

ACTIVITIES
Pick up a **pedalo** (per hour 20Lt) or **rowing boat** (per hour 15Lt) from boatmen near the footbridge leading to the Island Castle.

The tourist office can inform you on a plethora of activities, including horse riding, air ballooning and sailing. It also hires out **bicycles** (per hour/day 5/30Lt) and has information on the 14km **bicycle route** around the main sights. Kempingas Slėnyje (below) hires out bicycles (6/25Lt per hour/day) too, along with canoes and boats (8Lt per hour). The Trakai National Sports & Health Centre (below) reputedly hires out rowing boats and canoes but often its staff aren't aware of the fact. Those who prefer a quiet stroll in nature can head for the **Varnikai botanical-zoological preserve** 4km east of the Peninsula Castle. To get there, follow the signs marked 'Varnikų Gamtos Takas' across two lake bridges.

Winter guests to Trakai can expect to enjoy horse-drawn sled rides, skiing and ice-fishing.

SLEEPING
Trakai is an easy day trip from Vilnius, but it's worth staying overnight to experience the place minus the tourist hordes.

Kempingas Slėnyje (☎ 53 380; www.camptrakai .lt; Slėnio gatvė 1; sites per adult/car/tent 18/8/9Lt, d/tr/q without bathroom 70/90/100Lt, cottage for 2-6 people 220-300Lt, d in guesthouse 140Lt; ℗) Some 5km out of Trakai in Slėnje, on the northern side of Lake Galvė off the road to Vievis, this camp site has accommodation to suit all budgets and comfort requirements. Basic summer houses (sleeps three, 90Lt) are fine providing you have mosquito repellent. There are plenty of activities on offer, including a sauna and steam bath, barbecues to use, bikes to hire, folklore evenings to enjoy and a sandy beach to sprawl on.

Trakai National Sports & Health Centre (Trakų Poilsio ir pramogų centras; ☎ 55 501; sportocentras@mail .lt; Karaimų gatvė 73; s/d 110/130Lt; ℗ ☒) Despite often being full of Lithuania's overly healthy sport stars of the future, this enormous sports complex normally has enough places to accommodate travellers. Its simple and clean rooms have touches of comfort, such as

LITHUANIA

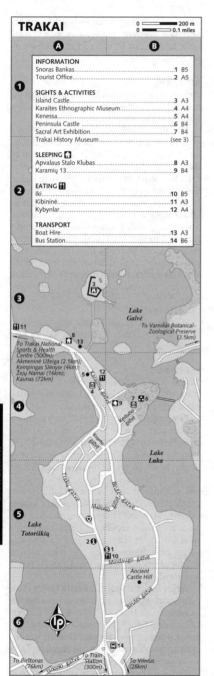

TRAKAI

0 |———————| 200 m
0 |———————| 0.1 miles

INFORMATION	
Snoras Bankas.....................................**1** B5	
Tourist Office......................................**2** A5	

SIGHTS & ACTIVITIES	
Island Castle.......................................**3** A3	
Karaites Ethnographic Museum............**4** A4	
Kenessa...**5** A4	
Peninsula Castle **6** B4	
Sacral Art Exhibition **7** B4	
Trakai History Museum.....................(see 3)	

SLEEPING 🏠	
Apvalaus Stalo Klubas..........................**8** A3	
Karamių 13...**9** B4	

EATING 🍴	
Iki...**10** B5	
Kibininė...**11** A3	
Kybynlar...**12** A4	

TRANSPORT	
Boat Hire...**13** A3	
Bus Station..**14** B6	

heated towel rails and fluffy duvets; a handful have castle views. The cafe/restaurant serves adequate fare and its massive terrace looks directly onto the lake. The centre is located only 500m west of Kibininė restaurant (see below).

ourpick **Akmeninė Užeiga** (Lake Stone Inn; ☎ 8-699 20510; www.akmenineuzeiga.lt; standard/lux/superluxd 295/640/675Lt, villa 795Lt; P ✗) Nothing short of gorgeous, this lakeshore retreat comprises several luxury thatched cottages with fireplace and kitchen, and a main building where terraced rooms peep onto the water. Stylish dining (mains 20Lt to 50Lt) is beneath thatch or on a wooden jetty above the water. Ladders lead into the water for swimming, you can fish from a rowing boat and self-pamperers can watch DVDs in bed, sweat in a sauna or wallow in an outdoor Jacuzzi above the lake shore. Ice-fishing with hot rum tea is the thing to do in winter. This unique hide-out (there are no signs) is located 2.5km north of Trakai; follow the road north (signposted Vievis) out of central Trakai and almost immediately after passing Galvės (right) and Lakes Akmenos (left), turn left towards the thatched rooftops.

Also worth mentioning:

Karamių 13 (☎ 51 911; www.karaimai.lt; Karaimų gatvė 13; s/d 150/200Lt; P ✗ 💻) Renovated Karaite house with six lovely rooms and cafe serving Karaite food.

Apvalaus Stalo Klubas (☎ 55 595; www.ask lubas.lt; Karaimų gatvė 53a; s/d from 290/340Lt; P ✗ 🐾 💻) Sparkling new hotel with elegant rooms directly across from the Island Castle. Perfect for a romantic weekend.

EATING

Akmeninė Užeiga (above) and Apvalaus Stalo Klubas (above) offer great dining.

Kibininė (☎ 55 865; Karaimų gatvė 65; mains 10-25Lt) This green wooden house with Karaite kitchen is *the* spot to munch on traditional Karaite pasties called *kibinai* (like a Cornish pasty, served with a bread-based drink similar to *gira*). But beware that first bite – scalding-hot juices pour out. A hole in the wall doles out meat- or veg-stuffed *kibinai* (3.80Lt to 5Lt) to take away.

Kybynlar (☎ 55 179; Karaimų gatvė 29; mains 15-30Lt; ✗) There is a definite Turkic feel to Trakai's other Karaite-driven restaurant, where piping-hot pastries are likewise cooked up alongside predominantly meat-based fare. The writing on the wall in Arabic is native Karaim, a language belonging to the Kipchak branch of Turkish languages and spoken as mother tongue by 535 people worldwide.

Žejų Namai (☎ 26 008; trout per kg 42Lt) If you have your own wheels and a hankering for fresh fish, travel 16km north of Trakai to Žejų Namai. On arrival, pick up a rod, bait and bucket and head for one of the pools filled with live trout. Staff are on hand to weigh, fillet and cook the fish in a choice of spices, and then bring it to your table on a platter. Žejų Namai is signposted off the road to Vievis; fish must be caught before 9pm as they take around 30 minutes to cook.

Buy picnics at **Iki** (☎ 54 628; Vytauto gatvė 56).

GETTING THERE & AWAY
Up to 10 daily trains (3.40Lt, 40 minutes) travel between **Trakai station** (☎ 51 055; Vilniaus gatvė 5) and Vilnius.

Centre of Europe
Lithuania is proud of its supposed geographic Europos centras (centre of Europe), 25km north of Vilnius off the Molėtai highway. Despite contrary claims, the French National Geographical Institute pronounced this central position – at a latitude of 54° 54' and longitude of 25° 19' – in 1989, marking it with a boulder inscribed with the points of the compass and the words 'Geografinis Europos Centras'. In 2004 Lithuania brightened up this rather unexciting spot with 27 fluttering flags (the EU flag plus that of each member country), a wooden decking stage and a phallic white granite obelisk with a crown of gold stars. Around it the hills were landscaped and a wooden house marked 'tourist information' set up to issue tacky 'I've been to the centre of Europe' certificates (5Lt) and sell souvenir T-shirts. Surrounding the centre is an 18-hole **golf course** (☎ 8-616 26 366; www.golfclub.lt; club hire 40Lt, round 140Lt) and sparkling restaurant.

Most people will find the **Europos parkas** (☎ 237 7077; www.europosparkas.lt; adult/student/child 21/14/7Lt; ☺ 10am-sunset), some 17km from the centre of Europe off the Utena road, more appealing. Leading contemporary sculptors, including Sol LeWitt and Dennis Oppenheim, show works in wooded parkland (bring mosquito repellent in summer). The latest inclusion is the largest sculpture in the world made entirely of TV sets; constructed as a maze, it consists of 3000 TVs and is centred on a fallen statue of Lenin. The sculpture park was the brainchild of Lithuanian sculptor Gintaras Karosas in response to the centre of Europe tag. Every year international workshops are held here, attracting artists from all over the world.

GETTING THERE & AWAY
Travelling north on the Vilnius–Molėtai road from Vilnius, the centre of Europe is to the left and marked by the sign 'Europos Centras'. Getting there by public transport requires two bus changes and plenty of patience; the Vilnius tourist offices (p296) have more information if you're dead keen.

From Vilnius, minibuses marked 'Skirgiskes' leave from the bus stop on Kalvarijų gatvė for the Europos parkas (2Lt, 30 minutes) at least three times daily. By car, head north along Kalvarijų gatvė until you reach the Santasriskių roundabout, then bear right towards Žalieji ežerai, following the signs for 'Europos parkas'.

Kernavė
Deemed an 'exceptional testimony to 10 millennia of human settlements in this region' by Unesco who made it a World Heritage site in 2004, Kernavė (ker-na-vey) is a must-see. Thought to have been the spot where Mindaugas (responsible for uniting Lithuania for the first time) celebrated his coronation in 1253, the rural cultural reserve comprises four old castle mounds and the remains of a medieval town.

The fascinating heritage of the **Kernavė Cultural Reserve** (Kernavės kultūrinio rezervato; www .kernave.org; admission free; ☺ dawn-dusk) can be explored in the **Archaeological & Historical Museum** (Archeologijos ir istorijos muziejus; ☎ 382-47 385; Kerniaus gatvė 4a) after spring 2010, when it was due to reopen following extensive renovations. Guided tours (12Lt) of the area are still available by prior arrangement between 9am and 5pm Tuesday to Saturday, April to October; otherwise the area is free to explore at your leisure.

Medieval fun and frolics – axe throwing, catapulting, mead making, medieval fights, music making and so on – fill Kernavė with festivity on 23 June and during the three-day **International Festival of Experimental Archaeology** (lots of fun despite the deadly name) in mid-July.

LITHUANIA

To reach Kernavė, 35km northwest of Vilnius in the Neris Valley, follow the road through Dūkštos from Maisiagala on the main road north to Ukmergė.

EASTERN & SOUTHERN LITHUANIA

The deep, magical forests of Lithuania's eastern and southern corners are a tree-hugger's paradise. Some of the most spectacular scenery in Lithuania is found in these wildernesses, with a lake district that extends into Belarus and Latvia.

Aukštaitija National Park is Lithuania's oldest park, framed by the 900-sq-km Labanoras-Pabradė Forest. Outdoor purists will have a ball here, pursuing canoeing, hiking, windsurfing, sailing, birdwatching and, in winter, ice-fishing and even skiing. Dzūkija in the far south is the biggest national park, surrounded by the 1500-sq-km Druskininkai-Varėna Forest. Both parks are blessed with an abundant berry crop in early summer, while mushrooms of all shapes and guises sprout by the bucketful from early spring until late autumn.

Close to the Dzūkija National Park is the spa resort of Druskininkai, where rich Lithuanians indulge in winter breaks and the likes of warm honey massages. Next door at Grūtas sculpture park reside Lenin, Stalin and co – the main reason most people travel here.

A few words of warning: mosquitoes are a menace so bring insect repellent; only pick mushrooms with a local guide and be aware that the stomach of the guide – reared on mushrooms since birth – is substantially more tolerant of certain species than your own.

AUKŠTAITIJA NATIONAL PARK
☎ 386

In beloved Aukštaitija (owk-shtai-ti-ya) National Park it's clear where Lithuania's love for nature arose. The natural paradise of deep, whispering forests and blue lakes bewitched this once-pagan country.

Around 70% of the park comprises pine, spruce and deciduous forests, inhabited by elk, deer and wild boar. Its highlight is a labyrinth of 126 lakes, the deepest being **Lake**

Tauragnas (60.5m deep). A footpath leads to the top of 155m **Ice Hill** (Ledakalnis), from where a panorama of some seven lakes unfolds. Particularly pretty is **Lake Baluošas**, ensnared by woods and speckled with islands. White-tailed and golden eagles prey here and storks are rife. The **Trainiškis Wildlife Sanctuary** and **Ažvinčiai Forest**, home to 150- to 200-year-old pine trees, can only be visited with park guides.

The main jumping-off point for the park is the sleepy town of **Ignalina**, which has a supermarket and post office. There are 100 settlements within the park itself: **Šuminai, Salos II, Vaišnoriškės, Varniškės II** and **Strazdai** are protected ethnographic centres. **Palūšė**, on the banks of Lake Lūsiai (literally 'Wild Cat Lake'), is Aukštaitija's largest community. Ginučiai has a 19th-century **watermill** (☎ 8-616 29366; adult/student 2/1Lt; ⏱ 10am-6pm Tue-Sun May-Sep) with a small exhibition on its flour- and electricity-producing history. Stripeikiai's **Ancient Bee-keeping Museum** (Senorinės bitininkystės muziejus; ☎ 36 210; adult/student 3/1Lt; ⏱ 10am-7pm Tue-Sun May–mid-Oct) spins the story of beekeeping through a merry collection of carved wooden statues and hives.

The park has several ancient *piliakalnis* (fortification mounds) such as the **Taurapilio mound** on the southern shore of Lake Tauragnas, and some quaint wooden architecture, including a fine **church** and **bell tower** at Palūsė. Around Lake Lūšiai a **wooden sculpture trail** depicts Lithuanian folklore.

Unaccompanied children under 16, littering, lighting fires and drunken behaviour are forbidden in the park.

Information
Both Ignalina's **tourist office** (☎ 52 597; www .ignalina.lt/tic; Ateites gatvė 23; ⏱ 8am-6pm Mon-Fri, 10am-3pm Sat Jun-Aug, 8am-5pm Mon-Fri, 8am-3.45pm Sat Sep-May), on the town's central square, and the **Aukštaitija National Park Office** (☎ 53 135, 47 478; www.anp.lt; ⏱ 9am-6pm Mon-Sat), in Palūsė, have information on the park's activities and accommodation and sell park maps (15Lt). The latter also provides free internet access.

Activities
Boating and **trekking** are the main activities in the park. The national park office ar-

EASTERN LITHUANIA

LATVIA

To Biržai (25km);
Riga (125km)

To Riga
(225km)

To Rēzekne
(65km)

Juodopė

Pandėlys

Subate

Ilūkste

Rokiškis

Obeliai

DAUGAVPILS

Kupiškis

Kamajai

Lake
Sartai

Jūžintai

To Panevėžys
(40km)

Dusetos

Zarasai

Svėdasai

Sudeikiai

Lake
Antalieptė

Bikėnai
Lake
Luodis

Salakas Paukščiu Sala

Ignalina Nuclear
Power Station

Visaginas

Anykščiai

Širutėnai

See Aukštaitija National
Park Map (p328)

Dūkštas

BELARUS

Utena

Aukštaitija
National
Park

Molėtai Astronomical
Observatory &
Lithuanian
Ethnocosmology Museum

Palūšė

Ignalina

To Ukmergė (25km);
Kaunas (100km)

Lake
Antaliepте

Labanoras

Kaltanėnai

Didžiasalis

LITHUANIA

Molėtai

Siesartis
Labanoras
Regional
Park

Baltieji
Lakajai

Švenčionėliai

Adutiškis

Giedraičiai

Šventoji

Švenčionys

Širvintos

To Vilnius
(45km)

To Vilnius
(45km)

To Vilnius
(40km)

Pabradė

0   30 km
0   20 miles

ranges treks and backpacking trips by boat, English-speaking guides (45Lt per hour), and skiing, fishing (summer and winter) and sledging.

Palūšė valtinė (☎ 8-686 90030; www.valtine .lt; ☉ May-Oct) on the lakeshore in Palūšė hires out rowing boats (7/35Lt per hour/day), canoes and kayaks (10/60Lt per hour/day) and arranges canoeing trips, with or without guide.

Hire bicycles from **Piratų baras** (☎ 8-614 61321; ☉ 11am-10pm), on Palūšė's main drag, for 8/35Lt per hour/day.

Mushroom and berry picking (p330) is only permitted in designated forest areas. If you are unsure, please ask at the tourist office.

Sleeping

Pick up homestay lists from the national park office and Ignalina tourist office. The **Tourism Centre Palūšė** (☎ 47 430; www.paluse.lt) has its own very basic rooms (from 44Lt) in Palūšė village.

Lithuanian Winter Sports Centre (Lietuvos žiemos sporto centras; ☎ 54 102, 54 193; www.lzsc.lt; Sporto gatvė 3, Ignalina; s/d/apt 60/100/240Lt; P) Accommodation, which consists of presentable cottages overlooking the centre's own lake, plays second fiddle at this Soviet-era sports centre. In winter guests can wake up, hire skis (per hour/day 15/40Lt) and leap on the ski lift (per hour/day 15/40Lt). Summer activities include boating (15Lt per hour) on the lake or rollerblading along a 7.5km track. From Ignalina centre,

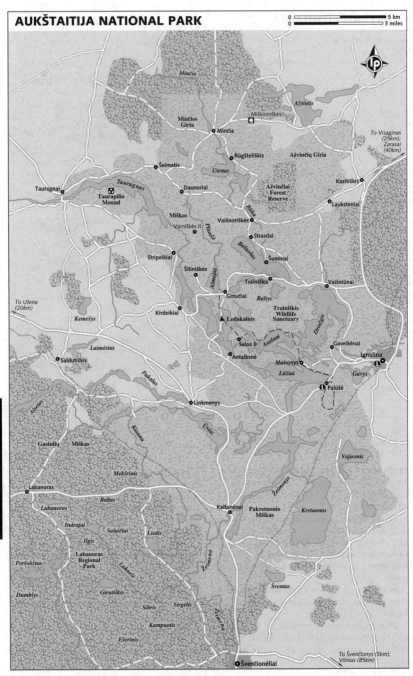

AUKŠTAITIJA NATIONAL PARK

0 — 5 km
0 — 3 miles

Minčia

Ažvintis

Minčios
Giria

Miškininkškės

To Visaginas
(25km);
Zarasai
(40km)

Minčia

Rūgšteliškis

Ažvinčių Giria

Šeimatis

Utenas

Tauragnas

Daunoriai

Ažvinčiai
Forest
Reserve

Kazitiškis

Tauragnai

Taurapilio
Mound

Vaišnoriškės

Lauksteniai

Miškas

Varniškės II

Plūtė

Strazdai

Stripeikiai

Almajas

Baluošas

Suminai

Šiliniškės

Trainiškis

Vaišniūnai

Ginučiai

Baltys

To Utena
(20km)

Kemešys

Kirdeikiai

Ledakalnis

Trainiškis
Wildlife
Sanctuary

Dringis

Laimėstas

Asalnai

Saldutiškis

Salos II

Gaveikėnai

Antalksnė

Meironys

Ignalina

Pakalas

Lūšiai

Palūšė

Gavys

Linkmenys

Ūsiai

Kiauna

Aiseitas

Gasiulių

Miškas

Žeimenys

Vajuonis

Mekšrinis

Labanoras

Baltas

Kaltanėnai

Pakretuonio
Miškas

Kretuonas

Labanoras

Indrajai

Salaičiai

Liedis

Ilgis

Labanoras
Regional
Park

Lakaldė

Peršokšna

Dumblys

Girutiškis

Žeimena

Sibris

Sirgėlis

Kampuotis

Šventas

Ešerinis

To Švenčionys (3km);
Vilnius (85km)

Švenčionėliai

LITHUANIA

cross the train track and follow Budrių gatvė for 2km.

Ginučiai watermill (☎ 8-616 29366; d/apt from 130/260Lt; P) Run by the Tourism Centre Palūšė, the watermill offers stripped-back rooms with clean wood interiors and as peaceful a surrounding as you'll ever find in Lithuania. Bring your own food to cook in the kitchen, and end the evening relaxing by the fire or in the sauna (200Lt).

Miškiniškės (☎ 8-612 33577; www.miskiniskes.lt; r 190-220Lt, 7-person cottages 590Lt; P ✗) This forest hide-out is a fabulous example of ecological living. Accommodation comprises rustic log cabins with fireplace and modern interiors, and meals served in the main house are homemade, using seasonal produce from local farmers (breakfast 15Lt to 25Lt, dinner 30Lt to 50Lt). Activities abound: try your hand at archery (85Lt), axe throwing (85Lt) or rock climbing (120Lt); hire a canoe (80Lt per day) or bicycle (per hour/day 10/40Lt); or simply wander the vast grounds. Miškininškės is best reached from Kazitiškis; follow the dirt road north out of the village through the Ažvinčiai Giria forest, then turn west (left) and follow the signs (about 7km).

Getting There & Away

Hop on a bus (14Lt, 1¾ hours, 10 daily) or jump on a train (13.10Lt, two hours, eight daily) from Vilnius to Ignalina; there's also one bus to/from Kaunas (33.50Lt, four hours) via Utena (11Lt, one hour). Three buses daily travel between Ignalina and Palūšė (2.50Lt).

VISAGINAS & IGNALINA NUCLEAR POWER STATION

☎ 386 / pop 28,250

Visaginas is as Soviet as you'll get outside the borders of Russia. Built in 1975 for workers at the nearby Ignalina Nuclear Power Plant, the town is packed with identical-looking blocks of flats amid forest and circled by a ring road. Attractive it ain't; bizarre it is.

Approximately 3000 shift workers are shuttled between Visaginas and the plant, 2km east of the town centre. In its heyday 5000 people worked at Ignalina. A Geiger counter records the day's radiation level and Russian remains the language spoken on the streets. Visaginas' future is uncertain, however – the plant is scheduled for shutdown in 2009 and a new one may, or may not, be built close by.

Those looking for a true Soviet experience can overnight in **Hotel Aukštaitija** (☎ 50 684; Veteranų gatvė 9; s/d from 40/60Lt; P), a stunningly ugly concrete block with little appeal apart from the price, or those looking to avoid it can try the spa-hotel **Gabriella** (☎ 70 171; www.gabriella.lt; Jaunystės gatvė 21; s/d from 150/230Lt; P ☎).

In mid-August Visaginas bizarrely rocks with a bunch of cowboys – hats, boots and all – who groove on into town from across Europe for the two-day international country music festival, **Visagino Country** (www.visagino country.lt).

From Vilnius to Visaginas there are daily trains (16.30Lt, 2½ hours, five daily) and plenty of buses (22Lt, 2½ hours).

LABANORAS REGIONAL PARK

West of Aukštaitija is 528 sq km of pretty parkland polka-dotted with 285 lakes. At its heart sits lovely **Labanoras**, home to the **Regional Park Information Centre** (☎ 838-747 160/142; www.labanoroparkas.lt; ☒ 8am-noon & 1-5pm Mon-Fri, 8am-3.45pm Sat), where information on the park can be gathered.

Canoeing is a grand pastime in Labanoras, particularly on the Lakaja River in the southern section of the park, and trips can be organised through **Plaukių** (☎ 8-676 11086; www.plaukiu.com; Kalno gatvė 32) in Švenčionėliai. One-day kayak hire during the week/weekend costs 40/60Lt plus 1Lt per kilometre for transportation.

Accommodation in the park is limited to a handful of homestays and one delightful hotel-restaurant in Labanoras village.

our pick **Hotel Restaurant Labanoras** (☎ 8-655 70917; www.hotellabanoras.lt; s/d 100/150Lt; P) has a pretty terrace overlooking the village square and, when in season, roosting storks. The wooden house and its six guest rooms are full of character and quirks, and jammed with all sorts of collectables. Homemade dumplings, cold beetroot soup, grilled trout, and crepes with wild berries and cream are just some of the divine choices on the menu (mains 15Lt to 30Lt). Guests can borrow a bike to explore the park.

Moletai

☎ 383 / pop 6970

A small town 30km west of the Aukštaitija National Park, Molėtai (mo-ley-tai) is un-startling apart from its lake surrounds, about

MUSHROOMING & BERRYING

Mushrooming is a, um, mushrooming business, particularly in the Aukštaitija and Dzūkija national parks, which, come August and September, are carpeted with little white and yellow buttons. The forests lining the Varėna–Druskininkai highway (A4) and the Zervynos forests – best known for sand dunes, beehive hollows and substantial *grybai* (mushroom) populations – make rich *grybaula* (mushroom-hunting grounds) too. For mushroom addicts, there's Varėna's September **mushroom festival** (www.varena.lt/en/events).

The crinkle-topped, yellow chanterelle and stubby *boletus* are among the edible wild mushroom varieties hunted and exported to other parts of Europe. The less common *baravykas*, with its distinctive brown cap, is a stronger-tasting mushroom that ends up stuffed inside a *cepelinai* or dried and stored until Christmas Eve, when it is served as one of 12 dishes (p290). Lithuania boasts 1200 mushroom species; 100 are poisonous and 380 edible.

Berrying is another trade and tradition. Red bilberries only ripen in August and cranberries in September, but most other berries – wild strawberries, blueberries, buckthorn berries, sloe berries and raspberries – can be harvested whenever they are ripe.

The roadside rate for mushrooms is around 15Lt to 20Lt per kg. Look for locals selling at roadsides, with glass jamjars overflowing with freshly picked forest goodies lined up on car bonnets. The mushroom season runs from early spring to late autumn.

which its **tourist office** (☎ 51 187; www.infomoletai .lt; Inturkės gatvė 4; 8am-6pm Mon-Fri, 10am-2pm Sat) has information.

There are spectacular views of Molėtai's lake-studded landscape and the stars above from the **Molėtai Astronomical Observatory** (Molėtų astronomijos observatorija; ☎ 45 444; www.astro.lt/mao) on Kaldiniai Hill (193m). The observatory boasts northern Europe's largest telescope; visits must be booked in advance. Next door, the **Lithuanian Ethnocosmology Museum** (Lietuvos etnokosmologijos muziejus; ☎ 45 424; www.cosmos.lt, in Lithuanian; adult/child 6/4Lt; 8am-4pm) explores the cosmos' connection to hell, heaven and earth in its bubble-shaped exhibition centre. Dwarfing it are two observation towers topped by a massive rugby ball; inside are two telescopes providing outstanding views of the surrounding Lakeland. Night tours with English-speaking guides (adult/child 10/6Lt), two hours after sunset, can be arranged in advance.

The hourly buses from Vilnius (15Lt, 1¼ to two hours) to Molėtai normally continue onto Utena (8Lt, 35 minutes). To visit the observatory and museum, catch a bus from Molėtai to Utena and ask to be let off at the *ethnokosmologijos muziejus* turn-off (signposted 10km north of town) and follow the road to the right for another 4km.

Utena
☎ 389 / pop 32,800
Utena, 34km north of Molėtai, is a quiet town in the centre of Lithuania's northeastern Lakeland

region. Its **tourist office** (☎ 54 346; www.utenainfo.lt; Utenio aikštė 5; 9am-noon & 1-6pm Mon-Fri, 9am-3pm Sat & Sun) can provide information on accommodation, activities and tours of the **Utenos Alus Brewery** (☎ 63 309; www.utenosalus.lt; Pramonės gatvė 12).

Alaušynė (☎ 66 047; www.abuva.lt; 4-person chalet 100-270Lt, s/d 280/350Lt; P) is a rural spot 12km northeast of Utena and immediately northeast of Sudeikiai village with a range of accommodation and leisure options, including simple log chalets sleeping up to four people and modern houses with fireplace. It offers a sauna for weary bones, boats and canoes to hire (5Lt per hour), and fishing excursions to enjoy. Alaušybė also cooks up a mean fish soup – swimming with six different fish (including eel and carp) and served in a brown loaf of bread.

Geltonasis Submarine (☎ 50 223; Basanavičiaus gatvė 55; small/medium/large pizza 10/12/14Lt), a Beatles-inspired pizzeria that serves *pica su karka* (pizza with smoked pigs' trotters), is the cheeriest place to eat.

Iki (Basanavičiaus gatvė 55) next door sells the makings of a lovely lakeside picnic.

From Utena **bus station** (☎ 61 740; Baranauskas gatvė 19) there is one daily bus to/from Ignalina (11Lt, one hour), hourly buses to/from Vilnius (20Lt, 1½ to two hours), some via Molėtai (8Lt, 35 minutes), and seven daily buses to/ from Kaunas (20Lt, 2½ hours).

Around Utena
Dusetos, some 34km northeast of Utena, is famous for its annual **horse race** (www.zarasai

.lt) held on the first Saturday in February on frozen **Lake Sartai**. The race dates from 1865 and attracts horse enthusiasts, musicians and folk artists from all over the region, who pour into the small village to watch the race and slug local Čižo beer (see right).

A fun spot to stay and play is **Bikėnų Uzeiga** (☎ 8-685 44450; www.degesa.lt; ☺ 10am-10pm Apr-Sep; Ⓟ), in Bikėnai on the eastern shore of **Lake Antalieptės**. The bar hires out rowing boats, canoes and kayaks for 6Lt per hour, offers a 10-person speedboat for charter (250Lt per hour) and has a water slide that snakes into the lake. The centre also organises two-day canoeing expeditions (80Lt for a two-person canoe and tent hire) on the Šventoji River and has rooms to rent in lakeside houses for 100/200Lt per double/quad.

Bikėnų Uzeiga has a number of sister sites in the lake region, including the newly built **Paukščių Sala** (☎ 8-685 44450; s/d Mon-Fri 50/100Lt, Sat & Sun 100/150Lt; Ⓟ Ⓧ) 1km east of Salakas on the shores of Lake Luodis. Rooms inside the wooden house are smallish but they're all en suite, super clean and good value. The restaurant on-site will cook fish caught in the fish pond nearby (25Lt per kg), and it's 'activity central' here, with bicycles (10/30Lt per hour/day) and canoes (10Lt per hour) for hire, plus sailing, wind surfing and, in winter, ice-fishing options.

ourpick Užeiga Prie Bravoro (☎ 385-56 653; www .cizoalus.lt, in Lithuanian; Dusetų homestead; ☺ 10am-10pm Tue-Sun) is not much to look at, but the story behind this brewery creates its soul. Four generations have brewed the light, thirst-quenching Čižo *alus* (beer) since 1863, teenage daughters Miglė and Rūta being let into the family secret on their 16th birthdays. The girls are now frequently found behind the bar at their family-run village inn, pulling a pint of the cloudy unfiltered beer (10/25Lt per 2/5 litres), cooking up winter-warming beer soup (mains 15Lt to 20Lt) or showing punters the old beer-making equipment their grandfather used to grind hops upstairs. Preservatives are a strict no-no and honey made by forest bees is the only sweetener. Their father, Ramūnas, gave up his day job to run his brewery full time in 1995: brewing and selling beer was forbidden in the USSR, forcing the fourth-generation brewer to concoct in secret while working as an economist. Today he produces 12 tonnes annually – which peaks at half a tonne per week in summer – and tours craft fairs and folk celebrations. He always travels to Kernavė on 6 July, the nation's Statehood Day, commemorating the coronation of Grand Duke Mindaugas in Kernavė. Find his brewery on the 178 road to Obeliai heading north out of Dusetos village.

IGNALINA

Ignalina (named after Ignalina region) looks uncannily like Springfield's nuclear power station in *The Simpsons* and it's just as safe, say scientists. Unlike reactors in the West, its one remaining online reactor, Reactor Bolshoi Moschnosti Kanalynyi (RBMK) – the same design as Ukraine's Chernobyl reactor, which suffered a meltdown in 1986 – is graphite-cooled and has no containment system.

Enormous pressure from the EU forced a reluctant Lithuania to shut down the first reactor on 31 December 2004; the second is scheduled to discontinue operation on 31 December 2009. Millions of euros have been pumped into Ignalina to improve safety, and its eventual closure and the disposal of redundant radioactive material – the complete decommission process will take 25 years – will consume billions of euros more.

The plant regularly meets around 70% of Lithuania's energy needs, a factor which has forced the government to consider the construction of a new station. In July 2006 Lithuania invited its neighbours Poland, Latvia and Estonia to join in doing just that – potentially at Visaginas – and in February of the next year the four countries agreed to go ahead with the €6.7 billion project. At the time of writing, the lengthy negotiations between the partners were still continuing, yet the world press and nuclear watchdogs agree the new plant could be operational as early as 2015. Up-to-date news on the project can be found online at www.vae.lt.

To visit the site, see a video in English about Ignalina and play with a scaled-down model of the plant, ring Ignalina AE's **Information Centre** (☎ 29 911; www.iae.lt; ☺ 8am-4pm Mon-Fri).

DRUSKININKAI

☎ 313 / pop 16,450

Nineteenth-century spa town Druskininkai (drus-ki-nin-kai) on the Nemunas River is Lithuania's oldest and most chic. Today it attracts plenty of investment and young, hip and wealthy Lithuanians seeking a quick detox from city life. Tourists also flock here, not so much to take the waters but to visit one of the Baltic's more unusual sights, the Soviet sculpture park just outside the town.

During the days of the USSR, the old and ailing flocked to this famous health resort in search of miracle cures for all sorts of ailments, and some of the vast dinosaur sanatoriums still remain today.

Information

Iki Internet (Čiurlionio gatvė; per hr 3Lt; ☼ 9am-8pm) Inside an Iki supermarket on the road to Vilnius.

Post office (Kudirkos gatvė)

SEB Bankas (Čiurlionio gatvė 40) Currency exchange inside, ATM outside.

Tourist office Former train station building (☎ 60 800; Gardino gatvė 3; ☼ 8.30am-12.15pm & 1-5.15pm Mon-Fri; Town Centre (☎ 51 777; www.info.druskininkai .lt; Čiurlionio gatvė 65; ☼ 10am-1pm & 1.45-6.45pm Mon-Sat, 10am-5pm Sun)

Sights

Druskininkai has a strong connection to Lithuania's most talented painter-musician, MK Čiurlionis; he spent his childhood in what is now the **MK Čiurlionis Memorial Museum** (☎ 52 755; Čiurlionio gatvė 41; adult/student 4/2Lt; ☼ 11am-5pm Tue-Sun), and the town has honoured him with a **statue** at the northern end of Kudirkos gatvė. Both the museum and the open-air stage in front of the **Cultural Centre** (Vilniaus alėja 24) host beautiful classical concerts during the 'Druskininkai Summer with Čiurlionis' festival (June to September). On the top floor of the Culture Centre is the small but worthwhile **Museum of Armed Resistance** (☎ 8-656 08373; admission free; ☼ 1-5pm Tue-Sun), detailing the partisan movement and cultural resistance to Soviet rule.

To see Druskininkai past and present, take a walk around the town, starting from Laisvės aikštė. On this vast tree-shaded square, one of the USSR's biggest and best, 10-storey **Nemunas Sanatorium** overlooks the striking multidomed 19th-century **Russian Orthodox church**. Not far east rises the Druskininkai **Aqua Park** (p335), the boldest

and brightest project to hit the town for years.

The magical powers of local mineral water can be tested at the Dzūkija Fountain inside the **Mineralinio Vandems Biuvetė** (per cup 0.30Lt or per 10/20 days 5/9.50Lt; ☼ 11.30am-1.30pm & 4-7pm Mon-Fri, 10.30am-1.30pm Sat), a round green building with mosaic floor and stained-glass windows on the footpath running along the Nemunas. Continue north to the **Fountain of Beauty** (Grožio šaltinis) – one slurp of the shockingly salty water promises eternal beauty.

Heading 2km east of town, **Girios Aidas** (Echo of the Forest; ☎ 53 901; Čiurlionio gatvė 102; adult/child 5/2Lt, sculpture trail only 1Lt, camera 2Lt; ☼ 10am-6pm Wed-Sun) is home to a pagan collection of wood carvings and a nature museum. More lovable folk characters fill the **Windmill Museum** (Vėjo malūnas; ☎ 52 448; adult/child 5/2Lt; ☼ 10am-6pm Wed-Sun), about 5km southeast of the centre in Naujasodė.

Activities

Spas (p335) aside, cruising around by pedal-power is the way to go. Bicycle and two- or four-seater buggy **hire** (☎ 8-686 87022; ☼ 8am-9pm May-Oct) is available from the corner of Vilniaus and Laisvės alėjas, Vilniaus alėja 10 or opposite the tourist office at Čiurlionio gatvė 52. Expect to pay 4Lt to 6Lt per hour or 20Lt to 30Lt per day for a bicycle and 15/25Lt per 30/60 minutes for a buggy.

The tourist office sells cycling maps (5Lt) covering three local cycling trails: the south-bound riverside **Sun Path** (Saulės takas; 24km) – also a footpath – goes to the windmill museum (above), **Stars Orbit** (Žvaigzdžių orbita; 24km) snakes south into the Raigardas Valley, and the forested eastbound **Žilnas Path** (Žilvino takas; 20km) links Druskininkai with Grūtas Park (p336) 8km east – a great day trip.

Water-bound activities include **rowing boats** (per hr 15Lt) or **pedalo** (per hr 20Lt) on Lake Druskonis or taking a **steamboat cruise** (☎ 8-612 26982; adult/child 32/16Lt; ☼ 2.30pm Tue-Sun May-Oct) along the Nemunas River to Liškiava in the Dzūkija National Park (p334). Journey time is 45 minutes each way and passengers spend 1½ hours in Liškiava before sailing back to Druskininkai. Kids – both young and old – will have a ball in the **Aqua Park** (p335). The complex sports six water slides, a wave pool, flow pool and

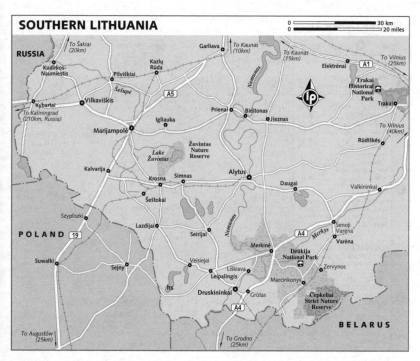

SOUTHERN LITHUANIA

massive outdoor pool. Admission prices for a full day: adult 77Lt, child 3-7/7–18 years old 35/57Lt.

Sleeping

Prices increase on weekends and in July and August; consult the tourist offices if you need help.

Medūna (☎ 58 033; www.meduna.lt; Liepų gatvė 2; s/d/apt from 80/120/350; **P** ✗) Associated with the Aqua Park, and a bold example of contemporary architecture in the middle of town. Interior furnishings are tidy but less inspiring.

Galia (☎ 60 510; www.galia.lt; Maironio gatvė 3, Dubintos gatvė 3 & 4; s/d from 110/160Lt; **P**) Galia surprises with a rainbow of colours. The hotel is spread over three buildings, all of which are in good condition; confirm before you check in as prices vary between the houses.

Aqua Medūna (☎ 59 195; www.aquameduna.lt; Vilniaus alėja 13-1; s/d/apt from 150/230/599Lt; **P** ✗) Filling one third of the Aqua Park, this new hotel has spacious rooms coloured in pleasing shades of brown. Little extras, such as flat-screen TVs, big fluffy towels and welcome robes make the stay here all that more worthwhile.

Hotel Druskininkai (☎ 52 566; www.hotel-druski ninkai.lt; Kudirkos gatvė 43; s/d/ste from 210/300/430Lt; **P** ✗ ✗ ☐) Despite its Soviet block past, Druskininkai is one of the most stylish hotels in town. Behind its striking glass-and-wood facade are modern rooms bathed in subdued light, a Turkish bath, Jacuzzi bubbling with Druskininkai mineral water, and hotel gym.

Other options:

Druskininkai Camping (☎ 60 800; camping@drus kininkai.lt; Gardino gatvė 3a; site per adult/tent 5/15Lt, tepee 40Lt, cabins 120Lt; **P** ☐) Large, well-organised camp ground near tourist office and bus station. Tepees and cabins sleep up to two people.

Regina (☎ 59 060; www.regina.lt; Kosciuškos gatvė 3; s/d from 150/220Lt; **P** ✗ ☐) Solid bet for those looking for large, comfortable rooms at a reasonable price. If you're looking for character, look somewhere else.

Eating

Unfortunately, the dining scene leaves a little to be desired.

LITHUANIA

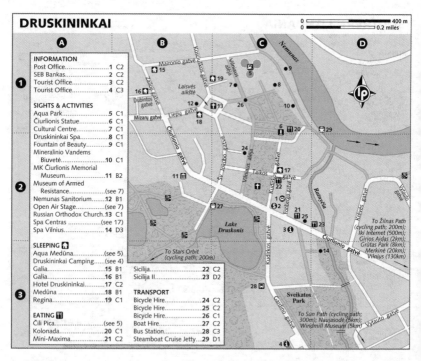

DRUSKININKAI

0 — 400 m
0 — 0.2 miles

To Stars Orbit
(cycling path; 200m)

To Žilnas Path
(cycling path; 200m);
Iki Internet (500m);
Girios Aidas (2km);
Grūtas Park (8km);
Merkinė (20km);
Vilnius (130km)

To Sun Path (cycling path;
300m); Naujasodė (5km);
Windmill Museum (5km)

Sicilija (pizzas 10-20Lt, mains 12-20Lt) Main branch (☎ 51 865; Taikos gatvė 9); Sicilija II (☎ 57 258; Čiurlionio gatvė 56) Pizza – over 40 varieties – is the speciality of this massively popular dining spot, which fills to overflowing at lunch time. Its second, industrial-styled outlet, Sicilija II, serves much the same fodder.

Čili Pica (☎ 8-612 22462; Vilniaus alėja 13; pizzas 10-40Lt) Lithuania's version of Pizza Hut has struck gold once again – this time in Druskininkai. Locals and tourists flock to this pizza joint in the Aqua Park for surprisingly decent pizza and Lithuanian choices.

Kolonada (☎ 51 222; www.kolonada.lt, in Lithuanian; Kurdikos gatvė 22; mains around 20Lt) A diamond in the rough, this renovated late-1920s music hall combines atmosphere with fine Lithuanian cuisine, a huge patio overlooking the central park, and live music (jazz, classical, rock 'n' roll) on a regular basis.

Self-caterers can stock up at **Mini-Maxima** (Čiurlionio gatvė 50).

Getting There & Away
From the **bus station** (☎ 51 333; Gardino gatvė 1) there are up to 10 daily buses (25Lt, two

hours) to/from Vilnius; hourly buses to/from Kaunas (25Lt, two to three hours), two of which continue to/from Palanga (68Lt, 5½ to seven hours); one to/from Panevėžys (46Lt, 4¼ hours) and one to/from Šiauliai (52Lt, 5¼ hours).

DZŪKIJA NATIONAL PARK
☎ 310

The 555-sq-km Dzūkija (dzoo-ki-ya) National Park (Lithuania's largest) is a nature-lovers paradise. Four-fifths of it is covered by dense pine forest, and 48 lakes can be found within its borders. The Ūla and Grūda Rivers, perfect for a days' canoeing, flow through it, and an abundance of mushrooms and berries grow here during the season. And, to add the icing to the cake, squeezed between Marcinkonys and the Belarusian border is the **Čepkeliai Strict Nature Reserve**, which safeguards the country's largest marsh.

Several villages, including **Zervynos**, between Varėna and Marcinkonys, are ethnographic reserves. **Liškiava**, 10km northeast of Druskininkai, has remnants of a 14th-century hill-top castle. The village church and former Dominican monastery is famous for its seven rococo-style altars and its crypt with glass coffins. **Merkinė**, 10km further down the Nemunas, is the starting point for a 12km **black potters' trail** around workshops where pots as black as soot are made from red clay. The extraordinary colour comes from pine-wood resin fired with the pot in an outdoor kiln. Other traditions such as woodcarving, weaving, basket-making and beekeeping come to life in Marcinkonys' **Ethnographic Museum** (Marcinkonių etnografijos muziejus; ☎ 39 169; Miškininkų gatvė 10; adult/child 2/1Lt; ☿ 9am-4pm Tue-Sat May-Sep, 10am-4pm Tue-Sat Oct-Apr).

Two **visitor centres** Marcinkonys (☎ 44 466; www .dzukijosparkas.lt; Miškininkų gatvė 61; ☿ 8am-5pm Mon-Fri, 8am-3.45pm Sat); Merkinė (☎ 57 245; merkine@dzukijosparkas.lt; Vilniaus gatvė 3; ☿ 8am-noon & 1-5pm Mon-Thu, 8am-3.45pm Fri) advise on walking, cycling, canoeing and arranging English-speaking guides (50/200Lt per hour/day) for mushrooming or berrying. The centres also have information on the 14km **Zackagiris Sightseeing Route** (Zackagirio Takas), with shorter 7km and 10.5km routes, which starts outside Marcinkonys visitor centre. At Marcinkonys, staff can arrange bicycle and canoe hire, but they must be booked one day in advance.

Falling just outside the boundaries of the park, 22km northeast of Marcinkonys and 58km northeast of Druskininkai, is **Varėna** (www.varena.lt). Founded in the 15th century when Grand Duke Vytautas built a hunting lodge here, it is the birthplace of Čiurlionis. The main road (A4) leading from Varėna to Druskininkai is lined with sculpted wooden 'totem' poles and sculptures, erected in 1975 in commemoration of the 100th anniversary of his birth.

Sleeping

The visitor centre at Marcinkonys has its own simple **guesthouse** (s/d/tr/q with breakfast 90/140/180/210Lt; Ⓟ ☒ ⌨) with en suite rooms, along with a list of homestay accommodation (around 70Lt per person) but doesn't make bookings; camping is only allowed in designated areas.

Zervynų (☎ 8-687 50826; camping 5Lt; dm 20Lt) A rural idyll with two wooden turn-of-the-20th-century cottages, one with wood-burning stove, the other with no heating. Both have basic bunks and no running water

---

TOP DRUSKININKAI SPAS

Druskininkai is spa-riddled. But beware. Not all are swish. Step into the wrong place and you could be slapped around by a formidable babushka straight out of a horror movie. Here's a quick guide to help make the right decision:

Aqua Park (Vendens parkas; ☎ 52 336; www.akvapark.lt; Vilniaus alėja 13; ☿ 10am-10pm Mon-Thu, 10am-11pm Fri, 9am-11pm Sat, 10am-9pm Sun) Magnificent Soviet complex transformed into a fabulous modern spa. The list of wellness treatments seems endless, and includes body scrubs (60Lt), Thai and classic massages (60Lt to 250Lt) and all manner of facial and body beautifying programs. Saunas and steam baths are a dime a dozen.

Spa Centras (☎ 52 566; www.hotel-druskininkai.lt; Kudirkos gatvė 43; ☿ 9am-6.30pm Mon-Sat, 9am-4.30pm Sun) This spa is inside Hotel Druskininkai. Expect separate bubbling pools, filled with the likes of local mineral water or good old tap water (30Lt per hour). On the massage front (from 50Lt per hour), the body pummel with warm honey – a stronger massage than with regular or aromatic oil – wins hands down, although the massage with silky-smooth hot Hawaii stones is heavenly.

Spa Vilnius (☎ 53 811; www.spa-vilnius.com; Dineikos gatvė 1; ☿ 8am-10pm daily) Located inside an eight-storey hotel, it includes a clutch of baths, such as an indoor swimming pool (filled with local mineral water), one with seaweed (29Lt) and another with mud (25Lt). It also offers the full range of massages, including underwater body (39Lt per 20 minutes) and Shiatsu foot (59Lt per 30 minutes), along with scary-sounding things like gynaecologic irrigations (25Lt).

Druskininkai Spa (Druskininkų gydykla; ☎ 60 508; www.gydykla.lt; Vilniaus alėja 11; ☿ 9am-6.30pm Mon-Sat, 9am-4.30pm Sun) Whirling, herbal, mineral, mud and even vertical (!) baths are among the wonderful watery delights on offer inside this peppermint-green riverside building. It likewise treats a mind-boggling array of diseases – cardiovascular, cutaneous, vestibular, endocrinal and more..

LITHUANIA

STALIN WORLD

Headline-grabbing **Grūtas Park** (Grūto parkas; ☎ 55 511; www.grutoparkas.lt; adult/6-15yr 15/7Lt, audio guide 40Lt; ⏰ 9am-8pm) opened amid controversy in 2001. Dubbed Stalin World, this collection of bronze sculptures once stared down Big Brother–style at oppressed Lithuanians in parks and squares countrywide. The former head of a collective farm, Viliumas Malinauskas made his fortune canning mushrooms then won the loan of the hated objects from the Ministry of Culture in 1999 and transformed part of his 2-sq-km estate into a Soviet sculpture park.

Built to resemble a Siberian concentration camp, the park entrance is marked by a Soviet–Polish border crossing with barbed wire, and red-and-white (Polish) and red-and-green (USSR) striped poles. Next to it is a single carriage in which Lithuanians were deported to Siberia. Once through the turnstile, Russian tunes blast from watchtowers; in the restaurant, visitors eat vodka-doused sprats and onions with Soviet-made cutlery. Tacky souvenir stalls are rife; there is a playground with old Soviet swings and a mini children's zoo – all of which lends itself to critics branding the park a diabolical version of Disney.

Yet the park's attention to detail – reflected in the reconstructed rural Soviet polling station where visitors can sign the park's visitors' book – is impressive. In another building Soviet art is displayed. Top of the bill are 13 Lenins, two Stalins, six Kapsukas and various other communist heroes.

Accused of trivialising Soviet horrors, Malinauskas, whose father spent 10 years in Siberian camps, said: 'This is a place reflecting the painful past of our nation which brought pain, torture and loss. One cannot forget or cross out history – whatever it is.'

Find Grūtas Park 8km east of Druskininkai; entering Grūtas village from the south, turn right (east) off the main road and follow the road 1km to its end. Bus 2 from the bus station (1.80Lt) regularly connects the park with the town.

(bathe in the river and pee in the bushes); rough camping is in the field and meals cost 15Lt. There is a sauna (100Lt for an evening) and it organises mushrooming, berrying and canoeing expeditions on the Ūla River (50Lt per day). Call in advance (no English is spoken) and someone will meet you at Zervynos train station. By car, Zervynų is at the end of a 3km road, signposted off the main Varėna–Marcinkonys road (take the right fork at the end).

Getting There & Away

In summer a steamboat (p332) makes trips between Druskininkai and Liskiava.

Buses to/from Druskininkai and Vilnius stop at the Merkinė intersection (Merkinės kryžkelė; 6Lt, 25 minutes), 2km east of Merkinė town centre. Three daily trains to/from Vilnius stop at Zervynos (12.10Lt, two hours) and Marcinkonys (12.90Lt, two hours).

CENTRAL LITHUANIA

Most people only give Central Lithuania a quick glance – generally from the seat of their bus or train travelling from capital to coast. This flat land between the country's big attractions is often written off as dull, but to jump to such a conclusion would be foolhardy, for here resides Lithuania's most bizarre sight, along with cities of substance and bucolic splendour as far as the eye can see.

Proud Kaunas, the alternative Lithuanian capital during the interwar period and current number two city, holds court in the heart of the country. Its Old Town is as intriguing as its mass of museums and art galleries, and there is no better place to base yourself for central-country forays. Within easy reach of Kaunas is Birštonas, a tiny town where pampering – in the form of spas and luxury hotels – is serious business. It's also home to the Baltic's biggest jazz festival and a crook of a nature park.

Still in the throws of reinvention is Šiauliai, once a closed city in Soviet times that sheltered the USSR's largest military base outside Russia. This northern city is full of surprises, proffering up the weird and the wonderful: not many places can boast a Museum of Cats *and* a Bicycle Museum. Yet most tourists make the pilgrimage here for the papal-blessed Hill of Crosses 10km to the north, and leave awed by the strength and devotion of the Lithuanian people.

KAUNAS

☎ 37 / pop 358,000

Kaunas (kow-nas), a sprawling city on the banks of the Nemunas River, has a compact Old Town, a menagerie of artistic and educational museums, and a rich history all its own. Its sizeable student population provides it with plenty of vibrant, youthful energy, and its rough edges give it that extra bit of spice lacking in many of Lithuania's provincial towns and urban expanses.

History

Legend has it that Kaunas, 100km west of Vilnius at the confluence of the Nemunas and Neris Rivers, was founded by the son of tragic young lovers. Beautiful maiden Milda let the Holy Eternal Flame go out while caring for her lover Daugerutis. They were sentenced to death by vengeful gods, thus they fled to a cave, where Milda gave birth to Kaunas.

Archaeologists believe the city dates from the 13th century and until the 15th century was in the front line against the Teutonic Order in Lithuania's west. Kaunas became a successful river trading town in the 15th and 16th centuries. German merchants were influential here, and there was a Hanseatic League office. During the interwar period it became the capital of Lithuania as Vilnius lay in Polish hands. Its strategic position is the main reason it was destroyed 13 times before WWII – when it once again received a battering.

Orientation

Rotušės aikštė, the square wedged between the Nemunas and Neris Rivers, is the historic heart. From here pedestrian Vilniaus gatvė runs east to meet the city's main axis, Laisvės alėja – also pedestrian. The bus and train stations are 900m and 1.25km respectively south of the eastern end of Laisvės alėja.

MAPS

Jāņa sēta publishes the *Kaunas City Plan* (1:25,000), sold in bookshops and supermarkets.

Information

BOOKSHOPS

Centrinis Knygynas (☎ 229 572; Laisvės alėja 81) Maps, English-language newspapers and magazines.
Humanitas (☎ 209 581; Vilniaus gatvė 11) English-language books.

INTERNET ACCESS

Kavinė Internetas (☎ 407 427; www.cafenet.ot.lt; Vilniaus gatvė 24; per hr 5Lt; ☉ 9am-9pm) Old Town internet cafe.

INTERNET RESOURCES

Kaunas (www.kaunas.lt) Official city website

MEDIA

Kaunas in Your Pocket Annual city guide sold in hotels, art galleries and news kiosks for 5Lt; download it in PDF format at www.inyourpocket.com.

MEDICAL SERVICES

Kauno Medicinos Universiteto Klinikos (☎ 326 375; Eivenių gatvė 2) University medical clinic for emergencies. Approximately 2.5km north of the New Town; catch trolleybus 1 from the Old or New Town.

MONEY

Banks have currency exchange inside. ATMs accepting Visa and MasterCard are located outside.
Hansa Bankas Laisvės alėja (Laisvės alėja 79); Vilniaus gatvė (Vilniaus gatvė 13)
Ūkio Bankas (Laisvės alėja 80)

POST

Post office (Laisvės alėja 102)

TOURIST INFORMATION

Tourist office (☎ 323 436; www.kaunastic.lt; Laisvės alėja 36; ☉ 9am-7pm Mon-Fri, 10am-1pm & 2-6pm Sat, 10am-3pm Sun Jun-Aug, 9am-6pm Mon-Fri, 10am-3pm Sat May & Sep, 9am-6pm Mon-Fri Oct-Apr) Books accommodation, sells maps and guides; arranges bicycle hire (50Lt per day plus 5Lt for lock) and guided tours of the Old Town (35Lt) at 4pm on Thursday from mid-May to September.

Sights

OLD TOWN

Rotušės Aikštė & Around

This large, open square at the heart of the Old Town is lined with pretty 15th- and 16th-century German merchants' houses and is centred on the 17th-century former town hall. The latter, now a **Palace of Weddings** where brides and grooms say *taip* ('I do')

LITHUANIA

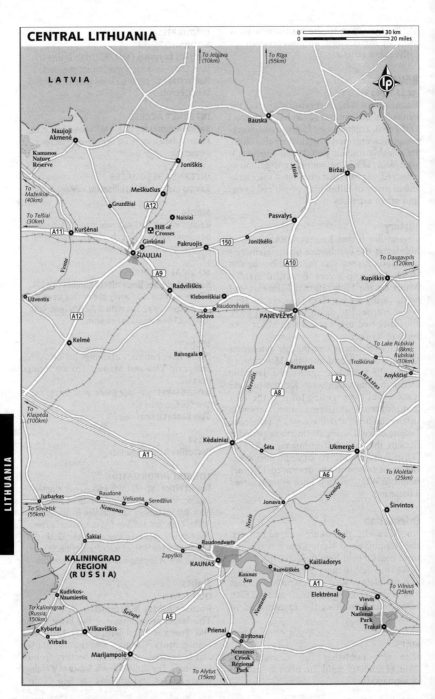

CENTRAL LITHUANIA

0 ____ 30 km
0 ____ 20 miles

L A T V I A

To Jelgava (10km)
To Rīga (55km)

Naujoji Akmenė

Kamanos Nature Reserve

Bauska

Mūša

Biržai

To Mažeikiai (40km)

Joniškis

Meškučius

A12

Gruzdžiai

Naisiai

Pasvalys

To Telšiai (30km)

A11   Kuršėnai

Hill of Crosses

Ginkūnai

Pakruojis

150

Joniškėlis

ŠIAULIAI

To Daugavpils (120km)

A9

Radviliškis

Kupiškis

Užventis

Klieboniškiai

Raudondvaris

A12

Šeduva

PANEVĖŽYS

Kelmė

To Lake Rubikiai (8km); Rubikiai (10km)

Baisogala

Troškūnai

Anykščiai

Ramygala

Nevėžis

A2

A8

Anykstas

Venta

To Klaipėda (100km)

Kėdainiai

Šėta

Ukmergė

A1

A6

To Molėtai (25km)

Jurbarkas

Raudonė   Veliuona

Seredžius

Šventoji

To Sovietsk (55km)

Nemunas

Jonava

Širvintos

Šakiai

Neris

Neris

Raudondvaris

Zapyškis

KAUNAS

Kaišiadorys

KALININGRAD REGION (RUSSIA)

Kaunas Sea

Rumšiškės

A1

To Vilnius (25km)

Kudirkos-Naumiestis

Elektrénai

Vievis

To Kaliningrad (Russia; 150km)

Šešupė

A5

Trakai National Park

Trakai

Kybartai

Vilkaviškis

Prienai

Birštonas

Virbalis

Marijampolė

Nemunas Cirook Regional Park

To Alytus (15km)

LITHUANIA

on Saturday, has a small **Ceramics Museum** (Keramikos muziejus; ☎ 203 572; Rotušės aikštė 15; adult/child 3/1.50Lt; ✆ 11am-5pm Tue-Sun) in its cellar. On the northern side of the square is the **Medicine & Pharmaceutical History Museum** (Medicinios ir farmacijos istorijos muziejus; ☎ 201 569; Rotušės aikštė 28; adult/child 3/1Lt; ✆ 11am-6pm Wed-Sun Apr-Oct, 11am-5pm Wed-Sun Nov-May), fascinating for its reconstructed 19th-century pharmacy, while the western side is filled by the late-Renaissance (1624–34), terracotta-roofed **Holy Trinity Church** (Rotušės aikštė 22).

In the square's southwestern corner is a **statue of Maironis** (1862–1932), a Kaunas priest called Jonas Mačiulis (Maironis was his nickname) who was the poet behind Lithuania's late-19th- and early-20th-century nationalist revival. Stalin banned his works. From 1910 to 1932 Maironis lived in the house behind, now the **Maironis Lithuanian Literary Museum** (Maironio Lietuvos literatūros muziejus; ☎ 200 410; Rotušės aikštė 13; adult/child 3/1Lt; ✆ 9am-5pm Tue-Sat). Those with a love of old telephones should take time for the **Communications Development Museum** (Ryšių istorijos muziejus; ☎ 424 920; Rotušės aikštė 19; adult/child 2/1Lt; ✆ 10am-6pm Wed, Thu, Sat & Sun), housed in the former post office nearby.

The square's southern side is dominated by the twin-towered **St Francis Church** (Rotušės aikštė 7-9), college and Jesuit monastery complex, built between 1666 and 1720. Only a few steps south of the church is the curious **House of Perkūnas** (Perkūno namas; Aleksotas gatvė 6), built in red brick in the 16th century as trade offices on the site of a former temple to the Lithuanian thunder god, Perkūnas. Beyond, on the bank of the Nemunas River, the Gothic-style **Vytautas Church** (Vytauto bažnyčia; Aleksoto gatvė 5) is the same red brick.

For rooftop views of the Old Town, cross the bridge by the Vytautas Church and mount the green hill via either the **Aleksoto funicular** (Aleksoto funikulierius; Skriaudžių gatvė 8 & Aušros gatvė 6; return ticket 0.50Lt; ✆ 7am-noon & 1-4pm Mon-Fri) or the steps beside it. A right turn from the top funicular station leads to a lookout point.

Kaunas Castle

A reconstructed tower, sections of wall and part of a moat are all that remain of Kaunas Castle, around which the town originally grew. Founded in the 13th century,

it was an important bastion of Lithuania's western borders.

Vilniaus Gatvė & Around

Vilniaus gatvė is the Old Town's charming main artery. Its eastern end is dominated by the former **Presidential Palace of Lithuania** (Lietuvos Respublikos prezidentūra kaune; Vilniaus gatvė 33; adult/student 3/1.50Lt; ✆ 11am-5pm Tue-Sun, gardens 8am-9pm daily), from where the country was run between 1920 and 1939. Restored to its original grandeur, the palace hosts a great exhibition on independent Lithuania. Black-and-white photographs are interspersed with gifts given to past presidents, collections of family silver and presidential awards. Statues of the former presidents stud the palace garden.

Nearby, the **Folk Music & Instruments Museum** (Lietuvos tautinės muzikos muziejus; ☎ 422 295; Zamenhofo gatvė 12; adult/child 2/1Lt; ✆ 10am-6pm Tue-Sat May-Sep, 9am-5pm Tue-Sat Oct-Apr) shows that almost any raw material can be turned into a musical instrument. The wonderful collection includes wood and bone flutes, unusual reed pipes, three-string cellos, and both basic and elaborately carved *kanklės* (zithers).

SS Peter & Paul Cathedral (Vilniaus gatvė 1) with its single tower owes much to baroque reconstruction, especially inside, but the original 15th-century Gothic shape of its windows remains. It was probably founded by Vytautas around 1410 and now has nine altars. The **tomb of Maironis** stands outside the south wall.

NEW TOWN

Kaunas expanded east from Old Town in the 19th century, giving birth to the modern centre and its striking 1.7km pedestrian street, **Laisvės alėja**, also known as Freedom Avenue.

Independent Lithuania's first parliament convened in 1920 at the **Kaunas Musical Theatre**, the former State Theatre Palace overlooking **City Garden** (Miestos Sodas) at the western end of Laisvės alėja, which was created in 1892. **Field of Sacrifice** (2002) – a name engraved on paving slabs in front of the garden – is a tragic tribute to the young Kaunas hero Romas Kalanta (p342), who set himself alight in protest at Soviet rule. Across the street is a **statue of Vytautas the Great** and a little west a stone turtle marks the entrance to the **Tadas Ivanauskas Zoological Museum** (Tado Ivanausko zoologijos muziejus; ☎ 229 675; Laisvės alėja 106; adult/child 5/3Lt; ✆ 11am-7pm

LITHUANIA

KAUNAS

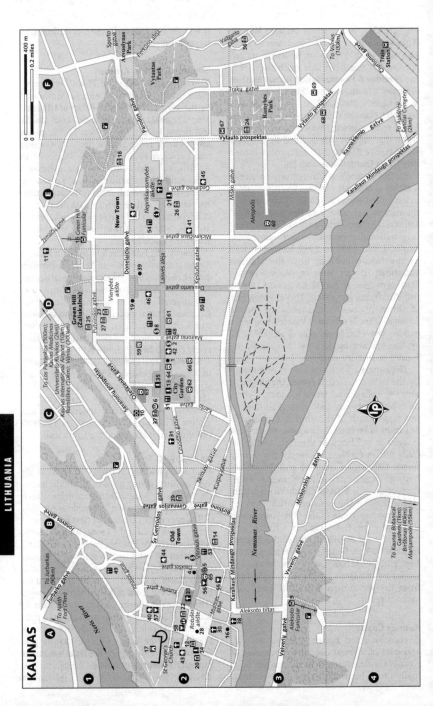

Tue-Sun). Inside, an incredible 13,000 stuffed animals jockey for attention.

A Gothic gem of a church is tucked in a courtyard off Laisvės alėja: **St Gertrude's Church** (Šv Gertrūdos bažnyčia; Laisvės alėja 101a) was built in the late 15th century. Its red-brick crypt overflows with burning candles, prompting a separate candle shrine to be set up in a shed opposite the crypt entrance.

Not far north of the zoological museum stands one of the few remnants of Kaunas' former Jewish community, the pale blue **Choral Synagogue** (Choralinė sinagoga; ☎ 206 880, 8-614 03100; Ožeškienės gatvė 17; admission free; 5.45-6.30pm Mon-Fri, 10am-noon Sat). Inside the functioning synagogue is a remarkable dark wood and gold bimah, and outside resides a memorial to 1600 children killed at the Ninth Fort (p342). The WWII Jewish ghetto was on the western bank of the Neris, in the area bounded by Jurbarko, Panerių and Demokratų streets.

The Soviets turned the blue neo-Byzantine **St Michael the Archangel Church** (Šv Mykolo Arkangelo igulos bažnyčioje; Nepriklausomybės aikštė 14), filling the skyline at the eastern end of Laisvės alėja, into a stained-glass museum. Built for the Russian Orthodox faith in 1895, the church was reopened to Catholic worshippers in 1991.

On the same square, **Man**, modelled on Nike the Greek god of victory, caused a storm of controversy when his glorious pose exposing his manhood was unveiled. The **Mykolas**

Žilinskas Art Gallery (Mykolo Žilinsko dailės galerija; ☎ 222 853; Nepriklausomybės aikštė 12; adult/child 5/2.50Lt; 11am-5pm Tue-Sun) behind boasts Lithuania's only Rubens.

Vienybės Aikštė & Around

Unity Sq houses **Kaunas Technological University** (Kauno technologijos universitetas) and the smaller **Vytautas Magnus University** (Vytauto didžiojo universitetas), first founded in 1992 and refounded in 1989 by an émigré Lithuanian.

The **Military Museum of Vytautas the Great** (Vytauto didžiojo karo muziejus; ☎ 320 939; Donelaičio gatvė 64; adult/child 4/2Lt; 11am-5pm Tue-Sun) covers Lithuanian history from prehistoric times to the present day with a strong emphasis on the country's military exploits. Of particular interest is the wreckage of the aircraft in which Steponas Darius and Stanislovas Girėnas died while attempting to fly nonstop from New York to Kaunas in 1933 (see the boxed text, p342).

In the same building (entrance at the back) is the **National Čiurlionis Art Museum** (Nacionalinis Čiurlionio dailės muziejus; ☎ 221 417; Putvinskio gatvė 55; adult/child 5/2.50Lt; 11am-5pm Tue-Sun), Kaunas' leading museum. It has extensive collections of the romantic paintings of Mikalojus Konstantinas Čiurlionis (1875–1911), one of Lithuania's greatest artists and composers, as well as Lithuanian folk art and 16th- to 20th-century European applied art.

LITHUANIA

KAUNAS HEROES

Beloved Lithuanian pilots Steponas Darius and Stanislovas Girėnas (featured on the 10Lt note) died on 15 July 1933, 650km short of completing the longest nonstop trans-Atlantic flight. Two days after the duo set off from New York, 25,000 people gathered at Kaunas airport for their triumphant return. They never arrived. Their orange plane *Lituanica* crashed in Germany; see the wreckage in the Military Museum of Vytautas the Great (p341). After being embalmed, then hidden during Soviet occupation, the bodies came to rest at **Aukštieji Šančiai Cemetery** (Asmenos gatvė 1) in 1964.

Kaunas-based Japanese diplomat Chiune Sugihara (1900–86) – with the help of Dutch diplomat Jan Zwartendijk – saved 6000 Jewish lives between 1939 and 1940, issuing transit visas to stranded Polish Jews who faced the advancing Nazi terror. When the Soviets annexed Lithuania and ordered that all consulates be shut he asked for a short extension. Dubbed 'Japan's Schindler', he disobeyed orders for 29 days by signing 300 visas per day, and handed the stamp to a Jewish refugee when he left. **Sugihara House** (Sugiharos namai; ☎ 423 277; Vaižganto gatvė 30; admission free; ✆ 10am-5pm Mon-Fri, 11am-4pm Sat & Sun May-Oct, 11am-3pm Mon-Fri Nov-Apr) tells his life story, and features video installations and stories of those he managed to save.

The **Museum of Deportation & Resistance** (Rezistencijos ir tremties muziejus; ☎ 323 179; Vytauto prospktas 46; adult/child 4/2Lt; ✆ 10am-4pm Tue-Fri) documents the Resistance spirit embodied by the Forest Brothers, who fought the Soviet occupation from 1944 to 1953. Led by Jonas Žemaitis-Vytautas (1909–54), anywhere between 50,000 and 100,000 men and women went into Lithuania's forests to battle the tyrannical regime. The museum staff estimates that one-third were killed, the rest captured and deported (in total 150,000 Lithuanians were sent to Soviet territory during this time).

One of the most desperate anti-Soviet actions was the suicide of Kaunas student Romas Kalanta. On 14 May 1972 he doused himself in petrol and set fire to himself in protest at tyrannical communist rule. A suicide note was found in his diary.

Diabolical is best word to descibe the collection of 2000-odd devil statuettes in the **Museum of Devils** (Velniukai; ☎ 221 587; Putvinskio gatvė 64; adult/child 5/2.50Lt; ✆ 10am-5pm Tue-Sun), collected by landscape artist Antanas Žmuidzinavičius (1876–1966). Note the satanic figures of Hitler and Stalin, performing a deadly dance over Lithuania.

The **Green Hill funicular** (Žaliakalnio funikulierius; Putvinskio gatvė 22; return ticket 0.50Lt; ✆ 7am-7pm Mon-Fri, 9am-7pm Sat & Sun) to the northeast of Vienybės glides up **Green Hill** (Žaliakalnis). Above the top station towers the strikingly white **Christ's Resurrection Basilica** (Kauno paminklinė Kristhaus Prisikėlimo bašničia; ☎ 200 883; Zemaicių gatvė 316; ✆ 10am-7pm), a piece of history that took 70 years to build. After being used as a Nazi paper warehouse and a Soviet radio factory, the church was finally consecrated in 2004.

Kaunas Picture Gallery (Kauno paveikslų galerija; ☎ 221 789; Donelaičio gatvė 16; adult/student 3/1.50Lt; ✆ 11am-5pm Tue-Sun) is an underrated gem with works by late-20th-century Lithuanian artists and a room devoted to Jurgis Mačiūnas, the father of the Fluxus avant-garde movement.

NINTH FORT

Lithuania's brutal history is at some of its darkest at the **Ninth Fort** (IX Fortas; ☎ 377 715; Žemaičių plentas 73; each museum adult/child 2/1Lt; ✆ 10am-6pm Wed-Mon Mar-Nov, 10am-4pm Wed-Sun Dec-Feb), built on Kaunas' northwestern outskirts in the late 19th century to fortify the western frontier of the tsarist empire. During WWII the Nazis made it a death camp where 80,000 people, including most of Kaunas' Jewish population, were butchered. Later it became a prison and execution site by Stalin's henchmen. The old museum covers the fort's history from its inception till the end of WWII, including exhibits on the Nazi horrors against Jews; the new museum deals with the Soviet occupation of Lithuania.

Take bus 38 from the bus station to the Mega Shopping and Leisure Centre, 7km out of town, from where it's a 1km walk west to the fort.

PARKS & GARDENS

Kaunas is a surprisingly green city, with parks around its fringes. **Vytautas Park** occupies the slope up from the end of Laisvės alėja to the stadium, behind which stretches a large majority of the lovely **Ažuolynas Park**. South along Vytauto prospektas is **Ramybės Park**, home to the Old City Cemetery until the Soviets tore up all the graves in the 1960s.

Gardening buffs will enjoy the **Kaunas Botanical Gardens** (Kauno botanikos sodas; Žilibero gatvė 6; admission 4Lt; ⏰ 10am-5pm Mon-Fri, 10am-6pm Sat & Sun), where university gardeners tend rare and wonderful plants in a 1920s manor-house garden. The gardens are around 2km south of the Old Town; to get there take bus 6 or 12 from anywhere along Kęstučio gatvė.

Festivals & Events

Kaunas' social diary highlights are April's four-day **International Jazz Festival** (www.kaunas jazz.lt) and the open-air **Operetta in Kaunas Castle**, held for two weeks in the castle ruins in late June–early July.

For classical fans, the **Pažaislis Music Festival** (p346) has concerts in the courtyards and churches of Pažaislis Monastery from June to August.

Sleeping

The tourist office has a list of farms outside the city where you can stay for 20Lt to 200Lt a night.

BUDGET & MIDRANGE

ourpick Kauno Arkivyskupijos Svečių Namai (☎ 322 597; kaunas.lcn.lt/sveciunamai; Rotušės aikštė 21; s/d/tr from 50/80/110Lt; P ✕ 🖳) This charming guesthouse, run by the Lithuanian Catholic Church, couldn't have a better location, sitting smugly between centuries-old churches overlooking the Old Town square. Rooms are spartan but spacious, and management employs a number of eco-friendly practices, including energy-saving light bulbs, recycling, and changing towels only once for guests. Breakfast is not included.

Metropolis (☎ 205 992; www.greenhillhotel.lt; Daukanto gatvė 21; s/d/tr/q 90/120/165/220Lt) This graceful old dame is looking a bit frayed these days, but it still displays strong overtones of past grandeur. Sculpted-stone balconies overlook a leafy street; a hefty wooden turnstile door sweeps guests into a lobby with moulded ceiling; and age-old furnishings only add to the charm. As the name in Lithuanian and Russian outside says, it was called Hotel Lietuva in the USSR.

Litinterp (☎ 228 718; www.litinterp.lt; Gedimino gatvė 28/7; s/d/tr from 120/160/210Lt; ⏰ 8.30am-7pm Mon-Fri, 9am-3pm Sat; P ✕) Not a lot of character, but rooms are cheap, clean and highly functional, and staff are super-friendly and knowledgeable about the town. Take trolley-bus 7 or 1 from the bus station and get off at the third stop.

Apple Hotel (☎ 321 404; Valančiaus gatvė 19; www.applehotel.lt; standard s/d 150/210Lt, lux s/d 170/230Lt; ✕ 🖳) Set on the Old Town's edge in a quiet courtyard, this budget hotel is inspired by a cheap, tasty green apple. Its 14 rooms are stylishly furnished with white linens, modern white-tiled bathrooms with the odd dash of bold colour and minimalist white blinds. Staff – recognisable by the apple-motif ties they sport – go out of their way to please and bring breakfast (6.50Lt) on a tray to your room. A computer sits in reception for guests to use.

Reval Hotel Neris (☎ 306 100; www.revalhotels.com; Donelaičio gatvė 27; s/d from 260/330Lt; P ✕ 🖳) This smart new business hotel fills eight floors of a recently renovated building in the New Town. Service is slick and professional, and rooms are standard business class, with a few added extras such as heated bathroom floors and free tea and coffee. Count on the restaurant, bar and huge conference centre on-site.

Also recommended:

Kaunas Apartments (☎ 8-687 01233; www.kaunas-apartments.lt; Laisvės alėja 50-4; apt 80-250Lt; ✕) Excellent budget option for a few nights' stay. Most apartments are supremely central.

Kunigaikščių menė (☎ 320 877; www.hotelmene.lt; Daukšos gatvė 28; s/d from 180/250Lt; P 🖳) Small, sweet and in the heart of the Old Town. Rooms are basic but highly adequate for a good night's sleep.

TOP END

Daniela (☎ 321 505; www.danielahotel.lt; Mickevičiaus gatvė 28; s/d/ste from 290/360/550Lt; P ✕ 🖳) A retro-chic hotel owned by basketball hero Arvydas Sabonis, Daniela is a fun and bold place, with soft pink chairs, steely mezzanines and extra-large bouncy sofas. Its standard rooms are well above par, and staff do their best to cater to guests needs. Parking is extra.

Kaunas Hotel (☎ 750 850; www.kaunashotel.lt; Laisvės alėja 79; s/d/tr/ste from 360/440/600/600Lt; P ✕ 🖳 🖳) This swanky five-floor, four-star pillow parlour dates from 1892 and is top dog in town. Glass fronts the top floor where room 512 sports a peek-if-you-dare glass-walled bathroom overlooking

Laisvės alėja. The hotel is a free wi-fi zone and guests can use the business centre for 20Lt per hour.

Eating

Dining has improved in recent years, but has yet to match the capital.

Žalias Ratas (☎ 200 071; Laisvės alėja 36b; mains 7-30Lt) Tucked away behind the tourist office is this pseudo-rustic inn where staff don traditional garb and bring piping-hot Lithuanian fare to eager customers. Choose from simple wooden benches and tables outside or a more intimate and formal setting inside.

our pick **Morkų Šėlsmas** (☎ 425 439; Laisvės alėja 78b; mains 10-12Lt; ⏱ 8am-7pm Mon-Fri, 11am-7pm Sat, 11am-5pm Sun) Looking at this small café's fridge jammed with bags of carrots, you'd think 'Carrot Party' only has time for carrot-based dishes. Fortunately not. Its selective menu has room for imaginative vegetarian mains, tasty salads, home-baked muffins and carrot-based smoothies – all using local organic produce when available. Look for the tiny patio tucked away in a private courtyard.

Senieji Rūsiai ('Old Cellars'; ☎ 202 806; Vilniaus gatvė 34; mains 18-40Lt) Hands down the tastiest street terrace at which to dine, drink and soak up the Old Town, this fashionable spot with candlelit 17th-century cellar grills great meats and serves a wide selection, which includes frogs' legs, trout and the ubiquitous potato pancakes.

Avilys (☎ 203 476; Vilniaus gatvė 34; mains 20-40Lt; ⏱ 11am-midnight Mon-Thu & Sun, to 2am Fri & Sat) Sharing the same terrace as Senieji Rūsiai, Avilys is an offshoot of the award-winning brewery in Vilnius. It serves unusual beers alongside Lithuanian standards and international dishes to a discerning crowd, street-side or underground in a brick cellar.

Geras Vyno Rūsys (☎ 207 233; Laisvės alėja 75; mains 20-40Lt) This cellar hideaway is a grand choice for an evening meal. Pick an intimate corner, then settle back to sample the gamut of meat options proffered by the menu (vegetarians should go elsewhere, unfortunately). The wine selection, which the owners know inside out, is lengthy.

Central supermarkets include **Iki** (Jonavos gatvė 3) and **Maxima** (Kęstučio gatvė 55).

Also recommended:

Miesto Sodas (☎ 424 424; Laisvės alėja 93; meals 20-30Lt) As personal as an Ikea couch but, like the Swedish furniture, seems to satisfy a wide variety of people. Huge terrace and plenty of choices.

55° (☎ 750 861; Laisvės alėja 79; mains 30-50Lt) Kaunas Hotel restaurant; funky and fun outside, cool and styled inside. Fine international cuisine.

Drinking

BO (☎ 206 542; Muitinės gatvė 9; ⏱ 9.30am-2am Mon-Thu, 9.30am-3am Fri, 3pm-3am Sat, 3pm-2am Sun) This laid-back bar attracts a student/alternative set and gets rammed to overflowing on weekends. Its own brew is a tasty offering, but rather potent.

Kavos Klubas (Coffee Club; ☎ 229 669; Valančiaus gatvė 19; ⏱ 9am-11pm Mon-Sat, to 7pm Sun) There's a definite bookish air to Coffee Club, a cosy winter hide-out in Old Town where fresh, aromatic coffee beans rule. Thirty-odd coffee types straddle the central bar and seating is around small tables that almost shout 'sit up straight, shoulders back'.

Skliautas (☎ 206 843; Rotušės aikštė 26; ⏱ 10am-midnight Mon-Thu, to 2am Fri & Sat, 11am-11pm Sun) Skliautas bursts with energy most times of the day and night, and in summer its crowd basically takes over the small alley it occupies off Rotušės aikštė. Also good for coffee and cake.

Crazy House Užeiga (☎ 221 182; Vilniaus gatvė 16; ⏱ 11am-midnight Mon-Thu & Sun, to 2am Fri & Sat) For all intents and purposes, this basement bar with pavement terrace is lame, but locals seem to love it, at least on weekend evenings. Join them and wonder at the moving furniture and toilet humour.

Entertainment

Check daily newspaper *Kauno diena* (www.kaunodiena.lt, in Lithuanian) for listings.

NIGHTCLUBS

Admission prices range between 10Lt and 30Lt for all the clubs.

Ex-it (☎ 202 813; www.exit.lt; Maironio gatvė 19; ⏱ Tue-Sat) Arguably the best club in town, with a thumping sound system, huge dance floor and quality DJs. However, the toilets are tiny, so don't arrive with a bursting bladder.

Latino Baras (☎ 8-685 28117; Vilniaus gatvė 22) Latin music, occasional dance lessons, multiple rooms and beautiful young things combine to make Latino Baras a stand-out club for many locals.

LITHUANIA

Other clubs:

Siena (☎ 205 454; www.siena.lt; Laisvės alėja 93) Below Miestos Sodas, brick cellar joint with regular crowds.

Los Patrankos (☎ 338 228; www.lospatrankos.lt; Savanorių prospektas 124) Young patrons. About 500m uphill walk from Old Town along Savanoriu prospektas.

CINEMAS

Catch films in their original language with Lithuanian subtitles at **Forum Cinemas** (☎ 1567; www.forumcinemas.lt; Karaliaus Mindaugo prospektas 49) in the Akropolis shopping complex.

THEATRE & CLASSICAL MUSIC

Original dramas take to the stage at the innovative **Kaunas Academic Drama Theatre** (Akademinis dramos teatras; ☎ 224 064; www.dramosteatras.lt; Laisvės alėja 71) and the **Youth Chamber Theatre** (Jaunimo kamerinis teatras; ☎ 228 226; www.kamerinisteatras.lt; Kęstučio gatvė 74a). Puppets enchant at the **Kaunas Puppet Theatre** (Kauno valstybinis lėlių teatras; ☎ 221 691; www.kaunoleles.lt; Laisvės alėja 87a).

The **Kaunas Philharmonic** (Kauno filharmonija; ☎ 222 558; www.kaunofilharmonija.lt; Sapiegos gatvė 5) is the main concert hall for classical music, and operas fill the **Kaunas Musical Theatre** (Muzikinis teatras; ☎ 200 933; www.muzikinisteatras.lt; Laisvės alėja 91).

Getting There & Away

AIR

From **Kaunas International Airport** (☎ 399 307; www.kaunasair.lt; Savanorių prospektas), 10km north of Kaunas, Air Lithuania flies to/from Antalya once a week in summer, while no-frills airline **Ryanair** (☎ 750 195; www.ryanair.com) handles the bulk of the airport's traffic, operating flights to/from Birmingham, Liverpool, Dublin, Frankfurt and London's Stansted Airport.

BOAT

Nemuno Linija (☎ 8-615 30155; www.nemunolinija.lt) has been planning scheduled boat trips between Kaunas, Rusnė (Nemunas Delta) and Nida (Curonian Spit) for years but at the time of writing nothing had come to fruition. Fingers crossed, hydrofoils, which can complete the journey in four hours, will be up and running by the time you read this.

BUS

At the **long-distance bus station** (☎ 409 060; Vytauto prospektas 24), information is available from the timetable on the wall or from the helpful information desk (open 7am to 8pm). Buy tickets for domestic destinations in the main booking hall and tickets for international journeys at **Eurolines** (☎ 322 222; ⏱ 8am-7pm Mon-Sat, 8am-3pm Sun), also in the main booking hall. **Ecolines** (☎ 202 022; Vytauto prospektas 23; ⏱ 9am-6pm Mon-Fri, 9am-3pm Sat), across the road, also sells tickets for international destinations.

Daily services within the Baltic include the following:

Druskininkai (25Lt, two to three hours, hourly)
Klaipėda (44Lt, 2¾ to four hours, over 20 buses a day)
Marijampolė (12Lt, one hour, every 30 minutes)
Palanga (48Lt, 3¼ hours, about 14 buses a day)
Panevėžys (23Lt, two hours, 22 buses daily)
Rīga (42Lt, five hours, one bus departs 8.30am)
Šiauliai (30Lt to 35Lt, three hours, 23 buses daily)
Tallinn (106Lt, nine hours, one bus departs 8.30am via Rīga).
Vilnius (20Lt, 1¾ hours, at least every 30 minutes)
Visaginas (40Lt, four hours, two buses daily at 7am and 1pm)

CAR

Autobanga (☎ 8-645 64444; www.autobanga.lt; Savanorių prospektas) provides car hire at the airport.

TRAIN

From the **train station** (☎ 221 093; Čiurlionio gatvė 16) there are up to 17 trains daily to/from Vilnius (12Lt, 1¼ to 1¾ hours).

Getting Around

Buses and trolleybuses run from 5am to 11pm and tickets cost 1.20Lt from newspaper kiosks or 1.50Lt from the driver. Minibuses shadow routes and run later than regular buses; drivers sell tickets for 2Lt. The tourist office sells a public transport map detailing all routes for 3Lt.

To get to/from the airport, take minibus 120 from the local bus station on Šv Gertrūdos gatvė or bus 29 from the stop on Vytauto prospektas. Buses depart at least once an hour between 7am and 9.30pm.

Trolleybuses 1, 5 and 7 run north from the train station along Vytauto prospektas, west along Kęstučio gatvė and Nemuno gatvė, then north on Birštono gatvė. Returning, they head east along Šv Gertrūdos gatvė, Ožeškienės gatvė and Donelaičio gatvė, then south down Vytauto prospektas to the bus and train stations.

Ordering a **taxi** (☎ 366 666) is safer than hopping into a car on the street.

LITHUANIA

Outside the Old Town, driving in Kaunas is a relatively simple affair; parking is plentiful and there are only a handful of one-way streets. The Old Town is a warren of small cobbled alleys, however, and can prove hard to navigate.

Around Kaunas

PAŽAISLIS MONASTERY

A fine example of 17th-century baroque architecture, **Pažaislis Monastery** (☎ 37-456 485; Masiulio gatvė 31; adult/child 3/1Lt; ☼ 10am-5pm Tue-Sun) is 9km east of the centre, near the shores of **Kaunas Sea** (Kauno marios), a large artificial lake. The monastery church, with its 50m-high cupola and sumptuous Venetian interior made from pink and black Polish marble, is a sumptuous if shabby affair. Passing from Catholic to Orthodox to Catholic control, the monastery has had a chequered history and was a psychiatric hospital for part of the Soviet era. Nuns inhabit it today. The best time to visit is between June and August during the **Pažaislis Music Festival** (www.pazaislis.lt). Take trolleybus 5 from the town centre to the terminus on Masiulio gatvė, a few hundred metres before Pažaislis Monastery.

RUMŠIŠKĖS

Go back in time at the **Open-Air Museum of Lithuania** (Lietuvių liaudies buities muziejus; ☎ 346-47 392; Nėries gatvė 6; adult/child 6/3Lt; ☼ 10am-6pm Wed-Sun May-Oct, upon request only Nov-Apr), where four villages of 18th- and 19th-century buildings represent Lithuania's four main regions. Potters, weavers and joiners demonstrate their crafts in the museum workshop. Rumšiškės is 20km east of Kaunas, about 2km off the Kaunas–Vilnius road. Direct buses (5Lt, 30 minutes, five daily) leave from platform 26 at the station.

BIRŠTONAS

☎ 319 / pop 3100

Birštonas (bir-shto-nas), some 40km south of Kaunas, resides on a pretty loop of the Nemunas River. It's famous as a spa town and for hosting **Birštonas Jazz** (www.jazz .birstonas.lt) – Lithuania's top jazz festival – in even-numbered years.

The extremely helpful **tourist office** (☎ 65 740; www.visitbirstonas.lt; Jaunimo gatvė 3; ☼ 9am-6pm Mon-Fri year-round, plus 10am-6pm Sat & Sun Jun-Sep) has a wealth of information on accommodation, activities, festivals and the town's spas.

Sights & Activities

Birštonas' handful of tiny museums and extensive spa treatments are sufficient attractions in themselves, but the real action is on the water. Much of the rural expanse surrounding Birštonas falls within the **Nemunas Crook Regional Park** (Nemuno kilpų regioninio parko), and its **visitors centre** (☎ 65 610; www .nemunokilpos.lt; Tylioji gatvė 1; ☼ 8am-5pm Mon-Thu, 9am-3.45pm Fri) is a good source of information on riverside activities.

The fast-flowing Verknė River provides excellent opportunities for **canoeing**, particularly in spring when the water is high. Half-day, day and two-day trips are possible, and can be arranged through the tourist office; canoes (5/25Lt per hour/day) can also be hired from the **Birštonas Sport Centre** (☎ 65 640; Jaunimo gatvė 3; ☼ 9am-7pm). **River trips** on the Nemunas include one-hour excursions (adult/child 10/20Lt) at 3pm on Sunday, on the *Vytenis*, a two-levelled pleasure boat, and more exhausting – and probably fun – trips in **Viking ships** (☎ 56 360; adult/child 10/15Lt; by appointment only) used for the filming of *Elizabeth I*.

Bicycles (per hour/day 5/25Lt) can be hired from the sports centre, and the guesthouse Audenis arranges **air ballooning trips** (1/2/3 people 350/600/800Lt).

Sleeping

For such a small town, Birštonas has some fine, and unusual, accommodation:

Audenis (☎ 61 300; www.audenis.lt; Lelijų gatvė 3; s/d 150/190Lt; P ⊠ ☐) This very pleasant guesthouse has simple rooms in an array of pastel colours, friendly staff and ballooning trips. Its terraced cafe is a fine spot for a light lunch too

Sofijos Rezidencija (☎ 45 200; www.sofijosrezidencija .lt; Jaunimo gatvė 6; r from 230Lt; P ⊠ ☒) If you can't afford Nemuno slėnis, consider overnighting at Sofijos in the heart of Birštonas. Rooms here may border on kitsch but they win you over with pseudo-Renaissance splendour, four-poster beds, comfy couches and plenty of mod-cons. There's also a small wellness centre on-site.

Nemuno slėnis (☎ 56 493; www.nemunoslenis .lt; Verknės gatvė 8; r from 499Lt, royal ste 4500Lt; P ⊠ ☒ ☐ ☒) Located on the banks of the Nemunas away from the town centre and surrounded by forest, Nemuno slėnis offers seclusion and oodles of privacy. The interior is lavish beyond belief, with rooms individually decorated in plush, antique furniture and draped in deep, warm colours, while added extras include a gourmet restaurant and fitness room. Perfect for a romantic weekend.

Getting There & Away

From Kaunas bus station there are buses every half-hour to/from Birštonas (8.40Lt, 50 minutes).

ŠIAULIAI

☎ 41 / pop 128,400

Lithuania's fourth-largest city is a work in progress. Formerly a shabby place on the outskirts of a massive Soviet military airfield, Šiauliai (shyow-ley) has been cleaning up its act (and its main street) in the recent past and transforming into a city with a buzz. Its biggest drawcard is the incredible Hill of Crosses 10km to the north, but there's a handful of weird and wonderful museums in the centre that deserve attention.

Information

Left Luggage (24hr 2Lt) Bus station (☼ 6am-7pm Mon-Fri, 6am-6pm Sat, 8am-4pm Sun); Train station (☼ 7am-5.30pm)
Post office (Aušros alėja 42)
Šiauliai bankas (Tilžės gatvė 149)
Snoras bankas (Vilniaus gatvė 204)
Topos Centras (Tilžės gatvė; per hr 3Lt; ☼ 8am-midnight) Internet access in the Saulės Miestas shopping centre adjacent to the bus stop.
Tourist office (☎ 523 110; www.tic.siauliai.lt; Vilniaus gatvė 213; ☼ 9am-6pm Mon-Fri, 10am-4pm Sat, 10am-3pm Sun) Sells maps and guides, including cycling itineraries to the Hill of Crosses; hires out bicycles for 5Lt an hour; makes accommodation bookings.

Sights

TOWN CENTRE

Towering over Priskėlimo aikštė is the massive **SS Peter & Paul Cathedral** (Šv Petro ir Povilo bažnyčia; Aušros takas 3), whose 75m spire is Lithuania's second highest. It was constructed between 1595 and 1625 from the proceeds of the sale of four-year-old bulls donated by local farmers. Legend says that the hillock it stands on was created from sand and dust, which blew over a dead ox that wandered into Šiauliai, sat down and died. **St George's**

Church (Šv Jurgio bažnyčia; Kražių gatvė 17), on the other side of town, is an attractive Catholic church with an onion dome – a reminder of its Russian origins.

A distinctive city landmark is the mammoth **sundial** (cnr Salkauskjo gatvė & Ežero gatvė), topped by a shining bronze statue of an archer in what has become known as 'Sundial Sq'. It was built in 1986 to commemorate the 750th anniversary of the Battle of Saulė (1236), the battle in which local Samogitians defeated the Knights of the Sword and founded the town. A few steps north of the sundial is the city's rambling **cemetery** (☼ dawn-dusk), where wrought-iron crosses and flowerbeds rest peacefully under the shade of mature trees.

Šiauliai has an eccentric museum collection, including the **Radio & TV Museum** (Radio ir televijos muziejus; ☎ 524 399; Vilniaus gatvė 174; adult/child 2/1Lt; ☼ 10am-6pm Tue-Fri, 11am-5pm Sat & Sun) and **Photography Museum** (Fotografijos muziejus; ☎ 524 396; Vilniaus gatvė 140; adult/child 4/2Lt; ☼ 10am-6pm Tue-Fri, 11am-5pm Sat & Sun). Of equal interest is the **Bicycle Museum** (Dviračių muziejus; ☎ 524 395; Vilniaus gatvė 139; adult/child 6/3Lt; ☼ 10am-6pm Tue-Fri, 11am-5pm Sat & Sun), where glorious bone-rattlers and torturous bicycles with wooden tyres stand next to mean speed machines made by Lithuania's biggest bicycle manufacturer, Šiauliai-based Balti Vairas (Black Panther).

To the east of the town centre stands **Frenkelis Villa** (☎ 524 389; Vilniaus gatvė 74; adult/child 6/3Lt; ☼ 10am-6pm Tue-Fri, 11am-5pm Sat & Sun), built in Art Nouveau style in 1908 for the then leather baron of Šiauliai. It survived WWII unscathed and was used as a military hospital by the Soviets from 1944 until 1993, at which time it was turned over to the city. The exterior is still rather shabby, but the interior has been lovingly restored to its former glory, with dark-wood panelling and period furniture featuring heavily throughout.

Further east again is the unusual **Museum of Cats** (Katinų muziejus; ☎ 523 883; Žuvininkų gatvė 18; adult/child 4/2Lt; ☼ 10am-5pm Tue-Sat). It's filled to overflowing with feline memorabilia, although a few mice have crept under the front door, gifts from the Museum of Mice in Myshkin, Russia. It's also home to one live cat and a menagerie of other beasts, including a mongoose, albino python, monkey and a couple of owls – all abandoned

LITHUANIA

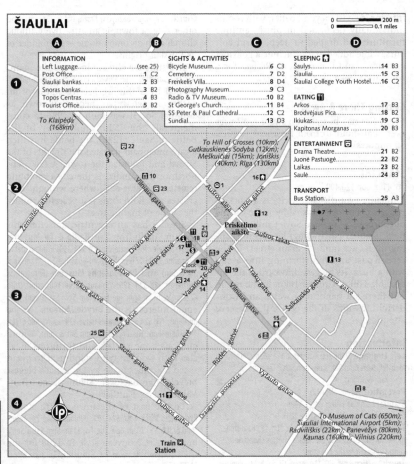

ŠIAULIAI

0	200 m
0	0.1 miles

INFORMATION
Left Luggage.................................(see 25)
Post Office...**1** C2
Šiauliai bankas.....................................**2** B3
Snoras bankas......................................**3** B2
Topos Centras......................................**4** B3
Tourist Office..**5** B2

SIGHTS & ACTIVITIES
Bicycle Museum...................................**6** C3
Cemetery..**7** D2
Frenkelis Villa.......................................**8** D4
Photography Museum..........................**9** C3
Radio & TV Museum...........................**10** B2
St George's Church.............................**11** B4
SS Peter & Paul Cathedral.................**12** C2
Sundial...**13** D3

SLEEPING
Šaulys..**14** B3
Šiauliai..**15** C3
Šiauliai College Youth Hostel.........**16** C2

EATING
Arkos...**17** B3
Brodvėjaus Pica..................................**18** B2
Ikiukas..**19** C3
Kapitonas Morganas **20** B3

ENTERTAINMENT
Drama Theatre....................................**21** B2
Juonė Pastuogė...................................**22** B2
Laikas..**23** B2
Saulė...**24** B3

TRANSPORT
Bus Station..**25** A3

To Klaipėda
(168km)

To Hill of Crosses (10km);
Gutkauskienės Sodyba (12km);
Meškuičiai (15km); Joniškis
(40km); Rīga (130km)

Priskėlimo
aikštė

Clock
Tower

To Museum of Cats (650m);
Šiauliai International Airport (5km);
Radviliškis (22km); Panevėžys (80km);
Kaunas (160km); Vilnius (220km)

Train
Station

LITHUANIA

by their owners and now looked after by
school children.

HILL OF CROSSES

A small hill north of Šiauliai is the location of
this strange and inspiring sight. Here stand
thousands upon thousands of crosses, planted
by countless pilgrims and, on Saturdays, one
newly wed couple after the next.

Large and tiny, expensive and cheap,
wood and metal, the crosses are devo-
tional, to accompany prayers, or finely
carved folk-art masterpieces. Others are
memorials tagged with flowers, a photograph or other mementoes of the deceased,
and inscribed with a sweet or sacred message. Traditional Lithuanian *koplytstulpis*

(wooden sculptures of a figure topped with
a little roof) intersperse the crosses, as do
magnificent sculptures of the Sorrowful
Christ (*Rūpintojėlis*). If you wish to add
your own, souvenir traders in the car park
sell crosses big and small.

An alternative view of the cross-swamped
hill is from inside the chapel of the modern brick **monastery**. Currently home to 10
Franciscan monks, it was built behind the
hill between 1997 and 2000 – allegedly upon
the wishes of John Paul II who said, after his
visit in 1993, that he wished to see a place of
prayer here. Behind the altar in the church,
the striking backdrop seen through the ceil-
ing-to-floor window of the Hill of Crosses
in place of a traditional crucifix is very

moving; Italian architect Angelo Polesello designed it.

The Hill of Crosses (Kryžių kalnas) is 10km north of Šiauliai, 2km east off the road to Joniškis and Rīga, in the village of Jurgaičiai. To get here, take one of up to seven daily buses from Šiauliai bus station to Joniškis and get off at the Domantai stop, from where it is a 2km walk to the hill. Look for the sign 'Kryžių kalnas 2' on the A12. By taxi, the return taxi fare is 40Lt, with a 30-minute stop at the hill (50Lt with a one-hour stop); ask Šiauliai tourist office or your hotel/hostel to order one for you by telephone to avoid being ripped off. By bicycle the Hill of Crosses is a 12km ride; allow at least three hours for the return trip. The tourist office hires out bikes and has route maps.

Sleeping

The tourist office has information on homestay accommodation around Šiauliai.

Šiauliai College Youth Hostel (Šiaulių Kolegijos Jaunimo Navynės Namai; ☎ 523 764; www.jnn.siauliu kolegija.lt; Tilžės gatvė 159; s/d/tr 50/70/90Lt; ☪ reception 7am-11pm; P ✗) This former college has been renovated with EU funds to create a spanking clean and sparkling hostel with kitchen and TV room. Reception staff don't speak English, but they do their very best to help.

Gutkauskienės sodyba (☎ 8-698 79544; www .horse-g.lt; Žačiai village; s/d 80/100Lt; P ☪) This century-old, renovated stud farm is perfect for those keen to skip Šiauliai's drab hotel scene for a taste of rural life. The farmhouse has six charming rooms, plenty of surrounding forest to explore and berries to pick in season – and lots of horses to ride. It's about 12km northeast of Šiauliai – head out of town on the eastbound 150 towards Pakruojis and after Ginkūnai turn left (north) towards Naisai. The place is signposted 5km along the road just before the village of Daunorai.

Šiauliai (☎ 437 333; www.hotelsiauliai.lt; Draugystės prospektas 25; s/d/tr from 95/170/195Lt; P) The town's old 14-storey Soviet hotel has enjoyed recent renovation both inside and out, leaving it with pleasant rooms dressed in pale yellow and brown. The views are still as great as ever.

Šaulys (☎ 520 812; www.saulys.lt; Vasario 16-osios gatvė 40; s/d/tr/apt from 230/280/400/575Lt; P ✗ ☪ ▭ ☪) This four-star establishment

is Šiauliai's swankiest choice. Hidden behind its deep-red facade are suitably plush rooms and staff who can organise paragliding, parachuting and biplane flights.

Eating

Juonė Pastuogė (☎ 524 926; Aušros 31a; mains 10-30Lt; ☪ 9am-1am) A country-and-western–style music club/tavern with an enormous garden, Juonė Pastuogė pulls the punters in with an imaginative menu including the likes of ostrich steak, hearty country stews and vegetarian pancakes. Live music features almost every evening.

Brodvėjaus Pica (☎ 500 412; Vilniaus gatvė 146; pizza 13-40Lt) This bustling joint has enough pizza choices (almost 40 in all) to satisfy everybody, including vegetarians. Securing a outdoor table in summer can prove difficult, however.

Arkos (☎ 520 205; Vilniaus gatvė 213; mains 15-30Lt) This refined cafe with brick cellar and summer terrace is just as good for a full meal as it is for beer or wine.

Kapitonas Morganas (☎ 526 477; Vilniaus gatvė 183; mains 20-40Lt) Come to Captain Morgan's jolly pirate ship to meet happy punters busily eating European fodder, drinking local beer and merrymaking on a great street terrace.

Ikiukas (Vilniaus gatvė 128) caters to food shoppers.

Entertainment

Spend the evening at the **Drama Theatre** (☎ 523 207; Tilžės gatvė 155), watching an English-language flick at **Laikas** (☎ 525 208; Vilniaus gatvė 172) or **Saulė** (☎ 524 983; Tilžės gatvė 140), or catching some live music at Juonė Pastuogė (above).

Getting There & Away

AIR

There are no scheduled passenger flights in and out of Šiauliai. **Šiauliai International Airport** (☎ 542 005; www.siauliai-airport.com), adjoining the Zokniai Military Airfield on the southeastern edge of town, is only used by cargo planes.

BUS

Services to/from Šiauliai **bus station** (☎ 525 058; Tilžės gatvė 109):

Kaunas (30Lt to 35Lt, three hours, 23 buses a day)
Klaipėda (30Lt, 3½ hours, five buses daily)

CROSS CRAFTING

Crosses were once symbols of sacred fervour and national identity, both Pagan and Catholic; cross crafting is the embodiment of Lithuanian contradiction.

Handed down from master to pupil, the crosses were carved from oak, the sacred pagan tree. They were made as offerings to gods, draped with food, coloured scarves (for a wedding) or aprons (for fertility). Once consecrated by priests, they became linked with Christian ceremonies in unmistakable sacred significance. The crosses, which measure up to 5m, then became symbols of defiance against occupation.

When it comes to explaining the origin of the Hill of Crosses, there are almost as many myths as crosses. Some claim it was created in three days and three nights by the bereaved families of warriors killed in a great battle. Others say it was the work of a father who, in a desperate bid to cure his sick daughter, planted a cross on the hill. Pagan traditions tell stories of sacred fires being lit here and tended by celestial virgins.

Crosses first appeared here in the 14th century. They multiplied after bloody antitsarist uprisings to become this potent symbol of suffering and hope.

During the Soviet era planting a cross was an arrestable offence – but pilgrims kept coming to commemorate the thousands killed and deported. The hill was bulldozed at least three times. In 1961 the Red Army destroyed the 2000-odd crosses that stood on the mound, sealed off the tracks leading to the hill and dug ditches at its base, yet overnight more crosses appeared. In 1972 they were destroyed after the immolation of a Kaunas student (see the boxed text, p342) in protest at Soviet occupation. But by 1990 the Hill of Crosses comprised a staggering 40,000 crosses, spanning 4600 sq metres. Since independence, they have multiplied at least 10 times – and are multiplying still. In 1993 Pope John Paul II celebrated Mass here (his pulpit still stands) and graced the hill a year later with a papal cross, adding his own message to the mountain of scribbled-on crosses: 'Thank you, Lithuanians, for this Hill of Crosses which testifies to the nations of Europe and to the whole world the faith of the people of this land'.

New crosses now stand to commemorate those who perished in the 2001 Twin Towers attack in New York and subsequent terrorist attacks elsewhere. The spirit continues, the hill grows and the sound of the crosses rattling in the wind becomes yet more sobering.

Palanga (29.50Lt, three hours, eight daily)
Panevėžys (15.50Lt, 1½ hours, around 20 daily)
Riga (28Lt, 2½ hours, four daily)
Vilnius (41Lt, three to 4½ hours, six daily)

TRAIN

Services to/from Šiauliai **train station** (☎ 430 652; Dubijos gatvė 44) include: Klaipėda (18.60Lt to 23.50Lt, two to three hours, five daily), Panevėžys (10.40Lt, 1½ hours, two daily) and Vilnius (28.70Lt, 2½ to three hours, three daily).

RADVILIŠKIS & AROUND

Grim, grimy **Radviliškis** (rad-vi-lish-kis; population 19,700), 22km southeast of Šiauliai, is notable only as the central hub of the rail network, but there are a couple of interesting stops on the 55km stretch of the A9 heading east towards Panevėžys.

Šeduva (she-du-va; population 3200), a 16th-century architectural monument 15km east of Radviliškis, is a large village with a faded yellow-and-white baroque church framed by cobbled streets. **Šeduvos Malūnas** (☎ 422-56 300; www.seduvosmalunas.lt; mains 10-20Lt), a windmill that's filled by a kitsch but fun restaurant, sits on its western outskirts. The structure, built in 1905, still retains the original central-core cog mechanism, and nowadays traditional Lithuanian cuisine is served on its four levels. The restaurant owners also run the pleasant hotel next door, housed in a modern building (double without breakfast 100Lt, parking available).

In **Kleboniškiai**, signposted 5km further east along the A9 to Panevėžys, is another windmill (1884) and – 1km down a dusty road – the **Kleboniškiai Rural Life Exhibition** (Kleboniškių kaimo buites ekspozicija; ☎ 422-42 005; adult/student 6/3Lt, camera 5Lt; ☺ 9am-6pm Tue-Sun). The beautiful farmstead, with 19th- and early-20th-century farm buildings, offers a picture-postcard peek at rural Lithuania. It is brimful with collectors' items, including wooden sleds, farming tools and a marvellous tractor dating from 1926 that's still in working order. The exhibition is part of the **Daugyvenė Cultural History Museum Reserve** (Daugyvenės kultūros istorijos muziejus-draustinis; ☎ 8-698 77973), which encompasses burial grounds, mounds and other local sights.

Plenty of buses between Šiauliai and Panevėžys stop at Radviliškis. There are buses every 30 minutes to/from Radviliškis and Šeduva (2Lt, 15 minutes) and six a day to/from Vilnius (30Lt, three hours).

There are two trains daily to/from Šiauliai and Šeduva (6.50Lt, 50 minutes), while three run between Vilnius (26.60Lt, 2½ hours) and Radviliškis and five between Klaipėda (25.70Lt, 2½ hours) and Radviliškis.

PANEVĖŽYS
☎ 45 / pop 114,600
Panevėžys (pa-ne-vey-zhees) is far from a tourist hot spot, and most people who venture to the town will do so en route from Vilnius to Rīga by bus. If you've time to kill there are a couple of sights to explore in this, Lithuania's fifth-largest city.

Orientation
At the centre of town is Laisvės aikštė, bordered at its northern end by east–west Elektros gatvė and at its southern end by Vilniaus gatvė. Basanavičiaus gatvė runs north to the Rīga road and south to Kaunas and Vilnius. The train station is 2km northwest of the centre; the bus station is on Savanorių aikštė.

Information
For ATMs and currency exchange, try the banks at Laisvė aikštė 18 and Ukmerges gatvė 18a.
Left Luggage (24hr 2Lt; ☺ 5.30am-7pm Mon-Fri, 7am-12.20pm & 12.50-4pm Sat & Sun) At the bus station.
Post office (Respublikos gatvė 60)
Tourist office (☎ 508 080; www.panevezystic.lt; Laisvės aikštė 11; ☺ 9am-6pm Mon-Fri & 9am-2pm Sat Apr-Sep, 8am-5pm Mon-Fri Oct-Mar)

Sights & Activities
Triangular-shaped **Laisvės aikštė** is a central tree-lined pedestrianised spot, pleasant for two months in summer and deadly grey the rest of the year. It is surrounded by a few uninspiring cafes and shops and the **Juozas Miltinio Drama Theatre** (☎ 584 614; www.miltinio

-teatras.lt; Laisvės aikštė 5), in action since 1940. By the river, a **small bridge** and **statues** make for a pleasant stroll.

The tiny **Museum of Regional Studies** (Kraštotyros muziejus; ☎ 461 973; Vasario 16-osios gatvė 23; adult/child 2/0.50Lt; ☺ 10am-5pm Tue-Sat) focuses on ethnography and hosts temporary exhibitions in

PANEVĖŽYS

INFORMATION	
Bank	1 B5
Bank	2 B5
Left Luggage	(see 13)
Post Office	3 A3
Tourist Office	4 B5

SIGHTS & ACTIVITIES	
Fairytale Train	5 A4
Juozas Miltinio Drama Theatre	6 B5
Museum of Regional Studies	7 A4
Oldest Building	8 A3

SLEEPING	
Hotel Panevėžys	9 B5
Hotel Romantik	10 B3

EATING	
Galerija XX	11 B5
Iki	12 B5

TRANSPORT	
Bus Station	13 B5
Eurolines	(see 13)

LITHUANIA

the city's oldest building, dating from 1614, at Kranto gatvė 21.

A great escape for the kids are the magical dolls and puppets in the **Fairytale Train** (Pasakų traukinukas; ☎ 511 236; Respublikos gatvė 30; admission 2-5Lt; ☼ 8am-5pm Mon-Fri) of the Wagon Puppet Theatre. Lithuania's only travelling cart theatre is rarely at home (it travels all summer), but the characters displayed inside this old narrow-gauge train carriage are enchanting.

Sleeping & Eating

If you're stuck overnight, **Hotel Panevėžys** (☎ 501 601; Laisvės aikštė 26; s/d from 80/120Lt) – a Soviet eyesore rising 12 storeys over the central square – should suffice; otherwise walk a little further to **Hotel Romantik** (☎ 584 860; www.romantic.lt; Kranto gatvė 24; s/d/ste 200/350/660Lt; P X X 🖳 🖾), housed in a converted old mill. Its rooms are suitably plush, and the restaurant terrace overlooking the park – definitely the best place in town to dine – is a delight (mains 20Lt to 55Lt).

Galerija XX (☎ 438 701; Laisvės aikštė 7; mains 10-15Lt), with a terrace on the main square, is as good an option as any; self-caters and snackerers can head to **Iki** (Ukmerges gatvė 18a) in the shopping centre adjoining the bus station.

Getting There & Away

Bus tickets for international destinations are sold at **Eurolines** (☎ 582 888; panevezys@eurolines.lt; ☼ 9am-6pm Mon-Fri, to 2pm Sat), at the bus station. Domestic and regional services from the **bus station** (☎ 463 333; Savanoriu aikštė 5) include buses to/from Vilnius (28Lt, 1¾ hours, hourly), Kaunas (23Lt, two hours, 22 daily), Šiauliai (15.50Lt, 1½ hours, around 20 daily), Rīga via Bauska (from 29Lt, 2½ to three hours, six daily) and Tallinn via Rīga (from 66Lt, 8½ hours, up to seven daily).

ANYKŠČIAI

☎ 381 / pop 12,000

Lovely Anykščiai (a-neeksh-chey), 60km southeast of Panevėžys, sits on the confluence of the Sventoji and Anyksta Rivers. Fanning eastwards are 76 lakes, the largest of which – **Lake Rubikiai** (9.68 sq km and 16m deep) – is freckled with 16 islands.

A pine forest 10km south of Anykščiai contains **Puntukas Stone** (Puntuko akmuo), a boulder 5.7m tall, 6.7m wide and 6.9m long, which legend says was put there by the devil. While trying to destroy Anykščiai's twin-steeple church, **St Mathew's** (1899–1909), a rooster crowed and the devil thundered to hell – prompting the boulder to hurtle down from the sky. The **tourist office** (☎ 59 177; www.antour.lt; Gegužės gatvė 1; ☼ 8am-5pm Mon-Sat, to 4pm Sun) can tell you precisely how to find it.

A steam locomotive is displayed at the **Narrow-Gauge Railway Museum** (Siaurojo geležinkelis istorijos ekspozicija; ☎ 58 015; www.baranauskas.lt; Viltis gatvė 2; adult/child 2/1.50Lt; ☼ 10am-5pm May-Oct, by appointment Nov-Apr), a fun museum for kids housed in Anykščiai's old station. Visitors can ride manual rail cars and, on weekends from May to October, travel along the line to Troškūnai (Saturdays) and Rubikiai (Sundays). Trains leave at 11am and return at 12.50pm and 2.20pm respectively; tickets in 2nd class cost 20Lt. More information can be found at www.siau rukas.eu.

Horse lovers will want to make the journey 6km north to Lithuania's only **Horse Museum** (Arklio muziejus; ☎ 51 722, 8-616 25124; www.arkliomuziejus.lt; adult/child 5/3.50Lt; ☼ 8am-6pm Jul-Aug, till 5pm Sep-Jun) in the tiny village of Niūronys. Set out as a traditional farmstead, the museum delves into equine matters from a Lithuanian point of view, displaying black-and-white photos of horse-drawn transport in Vilnius alongside a fine collection of horse-drawn fire engines, carriages and taxis. Horse (4Lt) and carriage (2Lt) rides are available and kids will have a ball mucking about on the big playground. Additionally, the museum has its own blacksmith, and traditional events are organised throughout the year. Join in by baking your own black bread Lithuanian-style (adult/child 13/7Lt; by appointment only). At least two buses daily (1.80Lt, 20 minutes) connect Niūronys with Anykščiai.

From the **bus station** (☎ 51 333; Vienuolio gatvė 1) opposite the tourist office there are buses to/from Panevėžys (12Lt, 1¼ hours, two daily), Vilnius (20Lt, 2½ hours, five daily), Kaunas (21Lt, 2¼ hours, 11 daily) and Utena (10Lt, one hour, two daily).

WESTERN LITHUANIA

It's easy to see why locals and tourists flock to Lithuania's western frontier. Its coastline, stretching 99km along the glistening Baltic Sea,

---

THE LAND OF BEER

Northern Lithuania is the land of barley-malt beer, ale-makers keeping to ancient recipes and rituals practised by their ancestors 1000 years ago. People here drink 160L of beer a year, say proud locals. The biggest drinkers in the world, the Czechs, consume around 160L per person per year. The Brits down around 100L per year, the Australians 110L.

Big-name brews to glug include **Horn** (www.ragutis.lt), brewed in Kaunas since 1853; Šiauliai-made **Gubernija** (www.gubernija.lt); and **Kalnapilis** from Panevėžys, whose **brewery** (☎ 505 219; www.kalnapilis.lt; Taikos alėja 1) is open for tours.

Lakeside Biržai, 65km north and the true heart of Lithuanian beer country, hosts the annual two-day **Biržai Town Festival** in August, a madcap fiesta where the town's breweries sell their wares on the street; expect plenty of beer swilling and general drunken behaviour. Its **Rinkuškiai Brewery** (☎ 450-35 293; www.rinkuskiai.lt; Alyvų gatvė 8) can be visited, and its beer – everything from light lager to lead-heavy stout – can be bought in bulk in its factory shop. A lesser-known label to look out for is the sweet **Butautų alaus bravoras**, an ale bottled in brown glass with a ceramic, metal-snap cap like Grolsch. It has been brewed in the village of Butautų since 1750.

---

is a mix of white sandy beaches backed by rising dunes and cities with vibrant energy, while inland lie pockets of magical parkland.

Topping the bill is the world-unique gem – Curonian Spit (Kuršių Nerija), a skinny leg of sand that stalks into Russia. So precious and extraordinary is this anorexic slice between the relentless Baltic Sea and lapping Curonian Lagoon that Unesco added it to its World Heritage list in 2000. Its historical fishing villages and East Prussian past are fascinating backdrops to the real attraction here – nature's own dense pine forests blissful beaches, all set to the echoes of crashing waves.

The gateway to the spit is Klaipėda, the country's third-largest city and only major port. This busy city with its tiny Old Town and constant flow of ferries exudes a definite grit. To the north is Palanga, a party town if ever there was; finding room to move here in summer can be a challenge.

Boggy wetland doesn't sound very appealing – until you clap eyes on the Nemunas Delta Regional Park. Sidling up to the Kaliningrad border where Lithuania's largest river spills into the lagoon, this oasis for birds and bird lovers is as peaceful as it is remote, and the local fish soup will have you offering all sorts of promises in exchange for the recipe. Not to be outdone is the Žemaitija National Park, where the combination of disused nuclear missile silos and sunsets over lake and pine woodlands manages to create one of the top attractions in the country.

KLAIPĖDA
☎ 46 / pop 186,000

Lithuania's third-largest city is a mix of old and new. This former Prussian capital – when it was named Memel – has retained a distinct German flavour in the architecture of its heavily cobbled Old Town and one remaining tower of its red-brick castle. It's also the only port of call for *Titanic*-sized cruise ships, and a vital sea link for cargo and passenger ferries between Lithuania, Scandinavia and beyond.

Most people will only catch a glimpse of Klaipėda (klai-pey-da) as they rush headlong for the ferry to Curonian Spit, but spend a few hours – or even better, a day – and you'll be justly rewarded.

History

Klaipėda was Memel until 1925. Founded in 1252 by the Teutonic Order who built the city's first castle, it was a key trading port from the 15th century until 1629, when Swedish forces destroyed it. After the Napoleonic wars it became part of Prussia and stayed in Prussian hands until WWI. The population at this time was an even split of Germans and Lithuanians.

Under the Treaty of Versailles, Memel town, the northern half of Curonian Spit and a strip of land (about 150km long and 20km wide) along the eastern side of the Curonian Lagoon and the northern side of the Nemunas River were separated from Germany as an 'international territory'. It remained stateless until 1923, when Lithuanian troops marched in, annexed it and changed its name two years later to Klaipėda.

LITHUANIA

Klaipėda served as a Nazi submarine base in WWII, and was all but destroyed during the war. After much rebuilding and repopulating, it has developed into an important city on the back of shipbuilding and fishing. In 1991 its university opened, followed in 2003 by a new cruise terminal. In recent years the town has begun to focus its attention on the tourist trade, building smart new hotels and restaurants at an alarming rate. Few Germans remain today.

Orientation

The Danė River flows westward across the city centre and enters the Curonian Lagoon 4km from the Baltic Sea. The key street axis is the north–south Manto gatvė (north of the river), Tiltų gatvė (for its first 600m south of the river) and Taikos prospektas.

The Old Town lies within the 400m south of the river, mostly west of Tiltų gatvė. Most hotels, the train and bus stations and Klaipėda University are north of the river.

Smiltynė, the northern tip of Curonian Spit, sits 500m off the mouth of the Danė, across the narrow channel that forms the northern end of the Curonian Lagoon.

MAPS

Jāņa sēta's *Klaipėda Neringa* map covers Klaipėda's northern beach suburbs, Smiltynė and Curonian Spit as well as central Klaipėda (1:10,000). Bookshops sell it for 8Lt.

Information

BOOKSHOPS

Akademija (Daukanto gatvė 16) Maps, guidebooks and English-language fiction.

Baltų Lankų (☎ 469 196; www.blt.lt; Taikos prospektas 61) Arguably the best bookshop in Klaipėda; south of the Old Town in the Akropolis centre.

Vaga (☎ 402 912; www.vaga.lt; Manto gatvė 9) Maps, travel guides and the *Baltic Times*.

INTERNET ACCESS

The tourist office has a couple of computers for surfing (4Lt per hour).

LEFT LUGGAGE

Train station (lockers 12/24 hr 4/5Lt; ☯ 6am-10pm)

MEDIA

Klaipėda in Your Pocket (www.inyourpocket.com) Annual city guide published locally and sold in hotels and news kiosks for 5Lt.

MONEY

Change cash or withdraw it with Visa or MasterCard at an ATM:

Bankas Snoras (Manto gatvė 9)

Hansa Bankas (Turgaus gatvė 9)

POST

Post office (Liepų gatvė 16) Gorgeous red-brick edifice.

TOURIST INFORMATION

Tourist office (☎ 412 186; www.klaipedainfo.lt; Turgaus gatvė 7; ☯ 9am-7pm Mon-Fri, 10am-4pm Sat & Sun Jun-Aug, 9am-6pm Mon-Fri, 10am-4pm Sat May & Sep, 9am-6pm Mon-Fri Oct-Apr) Exceptionally efficient tourist office selling maps and locally published guidebooks. It arranges accommodation, English-speaking guides (140/160Lt for one/two hours), hires out bicycles (10/40Lt per hour/day plus €100/300Lt deposit), and has a pet parrot named Rico.

TRAVEL AGENCIES

Krantas Travel (☎ 395 111; www.krantas.lt; Teatro gatvė 5) Kiel and Karlshamn ferry tickets (p361).

Mėja Travel (☎ 310 295; www.meja.lt; Simkaus gatvė 21-8) Excursions for cruise-ship passengers and amber-fishing.

Zigzag (☎ 314 672; www.zigzag.lt, in Lithuanian; Janonio gatvė 16) Specialises in student travel.

Sights

OLD TOWN

Little of German Klaipėda remains but there are some restored streets in the oldest part of town wedged between the river and Turgaus aikštė. Pretty **Teatro aikštė** (Theatre Sq) is the Old Town focus, dominated by the fine classical-style **Drama Theatre** (1857; under renovation). Hitler proclaimed the *Anschluss* (incorporation) of Memel into Germany to the crowd on the square from the theatre's balcony.

In front tinkles a fountain dedicated to **Simon Dach**, a Klaipėda-born German poet (1605–59), who was the focus of a circle of Königsberg writers and musicians. On a pedestal in the middle of the water stands **Äennchen von Tharau** (1912), a statue of Ann from Tharau sculpted by Berlin artist Alfred Kune (a replica; the original was destroyed in WWII) and inspired by a famous German wedding and love song originally written in the East Prussian dialect.

West of Pilies gatvė are the remains of Klaipėda's old moat-protected castle. The **Klaipėda Castle Museum** (Klaipėdos pilies muziejus;

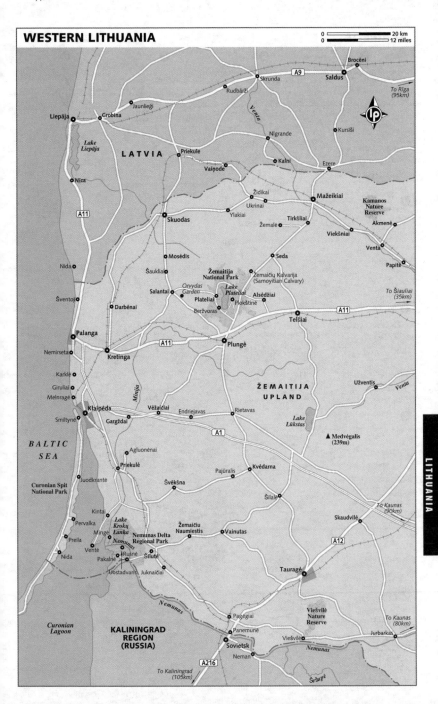

WESTERN LITHUANIA

| 0 | 20 km |
| 0 | 12 miles |

To Rīga (95km)

Broceni
Skrunda
A9
Saldus
Rudbārži
Jaunlieģi
Liepāja
Grobiņa
Kursiši
Nīgrande
Ezere
LATVIA
Priekule
Vaiņode
Kalni
Nīca
Židikai
Mažeikiai
Ukrinai
Kamanos Nature Reserve
Skuodas
Ylakiai
Tirkšliai
Akmenė
A11
Žemalė
Viekšniai
Mosėdis
Seda
Venta
Šaukliai
Papilė
Žemaitija National Park
Žemaičių Kalvarija (Samoyitiah Calvary)
Nida
Orvydas Garden
To Šiauliai (35km)
Salantai
Lake Plateliai
Alsėdžiai
Šventoji
Plateliai
Plokštinė
Darbėnai
Beržvoras
A11
Telšiai
Palanga
A11
Plungė
Nemirseta
Kretinga
ŽEMAITIJA UPLAND
Karklė
Užventis
Venta
Giruliai
Melnragė
Vėžaičiai
Endriejavas
Rietavas
Klaipėda
Minija
Lake Lūkstas
Smiltynė
Gargždai
A1
BALTIC SEA
▲ Medvėgalis (239m)
Agluonėnai
Priekulė
Pajūralis
Kvėdarna
Curonian Spit National Park
Juodkrantė
Švėkšna
Šilalė
To Kaunas (90km)
Kintai
Lake Kroku Lanka
Žemaičiu Naumiestis
Vainutas
Skaudvilė
Pervalka
Preila
Minge
Nemunas Delta Regional Park
A12
Nida
Ventė
Nemunas
Pakalnė
Rusnė
Šilutė
Uostadvaris
Juknaičiai
Tauragė
Curonian Lagoon
Nemunas
Pagėgiai
Viešvilė Nature Reserve
To Kaunas (80km)
KALININGRAD REGION (RUSSIA)
Panemunė
Viešvilė
Jurbarkas
Sovietsk
Nemunas
Neman
A216
Šešupė
To Kaliningrad (105km)

KLAIPĖDA

0   200 m
0   0.1 miles

To Melnragė (1km);
Giruliai (2km); Karklė
(3km); Palanga (30km);
Kretinga (35km)

Klaipėda
University

Dariaus ir Girėno gatvė

Train
Station

Priestočio gatvė   15

54

27
Butkų

Jūzės gatvė

Jonono gatvė

7

29

42

Šaulių gatvė

Lietovninku
aikštė   19

Vilties gatvė

Nerios gatvė

Sodų gatvė

Martynas Mažvydas
Sculpture
Park

Daukanto gatvė

Manto gatvė

50

Kanto gatvė

Naujoji Uosto gatvė

Daukanto gatvė

Ligoninės gatvė

Šaulių gatvė

Mažvydo alėja

Kanto gatvė

Donelaičio gatvė

20

To
Kaunas
(213km)

Donelaičio
aikštė

33

37

4

6

55

23

Vytauto gatvė

Danės gatvė

Liepų gatvė

Naujojo Uosto gatvė

Puodžių gatvė

Bokštu gatvė

28

Šimkaus gatvė

Manto gatvė

Vytauto gatvė

21

12

Kuršių
aikštė

Naujoji Sodo gatvė

26

Atgimino
aikštė

51

Riverside
Park

16

8

Danė River

Harbour

Uosto gatvė

Danės gatvė

Old
Town

46

To Aribė
(100m)

45

24 40

32

49

To Mary Queen of
Peace Church (200m);
Kaunas (213km)

Kepėjų gatvė

Turgaus gatvė

Žvejų gatvė

14

43

22

52

Teatro
aikštė

47

2

5

38

36

41 53

Tiltų gatvė

Didžioji Vandens gatvė

Tomo gatvė

18

25

17

9

Aukštoji gatvė

Sukilėliu gatvė

Daržų gatvė

44

34

10

39

48

35

Curonian
Lagoon

Danės gatvė

30

31

11

Pilies gatvė

13

Market

Turgaus
aikštė

To Smiltynė (500m);
Neringa (500m)

To New River Port (3km);
International Ferry Port (6km);
Lisco Lines (6km); Šilutė (48km)

Taikos prospektas

To Eurolines (750m);
Baltų Lankų (1km)

☎ 410 527; www.mlimuziejus.lt; Pilies gatvė 4; adult/child 4/2Lt; ❧ 10am-6pm Tue-Sat) inside the one remaining tower tells the castle's story from the 13th to 17th centuries. To get to the museum, walk through the Klaipėda State Sea Port Authority building and a ship-repair yard. Incredibly, this rundown ramshackle yard is the first thing the 20,000 passengers a year who step off luxury cruise ships in Klaipėda see! The **cruise ship terminal** (☎ 490 990; www.ports.lt; Pilies gatvė 4) shares the castle site.

Some excellent modern art hangs in the **Klaipėda Art Exhibition Palace** (Klaipėdos Dailės paradų rūmai; ☎ 314 443; Aukštoji gatvė 3; adult/child 4/2Lt; ❧ 11am-7pm Wed-Sun). Next door, **Baroti Gallery** (Baroti galerija; ☎ 313 580; Aukštoji gatvė 3/3; admission free) is partly housed in a converted fish warehouse (1819). Its exposed-timber style, called *Fachwerk*, is typical of German Memel.

Around the corner, the **Lithuanian Minor History Museum** (Mažosios lietuvos istorijos muziejus; ☎ 410 527; Didžioji Vandens gatvė 6; adult/child 3/1Lt; ❧ 10am-6pm Tue-Sat) traces the early history of Lithuania Minor and includes fascinating bits and pieces, such as Prussian maps, labour-intensive weaving machines and traditional folk art. Lithuania Minor was the name given to the northeastern corner of Prussia until the end of WWII, and encompassed parts of Lithuania, Poland and Kaliningrad.

The cute **Blacksmith's Museum** (Kalvystės muziejus; ☎ 410 526; Šaltkalvių gatvė 2 & 2a; adult/child 3/1Lt; ❧ 10am-6pm Tue-Sat) displays ornate forged-iron works such as elaborate crosses transferred from the town's former cemetery (Martynas Mažvydas Sculpture Park).

Not far from the town's scruffy market stands the **Mary Queen of Peace Church** (Švč Mergelės Marijos Taikos Karalienės bažnyčia; ☎ 410 120; Rumpiškės gatvė 6a; adult/child 3/1Lt). Its 46.5m tower is one of the highest points in the city, and visits can be booked through the tourist office.

NORTH OF THE RIVER

A **riverside park** skirts the northern bank of the Danė. A little further north, Liepų gatvė – called Adolf-Hitler-Strasse for a brief spell – has a few attractions of its own. Adjacent to the neo-Gothic **post office** at No 16 is the **Clock Museum** (Laikrodžių muziejus; ☎ 410 413; Liepų gatvė 12; adult/child 4/2Lt; ❧ noon-6pm Tue-Sat, to 4.30pm Sun), where all manner of clocks – from Gothic to nuclear – just keep ticking; its sunny back yard alone is worth the entrance fee. At the street's northwestern end is the **P Domšaitis Gallery** (☎ 410 412; Liepų gatvė 33; adult/child 4/2Lt; ❧ noon-6pm Tue-Sat, to 5pm Sun) with works by Lithuanian expressionist painter Pranas Domšaitis (1880–1965).

Back towards the lagoon is Klaipėda's tallest building, the **K building** (Naujoji Sodo gatvė 1), which, appropriately, is shaped like a 'K'. It houses the Hotel Klaipėda and is topped by the Vivalavita bar.

SMILTYNĖ

Smiltynė (Map p362) is a hop, skip and five-minute ferry ride away across the thin strait that divides Klaipėda from its achingly beautiful coastal sister, Curonian Spit (p362). This strait-side patch of paradise – packed on summer weekends with Klaipėda residents – has

LITHUANIA

SCULPTURE SCAPE

In true Lithuanian style, Klaipėda is studded with great sculptures, including 120-odd from the late 1970s in the **Martynas Mažvydas Sculpture Park** (Liepų gatvė), the city's main cemetery till 1977. Not far from the park on Lietuvninkų aikštė is a monumental 3.5m one in granite of the geezer the park is named after – **Martynas Mažvydas**, author of the first book published in Lithuanian in 1547.

The red granite pillar propping up a broken grey arch of almighty proportions at the southern end of Manto gatvė is Lithuania's biggest granite sculpture. Engraved with the quote 'We are one nation, one land, one Lithuania' by local poet Ieva Simonaitytė (1897–1978), **Arka** (Arch) celebrates Klaipėda joining Lithuania in 1923.

Outside the train station stands **Farewell** (2002), a moving statue of a mother with a headscarf, a suitcase in one hand, and the hand of a small boy clutching a teddy bear in the other. It was given by Germany to Klaipėda to remember Germans who said goodbye to their homeland after the city became part of Lithuania in 1923.

Smaller works seem to pop up overnight in Klaipėda. Inside the Old Town are sculptures of a dog, cat, mouse, spider, and disturbing red dragon, while on its outskirts reside an apple, a row of oversized yellow chairs, and a boy with dog waving off the ferries. Discover them on your wanders.

beautiful beaches, sandy dunes and sweet-smelling pine forests.

Equally crowd-pleasing are the sea lion and dolphin shows at the **Lithuanian Sea Museum** (Map p362; Lietuvos jūrų muziejus; ☎ 490 754; www.juru.muziejus.lt; adult/student Jun-Aug 12/6Lt, Sep-May 10/5Lt, dolphin show Jun-Aug 18/9Lt, Apr-May 14/7Lt, camera 5Lt; ☺ 10.30am-6.30pm Tue-Sun Jun-Aug, 10.30am-6pm Wed-Sun May & Sep–mid-Oct, 10.30am-5pm Sat & Sun mid-Oct–Apr), 1.5km from the passenger ferry landing (for Old Castle Port ferries) at the tip of the peninsula. It occupies a former 19th-century fort, and houses seals that dance on the rocks and dolphins that perform incredible acrobatics to the glee of multitudes of children.

In July and August horse-drawn carriages (70Lt for up to eight passengers) carry tourists from the ferry landing to the museum. Otherwise, catch the electric **tourist train** (adult/7-10yr 3/2Lt) that covers the same ground, hire a **bicycle** (per hr/day 8/40Lt, ☺ 10am-8pm May-Sep), or cover the distance on foot. Additional, there is bicycle hire (per hour/day 8/40Lt, open 10am to 8pm May to September) available at the ferry landing. The granite boulder at the start of the path honours past winners of the three- and six-nautical-mile races run around Smiltynė on the second Saturday in October. Next port of call is the National Park Visitors Centre (p363) of Curonian Spit National Park and the **Curonian Spit National Nature Museum** (Map p362; Kuršių nerijos nacionalinis parkas gamtos muziejus ekspozicija; ☎ 402 256; Smiltynė plentas 12, 10 & 9; adult/

student 5/2Lt; ☺ 11am-6pm Wed-Sun May-Sep), spread across three wooden houses. There are plenty of stuffed examples of the birds and animals that normally roam the spit, including wild pigs, badgers, beavers, and elk, a large collection of insects, and information on measures being taken to protect the dunes.

About 700m further north are **old fishing vessels** (Map p362) to explore inside and out, including three Baltic Sea fishing trawlers built in the late 1940s and a 1935 **kurėnas** (a traditional 10.8m flat-bottomed Curonian sailing boat used for fishing). Next door, the **Ethnographic Sea Fishermen's Farmstead** (Map p362; admission free; ☺ dusk-dawn), with its collection of traditional 19th-century buildings (the granary, dwelling house, cellar, cattle shed and so on), proffers a glimpse of traditional fishing life.

Activities

Grab your speedos and hit Smiltynė, where footpaths cut through pine forests across the spit's 1km-wide tip to a bleached-white sandy **beach**. From the ferry landing, walk straight ahead across the car park, then bear left towards Nida; on your right a large sign marks a smooth footpath that leads through pine forest to a women's beach (Moterų pliažas; 1km), mixed beach (Bendras pliažas; 700m) and men's beach (Vyrų pliažas; 900m). Nude or topless bathing is the norm on single-sex beaches.

Melnragė, 1km north of Klaipėda, has a pier and beach to which city dwellers flock at sunset; **Giruliai Beach** is 1km further north. Buses 6 and 4 respectively link Manto gatvė with both. **Karklė**, another 1km north, is known for having amber specks washed up on its unusually stony beach after autumn storms and for the protected **Dutch Cap**, a 24m sea cliff.

Boat trips on the lagoon are arranged through the tourist office. **Sailing excursions** (3 hr 60Lt) on the Baltic Sea only take place during the Sea Festival; once again, contact the tourist office.

With its Turkish sauna, pool and masseurs, the **Sothys Spa Centras** (☎ 315 063; www.sothys.lt; Mažoji Smilties gatvė 2; ☯ 8am-9pm Mon-Fri, 9am-8pm Sat) will appeal to winter visitors. The tourist office can help with **ice-fishing** contacts.

Festivals & Events

Klaipėda celebrates its rich nautical heritage on the third weekend in July with a flamboyant five-day **Sea Festival** (www.juros.svente.lt).

Sleeping

Be prepared to book accommodation in advance during the Sea Festival. The tourist office has private rooms from 70Lt and can help with country stays.

BUDGET

Klaipėda Travellers Hostel (☎ 211 879; www.lithua nianhostels.org; Butkų Juzės gatvė 7/4; dm/d 44/88Lt; 🖳) This friendly hostel close to the bus station looks terrible from the outside but is very homey and pleasant inside. Two small dorms sleep 12 people and there's one double, as well as a kitchen and free tea and coffee.

Litinterp Guesthouse (☎ 410 644; www.litinterp .lt; Puodžių gatvė 17; s/d/tr 100/160/210Lt, without bathroom 80/140/180Lt; ☯ 8.30am-7pm Mon-Fri, 10am-3pm Sat; 🅿 ✗) This accommodation agency arranges B&B in and around Klaipėda. The 16 rooms in its own guesthouse are clean and nonsmoking. Light pine furnishings create a fresh contemporary look and breakfast is delivered to your room in a basket.

MIDRANGE

Aribė (☎ 490 940; www.aribe.lt; Bangų gatvė 17a; s/d 160/210Lt; 🅿 ✗ 🖳) This three-star establishment is a short 10 minute walk from the Old Town and hides behind an unassuming facade in an unassuming neighbourhood. Rooms are quiet, pleasant and dressed in light, bright colours, and staff couldn't be more helpful.

Preliudija Guesthouse (☎ 310 077; www.preliudija .com; Kepėjų gatvė 7; s/d from 180/210Lt; ✗ 🖳) Snug in an Old Town house dating to 1856, this guesthouse – a rare breed in Klaipėda – is charming. Despite its history, rooms are minimalist and modern; each has a single fresh flower in a vase and a sparkling bathroom.

Magnisima (☎ 310 901; www.magnisima.lt; Janonio gatvė 11; s/d/ste/apt 200/250/300/700Lt; 🅿 ✗ 🖳) Newly renovated in Italian rococo style and value for money. Don't let the gambling machines at the entrance put you off.

Hotel Euterpė (☎ 474 703; www.euterpe.lt; Daržų gatvė 9; s/d from 200/260Lt; 🅿 ✗ ⚒) Sidling up to former German merchant houses in the Old Town is this relatively new hotel. Rooms are bathed in earthy colours and have that neat, minimalist look about them. Downstairs is the hotel's courtyard cafe and (in the reception) a Renaissance-era tile of Euterpe, a Greek muse, uncovered during excavations.

Old Port Hotel (☎ 474 764; www.oldporthotel.lt, in Lithuanian; Žėjų gatvė 20/22; s/d from 260/290Lt; 🅿 ✗ 🖳) Split between two newly renovated fishing houses on the southern bank of the Danė River, the Old Port Hotel offers small but supremely comfortable rooms with views of the docks or Klaipėda castle. Those looking for Spit views should book rooms 46, 47 or 57.

TOP END

Hotel Klaipėda (☎ 404 372; www.klaipedahotel.lt; Naujoji Sodo gatvė 1; s/d/ste/apt from 320/400/540/1000Lt; 🅿 ✗ ⚒ 🖳) Choose from sturdy and comfortable rooms in the 12-storey red-brick monstrosity or their newer yet shabbier cousins in the celebrated K building next door. Naturally the latter have the best views (rooms reside on floors 6 to 17) and it's not as far to Vivalavita (see Drinking).

Europa Royale (☎ 404 444; www.europaroyale.com; Teatro gatvė 1; s/d from €100/120; 🅿 ✗ ⚒ 🖳) Slick sliding doors set the tone for this oasis of elegance overlooking Klaipėda's prettiest square. Rooms are refined. Note that Europa Royale goes against the grain and advertises its rates in Euro rather than Lita.

Eating

Pėda (☎ 310 234; Turgaus gatvė 10; mains 10-20Lt) A stylish cellar adjoining an art gallery (entrance around the corner), this old-timer is ideal for light evening snacks, sweet-centred *blyneliai* and live jazz at weekends. Count on streetside seating in summer.

Senoji Hansa (☎ 400 056; Kurpių gatvė 1; mains 15-25Lt) This cafe sits wedged on a wooden decking terrace in the middle of a cobbled street with enviable Theatre Sq view. Classic Lithuanian dishes fill the menu, but there's surprisingly few fish options.

Hämmerli (☎ 311 209; Galinė gatvė 16; mains 15-40Lt; ☾ Mon-Sat) Hämmerli specialises in Swiss cuisine, with equal portions of French, German and Italian flavours thrown in. It's a heavily meat-based menu but vegetarians will find something to keep them happy. Further bonuses include top-notch service, a bright and breezy atmosphere, courtyard seating and a superb lunch menu (25Lt).

Keltininko (☎ 474 764; Žėjų 20/22; mains 20-40Lt) Keltininko, the restaurant of the Old Port Hotel, offers silver-service dining in a large glass box overlooking the Danė River. Enjoy European cuisine while Spit ferries sail past.

our pick Kurpiai (☎ 410 555; Kurpių gatvė 1a; mains 20-40Lt; ☾ noon-3am) This Old Town jazz club has been a Klaipėda legend for years, opening way before the postindependence bars and restaurants mushroomed. Its cobbled terrace and dark old-world interior are not only the best place in town to catch live jazz, but also to sample ostrich steak, fresh trout, and a wide range of pork, beef and vegetarian dishes. Service is also well above par. Arrive before 9.30pm on weekends (entrance Friday/Saturday 10/15Lt) or you'll be fighting for standing space.

Friedricho (☎ 301 070; Tiltų 26a; mains 20-50Lt) What was once a dump of an alley close to the market has been transformed into a row of sparkling restaurants and bars that attracts all and sundry. Friedricho Restoranas wins the eating award with an attractive selection of international wines and creative Mediterranean dishes, but there's also fine pizzas (Friedricho Pizzeria) next door. Alternatively, just stop in for a pint.

Self-caterers can head for **Iki** (Mažvydo alėja 7/11) and **Ikiukas** (Turgaus gatvė) supermarkets.

Also worth considering:

Čili Kaimas (☎ 310 953; Manto gatvė 11; pizzas 10-20Lt) Atmospheric setting in a great Soviet-era cinema; average pizzas but good Lithuanian fodder.

Scandal (Skandalas; ☎ 411 585; Kanto gatvė 44; meals 40Lt) Brash American dream, part Wild West, part Mae West, with legendary charcoal-grilled steaks and spare ribs.

Drinking

Klaipėda is home to Švyturys, Lithuania's big beer brewed in the country's oldest operating brewery (since 1784). An alternative to slurping the stuff in a bar is to take a tour of the **Švyturys brewery** (www.svyturys.lt); organised by the tourist office, tours are 1½ to hours and cost 30Lt per person (including tastings), and leave any time between 10am and 4pm Monday to Friday. Reservations essential.

Don't overlook Kurpiai (left) and Senoji Hansa (left) for a good night out.

our pick Vivalavita (☎ 228 800; Naujojo Sodo 1; ☾ noon-3am) Occupying the 20th floor of the K building, Vivalavita offers up spectacular views of the swathe of docks along Klaipėda's waterfront, the spit's northern point, and the Baltic Sea beyond. To the east stretches Lithuania as far as the eye can see, and even lift A and B provide astounding views. It's debatable whether crossing cocktails at sunset or after dark is more preferable, but why not do both? Food is also offered.

Tappo D'Oro (☎ 8-620 81169; Sukilėlių gatvė 10) Tappo d'oro sticks to the winning formula established by its older sister in Vilnius – wine, cheese and ham from Italy, accompanied by a convivial atmosphere. Grab a terrace seat overlooking the main square and enjoy the show.

Friedricho Smuklė (☎ 411 076; Tiltų 26a) Cool, casual and crowded in summer, Friedricho Smuklė has what it takes to attract the punters. It's a little too bright and new to be truly comfortable, but no one seems to care. Located in the same alleyway as Friedricho restaurant.

Memelis (☎ 403 040; www.memelis.lt; Žvejų gatvė 4) This red-brick brewery-restaurant by the river has been in operation since 1871. The interior is old-style beer hall; outside is industrial-feel riverside terrace.

Take a peek:

Miesto Smuklė (City Pub; ☎ 8-647 44470; Tiltų gatvė 6) Cosy inside, inviting summer terrace outside.

Black Cat Pub 2 (☎ 411 167; Žėjų gatvė 21) Convivial spot to meet expats and catch bad martial arts movies on TV.

Entertainment

Catch high-brow entertainment at the **Klaipėda Concert Hall** (☎ 410 561; www.koncertusale.lt; Šaulių gatvė 36). Kurpiai (left) tops the live-jazz bill. The Klaipėda Philharmonic plays at the **Musical Theatre** (Muzikinis teatras; ☎ 397 402; www.muzikinis-teatras.lt, in Lithuanian; Danės gatvė 19).

NIGHTCLUBS

Cover charges for these clubs range from 10Lt to 30 Lt.

Relax (☎ 8-700 55555; www.pramogubankas.lt; Turgaus gatvė 1) This flashy basement club is a fun night out when there's a crowd around. Men should wear a collared shirt or the gorillas on the door may not let you in.

Elcalor (☎ 8-671 59899; www.elcalor.lt; Kepėjų gatvė 10) Elcalor in Old Town (enter by Jono gatvė) is Klaipėda's Latin soul. Bands play on Friday and DJs mix Latin, Latin pop and Latin House on Saturday.

Shopping

Klaipėda is known for its amber (stalls selling souvenirs dot Teatro aikštė), but it's also possible to pick up fine linen and artwork in town. Galleries worth seeking out include **Parko** (☎ 310 501; Turgaus gatvė 9), for contemporary paintings, sculptures and etchings and **Pėda** (☎ 310 234; Vežėjų gatvė), for designs by contemporary jeweller Jurga Karčiauskaitė-Lago.

Getting There & Away

BOAT

From Klaipėda's **International Ferry Port** (Klaipėdos Nafta; ☎ 395 051; www.lisco.lt; Perkėlos gatvė 10), **Scandlines** (☎ 310 561; www.scandlines.lt; Naujoji Sodo gatvė 1) sails to Århus and Aabenraa (Denmark); and **Lisco Lines** (☎ 395 051; www.lisco.lt; Perkėlos gatvė 10) runs passenger ferries to/from Kiel and Sassnitz (Germany) and Karlshamn (Sweden). For schedules and fares, see p408. On Friday and Saturday from July to September, **Jukunda** (☎ 300 700; www.jukunda.lt; Karklų gatvė 9) ferries passengers to Nida (60Lt, 4½ hours), calling at Juodkrantė (30Lt, 1½ hours) along the way. Boats leave from opposite the castle at 10am and begin their return journey at 5pm.

BUS

Ecolines (☎ 310 103; www.ecolines.lt; Mažvydo alėja 1; ⏰ 9am-6pm Mon-Fri, 10am-3pm Sat) sells tickets for international destinations (p404), as does **Eurolines** (☎ 415 555; www.eurolines.lt; Tiakos prospektas 41; ⏰ 9am-6pm Mon-Fri, 10am-4pm Sat).

At the **bus station** (☎ 411547; www.klap.lt; Priestočio gatvė) the **information window** (⏰ 4.30am-noon & 1-10.30pm) has timetable information. Most buses to/from Juodkrantė and Nida depart from the ferry landing at Smiltynė on Curonian Spit.

Services to/from Klaipėda bus station include the following:

Kaliningrad (40Lt, 4½ hours, one bus departing 6.30am daily via Nida)

Kaunas (44Lt, 2¾ to four hours, over 20 buses a day)

Kretinga (5Lt, 30 to 50 minutes, half-hourly between 6.25am and 9.30pm)

Liepāja (18Lt, 2¾ hours, one bus departing 9am daily via Palanga)

Nida (9Lt, 1½ hours, two buses daily from the bus station at 6.30am and 10.55am, plus buses every one to two hours from Smiltynė)

Palanga (4.50Lt, 45 minutes, at least half-hourly between 4.15am and 10.35pm)

Pärnu (98Lt, 8¾ hours, three buses daily via Rīga)

Rīga (65Lt, five hours, three buses daily)

Šiauliai (30Lt, 3½ hours, five buses)

Tallinn (from 122Lt, 10 hours, three buses daily via Rīga)

Vilnius (59Lt, four to 5½ hours, up to 15 daily)

TRAIN

The **train station** (☎ 313 677; Priestočio gatvė 1), 150m from the bus station, has an unusual helmeted clock tower and a moving sculpture (p358) in front.

Daily services include three trains to/from Vilnius (42.10Lt, 4½ to five hours) and five trains to/from Šiauliai (18.60Lt to 23.50Lt, two to three hours) and Kretinga (4.10Lt, 20 to 35 minutes).

Getting Around

BOAT

Everything about **Smiltynė ferries** (Smiltynės perkela; ☎ 24hr information line 311 117; www.keltas.lt) – timetables, fares, newsflashes – is online. Smoking on ferries is forbidden.

The passenger ferry for Smiltynė leaves from **Old Castle Port** (Senoji perkėla; ☎ 314 257; Žvejų gatvė 8). It docks on the eastern side of Smiltynė, at the start of the Nida road. Ferries sail at least every half-hour between 6.30am and midnight June to August (at least hourly until 11pm the rest of the year). The crossing takes 10 minutes and a return passenger fare is 2/1Lt per adult/child; bicycles and children under the age of seven sail for free.

Year-round, vehicles can use the **New River Port** (Naujoji perkėla; ☎ 345 780; Nemuno gatvė 8), 3km south of the mouth of the Danė River. Ferries sail half-hourly between 5am and 2am and dock on Curonian Spit 2.5km south of the Smiltynė ferry landing. Cars cost 40Lt to transport, motorcycles 18Lt. Bus 1 links Klaipėda city centre with the New River Port.

LITHUANIA

BUS

Buy tickets for local buses from news kiosks for 1.50Lt or from the driver for 2Lt. Bus 8 (known for pickpockets) links the train station with Manto gatvė, the city centre and the Turgaus stop, on Taikos prospektas. Bus 11 links the bus station with Manto gatvė. Minibuses, which follow the same route, can be flagged down on the street and cost 2.20/3Lt before/after 11pm; pay the driver.

CURONIAN SPIT NATIONAL PARK

☎ 469 / pop 3100

The western Lithuanian scent of ozone and pine is at its headiest on this thin tongue of sand. Waves from the Baltic Sea pound one side, the Curonian Lagoon laps the other. The winds and tree-felling have sculpted Curonian Spit (Kuršių Nerija) over time. But this precious natural treasure is by nature a fragile one – being made up of millions of grains of constantly shifting sand. As the dunes creep closer to the Baltic Sea there are fears it may one day disappear.

In 1991 the Curonian Spit National Park was created to protect the dunes, lagoon and surrounding sea. Lush pine forests filled with deer, elk and wild boar cover 70% of the park; the dunes make up 25% of it; and just 1.5% is urban, namely the four villages where fishermen smoke their catch according to an old Curonian recipe. The main industry is tourism, the double-edged sword that yields both its main source of income and biggest environmental threat.

The entire Curonian Spit was Prussian territory until WWI. It used to have a hugely magnetic attraction for German exiles, who returned to the spot where they once lived for holidays, but today dozens of world languages are heard among tourists.

The southern half of the spit belongs to Russia; a road runs the whole length to Kaliningrad (p383), in the neighbouring Russian-owned Kaliningrad Region. The main settlement on the Lithuanian side is Nida, a busy summer resort north of the border; other settlements include Juodkrantė, Pervalka and Preila further north.

Information

Online information can be gleaned from the websites for **Neringa tourism** (www.visitneringa.com) and the **national park** (www.nerija.lt); for accommodation, surf www.kopos.lt. On the

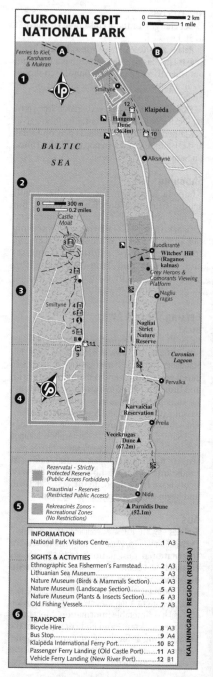

CURONIAN SPIT NATIONAL PARK

| 0 | 2 km |
| 0 | 1 mile |

Ferries to Kiel,
Karshamn
& Mukran

Smiltynė

Klaipėda

Hangeno
Dune
(36.4m)

BALTIC
SEA

Alksnynė

Castle
Moat

| 0 | 300 m |
| 0 | 0.2 miles |

Smiltynė

Juodkrantė
Witches' Hill
(Raganos
kalnas)
Grey Herons &
Cormorants Viewing
Platform

Nagliu
ragas

Nagliai
Strict
Nature
Reserve

Curonian
Lagoon

Pervalka

Karvaičiai
Reservation

Preila

Vecekrugas
Dune ▲
(67.2m)

Nida

Parnidis Dune ▲
(52.1m)

Rezervatai - Strictly Protected Reserve (Public Access Forbidden)

Draustiniai - Reserves (Restricted Public Access)

Rekreacinės Zonos - Recreational Zones (No Restrictions)

KALININGRAD REGION (RUSSIA)

INFORMATION
National Park Visitors Centre............................1 A3

SIGHTS & ACTIVITIES
Ethnographic Sea Fishermen's Farmstead..........2 A3
Lithuanian Sea Museum....................................3 A3
Nature Museum (Birds & Mammals Section)......4 A3
Nature Museum (Landscape Section)..................5 A3
Nature Museum (Plants & Insects Section)........6 A3
Old Fishing Vessels..7 A3

TRANSPORT
Bicycle Hire...8 A3
Bus Stop...9 A4
Klaipėda International Ferry Port.....................10 B2
Passenger Ferry Landing (Old Castle Port).......11 A3
Vehicle Ferry Landing (New River Port)...........12 B1

SHIFTING SANDS & DELICATE DUNES

Legend has it that motherly sea giantess Neringa created the spit, lovingly carrying armfuls of sand in her apron to form a protected harbour for the local fishing folk. The truth is as enchanting. The waves and winds of the Baltic Sea let sand accumulate in its shallow waters near the coast 5000 or 6000 years ago to create an original beauty found nowhere else.

Massive deforestation in the 16th century started the sands shifting. Trees were felled for timber, leaving the sands free to roam unhindered at the whim of the strong coastal winds. At a pace of 20m a year, the sands swallowed 14 villages in the space of three centuries.

It was soon dubbed the 'Sahara of Lithuania' due to its desert state; drastic action was needed. In 1768 an international commission set about replanting. Today this remains a priority of the national park authorities. Deciduous forest (mainly birch groves) covers 20% of the national park; coniferous forest, primarily pine and mountain pine trees, constitutes a further 53%. Alder trees can be found on 2.6 sq km (3% of the park's area). Lattices of branches and wooden stakes have pinned down the sand.

But the sands are still moving – at least 1m a year. Slowly the spit is drifting into the Baltic Sea. Each tourist who scrambles and romps on Parnidis Dune – the only remaining free-drifting dune – meanwhile pushes down several tonnes of sand. With 1.5 million people visiting the dunes each year, the threat posed by them wandering off designated paths – not to mention the risk of forest fire – is high.

The dunes are also shrinking. Winds, waves and humans have reduced them by 20m in 40 years. Its precious beauty may yet be lost forever.

spit itself, there are tourist offices at Nida and Juodkrantė.

National Park Visitors Centre Nida (Lankytojų centras; ☎ 51 256; nidainfo@nerija.lt; Naglių gatvė 8; ☯ 9am-noon & 1-5pm Mon-Thu, to 6pm Fri & Sat, to 4pm Sun May-Sep); Smiltynė (☎ 46-402 257; info@ nerija.lt; Smiltynės plentas 11; ☯ 9am-noon & 1-6pm Mon-Fri, 9am-6pm Sat, 9am-4pm Sun Jun-Aug, 8am-noon & 1-5pm Mon-Fri Sep-May). Arranges guides (30Lt per hour, minimum 10 people) and stocks an abundance of information on walking, cycling, boating and lazing activities in the park.

Festivals & Events

The summer season – early June to the end of August – ushers in the **Summer Extravaganza Neringa** (Vasaros pramogų kolekcijos; ☎ 5-212 7421; www.muzikosfrontas.lt), a fiesta of concerts, craft days and cultural events. The **International Folk Festival**, held on a weekend in late June, swamps Nida with visitors; contact the towns' tourist office for additional information.

Getting There & Around

The Klaipėda–Smiltynė ferry (see p361) is the main access route. A daily riverboat linking Curonian Spit with Kaunas (p345) should be under way by the time you read this.

You can also reach Kaliningrad (south) in Russia from here. The Russian border post is 3km south of Nida on the main road. Don't contemplate this without the necessary Russian visa and paperwork (see p399).

From Smiltynė, buses ply the route to/ from Nida via Juodkrantė. The odd bus stops in Pervalka and Preila too; see p370 for details. Alternatively, team up with fellow Nida-bound travellers in Smiltynė and share a taxi; a fare per person to Nida is around 10Lt. Cycling (p368) is the best way to explore the spit, and there is a well-marked trail running its entire Lithuanian length. Bicycles are for hire in Nida, Juodkrantė, and Smiltynė.

The spit has one **petrol station** (Smiltynės plentas 6) near the Lithuanian–Russian border.

Juodkrantė
☎ 469

The long, thin village of Juodkrantė (ywad-kran-tey) – Schwarzort to Germans – 20km south of Smiltynė is spread out along the lagoon. The pace of life here is slow even in the height of summer, and the sweet smell of smoked fish follows you wherever you go.

INFORMATION

The village's tiny centre is home to a pier, bus stop, post office and tourist office.

Pharmacy (Liudviko Rėzos gatvė 54; ☯ 9am-1pm & 5-7pm Mon-Fri) Located in Hotel Ažuolynas.

Post office (Kalno gatvė 3)

LITHUANIA

Snoras Bankas Only ATM in town; opposite Kurėnas cafe-bar.

Tourist office (☎ 53 490; juodkrante@visitneringa.lt; Liudviko Rėzos gatvė 8; ☒ 10am-8pm Mon-Sat, 10am-3pm Sun Jun-Aug, 9am-1pm & 2-5pm Tue-Fri, 10am-3pm Sat Sep-May) Located opposite the bus stop; has accommodation and activity information, and may have internet access.

SIGHTS

Contemporary stone sculptures and a silky-smooth promenade sidle up to the water's edge, while the main road – Liudviko Rėzos gatvė – is lined with holiday homes and quaint *žuvis* (fish) outlets.

At Juodkrantė's northern end is an area around a fishing harbour known as **Amber Bay** (Gintaro įlanka), recalling the amber excavated in the village in three separate clusters – 2250 tonnes in all – in 1854 to 1855 and 1860. The spit is about 1.5km wide at this point and the fine stretch of forest – good for spotting elk in the early morning and evening – is among the loveliest you will find on the peninsula.

A lazy stroll south from the centre brings you to the **Witches' Hill** (Raganos kalnas; Map p362), where devils, witches, ghouls and other fantastical and grotesque wooden carvings from Lithuanian folklore skulk along a sculpture trail careering from fairy tale to nightmare. It's located in the woods and signposted immediately south of Liudviko Rėzos gatvė 46.

The red-brick German **Evangelical-Lutheran church** (Liudviko Rėzos gatvė 56) built in 1885 and a **Weathervanes Gallery** (Vetrungių galerija; ☎ 53 357; Liudviko Rėzos gatvė 13), selling authentic weathervanes (opposite) and quality amber jewellery, mark the village's southern end.

SLEEPING & EATING

Kurėnas (☎ 53 101; kurenas@gmail.com; Liudviko Rėzos gatvė 10; r from 200Lt; **P**) Named after a flat-bottomed Curonian boat, this busy and bright cafe-bar with street-side terrace sports large, individually decorated rooms with wooden floors and clean white walls. Reserve one with a balcony overlooking the lagoon.

Vila Flora (☎ 53 024; www.vilaflora.lt, in Lithuanian; Kalno gatvė 7a; s/d 200/260Lt; **P**) Located in an attractive rust- and wine-red building, Vila Flora is filled with bright, stylish rooms, some of which sport balconies and conservatories. Its restaurant on the ground floor is the best in town, offering bog-standard Lithuanian

dishes with a twist. However, the service can be decidedly average at times.

Kogas (☎ 8-655 26949; Liudviko Rėzos gatvė 1; mains 20-40Lt) Board this pseudo pirate ship moored at Juodkrantė's harbour and chow down on a plethora of meaty dishes or simply rock up for a swashbuckling time and a few hearty ales.

Smoked fish is sold all along Liudviko Rėzos gatvė and self-caterers are limited to an expensive **store** (☒ 8am-10pm) near the start of the Witches' Hill trail.

Other options:

Hotel Ažuolynas (☎ 53 310; www.hotelazuol ynas.lt; Liudviko Rėzos gatvė 54; s/d/tr/q Jun-Aug 180/230/340/520Lt, May & Sep 110/150/220/280Lt, Oct-Apr 90/120/180/230Lt; **P** ☒ ☒) Characterless hotel with reasonable rooms. Facilities include a restaurant, tennis courts, billiard hall, gift shop, Turkish bath and sauna (110Lt per hour), swimming pool with curly-wurly water slide. Breakfast not included.

Pamario takas (Liudviko Rėzos gatvė 42; mains 15-30Lt) Fun, family-run restaurant in quaint wooden cottage with accompanying flower-filled garden.

Švejonė (Liudviko Rėzos gatvė 30; mains 15-30Lt) Much the same as Pamario takas.

Vela Bianca (☎ 50 013; Liudviko Rėzos gatvė 1a; mains 20-50Lt) Above-par cuisine, attentive service, smooth background tunes and sublime views of the lagoon.

GETTING THERE & AWAY

Buses to/from Nida (6Lt, 45 minutes) and Smiltynė (4Lt, 15 to 20 minutes) stop in Juodkrantė. Bicycle hire (8/30Lt per hour/day) can be found near the tourist office.

Juodkrantė to Nida

South of Juodkrantė is Lithuania's largest colony of grey herons and cormorants, observed here since the 19th century. Wooden steps lead from the road to a **viewing platform** where the panorama of thousands of nests amid pine trees – not to menton the noise of the 6500-strong colony – is astonishing. Cormorants arrive in early February (herons a little later) to pick and rebuild their nests. By May chicks are screaming for food. Starlings, thrushes, warblers, and grey, spotted and black woodpeckers can also be seen here.

Almost immediately afterwards, the road switches from the eastern side of the peninsula to the western. The 16.8-sq-km **Naglių Strict Nature Reserve** (Naglių rezervatas) here protects the Dead or Grey Dunes (named

---

SPIT RULES

▪ Neringa municipality entrance fee: motorbike July to Aug/September to June 7/5Lt; car 20/10Lt.

▪ Speed limit: 50km/h in villages, 70km/h on open roads.

▪ Don't romp in the dunes, pick flowers or stray off designated footpaths.

▪ Don't damage flora or fauna, mess with bird nests or light campfires.

▪ Don't pitch a tent or park a camper overnight anywhere in the park.

▪ Don't fish without a permit; purchase them at tourist offices.

▪ Beware of elk and wild boar crossing the road, and don't feed them!

▪ Break a rule and risk an on-the-spot fine of up to 500Lt.

▪ In case of forest fire, call ☎ 01, 112, Smiltynė 8-656 35025, Juodkrantė 8-656 34998, Prėila and Pervalka 8-687 27758, Nida 8-656 34992.

▪ To alert a lifeguard call ☎ 8-469 52239.

---

after the greyish flora that covers them) that stretch 8km south and are 2km wide; a marked footpath leads into the reserve from the main road.

Shifting sands in the mid-19th century forced villagers here to flee to **Pervalka** and **Preila** on the east coast, accessible by side roads from the main road. Pine-forested **Vecekrugas Dune** (67.2m), the peninsula's highest dune, south of Preila, stands on a ridge called Old Inn Hill – named after an inn that stood at the foot of the dune before being buried by sand; view it from the Juodkrantė–Nida cycling path (p368).

SEAFARING WEATHERVANES

Nowhere are Juodkrantė's and Nida's seafaring roots better reflected than on top of the 19th-century wooden cottages that speckle these spit villages. A ruling in 1844 saw weathervanes or cocks used to identify fishing vessels. They quickly became ornamentation for rooftops. Originally made from tin and later from wood, these 60cm x 30cm plaques were fastened to the boat mast so other fishermen could see where a *kurėnas* (Neringa boat) had sailed. Each village had its own unique symbol – a black-and-white geometrical design – incorporated in the weathercock and then embellished with an eclectic assortment of mythical cut-outs; see the different designs first hand in the Neringa History Museum (p366).

Accommodation and eating options are limited here; don't count on cash machines. **Neringos Luize** (☎ 8-614 91000; Pervalkos gatvė 29e; mains 20-40Lt), right on the lagoon at Pervalka, is a welcome respite for cyclists on the Nida–Juodkrantė trail (p368). At the southern end of Preila is **Kuršmarių vila** (☎ 55 117; 8-685 56317; www.kursmariuvila.lt; Preilos gatvė 93; r mid-Jun–mid-Sep/mid-Sep–mid-Jun 200/140Lt; ℗ ✗), which offers both sleeping and eating under its thatched roof. Run by a fishing family, it produces some of the finest smoked fish in the area in its old smokehouse in the garden. Roach and bream are the most frequent catch in the Curonian Lagoon – pike, perch, ling and eel are less common. It's also an excellent spot to try your hand at ice-fishing, if you can brave the Lithuanian winter.

Nida
☎ 469

Lovely Nida (Nidden in German) is the largest settlement on the Lithuanian half of Curonian Spit; it's also the spit's tourist hot spot. Remnants of a former life as an old-fashioned fishing village are plain to see in its pretty wooden cottages and harbour jammed with seafaring vessels, but these days Nida makes its money from holidaymakers and busloads of Germans exploring historical East Prussia.

Natural beauty abounds here, and white-sand beaches are only a 2km walk away through hazy pine forests. To the south is the most impressive dune on the peninsula,

LITHUANIA

Parnidis Dune (Parnidžio kopa), which has steps up to its 52m summit from where there are stunning views of rippling, untouched dunes stretching into Russia.

From the late 19th century a colony of artists drew inspiration from the area. Nida developed as a tourist resort and there were five hotels by the 1930s, when the German writer Thomas Mann (1875–1955) had a summer home built here. In 1965 French philosopher Jean Paul Sartre and companion Simone de Beauvoir were granted special permission by Khrushchev to spend five days on the dunes, Lithuanian photographer Antanas Sutkus being allowed to shoot the pair in the sand.

Nida is 48km from Klaipėda and 3km from the Russian border; the town stretches for 2km, but its centre is at the southern end, behind the harbour.

INFORMATION

Balt Tours (☎ 51 190; www.balttours.lt; Naglių gatvė 18; ☺ 9am-8pm May-Sep, 9am-5pm Oct-Apr) Books bus and ferry tickets, has information on Nemunas Delta boat trips, organises ice-fishing in winter, and can arrange visas for Kaliningrad (in one/four days €125/95, plus insurance).

Bankas Snoras (Naglių gatvė 27) Currency exchange and ATM opposite the bus station.

Curonian Spit National Park Visitors Centre (Lankytojų centras; ☎ 51 256; nidainfo@nerija.lt; Naglių gatvė 8; ☺ 9am-noon & 1-5pm Mon-Thu, till 6pm Fri & Sat, till 4pm Sun May-Sep) See p362.

Laundry (☎ 8-686 39223; Taikos gatvė 4a; per load 20Lt, soap 2Lt; ☺ 11am-5pm) Shock, horror! A self-service laundry in Lithuania!

Pharmacy (☎ 52 138; Taikos gatvė 11; ☺ 8.30am-8.30pm Mon-Sat May-Sep)

Police (☎ 52 202; Taikos gatvė 5)

Post office (Taikos gatvė 15) In the Palvė Hotel.

Tourist office (☎ 52 345; info@visitneringa.lt; Taikos gatvė 4; ☺ 10am-8pm Mon-Sat, to 3pm Sun Jun-Aug, 9am-5pm Mon-Fri Sep-May) Handy office sells maps, provides info on boat trips and guides, helps book accommodation (5Lt) and stocks loads of information (including photographs) about private rooms and flats to rent.

SIGHTS & ACTIVITIES

There's plenty to keep you occupied on land and water, or you could avoid it all and simply chill out. Outside the high season, scour the beaches for speckles of amber washed up on the shores during the spring and autumn

storms, and in the depths of winter brave the frozen lagoon and ice-fish for smelt and burbot.

At the harbour, opt for a 1½-hour boat trip aboard a handsome replica of a **kurėnas** (☎ 8-682 58595; per person 30Lt), a traditional 19th-century fishing boat operating in July and August; take a lagoon cruise on more modern boats (20Lt, one hour); or sail across the lagoon to the Nemunas Delta (120Lt, five hours). For more information on boat hire, organised trips and fishing expeditions in the lagoon, contact the tourist office.

There are outlets with bicycles to hire around almost every street corner in Nida centre, including a couple run by **Lucijos Ratai** (☎ 8-682 14798; www.liucijosratai.com; bicycle per hr/day/24hr 8/30/35Lt; ☺ 9am-sunset May-Oct) near the bus station. Lucijos also offers one-way hire between Nida, Juodkrantė and Smiltynė – a huge advantage if you don't have the legs for the return journey.

North of the Harbour

Breathtaking views of Parnidis Dune can be had at the harbour, from where a pleasant waterfront lagoon promenade stretches for over 1km to a flight of steps that leads up to the **Thomas Mann Memorial Museum** (Tomo Mano memorialinis muziejus; ☎ 52 260; www.mann.lt; adult/child 3/1Lt; ☺ 10am-6pm Jun-Aug, 10am-5pm Tue-Sat Sep-May). The German writer spent just two summers with his wife and six children in the peacock-blue cottage between 1930 and 1932, before returning to Germany.

B&W photographs of Nida in its more brutal spear-fishing, crow-biting days fill the thoughtfully laid-out **Neringa History Museum** (Neringos istorijos muziejus; ☎ 52 372; Pamario gatvė 53; adult/child 2/1Lt; ☺ 10am-6pm Jun–mid-Sep, 10am-5pm Mon-Sat mid-Sep–May), where Nida's tale from the Stone Age to 1939 is told. Particularly brilliant are the images of local hunters biting a crow's neck to kill the bird, followed by a taking a shot of vodka to dull the taste. Eating crows and seagulls' eggs was common on the spit in the 17th to 19th centuries, when continually drifting sands rendered previously arable land useless.

Back towards the town centre, a path leads to an 1888 red-brick **Evangelical-Lutheran church** (☺ Mass 11am Sun May-Sep). The church's peaceful woodland cemetery is pinpricked with *krikstai* – crosses carved from wood to help the deceased ascend to heaven more easily.

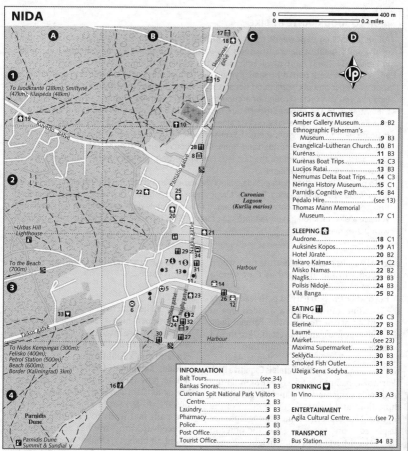

NIDA

0   400 m
0   0.2 miles

To Juodkrantė (28km); Smiltynė
(47km); Klaipėda (48km)

Curonian
Lagoon
(Kuršių marios)

Urbas Hill
Lighthouse

To the Beach
(700m)

Harbour

Harbour

To Nidos Kempingas (300m);
Feliisko (400m);
Petrol Station (500m);
Beach (600m);
Border (Kaliningrad) 3km)

Parnidis
Dune

Parnidis Dune
Summit & Sundial

LITHUANIA

Opposite is an **Amber Gallery Museum** (Gintaro galerija muzeijus; ☎ 52 712; www.ambergallery.lt; Pamario gatvė 20; ⏱ 10am-7pm mid-Apr–Sep) with a small amber garden and exceptional pieces of amber jewellery. It runs a second gallery, **Kurėnas** (Naglių gatvė 18c; ⏱ 9am-9pm mid-Apr–Sep), in a striking glass box encased in an old wooden boat near the harbour.

West of the Harbour

All westward routes lead to the beach. One way is to turn north off Taikos gatvė, opposite the post office. The street bends sharply left after 150m and climbs. A path leads up the hill to the 29.3m **Urbas Hill Lighthouse** (closed to visitors), at the highest point in the area. Continue 700m along the path behind the

lighthouse to come out on a straight path that leads back down to the main road and, 400m beyond that, to the beach.

A less adventurous option is to follow Taikos gatvė westwards until it meets the main Smiltynė–Nida road, then continue in the same direction along a paved footpath (signposted) through pine forest until you hit sand.

South of the Harbour

Heading south are two or three streets of fishing cottages with pretty flower-filled gardens. The **Ethnographic Fisherman's Museum** (Žejo etnografinė sodyba; ☎ 52 372; Naglių gatvė 4; adult/child 2/1Lt; ⏱ 10am-6pm May-Sep, 10am-5pm Tue-Sat Sep-May) is a peek at Nida in the 19th century, with

---

NIDA TO JUODKRANTĖ BY BIKE

An ab fab cycling path wends its way 30km from Nida to Juodkrantė, passing en route some of the spit's greatest natural treasures – Vecekrugas Dune (p365), an authentic fish smoker in Preila (p365) and footpaths leading from the cycling path in Karvaičiai Reservation where entire villages were buried by sand. Cycling the path also provides the perfect opportunity to spot wild boar and elk, something not so easily accomplished while seated in a car or bus. At Pervalka you can cycle through or around the village (the quicker route), arriving 4km later at the entrance to the Naglių Strict Nature Reserve (p364). Shortly afterwards, the cycling path crosses the main road to take cyclists along the opposite western side of the spit for the remaining 9km to Juodkrantė; the first 5km snake beneath pine trees alongside the main road and the final 4km skirt seaside sand dune. Once you're out of the reserve, leap into the sea for a quick cool down before the last leg – an uphill slog through forested dune to arrive in Juodkrantė behind the village.

To pick up the cycling path in Nida, follow the red-paved cycling track north along the lagoon promenade and, after passing Thomas Mann's house up top (left), follow the track left around the corner onto Puvynės gatvė. On the road, turn immediately right and follow it for 3.5km until you see a dirt track forking off left into pine forest: this is the start of the cycling path, complete with 0.0km marker.

---

original weathervanes decorating the garden, and rooms inside arranged as they were a couple of centuries ago.

Beyond Lotmiškio gatvė a path leads along the coastline and through a wooded area to a meadow at the foot of the **Parnidis Dune** (Parnidžio kopos), an unforested, 7km thread of golden sand that snakes south into Russia. In the meadow, dubbed 'Silence Valley', walkers can pick up the **Parnidis Cognitive Path** (Parnidžio pažintinis takas), a 1.8km nature trail with information panels highlighting dune flora and fauna. At the bottom of the flight of 180 steps, two dune photographs are displayed – one taken in 1960, the other in 2002. The difference in dune height – 20m in 40 years – is a warning to those keen to romp in the sand.

At the top of the spectacularly high bare dune, a panorama of sand, both coastlines, the forests to the north, and a mixture of sand and forests to the south is unforgettable. Park authorities have left the smashed remains of the granite **sundial** that stood 12m tall on the 52m dune peak until 1999, when a hurricane sent it crashing to the ground as a symbol of 'nature's uncontrollable forces' – another warning to wannabe sand rompers.

From here, the Kaliningrad border is 3km south – see the signs. If you stick to the designated wooden footpaths, you have no chance of wandering into Russia by mistake. From the dune, the Parnidis Cognitive Path continues past the lighthouse and pine forest to Taikos gatvė.

SLEEPING

Prices in Nida fluctuate wildly between winter and summer; high-season prices (June, July and August) are listed here. Camping is available at Nidos Kempingas (camping in the wild can land you a 500Lt fine).

Nidos Kempingas (☎ 52 045; www.kempingas .lt; Taikos gatvė 45a; site per tent 10-15Lt, per person 15-20Lt, car 10-15Lt, d from 230Lt, 4-/6-r studios with garden 350/490Lt; P ☏) Set in pine forest at the foot of a path that leads to Parnidis Dune, this spruced-up camp site has accommodation to suit all budgets. Double rooms have satellite TV and fridge, and apartments are fully equipped for self-caterers. There are also bikes for hire, and basketball and tennis courts to use.

Auksinės Kopos (☎ 52 387; www.auksineskopos .com; Kuverto gatvė 17; s/d from 95/150Lt; P ☒ ☏) A Soviet-era rest home still going strong, now as a hotel, thanks to the tour groups who flock to Nida. Golden Dunes surprises with its cathedral-hall lobby, stylishly pebbled outdoor-pool area and cool, crisp rooms. Bicycles and fishing equipment are available for hire.

Hotel Jūratė (☎ 52 618; www.hotel-jurate.lt; Pamario gatvė 3; s/d from 156/225Lt; P) This hotel looks and feels like a sanatorium but its supremely central position and cheap rooms help to balance things up. Soviet diehards will be thrilled to know that the hotel's most recent facelift didn't get rid of the kitsch glitter cement on the corridor walls. Austere rooms on the 3rd floor are not yet renovated.

Audrone (☎ 52 676; r withput/with balcony 200/300Lt; P) Located next to the Thomas Mann Museum, this guesthouse has enormous rooms, shared facilities (including a full kitchen) and really stunning views of the lagoon.

ourpick Misko namas (☎ 52 290; www.miskonamas.com; Pamario gatvė 11-2; r from 250Lt; P ✗) This unpretentious guesthouse is an appealing sky-blue cottage laden with flower boxes and oozing charm. Every room has a fridge, sink, and kettle and a couple have fully fledged kitchens and balconies. Guests can cook meals in a communal kitchen, hire bicycles, choose books from the small library, or laze in the garden. Jovita, the owner who turned what was once an outpatient facility into a wonderful accommodation option, is often on hand to help.

Inkaro Kaimas (☎ 52 123; www.inkarokaimas.lt; Naglių gatvė 26-1; d 250Lt; P) Blue pillars prop up this beautifully maintained red wooden house on the water's edge. The place dates from 1901 and a couple of pine-furnished rooms boast a balcony overlooking the lagoon. Look for the giant anchor in its small but sweet garden.

Poilsis Nidojė (☎ 31 698; www.neringahotels.lt; Naglių gatvė 11; d 250Lt; P ✗) Another wooden-house favourite, Poilsis Nidojė sports spacious yet cosy doubles with kitchenettes. Interior design is rustic, an optional breakfast (20Lt) is served in the kitchen around a shared table and guests can cook up dinner on a barbecue in the pretty garden.

Naglis (☎ 51 124; www.naglis.lt; Naglių gatvė 12; d/apt 250/300Lt; P) This charming guesthouse in a wooden house between the market, main street and harbour is full of smiles. Doubles comprise two rooms, and most have a door opening out to the table-dotted, tree-shaded garden. There's a dining room and kitchen for guests to share, one room has a fireplace and sauna (100Lt per hour), and the guesthouse hires out bikes (8/30Lt per hour/day).

Vila Banga (☎ 51 139; www.nidosbanga.lt; Pamario gatvė 2; d 250Lt, apt 350-460Lt) This pristine wooden house with bright-blue shutters and perfect thatched roof is a gem of a guesthouse. It has seven comfortable rooms in its pinewood interior and a sauna (100Lt per hour). Prices include breakfast.

EATING

Opening hours follow the Nida standard: 10am to 10pm daily May or June to September. Out of season, little is open.

Felisko (Taikos gatvė; mains 10-20Lt) This simple place in amongst the pines is the only real spot for lunch, dinner or a drink near the beach. The smell of smoking fish is a huge enticement.

Čili Pica (☎ 8-615 69665; Naglių gatvė 16; mains 15-40Lt; ☼ 9am-3am) It may be a chain but no one seems to care. Pop in for decent pizzas and Lithuanian cuisine, and take advantage of the pavement terrace overlooking bobbing boats. After sunset it transforms into a lively bar (for Nida at least).

Užeiga Sena Sodyba (☎ 52 782; Naglių gatvė 6; mains 16-25Lt) The selection of fish dishes at this delightful wooden cottage restaurant is impressive – and inviting – but it's the pancakes that win the day here. If you're here during berry season you'll be in gastronomic heaven.

Laumė (☎ 52 335; Pamario gatvė 24-3a; mains 17-30Lt) Towards the north of town is this simple eatery offering standard international fodder such as pizza and pasta. Better yet are the awesome views and fresh air provided by the delightful flower-bedecked terrace.

Ešerinė (☎ 52 757; Naglių gatvė 2; mains 20-40Lt) With its odd Hawaiian-style construction, Ešerinė looks completely out of place. However, its vast waterfront terrace and views of the Parnidis Dune make it massively popular for dining. Choose from a variety of fish dishes or mainland Lithuanian cuisine.

Seklyčia (☎ 50 000; Lotmiškio gatvė 1; mains 30-50Lt) Lovely, lovely, lovely. With a small terrace looking directly onto the lagoon and Kaliningrad beyond, there's no better place to chow down on Curonian fish while watching the sun set behind the dune.

Self-caterers have to make do with the **Maxima supermarket** (Taikos gatvė; ☼ 7am-midnight) in the centre of town. The one-stall **market** (opposite Naglių gatvė 17) sells plastic cups of wild strawberries, cranberries and other berries picked fresh from the forest, while Nida's **smoked fish outlet** (Rūkyta žuvis; Naglių gatvė 18; ☼ 10am-10pm May-Sep), next to the bus station, has *ungurys* (long slippery eel), *starkis*

LITHUANIA

(pikeperch), *stinta* (smelt), *ešerys* (perch) and *karšis* (bream).

DRINKING & ENTERTAINMENT

People don't come to Nida to party. Should you have the uncontrollable urge, try Čili Pica (p369) or In Vino (☎ 8-655 77997; Taikos gatvė 32), the only places showing any life after dark.

Agila Cultural Centre (Taikos gatvė 4), adjoining the tourist office, has the occasional disco, film and art exhibition.

GETTING THERE & AWAY

The Nida **bus station** (☎ 54 859; Naglių gatvė 20) has services every one or two hours to/from Smiltynė (9Lt, one hour) between 6am and 8pm, stopping en route in Juodkrantė (6Lt, 35 minutes); two daily from Klaipėda bus station (9Lt, 1½ hours); and one daily at 8.90am to/from Kaliningrad (22.60Lt, three hours), Kaunas (56Lt, 3½ hours) and Vilnius (72Lt, six hours).

For information on ferries to Klaipėda, see p361.

NEMUNAS DELTA

☎ 441

The low-lying, marsh-dotted eastern side of the Curonian Lagoon (Kuršių marios) could be the end of the world. Tourism has scarcely touched this remote rural and isolated landscape where summer skies offer magnificent views of the spit's white dunes across the lagoon. In winter ice-fishermen sit on the frozen lagoon – up to 12km wide in places – waiting for a smelt to bite.

The gateway into the extraordinary Nemunas Delta (Nemuno Delta), where the Nemunas River ends its 937km journey from its source in neighbouring Belarus, is **Šilutė** (population 21,000), a sleepy town an hour south of Klaipėda. The cluster of islands forms a savage but beautiful landscape protected since 1992 by the **Nemunas Delta Regional Park** (Nemuno Deltos Regioninis Parkas; www .nemunodelta.lt). One-fifth of the park is water – which freezes most winters, exposing hardy residents to extreme weather conditions. **Rusnė Island**, the largest island, covers 48 sq km and increases in size by 15cm to 20cm a year.

Boat is the main form of transport; villagers travel in and out of the park by an amphibious tractor from March to mid-May, when merciless spring floods plunge about 5% of the park under water. In 1994 flood waters rose to 1.5m in places, although 40cm to 70cm is the norm. From Nida there are seasonal boats (p366) across the lagoon to the delta settlement of **Mingė** (also called Minija after the river that forms the main 'street' through the village). No more than 100 people live in Mingė – dubbed the Venice of Lithuania – and only two families still speak Lietuvinkai, an ethnic dialect of Lithuanian distinct from the delta. The 19th-century riverside houses are made of wood with reed roofs and are protected architectural monuments. A good way to explore this area is by bicycle; from Mingė a cycling track runs around **Lake Krokų Lanka**, the largest lake in the park at 4km long and 3.3km wide.

Information

An influx of government and EU money to increase tourism is steadily making the region more accessible. The immensely helpful **Šilutė tourist office** (☎ 77 795; www.siluteinfo.lt; Lietuvininkų gatvė 10; ☻ 8am-6pm Mon-Fri, 10am-4pm Sat, 9-11am Sun Jun–mid-Sep, 8am-5pm Mon-Fri mid-Sep–May), on Šilutė's main road, should be the first port of call for those seeking information on accommodation, activities and transport. Among other things, it produces a handy cycling guide to the region and the annual newspaper *Šilutės kraštas*, which covers accommodation and cultural events in the delta. The **regional park headquarters** (☎ 75 050; www.nemunodelta.lt; Pakalne gatvė 40; ☻ 8am-noon & 12.45-5pm Mon-Fri) in the tiny village of Rusnė can also help, and additionally has rooms and bicycles for hire.

Sights & Activities

In the heart of the Nemunas Delta is **Rusnė**, 8km southwest of Šilutė, where the main stream divides into three: the Atmata, the Pakalnė and the Skirvytė. In this fishing village there's nothing to do except gawp at its two badly stocked food shops, regret not bringing a picnic to enjoy on its pretty riverbanks, and visit the tiny **Ethnographic Farmstead Museum** (Etnografine Sodyba Muziejus; admission by donation; ☻ 10am-6pm Fri-Sun mid-May–mid-Sep), signposted 1.8km from the village. Exhibitions of tools, furnishings and three farm buildings (in exceptional condition considering their age) reflect the harsh face of delta life centuries ago – and today.

Dike-protected polders (land reclaimed from the sea) cover the park, the first polder being built in 1840 to protect Rusnė. The red-brick water-pumping station (1907) near the lighthouse (*švyturys*) in Uostadvaris, 8km from the bridge in Rusnė, now houses the tiny **Polder Museum** (☎ 62 230; admission by donation; ☼ variable); you can swim in the river from the small beach here. Many lower polders are still flooded seasonally and serve as valuable spawning grounds for various fish species (there are some 60 in the park). Close by, on the shores of Lake Dumblė, is Lithuania's lowest point, 1.3m below sea level.

Ventės Ragas (World's Edge) is a sparsely inhabited area on the south-pointing promontory of the delta, which, with its dramatic nature and uplifting isolation, is beautifully wild. A Teutonic Order castle was built here in the 1360s to protect shipping, only for it to collapse within a couple of hundred years due to severe storms on this isolated point. The church was rebuilt, only to be storm-wrecked again in 1702. Its stones were used to build a new church at **Kintai**, 10km north on the regional park's northeastern boundary.

Bar a few fishers' houses and the lighthouse (1862), the main attraction here is the **Ventės Ragas Ornithological Station** (☎ 68 514; adult/child 2/1Lt; ☼ 10am-5pm daily Jun-Sep, 10am-5pm Mon-Fri Oct-May), 66km south of Klaipėda at the end of the Kintai–Ventė road.

The first bird-ringing station was established here in 1929, but it was not until 1959 to 1960 that large bird traps were installed. Today, around 100,000 birds pass through the station each migratory period; zigzag, snipe, cobweb and duck traps ensnare birds

to be ringed. Two exhibition rooms inside the station explain the birdlife (below) and an observation deck encourages visitors to spot species first-hand. The station or tourist office can put you in contact with local English-speaking ornithological guides.

Sleeping & Eating

Campers can pitch tents at designated spots in the park – the regional park office can tell you where – but bring food provisions with you. Wonderful farm accommodation is spread throughout the delta and can be organised through the regional park or tourist office; many also advertise their services. Beds cost on average 50Lt a night and meals can often be arranged for a little extra; a taste of delta life, though, is priceless. Šilutė itself has two decent hotels.

Ventainė (☎ 47 422; www.ventaine.lt, in Lithuanian; Ventės Ragas; camp site per adult/car/tent 10/10/10Lt, cabins 100Lt, d from 180Lt; Ⓟ ⊠ ☐ ⬚) This complex, a 20-minute walk from the ringing station, sits on the lagoon shore with views of the spit's sandy dunes. Comfy villa rooms have fridge and heated bathroom floors, and campers are well catered for with wooden huts, camp sites and a clean, modern shower-and-toilet block. Its restaurant serves imaginative Lithuanian cuisine (mains 18Lt to 40Lt), including outstanding fish soup.

Kintai (☎ 47 339; www.kintai.lt; d/tr/q from 140/180/240Lt; Ⓟ) This hotel-restaurant and boating complex attracts guests with comfort, seclusion and a plethora of water-bound activities. All rooms come with balcony, and some literally sit on water (located in a house boat). Fishing trips can be organised, as can tours of the delta by

---

NEMUNAS BIRDLIFE

This wetland is a twitcher's heaven. Some 270 of the 330 bird species found in Lithuania frequent the Nemunas Delta Regional Park and many rare birds breed in the lush marshes around Rusnė, including black storks, white-tailed eagles, black-tailed godwits, pintails, dunlin, ruff and great snipe. The common white stork breeds like there's no tomorrow in Ventė.

The Arctic–European–East African bird migration flight path cuts through the park, making it a key spot for migratory waterfowl. But it's not just a stopover or feeding site – the park is a breeding ground for around 170 species of bird, and some, such as the pintail, don't breed anywhere else in Lithuania.

Rare aquatic warblers, corncrakes, black-headed gulls, white-winged black terns and great crested grebes have their biggest colonies in the delta. In autumn up to 200,000 birds – 80% of which are tits and finches – fly overhead at any one time in the sky above Ventės Ragas Ornithological Station (above), and up to 5000 are ringed each day for research into world migration.

boat. Find Kintai 6km east of Kintai village on the Minija River.

Laimutès (☎ 59 690; www.laimutehotel.lt; per person 150Lt; P ✗ ☎) Laimutès is an all-in-one package, offering new rooms, a wellness and sauna centre, bicycle hire, boat and farm trips, winter lake fishing, and, despite all the activities, peace and relaxation. Its restaurant only uses organic produce from local farmers, and freshly caught trout from the nearby lake. The room price includes breakfast and dinner. Find Laimutès about 15km east of Šilutè in Žemaičių Naumiestis.

Getting There & Around

Getting to the area without your own wheels is tough. In summer Šilutè is served by 10 buses a day to/from Klaipėda (11Lt, one hour), nine to/from Kaunas (35Lt, 3½ hours) and five to/from Vilnius (40Lt, 5¼ hours).

Boats are the best means of exploring the delta (it's 8km from Pakalnė to Kintai by boat but 45km by road). The main routes follow the three main delta tributaries – the Atmata (13km), Skirvytė (9km) and Pakalnė (9km) Rivers – which fan out westwards from Rusnė.

Kintai, Ventainė and Laimutès hire out boats with a boatman-guide. The offices in Šilutè can also help.

PALANGA
☎ 460 / pop 17,600

Palanga is a seaside resort with a split personality – peaceful pensioner paradise in winter, pounding party spot in summer. Tourists from all over Lithuania and abroad flock to its idyllic 10km sandy beach backed by sand dunes and scented pines.

Despite the crowds and encroaching neon, Palanga, 25km directly north of Klaipėda, retains a semblance of its traditional charm with wooden houses and the ting-a-ling of bicycle bells and pedal-powered taxis adding a quaint air to red-brick Basanavičiaus gatvė – the pedestrian heart of the action.

History

Palanga has often been Lithuania's only port over the centuries; however, it was destroyed by the Swedish in 1710. It was a resort in the 19th century, and a Soviet hot spot. After 1991, villas and holiday homes nationalised under the Soviets were slowly returned to their original owners, and family-run hotels

and restaurants opened. In 2005 the city's main pedestrian street enjoyed a facelift befitting the sparkling reputation Palanga now enjoys.

Orientation

Vytauto gatvė runs parallel to the coast about 1km inland; the tourist office and bus station are a few steps east on Kretingos gatvė. Busy Basanavičiaus gatvė – pedestrian-only between 11am and midnight in summer and lined with bars and restaurants – heads west from amber stalls at its eastern end to Palanga's famous pier on the sea. Klaipėdos plentas, the main road between Klaipėda and the Latvian border, skirts the town to the east.

MAPS
Jāņa sēta's *Palanga* town plan (1:15,000), featuring Palanga and Šventoji, costs 8Lt.

Information

Bankas Snoras Basanavičiaus (Basanavičiaus gatvė); Jūratės (cnr Vytauto & Jūratės gatvė) Blue booths with currency exchange and ATM.

Hansa Bankas (Jūratės gatvė 15)

Laukinių Vakarų Salūnas (☎ 52 831; Basanavičiaus gatvė 16; internet per hr 6Lt; ☺ 9am-7am) Saloon bar with internet room.

Palangos vaistinė (Vytauto gatvė 33; ☺ 9am-8pm Mon-Fri, 9am-6pm Sat, 9am-4pm Sun) Pharmacy in the former KGB headquarters (1944–51).

Police station (☎ 53 837; Vytauto gatvė 4)

Post office (Vytauto gatvė 53)

SEB Bankas (Vytauto gatvė 61)

Tourist office (☎ 48 811; www.palangatic.lt; Kretingos gatvė 1; ☺ 9am-7pm Mon-Fri, 10am-4pm Sat & Sun mid-Jun–Aug, 1-5pm Mon, 10am-5pm Tue-Sat Sep–mid-Jun) Books accommodation and sells maps and guides; at Palanga bus station.

Sights & Activities
BASANAVIČIAUS GATVĖ

A stroll along Basanavičiaus gatvė is a sight in itself – and the way most holidaymakers pass dusky evenings. Stalls selling amber straddle the eastern end and amusements dot its entire length – inflatable slides, bungee-jump simulators, merry-go-rounds, electric cars, portrait artists, buskers and street performers with monkeys. A discordant note amid all this party madness is struck by the small photographic display inside the **Resistance Museum** (Basanavičiaus gatvė 21); check with the tourist office for opening times and prices as it was under reconstruction at the time of writing.

From the end of Basanavičiaus gatvė, a boardwalk leads across the dunes to the **pier**. The original wooden pier dated to 1888. By day, street vendors sell popcorn, *ledai* (ice cream), *dešrainiai* (hot dogs), *alus* and *gira* here. At sunset (around 10pm in July), families and lovers gather here on the sea-facing benches to watch the sunset.

From the pier end of Basanavičiaus, a walking and cycling path wends north and south through pine forest. Skinny paths cut west onto the sandy **beach** at several points and, if you follow the main path (Meilės alėja) south onto Darius ir Girėno gatvė, you reach the Botanical Park where cycling and walking tracks are rife.

BOTANICAL PARK & AMBER MUSEUM

Lush greenery and swans gliding on still lakes make Palanga's Botanical Park a haven of peace after the frenetic-paced beach and town centre. The 1-sq-km park includes a rose garden, 18km of footpaths and **Birutė Hill** (Birutės kalnas), once a pagan shrine. According to legend, it was tended by vestal virgins, one of whom, Birutė, was kidnapped and married by Grand Duke Kęstutis. A 19th-century chapel tops the hill.

The highlight is the **Amber Museum** (Gintaro muziejus; ☎ 51 319; Vytauto gatvė 17; adult/child 5/2.50Lt; ☺ 10am-8pm Tue-Sat, to 7pm Sun Jun-Aug, 11am-5pm Tue-Sat, 11am-4pm Sun Sep-May), inside a sweeping classical palace (1897). The museum showcases the world's sixth-largest collection of Baltic gold – 20,000-odd examples in all. Visitors are welcome until one hour before closing.

NORTH OF THE BOTANICAL PARK

Fascinating B&W photos of old Palanga fill the **Dr Jono Šliūpas Memorial House** (Jono Šliūpo memorialinė sodyba; ☎ 54 559; Vytauto gatvė 23a; adult/child 2/1Lt; ☺ noon-7pm Jun-Sep, 11am-5pm Tue-Sun Oct-May), the former home of the town's first mayor.

In the late 1880s Palanga was one of the largest amber-processing centres in the Baltic, its amber products being transported to Russia then mailed on to the Caucasus, Germany and France. The town was graced with a dozen or so amber workshops, but today only the **Amber Processing Gallery** (Gintaro dirbtuvės galerija; ☎ 8-652 36644; Dariaus ir Girėno gatvė 27; admission free; ☺ 10am-8pm

May-Sep, 10am-5pm Oct-Apr) remains. Run by the Palanga guild of amber masters, the gallery sells beautiful amber pieces (jewellery, sculptures, chessboards etc). The masters ply their trade in a workshop above the gallery, where it's possible to try your hand at fashioning your own piece of amber jewellery. You'll need some Lithuanian to communicate with the gallery staff, however. Exceptional works of the Baltic gold are also for sale at **Baltijos Aukas** (Vytauto gatvė 66; ☺ 10am-9pm).

The **Antanas Mončys House Museum** (Antonio Mančio namai muziejus; ☎ 49 366; Daukanto gatvė 16; adult/child 3/1Lt; ☺ noon-5pm Tue, to 9pm Wed-Sun) displays large wooden sculptures, collages and masks by Lithuanian émigré artist Antanas Mončys (1921–93).

Festivals & Events

The highlight of the summer season is the **Palanga Summer Festival** (www.palangosvasara.lt), which opens on the first Saturday of June and closes with a massive street carnival, song festival and pop concert on the last Saturday in August. It's one long merry-go-round of music concerts of all genres.

The three-day **Palanga Seals** (Palangos ruoniai) festival in mid-February sees thousands of hardy swimmers frolic and squeal in the freezing waters of the Baltic Sea.

Sleeping

Prices listed are for the high season (June to September) when everything gets booked up fast; winter sees rates slashed by up to 50%.

BUDGET

Try haggling with one of the many locals who stand at the eastern end of Kretingos gatvė touting '*Nuomojami kambariai*' (rooms for rent) signs. Most houses on Nėries gatvė and Birutės alėja tout the same sign. Count on paying 30Lt to 100Lt a night, room quality and facilities depending. Alternatively, check with the tourist office or with Litinterp (p359) in Klaipėda, or contact room-rental agency **Palbiuras** (☎ 51 500, 8-675 42500; www.palbiuras.lt; Kretingos gatvė 12; ☺ 9am-7pm Mon-Sat).

Seklytėlė (☎ 57 415; Jūratės gatvė 18; r 100-150Lt) Above the restaurant of the same name are large rooms going for a song in summer. The furniture and bedding may not entirely match but that doesn't distract from their homey feel. The cheaper variety have shared facilities.

MIDRANGE

Ema (☎ 48 608; www.ema.lt; Jūratės gatvė 32; r from 135Lt) This basic guesthouse has stripped-back rooms in every pastel colour known to man. A cactus marks the spot.

Vila Ramybė (☎ 54 124; www.vilaramybe.lt; Vytauto gatvė 54; d 180-250Lt; P) It is tricky to snag a room at this stylish, unpretentious standout. This 1920s wooden villa is the pick of the crop as far as Vilnius trendies are concerned. Pine-clad rooms come in soothing pastel hues of blues and greens, seven of the 12 have a terrace and most have a little lounge. Its terrace restaurant is equally hip.

Vila Žaigždė (☎ 49 012; Daukanto gatvė 6; r 200-250Lt; P ✕) Žaigždė may only be steps away from Basanavičiaus gatvė, but it's miles away in atmosphere. This lovingly renovated villa has massive yet cosy rooms with a touch of romance about them, and the ground floor is given over to a popular Ukrainian restaurant. Breakfast is an extra 20Lt.

Hotel Baltic Inn (☎ 30 400; www.balticinn.lt; Daukanto gatvė 10a; s/d from 200/340Lt; P ✕ 🖥) Well placed between the botanical garden and Palanga's party central, this new hotel has modern, minimalist rooms with balconies and immaculate bathrooms.

Hotel Alanga (☎ 49 215; www.alanga.lt; Nėries gatvė 14; d/ste/apt 250/360/480Lt; P ✕ 🖥) Families will love this hotel. It has a children's playroom, nanny care, billiard room and fitness centre alongside spotlessly clean and comfortable rooms. The decor is a bit bleak but balconies are livened up with bright red dahlias.

TOP END

Corona Maris (☎ 8-610 12000; www.coronamaris.lt; Darius ir Girėno gatvė 5; d/apt 280/500Lt; P) With thoroughly modern cottages and apartments, this smart guesthouse is worth noting. Doubles have microwave and fridge; apartments have proper kitchens. Guests can hire bikes for 5Lt per hour.

Palangos Vėtra (☎ 53 032; www.vetra.lt; Daukanto gatvė 35; s/d from 320/380Lt; P ✕ 🖥 🖥) An oasis of Scandinavian glass and wood, Palangos Vėtra accommodates every guest's need. Standouts include an ATM

in the lobby, the quick-service coffee bar and small wellness centre. It's situated in a quiet area of town.

Mama Rosa (☎ 48 581; www.mamarosa.lt; Jūratės gatvė 28a; s/d from 320/420Lt; P ✕ 🖥 🖥) The height of romance, Mama Rosa has eight sweet rooms, each cosily furnished English-style with fireplace, heated bathroom floor and wrought-iron bed-heads. There is a stylish lounge, restaurant, sauna complex (130Lt for first hour) and Jacuzzi (80Lt per hour) for guests.

our pick **Hotel Palanga** (☎ 41 414; www.palanga hotel.lt; Birutės alėja 60; d 600-700Lt, 1-/2-r apt 1200/1600Lt; P ✕ 🖥 🖥 🖥) This swish hotel of glass and wood wrapped inside 80-year-old pine trees is a stunner. Rooms peer out on blue sky and tree trunk, treetop or sea (in the case of the top floor), while furnishings are subtle and luxurious, with natural hues of amber, cream and sand predominating. Some even sport their own sauna or Jacuzzi. The outdoor pool is a sparkling expanse of blue between trees while the sauna complex (free to hotel guests between 8am and 2pm) is, as the hotel bumf phrases it, 'an oasis for body and soul'.

Also recommended:

Vasaros Ambasada (☎ 8-698 08333; Meilės alėja 16; r 345Lt; P) Grumpy staff but lovely villa in the dunes. The rooftop terrace has sea views.

Pusų Paunksnėje (☎ 49 080; www.pusupauksneje .lt; Dariaus ir Girėno gatvė 25; d 700Lt, apt 800-1500Lt; P ✕ 🖥 🖥 🖥) Owned by basketball hero Arvydas Sabonis. Beautiful wooden tavern, arranged around a courtyard big enough to host a full-sized basketball/ tennis court.

Eating

Basanavičiaus gatvė plays host to the majority of restaurants in town, but the focus here is on crap rather than quality. There are, however, a few diamonds in the rough. Don't pass over your own hotel's restaurant as it could be serving some of the best food in town. For instance Seklytėlė (mains 10Lt to 30Lt) has a wonderful selection of pancakes and granny quilts for chilly evenings; Vila Žaigždė (mains 20Lt to 35Lt) whips up a Ukranian storm in its kitchen; Vila Ramybė (mains 10Lt to 30Lt) has sweet service and formidable *cepelinai;* and Pusų Paunksnėje (mains 20Lt to 50Lt) specialises in silver service.

PALANGA

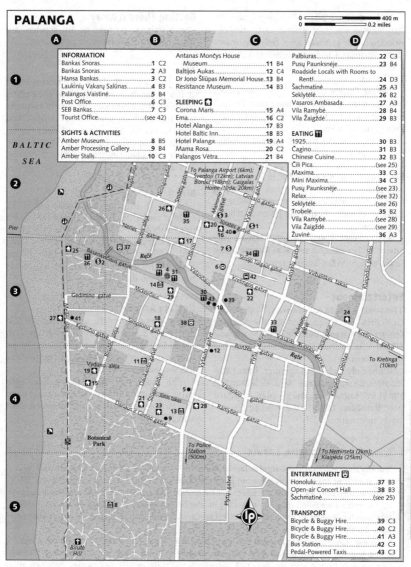

0   400 m
0   0.2 miles

BALTIC

SEA

Pier

LITHUANIA

Note: many places don't open in winter.

Trobelė (Jūratės gatvė 24; mains 10-20Lt) Drinkers and diners soak up a beer-garden atmosphere at this informal restaurant where kids run riot on swings, slides and cars while grown-ups munch herring with hot potatoes and the Lithuanian like.

Čili Pica (☎ 51 655; Basanavičiaus gatvė 45; 20/50cm pizza from 10/45Lt) This pizzeria is the face of Palanga, with its mixed crowd of kid-clad couples, noisy families and young beauties out to party. Find it propped up on candy-floss-pink pillars. Pizza delivery (☎ 1822) is also on the menu.

1925 (☎ 52 526; Basanavičiaus gatvė 4; mains 20-40Lt) Sunk down from Basanavičiaus, this old wooden house provides relief from the main-street madness. Cuisine is simple and its back garden with church view is the least Disneylike you'll find.

Chinese Cuisine (☎ 8-700 55555; Basanavičiaus gatvė 24a; mains 20-40Lt) The name may be naff but the food isn't. Take a pew on the ter-race gardens in front of a majestic villa and chow down on surprisingly decent Chinese a long way from Beijing.

Also on the main street, **Žuvinė** (☎ 48 070; Basanavičiaus gatvė 37a; fish 30-70Lt) has a reputation for fine fish dishes and **Čagino** (☎ 53 555; Basanavičiaus gatvė 14; meals 20-50Lt) for Russian cuisine. Both hide behind striking glass facades.

Self-caterers should check out **Maxima** (Plytų gatvė 9; ☼ 7am-midnight) and **Mini Maxima** (Senojo Turgaus gatvė 1; ☼ 8am-2am) supermarkets.

Entertainment

The tourist office knows what's on where. Concerts are often held at the **Open-air Concert Hall** (Vasaros Estrada; ☎ 52 210; Vytauto gatvė 43) and Vila Ramybė (p374) hosts regular live music evenings.

Clubs only kick on in summer: **Relax** (☎ 8-700 55555; Basanavičiaus gatvė 24a) and **Šachmatinė** (☎ 51 655; Basanavičiaus gatvė 45) play standard pop; **Honolulu** (☎ 8-618 57772; Neries gatvė 39) at-tracts international DJs.

Getting There & Away

Reach Palanga by road or air; services are substantially more frequent in summer.

AIR

Palanga Airport (☎ 52 020; www.palanga-airport .lt; Liepojos plentas 1), 6km north of the centre, handles twice-weekly flights in summer to/from Dublin and London Stansted Airport via Air Lithuania and daily flights to/from Copenhagen with **SAS** (☎ 52 300). There are also flights to Oslo, Moscow, and Antalya.

BUS

Services at the tiny **bus station** (☎ 53 333; Kretingos gatvė 1) include: Kaunas (48Lt, 3¼ hours, about 14 a day), Klaipėda (4.50Lt, 45 minutes, at least half-hourly between 4.15am and 10.35pm), Šiauliai (29.50Lt, three hours, eight daily) and Vilnius (63Lt, 4¼ to six hours, seven daily).

Getting Around

Bus 3 runs to/from the airport (adult/child 3/1.50Lt), roughly every hour from 7am to midnight. Timetables are posted at its town centre stop on Vytauto gatvė near the bus station.

The main taxi stand is on Kretingos gatvė in front of the bus station; a taxi from the airport into town costs between 25Lt and 30Lt.

A WACKY TRIP TO NIDA, LATVIA

Wackier than wacky is the **Gaigalas family home** (off Map p375), a crumbling homestead on a wild stretch of coastline with a garden decorated solely with trash washed up by the sea. Life rings, 'women only' signs from the beach, toothbrushes, hard hats, fishing nets, driftwood, buoys by the barrow-load: you name it, it's strung on the branch of a tree, studded on a bush, nailed to a wooden lean-to, or retooled as a sculpture. Carefully wrapped in plastic are letters washed up in bottles since 1995.

Totally ridiculous it might seem, but a visit here is a unique opportunity to peek into a local home and see the way in which far too many people in these tough postindependent climes live: water is from a well, the only sink is beneath the stars and Birute Gaigalas' only real in-come in the past 10 years has been from the odd camper she lets camp in her field, the 15kg of amber specks she's found on the beach after autumn storms, and the 100g bags of amber she sells for 20Ls.

Find the Gaigalas home in pinprick Nida, 20km north of Palanga and 2km north of the Lithuanian border in Latvia. After crossing, turn left after 200m down a mud track signposted Nida and follow it for 4km. All donations welcome: look for the orange buoy with the money-box slit.

FROM RUSSIA WITH LOVE

Deep in the forests of Žemaitija National Park resides a former secret Soviet underground missile base that once housed nuclear missiles with enough power to destroy most of Europe.

This terrifying arsenal – which consisted of 22m R12 rockets with 3m warheads – lay hidden from the Lithuanian people for at least two decades. The base, a circular underground centre, was flanked by four missile silos, only visible from the ground by their domed tops. The James Bond–style pad, which lies in Plokštinė, just a few kilometres east of the idyllic rural village of Plateliai, was equipped with electrical and radio stations, and control rooms. Ten thousand soldiers were secretly drafted in from USSR satellite states to construct the base in 1960, taking eight months to dig out the enormous 25m-deep silos. It was home to the 79th Rocket Regiment until 1978 – when the missiles mysteriously disappeared and the base was left to rot. During its history the base deployed rockets to Cuba during the crisis in September 1962 and was put on red alert during the 1968 Czechoslovakia aggression. The military town, once home to 320 soldiers, stands nearby: travellers can sleep in its barracks (p378).

In summer the base can be visited by **guided tour** (adult/child 5/2Lt; ☼ tours 10am, noon, 2pm, 4pm & 6pm May-Aug); at other times you need to ring **Žemaitija national park headquarters** (☎ 49 231; www.zemaitijosnp.lt; Didžioji gatvė 8, Plateliai; ☼ 8am-noon & 12.45-5pm Mon, 8am-6pm Tue-Fri, 10am-5pm Sat) in Plateliai to arrange a tour and/or book an English-speaking guide (30Lt per hour). Tours, which take about 30 minutes, explore the heart of the base: you see the control room, heating room, enormous diesel engine used to power the place and, most disturbing of all, one of the 27m-deep silos (6m across) where a warhead once stood ready. It is cold underground so bring a warm jumper. Sturdy shoes are also recommended; 30 years of abandonment renders the bat-infested site hazardous. A **3.2km nature trail** leads from the site into the surrounding forest and past the remains of security lines.

By car, take the road to Plateliai off the A11 (Kretinga–Šiauliai road), follow signs to Plateliai, then turn right (east) to Plokštinė following the 'Militarizmo Ekspozicija' (Military Exhibition) signs; find the base at the end of the gravel road, 5km from the Plateliai road turn-off. It's impossible to get to without your own wheels.

Pedal-powered taxis are at the eastern end of Basanavičius gatvė. From May to September, bicycle-hire stalls pepper the town. Hourly/daily rates are 8/30Lt for a bicycle, 25Lt for a four-wheel buggy for two and 25Lt for a kid's buggy.

Around Palanga

Brash **Šventoji**, 12km north, lacks the panache of Palanga but – with its inflatable fish that spit out kids, dodgem cars and merry-go-round of restaurant entertainers and fun-fair rides – it entertains. **Nemirseta**, a couple of kilometres south of Palanga, is known for its incredible sand dunes and for being the furthest east the Prussians ever got. Five buses daily run to Šventoji from Palanga, but to reach Nemirseta you'll need your own transport.

About 10km east of Palanga, the town of **Kretinga** is a sight for plant-lovers. A crumbling winter garden attached to the **Kretinga Museum** (Kretingos muziejus; ☎ 445-77 612; Vilniaus gatvė 20; adult/student 5/2Lt; ☼ museum 10am-6pm Wed-Sun, winter garden 10am-6pm Tue-Sun, cafe noon-10pm) houses a tropical mirage of 850 species of exotic plants. The museum itself is located in one of the many homes of the Tyszkiewicz family of Polish nobles.

Kretinga is connected to Palanga by frequent buses (3Lt, 15 minutes). Find the museum west of the centre in the Kretinga city park.

ŽEMAITIJA NATIONAL PARK
☎ 448 / pop 3500

After the kitsch of Palanga, arriving at Žemaitija (zhe-mai-ti-ya) National Park is equivalent to jumping into a cool and refreshing pool. The 200-sq-km park, a magical landscape of lake and forest, is as mysterious as it is beautiful, and it's easy to see why it is enshrined in fables of devils, ghosts and buried treasure. The presence of an underground Soviet missile base only adds to the park's magnetic attraction.

LITHUANIA

Information

In Plateliai the **national park headquarters** (☎ 49 231; www.zemaitijosnp.lt; Didžioji gatvė 8; ☺ 8am-noon & 12.45-5pm Mon, 8am-6pm Tue-Fri, 10am-5pm Sat) issues fishing permits (1/3Lt per day/month), arranges guides (30Lt an hour, must be booked in advance), has information on yacht, windsurfer and boat hire, and can direct you to the workshops of local folk artists. It also hosts a small exhibition on park flora and fauna and provides internet access (4Lt per hour).

Sights & Activities

Lake Plateliai (Platelių ežeras), renowned for its seven islets and seven ancient shore terraces, is the park's most stunning natural feature, and the site of midsummer celebrations on 23 and 24 June, when bonfires are lit and traditional songs sung. Legend says the lake was swept into the sky by a storm before being dropped where it lies now after the magic words *'Ale plate lej'* (the rain goes wide) were uttered.

Many traditional Samogitian festivals are celebrated in small-town **Plateliai** on its western shore, including the amazingly colourful **Shrove Tuesday Carnival**. See elaborate masks worn during the Shrovetide festivities in the old granary of **Plateliai Manor** (☎ 49 231; Didžioji gatvė 22; adult/child 2/1Lt; ☺ 10am-5pm Tue-Sat). Boats for excursions on the lake can be hired from the **Yacht Club** (☎ 8-682 42062; Ežero gatvė 40).

About 20km northeast is **Samogitian Calvary** (Žemaičių Kalvarija), built on the site of 9th- to 13th-century burial grounds. Pilgrims flock here during the first two weeks of July to climb the seven hills where 20 chapels form a 7km 'Stations of the Cross' route in commemoration of Christ's life, death and resurrection.

Plungė, 5km south of the park and the main gateway into it, is of no interest bar the modern Samogitian art (carvings, metal works, sun crosses) displayed at the **Žemaitija Art Museum** (Žemaičių dailės muziejus; ☎ 52 981; Parko gatvė 1; adult/child 2/1Lt; ☺ 10am-6pm Wed-Sun mid-May-Nov, till 5pm Nov–mid-May) inside the 19th-century Oginski Palace.

Sleeping & Eating

In July and August diehards can kip the night in the former military barracks: 15Lt gets you a bed (no hot water, no shower, one loo between everyone); the park headquarters can book you in.

Otherwise the park headquarters has a list of B&Bs (around 50Lt to 70Lt per person) in some fabulous farms and private homes in

---

A ROCKIN' GOOD TIME

A stony silence reigns over 'Lithuania's Stonehenge', as the **Orvydas Garden** (Map p355; ☎ 8-687 68325; adult/child 5/3Lt; ☺ 10am-7pm Tue-Sun) is known. Some say divine intervention was behind the prolific, obsessional carvings and fantastical creations of stonemason Kazys Orvydas (1905–89) and oldest son turned Franciscan monk Vilius (1952–92), which are packed into every nook and cranny of this unusual and peaceful garden.

Originally carved from stone and wood for the village cemetery in Salantai, the collection was hoarded at the Orvydas homestead after Khrushchev's wrath turned on religious objects in the 1960s. But most of the bizarre collection – which is not only Catholic but highly pagan – dates to the 1980s, the site being blockaded by the Soviets to prevent visitors getting to the persecuted Orvydas family. A reminder of the former Soviet presence can be seen today in the form of a rusting WWII tank in the car park. Stone and wood carvers' workshops are held at the farmstead on a regular basis, thus keeping the tradition alive. A traditional Samogitian roadside cross marks the farmstead entrance, 5km south of Salantai on the road to Plungė.

Amateur and professional geologists heading in the opposite direction can get stoned at the **Museum of Unique Stones** (☎ 76 291; Salantų gatvė 2; adult/child 5/2Lt, guide 20Lt; ☺ 10am-8pm summer, 8am-noon & 1-5pm Mon-Fri winter) in Mosėdis, 12km north of Salantai. Ranging from boulders to pebbles labelled with their origin from Scandinavia and the bottom of the Baltic Sea, the eclectic collection of stones spills out around the entire village.

Three daily buses between Kretinga and Skuodas stop in Salantai and Mosėdis. For the Orvydas Garden get off at the last stop before Salantai and walk about 1km.

the park, including the flowery lakeside home of **Marija Striaukienė** (☎ 49 152, 8-698 03485) in the village of Beržoras.

In Plateliai, **Morta Mikašauskienė** (☎ 49 117, 8-682 05059; Ežero gatvė 33; 4-bed cottages 200Lt; P) rents little wooden houses for four people; for more comfort, try **Hotel Linelis** (☎ 49 422; www.linelis.lt; Paplatelės; s/d/tr 110/140/160Lt; P ✖ ⬛), which has a fine restaurant and spa centre on the lake's eastern edge. Eating options are limited, but you could do worse than dine in Plateliai's **Yacht Club** (mains 10-20Lt), which has a limited menu but breathtaking lake views.

Getting There & Away

Plungė is best reached by train from Klaipėda (11.60Lt, one hour, up to five daily); from Palanga there are four direct buses (10Lt, 1¼ hours) daily. There are limited buses travelling on from Plungė to Plateliai and Žemaitija.

LITHUANIA DIRECTORY

For regional information pertaining to all three countries, see the Regional Directory, p389.

ACTIVITIES

Lithuanians love nature. People were still worshipping ancient oak trees a mere six centuries ago, and these days in their free time they make regular pilgrimages to their country's many luscious lakes and forests and long, sandy coastline. Boating, berrying, mushrooming, birdwatching and ballooning are uplifting pursuits. Travellers can walk and cycle into the wilderness, sweat in traditional lakeside saunas and enjoy ice-fishing in winter. For more details see the Great Outdoors chapter (p201) and individual destinations.

CUSTOMS

For pointers on customs regulations, see p393. The **Lithuanian Customs Department** (Map pp298-9; ☎ 5-266 6111; www.cust.lt; Jakšto gatvė 1/25; ◷ 8am-3pm Mon-Fri) in Vilnius has online updates.

From outside the EU you can import duty-free into Lithuania: 1L of spirits, 2L of wine or champagne, and 200 cigarettes or 250g of tobacco. Meat and dairy products cannot be brought in as hand luggage from outside the EU. Upon entering, you must declare foreign currency in cash above €10,000, and the same amount when exiting.

When travelling within the EU, there are no restrictions on what you can take in and out of Lithuania providing it's for personal use – with the exception of cigarettes, which are limited to 200 when leaving Lithuania for Austria, Belgium, Denmark, Finland, France, Germany, Ireland, Sweden and the UK (rule applies till the end of 2009).

Lithuania limits amber exports, but a few souvenirs should be OK providing the value doesn't exceed 3500Lt. You need a Culture Ministry permit, and pay 10% to 20% duty, to export artworks over 50 years old. Contact the **Committee of Cultural Heritage** (Map pp298-9; ☎ 5-273 4256; www.heritage.lt; Snipiškių gatvė 3, Vilnius) for info.

EMBASSIES & CONSULATES

Foreign embassies in Vilnius include the following:

Australia (Map pp298–9; ☎ 5-212 3369, emergency 8-687 11117; australia@consulate.lt; Vilniaus gatvė 23)

Belarus (Map pp298–9; ☎ 5-213 2255; www.belarus.lt; Muitinės gatvė 41)

Canada (Map pp298–9; ☎ 5-249 0950; www.canada.lt; Jogailos gatvė 4)

Denmark (Map pp294–5; ☎ 5-264 8760; www.amb vilnius.um.dk; Kosciuškos gatvė 36)

Estonia (Map pp298–9; ☎ 5-278 0200; www.estemb.lt; Mickevičiaus gatvė 4a)

Finland (Map pp298–9; ☎ 5-212 1621; www.finland.lt; Klaipėdos gatvė 6, 3rd fl)

France (Map pp298–9; ☎ 5-212 2979; www.amba france-lt.org; Švarco gatvė 1)

Germany (Map pp298–9; ☎ 5-210 6400; www.deut schebotschaft-wilna.lt; Sierakausko gatvė 24/8)

Latvia (Map pp298–9; ☎ 5-213 1260; www.latvia.lt; Čiurlionio gatvė 76)

Netherlands (Map pp298–9; ☎ 5-269 0072; www .netherlandsembassy.lt; Jogailos gatvė 4)

Norway (Map pp298–9; ☎ 5-261 0000; www.norvegija .lt; Mėsinių gatvė 5/2)

Poland (Map pp294–5; ☎ 5-270 9001; www.wilno .polemb.net; Smėlio gatvė 20a)

Russia (Map pp294–5; ☎ 5-272 1763; www.rusemb.lt; Latvių gatvė 53/54)

UK (Map pp294–5; ☎ 5-246 2900; www.britain.lt; Antakalnio gatvė 2)

USA (Map pp298–9; ☎ 5-266 5500; www.usembassy.lt; Akmenų gatvė 6)

PRACTICALITIES

- The *Baltic Times* (www.baltictimes.com; 5Lt) is published every Thursday, and has an entertainment guide that includes cinema listings.

- Listen to the BBC World Service 24 hours a day at 95.5 FM.

- For national news, pick up the most popular independent daily *Lietuvos Rytas* (www.lrytas.lt, in Lithuanian), its tabloid counterpart *Respublika* or quality business daily *Verzlio Žinios* (www.vz.lt, in Lithuanian).

- Lithuanian Airlines' in-flight magazine *Lithuania in the World,* sold in Vilnius bookshops (p293) and handed out free at Vilnius Airport, is an excellent source for insightful features on cultural and current affairs.

- Tune into state-run Lithuanian Radio (102.6 FM); M1 (106.8 FM; www.m-1.fm, in Lithuanian) for news and views; commercial channel Radiocentras (101.5 FM); or M1 Plus (106.2FM) for nonstop music.

- Public broadcaster Lithuanian TV (www.lrt.lt) puts up a good fight with LTV and its culture-driven Channel 2 against the stiff competition posed by the commercial channels, among them TV3 (www.tv3.lt, in Lithuanian), popular for American films, soaps and concerts; and BTV (www.btv.lt).

- Buy or watch videos on the PAL system.

- Plugs have two round pins; the electric current is 220V, 50Hz.

- Lithuania uses the metric system for weights and measures.

FESTIVALS & EVENTS

Lithuania's most important cultural events include its national song festival (the next will be in 2011; p34), midsummer celebrations and the Baltica Folklore Festival (p34). The **State Department of Tourism** (Map pp298-9; ☎ 5-210 8796; www.tourism.lt; Juozapavičiaus gatvė 13) posts a complete list online (in Lithuanian). See the Events Calendar, p18, for more.

HOLIDAYS

Lithuania also celebrates such days as the Day of the Lithuanian Flag (1 January), St Casimir's Day (4 March), Earth Day (20 March), Partisans' Day (fourth Sunday in May), Black Ribbon Day (23 August) and the Genocide Day of Lithuanian Jews (23 September). People still work on these days, but the national flag flutters outside most public buildings and private homes.

Public Holidays

New Year's Day 1 January
Independence Day (Nepriklausomybės diena) 16 February; anniversary of 1918 independence declaration
Lithuanian Independence Restoration Day 11 March
Easter Sunday March/April
Easter Monday March/April
International Labour Day 1 May
Mothers' Day First Sunday in May
Feast of St John (Midsummer) 24 June
Statehood Day 6 July; commemoration of coronation of Grand Duke Mindaugas in the 13th century
Assumption of Blessed Virgin 15 August
All Saints' Day 1 November
Christmas (Kalėdos) 25 and 26 December

INTERNET ACCESS

Internet use has developed at a staggering pace in Lithuania (at least in the country's larger urban centres), outstripping much of Western Europe. With the introduction of wireless technology, and more affordable PCs and laptops, an ever-increasing number of Lithuanians are becoming internet savvy. What this means for travellers is a decrease in the number of internet cafes and an increase in wi-fi hot zones. Most major cities still sport a cafe dedicated to internet access (on average 4Lt per hour) but in rural areas you'll be hard pressed to find one; in these parts you might be lucky enough to find a tourist office or library with computers linked to the web. For a listing of wi-fi hot spots in Lithuania, check www.wi fi.lt.

Almost all top-end hotels, an ever-expanding number of midrange places, and even a few budget options advertise internet access in rooms. What is actually meant by internet access varies enormously, though. Many simply have a telephone plug in the room or provide you with a cable, while others are covered by wi-fi (either free or around 5Lt per hour). Of course you'll need your laptop to use such services. A small number of places offer laptops for hire or have computers in each room.

A couple of top-end hotels in Vilnius and Kaunas have computer-equipped business centres for guests to use at a fairly substantial fee. Many budget and midrange places, meanwhile, have a computer terminal in the lobby, on which guests can surf for free. Another option is to ask to use the hotel's computer to check email (sometimes possible, sometimes not).

INTERNET RESOURCES

Useful general Baltic websites are listed on p17. Recommended sites pertaining solely to Lithuania:

Bus Tickets (www.autobusubilietai.lt) Comprehensive national and international bus information.

Countryside Vacation in Lithuania (www.country side.lt) Key site for booking farm and homestay accommodation in rural Lithuania or contacting local folk artists.

Entertainment Bank (Pramogos Lietuvoje; www.eb.lt) Entertainment and culture website, jammed with invaluable info on what's happening when across the entire country; covers eating, drinking and Lithuania with kids too.

European Information Centre (www.eic.lrs.lt) Lithuania in Europe! Read all about it.

Lithuania Statistics (www.stat.gov.lt) Crunch figures with the national statistics office.

Lithuania Travel Information (www.travel.lt) Precisely what its name says; set up by the Lithuanian Tourism Fund.

Litrail (www.litrail.lt) Train timetable and information by Lithuanian Railways.

Museums of Lithuania (www.muziejai.lt) More information than you'll ever need on Lithuania's museums.

Parliament of Lithuania (www.lrs.lt) Read all about the latest laws.

President of Lithuania (www.president.lt) Brush up on who's ruling the country.

MAPS

For regional maps, see p396. For Lithuania nothing can beat the interactive and searchable maps covering the entire country at **Maps .lt** (www.maps.lt).

In print, Lithuania is best covered by the *Lietuva* (1:400,000) road map, published by Vilnius-based map publisher **Briedis** (www

.briedis.lt; Parodu gatvė 4) and sold by the publisher online. Bookshops, tourist offices and supermarkets in Lithuania sell it for 11Lt. Jāņa sēta's *Lietuva* (1:500,000) is also worth recommending, and is available for around the same price.

For stress-free navigation buy Jāņa sēta's *miesto planas* (city maps) covering Vilnius, Kaunas and Klaipėda at a scale of 1:25,000, with a 1:10,000 inset of the centre, and Palanga (1:15,000), Šiauliai and Panevėžys (1:20,000). They cost 6Lt to 12Lt apiece in bookshops and some tourist offices.

MONEY

The Lithuanian litas (Lt) will remain firmly in place until at least 2010 when Lithuania could possibly trade in its litas for the euro. Some hotels and restaurants already list prices in euros as well as litų, but payment is still in litų only.

The litas (plural: litų or litai) is divided into 100 centai (singular: centas). It comes in note denominations of 10Lt, 20Lt, 50Lt, 100Lt, 200Lt and 500Lt and coins of 1Lt, 2Lt and 5Lt alongside the virtually worthless centai coins. Since 2002 the litas has been pegged to the euro at a fixed rate of 3.45Lt; see the inside front cover for other exchange rates.

POST

Lithuania's **postal system** (www.post.lt) is quick and cheap. Posting letters/postcards costs 2.95/2.45Lt to other EU countries, 3.35/2.90Lt outside the EU, and 1.65/1.55Lt domestically. Mail to the USA takes about 10 days, to Europe about a week. State-run EMS is the cheapest express mail service; find it in Vilnius at the central post office (p296).

TELEPHONE

Lithuania's digitised telephone network, run by **TEO** (www.teo.lt), is quick and efficient, although knowing what code to dial can be confusing.

To call other cities from a landline within Lithuania, dial ☎ 8, wait for the tone, then dial the area code and telephone number.

To make an international call from Lithuania, dial ☎ 00 followed by the country code.

To call Lithuania from abroad, dial Lithuania's country code (☎ 370), the area code and telephone number.

Then of course there are mobile telephones. No self-respecting Lithuanian would be seen without a mobile surgically attached to their

LITHUANIA

ear, and indeed, many a hotel and restaurant – especially in more rural parts – lists a mobile telephone as its main number. Mobile numbers comprise a three-digit code and a five-digit number.

To call a mobile within Lithuania, dial ☎ 8 followed by the three-digit code and mobile number. To call a mobile from abroad, dial ☎ 370 followed by the three-digit code and mobile number. This guide lists full mobile numbers; ie ☎ 8-xxx xxxxx.

Mobile companies **Bitė** (www.bite.lt), **Omnitel** (www.omnitel.lt) and **Tele 2** (www.tele2.lt) sell prepaid SIM cards; Tele2 is the only one to offer free roaming with its prepaid cards, making it the best choice for those travelling in Estonia, Latvia and Poland too. It also offers the cheapest rates.

Public telephones – increasingly rare given the widespread use of mobiles – are blue and only accept phonecards, sold in denominations of 50/75/100/200 units for 9/13/16/30Lt at newspaper kiosks.

TOURIST INFORMATION

Most towns have a tourist office with staff who usually speak at least a little English. Tourist offices range from the superbly helpful, useful and obliging to the downright useless and are coordinated by the Vilnius-based **State Department of Tourism** (Map pp298-9; ☎ 5-210 8796; www.tourism.lt; Juozapavičiaus gatvė 13). Details of tourist offices in cities and towns are given in the Information sections throughout the chapter.

For more info on Lithuania's four Unesco World Heritage sites – Neringa, Vilnius' Old Town, Kernavė, and Struve Geodetic Arcs – visit the Vilnius-based **Lithuanian National Commission for Unesco** (Map pp298-9; ☎ 5-210 7340; www .unesco.lt, in Lithuanian; Šv Jono gatvė 11, Vilnius).

Kaliningrad Excursion

Sandwiched by Poland to the south and Lithuania to the east and north, and with 148km of Baltic coastline to the west, Kaliningrad is a small Russian enclave that's intimately attached to the Motherland yet also a world apart.

In the last few years the region has started squaring up to its tourist-friendly Baltic neighbours by asserting its potential as a holiday destination. In this 'Little Russia' you'll find plenty of fine hotels and restaurants, a youthful outlook, plus all the traditions of the big parent, wrapped in a manageable package of beautiful countryside, splendid beaches and fascinating historical sights.

Annexed by Russia in 1945 (after one of the fiercest battles of WWII), Kaliningrad was previously the German kingdom of Prussia, its roots stretching back to the Teutonic Knights who ruled the Baltic in the Middle Ages from the city of Königsberg (now Kaliningrad). While Stalin ethnically cleansed the land of all Germans, centuries of Germanic culture and a legacy of castles, fortifications and domestic architecture were not as easily removed. In the go-ahead capital Kaliningrad, beside glitzy new shopping malls, the old cathedral has been rebuilt and there are plans to resurrect the castle and obliterated medieval core of the city.

If you plan to visit areas outside the region's capital, pick up a copy of Lonely Planet's *Russia & Belarus* guide.

FAST FACTS

- **Area** 15,100 sq km (region)
- **Birthplace of** Immanuel Kant; numerous cosmonauts
- **Country** Russia
- **Country code** ☎ 2 within the region, ☎ 4012 from elsewhere
- **Departure tax** none
- **Money** rouble; €1 = R39.25; US$1 = R28; UK£1 = R42.15
- **Population** 423,000
- **Official language** Russian
- **Visa** You need a Russian visa to enter Kaliningrad (see p399). Citizens of Schengen countries, the UK, Switzerland and Japan can enter with an on-demand 72-hour tourist visa. These need to be arranged via local tourist agencies, such as those listed on p384.

KALININGRAD

Pop 423,000 / ☎ 4012

A fascinating, affluent city that's clearly going places, Kaliningrad is an excellent introduction to Russia's most liberal region. Interesting museums and historical sights sprout in between shiny new shopping centres and the leafy parks and landscaped areas that soften swathes of brutal Soviet architecture. Plentiful transport options and good hotels mean you can use the city as a base to see the rest of the region.

Old photos attest that the former Königsberg was once a Middle European architectural gem equal to Prague or Krakow. The combined destruction of WWII and the Soviet decades put paid to all that. However, there are lovely prewar residential suburbs that evoke the Prussian past and make for rewarding exploration. The authorities also have big plans to remodel Kaliningrad with a mix of futuristic and heritage-inspired building projects – watch this space!

ORIENTATION

Leninsky pr, a north–south avenue, is the city's main artery, running over 3km from the bus and main train station, Yuzhny vokzal (South Station), to Severny vokzal (North Station). About halfway it crosses the Pregolya River and passes the cathedral, the city's major landmark. The city's modern heart is further north, around pl Pobedy.

INFORMATION

Baltma Tours (☎ 931 931; www.baltma.ru; pr Mira 94, 4th fl) The efficient, multilingual staff here can arrange visas, hotel accommodation, tailored city tours and a surprising array of local excursions, including one to Yantarny (42km northwest of the city), home to a huge amber mine.

Emergency Hospital (☎ 466 989; ul Nevskogo 90; ☻ 24hr)

Kaliningrad Regional Informative Educational Centre of Tourism (☎ 655 055; www.tourismkalinin grad.ru; Fish Village, ul Oktyabrskaya 2; ☻ 10am-8pm) Staffed by helpful, English-speaking staff.

King's Castle (☎ 350 782; www.kaliningradinfo.ru; Hotel Kaliningrad, Leninskiy pr 81; ☻ 8am-8pm Mon-Fri, 9am-4pm Sat) A private tourist agency that also operates as a very efficient tourist office. You can access the internet here and book city tours.

Königsberg.ru (www.konigsberg.ru) Web-based tour agency through which you can arrange visas, including the 72-hour express visa, and book hotels.

Post office (ul Chernyakhovskogo 32; internet per hr R50; ☻ post office 10am-2pm & 3-7pm Mon-Fri, 10am-2pm & 3-6pm Sat, internet room 10am-2pm & 3-10pm Mon-Sat) Internet access and postal services.

PVU (☎ 563 809, 563 804; Sovetsky pr 13, room 9) For questions or problems regarding Russian visas during your stay.

Russkaya Evropa (www.russeuropa.com) Publishes the free quarterly listings magazine *Welcome to Kaliningrad*, available in hotel lobbies, which has useful information in English on the city and region; see the website for more information.

Telekom (ul Teatralnaya 13; internet per hr R50; ☻ 9am-7pm) For long-distance calls, fax and internet access.

University Guides (foreign.lit.dep@gmail.com) Drop an email to these guys if you're looking for a student guide to show you around town.

SIGHTS

Cathedral & Around

A Unesco World Heritage site, the majestic red-brick Gothic **cathedral** (☎ 646 868; adult/student R100/50; ☻ 9am-5pm) dates back to 1333. For decades after WWII its ruins rose above the once densely populated Kant Island – now all parkland dotted with sculptures. Rebuilt during the 1990s, the cathedral is occasionally used for concerts and its ground floor has small Lutheran and Orthodox chapels. Upstairs you'll find the reconstructed carved-wood Wallenrodt Library, interesting displays of old Königsberg and objects from archaeological digs. On the top floor is an austere room with the death mask of Immanuel Kant, whose rose-marble **tomb** lies outside on the outer north side.

Crossing the nearby **Honey Bridge**, the oldest of the city's bridges, you can ponder the many padlocks that hang off its iron railings: it's customary for newlyweds to hang locks carved with their names off bridges. On the other side of the bridge is the half-timbered riverside development known as **Fish Village** (Ribnaya Derevnya). Disneylandish it may be, but this collection of hotels, tourist office, shops and restaurants is a laudable attempt to reprise some of the city's destroyed architectural heritage. The village's first phase, including the handsome new **Jubilee Footbridge**, is complete.

Königsberg's majestic castle, dating from 1255, once stood on Tsentralnaya ploshchad, north of the cathedral. Severely damaged during WWII and dynamited out of existence in the late 1960s, it was replaced by the

KALININGRAD

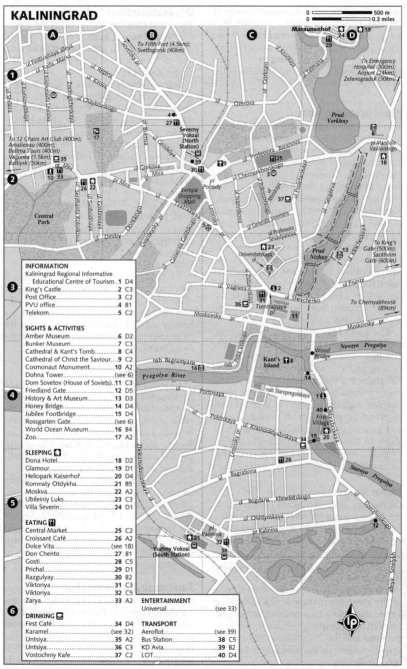

KALININGRAD EXCURSION

outstandingly ugly Dom Sovetov (House of Soviets). During the eyesore's construction it was discovered that the land below it was hollow, with a (now flooded) four-level underground passage connecting to the cathedral. The decaying half-finished building has never been used.

World Ocean Museum

Two boats and a submarine can be explored at the excellent World Ocean Museum (☎ 538 915; www.vitiaz.ru; nab Petra Velikogo 1; adult/student R200/120, individual vessels R120/80; ☺ 11am-6pm Wed-Sun Apr-Oct, 10am-5pm Wed-Sun Nov-Mar) strung along the banks of the Pregolya River. The highlight is the handsome former expedition vessel *Vityaz*, which during its heyday conducted many scientific studies around the world. It's moored alongside the *Viktor Patsaev*, named after one of Kaliningrad's famous cosmonauts; once part of the 'space flotilla', its exhibits relate to space research. Inside the B-413 submarine you can get an idea of what life was like for the 300 submariners who once lived and worked aboard.

Also part of the complex is the Maritime Hall in a newly restored old storehouse building, housing interesting displays on fishing and the sea-connected history of Kaliningrad as well as the remains of a 19th-century wooden fishing boat. There's also a pavilion with the skeleton of a 16.8m-long sperm whale, and halls with small aquariums and general information about the ocean. Visits to the *Vityaz* and *Viktor Patsaev* are by guided tour (every 45 minutes or so); you can wander freely through the sub.

Amber Museum

On the edge of Prud Verkhny (Upper Pond), the Amber Museum (☎ 466 888; www.ambermuseum .ru; pl Marshala Vasilevskogo 1; adult/student R90/60; ☺ 10am-6pm Tue-Sun) has some 6000 examples of amber artworks, the most impressive being from the Soviet period. In addition to enormous pieces of jewellery containing prehistoric insects suspended within, some of the more fascinating works include an amber flute and a four-panelled amber-and-ivory chalice depicting Columbus, the *Niña*, the *Pinta* and the *Santa Maria*. You can buy amber jewellery in the museum or from the vendors outside.

City Fortifications and Gates

The Amber Museum is housed in the attractive Dohna Tower, a bastion of the city's old defensive ring. The adjacent Rossgarten Gate, one of Königsberg's city gates, contains a decent restaurant.

Several other bits of the fortifications and gates remain scattered around the city. The impressively restored King's Gate (☎ 581 272; ul Frunze 112; adult/student R80/40; ☺ 11am-6pm Wed-Sun) houses a museum with cool models of old Königsberg and exhibits on the personalities who shaped the region's history. A little south of here is the twin-towered Sackheim Gate (cnr pr Moscovsky & Litovsky Val).

Newly restored Friedland Gate (pr Kalinina 6; adult/child R20/10; ☺ 10am-5pm Tue-Sun) contains a small museum with a great map plotting the locations of the 13 original city gates. There's an intriguing arms display, and the original cobblestone road that ran through the gate is visible inside.

At the city's northern border, along Sovietsky pr, is the Fifth Fort (Pyaty Fort). One of the city's 15 forts constructed between 1872 and 1892 as a second line of defence, it's a heavily wooded ruin that's fun to explore for its hidden passages. Take trolleybus 1 to the Pyaty Fort stop.

Other Museums

The History & Art Museum (☎ 453 844; ul Klinicheskaya 21; adult/student R70/50; ☺ 10am-6pm Tue-Sun), housed in a reconstructed 1912 concert hall by the banks of the pretty Prud Nizhny (Lower Pond), is worth a visit. Though it mainly focuses on Soviet rule, the German past is not ignored in the many interesting displays. There are chilling posters of the castle's destruction.

Cross the footbridge over Prud Nizhny and walk west towards the university to discover the fascinating Bunker Museum (☎ 536 593; Universitetskaya ul 2; adult/student R70/50; ☺ 10am-4pm Tue-Sun), the buried German command post in 1945, where the city's last German commander, Otto van Lasch, capitulated to the Soviets.

Amalienau & Maraunenhof

Casual strolls through the linden-scented, tree-lined neighbourhoods of Amalienau to the city's west along pr Mira, and Maraunenhof at the north end of Prud Verkhny, are the best way to get an idea of genteel pre-WWII Königsberg. Amalienau is particularly lovely, with an eclectic range of villas along ul Kutuzova and the streets connecting prs Pobedy and Mira. In Maraunenhof you'll find several appealing small hotels as well as the German consulate with its strikingly colourful visa section.

Ploshchad Pobedy & Prospekt Mira

Pl Pobedy is the site of several modern shopping centres and the new **Cathedral of Christ the Saviour**, its gold domes visible from many points in the city.

Extending west of the square is pr Mira, lined with shops and cafes leading to some of the city's prettiest areas. Along here you'll find the **Zoo** (☎ 218 924; pr Mira 26; adult/student R100/40; ⏱ 9am-9pm Jun-Aug, 10am-5pm Sep-May), which before WWII was considered the third best in the world, but is now in a sorry state.

Further west is the striking **Cosmonaut Monument**, a gem of Soviet iconography. This honours the several cosmonauts who hail from the region. Just west, as pr Pobedy branches out from pr Mira, is the entrance to **Central Park**, a splendid, forest-like park on the grounds of an old German cemetery.

SLEEPING

Kaliningrad is well served with midrange and top-end hotels but it's crying out for a decent hostel or budget accommodation.

Komnaty Otdykha (☎ 586 447; pl Kalinina; r R800) Inside the south train station, the 'resting rooms' are surprisingly quiet and clean, with OK shared bathrooms. Find them by turning right down the corridor after the ticket hall and walking up to the 3rd floor.

ourpick Villa Severin (☎ 365 373; www.villa-severin.ru; ul Leningradskaya 9A; s/d from R950/1900; ✗ 🖥) There's a homely atmosphere at this pretty villa, set back from Prud Verkhny, with nine comfortably furnished rooms including simple student rooms. There's also a small sauna and cafe.

Moskva (☎ 352 300; www.hotel.kaliningrad.ru; pr Mira 19; s/d from R1950/2400) Kaliningrad's oldest hotel has been reborn after extensive renovations and boasts bright spacious rooms, friendly atmosphere and a good location.

Glamour (☎ 340 000; www.glamour-hotel.ru; ul Verkhneozernaya 26; r incl breakfast from R2300; ✗ 🖥) Aspiring to boutique hotel status, the Glamour offers romantically decorated rooms, some with balconies overlooking Prud Verkhny.

Ubileiniy Luks (☎ 519 024; www.ubilejny-lux.ru; ul Universitetskaya 2; r/apt from R2500/3800; ✗ 🖥) Atop a business centre, this hotel's central, quiet location is ideal. Its 13 rooms are all enormous, and most have kitchens. Wi-fi available.

Dona Hotel (☎ 351 650; http://dona.kaliningrad.ru; pl Marshala Vasilevskogo 2; s/d incl breakfast from R2550/3050; ✗ 🖥) Featuring design touches worthy of a Philippe Starck protégé, the Dona is a tribute to sleek modernism. It has friendly English-speaking staff, buffet breakfasts, and Dolce Vita (p388), one of the city's best restaurants.

ourpick Heliopark Kaiserhof (☎ 592 222; www.heliopark.ru/eng; ul Oktyabrskaya 8; s/d incl breakfast from R3350/4150; ✗ 🖥) Anchoring Fish Village, this is a nicely designed and furnished hotel, with a central atrium and superstylish rooms.

EATING

ourpick Croissant Café (pr Mira 24; meals R100; ⏱ 9am-11pm Sun-Thu, 24hr Fri & Sat) A chic baked-goods heaven. Indulge in flaky pastries, quiches, muffins, biscuits and cakes, as well as omelettes and *bliny* (Russian-style pancakes) for breakfast.

Don Chento (☎ 937 672; Sovetsky pr 9-11; meals R100-200; ⏱ 11am-11pm) No need to endure a depressing Soviet-throwback *stolovaya* (cafeteria) for budget meals when you can dig in at the self-serve salad bar or pick a slice of pizza at this stylish chain with several branches across the city.

Razgulyay (☎ 533 689; pl Pobedy 1; meals R100-200; ⏱ 8am-10pm) The extensive buffet here features roasted meats, salads, fresh juices and other tasty selections in a cheery, folk-style setting. There's also a more formal restaurant on-site.

Zarya (☎ 213 929; pr Mira 43; meals R200-300; ⏱ 10am-3am) Fashionable brasserie in the lobby of the Scala cinema that also has an attractive outdoor area. Service can be hit-and-miss but the food is reliable.

Prichal (☎ 703 030; ul Verkhneozyornaya 2A; meals R200-500; ⏱ noon-1am Sun-Thu, noon-2am Fri & Sat) Private huts in a pretty garden overlooking Prud Verkhny make this spruced up Soviet-era Georgian restaurant a memorable dining experience.

ourpick Gosti (☎ 384 747; Maliy per 32; meals R400-800; ⏱ noon-midnight) Attached to the city's technical college, this charming restaurant has a wonderful homely atmosphere, inventive food and attentive service. At lunch everything is half-price.

Dolce Vita (☎ 351 612; http://dolcevita.kaliningrad.ru; pl Marshala Vasilevskogo 2; mains R500-1000; ⏱ noon-midnight) Bust your budget for the fantastic food at this elegant restaurant next to the Dona Hotel. The melon-and-mint gazpacho is inspired.

Self-caterers should visit the lively central market on ul Chernyakhovskogo or **Viktoriya** (Kaliningrad Plaza, Leninsky pr 30; ⏱ 10am-10pm), a large Western-style supermarket that also has a handy branch opposite the bus and train station at pl Kalinina.

DRINKING

First Café (☎ 644 829; ul Yepronovskaya 21) Kaliningrad's answer to Starbucks has three other locations in the city besides this branch opposite Fish Village. It's a stylish cafe-bar operation with a wide range of drinks, snacks and free wi-fi.

Untsiya Zhitomirskaya (ul Zhitomirskaya 22) Mira (pr Mira 58-60) Two outlets of an elegant old-world teashop and cafe serving all manner of black, green, white and fruit-flavoured teas and infusions.

Vostochniy Kafe (☎ 147 121; ul Proletarskaya 3a; meals R150-300) Paper lanterns, cushions and New Age music set the scene for lounging over pipefuls of flavoured tobacco and potfuls of green tea at this basement spot.

12 Chairs Art Club (☎ 955 900; pr Mira 67; mains R200-300) Dark and atmospheric, this arty cellar with mismatched furniture in an old German house serves cocktails, coffee and tea as well as food.

Karamel (Kaliningrad Plaza, Leninsky pr 30; ⏱ 24hr) On the 7th floor of a shopping centre, Karamel offers splendid city views, a DJ spinning top sounds and a wide range of drinks and dishes.

ENTERTAINMENT

Major DJs from Russia and Western Europe jet in for gigs at Kaliningrad's many clubs. Top picks include:

Universal (☎ 952 996; www.club-universal.com; pr Mira 43; admission from R300) Kaliningrad's classiest club.

Vagonka (☎ 956 677; www.vagonka.net; Stanochnaya ul 12; admission from R150) Best option for the under-21 crowd; drinks are cheap.

GETTING THERE & AWAY
Air

Kaliningrad's **Khrabrovo Airport** (☎ 459 426), 24km north of the city, is the hub of **KD Avia** (☎ 355 815; www.kdavia.eu; pl Pobedy 4) which has flights to 12 destinations in Russia, including Moscow and St Petersburg, as well as to France, Germany, Italy, Spain, the UK and Ukraine. Russia's largest airline, **Aeroflot** (☎ 954 805; pl Pobedy 4), flies four times daily to/from Moscow. Other airlines serving Kaliningrad include **Air Baltic** (☎ 890-6216 6872; www.airbaltic.com) serving Rīga, and **LOT** (☎ 592 121; www.lot.com; ul Oktyabrskaya 4) with flights to Warsaw.

Bus

The **bus station** (☎ 643 635; ul Zheleznodorozhnaya 7) has services to every part of the region. International destinations include: Klaipėda (R240, three hours, four daily), Kaunas/Vilnius (R465/640, six/eight hours, twice daily), Rīga (R660, nine hours, twice daily), Tallinn (R1192, 14 hours, daily), Olshtyn/Gdansk (R350/500, four/five hours, twice daily) and Warsaw (R650, nine hours, daily).

Train

There are two stations in the city: **Severny vokzal** (North Station; ☎ 601 838) and the larger **Yuzhny vokzal** (South Station; ☎ 600 888). All long-distance and many local trains go from Yuzhny vokzal, passing through but not always stopping at Severny vokzal. It's important to note that *all* trains, including local ones, run on Moscow time (minus one hour), so if a train is scheduled to depart at 10am on the timetable it will leave at 9am Kaliningrad time.

There are four trains daily to Vilnius (R1700, six hours), one daily to Berlin (R2900, 14 hours), three daily to Moscow (R2700, 23 hours) and one daily to St Petersburg (R3000, 26 hours); and every other day to Kyiv (R2500, 25 hours).

GETTING AROUND

To get to the airport, take bus 138 from the bus station (R30). Taxis ask at least R700 from the airport, and less to the airport.

Tickets for trams, trolleybuses, buses and minibuses are sold onboard (R10).

KALININGRAD EXCURSION

Regional Directory

CONTENTS

This chapter contains the nuts and bolts of travelling in the Baltic. Country-specific information can be found in the directories for Estonia (p164), Latvia (p272) and Lithuania (p379).

ACCOMMODATION

Finding a decent place in the Baltic to lay your head is generally not a problem. Tallinn, Rīga and Vilnius all have stylish choices among the many top-end hotels, with fewer midrange and budget options. Outside the capitals you'll find a wide range of guesthouses, hotels and hostels. Many old-school sanatoriums have been renovated and reopened as spa resorts; there are still a few grey, concrete Soviet mon-

---

> **THINGS CHANGE...**
>
> While prices quoted in this guide were correct at the time of research, visitors should be aware that the business situation in the region is quite volatile. Booming economies have seen high levels of inflation in recent years, and the slowing of these economies will no doubt have interesting results. Changes can also occur depending on season, demand, competition, big events and so on; some places listed may not be able to ride out the economic storm and may well be closed when you visit. Our best advice when it comes to accommodation: check the hotel website for up-to-date prices, ask the hotel for its best rates, and do some hunting around for internet bookings to find good deals.

sters lurking about (mostly in Latvia), but the Eastern Bloc blues are largely a thing of the past.

In this book, accommodation is ordered by ascending price under Budget, Midrange and Top End headings. In the Budget category (double rooms under €30), you'll find backpackers lodgings, hostels and pretty basic guesthouses and hotels (many with shared bathrooms). Our midrange listings (€30 to around €75) run the gamut from family-run guesthouses to large hotel rooms. Most rooms in this category will have private bathroom; some include breakfast in the price. Top-end listings (over €75) comprise historically set hotels, spa resorts and charming places offering something particularly unique (like antique-filled rooms or ocean views). You can expect good service, a prime location and a spacious room in tip-top shape.

The peak tourist season is from June through August. If you come then, you should book well in advance. This is essential in Tallinn, Vilnius and Rīga – and in popular summertime destinations, including the Estonian islands and all coastal resorts.

Rates published in this guide reflect peak prices. From October to April (and possibly

BOOK YOUR STAY ONLINE

For more accommodation reviews and recommendations by Lonely Planet authors, check out lonelyplanet.com/hotels. You'll find the true, insider lowdown on the best places to stay. Reviews are thorough and independent. Best of all, you can book online.

September and May), room prices typically go down by about 30% – sometimes substantially more depending on your powers of persuasion. Also keep in mind that popular seaside spots and other weekend getaway destinations are pricier on weekends than on Monday to Thursday.

B&Bs

Sharing the breakfast table with your host family each morning will give you a keen insight into local life. Sampling traditional cooking is another joy, and one that can be hard to find elsewhere.

Several agencies, both within and outside of the Baltic, arrange accommodation in private homes in several cities across Estonia, Latvia and Lithuania.

American-International Homestays (☎ 303-258 3234; www.aihtravel.com/homestays) US-based company offering homestay accommodation with dinner, transport and an English-speaking guide in any of the Baltic capitals for US$100/175 per single/double.

Litinterp (☎ 5-212 3850; www.litinterp.com; Bernardinų gatvė 7-2, Vilnius, Lithuania) As well as offering guesthouses and apartments, this company can arrange B&B accommodation with local families in Vilnius, Trakai, Kaunas, Klaipėda, Nida and Palanga; single/double from €23/41.

Rasastra Bed & Breakfast (☎ 661 6291; www .bedbreakfast.ee; Mere puiestee 4, Tallinn, Estonia) Rasastra can set you up in homes in Estonia, Latvia and Lithuania; single/double from €22/37.

Camping

In the Baltic, camp sites are found in some gorgeous natural settings – overlooking a lake or river, or tucked away in the forest – but most are difficult to reach unless you have a private vehicle. Some camp sites have permanent wooden cottages or, occasionally, brick bungalows. Cabins vary in shape and size but are usually small one-room affairs with three or four beds. Showers and toilets are nearly always communal and vary dramatically in cleanliness. Bigger camping grounds have a bar and/or cafeteria, and sauna.

Camp sites usually open in May or June and close in mid- to late September. A night in a wooden cottage typically costs €10 to €20 per person.

Estonia, in particular, has an extremely well-organised outfit overseeing camping. **RMK** (☎ 676 7532; www.rmk.ee) maintains dozens of free basic camp sites all over the country. You can pick up information from their information desk at the west gate of the Tallinn zoo (p75); the desk is open daily from mid-May to mid-September.

Farmstays

Staying in a private room in a farmhouse, rural manor or cottage is one of the region's most attractive sleeping options. Host families can provide home-cooked meals and arrange fishing, boating, horse riding, mushrooming and berrying, and other activities – for a fee. Each of the Baltic countries has its own rural tourism association through which rural accommodation can be booked.

Baltic Country Holidays (Lauku Ceļotājs; ☎ 761 7600; www.traveller.lv; Kuģu iela 11, LV-1048 Rīga) Arranges B&B accommodation in a variety of rural settings all over Latvia; it also lets whole farmhouses and cottages, and takes advance bookings for camping grounds, hotels and motels across Latvia.

Countryside Tourism of Lithuania (☎ 3740 0354; www.countryside.lt; Donelaičio gatvė 2-201, Kaunas) Arranges accommodation in farmhouses and rural cottages throughout Lithuania. A worthwhile investment is the hefty, illustrated catalogue of the extensive offerings, available in Lithuanian bookshops.

Estonian Rural Tourism (☎ 600 9999; www.maa turism.ee; Vilmsi 53b, Tallinn) An umbrella organisation for 320-odd rural tourism organisations in Estonia. The full range of accommodation – from camping and farm-based

COTTAGE RENTAL

Baltcott (www.baltcott.com) Estonia (☎ 648 5788); Latvia (☎ 6756 9435) is an Estonian company with dozens of cottages and apartments on its books, throughout Estonia and Latvia. Scour its website for a log cabin in Lahemaa National Park, a farmstead on Saaremaa, a beachside apartment in Pärnu or Jūrmala, or a city base in Tallinn or Rīga.

B&B to palaces and castle hotels – can be booked through it. The company's *Estonian Nature Travel Guide* is worth tracking down (available through the website).

Guesthouses

Small private guesthouses are a good bet for affordable travel in the Baltic. Priced somewhere between hostels and standard hotels, guesthouses typically have less than a dozen rooms and usually offer a cosier, less formal setting than other places.

Hostels

There's a growing number of hostels scattered across the Baltic, mostly concentrated in the capitals and larger cities. You'll find HI hostels (www.hihostels.com) in all of the countries. Wherever you decide to stay, book your bed well in advance if you come in the summer; you can usually score a bed in a dorm for as little as 150Kr/7Ls/34Lt (€10) in a Tallinn/Rīga/Vilnius hostel.

For a list of hostels (not comprehensive) in each country visit www.hostels.ee, www .hostellinglatvia.com and www.lithuanian hostels.org. A better source of information, especially for backpackers keen to get word-of-mouth recommendations and the nitty-gritty low-down on a place, check out Hostelworld (www.hostelworld.com), which has become the unofficial go-to website for choosing budget digs in the Baltic (especially the capitals, where competition is sometimes fierce).

Hotels

There are hotels to suit every price range, although budget hotel accommodation in the increasingly glam capitals has become dishearteningly scarce. As more cheap hotels make the effort to brighten up their image, so nightly rates are being yanked up too.

That's not to say, however, that delightfully horrible relics from the Soviet era don't exist – they do, and though they may retain that blocky, twilight-zone exterior, the interior is usually (but not always) modernised to within an inch of its life.

The midrange option – both in and outside of the capitals – is marked by a refreshing breed of small, family-run hotels. The only downside of these places is that they get booked up quickly, given the limited number of rooms they offer.

WHICH FLOOR?

Before you start traipsing up the stairs, note that in the Baltic countries the ground floor is referred to as the first floor.

Top hotels are a dime a dozen. Many are under Western management or are part of a recognised international hotel chain, while others – such as Europa Royale in Rīga, the Radisson SAS Astorija in Vilnius and the Three Sisters in Tallinn – are housed in exquisitely renovated, historic buildings dating from the 13th to 19th centuries. Tallinn has plenty of other places to relish the medieval splendour, plus there are other alluring options such as Muhu's exquisite Pädaste Manor, or the luxurious art-deco masterpiece Ammende Villa in Pärnu.

Spa Hotels

One of the newest attractions in the region, spa hotels, are an excellent place to be pampered. Even if you don't stay, you can pop in for treatments – mud baths, massages, herbal baths, and dozens of other options. Estonia has the most selections, and you'll find them in Tallinn, Saaremaa, Muhu, Pärnu, Haapsalu, Narva-Jõesuu and assorted other places. Druskininkai is Lithuania's premier spa connection, with Birštonas also popular. Latvia's spa central is Jūrmala, although Rīga has its fair share of pampering retreats.

ACTIVITIES

You'll never run out of options for outdoor amusement in the Baltic. Cycling across the picturesque countryside, hiking through lush forests, canoeing down meandering rivers, bird-watching, swimming in refreshing lakes, plus cross-country skiing in the winter are some of the region's offerings. For complete details see The Great Outdoors chapter, p201.

BUSINESS HOURS

Latvia and Lithuania follow similar hours:
Banks 9am to 5pm Monday to Thursday and 9am to 4pm Friday
Bars 11am to midnight from Sunday to Thursday, 11am to 2am Friday and Saturday
Cafes 8am to 11pm daily
Nightclubs 10pm to 5am Thursday to Saturday

Post offices 8am to 7pm Monday to Friday, 8am to 3pm Saturday
Restaurants noon to 11pm daily
Shops 10am to 7pm Monday to Friday, 10am to 4pm Saturday
Supermarkets 8am to 10pm daily

Estonia marches to a slightly different beat:
Banks 9am to 4pm Monday to Friday
Bars noon to midnight Sunday to Thursday, noon to 2am Friday and Saturday
Cafes 9am to 10pm or later daily
Nightclubs 10pm to 4am Thursday to Saturday
Post offices 8am to 6pm Monday to Friday, 9am to 3pm Saturday
Restaurants noon to midnight daily
Shops 10am to 6pm Monday to Friday, 10am to 3pm Saturday
Supermarkets 9am to 10pm daily

Reviews in this book generally won't include opening hours unless they deviate from those listed above.

CHILDREN
Travelling through the Baltic region with children in tow isn't as daunting as it used to be. Hotels generally do their best to help make kids feel at home; many have family rooms designed for parents travelling with kids, or if not most will gladly place an extra bed in the room. A number of restaurants have kids' menus. Nappies (diapers) and known-brand baby foods, including some organic ones, are widely available in big supermarkets in the capitals. Unfortunately, you won't find many high chairs, and restaurant changing rooms are yet to be invented here.

Good places to go with kids are the stretches of western coastline found throughout the region. In Estonia, Pärnu (p127) is a magnet for families, with its leafy parks, waterpark and lovely sandy beach, while two excellent kid-oriented museums are Haapsalu's Ilon's Wonderland and Tartu's Toy Museum. In Latvia, Jūrmala's shallow beaches are great for kids, and there are a couple of waterparks in the area. Sigulda (p253) is a kid-friendly destination – it's known for high-adrenaline sports but there are tamer versions for tots. Artisan houses and workshops offer a great way for kids to learn about the culture in a hands-on environment – the Ludza Craftsmen Centre and Ventspils' House of Crafts are among the more memorable.

In Lithuania the entire coastline is a playground for kids, be it the funfair amusements and in-house restaurant entertainers in Palanga and Šventoji, the dolphin and seal shows of Klaipėda's Sea Museum, or the bikes and boats to rent on the Curonian Spit. See also the sections on kids' activities in Vilnius (p311), Tallinn (p77) and Rīga (p211).

For tips and anecdotes on successful travel with the underage crowd, check out Lonely Planet's *Travel with Children*.

CLIMATE CHARTS
The Baltic climate is temperate but on the cool and damp side. It verges on the continental as you move inland where, in winter, it's up to 4°C colder than on the coasts but in summer may be a degree or two warmer. From May to September, daytime highs are normally between 14°C and 22°C. It's unusually warm if the temperature reaches the

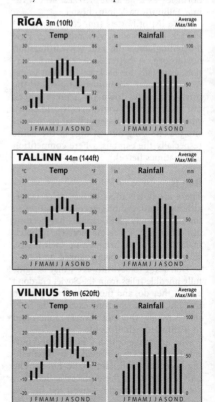

high 20s. At these northern latitudes, days are long in summer, with a full 19 hours of daylight around midsummer in Estonia. April and October have cold, sharp, wintry days as well as mild spring or autumn ones.

In winter, from November to March, temperatures rarely rise above 4°C and parts of the region may stay below freezing almost permanently from mid-December to late February. Winter hours of daylight are short, and sometimes it never seems to get properly light at all. The first snows usually come in November and there's normally permanent snow cover from January to March in the coastal regions – but up to an extra month either side in the inland east.

Annual precipitation ranges from 500mm to 600mm in the lowland areas to 700mm to 900mm in the uplands. About 75% of it falls as rain, 25% as snow. Winters can be foggy.

Coastal waters average between 16°C and 21°C in summer – July and August are the warmest. The Gulfs of Finland and Rīga freeze occasionally, and the straits between Estonia's islands and the mainland usually freeze for three months from mid-January. The open coast almost never freezes.

See also p13.

COURSES
Languages

In Lithuania, Vilnius University runs Lithuanian-language courses. An intensive two-/four-week summer course (50/100 hours) costs 1000/2000Lt, plus 100Lt registration fee. Accommodation in a student dorm or with a local family can be arranged for a fee. One-year courses are also available. For more details contact the Department of Lithuanian Studies at **Vilnius University** (☎ 5268 7215; www.lsk .flf.vu.lt; Universiteto gatvė 5, Vilnius).

In Estonia, the Tallinn University summer school has a range of language and cultural courses (see p48). In the university town of Tartu, intensive two-week courses are available for 5600Kr during summer. Contact the Language Centre of the **University of Tartu** (☎ 737 5358; www.isu.ut.ee; Näituse 2, Tartu).

Those wanting to twist their tongue around Latvian can contact the **International Language Services** (☎ 6732 5641; www.ilsriga.lv) in Rīga, or the School of Languages at the **University of Latvia** (☎ 6703 4630; www.lu.lv; Aspazijas bulvāris 5, Room 132, Rīga). At the latter, 36-hour summer courses over three weeks cost 99Ls to 124Ls.

Sculpture

Lithuania has the unique **Centre of Europe Museum** (Europos centro muziejus; ☎ 5-237 7077; www .europosparkas.lt), which runs an artists' residency program whereby artists from around the world can brainstorm with one another at the open-air sculpture park near Vilnius. Several programs are held each year and are open to anyone with an interest in applied art or sculpture. Applications must be accompanied by a CV and must be submitted two months before courses start.

CUSTOMS REGULATIONS

If you think that a painting or other cultural objects you want to buy in one of the Baltic countries may attract customs duty or require special permission to export, check with the seller before purchasing. You may have to get permission from a government office before it can be exported. For country-specific customs information see Estonia (p164), Latvia (p272) and Lithuania (p379).

DANGERS & ANNOYANCES
Theft

Crime is on the rise in the Baltic, though it's rarely of a violent nature. Pickpocketing and petty theft (bag-snatching) is a risk in all of the Baltic capitals, particularly in the busy summer season. Keep an eye out when you're exploring those enchanting old quarters. Late at night there are occasional muggings on the street. Always be mindful of your surroundings, and be sensible about where you go and who you travel with.

No matter which country you're travelling in, you should call a taxi rather than hail one on the street. You will definitely save money, and worry less if you call first. Be especially mindful of taxi drivers at airports, train stations and outside the main tourist hotels, who have a reputation (sometimes warranted, sometimes undeserved) for overcharging.

If you're driving, don't leave anything of value in your car. Car theft is less of an issue in Estonia, it's a moderate risk in Lithuania, and it's an integral part of the economy in Latvia: Rīga has one of the highest rates of car theft in the world.

Ethnic Attitudes

Some Estonians, Latvians and Lithuanians have a send-'em-home attitude towards Russians and other ex-Soviet nationalities in their midst. Racist and anti-Semitic statements are likewise not unknown to pass from some Balts' lips.

Some people might be surprised to find a certain level of hostility towards travellers attempting to communicate in Russian (patchy or otherwise).

Mosquitoes

Estonia, Latvia and Lithuania have vast stretches of forest, and yes, swampland, which is home to the mighty Baltic mosquito. Although disease is not a concern here, that may be of little consolation to you as you're being eaten alive on a late summer afternoon. Bring strong repellent (containing at least 20% DEET).

Other Creatures

Ticks are a greater health hazard than mosquitoes, as these can carry lime disease. If you're going hiking in the forest, try to cover up. See p417 for more tips.

DISCOUNT CARDS
City Discount Cards

Both Tallinn (p69) and Rīga (p191) offer discount cards to visitors; the Latvian town of Sigulda has a similar offer (p256). See the relevant sections for details.

Hostel Cards

A HI card yields discounts of up to 20% at affiliated hostels (though there are many non-HI hostels throughout the Baltic). You can buy one at some hostels en route; or purchase it before you go, via the national **Youth Hostel Association** (YHA; www.iyh f.org).

Seniors Cards

There are some discounts available to older people – museums often reduce the entrance fee, and concert and performance tickets may also be reduced for seniors, so it's always worth asking. Ferries, airlines and long-distance buses will often have seniors fares (discounts of around 10%).

Student & Youth Cards

An International Student Identity Card (ISIC) can pay for itself through half-price admissions, discounted air and ferry tickets, and cheap cinema and theatre tickets. Many stockists – generally student-travel agencies – stipulate a maximum age, usually 25. If you're aged under 26 but not a student, you can apply for an International Youth Travel Card (IYTC), which entitles you to much the same discounts as the ISIC. Both cards are administered by the **International Student Travel Confederation** (www.istc.org) and issued by student travel agencies. The ISTC website can direct you to agencies in Rīga, Tallinn and Vilnius that can issue the relevant cards.

EMBASSIES & CONSULATES

Estonia, Latvia and Lithuania each have numerous diplomatic missions overseas. Likewise, many countries have their own embassies or missions in the Baltic capitals. See Estonia (p165), Latvia (p272) and Lithuania (p379) for details.

It's important to realise what your own embassy can and can't do for you if you get into trouble. Remember that you are bound by the laws of the country you are in. Your embassy will not be sympathetic if you end up in jail after committing a crime locally, even if such actions are legal in your own country.

FESTIVALS & EVENTS

Estonia, Latvia and Lithuania all enjoy fat festival calendars encompassing everything from religion and music, to song, art, folk culture, handicrafts, film, drama and more. Summer is the busiest time of year, although each of the three Baltic countries celebrates a couple of truly magical festivals at other times of the year, too.

Most festivals are annual, others are one-off. For a comprehensive list of what's happening in the Baltic see the Events Calendar, p18.

FOOD

For details on the variety of cuisines on offer, and how to embrace/avoid the ubiquitous pork and potatoes, see the Food & Drink sections of Estonia (p57), Latvia (p185) and Lithuania (p289).

GAY & LESBIAN TRAVELLERS

When it comes to gay rights, the Baltic are still stranded in the shadows of the Dark Ages. While there is a small gay scene in Tallinn, Rīga and Vilnius, there's almost nothing elsewhere. Being 'out' here is largely out of the question, as small displays of public affection can provoke some nasty responses. Tallinn has the most progressive scene (with a couple of Old Town venues openly identifying themselves as gay clubs). Meanwhile, in the Latvian parliament, legislation has been ratified strictly banning same-sex marriage, and pride parades have been the target of homophobic protesters.

If reading all this has you yearning for a drink, you'll find permanent gay and lesbian bars listed under Entertainment in Tallinn (p88), Rīga (p222) and Vilnius (p312).

Organisations

The website of the International Lesbian and Gay Association (ILGA) of Europe (ILGA-Europe; www.ilga-europe.org) has excellent country-by-country information on gay life and acceptance in all of Europe, including the Baltic countries.

The **Gay and Lesbian Infocenter** (GLIK; ☎ 645 4545; glik@gay.ee; 2nd fl, Rüütli 16, Tallinn; ✆ 4-8pm Mon, Tue, Thu, Fri, noon-5pm Wed & Sat) is also a good source of info. The website www.gay.ee lists Tallinn's gay venues and events.

The Latvian association **Latvian Gay & Lesbian** (☎ 6959 2229; www.gay.lv in Latvian; Pastkaste iela 380, Rīga) offers advice on gay issues.

For general information, chat rooms and guides, contact Vilnius-based **Lithuanian Gay League** (☎ 5-233 3031; www.gay.lt; PO Box 2862, LT-2000 Vilnius), which publishes a solid entertainment guide in English online. Gals can befriend the Lithuanian lesbian league **Sappho** (☎ 244 0166; www.is.lt/sappho; PO Box 2204, LT-2049 Vilnius).

HOLIDAYS

Public holidays vary between countries; see the holiday information in the directories of Estonia (p165), Latvia (p273) and Lithuania (p380).

INSURANCE

A travel insurance policy to cover theft, loss of property and medical problems is a good idea. Worldwide travel insurance is available at www.lonelyplanet.com/travel_services. You can buy, extend and claim online anytime – even if you're already on the road.

Some policies offer lower and higher medical expense options. Policies can vary widely, so be sure to check the fine print. Some insurance policies will specifically exclude 'dangerous activities', which can include hiking.

You may prefer a policy that pays doctors or hospitals rather than you having to pay on the spot and claim later. If you have to claim later make sure you keep all documentation. Some

policies ask you to call back (reverse charges) to a centre in your home country where an immediate assessment of your problem is made. Check that the policy covers ambulances and an emergency flight home. For more information on health insurance, see p416.

For information on car insurance see p412.

INTERNET ACCESS

Internet use has developed at a staggering pace in the Baltic, outstripping much of Western Europe. With the introduction of wireless technology, and more affordable PCs and laptops, an ever-increasing number of locals are becoming internet savvy. What this means for travellers is a decrease in the number of internet cafes and an increase in wi-fi hotspots – Estonia in particular is virtually blanketed in wi-fi. Most major cities still sport a cafe or two dedicated to internet access (around €2 to €3 per hour), but in rural areas you'll be hard pressed to find one; in these parts you might be lucky enough to find a tourist office or library with computers linked to the web.

Almost all top-end hotels, an ever-expanding number of midrange places, and even a few budget options advertise internet access in rooms. What is actually meant by this varies enormously, though. Some simply have a telephone plug in the room or provide you with a cable, while many others are covered by wi-fi (either free or with a small charge). Of course you'll need your laptop to avail of such services. A small number of places rent laptops or have computers in each room. Many budget and midrange places, meanwhile, have a computer terminal in the lobby, on which guests can surf for free. Another option is to ask to use the hotel's computer to check email (sometimes possible, sometimes not).

Each of the countries maintains lists of hotspots you can tap into, with the vast majority of them in Estonia. See Estonia (www.wifi.ee), Lithuania (www.wifi.lt) and Latvia (www.lattelekom.lv) for details.

For excellent preplanning resources on the internet, see p17. Additionally, you'll find country-specific sites for Estonia on p166, Latvia on p273, and Lithuania on p381.

LEGAL MATTERS

If you are arrested in the Baltic you have the same basic legal rights as anywhere else in

REGIONAL DIRECTORY

LEGAL AGE

	Estonia	Latvia	Lithuania
Drinking	18	18	18
Driving	18	18	18
Sex	14	16	14

Europe. You have the right to be informed of the reason for your arrest (before being carted off to the police station) and you have the right to inform a family member of your misfortune (once you have been carted off). You cannot be detained for more than 72 hours without being charged with an offence, and you have the right to have your lawyer present during questioning.

In Rīga, you can be fined on the spot for straying from public footpaths onto the neatly mowed grass lawns in city parks. In Vilnius, you can sit/lie/sunbathe on the grass in city parks but you can't sleep; police patrol on horseback to check that your eyes aren't shut.

If you're travelling in Latvia, note that it's illegal to buy alcohol anywhere except restaurants, cafes, bars and clubs between 10pm and 8am; a similar law was in place in Tallinn (between 10pm and 10am) but was in a state of flux at the time of research.

From 2007, smoking is not permitted in restaurants, bars, nightclubs and cafes in all three countries, although it is permitted on outdoor terraces or in closed-off smoking rooms (with proper ventilation).

See also p411 for information on rules of the road.

MAPS
Decent regional and country maps are widely available outside the region, as are quality city maps in each country. A map covering the region is useful for planning: *Estonia, Latvia, Lithuania* (Cartographia; www.carto graphia.hu) has a 1:850,000-scale map of the three countries, and many publishers produce something similar. Insight Travel Maps has a useful 1:800,000 *Baltic States* map, with city plans of the three capitals.

Good maps to look for in the region include *Eesti Latvija Lietuva* (1:700,000) published by Vilnius-based Briedis (www .briedis.lt). In Estonia, EO Map (www .eomap.ee) does a pretty mean *Baltimaad*

(Baltic States, 1:800,000), which is widely available in Estonian bookshops.

In Latvia, map publisher Jāņa sēta (www .kartes.lv) is the market leader, with its pocket-size, spiral-bound, 152-page *Baltic States Road Atlas* (1:500,000) containing 72 city and town plans as well as road maps covering the entire region (including Kaliningrad). Its *Baltic States* (1:700,000) road map is equally indispensable.

The website www.maps.com is a decent digital map resource. See also p166 for Estonia, p274 for Latvia and p381 for Lithuania.

MONEY
The local currencies are Estonian krooni (Kr), Latvian lati (Ls) and Lithuanian litų – or litai – (Lt). Since 1992 when the kroon was introduced and 1993 when the lats and litas were introduced (following the dumping of the Soviet rouble), all three have remained completely stable. See the inside front cover for exchange rates.

Regionwide, Western currencies are perfectly acceptable and can be exchanged easily. Exchange rates for Polish złoty, Russian roubles, Ukrainian hrivna and other Eastern European money remain poor. Within the Baltic, it is easy to change one Baltic currency into another.

For information on costs, see the Getting Started chapter, p13. For notes on individual currencies see the country directories, Estonia (p166), Latvia (p274) and Lithuania (p381).

Although some hotels and tour operators list prices in euros, payment is always in the national currency. In this book, prices are listed in the local currencies, unless otherwise noted.

ATMs
ATMs accepting Visa and MasterCard/ Eurocard are widespread in cities and larger towns. Some are located inside banks and post offices but the majority are on the streets, outside banks and at bus and train stations, enabling you to get cash 24 hours a day. Most ATMs are multilingual, using the main European languages.

Credit Cards
Credit cards are widely accepted in hotels, restaurants and shops, especially at the

upper end of the market. Visa, MasterCard/Eurocard, Diners Club and Amex all crop up. They are essential for renting a car. With the liberal spread of ATMs, fewer banks are prepared to give cash advances on Visa and MasterCard/Eurocard – those that do, mainly in cities and larger towns, tack a 2% to 5% commission onto the amount of a cash advance. Bring along your passport if you do want a cash advance.

Moneychangers

Make sure whatever currency you bring is in good condition. Marked, torn or very used notes will be refused. US-dollar notes issued before 1990 are not generally accepted either.

Every town has somewhere you can change cash: usually a bank, exchange office or currency-exchange kiosk. The latter crop up in all sorts of places, particularly transport terminals, airports, bus stations and train stations. Rates vary from one outlet to another. Exchange places are generally open during usual business hours.

Tipping & Bargaining

It's fairly common, though not compulsory, to tip waiters 5% to 10% by rounding up the bill. A few waiters may try to tip themselves by 'not having' any change.

Some bargaining (but not a lot) goes on at flea markets. Savings are not likely to be more than 10% to 20% of the initial asking price.

Travellers Cheques

A limited amount of travellers cheques are useful because of the protection they offer against theft. It is difficult to find places to exchange them though, once you are out of the cities; most banks charge 4.5% commission.

American Express (Amex) has a representative in each capital:

Estravel (☎ 626 6266; www.estravel.ee; Suur-Karja 15, Tallinn)

Estravel Vilnius (☎ 5212 5805; www.amextravel.lt; Liejyklos gatvė 3, Vilnius)

Latvia Tours (☎ 6708 5001; www.latviatours.lv; Kaļķu iela 8, Rīga)

POST

Letters and postcards from any of the three countries take about two to four days to Western Europe, seven to 10 days to North America and two weeks to Australia, New Zealand and South Africa. Occasionally, as in any other country, a letter or parcel might go astray for a couple of weeks but generally everything arrives.

You can buy your stamps at a post office (Estonian: *postkontor;* Latvian: *pasts;* Lithuanian: *pastas*) and post your mail there. In Estonia, you can bypass the post office, buy stamps in shops and slip the envelope in any post box.

Postal rates for individual countries are listed in the country directories (see p166 for Estonia, p274 for Latvia and p381 for Lithuania). You can also check the websites of the postal companies: **Eesti Post** (www.post.ee) in Estonia, **Latvijas Pasts** (www.riga.post.lv) in Latvia and **Lietuvos Paštas** (www.post.lt) in Lithuania. Expensive international express-mail services are available in the capital cities.

The way addresses are written conform to Western norms, for example:

Kazimiera Jones
Veidenbauma iela 35-17
LV-5432 Ventspils
Latvia

Veidenbauma iela 35-17 means Veidenbaum Street, building No 35, flat No 17. Postcodes in Estonia are the letters EE plus five digits, in Latvia LV- plus four digits, and in Lithuania LT- plus five digits. For people wanting to receive mail on the move, there are poste-restante services in the main post offices in Tallinn and Vilnius, and at the post office next to Rīga train station. All three keep mail for a month. Address letters to Estonia with the full name of the recipient followed by: Poste Restante, Narva maantee 1, EE10101 Tallinn, Estonia. Letters to Latvia should be addressed as follows: Poste Restante, Rīga, LV-1050 Latvia. Letters to Lithuania: Poste Restante, Vilnius ACP, Gedimino prospektas 7, LT-01001 Vilnius, Lithuania.

SHOPPING

For traditional handicrafts, Estonia has the best selection. In Tallinn and most major centres you'll find traditional items like hand-knitted mittens and socks, lace, leather-bound books, linen, ceramics, amber, silverware and objects carved from juniper wood or limestone. The syrupy sweet and surprisingly strong liqueur Vana Tallinn also makes a nice gift.

In Vilnius you'll find an excellent selection of amber jewellery as well as plenty of handicrafts. Beautiful linens and textiles are good choices, as are glassware, wood carvings and ceramics. Amber, while not as ubiquitous as in Lithuania, is still among Latvia's top souvenirs, while country-specific offerings here include Art Nouveau-related designs, Latvian music CDs and/or a bottle of Black Balzām.

SOLO TRAVELLERS

There are enormous advantages to travelling alone: solo travellers can see and do whatever they want, wake up in the morning and let the fates decide their next destination. They meet locals and socialise with people they'd probably never have spoken to if they were travelling with others. Estonia, Latvia and Lithuania are no less rewarding for those seeking the freedom of going alone. The only drawbacks are the sometimes lonely and frustrating moments on the road. All of the Baltic countries are fairly safe destinations – Estonia, particularly so – and there's a good network of hostels sprinkled about the region, where you can meet up with other travellers along the way. The lively expat bars in each of the countries are good social places for meeting travellers. You can also check out Thorn Tree postings on Lonely Planet's website (www.lonelyplanet.com), and possibly make a few connections before or even while you're on the road.

Solo women travellers should employ the usual precautions. Though the region has its dark elements, on the whole men aren't terribly aggressive towards foreign women, and travelling in the region is no less safe than travelling through Western Europe.

TELEPHONE

City codes are a thing of the past in Estonia and Latvia, meaning if you're calling from abroad just dial the country code then the listed number. In Lithuania things are a little more complicated. Precise details on calling as well as the low-down on the local phone scene (hint: it's mobile-centric in all three countries), can be found in the country directories (see Estonia, p166; Latvia, p274; and Lithuania, p381).

Speaking of mobile phones, Estonia, Latvia and Lithuania all use GSM 900/1800 – compatible with the rest of Europe and Australia, but not with the North American GSM 1900 or the totally different system in Japan. Assuming your phone is GSM 900/1800-compatible, you can buy a cheap SIM-card package from a choice of mobile-phone providers in all three countries, and get dialling. Again, see the country directories for more details.

TIME

Estonia, Latvia and Lithuania are on Eastern European Time (GMT/UTC + 2). All three countries adhere to daylight savings, which runs from the last Sunday in March to the last Sunday in October. At this time it's GMT + 3.

The 24-hour clock is used for train, bus and flight timetables, while letters (the initial letter of each day) or numerals (I or 1 = Monday, VII or 7 = Sunday) may indicate the days of the week in posted opening hours or timetables. Dates may be listed the American way: the month first, followed by the day and the year; ie 01/06/74 referring to 6 January 1974, not 1 June 1974. If you're in any doubt, it's best to ask.

TOILETS

Public toilets in the Baltic countries are wondrous things compared to the stinking black holes of the past. Today, you'll find mostly clean, modern systems (no grubby baskets in the corner, just flush the paper). That isn't to say that we recommend spending much time in the public restrooms of train or bus stations; they aren't the most inviting of places – but you should've been here 15 years ago! Although there are public toilets in some places, you can also stroll into large hotels in major cities and use the toilets without upsetting the staff too much. Or, do

---

ANSWERING THE CALL OF NATURE

We hope you're not busting for a pee, as working out which toilet door to enter may require some thinking time. The letter 'M' marks a men's toilet in Estonian, 'V' in Latvian or Lithuanian. 'N' indicates a women's toilet in Estonian, 'S' in Latvian and 'M' in Lithuanian. Some toilets sport the triangle system: a skirt-like triangle for women and a broad-shouldered, upside-down triangle for men. To add even more confusion, in Lithuania (as in neighbouring Poland), male toilets may be indicated by a triangle and female toilets by a circle.

what everyone else does and pop into the nearest McDonald's.

TOURIST INFORMATION

All three capitals, plus most cities, towns and seaside resorts, sport an efficient tourist office of sorts that doles out accommodation lists and information brochures, many in English and often delivered with a smile. These tourist offices are coordinated by each country's national tourist board, listed under Tourist Offices in the country directories (Estonia, p166; Latvia, p274; and Lithuania, p382).

TRAVELLERS WITH DISABILITIES

With its cobbled streets, rickety pavements and old (often elevator-less) buildings, the Baltic is not user-friendly for travellers with disabilities. That said, many city hotels have rooms equipped for disabled travellers; your first port-of-call for this information should be the tourist information centres of the capitals.

Able-travel (www.able-travel.org) has excellent guides to various parts of the world – Estonia is one of the destinations featured on the website (sadly there's no information for either Latvia or Lithuania). For Estonia, they recommend the website http://liikumisvabadus.invainfo.ee, dedicated to providing information about accessibility in Estonia for wheelchair-users and those with limited movement.

In Latvia, a good first contact is **Apeirons** (☎ 729 9277; www.apeirons.lv), an organization of people with disabilities and their friends. Latvia scores oodles of brownie points from disabled travellers for having the Baltic's most disabled-friendly hotel, adjoining Jūrmala's seaside **Vaivari National Rehabilitation Centre** (☎ 6776 6122; nrc3@nrc.lv; Asaru prospketas 61, Jūrmala), which acts as an information centre for travellers with disabilities. Room rates are exceptionally reasonable.

Some beaches on the western Lithuanian coast in Nida and Palanga have ramps to allow wheelchair access to the sand, as does the above-mentioned hotel.

VISAS

Your number-one document is your passport. Make sure it's valid for at least three months after the end of your Baltic travels. Only some nationalities need visas. Citizens from the EU, Australia, Canada, Japan, New Zealand and the US do not require visas for entry into Estonia, Latvia or Lithuania.

Other nationalities should check the relevant websites of the **Ministries of Foreign Affairs** for **Estonia** (www.mig.ee), **Latvia** (www.pmlp.gov.lv) and **Lithuania** (www.migra cija.lt).

Visa Extensions

Single-entry visas can sometimes be extended in the Baltic. In Estonia go to the Tallinn office or a regional branch of the **Migration & Citizenship Board** (☎ 666 2722; www.mig.ee; Endla 13, Tallinn). In Latvia visit the foreigners' service centre of the **Office of Citizenship & Migration Affairs** (☎ 6721 9656; www.pmlp.gov.lv; Alunāna iela 1, Rīga). In Lithuania your first port of call should probably be the migration department inside the **Ministry of Interior** (☎ 5271 7112, 271 7194; www.migracija.lt; Šventaragio gatvė 2, Vilnius).

Russian Visas

Lithuania's neighbour, Kaliningrad Region, is part of Russia; St Petersburg is just a train or bus trip from any of the Baltic capitals. All Western visitors need a visa to enter Russia.

Getting the visa can be time-consuming, and our strongest advice is that you obtain one before you leave home. A tourist visa requires an invitation, which can be issued from a hotel or some hostels in Russia or from online visa specialists (like www.visatorussia.com). You'll then present your invitation and application to a Russian consulate and receive your visa a few weeks later (or an agency can do that step too, for a fee – this is recommended, as they're experts in dealing with the bureaucracy).

If you didn't get the urge to enter Russia until arriving in the Baltic, you can try your luck in obtaining a Russian visa from one of the embassies in Tallinn, Rīga or Vilnius. There you'll get a heavy dose of bureaucracy and perhaps a visa – a recent tightening of regulations means that there are no guarantees, and this might come down to your nationality. You might also consider asking a local travel agency for help in arranging a visa – **Union Travel** (Map pp62-3; ☎ 627 0627; www.uniontravel.ee, in Estonian; Lembitu 14) in Tallinn told us they could help Schengen, Australian, Canadian and American passport-holders apply for a Russian tourist visa, but not UK or New Zealand passport-holders. And a visa would take at least 10 working days.

If you want to try your luck with a Russian embassy, see Embassies & Consulates in Estonia (p165), Latvia (p272) and Lithuania (p379).

Belarusian Visas

You will need a Belarusian visa, arranged in advance, even to transit the country. Visas are not issued at road borders. Belarusian embassies in all three Baltic capitals issue visas – see www.belembassy.org for contact details. For the low-down, see the **Ministry of Foreign Affairs of the Republic of Belarus** (www.mfa.gov.by).

WOMEN TRAVELLERS

The Balts have some fairly traditional ideas about gender roles, but on the other hand they're pretty reserved and rarely impose themselves upon other people in an annoying way. Women are not likely to receive aggravation from men in the Baltic, although unaccompanied women may want to avoid a few of the sleazier bars and beer cellars. Many women travel on overnight buses and trains alone but if you're travelling on a train at night, play safe and use the hefty metal lock on the inside of the carriage door.

WORK

The Baltic region has enough difficulty keeping its own people employed, meaning there's little temporary work for visitors. Most Westerners working here have been posted by companies back home. However, these are times of change, and there is some scope for people who want to stay a while and carve themselves a new niche – though, in Western terms, you shouldn't expect to get rich doing so. The English language is certainly in demand, and you might be able to earn your keep (or part of it) teaching it in one of the main cities. On the internet, there's a wide array of databases where you can search for posts teaching abroad (www.teaching-abroad.co.uk and www.teachabroad.com).

Various volunteer placements – teaching or working in a summer camp, for example – are occasionally advertised on websites such as www.escapeartist.com, an employment overseas index which advertises international jobs and volunteer placements. Estonia has started a WWOOF system (see p54), facilitating volunteer work on organic farms in exchange for accommodation and meals. Occasionally jobs for English speakers are advertised locally in the *Baltic Times* newspaper (online at www.baltictimes.com).

Transport

GETTING THERE & AWAY

There are numerous ways of travelling into the Baltic countries, and there is certainly no need to stick with the same form of transport. It's perfectly feasible to fly or take a bus to Warsaw and then enter Lithuania by train, or fly to Helsinki and sail from there to Estonia, for example. Within the Baltic, distances are relatively small.

Flights, tours and rail tickets can be booked online at www.lonelyplanet.com/travel_services.

ENTERING ESTONIA, LATVIA & LITHUANIA

Whether you arrive by bus, boat, plane or train, entering procedures are fairly quick and painless when coming to the Baltic countries. If you're travelling from within the Schengen border zone (ie, most countries of the EU, excluding the UK and Ireland), there are no longer any arrival formalities, since Estonia, Latvia and Lithuania all joined the zone in December 2007.

Passport

Travellers arriving from outside the Schengen border zone need a passport, valid for three months beyond the planned stay. Very few nationalities need a visa for entering Estonia, Latvia or Lithuania. See p399 for more information.

AIR
Airports & Airlines

International airports in the region:
Kaunas International Airport (KUN; ☎ 37-399 307; www.kaunasair.lt)
Palanga Airport (PLQ; ☎ 460-52020; www.palanga-airport.lt)
Riga Airport (RIX; ☎ 6720 7009; www.riga-airport.com)
Tallinn Airport (TLL; ☎ 605 8888; www.tallinn-airport.ee)
Vilnius Airport (VNO; ☎ 5-273 9305; www.vilnius-airport.lt)

The national carriers in the region:
Air Baltic (airline code BT; ☎ 9000 6006; www.airbaltic.lv)
Estonian Air (airline code OV; ☎ 640 1163; www.estonian-air.ee)
Fly LAL (Lithuanian Airlines; airline code TE; ☎ 5-252 5555; www.flylal.com)

AIRLINES FLYING TO & FROM ESTONIA, LATVIA & LITHUANIA

As well as major European carriers, budget airlines like Ryanair, easyJet, Germanwings and Norwegian Air Shuttle fly into the Baltic.
Aer Lingus (airline code EI; ☎ Latvia 6735 7736, Lithuania 5-265 2690; www.flyaerlingus.com) Serves Rīga and Vilnius.
Aeroflot (airline code SU; ☎ Latvia 6724 0228, Lithuania 5-212 4189; www.aeroflot.com) Serves Rīga and Vilnius.
Air Baltic (airline code BT; ☎ Estonia 640 7750, Latvia 9000 6006, Lithuania 5-235 6000; www.airbaltic.lv) Serves Tallinn, Rīga and Vilnius.

THINGS CHANGE...

The information in this chapter is particularly vulnerable to change. Check directly with the airline or a travel agent to make sure you understand how a fare (and ticket you may buy) works and be aware of the security requirements for international travel. Shop carefully. The details given in this chapter should be regarded as pointers and are not a substitute for your own careful, up-to-date research.

Austrian Airlines (airline code OS; ☎ Latvia 6750 7700, Lithuania 5-279 1416; www.aua.com) Serves Rīga and Vilnius.

City Airline (airline code CF; www.cityairline.com) Serves Tallinn.

ČSA (Czech Airlines; airline code OK; ☎ Estonia 630 9397, Latvia 6720 7636, Lithuania 5-215 1503; www.czech-airlines.com) Serves Tallinn, Rīga and Vilnius.

easyJet (airline code U2; www.easyjet.com) Serves Tallinn and Rīga.

Estonian Air (airline code OV; ☎ Estonia 640 1163; www.estonian-air.ee) Serves Tallinn and Vilnius.

Finnair (airline code AY; ☎ Estonia 626 6309, Latvia 6720 7010, Lithuania 5-261 9339; www.finnair.com) Serves Tallinn, Rīga and Vilnius.

Fly LAL (Lithuanian Airlines; airline code TE; ☎ Estonia 605 8887, Latvia 6271 0376, Lithuania 5-252 5555; www.flylal.com) Serves Tallinn, Rīga and Vilnius.

Germanwings (airline code 4U; www.germanwings.com) Serves Rīga.

KLM (airline code KL; ☎ Estonia 699 9696, Latvia 6766 1305; www.klm.com) Serves Tallinn and Rīga.

LOT (airline code LO; ☎ Estonia 605 8355, Latvia 6720 7113, Lithuania 5-273 9020; www.lot.com) Serves Tallinn, Rīga and Vilnius.

Lufthansa (airline code LO; ☎ Estonia 681 4630, Latvia 6750 7711, Lithuania 5-232 9290; www.lufthansa.com) Serves Tallinn, Rīga and Vilnius.

Norwegian Air Shuttle (airline code DY; www.norwegian.no) Serves Tallinn, Rīga, Vilnius and Palanga.

Ryanair (airline code FR; www.ryanair.com) Serves Rīga and Kaunas.

SAS Scandinavian Airlines (airline code SK; ☎ Estonia 16663, Latvia 9000 6006, Lithuania 5-235 6000; www.scandinavian.net) Serves Tallinn, Rīga and Vilnius.

Tickets

Some of the best deals can be found by buying directly from the airlines. This is a departure from the past, where discount agencies often undercut prices. You can buy one-way tickets on no-frills carriers for half the price of a regular ticket, which will give you much more freedom in planning your itinerary.

Australia & New Zealand

There are no direct flights to the Baltic countries from Australia or New Zealand. The best option will nearly always be flying to Western Europe and connecting to your destination from there, although some Asian and Middle Eastern gateways such as Bangkok, Dubai and Hong Kong may also offer good deals. The cheapest fares to Europe are routed through Asia.

Two well-known agents for cheap fares in Australia are **STA Travel** (☎ 1300 733 035; www.statravel.com.au) and **Flight Centre** (☎ 133 133; www.flightcentre.com.au), which have dozens of offices throughout Australia.

Try **Flight Centre** (☎ 0800 243 544; www.flightcentre.co.nz) and **STA Travel** (☎ 0508 782 872; www.statravel.co.nz) in New Zealand also.

CLIMATE CHANGE & TRAVEL

Climate change is a serious threat to the ecosystems that humans rely upon, and air travel is the fastest-growing contributor to the problem. Lonely Planet regards travel, overall, as a global benefit, but believes we all have a responsibility to limit our personal impact on global warming.

Flying & Climate Change

Pretty much every form of motorised travel generates CO_2 (the main cause of human-induced climate change) but planes are far and away the worst offenders, not just because of the sheer distances they allow us to travel, but because they release greenhouse gases high into the atmosphere. The statistics are frightening: two people taking a return flight between Europe and the US will contribute as much to climate change as an average household's gas and electricity consumption over a whole year.

Carbon Offset Schemes

Climatecare.org and other websites use 'carbon calculators' that allow travellers to offset the level of greenhouse gases they are responsible for with financial contributions to sustainable travel schemes that reduce global warming – including projects in India, Honduras, Kazakhstan and Uganda.

Lonely Planet, together with Rough Guides and other concerned partners in the travel industry, support the carbon offset scheme run by climatecare.org. Lonely Planet offsets all of its staff and author travel.

For more information check out our website: www.lonelyplanet.com.

The sites www.travel.com.au and www.travel.co.nz are good for online bookings.

Continental Europe

Budget airlines have revolutionised European air transport in the past decade. Although London is the travel discount capital of Europe, there are several other cities where you'll find a wide range of good deals, namely Amsterdam, Frankfurt, Munich and Paris.

STA Travel (www.statravel.co.uk) has offices throughout Europe where cheap tickets can be purchased and STA-issued tickets can be altered (usually for a small fee); check the website for contact details. **Nouvelles Frontières** (www.nouvelles-frontieres.fr) also has branches throughout the world.

Russia, Ukraine, Transcaucasia & Central Asia

There are up to four flights daily between Moscow and each of the Baltic capitals. In Moscow, flights use Sheremetyevo I airport. There are also three to five weekly flights between each of the capitals and Kyiv (Ukraine). You can also get to and from dozens of other places in Russia, Transcaucasia and former Soviet Central Asia via a connection at Moscow.

Scandinavia

TO/FROM ESTONIA

Estonian Air and Finnair codeshare on five to seven flights daily between Tallinn and Helsinki. Flying time is only 20 minutes but the trip often ends up being no quicker than a hydrofoil (which is substantially cheaper), due to the time spent getting to and through airports.

Estonian Air also has two or three daily flights to/from Copenhagen, and between one and four daily flights connecting Tallinn and Stockholm. One or two flights service Oslo from Tallinn. Direct flights with Estonian Air also connect Stockholm and Kuressaare on Saaremaa a couple of times a week, year-round (more frequently in summer).

TO/FROM LATVIA

Air Baltic flies up to five times a day between Rīga and Helsinki, while Finnair flies the same route once or twice a day. SAS and Air Baltic codeshare on daily Rīga–Stockholm, Rīga–Copenhagen and Rīga–Oslo flights (two or three services daily in each direction). Air Baltic also has connections a couple of times a week to destinations including Gothenburg (Sweden); Billund (Denmark); Ålesund, Bergen and Stavanger (Norway); and Oulu, Tampere and Kuopio (Finland). There's one daily Air Baltic flight between Liepāja and Copenhagen. Ryanair flies between Rīga and Tampere, and Rīga and Stockholm Skavsta.

TO/FROM LITHUANIA

Air Baltic flies once or twice daily between Vilnius and Helsinki; Finnair connects the two cities also once or twice a day.

SAS and Air Baltic codeshare on two or three daily flights on the Vilnius–Copenhagen and Vilnius–Stockholm route; one daily service connects Vilnius with Oslo. Fly LAL has three weekly services between Vilnius and Stockholm.

UK & Ireland

If you're looking for a cheap flight to or from Eastern Europe, London is Europe's major centre for discounted fares. However, if you are connecting in London, remember that some 'London' airports are a huge distance from the city – you need to check before giving yourself just a few hours in transit.

For destinations in the Baltic countries, Ryanair and easyJet offer some of the best deals (just be mindful of taxes, which can be high). Ryanair operates plenty of flights into and out of Rīga, and Kaunas in Lithuania. All the national operators (Estonian Air, Air Baltic, Fly LAL) connect the Baltic capitals with London and Dublin.

Plenty of budget travel agents advertise in the travel sections of weekend newspapers and also in the **TNT Magazine** (www.tntmagazine.com) and the entertainment listings magazine *Time Out*.

TRANSPORT

TRANSPORT

IN & OUT OF ESTONIA BY HELICOPTER

Until Copterline suspended services in late 2008 (a victim of the global financial crisis), one option of arriving in Estonia was by helicopter from Helsinki. **Copterline** (www.copterline.com; Helsinki ☎ 0200-18181; Hernesaari helicopter terminal, Hernematalankatu 2B; Tallinn Map pp62-3; ☎ 610 1818Linnahall, Mere puiestee 20) flew between the capitals hourly, with a flight time of 18 minutes and a hefty one-way price range of €89 to €198 (1390Kr to 3100Kr). There is a chance that services will resume in the future – check the website.

STA Travel (☎ 0871 230 0040; www.statravel.co.uk) has 45 branches throughout the UK and sells tickets to all travellers but caters especially to young people and students. Other recommended travel agents are **Trailfinders** (☎ 0845 050 5945; www.trailfinders.co.uk), which has branches in London, Manchester, Glasgow and other large British and Irish cities; and **Flightbookers** (☎ 0870 223 5000; www.ebookers.com).

USA & Canada

Any journey to the Baltic entails a flight to Scandinavia or another European transport hub, from where there are ferry or plane connections to the region. In addition to online booking sites like **Orbitz** (www.orbitz.com), **Travelocity** (www.travelocity.com), **Expedia** (www.expedia.com) and the name-your-price service of **Priceline** (www.priceline.com), you can also try the following agents:

STA Travel (☎ 800 781 4040; www.statravel.com) Has offices in Boston, Chicago, New York, Seattle, LA and other major cities.

Travel Cuts (☎ 866 246 9762; www.travelcuts .com) Based in Canada, this outfit has offices in all major Canadian cities.

LAND
Bicycle

Bicycles can be carried cheaply (or for free) on the ferries from Scandinavia and Germany to the Baltic; see p408 for ferry routes. Pedallers through Poland face the same choice of routes as drivers; see p406 for more information.

Border Crossings

Travelling from north to south, Estonia shares borders with Russia and Latvia; Latvia shares borders with Russia, Belarus, Estonia and Lithuania; while Lithuania borders Latvia, Belarus, Poland and the Kaliningrad Region (part of Russia).

Now that the Baltic countries are part of the EU, and part of the Schengen Agreement, border crossings between Estonia, Lithuania and Latvia have been abolished.

Travel to Belarus and Russia is another matter entirely. These borders continue to be rigorously controlled, and you'll need to get a visa in advance. Expect to wait up to an hour regardless. Entering Russia (including the Kaliningrad Region) or Belarus, you must fill in a declaration form, specifying how much cash (in any currency) and what valuables you are taking into the country.

At Narva-Ivangorod, on the Estonian–Russian border, particularly long queues form. The Kaliningrad Region enjoys quieter road borders with Lithuania at Panemunė/Sovietsk, between Kybartai (Lithuania) and Nesterov, and on Curonian Spit along the Klaipėda–Zelenogradsk road. Only Belarus' road-borders with Lithuania at Salčininkai, Medininkai and Lavoriskės are open to Westerners.

Bus

With a few exceptions, buses are the cheapest but least comfortable method of reaching the Baltic. There are direct buses to/from Austria, Belgium, Czech Republic, France, Germany, Netherlands, Poland, Russia, Ukraine and Belarus. From much of the rest of Europe you can reach the Baltic with a single change of bus in Warsaw.

International services to/from the Baltic are operated by **Ecolines** (www.ecolines.net) and **Eurolines** (www.eurolines.ee). See websites for route maps, prices, schedules, ticketing agents and more; you can also purchase tickets online. Eurolines has more services within the Baltic; Ecolines has more international routes. Both companies give 10% discounts for passengers under 26 or over 60. Return tickets cost about 20% less than two one-way tickets.

Eurolines ticketing offices:

Estonia Tallinn central bus station (Map pp62–3; ☎ 680 0909; Lastekodu 46); Tartu bus station (☎ 12550; Turu 2)
Latvia (Map pp196–7; ☎ 721 4080; Prāgas iela 1) Rīga international bus station.
Lithuania Kaunas long-distance bus station (Map p340; ☎ 37-20 2020; Vytauto prospektas 38); Vilnius bus station (Map pp294–5; ☎ 5-215 1377; Sodų gatvė 24f)

Ecolines ticketing offices:

Estonia Tallinn central bus station (Map pp62–3; ☎ 5637 7997; Lastekodu 46) Just outside the main bus station.

Latvia (Map pp196–7; ☎ 6721 4512; Prāgas iela 1) Rīga international bus station.

Lithuania Vilnius bus station (Map pp294–5; ☎ 5-213 3300; Sodų gatvė 24e)

POLAND & THE CZECH REPUBLIC

Eurolines runs six weekly buses in each direction between Warsaw and Tallinn (€49, 16 hours), stopping at Kaunas, Rīga and Pärnu en route (with a bus change in Rīga). Once a week this bus continues on to Krakow (Tallinn to Krakow is around €60, 23 hours).

For travel from Lithuania to Poland, Ecolines has the most services, with about a dozen journeys a week linking Vilnius and Warsaw (€41, 8½ hours). There is also an overnight bus between Vilnius and Gdansk (€49, 10 hours), run by **Toks** (☎ 1661; www.toks .lt) in affiliation with Eurolines.

In Warsaw, buses depart from the **Western Bus Station** (Dworzec Zachodnia; al Jerozolimskie 144). Tickets are sold at the *miedzynarodowa* (international) ticket window at the bus station.

The Czech Republic has two weekly bus links to Vilnius (€57, 20 hours) with Ecolines, and two with Toks (€61, 20 hours).

RUSSIA

Estonia, Latvia and Lithuania all have bus links with the Kaliningrad Region (Russia) and the Russian motherland.

From Tallinn, Eurolines runs one bus nightly to Kaliningrad, via Pärnu, Rīga, Šiauliai and Sovietsk (Tallinn–Kaliningrad around €30, 13 hours; Rīga–Kaliningrad €20, nine hours). From Vilnius and Kaunas, there's one bus daily with Toks (€8, seven hours). Buses also travel along Curonian Spit between Klaipėda and Kaliningrad – some even travel as far north along the coast as Liepaja.

Moscow and Rīga are connected by one daily direct Ecolines bus (€41, about 15 hours); there is also a daily Ecolines service connecting Vilnius and Moscow (€41, about 16 hours).

Six or seven daily Eurolines buses connect St Petersburg and Tallinn (€25, eight hours), passing through Rakvere and Narva en route. Eurolines also operates a daily Tartu–St Petersburg service (€25, 7½ hours), and a direct nightly service between Rīga and St Petersburg (€30 to €40, 12 hours).

UKRAINE & BELARUS

Vilnius has two daily buses to Minsk (€10, four hours), with Toks; daily buses run from Rīga to Minsk, via Daugavpils (€17, 10 to 12 hours). **Vares Reisid** (☎ 665 1020; info@varesreisid.ee) offers two buses a week from Tallinn to Minsk (€38, 12½ hours), via Pärnu.

Ukraine-bound buses also pass through Belarus. Ecolines runs a six-times-weekly service between Rīga and Kyiv (€53, 16 hours). Twice a week, the bus continues to Odesa (from Rīga €63, 25 hours). From Tallinn, Ecolines has two weekly buses to Kyiv (€50, 20 hours). Toks runs nightly between Vilnius and Kyiv (€37, 12 hours).

All Western travellers need a visa to travel through Belarus. Ukraine has eased visa restrictions for many nationalities (no visa is required for visits of less than 90 days for citizens of the US, Canada, Japan and the EU; Australians and New Zealanders require a visa).

Car & Motorcycle

If you do take your own vehicle to the Baltic, get it in good condition before you leave home. Motoring clubs like the **AAA** (www.aaa .com) in the US and **AA** (☎ 0870 600 0371; www.theaa .com) and **RAC** (☎ 0800 550 055; www.rac.co.uk) in the UK are worth contacting for information on regulations, border crossing, and so on, as are Estonian, Latvian and Lithuanian embassies. For information and tips on driving once you're in the region, see p411.

DOCUMENTS

You need to bring your vehicle's registration document. If you can get it in the form of an international motor vehicle certificate, which is a translation of the basic registration document, so much the better. Motoring associations should be able to provide one. An International Driving Permit (IDP; also obtainable from motoring associations) is recommended, but if you don't have one, your own licence will suffice in most situations. All three Baltic countries demand compulsory accident insurance for drivers.

Insurance policies with limited compensation rates can be bought at the Estonian, Latvian and Lithuanian borders, costing around €30 to €50 for two weeks' insurance. Remember that you'll also need appropriate documentation for all the countries you pass through on the way to or from the Baltics; motoring associations can advise you.

POLAND & GERMANY

Bringing a vehicle into the Baltic from the south entails either a ferry trip from the German ports of Kiel, Sassnitz, Rostock or Lübeck, to Klaipėda (Lithuania) or to Ventspils or Rīga (Latvia); ferry routes are detailed on p408. Alternatively there's a hassle-free crossing of the Polish–Lithuanian border at Ogrodniki-Lazdijai, or on the road from Suwałki, Szypliszki and Budzisko (Poland) to Kalvarija and Marijampolė. Now that Lithuania and Poland are both part of the Schengen agreement, border formalities are minimal to nonexistent. The third option is a hellish (albeit fascinating) trip through Belarus.

Suckers for punishment opting for the third – and least rosy – motoring option should not attempt to even approach the border or set foot in Lukashenko land without a Belarusian transit visa, only available at Belarusian embassies. No visas are sold at any Belarus border. Those sufficiently privileged to have their visa application accepted can then expect to wait several hours, at least, at the border. A possible route is from Białystok, Poland, to Grodno in northwestern Belarus, then on to Merkinė in Lithuania; other routes include Brest–Lida–Vilnius or Brest–Minsk–Vilnius.

SCANDINAVIA

If travelling from Scandinavia, you can put your vehicle on a ferry in Denmark, Sweden or Finland (see p408), or drive to the Baltics through Russia.

From the Finnish–Russian border at Vaalimaa–Torfyanovka to St Petersburg is about 220km; from St Petersburg to the Russian/Estonian border at Ivangorod–Narva is 140km. You could do it in a day but there's little point coming this way unless you want to look at St Petersburg on the way through. Don't delay on the road from the border to St Petersburg, as it's said to be plagued by bandits.

Train

Travelling by train can be an interesting way of reaching the region – cheaper than flying and less boring than bussing it. One of the world's most memorable rail journeys figures among the approaches to the Baltic: the Trans-Siberian. Unfortunately, train service both to and within the region has been cut back markedly in recent years. There is light at the end of the tunnel, however: the **Rail Baltica Project** (www.rail-baltica.net) envisages an upgraded rail link connecting Tallinn with Rīga, Kaunas and Warsaw, and on to Berlin. It won't be completed until at least 2013.

The *Thomas Cook European Timetable* is the rail-lover's bible, giving a complete listing of train schedules, supplements and reservations information. It is updated monthly and is available from Thomas Cook outlets or from www.thomascookpublishing.com. An independent website, with loads of excellent up-to-date tips on rail travel throughout Europe, is the brilliant **Man in Seat Sixty-One** (www.seat61.com).

On the internet, you can also search in English through the timetables of the Latvian (www.ldz.lv) and Lithuanian (www.litrail.lt) railways. The website of the Estonian domestic railway, operated by **Edelerautee** (www.edel.ee), is only in Estonian (on the Estonian-language page, click on Sõiduplannid jahinnad to access the timetables and prices). For full international schedules, check out http://bahn.hafas.de.

POLAND

Surprisingly, there is no longer a direct train route operating between Warsaw and Vilnius. You can make a daytime journey on local trains from Warsaw to Kaunas or Vilnius, changing trains in Šeštokai, in Lithuania (close to the Poland-Lithuania border). Timetables are designed to give a 15-minute window to transfer. Total journey time is about 9½ hours. Note, too, that this option doesn't pass through Belarus.

RUSSIA, UKRAINE & BELARUS

The old Soviet rail network still functions over most of the former USSR. Trains linking Moscow with all the main Baltic cities enable you to combine the Baltics with a Trans-Siberian trip or other Russian or Central Asian travels. If you can make sense of it, the website www.poezda.net allows you to search timetables for trains within the former USSR, but we prefer the simpler http://bahn.hafas.de for European train schedules, although prices aren't given.

The on-again, off-again Tallinn–St Petersburg service (phased out in 2004, reintroduced in 2007, cancelled in 2008) was off at the time of research. Estonia's only rail link to Russia is via Moscow, with overnight

TRANSPORT

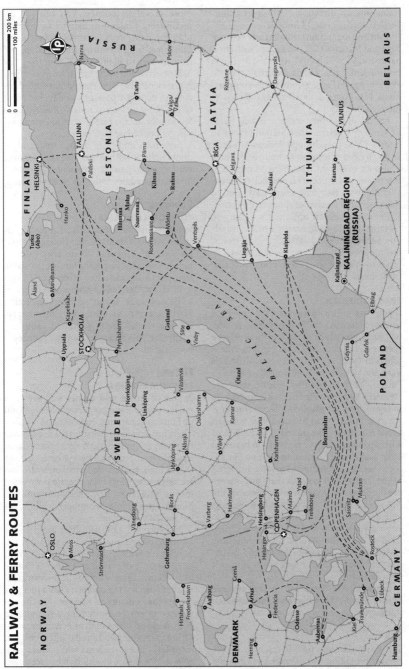

RAILWAY & FERRY ROUTES

trains in each direction (1500Kr in a four-berth compartment, 14 hours).

Two overnight trains trundle daily between Rīga and Moscow (68Ls in a four-berth compartment, 16 to 17 hours), while the overnight *Baltija* links the Latvian capital with St Petersburg (61Ls in a four-berth compartment, 12½ hours, daily). Neither train passes through Belarus.

From Vilnius, there are several daily trains to Moscow's Belarus train station (about 16 hours). These pass through Belarus, however, so you'll need a Belarusian visa (p400). There is also an overnight train from Vilnius to St Petersburg, which doesn't transit Belarus. From Vilnius, about four daily trains travel west to Kaliningrad (a journey of about seven hours).

There are several options for getting to Ukraine, but these generally involve travelling through Belarus and changing trains, meaning you'll need a visa. Your best bet is to travel to Warsaw and take a train to Ukraine from there.

TRANS-SIBERIAN

If you have the inclination and the time (and we mean lots of it), the Trans-Siberian railway will carry you much of the way between the Baltics and eastern Asia. The 9297km Trans-Siberian (proper) runs between Moscow's Yaroslavl station and Vladivostok on Russia's Pacific Coast. In summer at least, there are steamers between Vladivostok and Niigata in Japan. Straight through without stopping, the ride takes 5½ to 6½ days, but you can break it at places like Irkutsk, Ulan-Ude and Khabarovsk, and make side trips to beautiful Lake Baikal and interesting regions like remote Yakutia or Buddhist Buryatia. Branches of the Trans-Siberian with their own names are the Trans-Mongolian, which goes via the Mongolian capital, Ulaan Baatar, to Beijing; and the Trans-Manchurian, which goes to Beijing via Harbin and northeastern China. There's also the Baikal Amur Mainline (BAM), which splits from the Trans-Siberian west of Lake Baikal, running north of it, as it goes eastward.

For complete details of the journey, see Lonely Planet's comprehensive *Trans-Siberian Railway*.

SEA

There are numerous ways to reach the Baltics by sea, providing for a slower but certainly more nostalgic journey. You can sail directly from Finland to Estonia (a distance of only 85km); from Germany to Latvia and Lithuania; from Denmark to Lithuania; and from Sweden to all three Baltic countries. The Tallinn–Helsinki route has so many competing services that you should have no difficulty in getting a passage any day, but some of the other services – notably Tallinn from Stockholm and the cargo ferries to Denmark – can get booked up far in advance.

Schedules and fares change frequently – double-check both when you are planning your trip. Ferry and hydrofoil operators keep updated schedules and fares on the internet.

Denmark
TO/FROM LITHUANIA

Scandlines (www.scandlines.lt) sails twice weekly between Århus, Denmark, and Klaipėda, stopping also at Aabenraa (Denmark). Journey time is around 30 hours, the fare is €136 and to transport a car (including driver) costs €315.

DFDS Tor Line (www.dfdstorline.com) operates a 'BalticBridge' cargo service connecting Fredericia and Klaipėda, via Copenhagen, twice a week. There is limited cabin capacity for passengers to join the journey – book ahead.

Finland
TO/FROM ESTONIA

A fleet of ferries now carries well over two million people each year across the 85km Gulf of Finland separating Helsinki and Tallinn. There are dozens of crossings made each way every day (ships two to 3½ hours year-round; hydrofoils approximately 1½ hours). Note that in high winds or bad weather, hydrofoils are often cancelled; they operate only when the sea is free from ice (generally around late March/April to late December), while larger ferries sail year-round.

Shop around – the best deals are often for advance tickets purchased on the internet. Fares vary widely, depending on season, day and time of travel, and other factors – like whether there's a crisis in the world oil market (check if the company has a fuel surcharge that's included – or not – in the advertised price). Fares are generally higher at high-demand times such as Friday evening, Saturday morning and Sunday afternoon. On most ferry lines, students and seniors get a 10% to 15% discount, children between ages six and 17 pay half price and those under six sail for free. Most operators offer special deals for families and serial tickets for frequent passengers.

Operators include the following:

Eckerö Line (Map pp66-7; ☎ Tallinn 664 6000, Helsinki 0600 04300; www.eckeroline.ee) Operates the *Nordlandia* ferry, big enough to carry 2000 passengers and 450 cars. It sails once daily back and forth from Tallinn to Helsinki year-round (adult/car from €19/21, three to 3½ hours). It uses Terminal A in Tallinn and Länsi Terminal in Helsinki.

Linda Line (Map ppp62-3–00; ☎ Tallinn 699 9333, Helsinki 0600 0668970; www.lindaliini.ee) A small, independent, passenger-only hydrofoil company ploughing the waters (adult from €19, 1½ hours) up to seven times daily from around late March to late December (while the passage is ice-free). Linda Line hydrofoils arrive and depart from the well-hidden Linnahall Terminal in Tallinn, and Makasiini Terminal in Helsinki.

Nordic Jet (Map pp66-7; ☎ Tallinn 613 7000, Helsinki 0600 01655; www.njl.info) Runs two sleek, 430-seat jet catamarans, *Nordic Jet* and *Baltic Jet*, between Tallinn and Helsinki. They generally sail from May to September or later (depending on the weather); and there are up to seven crossings a day (adult/car from €28/35, 1¾ hours), docking at Terminal C in Tallinn. In Helsinki, Nordic Jet uses the catamaran harbour at Kanava Terminal.

Tallink (Map pp66-7; ☎ Tallinn 640 9808, Helsinki 09-18041; www.tallinksilja.com; Laikmaa 5, Tallinn) From Tallinn Terminal D; in Helsinki, Tallink uses Länsi Terminal. Runs at least five services daily in each direction. The huge *Baltic Princess* takes 3½ hours, the brand-new high-speed ferries *Star* and *Superstar* take two hours and operate year-round. One-way prices start at €23, with a vehicle adding an extra €20.

Viking Line (Map pp66-7; ☎ Tallinn 666 3966, Helsinki 0600-41577; www.vikingline.ee) Operates the giant car ferry *Rosella*, with two departures daily from each port (adult/car from €19/18, 2½ hours). The *Rosella* uses Tallinn Terminal A and Helsinki's Katajanokka Terminal.

Germany
TO/FROM ESTONIA
To reach Germany from Estonia you'll need to first travel to Helsinki. **Silja Line** (www.tallinksilja.com) has four weekly services between Helsinki and Rostock.

TO/FROM LATVIA
DFDS Tor Line (www.dfdstorline.lv) and **Lisco Lines** (www.lisco.lt) operate a joint service sailing three times a week between Lübeck and Rīga (car/pullman seat/berth from €123/63/83, 33 to 38 hours).

> **INTERCAPITAL TRAVEL**
>
> Buses provide the main link between each of the capitals (although there are also plenty of flights offered by the national carriers). For details on bus travel, see Tallinn (p91), Rīga (p224) and Vilnius (p320).

Scandlines (www.scandlines.lt) ferries sail between Rostock and Ventspils. Ferries depart from each port five times weekly (car/pullman seat/berth from €75/50/60, 28 hours).

TO/FROM LITHUANIA
Lisco Lines (www.lisco.lt) runs a service between Kiel and Klaipėda (car/pullman seat/berth from €78/46/75, 21 hours) six days a week. It also sails between Sassnitz and Klaipėda twice a week (car/pullman seat/berth from €64/46/73, 18 hours).

Sweden
TO/FROM ESTONIA
Tallink (www.tallinksilja.com) sails every night between Tallinn and Stockholm (car/cabin berth from €52/144, 16 hours), stopping at the Finnish island of Mariehamn en route. Ferries make the 16-hour crossing year-round, and leave from Terminal D in Tallinn and the Tallinn terminal at the Free Harbour (Frihamnen) in Stockholm.

Tallink also operates a daily ferry (predominantly for cargo) between Paldiski, 52km west of Tallinn, and Kapellskär, northeast of Stockholm.

Tallink's Tallinn–Stockholm services gets heavily booked, so make your reservation a month or two ahead.

TO/FROM LATVIA
Tallink (www.tallinksilja.com) also operates overnight services daily between Rīga and Stockholm (car/cabin berth from €52/103, 17 hours).

Scandlines (www.scandlines.lt) has a ferry connecting Ventspils and Nynäshamn (about 60km from Stockholm). Ferries depart five times weekly (car/pullman seat/berth from €85/50/70, 11 hours) from both ports.

TO/FROM LITHUANIA
Lisco Lines (www.lisco.lt) operates nightly ferries between Klaipėda and Karlshamn (car/pullman seat/berth from €61/70/95, 14 hours).

TRANSPORT

Yacht

The Baltics – particularly Estonia with its islands and indented coast – attract hundreds of yachts a year, mainly from Finland and Scandinavia. The best source on information is http://marinas.nautilus.ee, which has information on entry regulations, information on how to order the *Estonian Cruising Guide*, plus a database of all the local marinas. Another good reference is the website www.balticyachting.com, which covers southern Finland as well as western Estonia.

It's also possible to rent yachts throughout the region; see opposite for more information.

TOURS

A number of international travel operators specialise in travel to the Baltic region and can help you organise a trip. See also p415 for operators based in the Baltic. The following are recommended:

Baltic Holidays (☎ in the UK 0845 070 5711; www.balticholidays.co.uk) UK operator offering spa or city breaks, or beach, family or countryside holidays. There's even custom-made opera and ballet breaks, or help with genealogy research and trips.

Baltics and Beyond (☎ in the UK 0845 094 2125; www.balticsandbeyond.com) A UK-based company offering regular tours, self-guided options and tailor-made trips to the three Baltic countries and their neighbours (including Belarus, Russia and Poland).

Regent Holidays (☎ in the UK 0845 277 3317; www.regent-holidays.co.uk) A UK company with an array of Baltic options, including add-ons to visit the neighbours. Fly-drive, city breaks and cycling holidays are all offered.

Vytis Tours (☎ in the US 1800-778-9847, 718-423-6161; www.vytistours.com) A US company offering a range of tours, from an economical eight-day jaunt round the capitals, to a 17-day 'Grand Tour'. Add-ons include Helsinki and St Petersburg.

GETTING AROUND

AIR

There are plenty of scheduled flights between the three Baltic capitals, but within each country, domestic flights are minimal.

In Estonia, **Avies Air** (☎ 605 8022; www.avies.ee) flies daily from Tallinn to the island of Hiiumaa, while **Estonian Air** (☎ 640 1163; www.estonian-air.ee) connects Tallinn and Saaremaa. Light aircraft provide a wintertime link to the Estonian islands of Ruhnu and Kihnu from Pärnu.

In Latvia, **Air Baltic** (code BT; ☎ 9000 6006; www.airbaltic.lv) operates government-subsidised, inexpensive weekday flights between Rīga and Liepāja, and Rīga and Ventspils.

BICYCLE

The flatness and small scale of Estonia, Latvia and Lithuania, and the light traffic on most roads, make them good cycling territory. On the Estonian islands particularly, you will see cyclists galore in summer. Most bring their own bicycles but there are plenty of places where you can rent a bicycle, including each of the capitals and most major towns. See p202 for more information.

Cyclists should bring waterproof clothing, and perhaps a tent if touring: you may not find accommodation in some out-of-the-way places.

Several travel agencies and organisations, both within and outside the region, organise cycling tours (see p415).

BOAT
Ferry

The only ferry link between Baltic countries is the passenger and vehicle line travelling between Ventspils in Latvia and Mõntu on Saaremaa Island, Estonia. **SSCF Ferries** (☎ Estonia 452 4376, Latvia 360 7184; www.slkferries.ee) sails four or five times weekly from June to August (adult/child/car €27/18/38, four hours).

Estonia, with its many islands, has plenty of opportunities for sailing. Combined passenger and vehicle ferries sail from the Estonian mainland to the islands of Vormsi, Hiiumaa and Muhu (which is linked by causeway to Estonia's biggest island, Saaremaa). There are also ferry services between Saaremaa and Hiiumaa, and between Saaremaa and the island of Vilsandi. From Pärnu, you can travel by boat to the island of Kihnu; there are also summer ferries between Saaremaa and Ruhnu.

Boating opportunities within Latvia are few, although you can catch a slow boat between Rīga and Jūrmala.

Ferries make the short crossing from Klaipėda to Smiltynė in western Lithuania. In southeastern Lithuania, a steamboat ploughs the Nemunas River between Druskininkai and Liškiava. Soon, there should be a seasonal hydrofoil daily along the Nemunas River and the Curonian

Lagoon between Kaunas, Rusnė and Nida; in summer you can hire a boat along part of the hydrofoil route. It's possible to travel from Klaipėda to Nida via Juodkrantė by boat from July to September. You can also explore the Nemunas Delta by boat.

Yacht

Private yachting is a popular way to get around the Baltic Coast, particularly Estonia's coast with its many islands and bays. Yachts can be rented with or without a skipper from **Spinnaker** (☎ 5333 1117; www.sailing.ee; Regati puiestee 1, Tallinn). For information and advice on Estonia's dozens of harbours, check out http://marinas.nautilus.ee.

In Latvia, Rīga's **Andrejosta Yacht Club** (☎ 732 3221; Eksporta iela 1a, Andrejosta) hires yachts and assists sailors wanting to navigate the country's other ports. Detailed information on these can be found on the website of **Latvian Coast** (www.latviancoast.lv) and in the *Yacht Ports of Latvia* guide, sold at the **Jāņa sēta bookshop** (☎ 6724 0894; Elizabetes iela 83-85) in Rīga.

BUS

The region is well served by buses, although services to off-the-beaten track villages are infrequent. Direct bus services link the three capitals – Tallinn, Rīga and Vilnius – and there are plenty of other cross-border services between main towns.

Buses are generally faster than trains and, on the whole, slightly cheaper. Those used for local journeys, up to about two hours long, offer few comforts. Dating from some prehistoric time, many appear to be only fit for the scrap heap. To ensure semisurvival, avoid window seats in rainy, snowy or very cold weather; travel with someone you're prepared to snuggle up to for body warmth; and sit in the seat allocated to you to avoid tangling with a merciless babushka who wants *her* seat that *you're in*. Some shorter routes, however, are serviced by nippier and more modern microbuses, holding about 15 passengers and officially making fewer stops than their big-bus counterparts.

By contrast, buses travelling between the Baltic countries are equal to any long-distance coaches anywhere else in Europe. **Eurolines** (www.eurolines.ee) and **Ecolines** (www.ecolines.ee) have their appointed agents in each Baltic capital. Eurolines buses boast a higher standard than Ecolines, though tickets cost a bit more.

Regardless, both are clean and tout a heating system that functions and can be moderated. Most have a toilet, hot drinks dispenser and TV on board. Many scheduled buses to/from Tallinn, Rīga and Vilnius run overnight; a convenient and safe way of travelling, even for solo female travellers.

Tickets & Information

Ticket offices/windows selling national and international tickets are clearly marked in the local language and occasionally in English too. Tickets are always printed in the local language and easy to understand once you know the words for 'seat', 'bus stop' etc (see p419).

For long-distance buses originating from where you intend to leave, tickets are sold in advance. For local buses to nearby towns or villages, or for long-distance buses that are in midroute ('in transit'), you normally pay on board. This may mean a bit of a scrum for seats if there are a lot of people waiting.

Most bus and train stations in towns and cities have information windows with staff who generally speak some English.

Timetables & Fares

Timetables can be checked before leaving home on the respective bus company websites or, upon arrival in the region, by checking schedules at the local tourist office. The offices in Tallinn, Rīga and Vilnius in particular maintain up-to-the-minute transport schedules. The **In Your Pocket** (www.inyourpocket.com) city guides to the capitals include fairly comprehensive domestic and pan-Baltic bus schedules, updated every two months.

Comprehensive timetables are posted in bus stations' main ticket halls. A rare few need careful decoding. Most simply list the departure time and the days (using either Roman or Arabic numerals, the digit 1 being Monday) on which the service runs.

Fares vary slightly between the three countries, and between bus companies, reflecting the speed of the bus, comfort levels (Eurolines has a pricier 'lux express' service) and time of day it arrives/departs.

CAR & MOTORCYCLE

Driving or riding your own vehicle is an attractive option if you are able to bring or rent a car or motorcycle. It makes some of the region's most beautiful – and remote – places far more accessible, enabling you to discover spots that a bus or train would not get you to in a short time – or at all. Indeed, driving in the country is a world apart from the capital cities' manic motorists: zigzag along gravel roads, admire the movie-style dust trail in your mirror and wonder where on earth that solitary passer-by, you just passed, is walking to.

Main roads linking the cities and towns are generally good, and distances are not too great. In more remote areas there are many gravel roads and dirt tracks, but with a wide range of quality road maps with the different grade roads marked you can easily avoid the rougher roads if you don't feel your suspension is up to it.

Bring Your Own Vehicle

You can take your own vehicle to the Baltics by ferry from Finland, Sweden, Denmark or Germany; or by road from Poland and beyond, Belarus or Russia (see p405). Alternatively, you can hire a car once in the region.

Driving Licence & Permits

If you are planning to drive to or in the region, an International Driving Permit (IDP) will be useful, although, if you don't have one, your own national licence (if from a European country) should suffice. Note that licences not bearing a photograph of the holder have been known to upset traffic police, so try to get an IDP before you arrive. You will also need your vehicle's registration document. Accident insurance is compulsory in all three countries.

Fuel & Spare Parts

Petrol stations, run by major oil companies such as Statoil, Shell and Neste, are open 24 hours along all the major roads. Western-grade fuel, including unleaded, is readily avail-

able. As elsewhere in the world, the price of petrol fluctuated wildly in the Baltics during 2008, reaching highs around €1.20 per litre. At press time, you could count on paying around 15Kr/0.64Ls/3.10Lt per litre in Estonia/Latvia/Lithuania (that's approximately €0.90).

Hire

Tallinn, Rīga and Vilnius are naturally the easiest places to rent cars, although there are small outlets elsewhere. The major international car-hire companies all have offices in the capitals, often both in town and at the airport, listed in the city and town Getting There & Away sections. Some companies, such as Avis and Hertz, allow you to pick up a car in one city and drop it off in another. A variety of different packages and weekend specials is available, so it is worth shopping around.

DOCUMENTS

When hiring a car you need a passport and a suitable driving licence, normally an International Driving Permit (IDP), but a national licence from a European country is often acceptable. Some hire companies have minimum ages (usually 19 or 21, but 22 at some places in Estonia) and stipulate that you must have held your licence for at least a year. A major credit card is essential too, as some companies insist on it as the method of payment. Even if they don't, you'll have to leave a very large deposit or make a heavy cash prepayment. See p405 for more on licences and other documents you need if you bring your own vehicle.

Insurance

Third-party motor insurance is compulsory throughout Europe, and the same applies

---

DANGERS ON THE ROAD

One recent report that may get travellers thinking twice is that which placed Lithuania, Latvia and Estonia in the top three positions on the list of Europe's most dangerous drivers (Greece, notorious for its crazy drivers, came fourth).

Lithuania came out tops in the list, which calculated the number of road deaths per million inhabitants in 28 European countries (Lithuania's alarming statistic is over 200 fatalities per million; France, Germany, the UK and three Scandinavian countries have fewer than 75 road deaths per million inhabitants). As the report noted, the Baltic countries' burgeoning economies have increased consumer spending and placed more cars on roads, but without major improvements to infrastructure or increased awareness of dangerous driving.

We have to report that our experiences on Baltic roads were relatively good (and accident-free, thankfully), but it may be something to bear in mind when it comes to choosing your preferred mode of transport around the region. Now, about those buses...

Road Distances (km)

	Tallinn	Tartu	Pärnu	Narva	Valka/Valga	Riga	Liepāja	Daugavpils	Ventspils	Vilnius	Kaunas	Klaipėda	Panevėžys
Tartu	190												
Pärnu	130	205											
Narva	210	194	304										
Valka/Valga	276	86	140	268									
Riga	310	253	180	435	167								
Liepāja	530	473	400	655	387	220							
Daugavpils	540	377	410	559	291	230	450						
Ventspils	510	453	380	635	367	200	119	430					
Vilnius	600	543	470	725	457	290	465	167	584				
Kaunas	575	523	460	715	447	280	230	267	349	100			
Klaipėda	620	538	490	745	477	310	155	477	274	310	210		
Panevėžys	460	403	330	585	317	150	270	168	350	140	110	235	
Šiauliai	465	383	310	565	297	130	192	387	330	220	140	155	80

TRANSPORT

to the now-EU Baltic countries. For further advice and more information contact the **Association of British Insurers** (☎ 020-7600 3333; www.abi.org.uk).

You should get your insurer to issue a Green Card (which may cost extra), an internationally recognised proof of insurance, listing all the countries you intend to visit. You'll need this in the event of an accident outside the country where the vehicle is insured. The European Accident Statement (the 'Constat Amiable' in France) is available from your insurance company and is copied so that each party at an accident can record information. The Association of British Insurers has more details. Never sign accident statements you cannot understand or read; insist on a translation and sign that only if it's acceptable.

It's also wise to take out a European breakdown assistance policy, such as those offered by the **AA** (☎ in UK 0870 085 7253; www .theaa.com) or **RAC** (☎ in UK 0800 015 6000; www.rac .co.uk). Non-Europeans might find it cheaper to arrange for international coverage with their own national motoring organisation before travelling.

Road Rules

The whole region drives on the right. In Estonia and Lithuania, driving with any alcohol at all in your blood is illegal. In Latvia the legal blood alcohol limit is 0.05%. Seat belts are compulsory, and headlights must be on at all times while driving. Speed limits in built-up areas are 50km/h; limits outside urban areas vary from 70km/h to 110km/h – be on the lookout for signs, as these limits are often strictly enforced. Fines may be collected on the spot – the amounts vary and the only way you can ensure an officer is not adding a little pocket money for himself onto the official fine is to ask for a receipt.

Note that it is illegal to use a mobile phone while operating a vehicle (hands-free kits are allowed). Winter tyres are a legal requirement, usually from December to March every year, but if there are severe weather conditions outside these dates (likely in most years) the dates will change accordingly. You should therefore check local conditions if driving between October and April.

Parking meters are still found in some parts of the Baltics, though both Tallinn and

Vilnius have moved towards more advanced parking systems. Here drivers pay for parking via SMS, dialling a number and inputting the car's licence plate and location number (posted nearby).

There is an hourly fee of 5Ls to drive into the Old Town of Rīga, and you'll need to buy a *viedkarte* (a reusable card permit) for the privilege. Driving into the old towns in Tallinn, Vilnius and Kaunas is free, but parking is pricey, and often involves confusing regulations – ask at your hotel or the tourist office to avoid being fined. Motorists must also pay a small entrance fee to drive into Latvia's prime seaside resort, Jūrmala (1Ls per day, year-round). The Curonian Spit National Park in Lithuania also requires an entrance fee from motorists (20Lt in July and August, half that from September to June).

Take care driving near trams, trolleybuses and buses in towns. Passengers may run across the road to catch them while they're still in motion. Traffic behind a tram must stop when it opens its doors to let people in and out. Trolleybuses often swing far out into the road when leaving a stop.

HITCHING

Hitching is never entirely safe in any country in the world, and we don't recommend it. Travellers who decide to hitch should understand that they are taking a small but potentially serious risk. People who do choose to hitch will be safer if they travel in pairs and let someone know where they are planning to go.

Locally, hitching is a popular means of getting from A to B. The **Vilnius Hitchhiking Club** (VHHC; www.autostop.lt) provides practical information and contacts to travellers hoping to hitch a ride in all three Baltic countries. Hostel notice boards in capital cities are a good place to find or offer a ride-share; the website www.digihitch.com might also be able to help.

LOCAL TRANSPORT
Bus, Tram & Trolleybus

A mix of trams, buses and trolleybuses (buses run by electricity from overhead wires) provides thorough public transport around towns and cities in all three countries. All three types of transport get crowded, especially during the early-morning and early-evening rush hours.

Trams, trolleybuses and buses all run from about 5.30am to 12.30am, but serv-

ices get pretty thin in outlying areas after about 7pm. In Tallinn and Vilnius, the same ticket is good for all types of transport (but not minibuses); in Rīga a bus ticket must be purchased on board, but trolleybus and tram tickets are interchangeable. In all three countries, you validate by punching a flat-fare ticket in one of the ticket punches fixed inside the vehicle. Tickets are sold from news kiosks displaying them in the window and by some drivers (who are easier to find but charge a little more for tickets). Buy five or 10 at once; a single ticket costs 13Kr in Estonia (or 20Kr from the driver), 0.40Ls in Latvia (0.50Ls from the driver), and 1.10Lt in Lithuania (1.40Lt from the driver). Weekly and monthly travel passes are also available. The system depends on honesty and lends itself to cheating, but there are regular inspections, with on-the-spot fines if you're caught riding without a punched ticket.

Travelling on all trams, trolleybuses and buses requires a certain etiquette. If you are young, fit and capable of standing on one foot for the duration of your journey, do not sit in the seats at the front – these are only for babushkas and small children. Secondly, plan getting off well ahead of time. The moment the bus/tram rolls away from the stop prior to the one you are getting off at, start making your way to the door. Pushing, shoving, stamping on toes and elbowing are, of course, allowed.

City buses are supplemented by the route-taxi (*liinitakso* or *marsruuttakso* in Estonian, *marsruta taksobuss* or *mikroautobuss* in Latvian, and *masrutinis* in Lithuanian), minibuses that drop you anywhere along fixed routes for a flat fare.

All airports are served by regular city transport as well as by taxis.

Taxi

Taxis are plentiful and usually cheap: they officially cost 7Kr to 12Kr per kilometre in Estonia, 0.30Ls per kilometre in Latvia, and 3Lt in Lithuania; night-time tariffs, which generally kick in between 10pm and 6am, are higher. To avoid rip-offs, insist on the meter running. In any of the cities, it's always cheaper and safer to order a cab by phone.

Train

Suburban trains serve the outskirts of the main cities and some surrounding towns and villages. They're of limited use as city transport for visitors, as they mostly go to residential or industrial areas where there's little to see. But some are useful for day trips to destinations outside the cities.

TOURS

A number of local travel operators specialise in travel around the Baltic region and can help you organise a trip. The following are recommended; other useful local contacts are listed in the regional chapters, and tour operators originating from outside the Baltic countries can be found on p410.

Scanbalt Experience (www.scanbaltexperience.com) A backpacker-focused company offering adventure bus trips through Scandinavia and the Baltic region (including winter tours, although for now the emphasis is on Scandinavian destinations). The eight-day Baltic Explorer travel begins and ends in Tallinn, and takes in Rīga, Vilnius, Trakai and the west coast for €430.

TrekBaltics (☎ Tallinn 5623 3255; www.trekbaltics .com) An Estonian-based operator with a great range of camping treks, adventure and activities packages (eg, cycling tours), and spa breaks, taking in the three Baltic countries. The comprehensive 19-day Grand Baltics Trek can be done as a camper, or in more comfort (overnighting in cabins, farmhouses and hostels). The 10-day cycling trip from Tallinn to Klaipėda is a journey along the coast, including the Estonian islands.

TRAIN

Estonia, Latvia and Lithuania have railways, although services have been scaled back significantly in recent years and most long-distance travel within the Baltics is done by bus (or plane). A planned intra-country rail network is in the pipeline – the **Rail Baltica Project** (www.rail-baltica.net) envisages an upgraded rail link connecting Tallinn with Rīga, Kaunas and Warsaw, and on to Berlin. It won't be completed until at least 2013.

In the meantime, Baltic trains are slow and cheap, and not terribly comfortable. You can almost never open the windows, which can make things stuffy (and smelly, depending on your travelling companions), while you stand equal chances of freezing or baking, depending on whether the heating is turned on or not. Local trains, known as suburban or electric, are substantially slower and make more frequent stops than long-distance trains.

Routes

There are no direct train services running between the Baltic capitals – your best bet is

the bus. In the past, with perseverance, you could manage to travel from Tallinn to Vilnius by train, but the indefinite closure in late 2008 of the train service between Tallinn and Valga (on the Estonia–Latvia border) has put a halt to that. From Tallinn you can take a bus to Valga, then change there to a train on to Rīga. You can take a train from Rīga to Daugavpils, then change for a train on to Vilnius (this may involve an overnight stop in Daugavpils).

Routes within countries include Tallinn–Narva, Tallinn-Pärnu, Tallinn-Tartu, Tallinn-Viljandi; Rīga–Rēzekne, Rīga–Daugavpils, Rīga–Liepāja, Rīga–Sigulda; Vilnius–Daugavpils, Vilnius–Ignalina, Vilnius–Kaunas, Vilnius–Klaipėda, Vilnius–Šiauliai and Vilnius–Trakai. There are other local suburban railways fanning out from the main cities.

Tickets & Information

In Latvia and Lithuania, tickets can be purchased in advance and right before departure at train stations. In larger train stations, such as Rīga, you can only buy tickets for certain types of trains or destinations at certain windows.

Except for in Tallinn, Estonia's train stations are deserted places. There's no ticket agent and no services of any kind. You buy your tickets on the train, and don't head to the train station (which is usually quite far from the city centre) unless you know the exact departure time.

Tickets – upon boarding a long-distance train between the Baltics and elsewhere – must be surrendered to the carriage attendant, who will safeguard it for the journey's duration and return it to you 15 minutes before arrival at your final destination (a handy 'alarm clock' if you're on an overnight train).

Timetables

The railways of Latvia (www.ldz.lv) and Lithuania (www.litrail.lt) maintain updated train schedules on their websites, as does Estonia (www.edel.ee), though it's only in Estonian (on the Estonian-language page, click on Sõiduplannid ja -hinnad to access the timetables and prices). Those displayed at train stations generally list the number of the train, departure and arrival times, and the platform from which it leaves. Some list return journey schedules, the number of minutes a train waits in your station or the time a train left the place it began its journey. Always study the small print on timetables, too, as many trains only run on certain days or between certain dates.

TRANSPORT

Health

CONTENTS

Travel health depends on your predeparture preparations, your daily health care while travelling and how you handle any medical problem that does develop. The Baltic region is, on the whole, a pretty healthy place to travel around, though medical facilities, particularly outside the capital cities, are not entirely up to Western standards.

BEFORE YOU GO

Prevention is the key to staying healthy while abroad. A little planning before departure, particularly for pre-existing illnesses, will save trouble later. See your dentist before a long trip. Carry a spare pair of contact lenses and/or glasses, and take your optical prescription with you. Bring medications in their original, clearly labelled, containers. A signed and dated letter from your physician describing your medical conditions and medications, including generic names, is also a good idea. If carrying syringes or needles, be sure to have a physician's letter documenting their medical necessity.

INSURANCE

If you're an EU citizen, a European Health Insurance Card (EHIC, which replaced the E111 form in 2006) covers you for most medical care, but not for nonemergencies or the cost of repatriation. You can apply for one online in many EU countries via your government health department's website. Citizens from other countries should find out if there is a reciprocal arrangement for free medical care between their country and the country visited. If you do need health insurance, seriously consider a policy that covers you for the worst possible scenario, such as an accident requiring an emergency flight home. Find out in advance if your insurance plan will make payments directly to providers or reimburse you later for overseas health expenditure. The former option is generally preferable, as it doesn't require you to pay out of your own pocket in a foreign country.

RECOMMENDED VACCINATIONS

The World Health Organization (WHO) recommends that all travellers should be covered for diphtheria, tetanus, measles, mumps, rubella and polio, as well as Hepatitis B, regardless of their destination. Since most vaccines don't produce immunity until at least two weeks after they're given, visit a physician at least six weeks before departure. If you intend to spend a lot of time in forested areas, including by the coast where pine forest prevails, it is advisable to get a vaccine against tick-borne encephalitis.

ONLINE RESOURCES

The WHO's publication *International Travel and Health* is revised annually and is available online at www.who.int/ith. Other useful websites include www.mdtravelhealth.com (travel health recommendations for every country; updated daily), and www.fitfortravel.scot.nhs.uk (general travel advice for the layperson).

IN ESTONIA, LATVIA & LITHUANIA

AVAILABILITY & COST OF HEALTH CARE

Practically all pharmacies in the capitals and larger towns stock imported Western medicines. There are few alternatives to the local medical system, which is improving but is short on facilities and training should you have the misfortune to need serious attention. Private clinics offer Western-standard, English-speaking medical care in the capitals but they are often expensive. In an emergency seek your hotel's help first (if you're in one); the bigger hotels may have doctors on call. Emergency care is free in all three countries.

INFECTIOUS DISEASES

Spread by tick bites, tick-borne encephalitis is a serious infection of the brain. Vaccination is advised for those in risk areas who are unable to avoid tick bites (such as campers, forestry workers and walkers). Two doses of vaccine will give a year's protection, three doses give up to three years'.

TRAVELLER'S DIARRHOEA

Simple things like a change of water, food or climate can cause stomach upsets. If you develop diarrhoea, be sure to drink plenty of fluids, preferably with an oral rehydration solution (eg Dioralyte). A few loose stools don't require treatment, but if you start having more than four or five motions a day, you should start taking an antibiotic (usually a quinolone drug) and an antidiarrhoeal agent (such as Loperamide). If diarrhoea is bloody, persists for more than 72 hours or is accompanied by fever, shaking, chills or severe abdominal pain you should seek medical attention.

ENVIRONMENTAL HAZARDS
Heat Exhaustion & Hypothermia

Visitors to the Baltic region are not at excessive risk from either of these conditions. It is surprisingly easy, however, to become overexposed to the sun in a temperate climate, even on a cloudy day, and to become dangerously cold in mild, damp weather if out cycling or hiking.

Heat exhaustion occurs following excessive fluid loss with inadequate replacement of fluids and salt. Symptoms include headache, dizziness and tiredness. Dehydration is already happening by the time you feel thirsty – aim to drink sufficient water to produce pale, diluted urine. To treat heat exhaustion, replace lost fluids by drinking water and/or fruit juice, and cool the body with cold water and fans.

> **TRAVEL HEALTH WEBSITES**
>
> It's usually a good idea to consult your government's travel health website before departure, if one is available.
> **Australia** www.smartraveller.gov.au
> **Canada** www.hc-sc.gc.ca
> **UK** www.dh.gov.uk
> **USA** www.cdc.gov/travel

Acute hypothermia follows a sudden drop of temperature over a short time. Chronic hypothermia is caused by a gradual loss of temperature over hours. Hypothermia starts with shivering, loss of judgement and clumsiness. Unless rewarming occurs, the sufferer deteriorates into apathy, confusion and coma. Prevent further heat loss by seeking shelter, warm dry clothing, hot sweet drinks and shared bodily warmth.

Insect Bites & Stings

Mosquitoes are a problem in the region, and can cause irritation and infected bites. Use a DEET-based insect repellent.

Bees and wasps cause real problems only to those with a severe allergy to bee or wasp stings (anaphylaxis). These people should carry an 'epipen' or similar adrenaline injection.

Bed bugs lead to very itchy, lumpy bites. Spraying the mattress with crawling-insect killer after changing bedding will get rid of them.

You should always check all over your body if you have been walking through a potentially tick-infested area. Signs along the Lithuanian coast alert walkers and beachgoers to particularly rampant tick areas. If a tick is found attached, press down around the tick's head with tweezers, grab the head and gently pull upwards. Avoid pulling the rear of the body as this may squeeze the tick's gut contents through the attached mouth parts into the skin, increasing the risk of infection and disease.

Water

Official travel advisories all detail the need to avoid tap water and drink only boiled or bottled water, but locals insist the tap water is perfectly safe to drink (if not altogether pleasant-tasting). Some visitors may wish to take the necessary precautions or buy bottled

HEALTH

water simply because they prefer the taste (see p15). Do not drink water from rivers or lakes as it may contain bacteria or viruses that can cause diarrhoea or vomiting.

TRAVELLING WITH CHILDREN

If you are travelling with children, ensure that you know how to treat minor ailments and when to seek medical advice. Make sure the children are up to date with routine vaccinations, and discuss possible travel vaccines well before departure as some vaccines are not suitable for children under a year. If your child has vomiting or diarrhoea, lost fluid and salts must be replaced. It may be helpful to take rehydration powders for reconstituting with boiled water.

WOMEN'S HEALTH

Travelling during pregnancy is usually possible but always consult your doctor before planning your trip. The most risky times for travel are during the first 12 weeks of pregnancy and after 30 weeks.

SEXUAL HEALTH

Emergency contraception is most effective if taken within 24 hours after unprotected sex. The **International Planned Parent Federation** (www.ippf.org) can advise about the availability of contraception in different countries.

When buying condoms, look for a European CE mark, which means they have been rigorously tested to a high standard. Keep them in a cool dry place.

Language

CONTENTS

ESTONIAN

Estonian belongs to the Baltic-Finnic branch of the Finno-Ugric languages. It's closely related to Finnish and distantly related to Hungarian. The complex grammar of Estonian makes it a difficult language to learn – try your luck with 14 cases, declining adjectives and no future tense. Added to this is a vocabulary with no link to any other language outside its own group, save recent borrowings.

A comprehensive and radical reform of the language was undertaken in the early 1900s by Johannes Aavik, somewhat de-Germanising the grammar and adding thousands of new terms. Another language reformer, Johannes Veski, criticised Aavik's liberal borrowing from Finnish, and proceeded to augment the vocabulary by using Estonian roots to create new words. It's a process that is continuing to this day as new Estonian words are invented to suit modern needs. All the same, recent years have seen an increase in the liberal use of English words in place of their more complicated Estonian translations, or adding Estonian verb endings to English words, eg if you want to *surfima* the Web or *e-mailima* your friends, you'll need to *klikkima* the mouse often!

Most Estonians, especially the younger generations, understand some English and Finnish, but you'll find that Estonians are much more welcoming of visitors who make an effort to speak their language. So don't be shy – there's nothing to lose and much to gain. For trivia buffs, Estonian boasts the word with the most consecutively repeated vowel: *jäääär*, which means 'edge of ice'.

PRONUNCIATION
Vowels

a	ah	as in 'father'
ä	a	as in 'act'
ää	aa	as in 'Aaron'
äe	aeh	as the 'ae' in 'aesthetic'
e	e	as in 'ten'
ee	eh	as the 'e' in 'ten' but longer
i	i	as in 'tin'
ii	ee	as the 'ee' in 'see'
o	o	as in British English 'hot'
õ	y	roughly as the 'i' in 'girl' (without rounding the lips)
ö	er	as in 'fern' (rounding the lips)
oo	aw	as in 'dawn'
öö	err	as the 'yrr' in 'myrrh' (rounding the lips)
u	u	as in 'put'
ü	ü	as the 'oo' in 'too' said with a small, round opening of the lips
uu	oo	as in 'zoo'

Diphthongs

ae	ae	as the 'ie' in 'diet' (two sounds)
ai	ai	as in 'aisle'
ea	ea	as in 'bear'
ei	ay	as in 'pay'
oi	oy	as in 'ploy'
õi	yi	roughly as the word 'curly' leaving out the 'c', 'r' and 'l'
ui	uy	as the 'oui' in 'Louie', but shorter and clipped

Consonants

The letters **š** and **ž** are only used in foreign loan words. Consonants are pronounced as in English, with the following exceptions:

c	ts	as in 'tsar'
g	g	as in 'good', never as in 'page'
j	y	as in 'yes'
k	k	softer than in English
p	p	between English 'p' and 'b'
r	rr	always trilled, as the Italian 'r'
š	sh	as in 'she'
ž	zh	as the 's' in 'treasure'
t	t	between English 't' and 'd'

Stress

Word stress falls on the first syllable. There are very few exceptions to this rule, but there is one that's very conspicuous – the word for 'thanks' *aitäh* (ai·*tahh*) stresses the second syllable.

In the pronunciation guides included in the following words and phrases, stress is indicated with italics.

ACCOMMODATION
Where can I find a ...?
Kus asub ...?   kus *ah*·sub ...
  hotel
  hotell   ho·*tell*
  pension
  võõrastemaja   vyy·rrahs·te·mah·yah
  campsite
  kämping   kam·ping

I'd like a ...
Ma tahaksin ... tuba.   mah *tah*·hak·sin ... *tu*·bah
  single room
  ühe voodiga   ü·he vaw·di·gah
  double room
  kahe voodiga   kah·he vaw·di·gah
  room with a bathroom
  vannitoaga   vahn·ni·toa·gah

How much is it per person?
Kui palju maksab voodikoht?
kui *pahl*·yu *mahk*·sab vaw·di·koht
How much is it per night?
Kui palju maksab ööpäev?
kui *pahl*·yu *mahk*·sab err·paehv
Does it include breakfast?
Kas hommikusöök on hinna sees?
kahs hom·mi·ku·serrk on *hin*·nah sehs
May I see it?
Kas ma võin seda näha?
kahs mah vyin se·dah na·hah

CONVERSATION & ESSENTIALS
Use the polite 'you', *te* (te) or *teie* (*tay*·e), when addressing strangers or people you've just met. The informal *sa* (sah) or *sina* (si·nah) is reserved for children, family and friends. Except with children, don't use it until you are invited to.

Good ...
Tere ...   te·rre ...
  morning
  hommikust   hom·mi·kust
  afternoon
  päevast   paeh·vahst
  evening
  õhtust   yh·tust

Hello.
Tere. (inf & pol)   te·rre
Welcome.
Tere tulemast.   te·rre tu·le·mahst
Goodbye.
Head aega.   head ae·gah
Good night.
Head ööd.   head errd
Yes.
Jah.   yah
No.
Ei.   ay
Thank you.
Tänan.   ta·nahn
You're welcome.
Palun.   pah·lun
Excuse me/I'm sorry.
Vabandage.   vah·bahn·dah·ge
How are you? (How's it going?)
Kuidas läheb?   kuy·dahs la·heb
Fine.
Hästi.   has·ti
What's your name?
Mis te nimi on?   mis te ni·mi on
My name is ...
Minu nimi on ...   mu ni·mi on ...
Very nice (to meet you).
Väga meeldiv.   va·gah mehl·div

EMERGENCIES – ESTONIAN
Help!
Appi!   ahp·pi
Call a doctor!
Kutsuge arst!   kut·su·ge ahrrst
I'm ill.
Ma olen haige.   mah o·len hai·ge
I'm lost.
Ma olen eksinud.   mah o·len ek·si·nud
Go away!
Minge ära!   min·ge a·rrah

HEALTH
Where's the nearest ...?
Kus on lähim ...?
kus on la·him ...
  chemist   *apteek*   ap·tehk
  doctor   *arst*   ahrrst
  hospital   *haigla*   haig·lah

  antibiotics
  antibiootikumid   ahn·ti·bi·aw·ti·ku·mid
  condoms
  kondoomid   kon·daw·mid

painkillers
  valuvaigisti   *vah·lu·vai·gis·ti*
sanitary napkins
  hügieenisidemed   hü·gi·*eh*·ni·si·de·med
sunblock cream
  päevituskreem   *paeh*·vi·tus·krrehm
tampons
  tampoonid   tahm·*paw*·nid

LANGUAGE DIFFICULTIES
Do you speak English?
  Kas te räägite inglise keelt?
  kahs te *rraa*·gi·te *ing*·li·se kehlt
I don't understand.
  Ma ei saa aru.
  mah ay saah *ah*·rru
Please write it down here.
  Palun kirjutage see siia.
  pah·lun *kirr*·yu·tah·ge seh *see*·ah

SHOPPING & SERVICES
Where's (a/an/the) ...?
Kus on ...?
kus on ...

bank	*pank*	pahnk
chemist/ pharmacy	*apteek*	*ahp*·tehk
city centre	*kesklinn*	*kesk*·linn
... embassy	*... saatkond*	*... saaht*·kond
market	*turg*	turrg
police	*politsei*	po·lit·*say*
post office	*postkontor*	*post*·kon·torr
toilet	*tualett*	tua·*lett*
tourist office	*turismibüroo*	tu·*rris*·mi·bü·*rroo*

How much does it cost?
  Kui palju see maksab?
  kui *pahl*·yu seh *mahk*·sahb
Can I pay by credit card?
  Kas teil saab maksta krediitkaardiga?
  kahs tayl saahb *mahks*·tah krre·*deet*·kaahrr·di·gah
Where can I exchange money?
  Kus ma saan vahetada raha?
  kus mah saahn *vah*·he·tah·dah *rrah*·hah
I need to check my email.
  Ma pean vaatama oma elektronposti.
  mah pean *vaah*·tah·mah *o*·mah e·*lekt*·rron·pos·ti
What time does it open/close?
  Mis kell see avatakse/suletakse?
  mis kell seh *ah*·vah·tahk·se/*su*·le·tahk·se

TIME, DATES & NUMBERS
Excuse me, what time is it?
  Vabandage, mis kell on?
  vah·bahn·dah·ge mis kell on

It's ...	*Kell on ...*	kell on ...
eight o'clock	*kaheksa*	*kah*·hek·sah
one o'clock	*üks*	üks

in the morning	*hommikul*	*hom*·mi·kul
in the evening	*õhtul*	*yh*·tul
today	*täna*	*ta*·nah
tomorrow	*homme*	*hom*·me
yesterday	*eile*	*ay*·le

Monday	*esmaspäev*	*es*·mahs·paehv
Tuesday	*teisipäev*	*tay*·si·paehv
Wednesday	*kolmapäev*	*kol*·mah·paehv
Thursday	*neljapäev*	*nel*·yah·paehv
Friday	*reede*	*rreh*·de
Saturday	*laupäev*	*lau*·paehv
Sunday	*pühapäev*	*pü*·hah·paehv

January	*jaanuar*	*yaah*·nuahrr
February	*veebruar*	*vehb*·rruahrr
March	*märts*	marrts
April	*aprill*	*ahp*·rrill
May	*mai*	mai
June	*juuni*	*joo*·ni
July	*juuli*	*joo*·li
August	*august*	*au*·gust
September	*september*	sep·*tem*·berr
October	*oktoober*	ok·*taw*·berr
November	*november*	no·*vem*·berr
December	*detsember*	det·*sem*·berr

0	*null*	null
1	*üks*	üks
2	*kaks*	kahks
3	*kolm*	kolm
4	*neli*	*ne*·li
5	*viis*	vees
6	*kuus*	koos
7	*seitse*	*sayt*·se
8	*kaheksa*	*kah*·hek·sah
9	*üheksa*	*ü*·hek·sah
10	*kümme*	*küm*·me
11	*üksteist*	*üks*·tayst
12	*kaksteist*	*kahks*·tayst
13	*kolmteist*	*kolm*·tayst
14	*neliteist*	*ne*·li·tayst
15	*viisteist*	*vees*·tayst
16	*kuusteist*	*koos*·tayst
17	*seitseteist*	*sayt*·se·tayst
18	*kaheksateist*	*kah*·hek·sah·tayst
19	*üheksateist*	*ü*·hek·sah·tayst
20	*kakskümmend*	*kahks*·küm·mend
21	*kakskümmend üks*	*kahks*·küm·mend üks
30	*kolmkümmend*	*kolm*·küm·mend

LANGUAGE

40	nelikümmend	ne·li·küm·mend
50	viiskümmend	vees·küm·mend
60	kuuskümmend	koos·küm·mend
70	seitsekümmend	sayt·se·küm·mend
80	kaheksakümmend	kah·hek·sah·küm·mend
90	üheksakümmend	ü·hek·sah·küm·mend
100	sada	sah·dah
1000	tuhat	tu·haht

TRANSPORT

Where's the ...?
Kus on ...?
kus on ...

airport	lennujaam	len·nu·yaahm
bus station	bussijaam	bus·si·yaahm
ferry terminal	sadam	sah·dahm
train station	rongijaam	rron·gi·yaahm

Which ... do I take to get there?
Mis ... ma sinna saan?
mis ... mah *sin*·nah saahn

bus	bussiga	bus·si·gah
tram	trammiga	trrahm·mi·gah
trolleybus	trolliga	trrol·li·gah

What time is the next ...?
Mis kell on järgmine ...?
mis kell on *yarrg*·mi·ne ...

| bus | buss | buss |
| train | rong | rrong |

Please give me a ... ticket.
Palun ... pilet.
pah·lun ... *pi*·let

| one-way | üks | üks |
| return | edasi-tagasi | e·dah·si·*tah*·gah·si |

Directions

Excuse me.
Vabandage.   *vah*·bahn·dah·ge
Where is ...?
Kus on ...?   kus on ...

How far is it?
Kui kaugel see on?   kuy *kau*·gel seh on
Go straight ahead.
Otse.   *ot*·se
Turn left.
Vasakule.   *vah*·sah·ku·le
Turn right.
Paremale.   *pah*·rre·mah·le
Please show me on the map.
Palun näidake   *pah*·lun *nai*·dah·ke
mulle seda kaardil.   *mul*·le se·dah *kaahrr*·dil

LATVIAN

Latvian is one of only two surviving languages of the Baltic branch of the Indo-European language family. Even more than Estonians, the speakers of Latvian regard their language as an endangered species – only about 55% of the population, and just over 45% of the inhabitants of the capital, Rīga, speak it as their first language. Latvian and Lithuanian have a lot of vocabulary in common, but are not quite close enough to be mutually intelligible.

English is a popular foreign language in Latvia so you may find that local people will be more than pleased to practise their language skills with you. If you manage to grasp at least some basic phrases in Latvian you'll be received warmly.

Latvian uses feminine and masculine forms of words. In this language guide the masculine form appears first and is separated from the feminine form by a slash. All phrases are given in the polite form unless otherwise indicated.

PRONUNCIATION
Vowels

A line above a vowel (a macron) indicates that it has a long sound. It's important to make the distinction between short and long sounds as they can change the meaning of a word. For example, *istaba* (a/the room) and *istabā* (in a/the room). Note that there are two different ways of pronouncing the letters **e**, **ē** and **o**, so follow the pronunciation guides carefully.

a	uh	as the 'u' in 'fund'
ā	ah	as in 'father'
e	e	as in 'bet'
	a	as in 'fat'

ē	eh	as the 'ai' in 'fair'
	aa	as the 'a' in 'sad', but longer
i	i	as in 'pin'
ī	ee	as in 'beet'
o	o	as in 'pot'
	aw	as in 'saw'
u	u	as in 'pull'
ū	oo	as in 'pool'

Diphthongs

ai	ai	as the 'i' in 'dive'
au	ow	as the 'ow' in 'now'
ei	ay	as the 'ay' in 'may'
ie	ea	as the 'ea' in 'fear'
oi	oy	as the 'oy' in 'toy'
ui	uy	similar to the 'ui' in 'ruin'

Consonants

Consonants are pronounced as in English with the following exceptions:

c	ts	as in 'lots'
č	ch	as in 'chew'
dz	dz	as the 'ds' in 'beds'
dž	j	as in 'job'
ģ	jy	a 'dy' sound, similar to the 'dy' sound in British 'duty'
j	y	as in 'yellow'
ķ	ky	as the 'cy' sound in 'cute'
ļ	ly	as the 'll' in 'million'
ņ	ny	as in 'canyon'
r	r	a slightly rolled 'r'
š	sh	as in 'shop'
ž	zh	as the 's' in 'pleasure'

Stress

In Latvian, the stress is almost always on the first syllable. One notable exception is the word for 'thank you' *paldies* (puhl-*deas*). Stress is indicated in the pronunciation guides with italics.

ACCOMMODATION

I'm looking for a ...
Es meklēju ...   es *mek*·leh·yu ...
  cheap hotel
  lētu viesnīcu   *laa*·tu *veas*·neets·u
  good hotel
  labu viesnīcu   *luh*·bu *veas*·neets·u
  youth hostel
  jauniešu mītni   *yow*·nea·shu *meet*·ni

Do you have any rooms available?
Vai jums ir brīvas istabas?
vai yums ir *bree*·vuhs *is*·tuh·buhs

How much is it per night?
Cik maksā diennaktī?
tsik *muhk*·sah *dean*·nuhk·tee

I'd like a ...
Es vēlos ...
es *vaa*·laws ...
  single room
  vienvietīgu istabu   *vean*·vea·tee·gu *is*·tuh·bu
  double room
  divvietīgu istabu   *div*·vea·tee·gu *is*·tuh·bu
  room with a shower
  istabu ar dušu   *is*·tuh·bu uhr *du*·shu
  room with a bath
  istabu ar vannu   *is*·tuh·bu uhr *vuhn*·nu

CONVERSATION & ESSENTIALS

Hello. (inf)
Sveiks. (m)   svayks
Sveika. (f)   svay·kuh
Good morning.
Labrīt.   luhb·*reet*
Good day/afternoon.
Labdien. (also 'hello')   luhb·*dean*
Good evening.
Labvakar.   luhb·*vuh*·kuhr
Goodbye.
Uz redzēšanos.   uz·*redz*·eh·shuhn·aws
Good night.
Ar labu nakti.   uhr *luh*·bu *nuhkt*·i
How are you?
Kā jums klājas?   kah yums *klah*·yuhs
Fine, thank you.
Labi, paldies.   *luh*·bi puhl·*deas*
Yes.
Jā.   yah
No.
Nē.   neh
Please/You're welcome.
Lūdzu.   loo·dzu
Thank you (very much).
(Liels) paldies.   (leals) puhl·*deas*
Excuse me.
Atvainojiet.   uht·vai·naw·yeat
I'm sorry.
Piedodiet.   pea·doad·eat
What's your name?
Kā jūs sauc?   kah yoos sowts
My name is ...
Mani sauc ...   *muhn*·i sowts ...
Where are you from?
No kurienes jūs esat?   naw *kur*·ean·es yoos *as*·uht
I'm from ...
Es esmu no ...   es *as*·mu naw ...

LANGUAGE

EMERGENCIES – LATVIAN

Help!
Palīgā! — puh·lee·gah
Call a doctor!
Izsauciet ārstu! — iz·sowts·eat ahr·stu
I'm ill.
Es esmu slims/ — es as·mu slims/
slima. (m/f) — slim·uh
I'm lost.
Es esmu apmaldījies/ — es as·mu uhp·muhl·dee·yeas
apmaldījusies. (m/f) — uhp·muhl·dee·yu·seas
Go away!
Ejiet projam! — ay·eat praw·yam

HEALTH

Where can I find a/an ...?
Kur es varu atrast ...? — kur es vuh·ru uht·ruhst ...
  doctor
  ārstu — ahr·stu
  hospital
  slimnīcu — slim·neets·u

I'm allergic to penicillin.
Es esmu alerģisks/alerģiska pret penicilīnu. (m/f)
es as·mu uh·ler·jyisks/uh·ler·jyis·kuh pret pen·its·i·lee·nu

LANGUAGE DIFFICULTIES

Do you speak English?
Vai jūs runājat angliski?
vai yoos run·ah·yuht uhn·gli·ski
I don't understand.
Es nesaprotu.
es ne·suh·praw·tu
Please write that down.
Lūdzu pierakstiet to.
loo·dzu pea·ruhk·steat taw

SHOPPING & SERVICES

Where's the ...?
Kur atrodas ...? — kur uht·raw·duhs ...
  bank
  banka — buhn·kuh
  chemist/pharmacy
  aptieka — uhp·tea·kuh
  city/town centre
  pilsētas centrs — pil·saa·tuhs tsent·rs
  currency exchange booth
  valūtas maiņa — vuh·loo·tuhs mai·nyuh
  ... embassy
  ... vēstniecība — ... vehst·nea·tsee·buh
  market
  tirgus — tir·gus
  post office
  pasts — puhsts

How much is it?
Cik tas maksā?
tsik tuhs muhk·sah
Can I pay by credit card?
Vai es varu maksāt ar kredītkarti?
vai es vuh·ru muhk·saht uhr kred·eet·kuhr·ti
I'd like to change a travellers cheque.
Es vēlos izmainīt ceļojuma čeku.
es vaa·laws iz·mai·neet tsely·aw·yum·uh che·ku
I need to check my email.
Es vēlos pārbaudīt savu e-pastu.
es vaa·laws pahr·bow·deet suh·vu e·puhst·u
What time does it open?
No cikiem ir atvērts?
naw tsik·eam ir uht·vaarts
What time does it close?
Cikos slēdz?
tsik·aws slaadz
Where are the toilets?
Kur ir tualetes?
kur ir tu·uh·le·tes

  condoms
  prezervatīvi — prez·er·vuh·tee·vi
  sanitary napkins
  bindes — bin·des
  sunblock cream
  saules krēms — sow·les krehms
  tampons
  tamponi — tuhm·po·ni

TIME, DATES & NUMBERS

What time (is it)?
Cik (ir) pulkstenis? — tsik (ir) pulk·sten·is

It's ...	Ir ...	ir ...
two o'clock	*divi* (lit: it's two)	di·vi
five o'clock	*pieci*	peats·i
today	*šodien*	shaw·dean
tomorrow	*rīt*	reet
morning	*rīts*	reets
afternoon	*pēcpusdiena*	pehts·pus·dea·nuh
night	*nakts*	nuhkts
Monday	*pirmdiena*	pirm·dea·nuh
Tuesday	*otrdiena*	aw·tr·dea·nuh
Wednesday	*trešdiena*	tresh·dea·nuh
Thursday	*ceturtdiena*	tsat·urt·dea·nuh
Friday	*piektdiena*	peakt·dea·nuh
Saturday	*sestdiena*	sast·dea·nuh
Sunday	*svētdiena*	sveht·dea·nuh
January	*janvāris*	yuhn·vah·ris
February	*februāris*	feb·ru·ah·ris

March	marts	muhrts
April	aprīlis	uhp·ree·lis
May	maijs	maiys
June	jūnijs	yoo·niys
July	jūlijs	yoo·liys
August	augusts	ow·gusts
September	septembris	sep·tem·bris
October	oktobris	ok·to·bris
November	novembris	no·vem·bris
December	decembris	dets·em·bris

0	nulle	nul·le
1	viens	veans
2	divi	di·vi
3	trīs	trees
4	četri	chet·ri
5	pieci	peats·i
6	seši	sesh·i
7	septiņi	sep·ti·nyi
8	astoņi	uhs·taw·nyi
9	deviņi	de·vi·nyi
10	desmit	des·mit
11	vienpadsmit	vean·puhds·mit
12	divpadsmit	div·puhds·mit
13	trīspadsmit	trees·puhds·mit
14	četrpadsmit	chet·r·puhds·mit
15	piecpadsmit	peats·puhds·mit
16	sešpadsmit	sesh·puhds·mit
17	septiņpadsmit	sep·tiny·puhds·mit
18	astoņpadsmit	uhs·tawny·puhds·mit
19	deviņpadsmit	de·viny·puhds·mit
20	divdesmit	div·des·mit
21	divdesmitviens	div·des·mit·veans
30	trīsdesmit	trees·des·mit
40	četrdesmit	chet·r·des·mit
50	piecdesmit	peats·des·mit
60	sešdesmit	sesh·des·mit
70	septiņdesmit	sep·tiny·des·mit
80	astoņdesmit	uhs·tawny·des·mit
90	deviņdesmit	de·viny·des·mit
100	simts	simts
200	divi simti	di·vi sim·ti
1000	tūkstots	tooks·tawts

TRANSPORT

Where's the ...?
Kur atrodas ...?
kur uht·raw·duhs ...
  airport
  lidosta lid·aw·stuh
  bus station
  autoosta ow·to·aws·tuh
  ferry terminal
  pasažieru osta puh·suh·zhea·ru aw·stuh

train station
dzelzceļa stacija dzelz·ce·lyuh stuhts·i·ya
tram/trolleybus stop
tramvaja/trolejbusa truhm·vuh·yuh/trol·ey·bu·suh
  pietura pea·tu·ruh

I want to buy a ... ticket.
Es vēlos nopirkt ... biļeti.
es vaa·laws naw·pirkt ... bi·lyet·i
  one-way
  vienvirziena vean·virz·ean·uh
  return
  turp-atpakaļ turp uht·puh·kuhly

How much does it cost (to go to ...)?
Cik maksā (aizvest līdz ...)?
tsik muhk·sah (aiz·vest leedz ...)

boat (ship)
  kuģis ku·gyis
platform
  perons pe·rawns
ticket office(s)
  biļešu kases bi·lye·shu kuh·ses
timetable
  vilcienu saraksts vilts·ea·nu suh·ruhksts

Directions
How do I get to ...?
Kā es tieku līdz ...?
kah es tea·ku leedz ...
Is it far from here?
Vai tas atrodas tālu?
vai tuhs uht·raw·duhs tah·lu
Could you show me (on the map), please?
Lūdzu parādiet man (uz kartes)?
loo·dzu puhr·ah·deat muhn (uz kuhrt·es)
Go straight ahead.
Uz priekšu.
uz preak·shu
Turn left/right (at the ...)
Pa kreisi/labi (pie ...)
puh kray·si/luh·bi (pea ...)

LITHUANIAN

Lithuanian is another surviving language of the Baltic branch of the Indo-European language family (along with Latvian). As many of its forms have remained unchanged longer than those of other Indo-European languages (which cover most of Europe and a fair bit of Asia), Lithuanian is very important to linguistic scholars; it's said to be as archaic as Sanskrit in its grammatical forms. It is also open to free borrowings from other tongues when deemed necessary, particularly English, as phrases like *ping pong klubas* and *marketingo departamento direktorius* demonstrate.

Low Lithuanian (*Žemaičiai*), spoken in the west, is a separate dialect from High Lithuanian (*Aukštaičiai*), spoken in the rest of the country and considered the standard dialect.

Lithuanian has masculine and feminine forms of words, indicated in this language guide by (m) and (f).

PRONUNCIATION
Vowels

a/ą	ah	as the 'u' in 'cut' or longer, as the 'a' in 'arm'
e/ę	a	as the 'a' in 'cat' or longer, as the 'a' in 'amber'
ė	eh	as the 'e' in 'bed' but longer
i	i	as the 'i' in 'it'
y/į	ee	as the 'ee' in 'eel'
o	aw	as the 'aw' in 'law'
	o	as the 'o' in 'hot'
u	u	as the 'u' in 'put'
ū/ų	oo	long, as the 'oo' in 'poor'

Diphthongs

ai	ai	as the 'i' in 'bite' or longer as the 'ai' in 'aisle'
au	ow	as the 'ou' in 'ouch' or longer as the 'ow' in 'owl'
ei	ay	as the 'ay' in 'say'
ie	eah	as the 'ea' in 'ear'
ių	ew	as the 'ew' in 'new'
ui	wi	as the 'oui' in 'Louis'
uo	u·aw	as the 'wa' in 'wander'

Consonants

c	ts	as the 'ts' in 'ants'
č	ch	as the 'ch' in 'chicken'
ch	h	as the 'h' in 'hot'
dz	dz	as the 'ds' in 'roads'
dž	j	as the 'j' in 'jump'
g	g	as the 'g' in 'gas'
j	y	as the 'y' in 'you'
r	r	trilled like the Italian 'r'
s	s	soft, as the 's' in 'kiss'
š	sh	as the 'sh' in 'shop'
ž	zh	as the 's' in 'treasure'

Stress

Stress and tone variations are very subtle and complex in Lithuanian. You'll be understood without having to worry about this too much. The best way to learn is by listening. Stressed syllables are indicated by italics in the pronunciation guides.

ACCOMMODATION
I'm looking for (a) ...
Aš ieškau ...   ahsh *yeash*·kow ...
  hotel
  viešbučio   *veash*·bu·chaw
  somewhere to stay
  kur nors apsistoti   kur nors ahp·si·*staw*·ti

Could you write down the address, please?
Ar galétumét man užrašyti adresą?
ahr gah·*leh*·tu·met mahn uzh·rah·*shee*·ti ah·dras·ah
Do you have any rooms available?
Ar turite laisvų kambarių?
ahr tu·ri·ta lais·*voo* kahm·bahr·yew
How much is it per night, per person?
Kiek kainuoja apsistoti nakčiai asmeniui?
keahk kai·*nu·aw*·yah ahp·si·staw·ti nahk·chay ahs·man·wi
Does it include breakfast?
Ar karina įskaito pusryčius?
ahr kai·*nah* i·skai·taw pus·ree·chus
Can I see the room?
Ar galėčiau kambarį pamatyti?
ahr gah·*leh*·chow kahm·bah·ri pah·mah·*tee*·ti

I'd like a ...
Aš noriu ...
ahsh *nawr*·yu ...
  single room
  vienviečio kambario
  veahn·*veah*·chaw kahm·bahr·yaw
  double room
  dviviečio kambario
  dvi·*veah*·chaw kahm·bahr·yaw
  room with a bathroom
  kambario su prausykla
  kahm·bahr·yaw su prow·*seek*·lah

CONVERSATION & ESSENTIALS

Hello.
Sveiki.   svay·ki
Hi.
Labas.   lah·bahs
Good morning.
Labas rytas.   lah·bahs ree·tahs
Good day.
Laba diena.   lah·bah deah·nah
Good evening.
Labas vakaras.   lah·bahs vah·kah·rahs
Welcome.
Sveiki atvykę.   svay·ki aht·vee·ka
Goodbye.
Sudie.   su·deah
Good night.
Labos nakties. (pol)   lah·baws nahk·teahs
Labanaktis. (inf)   lah·bah·nahk·tis
Yes.
Taip.   tayp
No.
Ne.   na
Please.
Prašau.   prah·show
Thank you.
Dėkoju/Ačiū. (pol/inf) deh·kaw·yu/ah·choo
You're welcome.
Prašau.   prah·show
Excuse me.
Atsiprašau.   aht·si·prah·show
Sorry.
Atleiskite.   aht·lays·ki·ta
How are you?
Kaip gyvuojate? (pol) kaip gee·vu·aw·yah·ta
Kaip gyvuoji? (inf)   kaip gee·vu·aw·yi?
What's your name?
Kaip jūsų vardas?   kaip yoo·soo vahr·dahs
My name is ...
Mano vardas yra ...   mah·naw vahr·dahs ee·rah ...
Where are you from?
Iš kur jūs esate?   ish kur yoos a·sah·ta
I'm from ...
Aš esu iš ...   ahsh a·su ish ...

HEALTH

Where's the ...?
Kur yra ...?   kur ee·rah ...
doctor
gydytojas   gee·dee·taw·yahs
hospital
ligoninė   li·gaw·ni·neh

I'm allergic to penicillin.
Aš alergišk(as/a) penicilinui. (m/f)
ahsh ah·lar·gishk·(ahs/ah) pan·it·si·lin·wi

LANGUAGE DIFFICULTIES

Do you speak English?
Ar kalbate angliškai?
ahr kahl·bah·ta ahn·glish·kai
I don't understand you.
Aš jūsų nesuprantu.
ahsh yoo·soo na·su·prahn·tu
What's Lithuanian for ...?
Kaip lietuviškai ...?
kaip leah·tu·vish·kai ...

SHOPPING & SERVICES

I'm looking for the ...
Aš ieškau ...   ahsh yeahsh·kow ...
  bank
  bankas   ban·kas
  chemist
  vaistinė   vais·ti·neh
  city centre
  miesto centro   meahs·taw tsan·traw
  currency exchange
  valiutos   vah·lyu·taws
  embassy
  ambasados   ahm·bah·sah·daws
  market
  turgaus   tur·gows
  old city
  senamiesčio   san·ah·meahs·chaw
  police
  policijos   paw·lit·si·yaws
  post office
  pašto   pahsh·taw
  public toilet
  tualeto   tu·ah·lat·aw

How much is it?
Kiek kainuoja?
keahk kai·nu·aw·yah
What time does it open/close?
Kelintą valandą atsidaro/uždaro?
kal·in·tah vah·lahn·dah aht·si·dah·raw/uzh·si·dah·raw

I need to check my email.
Man reikia pasitikrinti elektronini paštą.
mahn *rayk*·yah pah·si·*tik*·rin·ti al·ak·*tron*·i·ni *pahsh*·tah

condoms
prezervatyvai   pre·zer·vah·*tee*·vai
credit card
kredito kortelė   kra·*di*·taw kor·*ta*·leh
sanitary napkins
bintai   *bin*·tai
sunblock cream
saulės kremas   sow·lehs *kram*·ahs
tampons
tamponai   tahm·*pon*·ai

TIME, DATES & NUMBERS

What time is it?
Kiek dabar laiko?
keahk dah·bahr *lai*·kaw

It's ... (o'clock).
Dabar ... (valanda).
dah·*bahr* ... (vah·lahn·*dah*)

two o'clock	*antra*	ahn·*trah*
half past five	*pusė šešių*	pu·seh shash·*yew*

today	*šiandien*	shan·*deahn*
tomorrow	*rytoj*	ree·*toy*
morning	*rytas*	ree·tahs
afternoon	*popietė*	paw·peah·teh
night	*naktis*	nahk·*tis*

Monday	*pirmadienis*	pir·*mah*·deah·nis
Tuesday	*antradienis*	ahn·*trah*·deah·nis
Wednesday	*trečiadienis*	trach·*ah*·deah·nis
Thursday	*ketvirtadienis*	kat·vir·*tah*·deah·nis
Friday	*penktadienis*	pank·*tah*·deah·nis
Saturday	*šeštadienis*	shash·*tah*·deah·nis
Sunday	*sekmadienis*	sak·*mah*·deah·nis

January	*sausis*	sow·sis
February	*vasaris*	vah·*sah*·ris
March	*kovas*	kaw·vahs
April	*balandis*	bah·*lahn*·dis
May	*gegužis*	gag·*uzh*·is
June	*birželis*	bir·*zhal*·is
July	*liepa*	leah·pah
August	*rugpiūtis*	rug·*pew*·tis
September	*rugsėjis*	rug·*seh*·yis
October	*spalis*	spah·lis
November	*lapkritis*	lahp·krit·is
December	*gruodis*	gru·*aw*·dis

0	*nulis*	nul·is
1	*vienas*	veah·nahs

2	*du*	du
3	*trys*	trees
4	*keturi*	kat·u·*ri*
5	*penki*	pan·*ki*
6	*šeši*	shash·*i*
7	*septyni*	sap·tee·*ni*
8	*aštuoni*	ahsh·tu·aw·*ni*
9	*devyni*	dav·ee·*ni*
10	*dešimt*	*dash*·imt
11	*vienuolika*	veah·*naw*·lik·ah
12	*dvylika*	dvee·lik·ah
13	*trylika*	tree·lik·ah
14	*keturiolika*	kat·u·*raw*·lik·ah
15	*penkiolika*	pank·*yaw*·lik·ah
16	*šešiolika*	shash·*yaw*·lik·ah
17	*septyniolika*	sap·teen·*yaw*·lik·ah
18	*aštuoniolika*	ahsh·tawn·*yaw*·lik·ah
19	*devyniolika*	dav·een·*yaw*·lik·ah
20	*dvidešimt*	dvi·*dash*·imt
21	*dvidešimt vienas*	dvi·*dash*·imt veah·nahs
30	*trisdešimt*	tris·*dash*·imt
40	*keturiasdešimt*	kat·ur·as·dash·imt
50	*penkiasdešimt*	pank·as·dash·imt
60	*šešiasdešimt*	shash·as·dash·imt
70	*septyniasdešimt*	sap·teen·as·dash·imt
80	*aštuoniasdešimt*	ahsh·tu·aw·nas·dash·imt
90	*devyniasdešimt*	dav·een·as·dash·imt
100	*šimtas*	shim·tahs
101	*šimtas vienas*	shim·tahs veah·nahs
500	*penki šimtai*	pan·*ki* shim·*tai*
1000	*tūkstantis*	tooks·tahn·tis

TRANSPORT

Where's the ...?
Kur yra ...?   kur ee·*rah* ...
  airport
  oro uostas   aw·raw u·*aws*·tahs
  bus stop
  autobuso stotelė   ow·*taw*·bu·saw staw·*ta*·leh
  ferry terminal
  kelto stotis   kal·taw staw·*tis*
  train station
  geležinkelio stotis gal·azh·*in*·kal·yaw staw·*tis*

SIGNS – LITHUANIAN

Įėjimas	Entrance
Išėjimas	Exit
Atidara	Open
Uždara	Closed
Dėmesio	Caution
Patogumai	Public Toilets

When does the ... arrive?

Kada atplaukia ...?	kah-*dah* aht-plowk-yah ...
boat	
laivas	*lai*-vahs
ferry	
keltas	*kal*-tahs
hydrofoil	
raketa	rah-*kat*-ah

I'd like (a) ...

Aš norėčiau ...	ahsh naw-*reh*-chow ...
one-way ticket	
bilietą į vieną galą	*bil*-eah-tah i *veah*-nah *gah*-lah
return ticket	
bilietą į abu galus	*bil*-eah-tah i ah-*bu* gah-*lus*

I want to travel to ...

Aš noriu nuvažiuoti į ...
ahsh *naw*-ryu nu-vah-*zhu-aw*-ti i ...

How much does it cost to go to ...?

Kiek kainuoja nuvažiuoti į ...?
keahk kai-*nu-aw*-yah nu-vah-*zhu-aw*-ti i ...

Directions

How do I get to the ...?

Prašom pasakyti, kaip patekti į ...?
prah-shom pah-sah-*kee*-ti kaip pah-*tak*-ti i ...

Is it far?

Ar toli?
ahr taw-*li*

Can you show me (on the map)?

Galėtumėt man parodyti (žemėlapyje)?
gah-leh-tu-met mahn pah-raw-dee-ti
(zham-eh-lah-pee-ya)

Turn left (at the ...)

Sukite į kairę (prie ...)
su-ki-ta i *kai*-ra (preah ...)

Turn right (at the ...)

Sukite į dešinę (prie ...)
su-ki-ta i *dash*-na (preah ...)

straight ahead

tiesiai
teah-say

Also available from Lonely Planet:
Baltic Phrasebook

Glossary

See the individual destination chapters for some useful words and phrases dealing with food and dining; see the Language chapter (p419) for other useful words and phrases. This glossary is a list of Estonian (Est), Finnish (Fin), German (Ger), Latvian (Lat), Lithuanian (Lith), and Russian (Rus) terms you might come across during your time in the Baltic.

aikštė (Lith) – square
aludė (Lith) – beer cellar
alus (Lat, Lith) – beer
apteek (Est) – pharmacy
aptieka (Lat) – pharmacy
Aukštaitija (Lith) – Upper Lithuania
autobusų stotis (Lith) – bus station
autoosta (Lat) – bus station
autostrāde (Lat) – highway

baar (Est) – pub, bar
babushka (Rus) – grandmother/pensioner in headscarf
bagāžas glabātava (Lat) – left-luggage room
bagažinė (Lith) – left-luggage room
bāka (Lat) – lighthouse
Baltic glint – raised limestone bank stretching from Sweden across the north of Estonia into Russia
baras (Lith) – pub, bar
bažnyčia (Lith) – church
baznica (Lat) – church
brokastis (Lat) – breakfast
bulvāris (Lat) – boulevard
bussijaam (Est) – bus station

ceļš (Lat) – railway track, road
centras (Lith) – town centre
centrs (Lat) – town centre
Chudkoye Ozero (Rus) – Lake Peipsi
Courland – Kurzeme

daina (Lat) – short, poetic oral song or verse
datorsalons (Lat) – internet cafe
dzintars (Lat) – amber

ebreji (Lat) – Jews
Eesti (Est) – Estonia
ežeras (Lith) – lake
ezerpils (Lat) – lake fortress
ezers (Lat) – lake

gatvė (Lith) – street
geležinkelio stotis (Lith) – train station
gintarinė/gintarinis (Lith) – amber

hinnakiri (Est) – price list
hommikusöök (Est) – breakfast

iela (Lat) – street
iezis (Lat) – rock
informacija (Lith) – information centre
internetas kavinė (Lith) – internet cafe
interneti kohvik (Est) – internet cafe

järv (Est) – lake

kafejnīca (Lat) – cafe
kalnas (Lith) – mountain, hill
kalns (Lat) – mountain, hill
kämping (Est) – camp site
katedrāle (Lat) – cathedral
katedra (Lith) – cathedral
kauplus (Est) – shop
kavinė (Lith) – cafe
kelias (Lith) – road
kempingas (Lith) – camp site
kempings (Lat) – camp site
kesklinn (Est) – town centre
kino (Est, Lat, Lith) – cinema
kirik (Est) – church
kohvik (Est) – cafe
kõrts (Est) – inn, tavern
krogs (Lat) – pub, bar
Kurshskaya Kosa (Rus) – Curonian Spit
Kuršių marios (Lith) – Curonian Lagoon
Kuršių Nerija (Lith) – Curonian Spit

laht (Est) – bay
Latvija (Lat) – Latvia
laukums (Lat) – square
lennujaam (Est) – airport
lidosta (Lat) – airport
Lietuva (Lith) – Lithuania
looduskaitseala (Est) – nature/landscape reserve
loss (Est) – castle, palace

maantee (Est) – highway
mägi (Est) – mountain, hill
Metsavennad (Est) – Forest Brothers resistance movement
midus (Lith) – mead

mõis (Est) – manor
muuseum (Est) – museum
muzejs (Lat) – museum
muziejus (Lith) – museum

nacionālais parks (Lat) – national park

õlu (Est) – beer
oro uostas (Lith) – airport
osta (Lat) – port/harbour

pakihoid (Est) – left luggage
parkas (Lith) – park
parks (Lat) – park
pastas (Lith) – post office
pasts (Lat) – post office
Peko (Est) – pagan god of fertility in Setu traditions
perkėla (Lith) – port
piletid (Est) – tickets
pilies (Lith) – castle
pils (Lat) – castle, palace
pilsdrupas (Lat) – knights' castle
pilskalns (Lat) – castle mound
plats (Est) – square
plentas (Lith) – highway, motorway
pliažas (Lith) – beach
pludmale (Lat) – beach
pood (Est) – shop
postkontor (Est) – post office
prospektas (Lith) – boulevard
prospekts (Lat) – boulevard
pubi (Est) – pub
puhketalu (Est) – tourist farm (ie a farm offering accommodation)
puiestee (Est) – boulevard
pusryčiai (Lith) – breakfast

raekoda (Est) – town/city hall
rahvuspark (Est) – national park
rand (Est) – beach
rātsnams (Lat) – town hall
raudteejaam (Est) – train station

Reval (Ger) – old German name for Tallinn
rezervāts (Lat) – reserve
Riigikogu (Est) – Parliament
rotušė (Lith)- town/city hall
rūmai (Lith) – palace

saar (Est) – island
sadam (Est) – harbour/port
Saeima (Lat) – Parliament
Seimas (Lith) – Parliament
Setu (Est) – ethnic group of mixed Estonian and Orthodox traditions
Setumaa (Est) – territory of the Setu people in south-eastern Estonia and Russia
sild (Est) – bridge
smuklė (Lith) – tavern
stacija (Lat) – station
švyturys (Lith) – lighthouse

Tallinna (Fin) – Tallinn
talu (Est) – farm
tänav (Est) – street
tee (Est) – road
tiltas (Lith) – bridge
tilts (Lat) – bridge
tirgus (Lat) – market
toomkirik (Est) – cathedral
trahter (Est) – tavern
tuletorn (Est) – lighthouse
turg (Est) – market
turgus (Lith) – market
turismitalu (Est) – tourist farm (ie a farm offering accommodation)

vanalinn (Est) – old town
vaistinė (Lith) – pharmacy
väljak (Est) – square
Vecrīga (Lat) – Old Rīga
via Baltica – international road (the E67) linking Estonia with Poland

žydų (Lith) – Jews

432

The Authors

CAROLYN BAIN
Coordinating Author, Estonia

Melbourne-born Carolyn got her first glimpse behind the Iron Curtain in Poland in early 1989, while a student in Denmark. It was the year communism unravelled throughout Eastern Europe, and thus began her fascination. In 1991, while studying Russian and politics at university, she was overjoyed when her 'Soviet Politics' class had to change its name to 'The Soviet Union & Beyond'. Since then, on regular visits to the Baltic region she has applauded the renewed independence and flourishing creativity here. Among other destinations, she has covered Sweden and Denmark for Lonely Planet; Estonia holds a special place in her heart for combining the best of Eastern Europe and Scandinavia and coming up with something heart-warmingly unique.

NEAL BEDFORD
Lithuania

Neal had ventured to the northeastern corner of Poland some summers ago and came into more contact with Lithuania than he'd expected. Many locals affiliated themselves with Vilnius rather than Warsaw and whenever he read about Poland's history, up would pop that country just across the border. His interest was sparked, and he decided to explore Lithuania from end to end. He found paganism and Catholicism comfortably sleeping in the same bed; dense, mysterious forests and glistening lakes; sweeping sand dunes; and curious, friendly people – once you broke the ice. He also found some of the most challenging restaurant service he'd ever come across. Neal has travelled much of Eastern Europe from his base in Vienna, Austria.

BRANDON PRESSER
Latvia

After a rainy stint back in 2005, Brandon was delighted to return to the region, especially since he's got a bit of Baltic blood in him. This time around his prayers to the weather gods were answered with blissful beach days along the Kurzeme coast, misty cricket-filled evenings in Latgale, and fiery sunsets off the tip of Cape Kolka. In Rīga, Brandon put his Harvard art-history degree to good use while checking out the city's surplus of evocative Art Nouveau architecture. When Brandon's not writing about himself in the third person, he likes to watch old Bond movies – especially the ones with crafty KGB agents.

LONELY PLANET AUTHORS

Why is our travel information the best in the world? It's simple: our authors are passionate, dedicated travellers. They don't take freebies in exchange for positive coverage so you can be sure the advice you're given is impartial. They travel widely to all the popular spots, and off the beaten track. They don't research using just the internet or phone. They discover new places not included in any other guidebook. They personally visit thousands of hotels, restaurants, palaces, trails, galleries, temples and more. They speak with dozens of locals every day to make sure you get the kind of insider knowledge only a local could tell you. They take pride in getting all the details right, and in telling it how it is. Think you can do it? Find out how at **lonelyplanet.com**.

GEORGE DUNFORD   Helsinki

wrote the Helsinki Excursion chapter. Having visited Helsinki several times,
George was thrilled to research the Finnish capital for Lonely Planet's *Finland*.
He's a freelance writer who has written for several publications including
Wanderlust, Life Coach and Lonely Planet's *The Big Trip*. He kept a blog while
travelling in Finland at http://hackpacker.blogspot.com.

CONTRIBUTING AUTHOR

Simon Richmond wrote the Kaliningrad Excursion chapter. He first travelled to Russia in 1994 and has
been working on Russia-related books for Lonely Planet since 2001 when he coauthored the 1st edition of the *Trans-Siberian Railway*. He thinks Kaliningrad is an ideal introduction to the world's largest
country. His website is www.simonrichmond.com.

Behind the Scenes

THIS BOOK

This 5th edition of *Estonia, Latvia & Lithuania* was researched by Carolyn Bain, Neal Bedford and Brandon Presser, with contributions from George Dunford and Simon Richmond. The 1st edition of this guide was written by Nicola Williams and she also coordinated the 2nd edition. In the 3rd edition she was joined by Debra Herrmann and Cathryn Kemp, and for the 4th edition by Becca Blond, Regis St Louis and Dr Caroline Evans. This guidebook was commissioned in Lonely Planet's London office, and produced by the following:

Commissioning Editors Fiona Buchan, Emma Gilmour, Michala Green, Jo Potts
Coordinating Editor Shawn Low
Coordinating Cartographers Hunor Csutoros, Herman So
Coordinating Layout Designer Indra Kilfoyle
Managing Editor Sasha Baskett
Managing Cartographer Mark Griffiths
Managing Layout Designers Sally Darmody, Laura Jane
Assisting Editors Janet Austin, Janice Bird, Alan Murphy
Assisting Cartographer Mick Garrett
Cover Designer Pepi Bluck
Colour Designer Vicki Beale
Project Managers Chris Girdler, Craig Kilburn
Language Content Coordinator Quentin Frayne

Thanks to Melanie Dankel, Mark Germanchis, Jennifer Garrett, John Mazzocchi, Trent Paton

THANKS
CAROLYN BAIN

Thanks first and foremost to my sterling coauthors, Brandon and Neal, for all their great work (and their company in Rīga and Vilnius, respectively). I am indebted to Simon Richmond for coming on board and sharing his Kaliningrad expertise. Other LP authors, past and present, gave freely of their tips and contacts – many thanks to Nicola Williams, Greg Bloom and Debra Herrmann.

In Estonia (and beyond), a huge *aitäh* to Steve Kokker for his friendship, kindness and immense local wisdom. Others who generously helped out with tips and company around the country include Pille Petersoo, Liina Laar, Geli Lillemaa, Hugo & Tim, Maido Rüütli, Sergei Iarovenko, Malcolm Russell, Madis Mutso and Varje Papp.

And finally, big bouquets and heartfelt thanks to fabulous friends who shared with me the pleasure of their company on parts of this trip: Sally O'Brien and George Dunford for the memorable weekend in Tallinn, and Amanda Harding and Graham Harris for the incredible Baltic City Blitz. Cheers guys!

THE LONELY PLANET STORY

Fresh from an epic journey across Europe, Asia and Australia in 1972, Tony and Maureen Wheeler sat at their kitchen table stapling together notes. The first Lonely Planet guidebook, *Across Asia on the Cheap*, was born.

Travellers snapped up the guides. Inspired by their success, the Wheelers began publishing books to Southeast Asia, India and beyond. Demand was prodigious, and the Wheelers expanded the business rapidly to keep up. Over the years, Lonely Planet extended its coverage to every country and into the virtual world via lonelyplanet.com and the Thorn Tree message board.

As Lonely Planet became a globally loved brand, Tony and Maureen received several offers for the company. But it wasn't until 2007 that they found a partner whom they trusted to remain true to the company's principles of travelling widely, treading lightly and giving sustainably. In October of that year, BBC Worldwide acquired a 75% share in the company, pledging to uphold Lonely Planet's commitment to independent travel, trustworthy advice and editorial independence.

Today, Lonely Planet has offices in Melbourne, London and Oakland, with over 500 staff members and 300 authors. Tony and Maureen are still actively involved with Lonely Planet. They're travelling more often than ever, and they're devoting their spare time to charitable projects. And the company is still driven by the philosophy of *Across Asia on the Cheap*: 'All you've got to do is decide to go and the hardest part is over. So go!'

NEAL BEDFORD

Thanks to my two coauthors, Carolyn Bain and Brandon Presser, for their fun, energy, and input – great working with you. A low bow of gratitude to Nicola Williams for her work on the previous editions and her tips, hints, and contacts in the country. To LP's language department, a big *ačiū* for their immense help with Lithuanian transliterations.

In the country, a huge thank you to Andrew Quested, the man in the know in Lithuania, for all his suggestions and shouts; Nomeda Navickaite and friends for their knowledge of the capital and the coast; Hans Bastian Hauck for the sailing trip of a lifetime and good company; Cornelis Oskamp and Lena Björkenor for the evenings out and random meetings; and the Lithuanian tourist office, bus station, and train-station staff for all the help they gave.

Lastly, to Karin, for spending a beautiful week with me, giving up her precious holiday time, and keeping me sane when the workload gets too much. Much love.

BRANDON PRESSER

A heartfelt *paldies* to Aleks Karlsons and Ellie Schilling for adding me to their Rīga posse, to Ojars and Irma Kalnins for an unforgettable trip to Kolkasrags, to Inese Loce – you were a lifesaver (literally!), and to Jūlija Minkeviča and Jānis Rutka for opening my eyes in Latgale. To my wonderful coauthors: Carolyn (the best CA ever) and Neal – thank you both for all of your wonderful advice and support, it was such a treat to work with you guys. Additional thanks to Vaira Vīķe-Freiberga, Aleks Čvakste, Jānis Jenzis, Mara Bergmane, Richards Baerug, Richard Kalnins and the ab-fab LP production staff.

OUR READERS

Many thanks to the travellers who used the last edition and wrote to us with helpful hints, useful advice and interesting anecdotes:

Federico Arrizabalaga, Cathie Au, Sally Banks, Normunds Barons, Evelin Bauman, M Beiers, Petter Bienrik, Elleke Bijsterveld, Herve Blumenthal, Leslie Burnett, Christian Byhahn, John Cartledge, Rajinder Chaudhary, Helen Corning, Monique Cuppen, Andrew Curran, Dandem Dandem, Carla De Beer, Bram De Bruin, Wouter De Valk, Andrew Dienes, Heinz Effertz, John El Basha, Sharon Ellwood, Olivia Faul, Mike Follows, Susan Fuller, Stefan Gemzell, Giorgio Genova, Sean Grove, James Harvey, Helen Jackson, Anne Jaumees, Ellen Kaptijn, Deirdre Keary, Miriam Kersten, Erik Kissa, Alan Law, Bethe Lewis, Darius Lith, Heike Matcha, Ettore Mazza, Robert Merkel, Dean Meservy, Arno Mikkor, William Miles, Kristian Miles, Linda Minke, Richard Orr, Rait Parts, David Paul, Michael Raffaele, Karlis Rozenkrons, Gerrit Schilder Jr, Gerhard Schweng, Anne Shand, Laurie Shervington, Ben Smethurst, Vic Sofras, Alister Somerville, Madolene Stap, A Swistechi, Martijn Van Best, Pim Van Wel, Lady Vanj, Jeff & Charlotte Vize, Chloe Wickenden, Frank Wurft, Eva Zichova

ACKNOWLEDGMENTS

Many thanks to the following for the use of their content:

Globe on title page ©Mountain High Maps 1993 Digital Wisdom, Inc.

SEND US YOUR FEEDBACK

We love to hear from travellers – your comments keep us on our toes and help make our books better. Our well-travelled team reads every word on what you loved or loathed about this book. Although we cannot reply individually to postal submissions, we always guarantee that your feedback goes straight to the appropriate authors, in time for the next edition. Each person who sends us information is thanked in the next edition – and the most useful submissions are rewarded with a free book.

To send us your updates – and find out about Lonely Planet events, newsletters and travel news – visit our award-winning website: **lonelyplanet.com/contact**.

Note: we may edit, reproduce and incorporate your comments in Lonely Planet products such as guidebooks, websites and digital products, so let us know if you don't want your comments reproduced or your name acknowledged. For a copy of our privacy policy visit lonelyplanet.com/privacy.

Index

INDEX

INDEX

INDEX

INDEX

GreenDex

In a region where the local populace has a deep and abiding love of the countryside, many people go about their business with a high regard for the environment as a matter of course, but the following accommodation options, cafes, restaurants, sights, tour operators and natural highlights have been selected by Lonely Planet authors because they demonstrate an obvious commitment to sustainability. Here we've selected some places for their support of local producers or devotion to the 'slow food' cause – serving seasonal, locally sourced and/or organic produce. In addition, we've covered accommodation options that we deem to be environmentally friendly (in Estonia, these hotels have fulfilled numerous criteria to be awarded the 'Green Key'; www.green-key.org). Attractions are listed because they're involved in conservation or environmental education or have been given an ecological award (for example, Blue Flag beaches in Latvia and Lithuania; www .blueflag.org). Some sights and artisans keeping alive rich folk traditions are also acknowledged; there are many more throughout the Baltic.

We want to keep developing our sustainable-travel content. If you think we've omitted somewhere that should be listed here, or if you disagree with our choices, send us feedback on our selection via www.lonelyplanet.com/feedback. For more information about sustainable tourism and Lonely Planet, see www.lonelyplanet.com/responsibletravel.

For more tips about travelling sustainably in the Baltic countries, turn to the Getting Started chapter, p14.

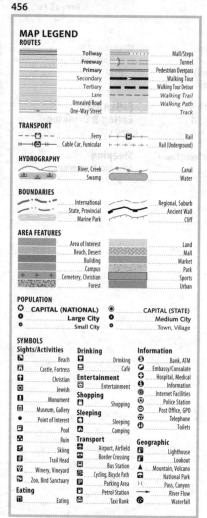

MAP LEGEND

ROUTES

Tollway	Mall/Steps
Freeway	Tunnel
Primary	Pedestrian Overpass
Secondary	Walking Tour
Tertiary	Walking Tour Detour
Lane	Walking Trail
Unsealed Road	Walking Path
One-Way Street	Track

TRANSPORT

Ferry	Rail
Cable Car, Funicular	Rail (Underground)

HYDROGRAPHY

River, Creek	Canal
Swamp	Water

BOUNDARIES

International	Regional, Suburb
State, Provincial	Ancient Wall
Marine Park	Cliff

AREA FEATURES

Area of Interest	Land
Beach, Desert	Mall
Building	Market
Campus	Park
Cemetery, Christian	Sports
Forest	Urban

POPULATION

⊛ CAPITAL (NATIONAL)	⊚ CAPITAL (STATE)
● Large City	● Medium City
○ Small City	○ Town, Village

SYMBOLS

Sights/Activities
- Beach
- Castle, Fortress
- Christian
- Jewish
- Monument
- Museum, Gallery
- Point of Interest
- Pool
- Ruin
- Skiing
- Trail Head
- Winery, Vineyard
- Zoo, Bird Sanctuary

Eating
- Eating

Drinking
- Drinking
- Café

Entertainment
- Entertainment

Shopping
- Shopping

Sleeping
- Sleeping
- Camping

Transport
- Airport, Airfield
- Border Crossing
- Bus Station
- Cycling, Bicycle Path
- Parking Area
- Petrol Station
- Taxi Rank

Information
- Bank, ATM
- Embassy/Consulate
- Hospital, Medical
- Information
- Internet Facilities
- Police Station
- Post Office, GPO
- Telephone
- Toilets

Geographic
- Lighthouse
- Lookout
- Mountain, Volcano
- National Park
- Pass, Canyon
- River Flow
- Waterfall

LONELY PLANET OFFICES

Australia
Head Office
Locked Bag 1, Footscray, Victoria 3011
☎ 03 8379 8000, fax 03 8379 8111
talk2us@lonelyplanet.com.au

USA
150 Linden St, Oakland, CA 94607
☎ 510 250 6400, toll free 800 275 8555
fax 510 893 8572
info@lonelyplanet.com

UK
2nd fl, 186 City Rd,
London EC1V 2NT
☎ 020 7106 2100, fax 020 7106 2101
go@lonelyplanet.co.uk

Published by Lonely Planet Publications Pty Ltd
ABN 36 005 607 983

Printed by Hang Tai Printing Company
Printed in China.

Mixed Sources
Product group from well-managed forests and other controlled sources
www.fsc.org Cert no. SGS-COC-005002
© 1996 Forest Stewardship Council

Although the authors and Lonely Planet have taken all reasonable care in preparing this book, we make no warranty about the accuracy or completeness of its content and, to the maximum extent permitted, disclaim all liability arising from its use.